History Man

FRED INGLIS

History Man

THE LIFE OF R. G. COLLINGWOOD

PRINCETON UNIVERSITY PRESS
PRINCETON AND OXFORD

Library of Congress Cataloging-in-Publication Data
Inglis, Fred.
History man : the life of R.G. Collingwood / Fred Inglis.
p.   cm.
Includes bibliographical references and index.
ISBN 978-0-691-13014-9 (hardcover : alk. paper)
1. Collingwood, R. G. (Robin George), 1889–1943. I. Title.
B1618.C74I54   2009
192—dc22
[B]   2008044647

British Library Cataloging-in-Publication Data is available

This book has been composed in Minion

Printed on acid-free paper. ∞

press.princeton.edu

Printed in the United States of America

1   3   5   7   9   10   8   6   4   2

For Quentin Skinner
and Susan James

Contents

Preface

A preface has always seemed a happy convention. For one treats a book something like the way one does another human, as being trustworthy or not, as being engaging or haughty or tedious or revisitable, as becoming a friend, a teacher, a bore, an old misery, a cheerful companion on long journeys, a master. So the author's preface bids the reader greet the book, tells him or her, briefly and with modest ceremony, what sort of person it is, and leaves the interlocutor to get on with it.

Yet readers mostly skip prefaces. This time I hope you won't. For I have adopted a particular device by way of dramatising one very important aspect of my subject's thought. In each chapter the biography is told, naturally, according to the chronology of the life, as well it might be. A biography is the story of how an individual came through time to be what he or she was. Disrupting biographical chronology in the name of postmodernism or literary theory is merely mannerism. However, each chapter is closed by a section in which assorted topics arising from a narrative of the past are reconsidered in the light of the present.

This minor dislocation of the history is intended by way of drawing attention to Collingwood's prime lesson, that the past, completed as it must be, nonetheless may be found living in the present, in his word, "encapsulated," and releasing its force into the later moment from within that capsule. The concluding sections, that is, are intended to dramatise such a contention, to keep in motion the surge and withdrawal of the tide of past time.

Acknowledgements

A recent piece in The *London Review of Books* started out with some malicious animadversions on the whole convention of prefatory acknowledgements, suggesting that they were merely a boastful record of the author's posh friends. It is to be feared that so sneering a note is not untypical of the present journal's rival conviction that anything of literary note can only take place in NW6.

As far as a biography of R. G. Collingwood is concerned, the pages of acknowledgement illustrate with numerical force the man's lifelong argument that all history is the history of the mind in action, and that it is made and remade by the thoughts of innumerable people thinking not in concert but, nonetheless, together consequentially and collectively.

This history of a thinker's thought as it was shaped by his life is therefore also a collective act of making, and each of the names now thanked, honoured, and listed here has contributed, sometimes largely, to the finished article.

My indebtedness is, first, most substantial to the Leverhulme Foundation, whose handsome Emeritus Fellowship, solicited on my behalf by two of the names appearing below, made the whole thing possible. Most retired scholars simply cannot afford on their own the quantities of travel (in this case including Italy and Greece, let alone Oxford and the Lake District) demanded by any biography, and it is one of the most cheering features of intellectual life in the present that Leverhulme is there to give such help quite untarnished by the inanities of the Research Assessment Exercise.

After that first, grand, and institutional name, all the many individuals who lent assistance follow alphabetically, on occasion with details of the help appended, particularly in those several cases in which my many appeals for succour were promptly responded to, quite without the irritation to which my rescuers were entitled by my importunate letters and emails.

Great gratitude, therefore to the Armitt Library Ambleside and to Ian Matheson and Tanya Flower for their curatorial help and details about the Collingwood family house, Lanehead; the Australian National University for a Visiting Fellowship in 2008 during which I was able to try out some of the finished version of this book on sympathetic and critical members of the Humanities Research Centre; Sir Roger Bannister, formerly master of Pembroke, for a long conversation in Coniston in 2005; Simon Bennett, old Rugbeian, for his omniscience about his old school; John Berra, friend and former student, who acted, with Leverhulme's help, as my faithful research assistant; David Boucher, who is given space to himself in the body of the text, but who was unfailingly generous with time, books, and his own unrivalled knowledge of Collingwood's life; Lord Melvyn Bragg for his local knowledge of the Lake District; Hilary Britland for her uncomplaining and handsome labours on the several sites of the life with her camera; Dennis and Mary Butts for affectionate support, bibliographic and literary critical help; Stefan Collini for friendly help in ensuring a contract; James Connelly, more knowledgeable than I shall ever be about Collingwood, for scholarly assistance; Colin Crouch for encouragement at an early stage; the European University Institute at San Domenico, in particular Anthony Molho and Arfon Rees, for hospitality at and admission to the institute in 2005 and 2006; my cherished friend the late, much missed Clifford Geertz for encouragement and support on the roads to Leverhulme and to a Princeton University Press contract; Maurice George for his irreplaceable knowledge of railway services; Janet Gnosspelius, Collingwood's niece, for four long, essential letters, sharp criticism of chapter 1, and many offprints; Chelly Halsey for supportive letters, encouragement, and reassurance; Colin Harris for many welcomes to the Reading Room at the Bodleian; Sir Brian Harrison, editor of the latest *DNB*, for prompt and personal provision from his huge files on the history of Oxford; David Hornbrook, well-loved friend and capable sailor, for much specific sailing lore as well as his nautical prose; Richard Honells, for loyal interest; Jim Hunter, as so many times before, for his caustic and critical reading; Wendy James for anthropological help; Roy Long, for ecclesiastical history; Ian Lowe, for hospitality, critical commentary, and his extensive files on Collingwood; Rusty Maclean, Rugby School's librarian, for ready and efficient help with school records; Magdalen College, Oxford, for hospitality and scholarly help from its former president, Tony Smith, Robin Darwall-Smith, and its accommodation officer, Catherine Hughes; Ian Malcolm, my incomparable and courteous editor at the Press; Carol Marks as ever, for her typing of a cussedly difficult manuscript; Professor Mathieu Marion for his handsome invitation to me to present a relevant chapter to his excellent conference on Collingwood's work held at the University of Quebec at Montreal in

2007; Tim and Karen Mathias for friendship and their spare bed in Cardiff; David McLellan for long friendship and important help; Jeremy Mynott, Cambridge University Press, for his indispensable help in obtaining a contract with a rival press; Tony Page for his knowledge of Arthur Ransome; James Patrick for friendly advice; Iain Paterson for encouragement, hospitality, and transport in Cumbria; Pembroke College, Oxford, also for hospitality, kindness, and efficient help from the master, Giles Henderson, Lucie Walker in the library, and Jane Osborne, admirable accommodation officer; Paul Pickering, for illumination of the problem of historical re-enactment; Michael Rae, old friend, for ready hospitality in Naples; Abby Sabey, my daughter, for help with the medical details of Collingwood's condition; Glenn Shipley, for encouragement, details about Margaret Lowenfeld, and a precious disk; Philip Smallwood for reassurance and recognition at the way I conceived this tale; the late Sir Peter Strawson for informative letters and a valuable conversation in 2005; Douglas Templeton for scholarly help; Eleanor and Kingsley Williams for bibliographic help, old friendship, and encouragement; Dr. Wilson, housemaster, for hospitality at Rugby School.

Finally, the two dedicatees must have a short paragraph to themselves. Not only did Quentin Skinner send me the first critical but enthusiastic response to my synopsis of the biography, he also supported with vigour, my proposal first to the Leverhulme Foundation, then to the publishers. But far more than that, he and his wife, Susan James, have been to me and countless others (in my case for all but fifty years) staunch friends of inexhaustible kindness, comedy, and generosity, and in their lives as in their scholarship models of selfless probity, excellent irreverence, and high intellectual distinction. Behind them, to whom all my own work is invisibly dedicated, stands Eileen, wise, acute, loving, who shared with me the seminar on *An Autobiography* three decades ago, and chose the name for our house.

Collingwood House
West Harptree

History Man

1

By Coniston Water

The mighty Roman road ran arrow-straight from Manchester, which was Mamucium, to Blackburn, swerved a little as it hit the fells, then straight again to meet Hadrian's great wall at Carlisle. At Penrith, the legionaries and their pressgangs laboured on the main thoroughfare east, their flagstones now somewhere below the A66, to meet the Great North Road at Scotch Corner. Southwest from Penrith, they built a smaller road, still pretty straight, bending round Ullswater, making camp at Ambleside, threading through Hardknott Pass and leaving a large fort there, and on to the estuary of the Esk where the iron ore lay and the raiders from Iceland or Ireland would land.

Lesser roads from the south, marking no doubt older patterns of marketing and migration, lead you variously up the coast, with glimpses of Morecambe Bay on your left, marked "Danger Area" on the Ordnance Survey map, until, passing through Ulverston, you reach Greenodd at the mouth of the river Crake. You are now four miles from the tip of Coniston Water, the first leading character in our tale.

The road winds up along the line of the river, until the vista wonderfully expands and the day is filled with the shining waters of the lake, shaped by the open, sunny Blawith Fells and Bethecar Moor on either side. As you advance northwards up the lake, the fells on the left begin unmenacingly to gather and rear up into a benign and powerful crag that sits familiarly athwart the rolling hills, a kindly 800 metres high, authoritative nonetheless, braced to break the great winds roaring in from the Atlantic and to turn the dark clouds to the Lakeland's steady rain.

This is the Old Man of Coniston, awful and reassuring by turns like all good father-figures, barometer to the sailors and farmers of the lake, endlessly the subject-matter of painters and photographers since tourism began here in 1770 or so.[1] His squat majesty presides over the little town, a plain gritstone Victorian street the product of the nineteenth-century railway and the smelters and holidaymaking sailors who took it.

As you enter the town, hardly more than a village, the road forks right after the humpbacked bridge and passes the Victorian Gothic church with its quiet graves about it, one short row of graves dominated by a copy of a tall pre-Norman Northumbrian cross, housing the body of John Ruskin, two respectfully lower, containing those of his friend, unpaid secretary, and lifelong admirer William Gershom Collingwood, and, next to him, Collingwood's son, our subject and object in this book, Robin George.

The road runs down to the ferry across the lake that will take you to Brantwood, Ruskin's house. If you continued by the road, then to find some of the Collingwoods at home any time between 1891 and the 1960s, you turned right at the top of the lake, briefly following the signs to Hawkshead, and after bending back down the east side of the lake took the narrow, ancient lane, clustered along the first mile or so to Brantwood by the solid, comfortable, unassertive family houses of Victorian romantics come to confirm themselves as Wordsworthians and Ruskinians by building suitably in front of a noble composition, the mountain just off centre, the blue and silver-grey lake in the middle ground, old firs and oaks on the long slopes of the garden down to the boathouse.

Among them, at the top of a modest rise, stands Lanehead, now rather changed by its role as an outdoor recreation centre for a couple of education authorities, but still rediscoverable as the family home it was for so many decades. WG, as he was commonly known, Gershom to his wife, moved to the house with his four children, Dora (born in 1886), Barbara (born in 1887), Robin (born on 22 February 1889), and his wife, christened Edith, even-handedly known as "Dorrie" or "Molly," pregnant with Ursula, who was born just before the move. William Gershom had moved them all by local carter from Gillhead, a cottage at Cartmel Fell, a few miles away, in order to be near his avatar and teacher, master and friend, John Ruskin, who since 1871 had lived another mile down the lakeside road at Brantwood, a plain, impressive, but not enormous house piled on a bluff with the finest view in the valley.

Lanehead was, and is, only a little smaller than Brantwood and although standing lower, it commanded a hardly less splendid view, the Old Man always in sight, the tall pines flanking the northwest of the building, the garden, and then the meadow sloping quite steeply to the lake. The house was built in 1848 on the site of an old pothouse once visited, WG tells us, by Turner, and extended three years later. The Collingwoods paid a substantial but intermittent rent of £100 a year (intermittent because they lived rent-free until 1894)[2] and for this enjoyed the safety, the happiness, and—near enough—the fiefdom of a dozen rooms, a conservatory known to the family as the Mausoleum, a loft, later made into a studio in the old stables at the back of the house, a sunny garden flanked with rhododendrons, the pinewood, and the boundless freedoms of the lake.

It isn't until the second half of the nineteenth century that one really finds widespread literary reference to the importance of the home as the key domestic value in the middle classes,[3] and it is at about the same time that, with the legalisation of the trade unions and their local victories in acquiring something like a living wage in the heavy industries (coal, steel, rail, shipping), working-class neighbourhoods settled into the close, companionable, well-fed, and coal-heated kind of family life that was to last a little over a century until it was torn apart by the tigerish economies of the 1980s.

The home the Collingwoods made was a long aesthetic journey from the Liverpool Gershom was born in. His father was a painter and lay preacher for the Plymouth Brethren, and his son, fired by Ruskin's genius as teacher and preacher at Oxford, was seized of a Ruskinian vision, shared with his wife, to live the good, self-supporting family life as artists, dedicated in their avocation to all forms of art. Such a life would be lived in pursuit of personal adequacy from art to craft, to competent making and repairing, in wood, stone, glass, to small sufficiencies in the herb and vegetable garden, the devout and diurnal round of egg-collecting, cabbage-cutting, fruit-picking, room-tidying, tea-making, book-learning; of study and scholarship and writing; of painting and sculpting; and, lastly, of sailing—sailing because it was the easiest way to fetch the groceries from Coniston on the west side of the lake, sailing because it too was art and craft and the livelihood of the many Collingwoods of the great north country family, including the mighty admiral, who had lived and died as naval officers, sailing finally because, especially for Robin, it lent itself to the rigours of solitary and extended meditation.

Almost every morning began with the sound of Mrs. Molly Collingwood playing the piano for an hour before breakfast at 8 a.m. The piano—a Broadwood grand—was in the morning room, part of the handsome extension to Lanehead built in 1851. It had then a high plasterwork ceiling and a window directly above the fireplace (the chimney flue bent around it) so that one could stay warm and look at the view south at the same time. The walls were hung with those of Molly's and Gershom's paintings which they approved at the time, dominated by the huge *Two Angels* by Edward Burne-Jones, a family friend and visitor.

Mrs. Molly played Beethoven above all, the full run of the sonatas, even the very hard opus numbers 109, 110, 111, Chopin, Mendelssohn, Mozart of course. As a schoolgirl, Wakefield tells us, she was taught by a well-known Dutch pianist, Willem Koenen, and under his instruction practised five hours a day. All the children learned to play proficiently, Ursula becoming as accomplished as her mother, Robin an excellent violinist, well remembered as such in his youth at Oxford. When, at times, Molly played in the evening and sang songs so beautifully—Schubert, Wolf (a new name), English madrigals, and folksongs—Gershom came out of his study to listen, and the children stole out of bed and sat together in the dark at the top of the stairs.

After breakfast, lessons by either parent in Gershom's study, which gave onto garden, lake, and the changeable face of the Old Man of

Coniston. The curriculum was intensely practical. Collingwood himself describes his father giving him "lessons in ancient and modern
history, illustrated with relief maps in papier-maché made by boiling
down newspapers in a saucepan,"[4] and it was according to his father's
curriculum that brother and sisters alike began Latin at four and
Greek at six, and the boy certainly and the girls surely, in so excellently egalitarian a household with senior sisters, learned to understand the working of pumps and locks, oil lamps and water-closets,
and "other mechanical appliances up and down the house."

Gershom, painter, writer, scholar, formidable handyman, and
practical pedagogue, had of course a large library, and the children,
equally precocious, eager to learn, read in it at will. It had become
the custom in many such families for one parent to read aloud to
spouse and children, Dickens often, Wordsworth in his home county,
Dumas; Kipling's *Stalky and Co*, the "best boarding school novel ever
written," proved so irresistible that Dora adopted the nickname of
"Beetle" from the Kipling-figure in the book, and the house rang to
its schoolboy slogans and insubordinate ditties. In their early years
of reading, the children thrilled not only to the new classic, *Treasure
Island*, but also to the grand and terrifying old English and German
fairy tales of *The Hobyahs, Tom Tit Tot, Cinderella* or its variant,
Catskin, Ruskin's own wonderful tale, *King of the Golden River*,
and, told aloud by Gershom, their father's passion, the fearful, cold
Icelandic sagas.

They were ardent pupils. Certainly there were days of reluctant learning, when the lake sparkled outside and when Euclid simply would
not come alive, even as illustrated with wooden trigonometrical symbols and Pythagoras's theorem tested in practical experience with
cartridge paper. The children peeled off into duos by age, Robin
and Ursula playing together, Dora the eldest taking charge of joint
operations for many years, editing the family journal, *Nothing Much*,
sometimes monthly, sometimes fortnightly.

Dora edited, everyone contributed. Indeed, Gershom thriftily collected his stories from *Nothing Much* and published them as *Coniston
Tales*. The elder girls provided pen-and-ink portraits; grandfather

William handed in one or two colour sketches; when she was little, Ursula's more pungent sayings were copied out as a list of aphorisms; Robin wrote accounts of trips with his father, sketching or elementary archaeologising at Hardknott Fort, and he wrote his own, serialised detective stories for which he had conceived a passion, beginning with Conan Doyle and taking E. W. Hornung's *Raffles* with him on the long train journey to boarding school. Dora and Barbara invented and peopled the land of Piwitee, and Robin and Ursula the nation-state of Jipandland, "which had a pretty formidable navy."[5]

Occasionally the older daughters attended the village school, smocked, pinafored, and wearing clogs, but the local children hooted at them for talking posh and seeming strange, so it didn't last. No more did the brief succession of governesses, and although Ursula was, after Robin went to Rugby, dispatched to boarding school, the education, both formal and customary, provided by the parents gave all four children the essential coding, the very ground and being of their lives.

There is something important and exemplary in the nature of such a childhood, something with a historical lesson in it for the future development of England, England rather than the different class and theological educations that shaped Scotland, Wales, both Irelands. The Collingwood family education was, one could say, anchored to that powerful tradition which inaugurated the Arts and Crafts movement and was commanded by Ruskin, the childless patriarch. The official content of its curriculum, as we saw, placed painting, music, classical, folk, and English literature as its heart, but it was above all practical, active, an education in studying by *doing*, doing painting, writing poems, building a little theatre for a drama with marionettes (as the children did at Lanehead), and leaving the schoolroom for the lived endeavour of archaeology on the very sites of Roman or Norse habitation, for the strenuous discovery of geological formation, fossil traces, or (also launched from Lanehead) copper ore. Learning to sail was then just another active art-and-science, and one learned it best out of the schoolroom, in the making of it in its proper place, on the water; where else?

Surrounding and pervading this rich, dense, and even at that date and to the village schoolchildren slightly strange and fey form of life was the calm, absolute, and loving authority of Dorrie and Gershom Collingwood. To say to contemporary managers of either state or private education in the twenty-first century that the first and cherished value of a human education must be love invites the glazed eye and wrinkled nostril with which the good professor or head teacher would consign the interlocutor to the barmy enclaves of Rudolf Steiner. But love and its authority was the first, unspoken principle of Collingwoodian education, and in this parents and children spoke for a tradition that inspired British progressive and experimental education for a century. It is a tradition that expressed itself in the strong psychoanalytic doctrines of such teachers as Melanie Klein and Susan Isaacs, which had in turn so marked an influence on the making of nursery education, and came to a brief official flowering in the government report on primary schools published in 1967 as the *Plowden Report*.[6]

It is no paradox that Collingwood himself recommended, in his farewell to the world, *The New Leviathan*, that all children are best raised and educated by their parents and within their family, and kept well away from any kind of formal or state-managed education. Implicit in all the pedagogy of progressivism was a vision of schooling dissolved naturally into learning-by-living. His own best tribute to the childhood he enjoyed until the age of thirteen was that earnest recommendation in his last book that those children will thrive best—find their own best lives—who are educated according to the natural rhythms of an upbringing in the perfect safety of a loving home, deliberately placed at the centre of orderly and exhilarating freedom. Collingwood knew and sternly admonished the inflexibility and fragmentariness of all forms of official education; he also knew and praised as exemplary the special genius of his own father and mother as creators of a miniature model of the good society, the culture of which would confirm wide and deep learning, build upright, truthful, and self-reliant character, transmit and renew its particular version of love and happiness and a steady courage in the face of the future.

These are not the terms in which official education was discussed then or is managed now. Yet my claim would be, on behalf of the Collingwoods' way of life, that it shook off the heavy piety and its sometime severity of the arch-Victorian family and emerged into the freer, sunnier air of a class generation happily, momentarily at poise between prosperity and thrift, liberty and discipline, recklessness and duty, belief and antinomianism.

Their corner of their class never had much money to spare, but they kept up a big house with an assortment of part-time servants chosen from the locals for readiness, ruggedness, friendliness, availability. Dorrie's version of motherhood is still a powerful one. She was daughter of a nonobservant, partly Jewish family, born Edith Isaac, had received extensive tuition as a painter (at the West London Art School) as well as a musician, and went on painting professionally long after marrying Gershom in 1883. She was elected member of the Society of Miniaturists in 1901, exhibited frequently at the Royal Academy, went abroad annually until the First World War broke out to paint larger landscapes in northern Italy, the Tyrol, Venice, and to charge between five and fifteen guineas for a painting.[7] Her pictures are quick, light, deft, with a lovely living line.

Gershom was, in his way, a pretty eminent Victorian, as well as one of those strong self-inventors who take the established conventions of personhood in a particular era and turn them to creative, novel, and admirable effect. He was born in 1854, son of a professional art teacher and fairly successful landscape painter who was also a devout member of the Open Plymouth Brethren, who still retain today a strong membership of biblical and antidenominational fundamentalists. Gershom's father, William, wanted his son to become prominent in the Brethren (who have elders but no ministers) and, having sent Gershom to Oxford, was very dismayed when the young man was converted by the irresistible ardour of John Ruskin's teaching to the rather different vocation of serving art, and the art of archaeology as well as the absolute art of creating a happy family.

Gershom announced his betrothal to a fiancée outside the Brethren and renounced the calling his father had chosen for him. There was a dignified family row, but Gershom would not give way. Ruskin had fired him with his own excellent idealism to revere the moral lessons of nature as she taught them in the everyday phenomena of rocks and stones and trees, clouds and waters and flowers, and to struggle on behalf of all working men to find creative fulfilment in labour and the hope of beauty in all aspects of life. Ruskin had moreover shown Gershom personal friendship as well as enlisting him in the undergraduate roadmaking *corvées* at Hinkley on the outskirts of Oxford whereby he taught the young volunteers the satisfactions as well as the hardship of physical work.

Gershom became Ruskin's devoted disciple. After marrying Dorrie, he moved first to the cottage at Gillhead, then became Ruskin's near neighbour a quiet mile's walk north of Brantwood. He had been an admirer not only of Ruskin but also of the British idealist philosopher T. H. Green, and taught by Green's pupil Bernard Bosanquet. They taught, and Gershom passed on to his son, not only that it is our ideas about the world that constitute our understanding of the relations between things rather than our empirical sense-experiences, but also Green's early and telling lesson of excellent civic-mindedness as well as of the English liberal principle that any extension of one person's freedom must be commensurate with the same freedom for others.

Public-spiritedness of this kind was an encompassing feature of Gershom's character and the British idealist inheritance; it was to be integral to the thought of the mature Collingwood. But Ruskin himself was far more than (as they say) an academic influence. Gershom moved to Lanehead to be as near as possible to his friend and master after Ruskin's mental health sharply deteriorated. As his most recent biographer also notes, Ruskin's enormous generosity ("As had always been the case with Ruskin family servants, no one was ever dismissed [when Ruskin was sane]")[8] meant that he was pouring away thousands of pounds of the family fortune and his own royalties "into wages, gifts, manuscripts, missals, gems, books, pictures, building projects, museums, psalters, continental trips and miscellaneous charities." He depended on half a dozen secretaries, Gershom at this time the busiest, but they gave their labours out of devotion and without remuneration.

Gershom walked down to Brantwood three or four mornings a week. Some years earlier, shortly before his marriage to Dorrie, he had accompanied Ruskin for a four-month trip to Italy, his own first visit to the country. It was September 1882 and they travelled via Switzerland to Turin, Genoa, and Pisa, spending most of their time in Lucca and Florence where the author of what became after its serial publication across 1875–77 an instant classic, *Mornings in Florence*, showed his former pupils the glories of Ghirlandaio and Fra Angelico. Gershom and Ruskin had together prepared extensive geological notes as they crossed Haute-Savoie on the way to Italy, which were published as *The Limestone Alps of Savoy*,[9] and it was then that Gershom first conceived the idea of writing Ruskin's biography.

By the time he moved to Lanehead, this work was well advanced and a kind of precipitate from it, witnessing just how full Ruskin's example filled Gershom Collingwood's mind, was published in 1891 as *The Art Teaching of John Ruskin*.[10] The biography, as Robin Collingwood wrote in his father's obituary many years later, "has remained the standard biography for the strict and severe selectiveness of its historical method, in spite of its great successor by E. T. Cook."[11]

Gershom continued to guard and sustain Ruskin's reputation long after the hero's death. But the household should not be imagined as living its life under Ruskin's shadow. For sure, when the children were old enough to make the walk to Brantwood and back, they were taken on visits or left to roam the wild gardens, for Ruskin loved to see children about him, however daunting his terrific beard and removed air were to them.

But their own house saw frequent visitors: the great Burne-Jones: A. W. Simpson, a Kendal furniture maker of an Arts and Crafts persuasion; admirers from University College, Liverpool, where Gershom had lectured on ornament; Thomas Ellwood, a local rector and philologist; Gershom's travelling companion from Iceland, Jon Stefansson; members of the Lake Artists Society of which Gershom became president; the numerous and active Viking Society (ditto);

and the dedicated amateurs of the Cumberland and Westmorland Antiquarian Society (which included Beatrix Potter Heelis) of which both father and son finally became presidents after many years as its moving spirits.

Gershom's prodigious energies never failed until the deadly lesions in the brain that his son inherited cut him down in the late 1920s and then paralysed him. As was necessarily the case, those energies had to be directed, along with his wife's no less signal efforts, to bringing in enough money to keep things plentiful where plenty rarely extended very many months ahead. Ruskin himself, the Vikings, the Antiquarians, and the Lake Artists all gave Gershom access to earnings, although his personal gusto for life, his charm and gentleness of manner, his invincible sense of duty committed him to a giving of himself far beyond what money he might make in return.

Typical of this zest was his voyage to Iceland in 1897, when his son was eight. That same son had recently, as he himself recalled in an astonishing revelation,

> been moved by curiosity to take down a little black book lettered on its spine "Kant's Theory of Ethics"; and as I began reading it, my small form wedged between the bookcase and the table, I was attacked by a strange succession of emotions. First came an intense excitement. I felt that things of the highest importance were being said about matters of the utmost urgency: things which at all costs I must understand. Then, with a wave of indignation, came the discovery that I could not understand them. Disgraceful to confess, here was a book whose words were English and whose sentences were grammatical but whose meanings baffled me. Then, third and last, came the strangest emotion of all. I felt that the contents of this book, although I could not understand it, were somehow my business: a matter personal to myself, or rather to some future self of my own. . . . I felt as if a veil had been lifted and my destiny revealed.[12]

This was the eight-year-old "Bobbin" to whom his father was writing in June and July of that year from Iceland, plainly but silently acknowledged by both parents as of rare genius. The happy, venturesome little boy was at the same time strikingly removed on occasions from the intent and boisterous family, pursuing thoughts that he could not yet clothe in words, but knowing them to be irresistible, thrilling also, summoning him from across a vast landscape of the mind to the long exploration at the end of which he would find them, the deep forests and dark hills would fall back, and he would be in a sunlit clearing and at peace.

II

Gershom had joined the local Archaeological Society in 1887 and instantly turned to the study of Roman and Nordic remains, subsequently publishing his *Scandinavian Britain*, the first such history, in 1908 and ultimately, copiously illustrated by his own hand, *Northumbrian Crosses of the Pre-Norman Age* in 1927.[13] Fired by his studies of the Norsemen's arrival in Cumbria (the Viking Society nicknamed him "the Skald," a Nordic bard or folk poet), he observed a correspondence between the politics of those early settlers and the tradition of North Country "statesman," that is, independent yeoman farmers, trading on equal terms with whomever turned up along the coast for peaceable exchanges, fierce and military in response to any unwanted irruption, absolutely refusing fealty to any of the many possessive barons and monarchs who tried to claim it. It was this same tough independence and courteous mutuality that Wordsworth celebrated in poems such as "The Old Cumberland Beggar," the section called "The Wanderer" in *The Excursion*, and made *Michael* one of Robin Collingwood's favourite poems.

The earliest incarnation of this local hero, the "statesman," was the origin of Gershom's most successful novel, *Thorstein of the Mere: A saga of the Northmen in Lakeland*, and it is not only its author's homage to the political tradition of his adopted locality, but also a careful historical reconstruction of the early settlement of Lakeland after the Roman Empire withdrew.[14] It is a plainly spoken, direct, and wholly dry-eyed novel, telling how young Thorstein, roaming north up the Crake from Greenodd on the estuary, finds the hidden mere Thorstein's Water, subsequently named after him, only later becoming Coniston. This is tenth-century Lakeland, and the hero lives in boyish rivalry with his older brothers, a pastoral but not unendangered idyll within the always trusted safety of his father's seagoing and his mothers's calm and beautiful provision.

As one would expect, the narrative manner is faithful as to dialect, teacherly as to the historical and geographical facts of husbandry, food, weather, and pathway. Gershom lingers over the details of artefacts he had drawn and loved well—the brooches, the door latches, the old carving knives—which would reappear at the heart of his son's theory of cultural suppression and resurrection. It is as if, looking down at the page, he sees something new or difficult, and looking up at his audience, he pauses in the story to explain it in a sentence or two and then resumes.

The pastoral splits open. There are raiders and abductions. Thorstein is kidnapped adventuring beside Thirlmere and forced to live as a serf with a harsh new master. Gershom describes straightly the filthy, reeking beehive huts he and his abductors inhabit. Thorstein falls in love with the daughter, "Raineach, that is Fern," escapes home, finds a bride, Raineach follows him, is lost, Thorstein marries the wrong, the right woman, Raineach returns, Thorstein, honour bound, kills his brother in mortal, rivalrous combat, goes on the run, is baptised in York, finds and marries Raineach in a tiny Christian ceremony, hides blissfully away with her on Peel islet in the middle of Coniston Water, has two children, builds a coracle exactly copied by Robin Collingwood a few years later. In the end he is killed while repelling soldiers, Raineach settles at the old homestead, and his people

> everywhere held to their old manners and their old speech, changing little of either, and that but slowly.
>
> For in these dales the dream of Unna came true, that saw love abiding and labour continuing, heedless of glory and fearless of death.

WG's novel is a little masterpiece, slightly awkward at times, pedagogic no doubt, but filled with that fine highmindedness, that realistic recognition of all it took to settle, defend, and perpetuate a hard way of life, that deep trust in family love and love of place as well as in an incipient democracy of the self-reliant, all of which shaped the politics and the historical vision of his son, the greatest English philosopher of such matters. *His* peers in the university thought it Collingwood's Tory picture of society; he himself called it "democratic" *tout court*; people at Oxford by 1938 thought he had become a communist, but what Robin Collingwood learned from his father was a reverence for Lakeland "statesmen," and his politics flowed from that.

Family life, however, is only political in a colloquial sense. What the son learned from both parents, as well as his artist-sisters with whom he painted in "the Mausoleum," crewed on the lake and picnicked on Peel Island, was how best to live the warm, welcoming, fully human, and richly varied life of a not too well-off, hardworking, and strenuously creative English middle-class family of that time, and in clearly derived forms, of the next century as well. Gershom's letters from Iceland express all this with great, inexplicit, and moving force. In a letter to Barbara, then ten years old, her father writes as he must have spoken to her, pitching his actual traveller's tale into the middle of her fanciful one as any fond parent still would, spotting the narrative with the painter's eye for colour which she shared, lining up Iceland and Cumbria side by side before turning to write punctually to "My darling Molly" and to his "dear father" in Bristol.

SS Laura—Klaksvig, Faero
June 8 1897
My duckie Bab,

This letter must be to you, being written from a fairy island quite as wonderful as Piwitee. Imagine (you can) a peeled walnut magnified into a range of mountains rather bigger than the Old Man—and set in a blue sea—so that all the crinkles and folds of the walnut are voes or long bays of the sea. In and out of them the steamer goes, winding about in streets as it were of mountains—with never a scrap of flat ground, nothing but basalt crags, grass slopes and sea water. And here and there in the ledges of the great peaked hills, near the shore are green spots, drained with lots of little dykes which are full of marshmarigolds, and rich with the greenest grass—and little brown wooden farmhouses with roofs of turf—and the grass growing green on them—so that the Silly could have fed her cow off it—and gardens with gooseberry and currantbushes—and heaps of primroses—and in the grass everywhere white daisies with never a blush of pink. And all the rest is moor—with ling and grey rocks like the back of Lang Crags, or anywhere above the tree level in our fells. At Thorshavn there were a few trees, small planes, planted in gardens, and evidently tended as we tend cactuses. But for the rest—never a tree or even a shrub; grass and ling everywhere—and rocks.

But the Piwitean part is the people and their doings.

The men are *the* real veritable actual *gnomes of fairy book. They are dressed exactly like dwarves; and if they were smaller they would be the creatures who have the house in the story of Snow White. Their houses are toy houses—and their town is a toy town, all little wooden houses— with grass on roofs—apparently pigstyes—up and down toy paths, very steep—all in rock just like Old Man hard and clear, daisies by the sides of the streets—which can't be bicycled or driven in, and—inside the houses, such jolly old quaint comfort—like the house described in Scott's "Pirate"—sort of cabins—good furniture and brass things and walls panelled and papered with exactly the patterns we should have liked for the Morningroom. The men wear blue breeches with lots of brass buttons at the knee—grey stockings and Iceland shoes with long laces tied round their ancles—sometimes clogs also or rather pattens and long wadmaal coats and jerseys and dwarfs caps all colours. The women have shawls over their heads and aprons of many colours.*[15]

"Bobbin, my boy" was sent details of a long ride, of birds, ptarmigans, lava and cave icicles, and his father enclosed for him verses for the August edition of *Nothing Much*. After sixteen letters, twenty-two paintings, and two hundred sketches, and a thousand miles by sea, pony, and on foot around Iceland,[16] he came back to a rare old homecoming.

The trip was exceptional but characteristic. WG returned to the same unslackening round of painting, writing, teaching, administering his societies, sailing, repairing his house. In what Robin described as his father's "finest piece of imaginative work," a new novel, *The Bondwomen*, he dealt, as he would, candidly but decorously with the historical fact that tenth-century bondswomen in the Lakeland would have had to render sexual as well as domestic services to their owners. The result, his son wrote, was

> such an outburst of obloquy for its immoral tendencies (it was the year after the same fate had befallen *Jude the Obscure*) that Collingwood never published another book except in the obscurity of a country printer's office where none but friends would see them, until, more than thirty years later, Messrs Faber and Gwyer published his great work on Northumbrian crosses.[17]

Ruskin died in 1900, after years of intermittent insanity punctuated by some of his noblest work in his autobiography, *Praeterita*. Gershom had taken Ruskin on a last holiday some years before, to Seascale on the Cumbrian coast, and thereafter had faithfully cherished the master and his reputation, published the biography, three volumes of very successful anthologies of Ruskin's writings, and an album of drawings, all without remuneration.[18] Now that he had done his duty, he was able to take up a chair of fine art at University College, Reading, with the result that for the first time there was a bit of money to spare. The family was able to take a small apartment in London just off the King's Road so that the two elder daughters could pursue their training in art (which both were to practise professionally, Dora for many years in Aleppo, Barbara a sculptor in London).

There was naturally no question of the family's leaving Lanehead for either Reading or London. The girls finished their studies at Cope's Studio, Gershom came home for every vacation. Before the new money could run to school fees, a nameless friend paid for Robin to attend Mr. Podmore's preparatory school in Grange-over-Sands. It had been concluded that since the boy was proving so formidably intelligent, he would have to learn the conventions of formal examinations suitable to his social class as well as to the extraordinary endowments of his mind. Gershom had done as much at the

Liverpool Collegiate Institute; Robin duly won a scholarship to Rugby School.

Perhaps the best and last of the tokens of this remarkable man, Gershom Collingwood's energy, vivacity, and loving kindness, is to be found in his guide *The Lake Counties*. It had many rivals, most famously Wordsworth's own *Guide to the Lakes*, in its fifth edition as early as 1838. But WG brought to the labour of love as well as a useful advance from a local publisher[19] unrivalled archaeological knowledge and a familiarity with the paths, climbs, and navigable waters to match his great predecessor's. He illustrated his own book with many little line drawings; he wrote, as always, plainly and precisely and without any Victorian afflatus. This is how he approaches his family's favourite refuge:

> and through Blawith and the picturesque hamlet of Wateryeat we reach the foot of Coniston lake, the view from which is one of the finest in the Lake District. The name of this lake in 1196 was Thorstanes Watter, in medieval Latin "Turstini Watra," evidently from some early owner with the Scandinavian name of Thorstein. Like Windermere, it is not one single rock-basin though the bar that breaks it into two deeps is not so apparent. The greatest basin is that which sinks to a depth of 184 feet a little above the rocky Peel Island, conspicuous from the waterfoot. On the right is the once wooded slope of Heald Brow: on the left is heathery Beacon Hill with Torver Moor beyond, and a background of peaks rising in a concert of tossed and tumbled breakers, varied in form but harmonious in the swing of their lines— Dow Crag, the Old Man, Wetherlam, Helvellyn, Fairfield. Down below "neuks and nabs" vary the shore, and beyond, the lake spreads into breadth with Peel Island, steep-sided and crowned with trees, "ornate and gay like some stately ship of Tarshish," lifted above the surface. When you come nearer, the resemblance to a ship of old times is increased by the little "calf-rock" like a boat in tow at its stern, joined to the main rock at low water by a narrow ridge, beside which there is a pretty little cove for harbour, and a well-blackened fire-spot where many a picnic kettle has boiled.[20]

Gershom and Dorrie, like all Lakelanders of the time, were of necessity prodigious walkers as well as sailors. The children learned to sail in *Swallow*, an old fishing boat, cumbersome to row, strong and slow under sail, in any case probably the best-known name of a small sailing boat in all the world. There was also, even heavier, "the tub" ("toob" in Cumbrian). After crossing to Peel Island's little harbour to boil up a kettle for tea and to spread marmalade on bun loaf, to roam the island, to swim and then to take advantage of the breeze darkening the water, it was hard to make it back home in time for supper; "becalmed off Brantwood" was the standard and accepted excuse.

III

One evening in the summer of 1903, a couple of months before Robin left home for Rugby, Gershom, who had been painting high on the slopes of the Old Man of Coniston, was walking back down beside the shouting waters of Copper Mines Beck, which tumbles in such a picturesque way into Levers Water by the Miners' bridge. To his horror he saw what he thought was a corpse washed up on a wide, flat rock between the torrents. When he called out, to his immense relief the corpse sat up and a lean and bespectacled nineteen-year-old with an incipient moustache introduced himself as "Arthur Ransome."[21]

He had, he said, been writing poetry, which his interlocutor seemed to think a sensible occupation, and he was much thrilled to discover that this stranger was author of *Thorstein of the Mere*, "the best-loved book of my boyhood." Ransome should know. The first of his children's books, *Swallows and Amazons*, was to become the best-loved book of a great many boyhoods and girlhoods also, in two dozen languages across the globe.[22] Although the novel was not to be written until 1932, its origins were rooted deep in that first meeting and the family friendships that grew from it.

Gershom invited Ransome to call at Lanehead, but Ransome had failed to acquire from his recently completed education at Rugby the class assurance the school assuredly was to teach young Collingwood. Out of deep-seated difficulties, he put off accepting the invitation until the last minute and then embarrassed himself utterly by interrupting a small dinner party attended by two of the innumerable honorary uncles and aunts appointed as such by Dorrie. And of course for Ransome also, "Mr and Mrs Collingwood were to become touchstones by whom to judge all other people that I met."[23]

Ransome had lost his father young. Gershom, "infinitely kind, infinitely encouraging,"[24] filled the gap. He and Dorrie melted Ransome's shyness and turned it into unselfconscious and happy devotion. When he returned to the Lakes the next year, as he had always done in the past with his brothers and sisters, WG appointed Dorrie "aunt" to Ransome and thereafter "those two gave me something I had not missed because I had not till then known that it could be. The whole of the rest of my life has been happier because of them."[25]

It is Ransome's account that makes it possible to fill in the picture of the Collingwood family life, to insist that it serves to us now as type and token of the best kind of English family life that the Victorian middle classes shaped for the emancipation of their children. It was braced by necessity, dignified by self-reliance, liberated by egalitarianism, ruled by justice and by trust. Ransome turned those abstractions, in the great children's novels, into images of aspiration and promises of happiness to subsequent generations a long way from the Lakes. But he caught and caused to live again not only the noble values but the geography and history that gave them their particular life. Gershom and Dorrie sprang strongly from the roots they had put down in what was not their home county. We all of us seek and most earnestly hope to find a place to love and be at home in. This was the lesson of Wordsworth and the Romantic movement, and Gershom and Dorrie taught it all their lives. Ransome learned the lesson from his full heart.

Collectively, as a family, they adopted me and I was delighted by each small happening that helped to make me feel that I was so adopted. I remember still my extreme pleasure the first time Mrs. Collingwood trusted me to go to the village to do an errand for her at Coward's, the grocer. I rowed across the lake and, just after I had left the hotel grounds and come out on the road, I passed a hawthorn tree that had shed its petals all about it, a patch of glittering snow on the dust. During all that time the leaves of the trees seemed more luminous than they are today and the hills had sharper edges. I would stand gaping at this or that as if I feared I should not remember it for ever. I need have had no such fear. On the lake or on the further side of it I used to look for the pale corner of the Lanehead house where it showed through the trees below the fell and tell myself that I could not really be one of that loved family. After meals we all helped in clearing away and I valued my right to share in this. My chair, after a meal was over, had its particular place against the wall, between the door and the sideboard, and many years later, when I came to Lanehead after long absence abroad, my aunt laughed as I got up from the table after dining there and without thinking pushed my chair back into the old place where it had stood in 1904.[26]

He became the family's elder brother. He learned from and shared with WG that common Victorian passion for folktales which was to be one thick thread in the tapestry of R. G. Collingwood's intellectual production. The boy, six years Ransome's junior ("those years shrank rapidly as he grew up")[27] became nonetheless his close friend and, naturally, his sailing instructor. Ransome's biographer, Hugh Brogan, is of the reasonable view that since Ransome never mentions sailing until he joins the Collingwood family, they must have taught him, and Robin was the best, the most intrepid sailor in that sailor family. Their boat *Swallow* gave its name both to his heroine craft and to the children who sailed it. When Ransome met another Lakeland family, also very close to the Collingwoods, and wrote *Swallows and Amazons* for and about them, he found that the story needed an elder brother, calm, authoritative, resourceful. In Ransome's masterpiece, *We Didn't Mean to Go to Sea*, the elder brother, John Walker, drags his anchor in a fog, is swept to sea in a borrowed yacht with his brother and two sisters, is dreadfully afraid, and, learning and mistaking all the way, brings his family bravely to safe harbour in Flushing. I do not doubt that when Ransome needed a model for such a boy, he drew on the unphilosophical but central characteristics of the boy he had known best for thirty years.

Ransome joined joyfully in the Collingwoods' storytelling. His gifts ran that way, Gershom encouraged him to believe he could become a man of letters, he loved folktales, and Dora remembered her mother's retelling one of Arthur's favourites:

> One of the stories was about a witch who put a spell on Anansi, so that if he said the word five he would drop down dead. His enemy made five piles of yams by the side of the road, and then lay in wait for him. Along came Anansi. "Please Anansi will you count these piles of yams for me, I am so blind I cannot see." Anansi was so small that he had to climb on to one of the piles. He began counting, "One, two, three, four ... *and* the one I'm sitting on." "No! no! that is not the way," but he went on, over and over again, till the witch was trembling with rage, but he never said "five." My mother, counting washing for the laundry, or dealing out fruit to us at lunch, would say "One two three four ..." "AND the one I'm sitting on," we would chant in chorus.[28]

Living in so dependable a whirl of happiness, in love with the whole family, it was inevitable that Ransome should wish to make himself even more a part of it by falling in love with Barbara to whom he called up, as she teased him while leaning on the sill of an upstairs window at Lanehead, "talking to you is like eating a strawberry ice." Barbara, as self-possessed as well as being as open to life as the rest of them, deliberated and turned him down. Ransome gloried in the full house, and so did all who dwelled there. He stayed in Robin's bedroom for the first summer term that its occupant was at boarding school, and between the incomparable safety of the embryo archaeologist's bedroom, sailing, Beethoven at breakfast, and these vigorous, plain-spoken, spontaneous, and cultivated girls, Ransome found, as Robin did, the composition of the good life all artists and thinkers must keep alive in their imaginations.

Ransome owed much of his greatness as a writer to what he learned from the Collingwoods. But all those who saw the life at Lanehead bore witness to its qualities. In the first sentence of *Anna*

Karenina, Tolstoy famously wrote that life in all happy families is much the same, but that was only his pretext to writing about a divided one. Happy families are as various as unhappy ones, and the Collingwoods were happy in a way peculiarly conducive to the making of a philosopher. The greatest philosophers, it might be added, are those for whom the crux of thought is the making out and making up of the principles that at once direct and *constitute* a life. The human constitution is a powerful phrase and connotes not only the rules that order the body politic, connect its members, and control its heartbeat, but also the codes that compel its very shape and are immanent in its forms of life.

So it was that to have two painter parents, one a fine pianist as well, the other novelist, antiquarian, palaeographer, classicist, "skald," and practical man as well as professional landscapist, was to be well blessed for Collingwood's vocation. Add to that a household with two elder sisters and one younger (always better in a too-masculine world to observe the authority of an elder sister) all situated in the loveliest Romantic landscape in England, redolent of that fine, instructive local democracy which bore up, fought off, and simply ignored assorted tyrants for a thousand years,[29] gather up all this and the deposits of experience are laid down in rich veins to be mined as future intellectual energy. This is the making of a thinker and, as it happens, the stuff of the art of biography.

Out of such a house, settled in a homeland, one could contrive a theory of the good life and a politics for a civilisation and its art. This was both Collingwood's vocation and his good fortune. The life of Lanehead was like that of the ideal university as John Henry Newman conceived it in Dublin in 1852. Its purpose and its function, that is, was not

> to result in nothing better or higher than in the production of that antiquated variety of human nature and remnant of feudalism . . . called "a gentleman," rather its first and chief and direct object was . . . some benefit or other, to accrue, by means of literature and science, to [its] own children; not indeed their formation on any narrow or

fantastic type as, for instance, that of an "English gentleman," but their exercise and growth in certain habits, moral and intellectual.[30]

Such habits were what Collingwood himself found enacted in the paintings by his parents stacked against the walls of his home. They were "a visible record of an attempt to solve a definite problem," and they took their place in a thronged household in which the conversation was not disputatious but more a reporting of what the interlocutors were about, what were the questions and problems upon which they were deliberating. This *conversazione* was joined by all the family, naturally, and by all the visitors, about whom it was naturally assumed that they too were addressing not the great mysteries (whatever *they* may be) but particular and more or less piercing questions alive in the present moment. Arthur Ransome was only the most visible as well as the most admiring of this throng. Behind him stand "Uncle Will" Carton, Icelander-philologists Stefansson and Eirik Magnusson, rector-antiquarians Calverley and Ellwood of Turner, master painter Edward Burne-Jones, legal scholar Alfred Willink, his wife Beatrice, a painter, and son Henry (later master of Magdalene College Cambridge), carver and Quaker Simpson, writers Helen Viljoen and Evelyn Underhill, farmer Stalker, engineer Herbert Severn, youngest of the family who took over the care of Ruskin and Brantwood, William Collingwood, painter and grandfather—all these people and many others still to be called came to the Collingwoods' house in the summer.

IV

At the very beginning of the long journey that one hopes will lead to a completed biography of R. G. Collingwood, one meets and is stopped by the stern and formidable figure of the subject himself. For during the long and recuperative sea voyage to Indonesia that he took at the end of 1938 and the beginning of 1939, he set himself certain prodigious tasks of writing and, in a letter to his son Bill, then at Balliol, suggested that the new book, to be entitled *The Principles of History*, of which he was to write 40,000 words on the voyage, would one day be considered his "masterpiece."

The work issued from a torrent of composition in 1938 and 1939, but it was in *The Principles of History* that Collingwood's frequently sardonic impatience surfaced on the very topic of biography in history.

> The biographer . . . includes in his subject a good deal which does not belong to the object of any historical study whatever. He includes some events which embody no thought on the part of his subject, and others which do no doubt embody thought, but are included not because they embody thought but because they have an interest, or what is better perhaps called an appeal, of a different kind.
>
> The biographer's choice of his materials, though it may be (and ought to be) controlled by other considerations, is determined in the first instance by what I will call their gossip-value. The name is chosen in no derogatory spirit. Human beings, like other animals, take an interest in each other's affairs which has its roots in various parts of their animal nature, sexual, gregarious, aggressive, acquisitive, and so forth. They take a sympathetic pleasure in thinking that desires in their fellow-creatures that spring from these sources are being satisfied, and a malicious pleasure in thinking that they are being thwarted. Biography, though it often uses motives of an historical kind by way of embroidery, is in essence a web woven of these two groups of threads, sympathy and malice. Its function is to arouse these feelings in the reader; essentially therefore it is a device for stimulating emotion, and accordingly it falls into the two main divisions of amusement-biography, which is what the circulating libraries so extensively deal in, and magical biography, or the biography of exhortation and moral-pointing, holding up good examples to be followed or bad ones to be eschewed.[31]

If all this is not written "in a derogatory spirit," one would not like to be Collingwood's victim of a passage which was. The biographer's riposte to the antibiographer must be, no doubt, the biography itself, as work of art and work of history. But there is inexplicable bad faith in the passage as well. Quite apart from the existence of such great works of history and art as Boswell's *Life of Johnson* or John Forster's *Life of Charles Dickens*, both of which Collingwood certainly knew, and his father's biography of Ruskin, which he certainly revered, there is the special category of biography to which he made his own utterly distinctive and compelling contribution in *An Autobiography*. For sure, he says there that "the autobiography of a man whose business is thinking should be the story of his thought,"[32] but it is one of Collingwood's most signal contributions to the "science of human affairs," so urgently needed when he invented the designation and even more urgently now, to show not just the mutual inextricability of thought and feeling, but their *identity* also. Calm of mind is a feeling; all passion's being spent may be the best condition for the exercise of reason, but it is not an emotionless state. It is merely, as we shall learn from that undoubted masterpiece, *The Principles of Art*, that state of mind in which comprehensive feeling permits clear judgement. Avoiding any theological distraction, one might say that such is the moment of poise at which objectivity and loving-kindness become synonyms, the point at which sympathy dissolves into historical understanding.

So there is something irascible and wrong when Collingwood follows up his strictures by asserting so baldly a little later, "Even when we sympathise with rational animals over matters connected with their rationality, it is not their rationality with which we sympathise but only the feelings in which their pursuit of rational ends has involved them."[33] Well! This is too brisk. It fixes the biographer at the early stage of moral sympathy and arbitrarily cuts him or her off from historical understanding. But the natural movement of sympathy is to try and overcome the incomprehension of (in Collingwood's unendearing example) the baffled wife sympathising with her scientist husband, himself baffled by a scientific problem, she being (naturally) unable to follow the science. The natural extension of this block is for each to try to plumb the difficulty, to replace defeat and dejection by exposition and further thought which, even if it does not result in enlightenment, may well change despondency into resolution.

By this stage, however, there is no stopping Collingwood's crotchet. Off he goes again.

> Now because sympathy and its negative counterpart malice are the strings on which a biographer plays . . . he must depict a definite and recognisable person, and emphasise the animal side of this person's existence. He must remind the reader that his subject was born and died, suffered diseases and recovered from them . . . desired certain women and succeeded or failed in his attempts to win them. . . . And because it will help the reader to individualise him, the biographer will be wise to include a portrait of him, or several portraits; a photograph of his house; and so on.[34]

No explanation is given for the biographical airs being confined to two strings, nor is the pleonasm acknowledged about biography's needing to individualise its subject, as though biography could fail to do this and still be biographical. The feeling grows, especially as Collingwood's always high high-spiritedness mounts, that he is warning people off writing *his* biography, especially when he comes to the topics of illness and womenfolk, and most of all when he concludes, quite without an argument or evidence to support him, that not only is all biography "scissors-and-paste history," that kind of history it was at the centre of his life's work to fight against, but also, no less inexcusably, that it depends for its attraction on snobbery, as deluding its readers that they are really students of history.

Even Collingwood's admiring editors of *The Principles* recoil a bit at this point and suggest that the *Autobiography* is not without what he here disdains as "exhortation and moral-pointing." Indeed, such exhortation, expressed in some of the most pungent and powerful commentary on moral and political affairs to be found in English in the whole century, is the very heart of the book and its incontestable purpose.

The rebuttal of Collingwood's animadversions upon the genre of biography is, however, more than a matter of this biographer's needful self-defence. It is the defence of an intrinsically historical form. Certainly there are any number of scissors-and-paste biographies, as there are quantities of such histories of thought or of irrationality or of art or science. Yet biography is so obviously the readiest and most intelligible way with which to capture something of significance in historical movement. This may of course be done either briefly or profoundly, or both. That is to say, a biographical subject offers itself to us as somehow significant. Following the precepts of Collingwood's methods as we shall discover them over these pages, the historical significance of a life reveals itself as, reenacting (the key verb in the business) the conduct of that life by way of the thoughts, passions, and beliefs made manifest in its actions, the biographer-historian situates the subject in as carefully reconstructed a context as he or she may contrive. Action, as we can see even beside Coniston Water, only means what it does in a context; human intention is expressible within the meanings convention lends it (including of course flouting the convention). Placing an interpreted life in a detailed and accurate context simply *is* to discover its significance. Such a significance may be modest enough as it is here at hand, or even, for instance, in so fine a recent biography as, say, Claire Tomalin's *Samuel Pepys*,[35] but it restores life to that greedy egotist and his unstoppable observation of seventeenth-century London. Doing so, it contributes its mite to the social history of the moral imagination. It brings off this little miracle of resurrection by providing a lens through which we see a different life from a strange epoch. The magic touch must be to make us see that familiar estrangement.

This is the common endeavour of the interpretative sciences, whose queen is history.[36] On this argument biography, well practised, is a thoroughgoingly historical form, essential to the discipline and source of wisdom to a people.

A biographical figure may surely be commended to us as a guide to conduct. Hagiography has a long reading list, let alone an even longer liturgical canon, and is not so very discredited by historical revelation. But to take our very own topic, and to biographise an always specialist scholar, one whose name is little known nowadays outside the academy and the archaeological dig, is naturally to invite the questions, "who was he?" and "why bother?"

The answer is then not to say, or at least not to say *tout court* (my admiration for him is intended to be plain and generous), "He lived well. Be like him." It is much more a matter of fixing and, in the writing, dramatising a tradition to which this individual belonged. Everybody seeks to do this—that is what "identity" means, even when used in cant. Not everybody can find a tradition, and some traditions are not worth belonging to.

There have been various efforts since the Romantic movement to dislodge the idea of a tradition. Nietzsche was one such explosive engineer, and in assaulting Christianity's "tyranny," its "denial of life," shook off tradition in the name of the "will to power," the "work," "whether of the artist or philosopher, [which] invents the person who has created it."[37] Half a century later, Jean-Paul Sartre sought to smash through the moral tradition that he came to see as utterly poisoned by Fascism armed only with the existential self, freely choosing but only free in the exercise of its own "good faith."[38]

There remain innumerable tradition-dissolvers, Marxism and managerialism among them, but in the nature of things sheer longevity turns dissolvers into traditionalists. This biography therefore stands in a tradition. It is the tradition of good lives, inaugurated by Aristotle, amplified by Aquinas, liberated from Christianity and given the doctrine of the "civil affections" by David Hume and Adam Smith. Our tradition is rooted deep in its own history by Hegel as being the only foundation it could possibly justify, and thereafter domesticated by the British tradition that made Hegel tolerable and culminates (for our purposes) in R. G. Collingwood.

This tradition teaches that a good life may be lived only in terms of those virtues which an individual truly possesses and is capable of. The trouble with the word "tradition" is that it has, damnably, been so monopolised by the political Right, which contrasts the stability of tradition with the crazy enthusiasms of revolutionary struggle. But a moral tradition is no less than the embodiment through time and in a place of those principles which permit that version of a good life to be lived, revised, challenged, and transformed in the biographies of the traditionalists.

On this definition, as Alasdair MacIntyre (a leading present advocate of Collingwoodian ethics) says,

A living tradition then is an historically extended, socially embedded *argument* and an argument precisely in part about the goods which constitute that tradition . . . the virtues find their point and purpose not only in sustaining those relationships necessary if the variety of goods internal to practices are to be achieved and not only in sustaining the form of an individual life in which that individual may seek out his or her good as the good of his or her whole life, but also in sustaining those traditions which provide both practices and individual lives with their necessary historical context . . . *an adequate sense of tradition manifests itself in a grasp of those future possibilities which the past has made available to the present.*[39] (italics added)

V

It won't therefore do to allow Collingwood himself to dismiss biography as moral exhortation, nor will it do to allow Nietzsche to get away with saying that the work invents the person. He may be right to complain that "the great," as they are venerated, are "subsequent pieces of wretched minor fiction" (not so very minor, some of them, either), but for each life, major or minor, the "work" is what constitutes it and is created by it.

A life's work is only to be found in books for those people who write them. The life and works of a nurse, a university administrator, a truck driver, a television camera operator, a policewoman, a soldier are assembled by time and chance and insofar as each character is capable of making such a thing into as decent, upright, and truthful a narrative as may seem credible. On this showing the practices that fill a life and that normally include the domestic contents parallel to a job—friends, spouse, parents, in Blake's words "the price of experience, all that a man hath, his house, his wife, his children"— are a life's work *in the same way* as are the philosopher's thoughts and books.

The story of a thinker's thought is then indistinguishable from the story of his life. The intensity of pleasure and absorption that Collingwood found in sailing, first on Coniston, later across the

English Channel, were intrinsic to the disciplines of his thought. His moral admonitions to his students as well as the generous recognition he gave them—which any teacher should give to his or her students as they advance towards their status as the next generation—are grounded in the unity of his theory and his experience.

Collingwood refused all his life to concede what a certain kind of liberal too comfortably claims about the moral life,[40] and that is that the fact of there being incompatible values and rival conceptions of the good life means that there can be no *one* such determinate picture of living well. But "what this contention is blind to is that there are better or worse ways for individuals to live through the tragic confrontation of good with good."[41]

A biography that has thrown away its scissors and paste is thereby committed to the reconstruction of the actions and eventualities that *were* the subject's living through the tragic (and comic) confrontation of good with good. There are consequently two grand themes to any serious and historically minded biography, and these call for the orchestration of more major chords in the human mind than Collingwood's thin restriction to "sympathy and malice."

The first such theme is, I suppose, the subject's representativeness. Each of us finds, as best we can, a way of living made available by time and chance, by culture and convention, which we match to our gifts and opportunities. This isn't really a matter of choice; we speak of choosing a career, but the choice is hemmed in by history, geography, social class, and local accident, until the best we can do (and it *is* the best) is find a way of life that seems to answer to certain imperious predispositions in our souls. Of course, it is very rare for these to match perfectly, or even well. But that remains the compelling hope directing our biggest decisions—what to study at school, whom or whether to marry, whom to befriend, where to live, what to do for a living, how to be happy, whether to be good.

The shape of possible answers to these questions may be glimpsed in the singularity of this or that representative of a social type. Our hero, Robin Collingwood, typified a complex and variegated character out of the drama of English history. First and foremost, no doubt, he was a *thinker*, and the ambitions and achievements of that thought compose the second theme of his life's music. But he also lived with rare dedication and fullness the life of the man brought up as he was by such a father and mother, such amazing and devoted sisters, shaped by a particularly beautiful landscape, skilled in a dozen arts and crafts—fiddling, drawing, sailing, studying, handicraft, carpentry, bookbinding, beekeeping, singing, modelling, archaeologising. All these forces were then to be gathered across the fifty stormiest years of European history into the complex avocation of scholar, intellectual, sportsman, artist, teacher, Oxford gentleman, and democrat, parent and lover, free "statesman" and patriot.

You cannot make a man from a list. But you can imaginatively spin these threads of a life together until they are strong enough to draw a later generation into its own versions of these figures. Evaluations of the British culture of the twentieth century are much thinned out at present by moral hypochondria and sanctimonious recrimination towards both past and present: about certain things ill done in empire and other things done to harm our native poor, our ill-treated Celtic liminals and derelict estuaries. Not much is said in praise of *anything*.

This book is conceived as a minor riposte to this chorus. It attempts a dramatisation of a certain kind of Englishman, his courage and colourfulness, his "spots of commonness" (in George Eliot's phrase), the tragedy of his failure, the comedy of his vision.

These last two terms modulate into our second theme. For Robin Collingwood indeed had a vision and, desperate as he was to fulfil it, failed to create either the speech or the time to bring his vision to realisation. He sought to discover the unity of a life in the multiplicity of its absorbing and creative practices, and to communicate the needfulness of such a unity to a sufficient audience and in the happy names of goodness and meaning. He wanted more. This oneness of action and vision (of practice and theory) could only be achieved, in a single mind, or in a whole society, that won its emancipation, and hence secular redemption, by a knowledge of itself as wrung from its history.

Such was the road to salvation. Collingwood's life, embodying his thought, had as its guiding purpose the discovery and invention of the freedom to be won by the supercession of instrumental science and the coming-to-maturity of a shared and radically historical self-awareness. This was the single end towards which he directed his extraordinary talents and his powers of dedication.

He failed. But he was not defeated. He failed because he could not break up the abstractions of a too-heavy philosophical language and rebuild them as a homely house for the habitation of a free people. And yet, in his work, and especially in his last quartet of great books, as well as in the style of his living, he met Nietzsche's test, in an observation of his to which we shall return, of "style" of character as being that unification of "necessity and freedom of will" such that "strength and weakness fit into the plan of artistry." Such and such are the meanings of his life—in an American's phrase, "now and in England."[42]

For all his great gift for happiness, Collingwood is a tragic hero. It was surely his own discovery of the absoluteness of historically contrived presuppositions that, really, in his own phrase, "broke up his pose of the detached thinker." Once that was done, he appears for us as the inheritor of certain powerful traditions in European thought and the English character. Taking on that complex, contradictory inheritance of the roles I have already called—scholar-genius, sportsman, intellectual, Lakelander-"statesman," gentlemanly Oxonian, public professor, local figure, lover, parent, sailor, mortal invalid, and a dozen more—he battles to integrate these in as well a lived story of a life as such a character could tell between 1889 and 1943. Insofar as his story is well told in these pages, the sympathetic reader is better able to grasp certain aspects of those momentous and world-historical years. Doing so, that same reader is also better able to see the looming future for what it will bring. He or she, that is, will then see and feel how certain key threads of narrative in the tapestry of a national tradition were taken up, recoloured, and extended by this one man's life. Sixty-odd years after his death, he joins us to the best of our Anglo-Victorian past and shows how it was transmuted into something of the best parts of contemporary life. Showing us these things, linking us to the resolution and independence of which this Lakelander intellectual was capable in the midst

of those terrible wars and delusive politics, there need be no exhortation to follow such an example; you couldn't even if you wanted to.
He offers a lead, that's all. Without that leadership, certain vitalising
continuities might be sundered and lost. This biography is a reminder of those, a way of picking them up before they vanish. No
one can copy this man's life; but you can ask what he would have
made of yours, and translate his words into your own.

That latter-day Collingwoodian, Alasdair MacIntyre, everywhere
present in these pages, proposed a difference between "that well-
established genre, the biography of philosophers, and that yet-to-be-
established genre, the history of philosophers." This book, unmistakably a biography, is nonetheless an effort to blend the two, and turn
biography into history, thereby confounding our great original's polemic. As was not infrequently the case, he was giving a bit too much
rope to his large talent for irascibility with the intellectual degrada-
tion everywhere visible, and in doing so not only belittled his own
Autobiography, but ignored the fact of his life's best endeavour, which
was to provide a moral theory of experience. For as MacIntyre goes
on, "authors and readers of such biographies and such yet to be
written histories would do well to attend to the relationship in the
life of each philosopher between her or his mode of philosophical
speech and writing and her or his attitude towards questions about
the ends of life."[43]

2

Brought Up by Hand: The Moral Point of English Public Schools

On the third Friday of September 1903, the Collingwood family assembled at seven in the morning on the platform at Coniston station to see Robin, now fourteen and a half, off on the 7:35 for his first term at Rugby School.

He was a stocky lad, not tall, with a distant gaze, sharp, pronounced nose, clear features mounted on high cheekbones, thick black hair, irresistible slow smile. In later years, after acquiring for public use what Arthur Ransome later called his "steel blue and polished manner,"[1] those same features blurred a little as a result of the medical prescriptions he had to take, while in his thirties he assumed a rather bank-managerial moustache and brilliantined hair. But to Rugby School he took the frank and cheerful manner, the quick observation and chased lineaments, the strong, capable hands that were his family inheritance. The station was familiar enough: the family saw father or mother off to Iceland, to Ireland, to Liverpool, to London, to France. They left from there to work in London themselves at the Art College, to see Grandfather Collingwood in Bristol and to go to his dentist, to sally off on such painting and palaeontological expeditions as could be afforded. This time, however, a thirteen-week separation impended, and it would no doubt prove hard to keep voices steady and eyes dry as the little local train chugged out of Coniston the few miles to Foxfield for the first change. Then London and North-Western Railway to Barrow-in-Furness, another shortish ride, Barrow to Carnforth, and then the London–Carlisle express via Wolverhampton and Birmingham, grandest city on the route, pause at New Street Station, before the last thirty-five miles, arriving at 2:14 p.m. at the great marshalling yards around Rugby junction.

Once piled out at the final station, the boys each supervised the safe unloading of their trunks and luggage (shirts, suits, starched collars, pyjamas, handkerchiefs, football gear, all regulation and enough to last three months by way of the weekly laundry). Then Collingwood joined those trooping into number 10 Hillmorton Road, the boarding house under the rule of Walter Noel Wilson, a scientist and mathematician with, inevitably, first-class honours from Oxford on his record.

Collingwood recollected Rugby at its most vivid in terms of "the pigsty conditions of our daily life and the smell of filth constantly in our nostrils." For a fastidious boy brought up in a home in which his mother kept the doors and windows open to the winds scouring the fells to the west, the enforced propinquity of forty-odd other boys would at first have been the torment that all "total institutions"[2]— prisons, asylums, military camps, monasteries, ruling class schools— impose upon their inmates. Later, no doubt, he got as used to these things as people do, and later in any case such schools conferred modest privileges of private space and time upon their senior members, by then enlisted as themselves custodians, magistrates, and executioners of their juniors. But to begin with, the jostling urinals with their streaming marble walls and open gutters, the row of doorless cubicles that housed the water closets (installed in Wilson's House only a short time before) and served as a kind of unofficial agora for the boys' scatological raucousness, must fairly have underlined those descriptions in the sixth and seventh canons of Dante's *Inferno* of the reek and slimy deposits of sewage and sex as Collingwood taught himself to read them four years later.

Collingwood bitterly deprecated "the living by a timetable expressly devised to fill up the day with scraps and snippets of information in such a manner that no one could get down to a job of work . . . and, in particular, devised to prevent one from doing that "thinking" in which, long ago, I had recognised my own vocation."[3] The sociology of this entire and tightly closed cultural system was, however, hardly "devised" to prevent searching thought or to ensure staccato minds. On the contrary, it was a system inaugurated by a clutch of convinced and compelling headmasters—Thomas Arnold first of all, at Rugby between 1828 and 1841 during which time he became nationally renowned, and, following his example, Percival at Clifton, Thring at Uppingham, Sanderson at Oundle, and from 1895 Herbert James at Rugby. These men, and a battalion of schoolmasters trained on the staff at Rugby and later fanning out across the country as headmasters of a series of this historically unprecedented kind of school, composed a new social and intellectual class.

Thomas Arnold deliberately invented a school intent not merely to make classical scholars of a few pupils and, for the rest, ruling-class leaders passingly familiar with Thucydides and Tacitus.[4] Arnold sought to inscribe the principles of a pious and clean-limbed, "muscular" Christian, of a cultivated Englishman always respectful of scholarly effort in others, in each and every one of the boys. He set the pattern for the extraordinary efflorescence of the public schools that blossomed all over the southern half of England after Arnold showed them how. They were "public" because they were not sealed off by the most senior of the ruling class as were the handful that preceded these innovations—Eton, Harrow, Winchester, and pre-Arnoldian Rugby itself. They were open to talent and money, and the newish mercantile class and the old small landowners rushed to populate them with their sons. Their fortunes had been jointly made by the colossal rise in land values towards the end of the eighteenth century,[5] and by the rapid invention of both industrial process and leisure consumerism at the heart of the amazing new cities—Leeds, Birmingham, Manchester, Norwich, Newcastle; the new kind of school would make gentlemen of their sons and, eventually, ladies of their daughters.

Rugby School straddled the gap in class-conscious Britain between old power and new money, and it did so in the name of both intellectual achievement and what a later sociologist of these motions was to name "the civilising process."[6] By this he meant, with all the irony at his disposal, the smoothing out of rough manners and dispositions, the restraining of ruling-class tendencies to get plastered and throw the pots about, the acquisition of dark suits, and the bottling up of the passions, the reflex assumption of what Collingwood himself saw at Rugby as "that pose of boredom towards learning and everything connected with it which is notoriously part of the public school man's character,"[7] as well as, correspondingly, the absurd overvaluation of the games, during which emotional licence and physical abandon were positively encouraged by the rules.

Learning to be this kind of person at Rugby in 1903 took all day, and no wonder a child with Collingwood's upbringing chafed at it. At the very beginning of his time, boys had lessons before breakfast at seven o'clock until the reforming head, Herbert James "the Bodger," eased these and other rigours in the name of emancipation, to the outrage of old stagers. All the same, the days were minutely specified for each of the aspects of the civilising process: for religion, house prayers once a day plus compulsory chapel every morning, Matins and Evensong on Sundays naturally, "divinity" a required subject in the curriculum; for formal study, four one-hour lessons in the morning, two forty-five-minute lessons in the afternoon, two hours of compulsory "prep"—that is, tasks of preparation or recapitulation set by the teachers for subsequent evaluation and re-testing. Science was taken seriously, but the ancient classics dominated absolutely: all boys wrote out a Greek and Latin prose or verse translation and a composition every week, just as those who studied classics at Oxford or Cambridge would weekly do when they became undergraduates.

Sporting lives revolved essentially around the seasonal team games: eponymous rugby, so-called because it was first devised at Rugby, in winter, with athletics added in the frosts of March, and cricket in the summer. The team games were the hothouse environment of important cultural intensities in the school—team and school "spirit," loyalty to the school's victories, and sanctification of its history of achievement by way of commemorative plaques; above all, the visible symbolisation of distinction in the ways of tasselled caps, florid blazers, ties, and scarves, and peculiar permissions such as walking on holy sporting turf forbidden to the masses.

God, sport, study: these were intertwined in the texture of every day and pressed like the atmosphere itself upon the bodies and minds of every little soul who arrived all strange and shy at the black, gaunt railway. This is culture at its most fierce and penetrative, and it is no surprise that the great anthropologist Sir Edward Evan Evans-Pritchard saw in the 1930s such a close resemblance between these customs and the ancestor worship, patriliny, slavery, endogamy, and so forth in the remote African tribes he studied.

The very geography of the school and its magnificent aesthetics enforce tribal self-awareness. The Close, a wide, empty field, is held in by very tall, cast-iron railings. This is the playing field (Old and New Bigsides) on which the tribe-defining rituals of sport are enacted against rival schools. At the north end, marking like fortresses the mutual boundary of school and town, stand the awful, historic, and beautiful offices of state: chapel, Old Quad, Headmaster's House, and the senior boarding house, School House. They offer a compact medley of English architectural styles, pivoting on the same small, windless, and domestic courtyards that make the two great universities so homely, dominated by the beauty of the red and white brick of the Victorian Gothic chapel, which grew organically from first beginnings in 1820 by way of transepts added in 1850 until the mighty Butterfield began his transformations in 1872, not finished until 1898.[8] Ruskin's study, *The Seven Lamps of Architecture*, was in its third edition by 1880, and the combination of bold massing and domestic brick at the north end of Rugby Close meets all his demands that architecture, the supreme public art, be lit by the lamps of truth, beauty, life; sacrifice, power, memory, and obedience.

This was the stage on which the universal dovetailedness of school life was enacted. It was, I suppose, a kind of Panopticon, in which the minutest detail of a boy's life was under surveillance. Collingwood himself approved of such ceremonies of subordination as "fagging," the use of the smallest members of the school by prefects to act as servants in trifling duties—polishing shoes, making toast. Such relations served to dramatise the structures of seniority, authority, and achievement, all of which shaped the central character of class leadership in England, Britain, and its vast empire.

Collingwood says nothing about the systems of punishment, especially the beating with a cane of junior offenders by more senior boys, although as a prefect of long standing he performed such floggings himself. Nor does he touch upon that other infamous aspect of public school life, its dreadful food. A near-contemporary wrote home complaining that he "went into what *they* called supper i.e. a hunc of stale bread, a piece of cold meat and a cup of miserable tea. . . . [Breakfast was] vile porridge, bad tea and huncs of bread and butter with dried haddock."[9] All the same, the lad went bravely on, "now I am not a bit homesick, in fact I am awfully happy here."

There must be a slightly forced note in that last sentence, and homesickness remained a fearful affliction for thousands of boys from happy, well-off homes in the first sixty years of the twentieth century, before boarding schools relaxed their regime and allowed easier transits between home and school, parents and teachers, in and out. In 1903 "crybaby," "mother's boy," "cissy" were the small change of fourteen-year-old abuse, bullying no longer on the scale of Tom Brown's enemy Flashman or Kipling's thug Sefton, but amply practised,[10] and a boy of Collingwood's natural independence, maturity, and scorn towards merely childish nastiness could not escape herd malignance, nor one of his sunny upbringing escape clenched tears leaking into his pillow.

He was, however, gifted with all the talents, until a wretched accident removed the one that would have commanded immediate respect from the other boys. Towards the end of his first term, he suffered an injury to his knee while playing rugby, which the surgery of those days rendered incurable. The injury, a familiar one on the football field, was to the cartilage. Removing some of it made torsion of the knee, and therefore easy running, impossible.

Injury of that sort was in such a school a liberation. Collingwood could still bicycle with little trouble, he was excused compulsory games, he became his own educator. It should be said at this point that Collingwood is guilty of bad faith in his own account of his schooldays. Sure enough, such schools—*all* schools—cut knowledge into scraps, employ sometimes boring teachers, are liable to administrative incompetence. But the Rugby School of his day had on its staff at any time a dozen or more masters with first-class honours from Oxford or Cambridge.[11] All boys were encouraged to "read round" their subject. We are impressed by Collingwood's uncomprehendingly reading Kant when eight; his schoolfellow, William Temple, later archbishop of Canterbury, was doing so at sixteen. The headmaster, Dr. James, mentioned a scientist pupil who taught himself Sanskrit; Geoffrey Keynes, a contemporary and later a remarkable combination of surgeon, naval hero, and celebrated literary bibliographer, appears in the records as giving a monograph-length duo of lectures with extensive photographs on a "Late Roman settlement near Somersham, Hunts." This was in 1905 to the Architectural and Archaeological Society, and the future author of the *Oxford History: Roman Britain and the English Settlements* was in the audience.

These trifling instances stand for something fine and permanent in the education given to its boys by a handful of notable schools for a century or so. (The girls' history is also a history of struggle against men, and therefore very different.) Intellectual life in Britain would have been a much frailer thing without it, and indeed many of those figures who later did much for more general emancipation and on behalf of egalitarian principles that throve in the unofficial off-duty culture of these schools acquired the principles of argumentative opposition and rational dissent from the thick, enclosed, contradictory texture of Rugby School and its imitators. After all, Collingwood was just preceded at the school by R. H. Tawney, secular saint of the British Labour Party, saw and heard the dazzling contributions made to the school's literary life by its brilliant boy-poet, Rupert Brooke, let alone Arthur Waley, the first Englishman to translate classical Chinese poetry; he was a couple of years ahead of Arthur Bliss, all-English composer and later master of the Queen's Musick, shared desks in the Upper Bench with a dozen future bishops and generals and fellows of university colleges.

Collingwood in his strictures on the school is not quite straight about the way in which its culture allowed such a variety of plants to grow. Of course the plants had a uniform look, of course they were products of unmistakable class privilege and certainty—the arrogance of manner he shared with them was taught as inseparable from a proper sense of the school's standing and its social purpose. Nor were these privileges without their ultimate duties. Of the 2,250 boys admitted to the school while Dr. James was head, 450 were killed in action between 1914 and 1918. The cultural, political, aesthetic, and scientific variety of the place took much of its kaleido-scopic colour and patterning from the life of the societies that both mirrored and gave a lead to the same multitudinous, private-communal life of societies in the society at large. Natural historians (divided into lepidopterists, botanists, entomologists, each with their own section), straight historians (archaeologists, medievalists, and architectural historians, particularly of local parish churches), clima-tologists (450 boys attended a lecture on "The History of a Storm" in November 1906), philatelists, photographers, water colourists, naturally, all are, as they say, on the record of this teeming variety.

They cycled out in dozens during the summer of, for instance, 1906: to Kenilworth Castle, to Lichfield Cathedral, to Coventry Ca-thedral, to the exquisite Elizabethan jewel at Compton Wynyates. They played and listened to music all week. Collingwood had turned his time released from sport to good musical account; he mastered the fiddle, discovered Bach after the long-standing devotion his mother had taught him to Beethoven, studied counterpoint, plainchant, and Elizabethan music at just the moment when culti-vated taste was moving back in that direction away from the great Romantics (Arthur Bliss, of course, was to be in the van of that same movement).

He was far from being musically alone. The regular school con-certs were given by visiting orchestras and by pupils, and the items played were the canonical works by Handel, Bach, Beethoven, Men-delssohn, in the summer of 1907 alone. The following March, in a curricular novelty initiated by several other public schools, an en-larged school choir performed, with the help of the then active and mostly amateur Rugby Philharmonia (staff members among others), Mozart's *Requiem*.

No doubt boys poured themselves into these multiple activities in part to escape the tedium of timetable, clattering boarding house, unceasing "prep." No doubt also some of this endless attitudinising in public roles—the drama performances, the concerts, the debating society—conduced to exactly those public school qualities we now look steeply down upon. The arrogance, surely, the narcissism, the covert sexuality always rippling below sixteen-year-old skin, all this was then part of what Jim Hunter, in a novel about the effects of such an education, sees as the public school's unstopping operatic drama: "a public school's like an opera with nothing but tenors, all trained up to sing passionate arias, trained to think and move as romantic heroes, with no-one to be noble for, and therefore a tendency to load fantastic burdens of devotion and loyalty upon one or two of themselves."[12]

One frequently played scene in these schools was and is set in the school debating society, which solemnly and precisely would mimic parliamentary convention by way of training that same Parliament's future leading players. So Collingwood is to be found, on 12 October 1907, opposing the motion "that socialism is a grave danger" and appealing (in vain) to the 165 boys present (out of a total of only 580 in the school) to support what he quoted the *Daily Telegraph* as calling this "wicked system," and preferring to commend it to his audience as, no less, "a social system based on justice, morality, truth and love." His maiden speech had been on defence of patriotism the year before. The school set down faithful records of all these doings, and the secretary notes that Collingwood invoked Thucydides on patriotism.

This will have been the wonderful passage in which the historian summarises Pericles's praise of Athens and her makers.

> Look on the city's real power day after day and fall in love with her, and if she seems great to you, remember that men built these things who knew what needed to be done and dared to do it, and if they fell short of their goal they never thought to deprive the city of that talent; they gave her their best.[13]

It is safe to say that Collingwood shared with Pericles such a view of what it is to love and labour for one's country for the rest of his life. Yet he depicts himself as an isolate, and no doubt he was. The knee

injury gave him unrivalled freedoms, and he used them to read omnivorously, as well as to play and compose music, to teach himself
Italian in order to read Dante and medieval history (in Latin) and the
poets of medieval Burgundy—Charles d'Orléans, François Villon's
Ballade des Pendus, Pierre de Ronsard, and company.[14]

He roamed across the map of knowledge, staying up half the
night—this during his last two years when he was a prefect, a sixth-
former, member of the "Levée," head of house, a *grand seigneur* of
the school whatever his disclaimers—learning to use the school's
astral telescope and study afresh the night sky he knew by heart
from night sailing. All these things the school not merely permitted but genially encouraged. Hence its strengths, hence also the
difficulty lesser men experienced in growing up beyond these close
affiliations, this packed and *given* life, these ardent friendships and
near authorities.

Collingwood names only two of his schoolmasters with approval
and never mentions Dr. James. Charles Paget "Tiger" Hastings,
"from whom I learnt a good deal of modern history,"[15] enjoyed con-
siderable renown as a history teacher (with an Oxford First, naturally) and during his time at Rugby nursed sixty pupils to scholarships at Oxford or Cambridge. "Robert Whitelaw," his admiring
pupil wrote, "touched nothing that he did not adorn." He remains,
even now, an honoured name in school mythology, still giving that
name to a boarding house once his own property, and for forty-three
of his forty-seven years on the staff, form-master of what was known,
in typical Rugby argot, as the Twenty. The Twenty were an incipient
elite, awaiting promotion first (another such phrase) to the Lower,
then to the Upper Bench, the most senior and cleverest sixth-formers
in training to win their scholarships, perched at once actually and
symbolically in the highest room in the school, at the further end of
a tight spiral staircase whence new members of the Upper Bench
issued to applause from the old.

Back in the Twenty, Whitelaw ruled in his sovereignty, "a very
great schoolmaster," Hope-Simpson declares, his classroom known
as "Paradise Lost," who taught pretty well everything to his Twenty,

but in particular the literature of England and, supremely, of the classical tongues that he loved with an infectious, compelling passion. He had the quirks and crotchets this enclosed, intense, inbred kind of life engendered in all those who stayed for a lifetime in its beloved and lethal confinement. The alliance of longevity, indulgence, and an irritable intelligence combined to pit him consistently against the routines of authority in general and "Bodger" James and his successor Dr. Albert David in particular. When he retired in 1913 he wrote to David to say, "of course it comes to this, that I do not recognise your right—your moral right—to return thanks for me in the presence of the school."[16]

For such a man, the school assumed an immanence of a quite mystical kind, much as "my country" did for so many of those Rugbeians who were to begin dying for it a year later. The vigour and passion of his teaching Catullus, Ovid, Thucydides—the poetry of sex and the prose of political power—stirred, it seems, almost every one of his pupils. A bit maliciously, Geoffrey Keynes and Rupert Brooke (Whitelaw's godson) wrote verbatim notes of Whitelaw's trying to coax his class to understand some bit of Shakespeare and took down only the teacher's petulance at "the atmosphere of stunned inertia which is apt to prevail when a lesson isn't going too smoothly"; Whitelaw had filled the awful and obdurate silence of an uncooperative class with stylised reproaches: "You are beyond endurance, you are intolerable for sheer carelessness."[17] But when Whitelaw died in 1917, *The Meteor* glowed with heartfelt and admiring reminiscence, gathering personal shortcomings ("his magnificent unpunctuality") into the special radiance with which all those lucky enough to meet an inspiring teacher during their schooldays recollect the moment at which their passion for poetry first caught fire.

> For what one remembers most, and honours most, was the passion of his teaching, and how it vitalised all his exact learning. It was the same passion which made up the noble soul of the man, and gave him the fire and sensibility and imagination which, as he read out—chanted rather, for there was an almost religious fervour in it—his translations

of great poetry, showed him to us "attired in sudden brightness." For his enthusiasm, when he called upon it, was lyrical. We did not always understand, but in listening we found something of the faith which is not less great than knowledge.[18]

Whitelaw is a crux in any estimation of the place of Rugby School in Collingwood's formation, let alone in judging the importance of the most elite public schools to the history of Britain up to, say, 1956. Such a teacher concentrated in an emulable lifetime in the one place the faithfulness and loyalty demanded by sheer length of service, the allegiance to classical scholarship and English literature that would last for only a few pupils, but which freed the man from a merely totemic belonging to the school, the ruggedness, gleeful irreverence, and well-nursed truculence of disposition, all of which spoke so directly to Collingwood's clearest sense of his own enormous talents.

Far more than the power exerted by the one great teacher, however, Collingwood owed equally to the school as to his family his unspoken ratification of the liberal and idealist tenor of British politics. This is where the *Autobiography* isn't quite straight. He became, after all, head of his boarding house, Wilson's, for two whole years. As he says, "for the first time, I tasted the pleasure of doing administrative work, and learnt once for all how to do it."[19] But to win (and want), the appointment in the first place abruptly qualifies the self-portrait he paints of a solitary, caustic, uncooperative outlaw who "refused to enter for the prizes which decorated the career of the good boy" (although he takes the trouble to point to those he won anyway), and whose undoubted arrogance was inseparable from the certainty that he proved a proper and public-spirited prefect and ally of his teachers. Indeed, W. N. Wilson, that same housemaster, saw and praised these qualities, and many more, without having been singled out in his turn by his pupil for any commendation. In a reference written in 1912, when Collingwood applied to Pembroke College for his first post at Oxford, Wilson wrote with unaffected regard that during the whole of the time in Wilson's House "he earned the respect and affection of all those with whom he came into contact, with Masters and boys, and continually developed in both power and influence."[20] Wilson notes in his letter that seniority usually determined succession in the appointment of a head of house, but in appointing Collingwood, at only seventeen, to the post, he passed over several of the seniors,

> yet all the boys in the House thoroughly approved of my choice which was justified by the complete success, courage and tact with which he carried out his duties. . . . This success was the more remarkable in that he had no athletics—which counts for so much in the eyes of boys—to help him: for in his first term here he injured a knee and was never again able to join in a school game. The injury, however, had one excellent result in that it gave him the time to cultivate his taste for music in which he made remarkable progress until stress of work at Oxford compelled him to put it aside.

Two years in the post, with the substantial duties of administration in the day-to-day running of the house, confirmed in the boy his natural authority and containment. The judicious exchanges with the housemaster on matters of house discipline, exercise, manners, the ordering of the "fagging" rosters in which, as we saw, small boys were assigned to minor servitude as a way of learning subordination, watching and counselling fellow pupils in trouble—cigarettes behind the fives court, too many detentions, homesickness, clandestine meetings with town girls—all these confirmed that strong official part of him, complement to his suppressed recklessness, solitary reserve, and sardonic eye.

This propriety and reserve, this imperturbable authority, were what the most prominent of these mighty schools were intended to bring about in the character of their most senior boys, those who certainly became the leaders of Edwardian Britain, its cabinet ministers, imperial bureaucrats, bishops, admirals, bankers, as well as its scholars, artists, writers, composers. Inasmuch as these leading figures fall into two groups, there would have been no doubt at Rugby that Collingwood belonged to the second. His music, his reading, his easy acquisition of French, Italian, German, in addition to the classical tongues that were his formal studies, marked him out as a bohemian in the class structure of the school. But English upper-class bohemians have mostly been a dark-suited bunch whose passionate and private ardour has been driven indoors by the hearty and gregarious ruthlessness of their costly boarding school lives.

John Henry Newman's famous theory of reserve issued in Collingwood in the persona he maintained for the bachelor side of his life in Pembroke College, in the severe dutifulness of the work at the Admiralty after 1916, and in certain aspects of his thought and writing—the once-admired *Essay on Philosophical Method* of 1933 is the work of this version of what Ransome called the "steel blue and polished" aspect of Collingwood's character, severe, ascetic, professional, and at this remove, of rather dated power. The other Collingwood (as he himself said, there were at least three) flashed out in negation, so to speak, in his bloodymindedness and rare insolence at Rugby.

This other Collingwood was also a charmer. He was to magic the podium when he lectured in Oxford; he was to be seen capturing not a few hearts among admiring young men and (as his future pupil, Sir Malcolm Knox, disapprovingly observed, good-looking) women students;[21] he returned to the front of Collingwood's face when he boarded the train for the seven and a half hour journey back to Lanehead.

From the end of that first term, he mostly made that journey in the company of one fast friend—there were few such—from Rugby. He was a fellow scholarship winner, Ernest Altounyan, son of an Anglophile Syrian doctor from Aleppo, future son-in-law of Gershom and Dorrie (he married daughter Dora, five years his senior), and a joyously welcomed guest, bosom friend, foster son, whenever he came home with Robin. Altounyan came to that home with a friend restored to his patrimony, a history and a geography compounded of the glowing warmth of Lanehead life, the beautiful sisters, the irresistible lake, and the extraordinary combination of Lakeland's natural beauty and its scattered population's vitality and keen aesthetic energy.

II

By the time the fourteen-year-old Robin had taken his first train to Rugby, the Ambleside-Coniston road had become culturally busy. Much was due to WG's efforts, but the Lakelander tradition had drawn a number of progressives who came not just to love and admire the landscape, although that was a prime reason for their exile, but also because they responded keenly to the implicit political tradition that may be said to begin at Furness and Grange-over-Sands and extend as far north, the border notwithstanding, as Dumfries and Galloway. This was the geographical tract, as it was Gershom's life's work to document, that was settled by the Scandinavians; for all the border marauding and attempts by regal warlords from York and further south to dominate its impossible mountains and waters, the Scandinavian settlement held, helped by a geography as unamenable to emperors as the Greece that gave birth to democracy.[22]

In the folk-politics (no disparagement) of the Lanehead and Brantwood households, the Lakeland "statesman" upheld a rough-and-ready democratic independence. Class politics may have come to the shipbuilding yards on the coast, and haughty landowners had long been housed at Langley Castle up by Haydon Bridge and on the vast but discontinuous estates of the earl of Lonsdale, but these interruptions did not displace the old self-reliance and truculent independence of, first, smallholder-fishermen, and then, during the nineteenth century, wood-carvers, coachbuilders, poets, painters, stonemasons, ornithologists, railwaymen, boatbuilders, photographers, as well as the new kind of women of whom Beatrix Potter Heelis and Charlotte Mason were the forceful, unobtrusive heroines. They serve to vindicate that alternative education which all his life drew Collingwood back from the official capitals of learning and were the essential, gregarious complement of his solitary philosophising. Beatrix Potter broke out of her stiflingly respectable London family and, having learned the genteel young lady's craft of botanising water-colours, proved an attentive genius and, turning craft into art, wrote and illustrated *The Tale of Peter Rabbit* in 1906, entering the pantheon of great writers for children as she did so.

Having taken holidays in the Lake District, like all cultivated young ladies of the time, when her fiancé, the youngest brother of her publishing house, Frederick Warne, died, she quit the family home to buy a Lakeland farm near Ambleside out of her satisfyingly grand royalties. She ran the farm, too, and joined the Cumberland and Westmoreland Archaeological and Antiquarian Society, of which WG was a prime mover and, from 1920 until his death in 1932, president.

There was an active, dissident cultural life scattered around the shores of the Lakes, and many of its members were part of that migration out of London and the black industrial cities by the progressive fraction of the middle classes, once Wordsworth, then, following Ruskin's advocacy, Turner, had gripped its imagination.

No doubt such mobility had more complex causes than the life work of a poet and a painter. But poems and pictures, as Gershom's hardworking career shows us, were intrinsic to that class fraction and its vision of the good life. For those who settled around the Lakes, there was also, as I suggested, the strong pull exerted by both the legend and the historical actuality of the Lakelander "statesman"-smallholder. Two and a half centuries before Ruskin arrived at Brantwood, the people of Lakeland showed themselves robustly indifferent to the Civil War being won and lost at Worcester, Edgehill, Naseby, and on the scaffold not so very far south. Court and Parliament were not, it seems, the sources of their allegiance and certainly not strong enough to draw them to the colours. Indeed, the present-day historian-anthropologist Alan Macfarlane, who is most responsible for reconstructing that tranquil location, goes a good deal further in finding the roots of English individualism in the Northwest. He claims for its configuration of market towns—Kirkby Lonsdale (where he begins and whose fair charter is dated 1227), Hawes, Penrith, Kendal, Ambleside (Roman fort), Keswick (Norse for "cheese dairy"),[23] Ulverston (founded 1211)—that they were the birthplaces of that powerful Anglo-political character, "the freeborn Englishman." This worthy, somewhere compounded of freedoms and citizenship won from the Romans before they left in the fifth century AD, and mingled with trading rights and rules of exchange inscribed in market charters dating from the thirteenth century, comes in this partisan narrative to represent stout and early intimations of the independence and self-reliance on which the English so long congratulated themselves as having bequeathed to world civilisation.[24]

The historical formation of the freeborn Englishman was long, slow, and, it was surmised, very early. By the time these high-minded Victorians arrived by train at Windermere, Coniston, and Cockermouth, one of the attractions was the strength of this character as concentrated in Wordsworth's tragic hero in *Michael*, in his famous "Solitary," and in the wonderful celebrations of his people in *The Excursion*. WG added to the same mythology with *Thorstein of the Mere*. Far more than his admirable novel, however, as contributory to the characteristic culture of the Lakelanders, were his inexhaustible labours on behalf of the popular and scholarly societies that beat at the heart of local life.

One might say that they marked the advent of the domestic economy of tourism, if that did not immediately sound like a putting-down. Mind you, it's more than time it didn't. Tourism, which Ruskin so inveighed against in the form of his dreadful enemy, the locomotive, not only brought the joyfulness and liberation of natural beauty to all who came to gaze at it, it was the engine that powered much of the life of this and all holiday locales, in their economy and, more largely, their community. Community, the great lost catchall value of modernity, forever imperilled, forever renewed, took its vitality in the Lakeland of the 1900s (as of the 2000s) from the sale of cows and pigs and cheese and milk for sure, but just as much from wood-carving, archaeologising, fell walking, lake ferrying, and the enormous productivity of the landscape painters.

A little biographical parable brings out the force of this conjunction in Cumbrian culture between class pastimes and a long, mostly implicit political tradition. In 1892 a youngish woman called Charlotte Mason (a little older than Beatrix Potter) opened the House of Education at the solidly gabled, sturdy residence on the edge of Coniston known as Springfield.[25] This was to be one of the first of what became known as training colleges, where young women would not only acquire an education for themselves but learn at the same time to pass it on to children, particularly girls, who had never been provided with an education that would permit them to make an independent way in the world. Gershom's great mentor at Oxford, T. H. Green, had been active as a local councillor in the cause of women's education before his premature death at forty-six in 1882, had sketched out for the first time a diagram of tripartite education in which intelligence would be the sole criterion of merit, and later became, in the imagination of the young R. G. Collingwood, *the* type of English scholar-intellectual, idealist in philosophy and in value-allegiance, public-spirited and civic-minded, a teacher for whom the point of the vocation was to give his students (Collingwood's own phrase, a motto for this book) "ideals to live for and principles to live by."

Green, one might say, inaugurated the tradition. His efforts and his wife's on behalf of women's education fired disciples such as Charlotte Mason and her like, Philippa Fawcett and Margaret Macmillan, each progenitors of a training college. The pedagogy Charlotte Mason espoused was well at home in Ambleside. It could have been written by the Collingwood family, who in any case expressed strong solidarity. Charlotte Mason's curriculum featured the arts and crafts as largely as one would anticipate. A national movement, led by William Morris, had issued in 1888 in the Arts and Crafts Exhibition Society and the Art Workers Guild of 1884. Morris and Ruskin and the hosts of their supporters had won the argument that affirmed the likeness of artists and craftspeople, had roused both working-class men and women and sympathetic progressives to detest the deathly routines of industrial labour and to see the struggle for fulfilment in work and for the making of beauty in production as an intrinsically human necessity as well as an endeavour joining men and women across the chasms of social class difference.

So Charlotte Mason's teaching her girls to draw and paint sorted happily enough with long-standing customs in genteel education. Teaching them to use the chisel and the handsaw was quite another matter. When she added, as she did, minute observation of natural history and hunting for shards of pottery on the site of the Ambleside fort known to the Romans as Galava (first opened in the 1860s but only comprehensively dug and mapped by Robin Collingwood after 1911), she was, controversially, turning young women into scientists and manual labourers and worse.

She had, moreover, an educational theory to ground this busy work, one for which the founding name of Maria Montessori is usually given credit, but which emerged just as much from the kind of disciplined observation and exquisite recording taught and exemplified across Coniston Water by the sage of Brantwood. Directness of response to nature, to art and to literature, together with a close, wholly unegotistical attention to the medium in hand, whether a beetle, a frog, the brushstrokes of a painting, or the words of a poem, were each covered in the pedagogy by the single, complex concept, "experience." As Collingwood gradually discovered his life's mission as being to understand how human reason shakes theory out of practice by way of making sense of the history of its past, present, and future, he was giving meaning to the pedagogy of experience his father fashioned out of relief maps made from papier maché, and which Charlotte Mason formalised just down the road in Springfield's House of Education. The precision and beauty of Beatrix Potter's illustrations in her magnificent oeuvre (let alone her drawings of Roman remains)[26] may serve us as illustrative textbooks of that educational moment.

The educational moment was, as always, caught up on a cultural tide. That tide swept up and was swept up by such strong thrusts as came from the many manifestations of the Arts and Crafts movement, the "Anti-Scrape" (Society for the Protection of Ancient Buildings), and suchlike, all joined to that no less passionate wave of democratisation whereby trade unions forced themselves upon government as necessary and legitimate and laid their noble and moving claim to an ancestry beginning with the medieval guilds.

Medievalism had long been an intimate feature of Englishness, and the fillip that Ruskin's good judgement and fierce prose gave to Victorian Gothic throughout Britain as well as all over the eastern seaboard of North America was deeply part of Collingwood's inheritance and made Rugby School recognisable to him when he first arrived. But medievalism met the new democracy and the rampant industrialisation that accompanied and battled with it, and gave birth to a multitudinous progeny of militant societies, clubs, scholarly alliances, new guilds with archaic titles, and a vast literature of pamphlets, proceedings, reports, formal and collectible correspondence, papers given, attended, appreciated, and published. The culture of Britain, electronic technology and runaway consumerism notwithstanding, was fired in the factories of the nineteenth century, as this was so for high-minded followers of T. H. Green in the senior bureaus of the Liberal Party as well as in the working men's institutes that sent out their invitations to fellow trade unionists to start the Labour Party.

In his great essay on "the English genius," *The Lion and the Unicorn*, George Orwell writes warmly of

> an English characteristic which is so much part of us that we barely notice it, and that is the addiction to hobbies and spare-time occupations, the *privateness* of English life. We are a nation of flower-lovers, but also a nation of stamp-collectors, pigeon-fanciers, amateur carpenters, coupon-snippers, darts-players, crossword-puzzle fans. All the culture that is most truly native centres round things which even when they are communal are not official—the pub, the football match, the back garden, the fireside and the "nice cup of tea." [27]

This is finely and movingly observed, but it's not quite right either about Lakeland in 1904 or most of Britain after the turn of the last millennium. The movements of the 1880s *were* official, noisy, combative; they were what we have come to call "civil society," and they protected their right to a timely incivility towards political power. Many of the societies that the flower-lovers, carpenters (DIYers they'd say now), trainspotters, old car conservationists, preservers of rural England (CPRE as they became), and rambler-painters founded a century ago and which still flourish, set themselves at odds with officialdom and the law. Perforce, they had to learn to cross the boundary between civil life and the polity. They had, as Aristotle taught the classicists among them, WG and RG Collingwood for sure, learned the terms of a *praxis* embedded in a tradition. In order to keep those terms and their language clean and serviceable, they had to band together and resist such modes of routinisation and bureaucratic formality as spelled death to their practice and the taken-for-granted rationality it enshrined.

Private life, like private language, is meaningless. These were less expressions of privateness than quick, small, vigorous (but general) assertions of quiddity and independence, germinating spontaneously from a local geography and history and, as Orwell notes, "to some extent *against* the existing order." So when in 1904 Gershom wrote to Robin at Rugby that he had finally established the Lake Artists' Society, he was reporting a little declaration of independence.

The Lake Artists' Society joined the long-standing, long-sounding Cumberland and Westmorland Antiquarian and Archaeological Society as two of the great monuments to Gershom's and his family's lives. Of course the CWAAS went back long before the Collingwood family arrived in Coniston; it was the result of the vision and energy of another sage of Lakeland, Chancellor Ferguson of Carlisle, but Collingwood father and son were keystone presidents and dedicated diggers, copiers, mappers, and lecturers as chronicled in the society's *Transactions* from the early 1890s until his ill health forced Robin's resignation in 1938.

Archaeology as an amateur and local passion was one leading manifestation of the Victorians' turn to history as the radical competitor against natural science for predominance on the map of knowledge. As both Collingwoods saw and felt, the tradition and practices of the discipline sorted well with their deep allegiances to place and the loved facts of local rocks and stones and the trees that had grown above them. The son learned from the father of the presence of the past in old stones scattered beside the path up the Old Man, in the shallow declivities of sometime lead workings, in the lumpy outlines of turf that announced the remains of empire at Hardknott, Watercrook, or Burgh-by-Sands forts. Slow, effortful digging, the brisk business of charcoal rubbing to take the impression of Roman or Norse inscriptions, the slow compilation of trace and shard in order to lend authority to the hand-drawn maps that made a site canonical—these were the practical methods that returned history to the course of a particular, to the final finding of the ear. This was the hard labour that made it possible for Collingwood, philosophic historian, to reject "scissors-and-paste" history, cutting up the work of prior historians and sticking it together in a new order, and instead, like the painter, the poet, or the botanist, to feel and think the life of that which gives life as it was and is.

The solid rows on the shelves of the *Transactions* of the Cumberland and Westmorland archaeologists stretch from 1870 to the present day. They rebut any easy endorsement of Orwell's ideas about the privateness of culture. They bear their dignified witness to the civic ideal of scholarship in the ordinary lives of the society's members, as well as to the vindication of his conception of theory-in-practice in the mind and work of their most distinguished intellect. They corroborate that sublime, collective venture of nineteenth-century minds, now our most important intellectual inheritance, to wring self-knowledge out of the past. That self, it cannot go without saying, is no individual's self-knowledge but the knowledge of a whole people about itself, discovering historically what it is and therefore how it best may act, on its own behalf and that of humankind.

Hegel was the first philosopher-historian to write in such an idiom, but it led him into strange ways. The British idealists, so-called, refused his airier flights and took care of a homelier notion of the common good as directing moral and political endeavour. Establishing the facts of Roman occupation on and around Hadrian's Wall, as reconstructed by gentlemen in knickerbockers and ladies in bonnets for a hundred years on Lakeland fells, is one powerful token of such self-discovery and self-invention. If this sounds a high-flown way to describe amateur archaeological digs, its justification is, one hopes, to be found in the life of R. G. Collingwood.

Perhaps the communal, even the political force of the English passion for local societies is easier to see at work in Gershom's other great memorial, the Lake Artists' Society.[28] He and his wife had given impetus to the founding of the society with a joint exhibition at Barrow-in-Furness in 1899; it had raised the respectable sum of eighty-four guineas. In the local metropolis of Carlisle, there was a more than worthy, a wholly serious Art School, with Colin Rae at its head, teaching the livelihood of painting the Lake District. Joseph Severn, father to Arthur, Ruskin's companion and legatee, who was a painter of some consequence, was a founder member, as of course was Dorrie Collingwood. John Hodgson, a painter and etcher of great promise, was a member for the first two years before his sudden death at the age of thirty-five, and Arthur Tucker, Gershom's age, who became vice-president, was probably the best of the founder-painters, with a fine directness of line and form, and a bright clarity of colour. Hubert Coutts exhibited with WG at a Kendal gallery, while Herbert Bell, whose name is still well known as one of the best photographers of Lakeland, a frequent guest at Lanehead, was present to show that the camera, the engraver's needle, and the brush were alike instruments of art. A little later, the Collingwood daughters, Dora the portraitist and Barbara the sculptor, were active members even when, in Dora's case, away in Syria.[29]

The longevity of the society and the throngs of its members testify to the importance of water-colour painting, specifically of the Lake District, in the national imagination. These painters, and their descendants who work in the same tradition, still command keen interest among those dealers and collectors who are concerned not with the crazy jostle of international art auctioneering, but with the keen, instantaneous pleasure of purchasing plain paintings of loved views, paintings one might have painted oneself if only one had learned the way of it, paintings of spots on which one has often stopped, maybe picnicked, where the children played, paintings that keep the promise of happiness and mark the milestones of the years.

This is the meaning of landscape painting. One cannot help feeling that Ruskin was much too hard on it when he wrote that the nineteenth-century preoccupation with landscape was "the result of mistakes in our social economy, and is the expression of a love of liberty which can no longer find satisfaction in the civic life." For Ruskin, as for Orwell, freedom has turned into a private possession; it is a place "where we can lose the company of our friends among the hills."[30] The little tale of the founding of the Lake Artists' Society (and its still vigorous centenarian life) serves to qualify this view. The Lake Artists do not lose the company of their friends among the hills; they find it. In the *Autobiography*, Collingwood remembers his parents' innumerable paintings (Gershom painted The Old Man of Coniston over three hundred times) stacked against the walls as well as on them. They were evidence not only of the extended interrogation of and inquiry into the world that all serious art embodies, but also of its collaborativeness, its intent communality, a company of friends deep in conversation at their common task.

When Ernest Altounyan arrived home with Robin for the lengthy holidays from Rugby (two lots of four weeks, and in the summer, a blissful eight), he discovered the everyday consequences of such creative liveliness. The house, first, and then the little towns were full of *visitors*. This is important. Lakeland had become a refuge, no doubt; it was also a redoubt. After another century of tourism to add to the first (which in any case began in about 1770), we have reckoned up some of the costs of our inveterate vacationing. But its essential points remain the same: we name certain places sacred, Lakeland supreme among them at least in Britain, and appoint them refuges from the grime, the crowds, the damnably hard and daily routine of sheer work against which the solace of nature, her beauty and spaciousness, along with the productive happiness of non-profitable effort under nature's own sun and rain, restores us so that we can return to the city and its satanic mills.

This same movement away from the city's labours and its love of money creates also a more permanent class of visitor to the refuge. This visitor, determined to break with city life, comes to the sacred place to live in such a way as to reject the city. He or she makes the tourist refuge into a creative centre of resistance by practising against the economic grain the slow, painstaking livelihoods of painting, woodcraft, mixed farming, archaeology, glass-blowing. The city can't be gainsaid, of course; the artist must sell pictures, the archaeologist needs go to the great universities. But the two kinds of visitor create, as they must, a new and by now long-established economy. In Lakeland, it had three interlocking components: the arts and crafts and scholarly segment, the farmers and hostellers (often the same families), and the sailors, walkers, and climbers whose effortful activities are not only good and happiness-making in themselves, but also antidotes for the city-worn body and spirit.

And the greatest of these latter three is sailing. The mysteries of sailing have a peculiar place in the moral imagination of a maritime nation. Sailing means so much in the people's culture: pastime, means of commerce, transport, means of warfare, the occasions of worship and of burial, the frail collusion of a craftsman's craft with the barely harnessable powers of sea and wind, or just a pleasant Sunday afternoon. It is a happy accident for a polyglot and multicultural people like the British that sailing remains a multiclass activity and that its long history provides a way of rejoining a people's history. The ghosts of popular history in Britain as in New England or the Caribbean are buccaneers, explorers, traders, naval officers. The greatest writer in English literature about the sea is Joseph Conrad, whose first language and nationality was Polish, his second French, his third English. He came to writing and a position as respectable London clubman by way of the rank, first, of rating and then commander in the Mercantile Marine. The Collingwood dynasty is a famous north country one, and famous above all for the admiral who was Nelson's deputy at Trafalgar, then his successor in charge of the fleet who abolished flogging and brought to life in the navy something like humane justice, until he died at sea of neglect of his own health. Collingwood the philosopher-historian knew that naval history by heart and, like all English boys of his and the next two or three generations, took great pride in it, such that sailing across from the Lanehead boathouse at the bottom of the long, steeply sloping garden to boil a kettle for tea on Peel Island carried with it traces of the sea and seagoing tradition. Even on *Swallow* and Coniston Water, a boy felt himself, in quite unspoken, unpretentious ways, the "latest representative of what for all intents and purposes was a dynasty; continuous not in blood, indeed, but in experience, in its training, in its conception of duty and in the blessed simplicity of its traditional point of view on life."[31]

So Robin, Dora, Barbara, Ursula, and Ernest Altounyan sang *Spanish Ladies* as they made the short crossing:

So we'll rant and we'll roar like true British sailors,
We'll range and we'll roam over all the salt seas,
Until we strike soundings in the channel of old England,
From Ushant to Scilly 'tis thirty-five leagues.

Thirty years later Arthur Ransome invented his famous children out of Dora's and Ernest's children, gave them the same names and the same song. Tens of thousands of visitors since then have dressed up as sailors (the right uniform is everything) and launched from the east coast into the west wind that blows so strongly across Coniston. Taking the wind to carry the boat northwards, the wake lengthening and bubbling astern, you pass the point, let out the main sheet so that it fills with a ripping, crackling noise, put the helm up, and, with the wind by now aft, steer straight for Peel Island, where long ago Gershom had excavated the Norseman's bothy and put it to be lived in by Thorstein of the Mere.[32]

It is for little expeditions like these, joining them, however slightly, to the years-long voyages of seafaring history, that all those thousands of sailor-visitors still arrive. It is to keep those sentiments lucid that nowadays, and quite rightly too, local authorities have banned power-launches and skijets on Windermere and Coniston. This is the heart of the visitors' moral economy, perhaps the most important thing Collingwood himself came home for and to. It was what he turned towards when his illness declared itself mortal; it was the context of solitude and thought, the succession of moments in which the reassurance of tradition collides with the amazement of the unforeseeable, and the past turns abruptly into the future.

III

Public school education has become a far more conscience-stricken issue for its beneficiaries than ever it was for Collingwood. Whatever his criticisms, which are harsh and discomfiting, he drew, as we have seen, signal benefits from his education. Rugby was a far less insolently ruling-class institution than Eton or Harrow in those days,[33] and it cherished the intellectual virtues much more sedulously than its bourgeois neighbours in the modest market towns of Oundle or Uppingham. The school endorsed and deepened the dedication to both history and art that Collingwood learned from his parents, even if in the classroom it had less vivid, practical, and continuous a form. And whatever he may have disparaged in a public school education, Collingwood nonetheless sent his son Bill to such a school at Shrewsbury, and his daughter Ursula (named after her aunt) to the most socially stylish of all girls' boarding schools, Roedean.

The point of such schools was to ensure a homogeneous ruling class, competent and cultivated enough to keep society moving intelligibly into the future. In the heyday of empire—and it was not until 1932 that the British Empire reached its maximum point of expansion[34]—a function of this kind seemed self-explanatory. Oxford and Cambridge then served the same continuity for the nation's elite sons when they reached nineteen.

As, however, the long revolution of the British century turned, the huge disparity between the schools of the rich—Rugby with its splendid Gothic buildings, its proprietorship of a whole middle-sized town, its network of alumni running the country, its library, laboratories, orchestra, the sheer arrogance of its certainties—began to loom larger in the conscience of social democrats and progressive liberals. In the 1970s a Labour government instigated a couple of royal commissions on the public schools to do what in those days such bodies did and advise governments how to proceed.[35] The commissions, plentifully staffed by former pupils of public schools as well as by worthy spokesmen and women from the state education, suggested various ways of mitigating the grosser of the inequalities upon which the schools depended, such as paying no local rates and possessing the status of charitable institutions(!), after which the schools proceeded serenely on their way. A few anxious leftists of the privileged classes sent their children to local state schools in the name of both communal membership and egalitarianism, and they were much accused by others of the well-off classes of sacrificing their children to their principles, as though one could ever do anything else. Very gradually, Labour Party ministers came to believe, rightly enough in my view, that they really must display solidarity with the people by sending their own children to the people's schools, taking the risk that the children's gains in popular cultural knowledge and street wisdom would be paid for in lower grades in their examinations.

For the public schools proved to be protean learners of a new social role. All those who believed that their old rigidities of custom and stratification, of curriculum and pedagogy, would simply splinter under the pressures of historical change were wrong. Sometime round about 1960, as the democratising wave released by the Second World War met the riptide of postwar prosperity, old deferences went down, and in the neologism of the day, a meritocracy was declared in which achievement and ability would be the criteria of social worth and advancement, and the inheritance of status would be annulled.

The public schools, protectors of status and custodians of inheritance, proved quickest of all to see that as long as family fortunes remained inheritable, they could charge as much as they wanted if they ensured that their pupils came first in the meritocratic race. Imperial destiny and world-historical power were replaced on the moral horizon of their boys (girls doing things a bit differently) by honest and dishonest money. They still produced academics and politicians, of course, but the purpose of the education offered by the public schools since the great change has become, over the past fifty years or so, to fit their pupils to make as much money as possible.

In this they are responsive to as well as shapers of the *Zeitgeist*. The juggernaut of a new kind of capitalism was to roar away in Britain after 1979 when, as the Labour Party's chief intellectual and pupil of Collingwood's, Denis Healey, put it, "the great she-rhino," Margaret Thatcher, came to power. The public schools, not without courage as well as with plenty of brass neck, rode the wave with a resourceful balance. They taught their pupils to be victorious on these buccaneering seas and sent them out to captain their corporate crafts in a spirit of perfect irresponsibility.

This is the most marked difference between Collingwood's Rugby when he left in 1908 and its decorous, informal, co-educational, and extremely hardworking successor today. Individual pupils may have their consciences stricken by the state of the globe, but all such schools at large present the same bland indifference to human misery as does the super-rich class their pupils will mostly join.

One indication of this is the rising number of boys and girls coming to the few most successful public schools from the future leaders of world economies in China and India. The schools are still educating the elite, but it is gradually becoming a world elite with only shallow roots in a national culture, with homes in three or four world-historical leisure zones (one of them floating), with friends, colleagues, tastes, and ignorance confined to that same tiny and transnational membership, and without ties of duty or allegiance to a specific history or geography.

The moral point of a biography is not to add a figure to some gallery of model lives for imitation, but to take from the bequests of the past *lines of force for transformation.*[36] The line of force that comes through Collingwood, in part, to be sure, from Rugby School, is given mass and energy by its civic-mindedness, its slightly stiff principles, the arrogance of its sense of vocation, as well as the application of its ideas. The break between the historical past and the political present of which a biography should take the measure is in this case complete. The line of force coming through Collingwood, seeking its transformation, no longer finds an institutional earthing in the public schools. Its charge has to go veering off, seeking what individual lives it may electrify.

3

Oxford and the Admiralty: The Science of Human Affairs; God and the Devil

At the end of the spring term (the Hilary term at Oxford) of 1908, Collingwood went to Oxford to sit for the scholarship examinations, the most successful entrants for which would win substantial contributions towards their fees. It was the custom then, and remained so for another seventy-five years, for the candidates to enter briefly into college residence and taste the pleasures of undergraduate freedom after the carceral conditions of boarding house and public school.

Each day of his stay, the nineteen-year-old Collingwood could get up much later than he would have done at Rugby, take coffee instead of tea, along with such manifestations of maturity and manly independence as bacon and egg rather than lumpy porridge for breakfast, and eat slices cut from a great saddle of lamb rather than sardines on toast for dinner in the evening. For the first week of his stay, Collingwood was sharing a room with a competitor in University College, his father's old college, and although he also applied to another group of colleges by way of lowering the odds, it was to University College—"Univ" in Oxford slang—that he was committed, and whose examinations he took very seriously ("in the second I decided to enjoy myself and behaved disgracefully").[1] Each day during his four-day sojourn, he walked the hundred yards or so from the college gate down the High Street to the examination schools, then a newish pile of Victorian Venetian Gothic, paved in clubland marble and much pillared within.

There, for three hours at a time, even six on some days, the candidates bent themselves to composing Latin and Greek verses, Latin

and Greek translations from the original, writing critical essays on
Tacitus, Livy, and Herodotus, and, in the so-called general paper,
making as fine a display as possible of one's individual cultivation
and breadth of knowledge—in Collingwood's case, answering one
question about Turner and another about Mozart. When Collingwood adds, "what boyish nonsense I put into my essays, I dare not
try to recollect," we may be sure that whatever it was, it would not
have been nonsensical, and that the years of living as neighbour to
Turner's greatest champion and listening daily to his mother's performances of Mozart would have been turned to dazzling account.
Then, when asked at interview what he would decide if offered the
choice between the best scholarship at another college or a lesser one
at University, he answered that University was his father's college
and he would go there if offered any scholarship at all. His interlocutors, in their turn, "did not seem like men who thought the worse
of me" for saying so.

When Collingwood went up to Oxford (with all the airiness of
upper-class prepositions) in October 1908, he was assigned rooms
high in the tower that protrudes into the handsome and enclosed
garden quadrangle. From the window—a privileged room, assigned
only to scholarship winners—he could look down on the quiet and
pedestrian life of the college, sport his oak by way of warding off
importunate intruders, "swill and booze Homer until the world contained no Homer that he had not read."

It was during these first years in the city that became one of his
two settled, lifetime, and inviolable homes that Collingwood began
to become aware that the speed and forcefulness of his mind were
not perfectly under his control; or rather, that he had little choice
but to let his mind run, that the only way of reining it back to a
manageable pace was to set down on the page verbal versions of the
thoughts that flitted ahead of the words which could hold them back
and down.

Not all thinkers are like this, one presumes, and in any case for
all of us, professional thinkers included, the everyday and ruminative
monologue that is our consciousness arises from a turgid depth of
preverbal stirrings, tides, and tumblings of the mind without form

or direction. In a fine essay, D. W. Harding seeks to move backwards into what he calls "the hinterland of thought" by way of some wonderful lines in Wordsworth's *The Prelude,* after the poet, as a boy, has become persuaded that a great black mountain is striding dreadfully in pursuit of him.[2] For days later Wordsworth's mind was oppressed by a darkness, a solitude of blank desertion:

> No familiar shapes
> Remained, no pleasant images of trees,
> Of sea or sky, no colours of green fields;
> But huge and mighty forms, that do not live
> Like living men, moved slowly through my mind
> By day, and were a trouble to my dreams.

Collingwood knew and feared such forms, and he knew also that the philosopher-historian's kind of thinking needs and waits on such forms as the stuff out of which the kind of thinking for which he is searching, clear, pure, perfect, will precipitate and crystallise. Hence Collingwood's passion for and trust in painting, poetry, music; hence also his long, ambiguous, and mistrustful attitude towards Freud and psychoanalysis, culminating in his own, full-blown psychoanalytic treatment in 1937–38.

As an undergraduate, however, the endless movement of his thought from unapprehensible shapes to clear words and pure sentences issued, as he read and read omnivorously, largely in sleeplessness. He became a chronic insomniac, and writing eventually turned into a refuge from the frustration and rage that necessarily boil up in all insomniacs, as well as the condition's being the expression of the vitality and of the unignorable call to thinking that so cut off sleep, the innocent sleep, in the first place.

His childhood and his life at Rugby confirmed Collingwood in solitude and in the satisfaction of only a few close friends, among his contemporaries Ernest Altounyan, Geoffrey Garratt, Edward Poole, Arthur Cockin (later vicar at St. Mary's who invited his old friend to preach in the University church), Robert Whitelaw his teacher at Rugby, Arthur Ransome, Collingwood's parents, and his beloved sisters at Coniston. Oxford, at the high point of Edwardian England, is still framed as an aquatinted pastoral in the history of the national imagination. Collingwood refers curtly to his own quickness to take offence, to being "not unready to give it." Then he goes on: "But, for all that, there were many long walks in the country, many idle afternoons on the river, many evenings spent playing and hearing music, many nights talking until dawn; and more than one lifelong friendship in the making."[3]

The punt is one of the happiest contrivances of the leisure industry founded in the nineteenth century. It evolved from the tiny barges designed for lightish loads on the new canals of the previous century,[4] but it took up its permanent place in the national imagination as a picknickers' conveyance confined to the rivers Cam in East Anglia and Cherwell and Isis, the local names for the Thames and its tributary, in Oxford.

The Oxford punts are mostly moored on the Cherwell just below Magdalen bridge, and although most colleges then and now had one or two punts of their own, there was a busy trade in private hire as well as, naturally, approved attire and accoutrements for going on the river in 1908. Edwardian England is now celebrated for the harmless efflorescence of its dandyism, and boaters and blazers for the chaps, yellow organdie, white stockings, and parasols for the young women, were its now time-honoured pastel petals in the prewar years. While Collingwood was an undergraduate, Max Beerbohm was writing his comic spoof *Zuleika Dobson*.[5] Spoof it is, but Beerbohm's chronicling of the dazzling beauty's amazing wardrobe and jewellery—"black satin gown, big black diamonds, in her hair gleamed a great raven's wing"—is, as he notes, corroborated by Sargent's portraits of the day. When Beerbohm dresses his hero, a duke of course, in the full rig of the Order of the Garter in order to bring him to his climactic doom, the white buckskin breeches and navy velvet cloak would have seemed at that date only faintly excessive among the crowds on the college barges come to cheer the "threadlike crafts" of the oarsmen in Eights week. Beerbohm, playfully disembodying himself in order to catch a God's-eye view of Oxford, floats out above the untenanted meadows. Over them was the usual coverlet of white vapour, trailed from the Isis right up to Merton Wall. The scent of these meadows' moisture is the scent of Oxford. Even in hottest noon, one feels that the sun has not dried *them*. Always there is moisture drifting across them, drifting into the Colleges. It, one suspects, must have had much to do with the evocation of what is called the Oxford spirit—that gentlest spirit, so lingering and searching, so dear to them who as youths were brought into ken of it, so exasperating to them who were not. Yes, certainly, it is this mild, miasmal air, not less than the grey beauty and gravity of the buildings, that has helped Oxford to produce, and foster eternally, her peculiar race of artist-scholars, scholar-artists.

The pageant of the Edwardian city is still, I suppose, what lives on as folklore, and an undergraduate of Collingwood's gifts, even one of his professed unsociability, did not miss it. When his father came to Oxford on one of his fairly frequent visits, father and son walked from University past Magdalen to the bridge, stepped carefully into the flat-bottomed, swaying craft, stowed a small hamper in the cupboard under the bows,[6] and, both being competent punters, were swung by whomever took the pole, northwards along the Cherwell past Magdalen's magnificent pile and its deer park, upriver past the wide, still unchanged cricket grounds of colleges and university until finding the right, quiet mooring spot below a willow.

For someone raised for walking up the Old Man of Coniston, Oxford walks came easily. One such took Collingwood along the High Street, briskly down St. Aldate's and westwards across the mill stream and the railway to Hinksey where his father had been taught road-building by Ruskin, north to the west side of Osney and up the lane to Binsey where, a little before Collingwood's birth, Gerard Manley Hopkins wrote his lament to the felling of Binsey Poplars, one of a collection of poems that was not to appear in Oxford until 1918 and when it did, to such *éclat*.

> To mend her we end her,
> When we hew or delve:

After-comers cannot guess the beauty been.
Ten or twelve, only ten or twelve
Strokes of havoc unselve
The sweet especial scene,
Rural scene, a rural scene,
Sweet especial rural scene.

The poplars had gone when Collingwood stood there, and the thousand yards or so towards the city, still a sort of meadowland today, was already disfigured by what Hopkins, in a second love poem to Oxford, called her "base and brickish skirt." But if he had turned around and walked upwards another quarter mile or so, crossing the present site of the A34, an early bypass, until he stood on the corner of Marley wood, he could lift up his eyes beyond the Isis and the railway and have his gaze filled by the loveliest skyline in England. Well to his left, the towers and spires of Keble and of Somerville, first fortress of women's university education, at the northern edge of the then city, traversing south by way of the great mass of the Ashmolean, on a clear day and his tiptoes he could pick out the green copper dome of Queen's, the twin towers of All Souls, the commanding spire of St. Mary's, the university's church, and, at the southwestern end of the old city, the magnificent bulk of Christchurch's cathedral and Tom Tower tolling, as dusk gathered, its nightly 101 strokes.

Oxford, like her immemorial rival, is first of all an architectural experience, and the love of the city that working at its ancient trade in thought and knowledge naturally engenders is felt by way of its haughty castellated and forbidding exteriors—Balliol, St. John's, University, Magdalen—and the loveliness with which the great walls admit the pedestrian through their low entrances to the delicate and domestic interplay of stone and grass and occasional water, of short low passages from whose shadows one emerges into sunshine, turning the grey stone honey-coloured, opening suddenly at one end on wide meadows and the river.

It is a risky business trying to fix the nature of deep attachment to a place, and that place Oxford where so many writers and painters have brought off the same thing. Nor did Collingwood write much in this vein himself. But when he did, in the lecture on Ruskin's aesthetics, in his extraordinary essay on the historical origins of the King Arthur legend, even in his *bien-pensant* but heartfelt invocation of agrarian life and labour as the root of the good society (if it's true, then the good society is done for), perhaps above all in his exposition of T. S. Eliot's *The Wasteland*, Collingwood's loving attachment to the land-and-townscape whose history was his livelihood is plain upon the page.[7] It is, however, strongest of all when inexplicit in his devoted attention to all the traces of the same necessary love of place that lay deposited in stone, mortar, bones, metal, pots, and fossils several feet below the ordinary lie of the twentieth-century land, once a stretch of Roman Empire.

Many of the men whose purposes and passions lay there to be reconstructed from rubble and shards must have felt utterly alien to the mist and rain on Hadrian's Wall, and homesickness needs no poetry to fill a Roman soldier's being with longing for the Rhone or the Rhine. But the archaeologist's patient and unsentimental copying of the stone inscriptions left on tombs and regimental plaques in forts and on the wall cannot fail to be tinged with a sympathetic speculation that the centurion, like the archaeologist, came to love the land whose stones he cut and piled. Kipling's account of the Roman Wall in *Puck of Pook's Hill* was historically wrong but, to Collingwood as a boy, completely gripping. Kipling's poem about the centurion's love of the place, a regard for which was shared by T. S. Eliot, held the archaeologist's heart.

I've served in Britain forty years, from Vectis to the Wall.
I have none other home than this, nor any life at all.
Last night I did not understand, but, now the hour draws near
That calls me to my native land, I feel that land is here.

Here where men say my name was made, here where my work was done;
Here where my dearest dead are laid—my wife—my wife and son;
Here where time, custom, grief and toil, age, memory, service, love,
Have rooted me in British soil. Ah, how can I remove?[8]

II

Collingwood belonged in Oxford and to the Lakeland. He learned the ways of Oxford swiftly, and in any case its social rules sorted well with his own disposition, however much he annoyed his elders by absenting himself from formal college functions. He accepted its polite conventions and, leaving them to run themselves at the outer edge of his consciousness, withdrew to an inwardness where he could pursue his thoughts in peace.

But there were also impolite conventions, where the rules of Oxford sanctioned a sharpness and a bluntness with the ways of argument that would have broken into pieces the small change of conversation at the college dining table. Collingwood started to read philosophy in 1910 as a natural extension of the authors who filled the syllabus of his degree course, Classical Moderations, in his first year. After Homer, Virgil, Cicero, Lucretius, he turned to the distinguished Oxford tradition of British idealism, dominated by T. H. Green, his inspiration, and his father's tutor, Bernard Bosanquet. These men counted themselves heirs of Hegel but broke with him radically on most of his more importunate demands on history and Absolute Spirit. These two men and their fellow idealists—F. H. Bradley, Robert Nettleship, J. A. Smith, and H. H. Joachim—were also deep in intellectual debt to John Stuart Mill and counted themselves less Hegelians than heirs of David Hume and the Scottish Enlightenment.

As we have seen, Green, who died of septicaemia aged only forty-six, took his liberal and his Enlightenment inheritance into public life. His pupils carried his teaching into active politics and the institutions of social reform. The key concept of the common good and its implications for the authority of the state, as well as for the necessity of systematic social bonds that will hold different social classes in common membership, would still strike many chords of sympathy and recognition, were it not the case that the entire old school of the Idealists took such a fearful intellectual hammering at the hands of a new generation of philosophers that only Collingwood survived in isolation to sustain that line of force into the present. For while there can be no doubt that he was held in enormous esteem even by those who rejected his arguments, he kept up his kind of philosophy pretty well alone, and the archaeologists to whom he taught his theory and his practice never knew that they shared a philosophical method that also enshrined a moral vision.

The hammering of idealism—the doctrine, as I said, that the world *is* our idea of it—was first administered by diverse hands, mostly at Oxford, who had started work as jobbing idealists, first swept into the current of idealism with its strongest sources in Glasgow, Edinburgh, and St. Andrews. Of course in Germany, where Hegel's heirs (including Marx and the Left Hegelians) were generally entrenched, the attack on idealism was only brought to a triumphant conclusion by the devastating work of Friedrich Nietzsche.

Nietzsche wrote with fierce contempt of the emptiness of contemporary moral conventions; he detested the Christian pietism of the German bourgeoisie and was the first philosopher to conceive of "perspectivism," or the theory that there are many lenses through which we may behold life, that none of them has priority, least of all the "God hypothesis," and that only by constructing a "genealogy" of moral and epistemological thought will humankind discover a philosophy for itself with which to grasp, control, and emancipate its nature.[9]

Nietzsche died insane in 1900. For many years afterwards, his name was known in Britain mostly as a danger[10] (although he mattered a good deal to F. H. Bradley), but he was first to declare the end of metaphysics (which followed from the death of God). One mark of Collingwood's membership of a subsequent generation is not only his slow and incomplete withdrawal from Christianity, but also and more centrally his turning metaphysics itself into a historical inquiry, a genealogy of "absolute presuppositions."

The diminuendo as one turns from the name of Nietzsche to that of John Cook Wilson is so steep as to bring on vertigo. But to recover the origins of Collingwood's thought, it is necessary to take a few moving pictures of the social production of Oxford philosophy in the last years up to 1914 (not that social-class context or mode of production changed much between 1914 and, say, 1968).

Making philosophy was then a matter of conversation. This is to use the word literally. Philosophic argument took place by way of the lecture, the tutorial, face-to-face altercation and exchange, personal letters (in 1935 Collingwood and Gilbert Ryle wrote to one another some 25,000 words in an exchange of letters on "the ontological proof"), and endless, silent soliloquy. The main characters in the debate published very little. In the case of John Cook Wilson, first protagonist of the doctrine of realism or the contention that the world-out-there needs no help from ourselves if it is to be there and that it is unaffected by our perceiving it, professor of logic at Oxford for twenty-six years, he published nothing at all apart from translations from Greek until the very end of his life.[11]

He was a man of force and complexity, and peculiarly exemplary of the Oxford don. That is to say, he was very clever, very inspiring, utterly unaware of the line between elaborate good manners and hard professional rudeness, and powerfully egotistical insofar as philosophy itself went. That said, one of many devoted pupils and distinguished successors, H. A. Prichard (modes of address were then all initials and surnames), spoke of him as "generous, loyal to a fault, warm-tempered for sure," an inexhaustible climber and fell-walker, as they all were—R. L. Nettleship, Green's loyal editor, was killed in the Alps—and his invalid wife's patient nurse for twenty years.[12]

Doing philosophy for such a man was a matter of putting error down as flatly and plainly as possible. In a phrase that presages Wittgenstein, he declared his philosophic purpose to be "disentangling the mind from the snares of verbal expression," "the ultimate gain being to find out what will *not do*" (Cook Wilson's italics), the centre of such contentious activity being the verb "to know." The convergence of all such argument at Oxford was upon establishing a theory of knowledge, and Cook Wilson, whose declared enemy was "the crime of slovenly thinking," was in the van of the movement that culminated in A. J. Ayer's logical positivist classic, *Language, Truth and Logic* in 1936. Cook Wilson's endeavour was to make knowledge as clear and definite as—well, the facts about things. He gave a lecture course entitled "Things in Space" and threw off the strains of idealism by a trenchant briskness of this sort: "the possession of an idea is useless unless we know it to be like the reality . . . and to know this we must already know the reality and so have no need of the idea."[13]

Cook Wilson's great strength was to insist on the variety of acts of mind, and to keep distinct from one another supposition, judgement, inference, proposition, and so forth. Knowledge itself, however, is for him the foundation of thought, and its ideal type is mathematics. Logic, therefore, just *is* the study of the principles of thinking. In saying this, he was the trumpet if not of his age then of his intellectual milieu at Oxford and Cambridge. For at the same time, Bertrand Russell was arguing for the primacy of mathematics as *the* type of knowledge, although by methods that Cook Wilson described, characteristically, as "puerile," "contemptible" ("where *was* the publisher's reader?" he adds).[14]

He was a dedicated teacher, fiery, fluent, widely read (he had first studied the theory of knowledge with the eminent German realist, R. H. Lotze). To a twenty-one-year-old just beginning contemporary philosophy, with the thrill that rightly brings of listening to the *dernier cri*, he was irresistible, even to the point at which he told off his young student, no less characteristically: "there are two kinds of damn fool: there are damn silly fools like X, and damn clever fools like Y; and if you're going to be a damn fool, you'd much better be a damn silly one."[15] Collingwood ends his anecdote by teasing us, "I am sorry I cannot think myself justified in naming the eminent contemporary philosophers whom I have called X and Y."

There is much of Cook Wilson the man in the tale; maybe one can see the point of his advice. More to our point, however, is how much it tells us of the intellectual weather in which Oxford philosophers ordinarily took their constitutionals. It was vehement, it poured down ruthlessly on all pedestrians, it provided the stuff of daily conversation, it was intensely *local*. It soon cleared up. It did not destroy careers or even sensibilities. A cheerful student could get a drenching in the name of the mistakes made by one philosopher and be amiably consoled and warmed through by his tormenter.

When the magi met in the same room, at the Oxford Philosophical Society (for graduates) or the Jowett Society (for undergraduates), the Oxford manner held up and put down, as it was designed to do.

Cook Wilson was the biggest personality on the philosophic map of Oxford. But it was a populous map, with other landmarks. H. A. Prichard proved of similar longevity and unignorability. His first book, *Kant's Theory of Knowledge* and a straightforward critique of Kant from a position of Cook Wilsonian realism, came out in 1909; he was still writing for *Mind* in the late 1940s. Like all Oxonians, until the divisions of intellectual labour were more strictly marked out in the 1960s, Prichard entered the fields as both moralist and epistemologist, before assuming the title of White's professor of moral philosophy.

Prichard, like his senior, delighted in controversy and was, in Collingwood's own words, "an extremely acute and pertinacious thinker." These qualities, along with the zest for controversy, were exactly those nourished by the trade and the social milieu of Oxford philosophy. The certainty of rightness was quite sublime and gave rise, to Collingwood's exasperation, to a routine professional error, which was to argue with past thinkers as though they all—Plato, Leibniz, Spinoza, Kant, and company—were there together in Oxford in 1912.

From this distance, the self-centredness looks extraordinary. But perhaps it only does so exactly because Collingwood was to intervene in the name of historical philosophising. In 1912 Prichard published a famous paper, assertive and polemical as all his papers were, as the house style was, entitled "Does Moral Philosophy Rest on a Mistake?"[16] The mistake was to suppose that morality had to do with any larger field of action than that marked out by the forbidding notice, "Duty." Prichard specified with uncompromising firmness the force of the words "ought" and "obligation" as its corresponding abstract norm. Where there are things we ought to do, neither our personal desires nor the exercise of such virtues as one may have and which may be productive of good have any bearing on our actions. The moral realm is the realm of duty.[17] Obligation is paramount and only a higher obligation can trump another (lower) one. This for

Prichard and, it can reasonably be added, for all the right-thinking and principled English gentlemen who were his audience, his students, or the slightly wider but still locally metropolitan circle of the best of his social class, "ought" possessed a clinching authority. You ought always to do what you ought to do, whatever the impediments.

Collingwood, not a man to baulk at his duty, was, however, mockingly censorious of Prichard for the very reason that such a use of "ought" does not appear in print until the late eighteenth century, and then not in Hume. Oxonian philosophers like Prichard supposed themselves to be discussing exactly the same timeless questions as all the philosophers on the Oxford syllabus. Prichard hit upon the Greek word which it suited him to translate by "ought" and then berated the Greeks for a mistaken theory of moral obligation. As Collingwood wrote a quarter century or so after he began to rumble the realists:

> It was like having a nightmare about a man who had got it into his head that trireme was the Greek for "steamer," and when it was pointed out to him that descriptions of triremes in Greek writers were at any rate not very good descriptions of steamers, replied triumphantly, "That is just what I say. These Greek philosophers" (or, "these modern philosophers," according to which side he was on in the good old controversy between the Ancients and the Moderns) "were terribly muddle-headed, and their theory of steamers is all wrong."

Given the closeness of college life, the propinquity of one to another, the little neighbourhoods of red brick houses clustered round the Parks or in Summertown, the diminutive splendour of the city itself, it is no surprise that tight little schools, factions, vendettas, alliances, should so have characterised Oxford's intellectual life. Good manners forbade anything other than light conversation about another man's discipline, trespassing was prosecuted, the hard talk of philosophy kept strictly for philosophers. And although these were men well travelled in mainland Europe and speaking two or three of its languages (German necessarily, French, Italian) as well as the two classical tongues, they were instinctively Anglocentric and delicately condescending to the many visiting Americans who brought their pragmatism and their Anglophilia to be looked over at Oxford—Henry Adams, William James often—and who went away leaving their hosts unmoved.

Collingwood's philosophy tutor was one E. F. Carritt, an admirer of Prichard[18] and another but more expansive realist, but nonetheless the man who effected a crucial introduction when he sent his pupil to read the work of Benedetto Croce, which had been put top of his reading list in J. A. Smith's inaugural lecture of 1910. Collingwood had taught himself Italian in order to read Dante at school. During the vacations of the year 1908–9, he had visited the cities of the Grand Tour—Venice, Florence, Siena, Rome, Naples—familiar to his parents and had then picked up a copy of Giambattista Vico's *Autobiography* and *The New Science*, the latter published in 1725. Vico was the first philosopher to enunciate a theory of history insisting on the difference of the past from the present together with the necessity for the historian to understand the past empathetically, and to repudiate the Cartesians' demands for rigorous proof.[19]

There could be no reconciling historicism and realism. Naturally enough, however, as Collingwood moved towards his final examinations, he called himself a realist and went to listen to Harold Joachim of Merton, later Cook Wilson's successor as Wykeham professor, who became a close friend. Tough-minded, cheerful, refreshingly informal, he practised an elegant scepticism even upon the premises of his own logic. No proposition, he affirmed in his lectures, was wholly true;[20] knowledge is always incomplete, the history of thought develops stage by stage out of itself. First to picture this process and then to validate it, Joachim trod uneasily back to Hegel, where he balanced himself on the Oxonian fulcrum between old idealism and new realism, and shrank the Absolute Spirit down to something personal.

So, too, did J. A. Smith of Balliol, Waynflete professor of metaphysics for twenty-five years, a gentle gentleman, even diffident amid the prevailing self-confidence, who, like many of his colleagues, published only occasional lectures and translations of Aristotle but was a mild, courteous, much respected presence-about-Oxford, rather submissive towards the toughs from the realist school, keeping up by way of his office and his devoted teaching a respectable front for a doomed idealism.[21] His quiet humanity and calm temper commended him to Collingwood, whose own disposition, at least externally, was of a piece with Smith's. Smith became his academic father, and when, in 1916, Smith gave the eponymous Hibbert Lectures, Collingwood took the train every week from London, where he was in Admiralty Intelligence, and made faithful notes of his friend's unexceptionable metaphysical ruminations.[22]

The *Hibbert Journal* was the house magazine of the metaphysicals and gave birth to a little society calling itself simply the Cumnor Group, which met either in Queen's, in members' houses on Cumnor Hill, or at Smith's dignified Victorian mansion at 6 Norham Gardens, in order to discuss turns in modern theology. Rather to the surprise of his father, who lapsed as a young man from membership of the Darbyite or "open" wing of the Plymouth Brethren, his son had decided to receive confirmation into the Anglican church at Rugby in 1906. He attended college chapel devoutly enough and, being the man he was, sought out modern heresy with an eye to accommodating it.

The metaphysicals and the realists clashed, co-existed, and compromised with one another. As his finals approached in the summer of 1912, Collingwood, his mind half made up for realism, the other half strongly coloured by Christianity, ardently responsive to the music of metaphysics, of the necessity of immanence, began to move towards limning for himself a definition of a life's work that would bring into a single perspective the love of art he had learned at home, a stern adhesion to the principles and practice of history as taught by archaeology, and a reconciliation of a theistic metaphysics with the methods of scepticism as conveyed by his strong-minded teachers.

The degree itself, for this born scholar, represented a formidable training for such a task. In the first year of Classical Moderations, the examinations demanded translations of Homer, Virgil, Demosthenes, and Cicero, detailed knowledge of the history of drama, Latin and Greek prose and verse compositions (mastery of the conventions and strange elisions that ensured a right metric reading of the twelve-syllable line), adequacy in deductive logic. In his second and third year of *Literae Humaniones* or "Greats" (Oxford patois for the Classics degree), the student worked his way through the small print of the Greek and Roman historians, in Collingwood's case with particular attention to the biography of Governor Agricola in Tacitus's mighty history of the empire. For Agricola, round about the year 78, conquered, pacified, and colonised Britain in one rigorous campaign. He built roads and chains of forts from Chester to Carlisle, from York to the Tyne at Corbridge. "The next event of which we have certain knowledge is the establishment of a properly organised frontier by Hadrian, about the year 122."[23]

At this point, the syllabus and Collingwood's own life intersected in one of those abrupt, thrilling moments at which one's heart is of a sudden too small to hold its blood and for which the scholar's search is endless. For during the long vacation of 1913 he assumed, with his sister Ursula's help, as it were his first archaeological command at Galava fort on the present edge of Ambleside. The earth and stone of Cumbria speckled the pages of Tacitus with the living dust of the dead empire. The suddenness with which the past arrives in the present turned into a vertigo it was then his philosophical quest to steady up and slow down until its dizzy transit became intelligible.

The rest of the syllabus he could turn to this purpose. After history, logic, and metaphysics with Plato and Aristotle, moral and political philosophy extending well beyond Rome and Athens in his "special subject," which was, naturally, philosophy, brought him by way of the high excitements of the Latin of Spinoza's *Ethics* and the English of Hobbes's *Leviathan* to accept his hospitable tutor's invitations to a "philosophers" tea' and listen to the quickfiring of Cook Wilson, H.W.B. Joseph, Harold Joachim, and company. Collingwood's tutor, E. F. Carritt, was an energetic, argumentative, generous sort of man with catholic tastes in philosophy who became a close friend and had, with J. A. Smith, introduced his pupil to the works and, in 1923, to the person of Benedetto Croce.

Collingwood punctually won First Class honours in June 1912 and, there never having been any doubt about the career he would follow, at once applied for a vacant fellowship in philosophy at Pembroke College.

He was interviewed while still wearing his undergraduate scholar's gown, and his rivals at interview were William Pickard-Cambridge, who later made a name as a classical historian of drama, and one F. R. Barry from Oriel, a churchman with theological prizes to his name about whom the college's grim old toad of a house classicist, Drake, ruled with pursed lips that "he wanted to look after young men's souls." Collingwood's referees were unanimous in their praise. His former housemaster at Rugby, W. N. Wilson, we have already heard from. The philosophy tutor and dean at University College, A.S.L. Farquharson, an admirer of Cook Wilson,[24] weighed in first and handsomely, and Carritt, in striking and affectionate terms, did the same.[25] Carritt is worth quoting at length; these days, references are rarely so well written (it is worth adding that the adjective "brilliant" had not then undergone any colloquial devaluation).

I am told by his other teachers that his studies and practical work in archaeology are brilliant, but his main interest is in philosophy, and in this I consider him the most promising and accomplished pupil I have had since Mr A. D. Lindsay. . . . He has read widely, and has scholarly habits, great power of mastering a subject, and remarkable industry. His clearness of thought, acuteness in discussion, and sympathetic understanding of others' points of view, should make him an excellent teacher, as I have reason to believe he has already been found, in the way appropriate to their relation, by his contemporaries.

His music and artistic gifts make him a valuable companion on other than academic grounds, and I am glad to be able to speak of him as a friend as well as a pupil.

The warmth and cordiality of this bring Collingwood's figure, at the age of twenty-three, glowingly up close to us. The self-styled solitude dissolves into a group of serious-minded young men listening to the high, fluent north-country voice issuing from the bony face with its sharp nose, high cheekbones, and thick hair shaken forward by the emphasis of his speech.

Cook Wilson, the most senior voice of the quartet, wrote from his eminence in New College:

> For a considerable time he has been a member of a class of mine in Logic and Metaphysics, attending with unwearying assiduity, two hours per week, term after term. . . . he has also attended a select and advanced class for the study of difficult problems in metaphysics. . . . he is sane and judicious, avoiding the rhetoric and verbiage which too often takes the place of thinking in this subject, attending to the essentials of the problems before him with something of the concentration of a mathematician, and too seriously interested in his subject to strain after paradoxes. At the same time his style is genial and refined . . . he has the root of the matter in him . . . and could develop into one of the most valued representatives of philosophy in our university.

Those difficult problems were set for the seminar by Leibniz at the beginning of the eighteenth century in the opening paragraphs of his *Monadology*. His bleak doctrine, which so appealed to Cook Wilson for its bare reduction of all creation to simple entities, ran as follows: "it must be said that there is nothing in things except simple substances, and in them, nothing but perception and appetite . . . matter and motion are not so much substances or things as they are the phenomena of percipient beings."[26] Sympathetic to the heart with such a view, Cook Wilson could teach that ontology, the science of being and of its existence, the science of the categorical structures of reality, should best dispense with such ideas as "spirit" or even "history," and move towards an account of the world as independent of human perceptions, one in which propositions are true or false even if we can never know which.

As Cook Wilson's cleverest student took up his new post, he was becoming ill at ease with counting himself a realist, above all because of the depth of his immersion in the history they so airily dissolved into substances and properties. The mistake, he began to think at twenty-three, was not the desert dryness of this doctrine, but its supposition that it was itself free from its own, philosophic history, that philosophy could invent its own reality for realism to be realistic about, in 1912.

These thoughts marked the beginning of his discovery of his vocational purpose. There is never much point, whether in aesthetic or philosophic criticism, in arguing for coherent patterns of thought in the life's work of a thinker or a poet. The history of all thought is broken up into new starts, blind alleys, reactionary retreats, fake advances, whether in one person's work or in a collective movement. Yet in a life, as in an epoch, we search out form and direction. A biography is an attempt to place a life against a moral horizon, to frame it with its recognisable landmarks and pathways. One such framing was for Collingwood the long journey to make philosophy and history synonymous.

At Oxford he was a philosopher. In the autumn of 1912 he began his teaching career as fellow and lecturer in philosophy and classics at Pembroke, not at all one of the more fashionable colleges. The *haut ton* attended Christ Church, Magdalen, and Trinity, the intelligentsia Balliol and New College, the evangelicals Keble, and, this being England, all the rest arranged themselves in a descending hierarchy of esteem measured by money, family, and intelligence, with Pembroke somewhere near the bottom on all indices.

It was of course much smaller than it is now, and so poor that in 1915 Magdalen sent it £200 to tide it over a very penurious patch (between 1916 and 1933 the college received in gift and legacies a trifling total of £16,000). It was and is packed into a little cul-de-sac at the end of Pembroke Street opposite Christ Church, at that time a maze of narrow medieval alleys impassable to traffic, each winding through one another, several tumbledown houses, mostly over four hundred years old, serving as residences for students and fellows, cycles or shoes the only vehicles of transport. Always short of cash, the college had at the time a mere handful of permanent teachers— a master, who did little teaching, a bursar, a couple of historian-classicists "handling Mods and Greats"[27] (Collingwood and a grim, long- and time-serving old warrior called Drake), a chaplain in charge of divinity (although in 1912 the master was one Bishop Mitchinson), a college dean; and that was pretty well that: no economist, no natural scientist, no modern linguist. Collingwood doubled as librarian, and his library was partly housed in the Junior Common

Room where an undergraduate served as inefficient deputy, and partly in an upper lecture room. The rare books collection, including all the volumes once belonging to the college's principal alumnus-genius, Dr. Johnson, was held in the master's lodgings. Fellows were required to remain bachelors and to dine in college during term-time. They were charged a nominal rent and ran an account (the "battel") for food, wine, the services of their scout.

At this distance, it is easy to forget the privations and even the squalor, which Collingwood had learned to detest at Rugby. The baths were all located in a large communal bathroom off the second quadrangle, the high, wide urinals alongside them. Nocturnal urination was a matter of either the chamber pot or a chilly walk. The social life of the fellowship was formal, often taciturn, deeply hierarchical, frequently malicious. Its topics were local, self-absorbed, narrow-minded. And yet, to step through the small door opening in the great portal of the college was and is to pass into an uplifting serenity, shaped to the interplay of grass and grey stone, the modest scale of the first quadrangle opening by way of the *sottopassagio* into the second larger one, closed at its further end by the high and dignified chapel wall, pierced with little late Gothic windows.

These are surroundings whose every association in our culture is with the high-minded and disinterested disciplines of the mind, with calm and careful scholarship, with the best that has been known and thought. From 1912 to 1939, "drunken Pemmy"[28] may have had a name, as its future master confessed, for never making its men *work*, for its easygoing admission of public school playboys, for the heady strength of its college-brewed beer, but it was a self-confident part of Oxford at a time when a tiny proportion of the nation's young men and scarcely any women at all went on to university, and Collingwood entered happily into its inheritance at a going rate of £6 per student taught.

The division in his life, however, between the plain, superb style of Duke Humfrey's library and the sheds and tarpaulins covering the holes in the ground of Borrans Field on the edge of Ambleside was more than geographical. In the summer vacation of 1913, he took over direction of the dig at Galava, having long been active in its excavations. Now he had the command of the labourers who did the heavy work, watchful that they did not damage whatever lay beneath turfs, rocks, spoil, dug out by hand and spade to a depth, frequently, of eight or nine feet.

The digging season lasted four summer weeks or so, interrupted and obstructed by Lakeland's heavy rainfall. The labourers themselves needed to become sharp enough of observation to call out for supervision when they struck what looked like a course of hand-laid stone or brick, or the merest traces of mortar and lime concrete, and sharper still to spot inside encrustations of earth a tiny, dull brown coin or a shard of pottery.

Surely the minutest of the human sciences is archaeology, far and away the most physically exacting, and demanding an absolute patience. At first sight, it is surprising that a man of Collingwood's quickness and restlessness of mind should have made himself an adept and an acolyte of so gradual a mystery. But the slow discipline of the dig is an analogy to the extended inquiry of the painting. It is the practice of a craft that may turn at any moment into the practice of an art. This is a key distinction in *The Principles of Art*, between craft, which is the direction of learned technique with specific tools towards a known end, and art proper, which, while undoubtedly demanding a mastery of technique, of "intelligent and purposeful labour, painful and conscientious self-discipline,"[29] is the successful discovery and expression of an end that was to begin with unenvisageable, and is now to be understood as an answer of sorts to the question the artist began by posing to his or her experience.

Archaeology is both art and craft for those who might be called the farmers among the human scientists. They are outdoor people, used even now to physical effort, content to reap their findings and then to cover up their crop and wait for its harvest in another year. There is a photograph of Collingwood taking a charcoal rubbing of a Roman inscription—it was a life's work; he made five thousand of them.[30] He is on his knees on stony, backward-sloping ground, his arms uncomfortably embracing a big Roman tombstone, as he tries to secure the paper around the stone in order to rub for an impression. The task would take well over an hour; the dry, crackling paper might tear and the whole thing need to be started again. When finished, he would draw or photograph it, his drawings of the inscriptions, like his plans and reconstructions of a whole site, being always clear, accurate, and exquisite, the line free and lovely, so that one longs for those countless drawings of his that are lost.

His tutor in archaeology, besides his father, was the great F. J. Haverfield, associate of Theodor Mommsen, doyen of German historians. Haverfield, who died in 1919 at the age of only fifty-nine, was professor of ancient history at Oxford for the last seventeen years of his life,[31] and Collingwood naturally attended his lectures and rapidly became his friend, ally, and co-worker. Haverfield started off the Galava excavations (he conducted five hundred such during his career) and handed them over to Collingwood after they had written a joint report together in 1913. They both delighted in the severe practicality of their science, the steady labour and close interrogation of the ground at their feet. As his biographer says, Haverfield turned a practical craft into a historical art, and Collingwood went away to transform that practice into theory.

The rubbing, the drawing, the digging, the careful breaking off of hard, dried earth from a coin or a piece of a pot, the sheer rarity of such a find, the painstaking and uncertain business of taping the lines of an encampment, this was the thick experience out of which Collingwood began to shape not so much—as people now mouthfillingly say—a methodology, but a theory of practice, or as it might with less glassy abstraction be put, a practical rationality, a way of making the world intelligible.

He began, as he tells us, by realising the pointlessness of digging a site while asking casually, "Let's see what's here." Nor was one much better off by asking a slightly more pointed question as one dug about hither and yon, questions such as "Is that black stuff peat or occupation soil? Is that a potsherd under your foot?" He discovered for himself what Bacon and Descartes had already told him, that knowledge is constituted of truthful answers to the right questions asked in the right order. The true historical genius was to think out what these questions and their right order were. It was his later discovery to see not only that answers to the questions were partial, but that the partiality was an inescapable function of the inquirer's historical location. The recovery of the past by way of understanding the purposes and intentions of a Roman legion and its commander would serve only this present corner of history, not all presents still locked up in their futures.

So it was that farming for history in the dig at Ambleside served the first stirrings of his resentful disagreement with the realists. Cook Wilson had once, characteristically, said to his pupil, "I will say one thing about you: you can see the obvious." But if it was obvious that knowledge was, so to say, a product more like a work of art (and therefore the unforeseeable end to certain difficult questions)[32] than (in Cook Wilson's term) the "apprehension" of what was simply there for the senses to apprehend, then Cook Wilson couldn't see it. Collingwood learned from Borrans Field that realist teachings could not resist attacks from their own troops, but the first glimmerings of what he came to call his "question-and-answer logic" did away with this all-confident knower of knowledge and replaced him with an interrogative *person*, not only intent upon sharpening a list of questions until they could cut open the evidence cleanly, but addressing them to the exact historical original in order to comprehend its answers. Hence,

> I therefore taught my pupils, more by example than by precept, that they must never accept any criticism of anybody's philosophy which they might hear or read without satisfying themselves by first-hand study that this was the philosophy he actually expounded; that they must always defer any criticism of their own until they were absolutely sure they understood the text they were criticising; and that if the postponement was *sine die* it did not greatly matter. This did not as yet involve any attack upon the realists' critical methods. When my pupils came to me armed with grotesquely irrelevant refutations of (say) Kant's ethical theory, and told me they came out of So-and-so's lectures, it was all one to me whether the irrelevance came from their misrepresenting So-and-so, or from So-and-so's misrepresenting Kant: my move was to reach for a book with the words, "Let us see whether that is what Kant really said."

In lecturing, I adopted a similar procedure. I had become something of a specialist in Aristotle, and the first lectures I gave were on the *De Anima*. My plan was to concentrate on the question, "What is Aristotle saying and what does he mean by it?" and to forgo, however alluring it might be, the further question "Is it true?"[33]

III

When war broke out in 1914, Collingwood, already fluent in German, in correspondence with its scholars, sailing off its northwestern coast, familiar at least with its Roman frontier, had, for all his Englishness, no taint of militarist fervour or anti-German hysteria in his bones. He kept on with his teaching duties and went back to finish at Galava in the summer vacation of 1915.

Popular opinion was still on the patriotic boil. There had been shocking news from Mons and Loos, but the hideous roll call was still fairly short. Self-righteousness would have its say, and, in A.J.P. Taylor's words, "The agitation crystallised around the demand for compulsory military service."[34] And although the director of national service later concluded that conscription added nothing effective to the war effort, it was widely believed that there were thousands of slackers, arbitrarily supposed to number 650,000, who were dodging the draft. Lloyd George, foaming with military zeal, pressed for formal conscription. Asquith, persuaded of the virtues of a voluntary system, found a compromise. Men of military age would "attest" their readiness to serve if and when called up. Two and a half million men obliged, among them, I guess, Collingwood.

His stiff knee would have kept him out of the infantry in any case. A second operation in March 1913 at Acland House in Oxford had made no great difference, his sight wasn't good, severe hay fever as well as congenital inheritance drove blood pressure, which would eventually prove lethal, too high. But the family name was an exalted one in naval annals, and, as his single-handed crossings of the English Channel testify, he certainly did not lack physical courage.

He was immune, however, to the waves of patriotic sentimentality that coursed through the nation and swept the first hundred thousand volunteers into uniform before the war was three months old. Roman history had more than familiarised him with the necessities of empire, and left him entirely hardened to the ruthlessness of subordination. But the new war was not just different, it was unprecedented. It fell quite outside any of the normal considerations of the practical politics he had studied in theory. Indeed, the only theorist in history whose work seemed adequate in both its pessimism of vision and its realism of remedy was Thomas Hobbes. Twenty-six years later, as the consequences of the First World War led to the outbreak of the Second, even more terrible and menacing, Collingwood sought, as he said, "to bend the bow of Ulysses"[35] and write a "new science of human affairs" capable of comprehending the causes of a monstrous barbarism and its effects upon the tough, capacious civilisation that would defeat it.

In 1915, however, his philosophic rejoinder to historical enormity was more conventional, and his practical response to the pressing question of how to act with the enemy at the gates accidentally expedient. So he turned his fluent pen to demanding of religion what it had to say about its adversary the devil, roaming abroad and seeking whom he might devour, and meanwhile volunteered for a deskbound appointment in Admiralty Intelligence, then operating out of the Royal Geographical Society.

His father was already voluntarily recruited, well over sixty, to the same department and it seems likely was instrumental in keeping his beloved son out of harm's way.[36] However this may be, Collingwood removed perforce to London, rented a room at 69 Kensington Church Street, and every morning walked to work past the splendours of Kensington Palace and into Kensington Gardens. On his right was the bulbous magnificence of the Albert Hall, ahead of him the shining surface of the Serpentine and, as he took the Flower Walk past the Queen's Gate he braced himself daily for the shock to his system rendered by the Albert Memorial, with the great consort seated beneath his spindly, overdecorated, and towering shelter, rather on the lines of the giant candle extinguisher carried by the Ghost of Christmas Past.

> Everything about it was visibly misshapen, corrupt, crawling, verminous; for a time I could not bear to look at it, and passed with averted eyes; recovering from this weakness, I forced myself to look, and to face day by day the question: a thing so obviously, so incontrovertibly, so indefensibly bad, why had Scott done it? To say that Scott was a bad architect was to burke the problem with a tautology; to say that there was no accounting for tastes was to evade it by *suggestio falsi.* What relation was there, I began to ask myself, between what he had done and what he had tried to do? Had he tried to produce a beautiful thing; a thing, I meant, which we should have thought beautiful? If so, he had of course failed. But had he perhaps been trying to produce something different? If so, he might possibly have succeeded. If I found the monument merely loathsome, was that perhaps my fault? Was I looking in it for qualities it did not possess, and either ignoring or despising those it did?

The memorial slowly turned into his ideal type of historical problem, one the solution of which would attain to that fuller conception of knowledge itself of which the realists were ignorant and which would hold together both the activity of knowing *and* what is known. Thus a new mathematical theorem or a new work of art is at once the discovery and the fashioning of new knowledge. It is a bit of disappointment to report that Collingwood never tells us what he decided that Sir George Gilbert Scott was up to in devising his extraordinary memorial, but the intellectual generalisation to which his puzzling gave rise is both clear and true:

> you cannot find out what a man means by simply studying his spoken or written statements, even though he has spoken or written with perfect command of language and perfectly truthful intention. In order to find out his meaning you must also know what the question was (a question in his own mind, and presumed by him to be in yours) to which the thing he has said or written was meant as an answer.

It must be understood that question and answer, as I conceived them, were strictly correlative. A proposition was not an answer, or at any rate could not be the right answer, to any question which might have been answered otherwise.

He goes on: "A highly detailed and particularised proposition must be the answer, not to a vague and generalised question, but to a question as detailed and particularised as itself." So a man investigating his car engine after a breakdown and before the coming of the computer has no use for the vagueness of "why won't it go?" but must make his (locally successful) inquiries of different stages of combustion, from determining one by one whether each plug is sparking, on to dismantling the carburettor in order to see if the butterfly is stuck, and so forth. Each stage represents a satisfactory answer to a specific question. Hence his minatory conclusion that "you cannot tell what a proposition means unless you know what question it is meant to answer. . . . No two propositions . . . can contradict one another unless they are answers to the same question."[37]

Some such thoughts were already in his mind in 1916–17 when he wrote a now destroyed manuscript to be called *Truth and Contradiction*.[38] But his main and prior efforts outside naval intelligence went into his first book, begun a year or two before he arrived at the Admiralty and now made ready for publication as *Religion and Philosophy*, "published . . . because, at a time when a young man's expectation of life was a rapidly dwindling asset . . . I wished to leave at any rate one philosophical publication behind me."[39] When he submitted it to Macmillan, the reader, a clergyman, wondered why its author didn't go into orders.

It is an impressively stylish piece of writing, but it is not an argument likely to retain its grip nearly a century later. Collingwood's purpose is to treat religion as a philosophical topic, to ask *what it is*, not how it might be superseded or in some way improved. In his first of several assaults on psychology as an intellectual discipline (and with a hostile eye here and elsewhere on William James's 1902 classic *The Varieties of Religious Experience*), he dispatches those who think that religion is a merely emotional matter with no thinking or willing content to it and offers an inclusive declaration of the imperium of philosophy as subsuming the peculiar methods of science but as doing so on behalf of "through and through homogeneous straightforward thinking," disdaining the scientist's philosophical helplessness as his being baffled by questions to which his methods supply no answers.[40] Religion and philosophy are alike views (we would now say "theories") of the nature of the universe but expressed in different vocabularies.

He is at pains to accommodate the varieties not of religious experience but of religious allegiance, without building any altars to a personal god. God is a name for the principle of the universe, and by this token the serious atheist—serious in the devout sense that the universe is "mysterious and august"—is nonetheless a religious person for whom the *givenness* of certain facts about the universe and their making issues in precepts for conduct, which are then constituted as social institutions, in particular those of practical (and moral) rationality.

Throughout the book Collingwood writes with the quiet fervour and in the serene assumption not merely of the theist, but of the Christian. "[T]he self-dedication of the will to God is not the end of the individual life, but the beginning of a new and indeed of a more active life,"[41] and he embellishes this liturgy with versicles and responses about "free and joyful acceptance" that in the succeeding millennium are likely to stick in the gorge of his unchurched admirers.

He had, after all, made quite a thing of his turn to Anglicanism. He had asked for the full ceremony of baptism which his father, lapsed from the Brethren, had disregarded, and Dr. James had duly performed it, giving him his second name only at the age of sixteen, at Rugby School on 4 July 1905.[42] He was then confirmed by the bishop the following March. Once at Oxford he had joined the informal theological meeting, the Cumnor Group, which foregathered either at J. A. Smith's or in a house on Cumnor Hill, a little eminence on the west side of the city. There he befriended an active Christian apologist, Canon B. H. Streeter, who commissioned Collingwood's powerful essay "The Devil," as well as meeting regularly such prominent churchmen as Ronald Knox (a contemporary undergraduate at Balliol while he was at University) and C. H. Dodd from his own college, five years his senior but very visible in Oxford.

The intellectual atmosphere of the academic class was still, in 1916, sustained by scepticism; doubt, of course, it knew and even cultivated. The shock of the war had already blown apart many people's beliefs as well as their bodies. Noisy heretics, in particular Bertrand Russell, wrote contemptuously of the established church and dismissed its authority. But one cannot overestimate the forces of local knowledge nor the pressure of moral *atmosphere*, sixteen pounds to the square inch, in shaping belief into what Collingwood himself finally identified as our "absolute presupposition."[43] It became therefore his life's work, nearly half a century before Foucault, to archaeologise the foundations of belief, and to do so by excavating the strata of belief-formation as these were made visible in the morphology of differing, adjacent, and interpenetrating disciplines of the mind.

Such a mammoth venture is sure to be discontinuous. It is the open secret of the unity and scope of Collingwood's thought. If *that* is your self-appointed task, there are no limits to its range, and you must roam the map of knowledge and its perilous seas in the hope of finding not only magnetic north but a historically reliable (if impermanent) projection of the spheres of thought.

Religion and Philosophy is a first essay in this new genre. It is like a slim novel before novelists realised what they had invented. For "the layman is as much bound as the priest by the ideals of the religion which in some form or other he cannot help professing."[44]

There is a yet profounder theme in all this. Collingwood knew himself, even in this youthful essay, to have come onto the field of tournament as champion of antipositivism. Positivism, still the bloody old mastodon plodding across the wastes of data-collectibles, is the doctrine of empirical fact-collection, sterilised laboratory observation, foolproof and thoughtless hypothesis-verification. It is dogmatic scientism and not of course what serious scientists themselves actually practise.

Rather, it was what his newly identified enemies, "the realists," practised when they announced with such self-satisfaction that knowing makes no difference to what is known (in which case, as Collingwood said, how did they know?). Further, in this early work, he caught out the psychologists of religion (with whom he lumped in anthropologists like Tylor and Frazer as well) in the same positivist error. The great academic debate of the thirty or so years up to the outbreak of the First World War about "the historical Jesus" was held over the origins of Semitic theologies and the way in which Jesus changed and added to them, at least according to his evangelical biographers writing in the decades after his execution. But "the true task of historical theology is to find out not only what was said, but what was meant,"[45] which would be—to anticipate the phrase—to re-enact the thoughts of Jesus as he thought them: to excavate the questions to which his teachings were the answers.

At this stage, Collingwood is happy to leave matters as equivalently in the hands of both history and philosophy. History accumulates, therefore philosophy improves. On page 51 he risks saying they are the same thing, and this is just as true and consequential for theology, whether conceived as history or as philosophy. This intellectual heresy he gathers up into religion. For Christianity, here simply taken for granted as the crucial form of local religion, must be historically factual if it is to work. The drama of the life of Christ enacts a parable about the meaning of life; only by living in history the terrible sequence of events from Gethsemane onwards could this religious knowledge provide its special answer to the question of how is my life to be part of the meaning of life.

This releases the twenty-seven-year-old author into the freedoms of metaphysics, just then becoming a risible term for philosophers (remaining so amongst most of them until the day before yesterday). Present-day atheists of a briskly scientific persuasion, however, will not find the young Collingwood easy meat. Beginning by pointing out that no attempt at a proof, whether of a mathematical theorem or of the existence of God, can begin from nowhere, Collingwood reminds us not only of the historical assumptions from which thought *must* start out, but also of the absolute necessity to accept a degree of authority from past experience. Proof of God's existence and the personal nature of his being—the so-called ontological proof of Anselm—must allow Christianity's boldest claims, that is, for the omnipotence of God and his goodness.

Collingwood does not lack this boldness himself. The hauteur of the late style is well on the way to maturity in this first book. His sympathies are with Anselm, whom Collingwood much later quotes with relish as saying "I believe in order that I may understand; for this I know, that unless I first believe, I shall never understand. (T. S. Eliot, by now Collingwood's acquaintance, used the same quotation in a letter written at this time; Collingwood stored it up for twelve years.)"[46] For his premedieval teacher, the concept of God was *necessarily* instantiated. Nine centuries later, Anselm's disciple concluded, first, that because there is a common, perhaps unconscious, purpose uniting every good man and woman, every seeker after truth (which has innumerable aspects and yet is still one), then God is nonhypothetically immanent about us; second, God is transcendently *personal*, which is to say he cannot be "an undefined Absolute" because "to suppose that the spirit of goodness of which we are conscious in our hearts has its being there and there alone is no less fantastic than to suppose that the friends with whom we converse are only the projection upon nothingness of our own imagination."[47] Collingwood, in the key phrase, absolutely presupposes God. This— following his methodical precept—is *what he meant*.

In a parallel essay however, written at about the same time, on "The Devil," while taking seriously the possible manifestations of Old Nick complete with the acrid reek of fire and brimstone, Collingwood settles for understanding him as a myth.[48] Demonology is a storehouse of typefications not of devils, but of the will-to-evil alive in many persons.

There is, in this essay, the slightest shift from the firm orthodoxy of *Religion and Philosophy* in the direction of a narratology of the good life. "Man's nature," he says, is "in the great phrase of an English philosopher [T. H. Green in point of fact],[49] in process of being communicated to him." Collingwood goes on, "in that incomplete shape it is incapable of being the standard of anything. It is itself in need of a standard, and that standard, which for science is reality, for religion is God."[50] This is close to saying that God is the meaning of life because the meaning of life is God.

Prayer is not the contemplation of the ultimate being because we don't *contemplate* persons, we commune with them. God becomes the infinitude of good persons we each strive to become. The way is open for a secularised conception of goodness.

But not yet, if ever, for Collingwood. It is worth recalling, at this point in our narrative, that in 1914 T. Stearns Eliot, as he then signed himself, having begun his thesis at Harvard on F. H. Bradley,[51] came to finish it at Merton with Joachim and got on famously with Collingwood, only one year his junior, who was later to praise *The Waste Land* as the greatest of modern poems.

There are surely marked likenesses between Eliot's and Collingwood's conception of the making of the human nature of either the great poet or the great philosopher, and of the relation each man pictured himself as having with God. F. R. Leavis, writing in 1945 with unstinted admiration of Eliot's masterpiece, *Four Quartets*, said:

> The great difference between the thought of the metaphysical treatise and the thought in *Four Quartets* lies in the genius which enables the poet to refuse with such hardly credible rigour and success the ready-made, the illusory and the spectral in the way of conceptual apparatus, and to keep his abstractions so fully charged with the concrete of experience and his thinking so unquestionably faithful to it.[52]

The thought in *Four Quartets* is no less unquestionably "the thought of the metaphysician." Leavis's observations provide the standard against which to judge metaphysical writing. *Little Gidding* first came out when Collingwood had only a year or so to live. The progress of his writing is from the confident pieties and rather blank orthodoxies of *Religion and Philosophy*—striking though the manner is—to the plainness and beauty of *The Principles of Art* and the *Essay on Metaphysics*, the conversational ease and majestic scorn of *An Autobiography*, and, at the end, the vision and ruined splendour of late style in *The New Leviathan*.

"Charging abstractions with the concrete of experience" and "keeping thought faithful" to that experience, that is the calling of philosopher and poet alike. This task was for Collingwood identical with the dual, stupendous effort to affirm the unity of all the forms of thought—art, religion, science, history, philosophy—and to reinvent out of such a unity that "science of human affairs" the conspicuous absence of which had led to the hideousness of the Great War and the stupidity of the short peace. The war, as he later put it, "was an unprecedented triumph for natural science . . . and an unprecedented disgrace to the human intellect."[53]

One decisive conclusion transpired from his first book and was carried forward to the later work. It was his conviction that to sort out the relations of history and philosophy was the way to the new science that Vico had inaugurated under that title 175 years before. The missing science was certainly not psychology; Collingwood's assault on that topic is only begun in *Religion and Philosophy*; it is a main theme for him over the next twenty years. The missing science was not only to be historical, it was to be reflexive; it would settle the practices of everyday life within the thoughtfulness that constitutes them. This is the intertwined helix of theory and experience, and mapping it the purpose of his life.

IV

If "all history is the history of thought," what was Collingwood thinking during his time at a desk in the Admiralty? He was first set, it seems, to study the passages of the river Schelde in Belgium, from the two estuaries east and west of the peninsula of Noordbeveland and inland across the flats to Antwerp. The seaways and the river gave rise to a number of problems, juridical and nautical, and the dry-sounding job fired his imagination more than one might expect.

In 1903 a twenty-four-year-old civil servant of high promise called Erskine Childers published a political thriller brimming with seafaring distractions, entitled *The Riddle of the Sands*. In it the two young heroes discover a German plot to use the shallow and treacherous waterways of the rivers Elbe and Weser, punctuated by the muddy flats of the East Frisian islands, as a launching point for an invasion of Britain by way of the Wash. The book caused quite a stir. The so-called Great Naval Race had been signalled by the appointment of the bellicose Admiral Tirpitz in 1897 with the charge to build up the German Navy to a strength capable of challenging the Royal Navy. By 1902 Lord Selborne, first lord of the Admiralty, was saying in public that "if the German Fleet becomes superior to ours, the German Army can conquer this country." There was an almighty hum and buzz in the press about the danger of defeat at German hands, the Dreadnought building programme was launched, and Childers's gallant young men suddenly seemed real.

Naturally they foil the plot by warning the government, getting the plans back to London by daring seamanship in fog, storm, shallows, and gunfire. All the sailors at Rugby School—the sons of admirals and the future naval officers, the small boat boys of Pin Mill and Coniston Water—read the book and heard its war drums beating, and so did parliamentarians of the day. When the long-presaged war finally broke out, Antwerp, which fell on 10 October 1914, was the site of a hesitant German victory. Churchill himself had arrived with a brigade of marines and failed to hold the line with the Belgians. Yet the Germans never rounded the British flank to the sea, and meanwhile the trenches were consolidated to the point of immobility in Flanders. The North Sea saw no grand engagement; even the famous battle of Jutland proved a trifle.[54] The idea of an invasion along the Schelde to capture Antwerp remained enticing. Collingwood redrew the charts in his delicate penmanship, sorted the intricacies of access and permission—there was only a tiny German garrison in the city, the population was mixed Flemish Wolloon-speakers, Belgians, Netherlanders, and there was no such thing as a passport—and waited for his call-up papers.

They never came. After the sudden successes of the Germans in the spring of 1918 were turned back with the arrival of twenty-seven American divisions, bit by bit—in Turkey and Palestine in the rear, on the Italian frontier and at the front at Cambrai—it became clear that the war was going the Allied way. Collingwood was, like the young John Maynard Keynes, assigned to the preparation of the peace conference and the famous "Fourteen Points," to be hammered in at Versailles.

At the end of the war he reckoned up his intellectual accounts. Back in 1913, after his first trip to Naples and his dazzled reading of Benedetto Croce, he had published his translation of Croce's *Philosophy of Giambattista Vico* and henceforth counted himself heir to Vico (more so than Hegel) and apologist in public for Croce. Vico was his historical anchor, Croce his aesthetic one. But he was persuaded that something tidal and strong-running was happening to the intellectual weather, and that just as the moment of Galileo declares such a change in the breadth and depth of purely scientific thought, so there was similarly incipient a change in the conception of history as a feature of human conduct.

He dashed off, in his dashing way, a little book in three days, speaking a curse over the realists and their refusal to see that mind and its knowledge are jointly a matter not of fixity nor of being, but of becoming. He never intended to publish it—it was just intended to clear his mind. He called it, as a private joke, *Libellus de Generatione* and posted it to his friend and philosophical ally, Guido de Ruggiero, who gave it, years later, as a wedding present to Collingwood's son, Bill. But it was a first stone laid in the foundations of a future that would look for the regulation of politics not to science, still less to psychology, but to history.

V

A century later, now that comparative historicism runs in our bloodstream, people make the reflex argument that *all* moral schemes are culture bound and therefore incommensurable; horrible practices are just what people do and not what they ought not to do, and the whole concept of obligation needs rewriting once again.

When it is, any account of ethics adequate to modernity must start from Collingwood's own intimations that codes of conduct can only be fashioned from the inheritance of the past, then to be transformed by what seems best to match our later principles of ethical rationality. He set his face, after all, against what he called "the undischarged bankrupt of modern philosophy," the doctrine of realism whether in morality or epistemology. The exhilaration of listening to the realists beating up the earnest worthies of idealism must have been keen around 1910, but even then Collingwood's own roots in his father's teaching and Ruskin's shadow caused him to recoil from these fluent and attractive ideologues.

Yet whatever upheaval in thought this dark-suited revolutionary began to prefigure, realism may have lapsed in its more flat-footed forms, but it converged with and gave speed and energy to the tides of scientism, which were to dominate not only academic thought but political thoughtlessness, for the rest of the century. Whether one calls it scientism or positivism, "it" is the belief in the universally applicable principles of empirical research, of hypothesis-formation and refutation in terms of the careful garnering of observable data from the natural world and its explication of behaviour as the result of causes. "Don't classify, count," wrote the first prophet of this mode of thought, A. N. Whitehead, a mathematician like Russell nonetheless determined to write a metaphysics faithful to the colossal achievements of science, for "natural knowledge is exclusively concerned with relatedness."[55]

In some hands, the slogan "count, don't classify" turned into the rigidities of a new kind of theory of all causes and effects, which indeed taught the indisputable authority of collectible data and, even in the human sciences, the severance in inquiry between human oddity and simple facts. At its most inane, this way of thinking has led to the exclusion of human reasons and motives from the vision of the human scientist and still commands the big cheques in the competition of social research. But this tendency is only an aspect of the general conviction in intellectual culture that if philosophy is to justify its position as queen of the sciences, it can only be as grand theoretician of a truly scientific vision of everything.

A dozen schools have competed to find such a perspective. In the 1920s the logical positivists under Carnap were beginning their work in Vienna, which in Britain would come to a thunderclap with A. J. Ayer's *Language, Truth and Logic.* Indeed one theory of language, promulgated by Wittgenstein's *Tractatus Logico—Philosophicus*,[56] so knocked out the impulsive Russell that he arranged an instantaneous fellowship for its author at Trinity. Language itself, the expressive relation between mind and world, idea and object, seemed to some philosophers the location of a fully scientific theory of nature and knowledge.

These were the international developments that waited on the slow expiry of realism to terminating which the young Collingwood began to dedicate himself as the war ended. One way of conceiving this biography is as a narrative of the first hero of antipositivism. Certainly, realism mutated into a number of much more powerful philosophic pachyderms, plenty of them still trampling the campus. The readiest way to grasp the philosophic contest of the twentieth century is as a struggle between a victorious and polymorphous scientism presently incarnated in the ideology of scientific management, and the stalwart, undefeated guerrilla of the historicists, led by Collingwood's ghost.

It is, as I say, the significance of the rest of his life as well as of the weighing up of his bequests to fill out exactly what this historicism means. It has been both ignored and, by the twentieth century's most distinguished philosopher-of-science-turned-political-nostrum-doctor, Karl Popper, vilified, at least as recommended by Hegel and Marx.[57] In one respect, moreover, the intellectual atmosphere pressing on historically minded theorists has changed greatly. Only a small minority are still believers in God, and most of these are in North America. If anything, this gives greater force to Collingwood's ideas, even though this dissolution of theism in the academies coincides with the return or intensification of religious belief across the globe, especially in the church of Islam.

At the same time, the conviction that Collingwood consolidated around about 1919 when he went back to Oxford—that philosophy must break out of its little university cell into the big world, must teach to all those who could be made to listen the reunification of thought and action and the restoration of disjoined specialisms to a comity of disciplines—needs his prophetic magniloquence more than ever. The only sciences of human affairs in common circulation are either the dismal science of economics or its dependent and morally infantile halfling, scientific management. The frequency of international recourse to murder or militarism takes the measure of historical ignorance and corrigible stupidity in the world's political leadership. It was Collingwood's tragedy that the missing science was only half-formed when he died. As the apocryphally awful peace conference at Versailles wrote out its charter for another ninety or a hundred years of unhistorical and avoidable disasters, he went to work on "the foundations of the future."

4

Against the Realists:
Liberalism and the Italians

Just as he was assigned to duties in preparation for the scurrilous peace conference, Collingwood was married. He had met Ethel Winifred Graham while turning over the ancient stones of Skipness Castle in Argyllshire, at the further end of the Northmen's settlements on the northwest coast of Britain. He and his brother-in-law-to-be, Angus Graham, shared their interest, common in their class, in palaeography, and Collingwood published an archaeological report with Angus, who was much his age.[1] Ethel was four years his senior (but he was used to that in his womenfolk), could give him an inch or two in height, was a tall, pleasant-faced, capable young woman, a student for the year 1912–13 at Somerville when that was indeed a rarity, and a ready hand with trowel or sandwiches at the nearest dig. They were married at Skipness on 22 June 1918 in a modest ceremony; it was wartime and in any case the Graham family, although an old and honoured Scottish name, was far from being wealthy. The Collingwoods' first child, William Robert, arrived punctually forty weeks later.

Immemorially, the fellows of Oxford colleges were required to remain if not perfectly celibate then certainly bachelors. Assorted colleges had waived this grotesque regulation as the nineteenth century advanced, Balliol first among them, but backward old Pembroke had not. Accordingly, Collingwood had to reapply for his job when released from the Admiralty. There was no demur. He and Ethel took a house at 5 Fyfield Road in pleasant, inevitably red brick (Oxford's "brickish skirt" but not in the least "base"), just around the corner from J. A. Smith's rather grander place in Norham Gardens, where the remaining metaphysicians came to tea and tournament with the realists.

Bishop Mitchinson having died during the war, the master of Pembroke was now the awful figure of one F. Homes Dudden, doctor of divinity of course, former chaplain at Lincoln College, a redoubtable scholar with a massive tome on Gregory the Great to his credit, and a severe, unforgiving protector of collegiate customs and duties, including a strong tradition in favour of the rich, the dashing, the titled, and a style, so much associated with Oxford folklore, of playboyish and wildly inebriated attractiveness. As if these grisly and contradictory attitudes were not enough, they were allied to that reflex British racism that was just in line for scarifying (in 1924) at the hands of E. M. Forster in *Passage to India*.

Homes Dudden cared nothing for the Forsters of this world. As he wrote with distaste in a letter, "We already have enough Americans, Orientals and other such persons," and as his successor, a Scots pioneer of psephology called Ronald Buchanan McCallum, observed, the master and his colleagues recoiled from what they thought of, in a period algebraic sign, as "unpleasantness," "by which," McCallum goes on, "was usually meant boorish manners, plebeian origins, wrong accent . . . looking back on it now, what impresses me was the great importance given to good looks and general attractiveness of appearance and manner."[2]

The contradiction between the grim and masculine conservation of custom and ceremony in all collegiate regulation including scholarship and the debonair fecklessness in the everyday culture of college life marked the British elite very deeply. To take writers as signposts, between *Zuleika Dobson*, *Brideshead Revisited*, and *Gaudy Night*, on the one hand, and the arrival as undergraduates of such as Iris Murdoch, Dennis Potter, and Stuart Hall, on the other, there corresponds a jagged tear in the sensibilities of all those thousands who discovered gypsy happiness and the fulfilments of scholarly seriousness on the narrow peninsula dividing Isis from Cherwell.

Collingwood healed the split by living his gypsy life as an archaeologist. He retired early from the desolations of bachelor existence in college. Or rather, he withdrew as far as college regulations permitted. On 21 October 1919, having been reinstated as a married fellow, he wrote to Homes Dudden, requesting permission, in the argot, to "pernoctate" as follows:

> having now a house at 5 Fyfield Road and feeling it undesirable never to sleep there during full term, I wish to apply for [leave to reside elsewhere].... At the same time, I consider it against the interests of the College that any tutorial Fellow should reside altogether outside its walls . . . and therefore undertake . . . to spend at least half my nights in College, never sleeping out for more than two consecutive nights.[3]

Homes Dudden conceded the request, much later growling to McCallum, who had pleaded Collingwood's eminence as a scholar, "Yes, but he does nothing for the college." Not that Homes Dudden himself "did" much. The colleges in 1919 were very pure examples of Durkheim's "mechanistic" societies. That is to say, their principles of solidarity were entirely implicit and unspoken, their means of production and subsistence shared and unspecialised, their "group emotions" formed and inescapable outside individual consciousness, such exotica as a development plan or the management and diversification of college curricula and finances lying the other side of 1979.

These social and moral forms issued in, for some, a dismal and desperately boring way of life. When the garrulous McCallum was appointed from Worcester as a fellow (to teach history) in 1925, he later recalled the life of the Senior Common Room as a dateless sequence of joyless dinners. The long silences were broken only by dry exchanges and the wince and scrape of knives and forks on college china. A dinner-jacketed servant served the dishes and poured the wine. There were two guest nights, Wednesday and Sunday, and the master took it very amiss that Collingwood always refused to attend guest night on a Sunday.

He had a domestic life to live; in May 1921 his daughter, Ursula Ruth, was born, and a little later he put a symbolic as well as a geographical distance between himself and the college by moving out to Stapleton's Chantry, a Jacobean house of eccentric construction in the village of North Moreton, some twelve miles southeast of Pem-

broke College, a forty-minute journey by local train and on foot to
and from the station.

The fellows made a soulless little party of an evening, a group
portrait from this distance always incipiently comic. Herbert Drake,
classicist, was so to speak the senior professional, fielding all matters
of administration and tutorial timetabling to whose "mediocre and
narrow mind." McCallum reports in a baffled manner, "Collingwood, a man of superb intellect and marvellous learning, would submit himself . . . if Collingwood, in an expansive mood, continued
animated discussion, Drake would often terminate it with one of his
dry but repressive remarks." And McCallum asks, in a self-parody
beyond parody, "could Apollo really serve Admatus?" He lets Apollo
off, however.

> He was a man of immense intellectual industry . . . his life was full.
> Perhaps he had early summed up the situation and decided he must
> not waste his time . . . trying to improve the intellectual standards of
> the college. There was always the Faculty, the university, the world of
> learning. There he counted, there he was, if not liked, then re-
> spected. . . . Moreover his natural Toryism may have made him averse
> to setting out as a "reformer."[4]

Toryism? As I suggested, Collingwood belongs rather to an older,
more blurred and much less dishonoured British tradition of political continuity. His national heroes are St. Anselm and William of
Ockham; King Arthur and Robin Hood; Chaucer and Shakespeare
(*Hamlet* his favourite play); Hobbes and Hume and Mill; Wordsworth, Ruskin, Turner. These are the "lines of force" that gather in
Collingwood's breast and concentrate themselves in the new character and wholeness of the "freeborn Englishman" battling to wring
from a new history an answer to the question of how to live well by
thinking one's best thoughts.

It doesn't sound as if the Pembroke Senior Common Room was
much help. The master, Homes Dudden, dined in only on guest
nights. "His lack of interest in the academic improvement of the
college . . . his inability to know what anyone was reading, even the
better sort of scholar, was so remarkable that it must be regarded

almost as an effort of will . . . he was so easily bored, so easily bored."
Only his deep antipathy to Collingwood, keenly returned, gave him
any relish, and with his lowering colleagues—the narrow, punitive
Drake; Burrowes the dean, witty and waspish; Salt the arid little bursar—maintained without question an undergraduate population in
which "overwhelming weight was given to gentility, the right accent,
bearing and school," all these "bland assumptions" frankly held as
being the proper view of all reasonable persons, although, to give
him his due, McCallum himself objected, if without effect.

In 1926 things cheered up a little, at least for Collingwood, when
J.R.R. Tolkien was appointed fellow, and the two met on the mutually
sympathetic grounds of philology and folklore, a passion for which
ran in a strong, lifelong current stemming from his father through
Collingwood's imaginative life. But a little cameo from an interview
committee provided by McCallum suggests well enough that Tolkien
also could fend for himself in the tart, dreary exchanges of college
life.

> *Homes Dudden*: I have a prejudice against Welshmen.
> *Tolkien*: For that matter, I have a prejudice against Scotchmen.
> *McCallum*: And I have a pretty strong prejudice against Englishmen.

The war had no doubt made a difference to Oxford, but not so
very big a one. Robert Graves, for example, arriving in 1919 as a
married student of twenty-four after four full years on active service
with the Royal Welsh Fusiliers, went to live in a cottage owned by
John Masefield on Boar's Hill, five miles out of the city. A little colony
of poets as well as Graves and Masefield (then writing *Reynard the
Fox* with an empathy developed by four years as a Red Cross orderly)
flourished on Boar's Hill—Edmund Blunden, Robert Bridges (just
about to publish Gerard Manley Hopkins for the very first time)
among them. Down in the town:

> We found the University remarkably quiet. The returned soldiers did
> not feel tempted to rag about, break windows, get drunk, or have tus-
> sles with the police and races with the Proctors' "bulldogs," as in the
> old days. . . . G. N. Clark, a history don at Oriel, who had got his degree

at Oxford just before the war and meanwhile been an infantryman in France and a prisoner in Germany, told me: "I can't make out my pupils at all. They are all 'yes, sir' and 'no, sir,' They seem positively to thirst for knowledge and scribble away in their note-books like lunatics. I can't remember a single instance of such stern endeavour in pre-war days."

The ex-service men, who included scores of captains, majors, colonels, and even a one-armed twenty-five year old brigadier, insisted on their rights. At St. John's, they formed a "College Soviet," successfully demanded an entire revision of the scandalous catering system, and chose an undergraduate representative to sit on the kitchen-committee.[5]

McCallum noticed the same thing about

the terrifying generation who poured out of the schools in 1921 . . . of whom I suppose Evelyn Waugh is the most terrifying. They were brighter than we were, intellectually brighter, really on the spot and able to keep up with modern currents. Some of the mud of Flanders seemed to stick to our minds. These boys came up with the whole doctrine according to Keynes at their fingertips; they knew about Marx, they were getting on to Freud.

Collingwood had agreed to teach the philosophy students from Lincoln College as well as his own. He only had his salary to spend, earning Pembroke £6 per pupil, and taking home as salary 29 percent of the tutorial kitty (Drake got 39 percent). By the mid-1920s he was teaching or lecturing, he reckoned, forty hours per week in term-time. He was an immensely popular lecturer: the lecture theatre was packed, "his exposition and delivery (his voice itself as well as its audibility, for no one can really concentrate on an ugly voice) were flawless. He believed that the voice ought to be *produced* if one was to lecture at all and he enacted his belief. Let them who now study the content of his work remember this."[6] To this end, Collingwood took voice production lessons from a singing teacher.

It doesn't seem likely that Collingwood was one of those who didn't make their students *work*. Yet there was still more than enough of the world of *Zuleika Dobson* surviving the Somme. *Brideshead*

Revisited wasn't written by the "terrifying" Evelyn Waugh until 1944, and at that date it was avowedly a work of wistfulness, plangent, lubricious, greedy, and heavy with longing. But the chords Waugh strikes in his evocation of Oxford on arriving in 1923 not only capture an aspect of its partisan enchantment at that date, they tremble still in the recollections of anyone who has been young at the university and fired for good by its beauty, its luxuriousness of spirit, its sheer advantage.

> Oxford, in those days, was still a city of aquatint. In her spacious and quiet streets men walked and spoke as they had done in Newman's day; her autumnal mists, her grey springtime, and the rare glory of her summer days—such as that day—when the chestnut was in flower and the bells rang out high and clear over her gables and cupolas, exhaled the soft airs of centuries of youth. It was this cloistral hush which gave our laughter its resonance, and carried it still, joyously, over the intervening clamour. Here, discordantly, in Eights Week, came a rabble of womankind, some hundreds strong, twittering and fluttering over the cobbles and up the steps, sight-seeing and pleasure-seeking, drinking claret cup, eating cucumber sandwiches; pushed in punts about the river, herded in droves to the college barges; greeted in the *Isis* and in the Union by a sudden display of peculiar, facetious, wholly distressing Gilbert-and-Sullivan badinage, and by peculiar choral effects in the College chapels.[7]

This is music to guard against, but one would think unfortunate anyone who had been an undergraduate there and whose caution on hearing Waugh's siren voice was not caused by first softly melting towards him. The more so when it was soon followed by this second binding of the spell (Ryder, the main character, has been invited to lunch by Lord Sebastian Flyte as an act of contrition after Flyte, a stranger to him, has thrown up through an open window onto the floor of Ryder's room):

> I went there uncertainly, for it was foreign ground and there was a tiny, priggish, warning voice in my ear which in the tones of Collins told me it was seemly to hold back. But I was in search of love in those days, and I went full of curiosity and the faint, unrecognised

apprehension that here, at last, I should find that low door in the wall, which others, I knew, had found before me, which opened on an enclosed and enchanted garden, which was somewhere, not overlooked by any window, in the heart of that grey city.

Sebastian lived at Christ Church, high in Meadow Buildings. He was alone when I came, peeling a plover's egg taken from the large nest of moss in the centre of his table.

"I've just counted them," he said. "There were five each and two over, so I'm having the two. I'm unaccountably hungry today. I put myself unreservedly in the hands of Dolbear and Goodall, and feel so drugged that I've begun to believe that the whole of yesterday evening was a dream. Please don't wake me up."

He was entrancing, with that epicene beauty which in extreme youth sings aloud for love and withers at the first cold wind.[8]

Both extracts come early in a novel that, despite its effortful piety and its inexorable advance to the tomb, is suffused with longing for the coincidence of love as it bursts open at the centre of a friendship, and love as discovered in the beauty of art. The love of art and of Oxford are interchangeable in Charles Ryder's memory, and it is worth surmising that this was also the way that Collingwood, the young teacher of thirty, saw and felt the city. For *Brideshead*, especially after the slow, magnificent television adaptation of 1981, is wrongly associated with the playboyish, drunken, gaily irresponsible folklore of the antique universities (sports cars, Going Up to Town, and climbing into college). Certainly there was plenty of all that. But Ryder very quickly becomes a serious architectural painter of the noble houses of England, his beloved friend is thrown out of the university, and the overwhelming snobbery of the place that Waugh endorses so nonchalantly (that snobbery still had forty-odd years of life left in it) throve happily alongside the intense and life-giving heat of philosophic and aesthetic expression.

Harold Acton's cosmopolitan experience, old Etonian tie, youthful exhibitionism, and precocious aesthetic knowledge provided Waugh with half a dozen details for the character of Anthony Blanche—"part Gallic, part Yankee, part, perhaps, Jew; wholly exotic."[9] Acton came up to Christ Church in 1922 as a conscientious aesthete and follower of Wilde. He wrote prodigiously, edited an undergraduate arts journal called *The Oxford Broom* which was to sweep away deathly Victorianism, and published his first volume of poems, *Aquarium,* in his second term:

> In some ways *Aquarium* was in advance of its period, and for all its immaturities I have no cause to regret it. My poems made many friends. I was prolific and none too critical, and scattered them on the Oxford breezes. I read them from my balcony to groups in Christ Church meadow. They were always in demand. Certainly, looking back, they have had their day.
>
> Literary clubs and societies throve at Oxford as in Florence during the seventeenth century, and at first I was drawn to them like a moth. I fluttered my wings at the Italian Circle, the Spanish Society, the Ordinary, which invited me to read papers and join their discussions, and there were dining clubs as well. I read papers on El Greco, on Medician Villas, and listened to poets, critics and learned professors who favoured us with visits. At "The Ordinary" the members recited their own compositions. So nervous was each when his turn came that the process was more of a pain than a pleasure. How unlike the young poets of Italy or France! Here was ample opportunity to give each line its proper expression and each word its value: surely nobody could interpret a poem as well as its author? Yet nobody seized it. The poems were read in a self-deprecatory manner, amid stammerings and blushes. This irritated me at the time, but in retrospect I am touched by their shyness, so English, so free from conceit. It gave their readings a vibrant sincerity.[10]

Allowing for one's brief tremor of revulsion at some of the self-display as well as bits of shy-making diction, this is a bracing reminder of the high seriousness of Oxford life as youngsters like Acton and the travel writer Robert Byron joined half-crazy old soldiers of twenty-four like Robert Graves and Edmund Blunden and the rough trade of the local Communist Party at the Hypocrites' Club in St. Aldates, at the Railway Club, and then in London at (where else?) the Café Royal. For "at Oxford you could lead a hundred lives and discover more friends and sympathies than anywhere else,"[11] and philosophers, politicians, mathematicians, actors, aesthetes, sportsmen, and tweedily solid citizens who ate in the Bullingdon, took Third Class degrees with unmoved contentment, and went back home to follow their fathers into the solicitor's and doctor's practices were easy, overlapping neighbours and friends in an irreplaceable community that provided for life a glowing image of the good society.

It was good because communal, and communal because drawn almost entirely from the same social class. The Collingwoods may not have had much money, Ethel Graham didn't bring a fat dowry with her, and he never really lost, even after his lessons in elocution, a trace of the northwest counties in his voice, but one faces up to Collingwood, even at thirty, as to a patrician figure, Old Rugbeian, "steel blue and polished manner."

Yet that's not enough with which to enclose his carriage in the world. In 1913, just after he got the job at Pembroke, Arthur Ransome was sued by Lord Alfred Douglas for defamation in Ransome's (entirely delicate and discreet) book about Oscar Wilde. Ransome faced ruin if he lost. Calling on the very young Collingwood in no supplicant spirit, Ransome was staggered by Robin's offering him all his small savings.

There is much in the anecdote. Collingwood was not only generous, he was reckless. As his lecturing style developed in the 1920s, he won a cohort of strong admirers. His delivery, as we heard, was flawless, his prose not just eloquent but rousing; he was intensely serious and, inseparable from that, funny, mocking, allusive—his prose is thick with suppressed quotation, especially from Shakespeare and the Bible, but also from Wordsworth, Browning, Francis Thompson, Pope (often), Hardy—he bound his student audience in a spell and could do the same for local archaeological societies and antiquarian lectures. What is more, he set out to charm them, recklessly enough. T. M. Knox, always one of his most favoured pupils and who arrived from Scotland in 1924, wrote—as I mentioned—disapprovingly of Collingwood's preference for good-looking women students, but there are plenty of witnesses to come—Isaiah Berlin, Dorothy Emmet, Tom Hopkinson, Bernard

Miles, Michael Foot, J. D. Mabbott—who testify to the popularity of the man as a teacher, to his gripping presence, his formal, even mannered courtesy, suddenly flashing out as seductive warmth and the invitation to intimacy. Nobody can pretend that the relationship between a teacher and a pupil is without a strong sexual element;[12] we have known that since Heloise and Abelard; it's just that the very latest kind of prudery wants to expel it, greatly to the disadvantage of good teaching.

II

Handsome was as handsome did among the students in the town. But Collingwood had very deliberately quit Fyfield Road for North Moreton and a life in the beauties of an ordinary village near enough to the Bicester cut-off, which after 1920 allowed the Great Western expresses to miss Oxford and go directly to Birmingham. This would mean that the family could leave North Moreton around 8:00 in the morning for the 8:30 from Didcot, and get to Coniston about 6:30 that evening.

Stapleton's Chantry, with its odd little tower, sits athwart a bend in the deep lane that swerves through the hamlet on its way to Streatley, Goring, and the Thames. The sides of the lane are too deep for an entrance close to the house, and the gate is placed some yards further up the slope, where the road flattens out. North Moreton is unremarkable enough—two or three notable bits of Jacobean building, a dozen cottages, some pleasant Victorian additions, like enough to Eliot's ancestral village at East Coker to be sure that when Collingwood read Eliot's poem in 1940, it would have called up an image of the light falling across the open fields around Stapleton's Chantry,

> leaving the deep lane
> Shuttered with branches dark in the afternoon,
> Where you lean against a bank while a van passes,
> And the deep lane insists on the direction
> Into the village, in the electric heat

> Hypnotised. In a warm haze the sultry light
> Is absorbed, not refracted, by grey stone.
> The dahlias sleep in the empty silence.
> Wait for the early owl.[13]

Collingwood's metaphysics and his theology, born of Oxford and Coniston, kept step with Eliot's, born of St. Louis and Harvard, and Eliot's last great poem coincided with Collingwood's last great book.

Down at the further end of the garden, beyond the dahlias, were the beehives. He had picked up the craft of beekeeping above Coniston; it served in his lectures not only to distinguish between art and craft (there is an imaginative artistry in sensing the rhythms of bee-flights and nectar-gathering as those vary according to the time and temperature of the day or season); it was a pastime as contemplative as the sailing that was far away from Oxfordshire; it opened up two realms of thought, the precise and practical handling of the bees, and the parallel movement of the mind upon the near surfaces of speculation. The care of the hive was the happy occasion for Collingwood's applying his unfailing neatness of hand and eye to the cutting and fitting of the honeycomb frames, the repair of the weatherworn sections of the hive itself or of the slatted ramp upon which the heavy-laden squadrons landed with an almost audible plump. Then came the thrilling day in late summer when the roof of the hive was lifted, the bees sedated mildly with a smoking insufflator, the comb frames lifted out and set in racks in the heavy drum, their waxy surfaces slit and lifted off with a knife, the lid closed down, and the solid, silent, well-oiled wheel strongly spun until the centrifuge came up to speed and whirled the sumptuous, viscous, golden honey into the sump, to be poured off into the squat, familiar, one-pound jars.

For those with the nerve to accept a few stinging intrusions (remember, if a bee makes its way up your sleeve, it will always travel upwards; raise your arm and give it time to exit), the care of bees, as Virgil taught in the second Eclogue, expresses the plenitude of *dwelling*. The bees' hum is the sound of home.

Rebuilding an English home after the end of the war took some faith, and took some learning also. As he later wrote, that war was "one in which everyone was defeated, for the one thing about it of which everyone is conscious is the losses he has suffered in the course of it."[14] It is a desolate judgement, and the voracious devil in this bit of history is positivism. For the thinking that ought to have been done for the previous half century had been neglected and could not be thought in a hurry. Consequently there was no historically discovered statement possible as to what were the fundamental principles at stake in the war. The only general assertions made were wholly inane:

> e.g. the assertion that this was a war to end all wars, as if any war could do anything other than make more wars more probable; or that this war was "to make the world safe for democracy", as if the world could ever be made safe for anything, let alone by fighting.
>
> The intellectual bankruptcy of the peace treaty was a direct and inevitable consequence of the intellectual history of the 19th century.

Collingwood has sharp things to say about the notion that philosophers (or artists) may be divided into the camp of either the pessimist or the optimist; to be characterisable as either is to be in thrall to "a hopelessly false philosophy." The task as he set up his house was to enact his particular view of the good life as it might be lived postwar and by a man of his formation. Hence, it was to build out of that house and its quiet hills, this wife, these two children, this college and university, its library and junior and senior members, dire or decent as they might be, a theory of practice, a discipline of the mind as won from history that might conduce to the solidarity of the human spirit.

Shortly after the war, just before he removed with Ethel Collingwood to Fyfield Road, he had been asked, on 10 May 1919, to speak to a conference of Belgian students, several of them ex-soldiers, held at Fladbury near Evesham. The Belgians' invitation followed from Collingwood's wartime cartography west of Antwerp; his chosen topic was "The Spiritual Basis of Reconstruction."[15]

He started, typically, with the early music then just returning to prominence, and the collaboration of the great Fleming composers at the Burgundian court—Jean Ockeghem, his pupil Josquin des

Pres, Orlando di Lasso—with the Englishmen John Dunstable in the fifteenth century and William Byrd in the sixteenth. He praises Belgium, with his usual slightly elaborate courtesy (a trait that makes his not infrequent harshness the more severe) as alone in 1919 in "not lifting up her voice in greed and arrogance," contrasting this acknowledgement with the shame he felt at times towards his own country. Then he broaches a subject to which he returned several times during his career. There can be few of his opinions that pose more starkly to us now the question as to whether a thinker's view in some important matter is become a dead historical record or a live electric current capable of charging up new political passions. He told his Belgian audience: "There is a good deal of talk going on to the effect that imperialism . . . is fundamentally evil. It is not. The right imperialism—the rule of the more civilised over the less—is a necessary element in the education of mankind. Imagine what Europe would be like without the discipline of Roman rule and the legacy of Roman laws." This is the argument made telling and popular for the 1970s by actually answering the rhetorical question taken from the comic but deadly serious *Monty Python* movie. "What did the Romans ever do for us?" demands one of the little group of protesters that makes up the People's Front of Judea. The replies don't in any way impair their nationalist fervour. "Roads, drains, law and order, medicine, education. . . ." "Well, yes, of course, but. . . ."

Ninety years after Collingwood's address, the *bien pensant* wisdom is that imperialism can be used only as a swearword. Collingwood was less sentimental. Empires had not only proved historically inevitable—Chinese, Egyptian, Greek, Roman, Holy Roman, Spanish, Dutch, British—they were motors of economic and cultural development and as morally various as numerous. Contemporary relativism is convinced not only of the absolute wrongness of all imperial intervention, but of the difficulty (perhaps the impossibility) of coming-to-judgement on the life of another place or time. The puzzle for a thinker of Collingwood's ambition became to acknowledge particular embodiments of historical self-making as being the thing they are, good, bad, or indifferent, but always to place them in relation to "the principle of the unity and indivisibility of the spirit."

The phrase comes from a lecture Collingwood gave in August of
the same year of 1919, as the exhausted and bloodstained continent,
with revolution going horribly forward in Russia and apparently im-
minent in Germany, struggled to find the sources of its self-renewal
by way of the blind and stupid bigotry of the peace conferences.
Collingwood had reminded the Belgian students that if the League
of Nations was to be effective, "it must ensure the abolition of tyranny, of race and class war . . . for once the class war begins, it will
not matter who wins, the result will be death and disaster, the destruction of civilisation . . . desolation is certain if we allow ourselves
to believe that our State has no duties or responsibilities towards the
rest of the world."

These commonplaces needed the complement of intellectual posi-
tives it then became Collingwood's life-purpose and avocation to
provide. The biography of a thinker is the story of his thought, as he
almost said, and the conventions of narrative are such that biography
naturally seeks coherence, dovetailedness of books and arguments,
the life's work as an open road leading to a clear destination, the
lovely boulevards of the city of reason.

Well, fine if you can find it. More likely, the story of the thought
is broken, arduous, and irregular, like John Donne's truth-mountain:

> On a huge hill
> Cragged and steep, Truth stands, and hee that will
> Reach her about must, and about must goe;
> And what the hills suddenness resists, winne so . . .[16]

And yet to discover the order of a thinker's thought—its shape, direction, and meaning—is what we go to thinkers *for*; his biography
is just one means to meaning, to finding in the actuality of the life
the blessed concrete of its universal significance.

There is something as solid as that in Collingwood's address to
the faithful, given at the centenary celebration of the birth of John
Ruskin in Coniston on 8 August 1919.[17] His title was "Ruskin's philosophy" and by this he meant the colloquial usage that speaks of
someone's "philosophy" as that body of assumptions and allegiances
the integrity of which give point, firmness, and, if not consistency,

since the only utterly consistent individual would be a lunatic, then a predictability of patterned virtues in the passage of a life. Collingwood remarked that the question that most beset his mind was "what is philosophy," and this everyday usage is certainly part of his answer.

The exemplary aspect of Ruskin's philosophy was for the thirty-year-old speaker the same as it would be twenty-three years later at the premature end of his life. It was that principle of the unity of the spirit that "Ruskin never questioned and never attempted to prove." This was the "absolute presupposition" (not yet a phrase Collingwood had coined) that impelled Ruskin when talking of art to connect it at once to questions of morality, politics, religion, the justice and well-being of the social order. Ruskin is presented as admirable because he insisted that

> each form of human activity springs not from a special faculty—an organ of the mind, so to speak—but from the whole nature of the person concerned: so that art is not the product of a special part of the mind called the "aesthetic faculty," nor morality the product of a special "moral faculty," but each alike is an expression of the whole self. Thus, if the ancient Greek was a man of a definite type and character, his art exhibited this character in one way, while his political systems and his religious beliefs exhibited the same character in another way, translated, as it were, into another language, but otherwise identical.[18]

This is Ruskin's historicism. It follows, as Collingwood goes on to say, that understanding and evaluating Greek philosophy or Greek sculpture is a matter of setting Plato side by side with Phidias and Praxiteles (and Aristotle and Aeschylus and Euclid) rather than with entering him into a timeless conversation, uninterrupted by history, conducted by the company of philosophers for the next two and a half thousand years.

Historicism therefore broke with the eighteenth century, which argued, roughly speaking, for the profitability of the mind as depending on specialisation and multiplying the divisions of intellectual labour. Hegel breathed into the intellectual air his contention that this "unity of the spirit" must prove the key that will unlock the mystery of the *Zeitgeist*, and Ruskin, who didn't read Hegel, drew his oxygen into his bloodstream.

It followed from such a reading of Ruskin that the professional philosopher had two tasks: first, to understand history not as the positivists would, as "a mere succession of events, fact following fact with little or no internal cohesion," but on the contrary, to interpret history "as a drama, the unfolding of a plot in which each situation leads necessarily to the next." Second, it is the business of the philosopher to contrive, in a key phrase, "the scale of forms," the sequences of which frame the method and the moral vision carried in each of the modalities of knowledge and inquiry: art, religion, science, history, philosophy.

The lecture on Ruskin, "our super-ancestor," as Altounyan's daughter, Taqui, called him, announced these imperial themes, and the great nonphilosophising philosopher is one grand, implicit presence behind all of Collingwood's thought, present less in the conventional sense of an "influence" than as paragon of a characteristically English character, for all his oddities and craziness, a mightily capacious man, responding to life, to science and art, with his whole being. The pair of them were as ready with an exposition on natural historical as on human-scientific method or on the principles of art, and ready also to meet the charge of self-contradiction always glib on the tongues of "that levelling, rancorous kind of a mind" that lay in wait to catch them out.

III

The most direct influences on Collingwood as he braced himself to his self-appointed tasks in Oxford in 1919 were threefold Italian. The name of Benedetto Croce was well-known to Harold Joachim and much revered by J. A. Smith and Carritt,[19] who had first loaned his eager student Croce's book on Vico in 1912. Collingwood read Croce's *Logica* in 1912, and during the first six months of the following year, he had translated Croce's book on Vico, approved and very slightly emended by Croce in October of the same year.[20] (It is an odd detail of Collingwood's occasional brusqueness that, although he went on to translate during the 1920s Croce's *Autobiography* as well as Guido de Ruggiero's stout volume, *The History of European Liberalism*, he told a student who commented on his fluency in Italian that he certainly couldn't speak the language.)

Croce, who lived on to a venerable old age and died in 1952, is now modestly beatified as one of the first intellectuals to see plainly the potential horribleness of Mussolini's Fascism. At first, when *Il Duce* came to power in 1921, he had thought, as everybody did, "Well, give him a chance."[21] Modernising postwar Italy, a single nation for only a few decades, perhaps needed his kind of energy. Mussolini himself courted the favour of Italy's most celebrated philosopher, offering him a ministerial post in education. But Croce, unlike his acolyte and the third Italian presence in Collingwood's mind at the time, Giovanni Gentile (who, it must be added, brought about perfectly respectable and liberal reforms in Italy's sclerotic educational system), saw which way the Fascists tended, and he withdrew to a distance.

Croce's strongest philosophy is in aesthetics and its relation to history. For Croce, the aesthetic is the paramount realm of experience and the senior form of knowledge. But Collingwood, whose letters to Croce are models of courteous, slightly fulsome approbation ("I shall never cease to test my work by reference to yours")[22] was often sardonic at his master's expense. In his undergraduate lectures given at Oxford in 1924 on the philosophy of art,[23] although he begins from Croce's view of art as lyrical intuition synthesising image and feeling, he writes of Croce's "unintelligent and pigheaded rejection of the didactic theory of art" and a little later, in a good joke, blamed Croce for "the loafer's theory of art," according to which works of art are attended to "as finished products," "contemplated with hands in pockets."[24] The antithesis of this is Ruskin's, his parents,' and his own aesthetic, the "ascertaining by labour and no otherwise," as he quoted Ruskin as saying, "of the laws of truth and right in painting."[25]

Disagreement with Croce was the occasion for arguing that the forms of experience, formalised and given statutes by the forms of knowledge, align themselves in a single scale. For Croce art was top of the scale, the zenith of the imagination. For Collingwood, art was the primordial foundation of experience, the bedrock of identity in the child, but, as he was to work it out in the first major work, *Speculum Mentis*, which he began as soon as he arrived at Stapleton's Chantry, art was by definition "self-transcending."

> Art is not attacked and destroyed by philosophy as by an external enemy; it destroys itself by its own inner contradiction, by defining itself as at once pure intuition and also expression, imagination and thought, significance without definable signification, the intuitive concept. This contradiction is not irreconcilable. On the contrary, its reconciliation is the whole life of thought.[26]

This tussle with Croce lived on in Collingwood's mind, and was the source of his long dialectic between history and philosophy. Finally, resolving by dissolving, he melded one with the other. Vico, and Croce on Vico, had first revealed to him the mutual identity of each. This is the thread of his life. The life of thought and the life of practice are alike theoretic and historical. They are answers to those questions a man or a woman must put to experience in the expectation that they are answerable. For, as he wrote, "To ask questions you see no prospect of answering is the fundamental sin in science, like giving orders which you do not think will be obeyed in politics, or praying for what you do not think God will give in religion."[27]

Vico had set himself against Descartes' certainty that knowledge must begin from truths so clear and distinct that they can only be denied on pain of absurdity; that mathematics provided the rules for establishing these clarities; that the application of numbers to the natural world would issue in the conquest of nature. Vico argued that these methods were roundly inapplicable to human activity, that, in a famous distinction, knowledge of (natural) causes was intrinsically different from knowledge of (human) reasons, and that to treat all human behaviour as though it were the product of strictly physical causes debars us from saying some of the most natural and necessary things we *do* say about our fellows. The proper study of humankind, which is of internal reasons rather than external causes, is historical (factual therefore) and yields self-knowledge. In Vico's own noble and famous dictum from the *Nuova Scienzia*:

> In the night of thick darkness enveloping the earliest antiquities, so remote from ourselves, there shines the eternal and never failing light of a truth beyond all question: that the world of civil society has certainly been made by men, and that its principles are, therefore, to be found within the modifications of our own human mind. Whoever reflects on this cannot but marvel that the philosophers should have bent all their energies to the study of the world of nature, which, since God made it, He alone knows: and that they should have neglected the study of the world of nations or civil world, which since men had made it, men could come to know.[28]

Vico, first brought to Collingwood by Carritt, Smith, and Joachim, was always refracted through the spectacles of Croce, and Croce himself was always a venerably disregarded figure in the most active studios of Oxford philosophy. Croce was in all his work conscientiously historicist in a manner quite distinct from Vico's catholic tableaux of classical antiquity. This assumption tied Collingwood to his name and bound him, with an impressive selflessness, to translate, first, the book on Vico, later the long entry on "Aesthetics" that Croce wrote for the fourteenth (1929) edition of the *Encyclopaedia Britannica*, and during 1925, Croce's brief *Autobiography*, which was published a couple of years later.

There are arresting moments in this work for someone of Collingwood's piety and affiliations. Croce speaks at one point of "my contempt for the cant of Liberalism,"[29] which his translator was reading at just the moment in 1925 when he was also at work rendering his great friend Guido de Ruggiero's classic *History of European Liberalism* into English.[30] Croce, born in 1865 and orphaned in 1883 by the earthquake outside Naples in Casamicciola, moved to the house in Rome of the politician Solvio Spavento, prominent in the misleadingly named, more-or-less Christian Democrat party, The Right. There, over the next few years, "little by little, I let even [habits of church attendance] drop, and a day came when I saw, and told myself plainly, that I was done with my religious beliefs."[31]

This was a jolt to Collingwood in 1925, still writing Christian apologetics for *Theology* and the *Hibbert Journal*, and attending "the Group" in Cumnor. Croce filled his unslaked religious longings by a very particular and, to Collingwood, revelatory saturation in "the great philosophers" and an understanding that "cannot be acquired by reading their books but only by re-enacting their mental drama in one's own person, under the stimulus of actual life."[32]

This is, I think, the first sighting of Collingwood's key term, the "re-enactment" of past thoughts in the historian's own life. Four years before, he had written a review of Croce's *History: Its Theory and Practice*[33] in which Collingwood first reproaches his master sharply for separating the political theorist and the practical politician in "a dualism between thought and life" when he should have stood by the truth that "thought is life," and then anticipates Croce's own, perhaps passing point in the *Autobiography*, that understanding past thoughts must be a matter of living the thought again, however different that present will be in which the thoughts revive.[34] But the two men were joined in the belief that the second half of the nineteenth century saw the general coming-to-consciousness, at least among scholars, of the momentousness of the historical sense, and that this signalled a deep change in the search for a human order derivable from human nature. "Whenever we take a step," Croce wrote memorably, "everything moves."[35] Thus truth may be grasped "as history," as long as he, Croce, remains (with all historians) "on guard against falling into a half-naturalistic and half-mystical Hegelianism"[36]—the danger, in so many words, of which Collingwood warned him in his 1921 review.

Croce and Ruggiero were guides and companions to Collingwood when he couldn't have found similarly robust and appealing minds at work in Britain. It must be added that Gentile was also prominent in Collingwood's mind at that moment. Smith, who owned all thirty volumes of Gentile's work, had pressed them on his pupil, and Collingwood found much in Gentile that was congenial to his cartography of the forms of knowledge. He was later introduced to Gentile while staying with Ruggiero in Rome in 1927, and although Gentile's name appears nowhere in the index of *Speculum Mentis*, there is surely his influence detectable in the pages on art and history.

Gentile did for himself by joining the Fascists, and Collingwood says so in the *Autobiography*. Ruggiero, cordial, colourful, voluble Italian, was a close friend and gave Collingwood much more—more of the human warmth and vividness Pembroke lacked, as well as practical instances of political commitment (to liberalism and to principle—Ruggiero was briefly imprisoned).[37] Italy gave him his lead in the 1920s, Mussolini notwithstanding. There were potential allies elsewhere—Dewey might have called to him from across the Atlantic, but no Americans except Eliot and Santayana appear in the indices of Collingwood's books, and Michael Oakeshott was still to come. So Ruggiero, more straightforwardly historical and po- litically practical than Croce, was a happy choice of ally, and it is typical of Collingwood's generosity and, the gentlemanly reticence notwithstanding, impulsiveness, that with so much work on hand, he undertook translation of 460 pages of *European Liberalism*, having already done the same with his friend's workmanlike textbook *Modern Philosophy*.

The study of liberalism remains a striking work. Collingwood called himself a democrat and acknowledged that mainland Europe- ans would say "liberal"; today we would probably add the adjective "social," by way of indicating his proper respect for the principle of equality inseparable from questions either of justice or of liberty. But his larger concern was with the conditions of the principle of civility, and its turning of itself into actuality, which is to say, civilisation.

These grand themes had some way to travel in his mind before they emerged explicitly in the work, and they were always to be hampered in that partition by the acute limitations of Oxford life, the detestable stiffness of social class, the excellent peaceability of England between the wars. Croce, after all, was offered ministerial office by Mussolini, and when he rebuffed the Fascists and kept up intellectual life against them from his townhouse in Naples' centre and in the pages of his journal *La Critica*, he was pretty well isolated in unofficial house arrest. Ruggiero was briefly incarcerated. Gentile joined the Fascist Party at the same time as Martin Heidegger joined the Nazis, ill-advisedly assuming the good Bavarian's uniform of Lederhosen and Tyrolean hat, and the pair of them were dismissed from the company of serious philosophers. Serious philosophers in Oxford were a damn sight safer.   •

Not that Ruggiero foresaw how acute the dangers were. Even by the time *Liberalism* was published, he was still speaking optimistically of his hopes for Italian democracy, although this may only be his grace-note.[38] But the great strength of the book for our purposes is to vindicate its translator's endorsement of a nationally conceived and constructed liberalism as the remaining best hope for European parliaments.

In this hopefulness, Ruggiero exhibited a historical insistence largely missing from the Anglophone tradition of political theory. Collingwood's immediate predecessors and contemporaries in Britain—figures like L. T. Hobhouse, J. A. Hobson, Graham Wallas, admirers of T. H. Green to a man and mostly sympathetic to what was to become the intellectual arm of the Labour Party, the Fabian Society—put their faith in appeals to moral collectivism to be expressed by a supple, cooperative, and benignant state.[39] Ruggiero, on quite another hand, placed liberalism in the practice of historical politics within parties. The version of democracy that each nation— England [sic], France, Germany, Italy—devised was then the product of local argument and national standards of rationality and permissible altercation.

That is to say, that politics and its theories were and necessarily are *constituted* by "practical rationalities as social structures." The phrase is Alasdair MacIntyre's, a present admirer of Collingwood to whom I shall turn in the last chapter.[40] MacIntyre's contention is that what counts in a culture as the "practical rationality" that directs, explains, and justifies action turns into an ideal social structure of its own accord. (Crisis impends when such practical habits of mind are no longer agreed upon.)

For MacIntyre, rationality in the present century has been thinned out until it is no more than the personal preferences of individuals, which are then grouped and ordered by the forces of the market. It is then the concern of (successful) political parties to match these preferences to policies, thereby ratifying "choice" (the key value of liberalism) as the fulfilment of freedom.

Neither Ruggiero nor Collingwood would have countenanced this degree of individualism as anything other than decadent. Ruggiero certainly foresaw the danger of the "democratic worship of the state," of "a lack of education on the part of the masses" as leading to democratic tyranny, and urged the lessons of liberalism, for all its drastic shortcomings which he firmly enumerated, as teaching the duties of the citizen as self-conscious maker of a polity in which freedom would only attend upon true self-government.[41] Both men—Ruggiero in the translation at hand, Collingwood many times elsewhere—repudiated socialism as "degrading political conflict into economic conflict" and suppressing even while invoking solidarity of the human spirit. Socialism duly attempted as a result of its instincts rather than its arguments to repair the damage thus done to its own universality of appeal by recourse to an all-powerful bureaucracy and "its blind worship of the technical expert."[42] (The deadly vindication of Ruggiero's criticism by the advances of Stalinism in Russia was only just becoming apparent.)

In the end, Ruggiero concedes to socialism in its practical forms the possibility of its absorbing the best lessons of liberalism. He acknowledges a bit too blithely that liberalism has its inevitable partisanship towards middle-class life and its values of self-criticism and other-awareness. But he concludes that its "moral energies, which are the great reservoir of liberalism" and its definitional faith in the individual as the realm and fount of value remain the likeliest and most resolved resource of political possibility with which to tide Europe over the turbulence ahead.[43]

Translation—of which Collingwood did so much between 1913 and 1927—is a dialogic activity. Ruggiero's original, like Croce's, is a rousing and eloquent, as well as clear and firm document; Collingwood's prose is every bit his match. But as he worked at the translation, strong as was his support for the argument, the mind of the translator stopped, checked, qualified, and dissented. *The History of European Liberalism* is, obviously and strictly, a work of political theory as well as history, and politics has by now become the religion of the intelligentsia. Politics is in the twenty-first century the natural frame of reference for immediate conversation between scholars and intellectuals wherever they may meet, in a way that would simply not have been true in 1924 when Collingwood published *Speculum Mentis*. Indeed, one may counterpose this still powerful and impressive book to Ruggiero's *Liberalism* by understanding it in two ways: first, as a theory of the liberal intellectual's curriculum after the hideous detonation of the war; second, as a historical evaluation of those forms of knowledge whose different forces led different epochs to their destinies, but which may yet be gathered into a single, mutually embedded instrument of inquiry capable of realisation as "the science of human affairs."

IV

Collingwood wrote it, as he wrote everything, with astonishing speed and at home, at Stapleton's Chantry. He had barely finished his gripping little textbook, *Roman Britain*, to which we return in the next chapter. He had assumed duties as philosophy tutor for Lincoln College as well as Pembroke; he was giving lectures on the philosophy of art as well as his other philosophical and classical archaeological lectures; he wrote out every lecture word-for-word in longhand; he was a regular visitor at the digs on Caerleon and Verulam as well as in the North, and a regular lecturer on his copious reports of the period (120 in all, during his twenty-five years as practising archaeologist in the field); he was taking his regular lessons in voice-production; it is no wonder that he was insomniac and that this condition, which so often angered and frustrated him, was intensified by the ceaseless habit of internal philosophic soliloquy at the same time as it extended his long working day.

The Oxford terms, after all, occupied only twenty-four weeks of the year, with a crowded couple of weeks in addition at the end of the Trinity term when all the examining had to be done. Nonetheless, it is worth—with Henry James's injunction to the novelist in mind, "Dramatise, dramatise!"—enumerating a little of Collingwood's workload and his extreme conscientiousness in carrying it. These were days long before sabbatical leave-of-absence, regular transatlantic trips, taken-for-granted fees and expenses for outside lectures. They were also days in which fellows and lecturers, if they so chose, might live the life of scholarly tramps or playboys, conducting tutorials while half-asleep, giving few lectures, rewriting none.

These charges could hardly be laid at the door of the philosophers; Cook Wilson, J. A. Smith, Harold Joachim, E. F. Carritt, and all, as we watched them, kept up the liveliest of Oxford academic conversations in societies, tutorials, discussion groups over tea, and voluminous correspondence. They rewrote their lectures—which *were* their publications, published to the only audience they and their university cared about, their students and their competitors—and rewrote them again. Collingwood outdid them all. For as he wrote of himself, "there is in me something that craves expression, and knowing that if I am to express it at all, I must express it through that pen-driving ritual which is the custom of my tribe."[44]

So one leafs through his intellectual duties and engagements discharged during the 1920s, the years of his best, though never trustworthy, health; his knee was always troublesome, in February 1924 he succumbed to exceptionally severe flu, a little after-eddy from the dreadful flu epidemic of 1918–19, reading Duns Scotus on his sickbed, and in September of the same year was seriously unwell once again.[45] But whatever his daily health, he was young, sleepless, and energetic. On the vacations, he went visiting Roman sites, the front line of the empire in Germany in 1922 and 1923; Avignon, St. Remy and (though not really Roman) Les Baux in March 1924; with regular visits taken for granted to Cumbria, Argyll, Northumberland. Meanwhile, he gave what his notes describe as "elementary lectures," which he doesn't specify but were his introductions to the works on the Classical Moderations syllabus which he had studied himself. He completely rewrote his seven-lecture course on the theory of knowledge (tussling with the realists) in March 1920 while in Coniston—say, 45,000 words—and delivered them in the Trinity term for the next four years. He rewrote the same number of words and lectures on the philosophy of religion in December 1922 to give in the Hilary term of 1923; he also gave eight unprompted lectures on Ruggiero's work as a special topic not formally part of the syllabus in the Michaelmas term of 1920, plus a series of the same length on the Roman wall in Britain given from 1921 to 1923, a new set of lectures on moral philosophy entirely and verbatim prepared in September 1923 (45,000 words again). He had "written out more or less fully" his seven lectures on the philosophy of art (subsequently published as his *Outline*) during May and June 1924,[46] and in January 1926 he wrote as another seven-lecture course his first substantial statement on the philosophy of history, to be given at once in the Hilary term.

It would be tedious to go on with what are at first blush no more than instances of an exceptionally punctilious teacher. But the output bears enumeration. It seems that he must have written half a million words in the first four years of the decade, and this without counting the translating of Croce's *Estetica*, for which Macmillan paid a welcome £100, or Ruggiero's *Modern Philosophy*, nor adding to this total the numerous invitations received and accepted to lecture nationwide on archaeology, religion, philosophy, and—to the Johnson Society in Pembroke, Johnson's College, on 27 November 1921, his favourite novelist, Jane Austen.

Except "favourite" won't quite do. For Collingwood begins by saying "strange influences were abroad in the years 1770 to 1775" and goes on, unforgettably: "Here, falling within half a dozen years, are the births of Beethoven, the greatest man who ever wrote music: Turner, the greatest man who ever painted a landscape: Hegel, the supreme philosopher: and—Jane Austen."[47] There is no diminuendo here. For her greatness precisely summarises Collingwood's philosophy of successful art, that it shall find "a mid-point of equilibrium, where the intellect is perfectly pitiless in its clear vision of truth, and the feelings are perfectly fresh in their ecstatic enjoyment of it . . . the attainment of this perfect poise is the rarest thing in life."[48]

This is more than favouritism. Jane Austen prefigures Collingwood's definition of the greatest literary art, on a level with Shakespeare, and proving to us not only the triumph of art, but a theory of life, a complete rejection of what Collingwood later called "the corruption of consciousness" to which our misunderstood emotions lead us so often, replaced as it should be by a firm understanding of and delight in the best person our passions can make of us.

The little lecture, filled as it is with its author's own delight in his subject, serves to indicate the manner of his innumerable such contributions to the conversation of public-private culture in the early 1920s. We have just heard his celebration of Ruskin at Coniston in August 1919 and of Jane Austen in Oxford in 1921. In addition, Collingwood gave the Ruskin lecture again in Burlington House the autumn of the same year of the Ruskin centenary, spoke on "the Church" to the Group in Oxford, on "the Catalogue Habit" to the Beaumont Society, on "the intellectual basis of prayer" in Christ Church, on realism to the Oxford Philosophical Society, all in 1920. The following year, his extramural vaudevilles numbered at least seven, three of them archaeological—one to the Cumbrian anti-quarians, two more in Newcastle in August, one to the Shakespeare Institute (on religion and science), and, in a crowded November, the paper on Jane Austen to the Johnsonians and an address in paral-lel to his paper on religion and science, the new one called "history and science," at Exeter College, a couple of weeks before his hymn to the novelist.

One's instinctive comparison is with the prodigious energies of his two intellectual ancestors, William Morris and John Ruskin, each of whom drove himself unyieldingly to accept every one of the countless invitations that fell through the letterbox.[49] Collingwood was no national figure like those two, but he inherited the zeal and the sense of obligation to his two disciplines and to the solidarity of the unknown hundreds who counted themselves avowed and practi-cal members of the same guild, whether of art, philosophy, or ancient history. The sheer prodigality of this self-dedication, as well as its joyfulness, comes out best in Collingwood's life as archaeological traveller. Goodness knows, his father and his mother too had shown him just such a way of life, home in Coniston, the loved redoubt from which constantly to sally out, to Iceland, Savoy, Norway, Ger-many, Italy, as well as to work at University College at Reading, to pursue art and music in London, filling the enormous time of railway journeys with loved labour, sandwich tin on the seat beside you, the shiny greaseproof paper enclosing anchovy paste or mashed sardines inside the thick white slices of bread.

The purpose of such a life is then as simple as it is vast. It is to invent the form of the integrity that will hold all this activity in a single frame and will then confer upon it a sufficient beatitude. The religious language comes naturally even now, when university life has long severed its official connections with doctrine or liturgy. The sense the scholar makes of his or her life is compounded of answers to specific questions about the place of this or that inquiry in the architecture of human thought, the contribution of a given aspect of one's teaching to the quotidian maintenance of that building, the small, brief part played by any bunch of students during their three or four years' study (let alone what they might do with those years thereafter) in the commonplace rituals, services, and keeping of the calendar. What for? What ultimately *for*? These terrible and familiar questions hover above the everyday life of any university teacher, and the answers are fashioned out of that teacher's feeling for the discipline, its idiom, membership, sacred books, and places. The rhythm of such a life still moves to certain echoes from its monastic past, dim as these are. The force of that history comes through in particulars.

The monastic echoes were more sonorous at Oxford in the 1920s, and when Collingwood first set himself, in 1922, to make a model of what I have called the architecture of human thought, all his formation as well as his talents impelled him to create a single, multiplex edifice, one whose foundations were common to all its parts, whose nave and chancels, apse and transepts opened one into the other, whose vaults and arches, historical and philosophical alike, were built on the massive originals of art, religion, and science.

This is my fancy for the description of *Speculum Mentis*, which he had projected to himself as soon as he moved out to North Moreton, and began as soon as the textbook *Roman Britain* was out the way. It is a young man's book: three hundred pages, brief enough for something as ambitious as "the map of knowledge" (note the definite article), couched in an idiom both plain and eloquent, addressed, as it were, to all common and sympathetic readers, and offering a narrative account of the origin of each species of thought, finally presenting to us the whole possibility of vision implicit in the achievements of mind. In a characteristic gesture of levelling, Collingwood hands over the moment of epiphany to all the people:

> This absolute experience of concrete knowledge has nothing to do with any professional distinctions, any more than with distinctions of social class or physical race. The enjoyment of it has nothing to do with that "philosophy," a confused mixture of scientific abstractions and historical facts, which is professionally expounded by people called philosophers. It lives in a unity above all professional distinctions, and the philosopher may well achieve it in greater perfection when sailing a boat or telling stories to a child than when discoursing technicalities to a class. But it is not an intuitive or emotional experience, a mood whose precious visits illuminate the waste of life: it is just life itself in its infinite self-conscious development, a development which sees every detail of itself as organic to the whole.
>
> This life has no map and no object other than itself: if it had such an object, that would be its map, for the features of the object would be its own features. Thus the external world, whose origin, growth and structure we have been, throughout this book, investigating, is the Mirror of the Mind and the Map of Knowledge in one.[50]

Inquiry invents or discovers knowledge (the etymology of "invent" starts from "find"),[51] the ultimate value of which is its bringing the collective human mind and spirit to self-knowledge. No doubt Hegel's immense presence looms behind the book, but it is better grasped as an act of dissenting homage to his father, to Ruskin and Bosanquet, and to Shakespeare, as much as to Croce and Ruggiero.[52] Collingwood easily rebuts the "farcical refutations" of idealism (those who sneer by asking whether a table is in the room when nobody is there to have an idea of it). He leans on Green to affirm a spiritual principle in knowledge and in nature,[53] and then he summarises his argument as avoiding the assumption that *any* "form of experience" is wholly free from error. Thus, the world is

> implied but not asserted in art; asserted, but not thought out, in religion; thought out, but only as subject to fictitious assumptions in sci-

ence; and therefore in all these we found an ostensible object—the work of art, God, the material universe—which was confessedly a figment and not the real object. The real object is the mind itself, as we now know.[54]

Not many people talk like this any longer. The historical hiatus in philosophic idiom causes awful indigestion. But the effort so to theorise the human and natural sciences that they indeed stand in coherent relation to one another and replace mutual incomprehension and rancorous competition with a common pursuit of true judgement and reliable knowledge is the crux of rational thought for each intellectual epoch.[55] Collingwood's idiom is directly continuous with Green's and F. H. Bradley's. But at some point in the same decade the break in idiom was made, metaphysics was suspended for a generation, Hegel derided as late as the 1950s as " a servile lackey" [of the Prussian State], "a charlatan," "a clown," and such terms as "absolute," "spirit," "the ideal," "soul" rendered unspeakable.[56]

Such a change is far more than a mere movement in fashion; or perhaps better to say that changes in fashion, whether of clothes and cosmetics or forms of thought and belief, go deep. This being so, there are two ways to treat *Speculum Mentis*: the first as being a set of historical answers to questions we would no longer put like that. This would be to respect Collingwood's own injunction to determine what a thinker was trying to do in the context of his own times. The second treatment, an extension of the first, is to translate without violation the answers proposed in 1924 to a language permissible three generations later. Somewhere on the hinge between the two readings comes a judgement as to whether this thinker is now consigned if not to the dustbin then to the basement stacks of the library of history, or whether he anticipates the future and may be retrieved from 1924 in order to be rediscovered, found in a translation sounding out clearly to his great-grandchildren.

Collingwood's venture in the book is, as I say, an intrinsic necessity to every epoch. It is to discover how the forms of thought emerge one from the other and yet remain mutually embedded. He is firm in saying that his "scale of forms" advances in a progress. Art for him, unlike for Croce or Ruskin, is not the supreme but the most primitive because the earliest form of thought. Even the earliest societies have art. It is the theory of experience that stands closest to that experience in its unstoppable flow. For example, James Joyce's amazing *Ulysses* takes the one day in Bloom's life in Dublin in 1906 with as much of its meandering soliloquy, trifling loves and encounters, its glowing epiphanies and mean streets, as the novelist can cram in and still shape into something comely and readable. The shape of the book gives the experience its theory. Like all art, it must keep faith with the concrete of particular life. Aesthetic experience just *is* the making of works of art, and as children begin to learn life by imagining in their games and scribblings that are the art of early childhood, so societies work out their meanings by beginning with art. And "the law of this process, its guiding principle, is beauty."[57] But the artist's world, like the child's, is "not the world of facts or laws, it is a world of imaginations,"[58] and Collingwood scorns the idea, emerging then and clichéd now, that art must perspire to prove its social utility (another way in which this great book is due for resurrection is its complete and relentless hostility to utilitarianism). Every work of art is its own end and leads nowhere. The artist poses a problem (asks a question) and then solves it. Question and answer live in the imagination, and for the artist (as for the child, or for a society that has not progressed beyond art) what is imagined cannot be distinguished from what is known.

This has tricky consequences for those many teachers and moralists who were fired by the blaze of Romanticism to treat art as the source of pedagogic truths. Collingwood won't have it. To permit this latitude would be to crack open the scale of forms: "Art makes for itself two claims. First, that it is the activity of pure imagination; secondly, that it somehow reveals the truth concerning the ultimate nature of the real world."[59]

This is too much for the most primitive form of thought to get away with. Of course, art having the grip on us it has (and quite right too), we can't stop ourselves asking what it means. Well, "True, we cannot say what precisely it purposes or signifies. *But that is because art is only art and not philosophy*" (my italics). Philosophy in this book is crowned queen of the sciences; art, absolutely necessary to us as the first vehicle of explanation of ourselves to ourselves, cannot get beyond its own contradictions, standing as it is athwart our intuition of the world and our expression of our feelings about it (which is which, for heaven's sake?), defying us to tell the difference between imagined circumstances and our substantive thought.

In an early sighting of the phrase, Collingwood speaks of "the rhythm of question and answer as constituting the very life of the spirit" and concludes, "all life is art, but no single moment of life is mere art."[60] Knowledge begins in the playfulness of art, hence the prominence in Collingwood's aesthetics of children, about whom he always writes so well. But after the songs of Apollo, the words of Mercury.

Religion necessarily emerges from art. This is a law of the progress of mind. In a longish footnote, Collingwood refers us to *Religion and Philosophy* with which he remained more or less in agreement, much as he now purposed to think more dialectically. This being so, this is the chapter in the book hardest to find in translation. All is well for our secular academic as long as religion is treated as the form of thought essential if the superstitions of art were to be transcended. All remains well when the Christian religion is commended to us as providing humankind with its most compelling narratives with which to frame and explain the passage of human life. Sinfulness and salvation, the long journey from fall to redemption, are the most fulfilling metaphors with which to test the meanings of experience (and a metaphor, I might add, is hypothesis awaiting historical experiment). In Collingwood's beginning to his discussion of religion, the social equivalent of the child's crisis of learning after which she no longer believes in fairies marks the emergence of religion from art, and this emergence is complete only when religion grows out of polytheism into the conception of a single, supreme Godhead.

This progress leads directly to the victory of Christianity over other churches. In a crisp aside, Collingwood presages the contemporary criticism of the Church of Islam that it has never had its Enlightenment. He remarks that a religion that "makes of its God a mere abstract unity does violence to its own nature as religion and falls back from religion into art."[61] Hence the unresolved hatred of

Islam for such aspects of art as picturing the Prophet and the forbidding of the category of poetry as a blasphemous rival to the Quran.[62]

The chapters on art and religion are instinct with the strength of Collingwood's feelings for the world of both forms. The movement of transcendence to science is at first regretful, a deliberate exit from the Garden of Eden. Art and religion give the mind glimpses of the beauty and holiness to which it aspires. Religion is partial revelation; science the effort to connect these visionary flashes to the world of fact. The man is struggling for a "less abstract and over-intellectualised" way of thinking.

At pretty well the same time as Collingwood was writing this, Max Weber had been propounding in Munich (just before his death in 1920) his theory of the progressive "disenchantment" (*Entzauberung*) of the world by the forces of rationalisation and scientific inquiry.[63] Collingwood disciplined himself strenuously to keep faith with the forces surging through art and religion—"if the rationalist had any intelligence he would see that his attacks on religion are too easy to be sound, and that there must be a catch somewhere."[64] Science is then acknowledged for its triumphs but rebuked for the specific character of its method, the abstractness that is the source of its success and its inheritance from religion.

The concepts of science are at the further remove from art. $E = mc^2$ is at the remotest abstraction from the bombarding particles that the equation compacts. Science affirms the abstract as material. Given that "every phase of experience is implicit in its predecessor,"[65] this affirmation is taken from religion's theory of order. Science substitutes structure in its most abstract form for God.

In a bold extension of this diagram, Collingwood identifies in modern culture the scientist as being the dominant man of thought, where abstractness wins the day, the corresponding man of action being the businessman, as supreme utilitarian. For "it is a commonplace to point out such morbid symptoms in the fabric of an acquisitive society based on the concept of utility."[66] R. H. Tawney's stern philippic of that title came out in 1921,[67] and Collingwood repudiates Tawney's socialism as allowing the economic to swallow up the political realm but sees the deathliness at the heart of the capitalists' "business." Business needs science and pays for it. Competition, supposedly cut-throat, needs the reassuring framework of law and order. Hence the doctrine of the social contract.

Only when the social is acknowledged as a necessity in the teeth of piratical demands for profit can history replace science as the form of thought demanded by social development. The intellectual arena of the nineteenth century was site of the protracted, still inconclusive struggle between science and history.

"Science is not true, but useful." Collingwood does not endorse the aphorism but sees it as necessary. (It might have been coined by Richard Rorty, sixty years later.)[68] Rather, science is the question whose answer is history. It has done its job by sweeping away the nightmares of mythology; in 1924 we can see—and this more than half a century before Thomas Kuhn and Bruno Latour—that history rejoins the abstract to the concrete, the factual to the universal. "The way to philosophy from science lies through history," whatever fuss science is certain to kick up about the loss of its power.

It is still the case in the ordinary discourtesies of the academies that history is assigned its space in the humanities according to the subject boundaries marked out on the campus. But this, in the first appearance of one of Collingwood's favourite metaphors of abuse, is an attempt "which may easily be successful, by the tailless foxes for a general decaudation of their brethren."[69] The historical consciousness asserts the hardness of the facts and, restoring them to the drama of their making, tells a story that is true, subordinating immediacy to reflection, adjusting necessity to accident, speaking the poetry discoverable in the facts, replete "with a sense of obscure and mighty forces working for ends which no-one completely sees."[70]

History discovers the organised individuality and concreteness of life (there are no future facts). Art plays with the facts; religion in the form of Christianity attempts (and, as Collingwood says candidly, fails) to historicise the absolute, science can hold down nature but only in the terms confected by different epochs. Unaware of itself, separating, counting, classifying, it rejects unity as a consequence of its method, and cut off from its own historical self-making, it cannot contribute anything to the noblest goal of inquiry, the knowledge of a knowing mind by itself.

This is the point to which the whole book, perhaps the whole life, tends. In its extended coda, Collingwood, still with twenty years to go of his meditations on the pressing need for a science of human affairs that would have to be historical, there being nowhere apart from the past from which to derive both subject and object of thought, pretty well identifies history with philosophy. This marks his earliest effort to prevent the supposition that there is any distinction other than a rhetorical one between the categories of subjective and objective enquiry (compare the meaningless opposition of today between quantitative and qualitative research). His trade union loyalty is to philosophy, so philosophy is, at the end of the book, given its coronation.

He takes time to define a commonsensible version of idealism; he inaugurates a later philosophic movement by placing the interpretation of meaning rather than the passivity of observation at the heart of method and its morals; and he tells us, only a very few years after the doomed end of the war to end all wars, that the responsibility for its successful murderousness may be laid at the door of a blind, hubristic scientism and its attendant demons of materialism and superstition. Only history, remoralised as the philosophy of the human mind in its self-knowing, can teach a runaway world the cardinal virtues: prudence, justice, fortitude, temperance.

VI

These latter names are not much heard of in the academies these days. All the same, the vast mutations in the life of universities in general and Oxford in particular have not all led downhill. The leathery old snobberies have gone, and so has the flaccid indolence of playboy and sporting undergraduates towards their studies. The menaces of meritocracy may include all that Michael Young threatened us with sixty years ago,[71] and it cannot be doubted that its most revolting disinhibition—that it assures the successful they entirely merit their success and that the social failure of others is their just dessert—has been fully learned. But nearly all the students who now arrive in Oxford come with some dedication to scholarship and some understanding of its demands and fulfilments. Moreover, the sheer variety of language, physiognomy, skin, and shape, not to mention the multitudes of women students to be seen in any college, bears witness to the fact that here at least the community of learning has lost its ancient and horrible racism, has admitted the two genders with a now full heart (and lost its institutional and pubescent horror of sex as well), and assumed with ease its eminence as an international citadel of rational inquiry and disinterested originality.

It is damnably hard, however, to rescue such terms of approbation from the mess of corruption that has, at the hands of the chefs of university management, stewed together sacred terms like "creativity" and "excellence" with the lies of self-advertisement and the bullying of such fatuities as research assessment and performance targeting. God knows what Collingwood would have made of "module managers" of his lecture courses in morals and metaphysics, or of the criterion of market demand for Roman-British history. Yet the requirement in British academic life inaugurated during the Thatcher years that universities be allocated their cheques on the basis of four research papers published every four years by each member of staff—a regime subject to endless variation thereafter—was not only a matter of inane productivity regardless of its producing some terrible tripe. The stipulation also joined writing to thoughtfulness as an acute presence in the lives of the much increased force of intellectual labourers. It introduced a common measure of seriousness whether the academic concerned was one of the ancient, one of the civic, one of the plate-glass, or one of the quondam polytechnic universities sprinkled across the individual conurbations.

Collingwood long predated the day of the intellectual celebrity, the utterly invaluable global institutes of advanced study, and the foundation grants to permit sabbatical leave with impunity. But the intellectual celebrities of today, by their combination of recognisability and renown, take in the charge of energy deposited in the

veins of the culture by lives like Collingwood's, so much more paro-
chial and confined. Known directly to his students, to his numerous
admirers in the world of amateur archaeology, to the tiny readership
of professional journals and such neighbourhood weeklies as the *Oxford Magazine*, and to the unknowable, uncoordinated, and modest
crowd of those who bought or borrowed his books, Collingwood as
life-and-work is transmitted as a line of force to the far wider circuits
of intellectual life today.

What happens to all that applied and concentrated energy, packed
as it was with the small cells and batteries of English academic life
in the 1920s? Many of the names called over here—Cook Wilson,
Prichard, Ruggiero—have leaked away into forgetfulness. They have
no charge left. In the electronic connections and busy chatter of
modern communication, their energies have dispersed and faded.

Collingwood's haven't. More than that, his particular line of force
has begun, for the past generation or so, to come through with a
new iridescence. Something in him then connects with something
in us now with a brighter glow. The point of this biography is, so far
as it is convincing and true, to bring up that light some more. The
painfully difficult search by scholars and intellectuals for the self-
understanding and the forms of the good life that it is the duty of
universities to sustain is not so lost that Collingwood's way of living
his search and research no longer blazes out, making the nocturnal
money-grubbers recoil and hide their eyes.

5

On Hadrian's Wall:
"Question-and-Answer Logic"

In the verbatim notes he wrote in 1928 for his lectures on moral philosophy, Collingwood remarked that the "old name" for his subject, "practical philosophy," deserves attention, and in passing he voiced what was to become an intellectual emphasis for the rest of his life, namely, that judgement and inference are the same thing.[1] Every thought is at once an affirmation *and* a denial; that is, a thing is this and therefore not that. These remarks are of a piece with his dictum in *Speculum Mentis* that "questioning is the cutting edge of knowledge," later elaborated in one of his most characteristic flashes of combative swordplay:

> When Socrates taught his young pupils by asking them questions, he was teaching them how to ask questions of themselves, and showing them by examples how amazingly the obscurest subjects can be illuminated by asking oneself intelligent questions about them, instead of simply gaping at them, according to the prescriptions of our modern anti-scientific epistemologists, in the hope that when we have made our minds a perfect blank we shall apprehend the facts.[2]

He didn't yet put it like this, but his most severe objection to the practice of history as it consolidated itself throughout the nineteenth century at the hands of de Tocqueville in France, Mommsen and von Ranke in Germany, Burckhardt in Switzerland, Spencer, Froude and Acton in Britain was to the unreflective, uninterrogative habit of "scissors-and-pastework." Hunting for the facts, confident that they would be certain of what the facts were when they came across them, these men and those who followed them sought out the records and testimonies, decided which to believe, and arranged them in a more or less causal (because chronological) order in a narrative.

Scissors-and-paste history (now an electronic instrument and an academic habit of mind confirmed by computer devices) is a way of cutting up history in order to cut out thought. Insisting on the primacy of mind in the actions of human progress or regress makes for difficulties. To treat historical events in the same way as natural events and to seek for natural laws in human conduct not only lends the historian the terrific authority of scientific practice, it provides a noncognitive method of inquiry with which to fix the determinate structures of human passages. The history of ideas is dispatched to the sidelines as an individualistic kind of hobby, and the serious business of narrating the sum of things handed over to the scientists of management, the determinists of structuralism, the calm therapists of psychoanalysis.

Putting things this way makes it plain how wholly caught up we still are in the revolution of thought that started out in Collingwood's hands as an act of single-handed resistance after the dazzling *coup de théâtre* that was *Speculum Mentis*. As I have already suggested, that resistance is best felt in the long and thrilling tedium of archaeological excavation. Even now, the ordinary visitor to Housesteads or Chesters on the Wall, paying his or her not unkindly, not very attentive homage to the efforts of two centuries of heavy digging, is mostly at a loss to turn low stone courses, neat rectangles of grass, and a few bits of metal and pottery into an intelligible military encampment, vigilant for danger, cherishable as a home, a meeting place for trade, for settlement, for agriculture.

The interpretation of cultures that must take place at such a site, and which has been so slowly accrued by half-a-dozen generations of archaeologists, is at once peculiar and exigent. Reading books in order to perform scissors-and-paste history is on the other hand so familiar a scholarly practice. Print on a page (or a screen) reassures the scholar by its easiness, especially if written in one of the scholar's own languages. It is then a ready business to treat what is said as being said in that very room; to suppose one is joining a timeless conversation of simultaneous thinkers, like Raphael's famous *Stanza* in the Vatican, where Aristotle and Plato are striding together through a Renaissance city, teaching their admiring students, while Michelangelo, dressed as a stonecutter, sits truculently on the steps below them.

It is so obviously much *stranger*, as well as (at first) less exhilarating, laboriously to uncover a drain, a post-hole, a grain store, a gate; not to know the reach of the site, only roughly to ascertain its purpose (a principal fort or a minor sentry station? a guard room or a dormitory? a gate as thoroughfare or as attacking point?). Even more unignorable is the presence of previous historians on the site. The collective nature of the undertaking is the most moving thing about it, the correction of past error its most thrilling fulfilment, the unacrimonious collaboration of so many questioners, scattered along the wall, certainly, but scattered also across the country—Verulam, Caerleon, Winchester, Silchester, Aquae Sulis—and then across the old bone heap of Europe and Asia Minor, the further frontiers of empire in Germany, Syria, Libya, its ringing vindication. Archaeology pretty well forces upon its disciples not only the strenuousness of the discipline, but its equitable sharing out of intellectual and physical labour. Collingwood usually hired four to six diggers for a day lasting from eight until four-thirty, but it was in the nature of the work that the historian was as much a labourer as the men he hired.

Travel and travail went together. We can follow his physical labours criss-cross over England by listing a few of the papers in which he reported what was to be found. It is an agreeable convention of archaeological societies that frequently, and as long as the weather permits, the member of the society in charge of a dig will take the fellow members back to the very spot in order to give the summary of the latest discoveries. In the first five months of 1925, Collingwood gave six such addresses, a couple in Newcastle in January (to the Historical Association and that admirable national fraternity, the Lit and Phil, in its Geordie incarnation), another at the end of the month in Birmingham at the Martineau Centre below the Bull Ring (Harriet Martineau yet another Ambleside educationist), to the Classical Association in London in March, in Bournemouth in

April, and to a sixth-form conference of schoolgirls in south London in May.

The subject on all of these occasions was some aspect of Roman Britain. His classic little textbook, *Roman Britain*, was first published in 1923 and became modestly well selling. The larger conspectus in which he placed his provincial history had already been laid out also for the excellent worthies of the Lit and Phil in Newcastle, on 1 October 1922 when he addressed the Society on "Roman Frontiers": "What I want to do this evening is give you some rough idea of how the 4,000 miles of frontier were defended and manned, and to take you in imagination from Solway and Tyne to the Danube, the Euphrates, the Red Sea, and the riverless shores of the desert of Sahara."

The book emerged from a series of "extension" lectures given for the extramural department of the university, which paid a not insignificant fifteen guineas for sixteen such performances given to the voluntary class of students for no degree or qualification who met in a bare room in Wellington Square, Oxford. The same lectures formed the basis of those Collingwood gave yearly to undergraduates once the terms of his university lectureship were enlarged (uniquely) to take in both philosophy and Roman history. The same effortful labours provided the compressed material for half a dozen pamphlets by his hand over the same period, one on the Roman fort published in Ambleside, another on the Roman signal station there published in Scarborough, and sixpennyworth of *Guide to the Roman Wall* published in Newcastle.

Collingwood was the name the readers knew, but as he and I insist, it is the essentially collaborative and collective nature of archaeological research that is present in every line of its records. As he wrote in 1936 in his final volume on the subject with a more than conventional force: "this book could never have been written without the cooperation of innumerable scholars who, for the last twenty-five years, have helped me to form my ideas by explaining to me their own. Every page, as I wrote it, has recalled the generous friendship of these colleagues and the happy relations with them I have enjoyed."[3]

By the time he wrote *Roman Britain* in its first version, these friends included, of course, the doyen of the subject for the first twenty years of the century, Francis Haverfield, together with one of the most prominent of the gentlemen archaeologists, Frank Gerald Simpson, who worked and published extensively in the subject and acted as director of field studies at the University of Durham while keeping the family firm going, a chain of shoe shops called Stead and Simpson, the name still visible on high streets.[4] Simpson, a familiar figure at all the north country digs for thirty years, wearing the thick uniform of the trade—ankle boots, knee socks, knee breeches, bulky tweed jacket with laden pockets, waistcoat, and tie with a soft collar—became a close and respected friend of Collingwood's. So too did a very vivid pupil of his, Mortimer Wheeler, later the first television archaeologist and senior lecturer on Swan's Hellenic cruises, eventually to be knighted for his pains.

He in turn was joined by Eric Birley, probably Collingwood's most distinguished archaeological heir and another close friend. Birley went up to Oxford in 1924, joined the staff of the University of Durham at Armstrong College in Newcastle in 1931, and, taking over directorship of field studies from Simpson, lived pretty well alongside Hadrian's Wall at Chesterholm, Corbridge, Durham itself, and Carcoran until he died at the age of eighty-nine.[5] Birley, the great Italian classicist Momigliano once said, could "reconstruct history from a pair of used railway tickets" and in doing so would be applying his teacher's question-and-answer logic. Birley here takes his place as one ideal type of Collingwood's closest friends: genial, a bit tweedy, and pipesmoking, utterly serious about the discipline of archaeology; generous to a fault towards his pupils and collaborators; internationalist in taste, in politics, and by instinct; colonel of military intelligence during the Second World War; ardent, selflessly extravagant enthusiast for his subject, buying up (at twenty-three) the house, farm, and Roman fort that gradually became the Vindolanda Trust, subsequently in the care of his archaeologist sons, one of them named Robin.[6]

The lives and work of these men are woven into all Collingwood wrote and spoke about Roman history. This is, I realise, a large claim, but archaeology solidly symbolises in material form much of what Collingwood was to claim about history as the product of the collective mind of humankind, and the mirror of its self-knowledge.

Roman Britain opens with a frontispiece drawn in pen-and-ink by Gershom Collingwood. It is of a restored Hardknott Fort, a solitary outpost built by the legionaries below the western flank of the Old Man of Coniston, poised high in the pass that takes the river Esk to the sea. Patrols left the fort to watch the coast for piratical intruders from Ireland and the North, to maintain contact with troops stationed at Ravenglass, to send reports eastwards over the fells to Galava in Ambleside. It was, like all such forts, a miniature garrison city, with neat ranks of housing, stabling, central administrative offices, grain stores, all circumscribed by castellated walls slightly higher than a man and overlooking a deep ditch. Outside the walls were a parade ground and the baths.

Baths, you could say, were as much the distinguishing mark of Roman civilisation as its law. The bathhouse at Hardknott is naturally a much smaller affair than that along the wall itself at the much bigger fort at Chesters, but Hardknott, one of the sites at which Gershom had done early work, was perhaps his son's favourite archaeological spot in his home Lakeland. It is bleakly picturesque: empty rolling fells, the steep becks dropping vertically down the hillsides, a glimpse of the sea on the far horizon, the big sky, and, eighty yards up from the road, truly in the middle of nowhere, the trim little bathhouse, changing room, latrine with a sewage outlet to the stream close below it, warm bath heated by a wood or charcoal stove and hot air conducted below the floor by hypocaust, cold bath and then back to the changing room.

Puzzling out the few remnants of its walls discovered two or three or more feet below the turf takes all the patient alertness of which you are capable, as well as years to complete. As at Galava, so at Hardknott, the little teams of diggers and scholars come to work for their summertime sojourn, rarely more than a few days, then lightly cover over what they have found in order to protect it, and return probably a year later. Hardknott yielded its answers to the question put to it only with inevitable grudgingness. Where was the entrance?

What prospect must it command for military purposes? Was this a fighting or a watch garrison? Were any creatures kept here as well as horses? Where was drinking water drawn? How was the sewage dispersed? How senior was the commanding officer? What was the size of the command? Was the fort permanently manned? Where did they quarry the stone? Where (indeed) did they recruit the local labour to carry it to the site?

The long life of Hardknott, and of very many other such redoubts, from the big encampments by the wall itself at Chesters, Housesteads, and Segedunum (Wallsend) to the small stone forts that punctuated the wall at every mile and served as shelters and stores and beacon stations for the guards on duty, was thus gradually assembled across the century before *Roman Britain* was written. Haverfield had been field marshal of the past two decades in Cumbria, and each of his excavations cost less, his pupil tells us, than "thirty or forty pounds a year."[7]

Further south, as is usual in England, there was much more money spent, but much less intelligently and to much less purpose. Haverfield is canonised by Collingwood because, entirely unphilosophical as he was, he stuck severely to a clear list of questions addressed not just to the site in question, but to the particular problems of the trench in front of him. He and his men always "knew exactly what information they were looking for; they knew both that this information was the next thing they needed for the progress of their study and also that this trench would give it them."[8]

If this sounds improbably cut-and-dried to you, imagine the circumstances. The trench is open at your feet. Its composition shows plainly that it is a barracks wall. You want to know how many men it housed. You are therefore looking for its corner in order to fix its dimensions. You find cornerstones. But they have been roughly cut short. The building proceeds a little further to new cornerstones. Carbon dating came after Collingwood's day and is the process whereby the radioisotope in wood or any other organic material originally absorbed from the atmosphere is measured against the extreme slowness with which it is discharged (half-life = 5,730 years). It can answer much sharper questions than Collingwood, Birley, and

Ian Richmond, another eminent pupil and successor, could put to a trench. Even without the help of carbon-14, it's easy enough to see that in our imaginary excavation the building was enlarged. When? Answering this takes us back, perhaps, to written records. The garrison had been diminished by withdrawal after the date at which we know the barracks was first built. Subsequently there was military action in the area. The garrison was sent back in larger numbers, and the barracks enlarged.

II

Thus and thus the slow accumulation of an intelligible narrative. Collingwood is strongly reproachful of the "pre-Baconian" lack of method in the digs of southern England unsupervised by Haverfield. At Silchester (Calleva Arebatum), a tiny place some thirty miles southeast of Stapleton's Chantry, there was a hundred-acre tribal capital flourishing for the whole period of Roman occupation. But Collingwood reports incredulously that it was not until the 1920s that Haverfield's Baconian methods replaced those of Pitt-Rivers who, great pioneer of scientific archaeology as he nonetheless was, dug merely in order to see what he could find out. He neglected Acton's advice, "study problems not periods," and as a result was overwhelmed with finds; but he had never taught his Society of Antiquaries to date anything in the town, either its beginning or its end, nor to map its development, so that "the whole analysis is historically useless."[9] By the time the revised edition of *Roman Britain* appeared in 1934, the map and the history were complete according to Collingswoodian principle:

> There is no doubt that, many years before the Romans came, Silchester was a flourishing town and capital of the British Atrebates, as Arras was capital of the Gaulish. It already imported Italian pottery, and struck its own coins; in short, it was a civilized Celtic town, already much affected by that Romanizing movement which, as we have seen, began some time before the conquest. After the conquest, it was al-

lowed to develop along the same lines, until some one, perhaps Agricola (for the dates fit, and we know that Agricola was interested in
town-planning), induced the Atrebates to lay out a chess-board street-
plan and to build a square forum, two acres in extent, in the middle.
The forum was a market-square surrounded by colonnades containing
shops and giving access to what we should call a fine county hall with
county offices attached. Other public buildings were a bath-house,
temples, a tiny Christian church—this, of course, a late addition, probably of the fourth century—and what appears to have been a public
guest-house or inn. And at some date which we cannot exactly fix,
perhaps in the second century, walls were built.[10]

The writing, graceful, easy, courteous, is representative of this
minor classic, couched in the language of the antiquarian lecture-
meeting. Collingwood's style, until we reach the late works, is dateless. It springs pretty well formed by his education and his talents;
in *Speculum Mentis* it ascends without effort to the diapason of the
best philosophic music of the day; in *Roman Britain* he shows himself
master of the plain style.

As always, however, Collingwood is sharpening a polemical point,
one to be stuck fiercely into the trivial and inaccurate folk-history
with which most people frame their conception of Roman Britain.
Just as his father, in *Thorstein of the Mere*, was at pains to dramatise
the living culture of the Norse settlers in Lakeland, their weapons,
ornaments, independent politics, and horticulture, so Collingwood's
little history seeks to dispatch to the dustbin the vulgar folk-history
that believes that before the Romans the Celts lived barbaric lives
of mutual slaughter, before being put in order by Romans from
Rome who lived in villas and then went home when the Goths sacked
their city.

Their armies were recalled, their civilian immigrants left a country in
which, in the absence of armed protection, they were no longer safe
from the natives, and the Celtic barbarians once more had the island
to themselves, having learnt nothing and forgotten nothing in the
meantime. The Romans came, conquered, and departed, and left no

mark except the ruins of their buildings. When the Saxons landed, Britain was once more a country of Celtic tribes living in a state of barbarism and mutual warfare.[11]

This little cameo would easily slip into the pages of *1066 and All That*, but nor, as the author says, would it be out of place in the older histories of England, among which even David Hume's great classic dilates on the cruelty of the Druids and the relapse of the Britons into barbarism when the Romans left.[12]

Collingwood's purpose is to ramify and complicate the folk-history out of all recognition, and in doing so to acknowledge the necessary truth in the heresy (never more shocking than to twenty-first-century ears) that imperialism is everywhere and inevitable in history, and that the Roman incursion at least brought many and (as they say) multicultural benefits to the varied Celtic tribes living in Britain when the soldiers of empire, recruited from Gaul, Spain, Tuscany, Lombardy, Syria, North Africa, arrived to put in train the efficient work of colonisation. They spoke their mother tongues and they spoke Latin; they belonged to their blood race and they were Roman citizens. They were bound by Roman law and formed by Roman civilisation.

This latter—as against the inanities of folk-history, especially on television[13]—was a complex thing, much more porous and capacious, as Collingwood says, than Britishness in early twentieth-century India. The British, therefore, were not a subject race held down by the Romans, no more than were the African Berbers or the Mesopotamian Anatolians, both at that date uninvaded by Arabs or Ottomans, both unscorched by the flame of Islam: "The Romans, compounded of Celtic and Mediterranean elements, could claim kinship, physical and spiritual, with everyone from the Tyne to the Euphrates and from the Sahara to the Rhine. . . . Hence all attempts to understand the Roman Empire by comparison with, say, the British rule in India or the French in Algeria are frustrated by a false analogy.[14]

Here, in this early textbook, are the beginnings of Collingwood's theory of culture, one of his most radical and, for us, opportune contributions to the science of human affairs. He recalls a tombstone (which he draws for us) found at Corbridge (Corstopitum) on the Tyne. It is of the tomb of the Syrian Barates from Palmyra, to whose British wife Barates, when he became a widower, had already put up a splendid tombstone of her own. These geographical (and therefore cultural) differences, now so important to us, had no salience in the days before nationalism. Identity was not a concept.

> The Britons, then, became Romans; Romans in civilization, in speech, in patriotism and sentiment. At the same time, they did not cease to be Britons; their participation in the cosmopolitan life of the Empire was not of such a kind as to swamp or obliterate their original character and peculiarities. The business of this book is to show how this happened, to show in what ways the Britons became Romans and in what ways they remained Britons.[15]

Collingwood respectfully reviews the standard political constitution of the British province under Roman rule, with its principal military musters at York, Chester, and Caerleon, 17,000 regular troops and 25,000 auxiliaries, and the little local capitals of civilisation—London, Colchester, Dorchester, Winchester, for example—mostly lying southeast of the Fosse Way, a line drawn across England from Lincoln to Gloucester, petering out beyond Exeter on the Dumnomian peninsula. Beyond these limits, the Roman preserve was military and its biggest monument the wall.

As we would expect, Collingwood has much to tell about the wall, summarising his and Haverfield's discovery that it wasn't a defence but both a limit and "an elevated sentry walk," that its garrison members were more policemen than soldiers, demolishing as he went Kipling's marvellous imaginings in *Puck of Pook's Hill* where Parnesius with his century holds the wall as one would hold a besieged fort against the anachronistically premature hordes of the Vikings. But it is in the chapter "Art and Language" that Collingwood adumbrates his theory of culture, recognising as he does so that "the history of art is not the entire history of civilisation," whatever Ruskin might have said.

His analogy is bloodstock breeding: first crosses are vigorous, sharing the merits of both parents; later strains deteriorate. When

British artists, traceable in pottery, medallions, brooches, tomb inscriptions, floor mosaics, and wall paintings, met Graeco-Roman work, it seemed as if a new art expressing the vigour of one and the refinement of the other might arise. But it didn't. Roman-British art and craft settled down into forms of expression to match and adorn the domestic comforts and conveniences of "a culture somewhat like our own"[16] with third-rate art of an easy and accommodating kind to suit life in the villa and the market town.

Working from the reassembled fragments of plates and vases scattered in tiny deposits across the English landscape, Collingwood decides, with the boldness and certainty that characterise his signature and render his arguments so confidently assertive, that after the period from 50 to 100 CE when Roman design was the *dernier cri*, aspects of native Celtic taste began to reappear to produce a hybrid, which then very slowly reverted to its original forms but without ever recovering its original zest and gusto.

Somewhere in the lines drawn on Glastonbury ware and tribal brooches is to be found the crux of art history, at the moment perhaps the most popular as well as the most robust of the historical sciences. So: "Any process involving an historical change from P1 to P2 leaves an unconverted residue of P1 encapsulated within an historical state of things which superficially is altogether P2."[17]

This is the secret of cultural change, and for better or worse it discloses itself in Celtic ornaments, Roman-British vases, Florentine frescoes at the moment at which mannerism captures and corrupts the spirit of the Renaissance, or in the grand reanimation of British architecture that Victorian Gothic (never more so than in Ruskin's propaganda) brought to the new industrial cities. What has happened in each case is that the tides of war or of marketing or of religion sweep over a people and bring new forms of expression with them. The people respond by adopting the new forms, and allowing them, either because of fashion or because of compulsion, to overlay the old forms. Insofar as the old forms correspond with suppressed but still mobile passions and ideas, they do not die out but survive, not in some historical subconscious (this is not a psychological explanation) but in the continued, unofficial presence of such passions and ideas, living on in a thousand details of everyday life.

So it is that today the principles of solidarity and mutuality that gave rise to the British trade union movement, now pretty well forbidden by law and dissolved by the disappearance of its class constituency, survives not only in antique banners and annual galas, but in sudden demonstrations of mass dissent, in the march, the platform, the badge, in men and women crowded by common cause in the street, making friends with strangers. Of course, traditions may die out; new ways of life may be victorious because simply more fulfilling or more brutally enforced. But where eradication depends on force—think how orthodox religion survived in Russia—it is likely that the lost ways and means of expression are kept alive, whether in practice or in desire.

These lessons are there to be read in the many museums in Britain that house the scraps and relics of Roman times.

III

In 1926 a clever young woman called Dorothy Emmet, reading *Literae Humaniores* at Lady Margaret Hall, joined Collingwood's audience in his lectures. "As a lecturer he was a spell-binder. I attended his course on the Philosophy of History, and the finished polish of what he was saying was such that I tried to scribble it down verbatim for consideration at a later time."[18]

He was much talked about, remembered in a sprinkling of cameos in the many volumes of memoirs that Oxford so readily released in her students of the period. There was, for instance, the mischievous and flirtatious Collingwood, of whom Sir Malcolm Knox, much as he loved and admired his tutor, disapproved. This version of the man is caught by one pupil, Tamara Talbot Rice, as he was winding up a clockwork mouse and setting it to run across the carpet to bump into his student's feet. Since she thought of him as "aloof, less inclined to digress, far less considerate" than her other philosophy tutor, she was understandably unnerved by the confounded mouse; "Although I half came to expect it, it always startled me and made me forget what I had been going to say."[19]

Not that it will do to leave Malcolm Knox, who became Collingwood's student shortly before Dorothy Emmet, tutting away with Presbyterian rectitude in St. Andrew's. He too commemorates his teacher's gifts, "the thin but clear voice"—that Oxford accent so many people have parodied and disparaged (not to be confused with the old ruling-class staccato), still, it seems to me, one of the most beautiful products of English culture—"in the company of friends never aloof" even if that "aloofness was apt to inhibit affection." But the Scots reserve dissolves before "the affection inspired . . . by the man, the stimulus derived from the tutor, or the admiration evoked by the gifts of the philosopher and historian from whom I have learnt 'more than I can hope to acknowledge.' "

Well, Collingwood always scorned a cliché, fond as he remained of Knox. But the clockwork mouse sorts well enough with what Isaiah Berlin, in a letter written while still a student in 1932 to Shiela Grant Duff (later of the BBC), saw as the man's audacity, even the raffishness behind the subfusc correctness of mien and spectacles.

> Collingwood is very exciting and risky. He is a very sly lively continental sort of philosopher: if he takes an interest in you you will, I think, find him interesting and even sensational. I know really very little about him save that I always found him entertaining, enormously ingenious and frequently deceitful and unsound. He is the only philosophy tutor in Oxford who is also a man of genuine culture. This is all very good and I wish he taught me too.[20]

This is very shrewd. Berlin saw Collingwood's vivid delight in eristic misrepresentation, the passion to win the day over the forces of unreason as marching with the "minute philosophers," with their tormented fastidiousness over what it is possible to say, their triviality of instance, the resulting constipation of mind. Contrariwise, however, Ian Richmond, another pupil later to become an archaeological knight, had, as we shall hear, quite searching animadversions to make of Collingwood's summary ways with an excavation. He too recalls "the high-pitched, incisive tones, the spoken thoughts as clear cut as his beautiful written prose, the enthusiasm for the subject at concert pitch, but the ardent conviction, the sheer celerity of argument went with the tendency to drive the evidence hard, producing conclusions whose very artistry disguised the inherent weakness of foundation."[21] This was the figure he cut on the lecture podium or at the centre of the dig, not the "sensitive and kindly" critic at home offering to his students "a haven of refuge when in difficulty."

There again, Richmond is much disagreed with in this criticism of Collingwood. Gerald Simpson's archaeologist daughter, Grace, fiercely and in detail rebuts Richmond's strictures in his British Academy obituary for his teacher. She remarks disdainfully that "last year [1997] I was told that people in Oxford, who are not archaeologists, were telling philosophy students that Collingwood was a bad excavator. Where did this malign attitude come from?"[22] Grace Simpson leaves us with a more familiar Collingwood, amazingly swift with plausible conjecture, his mind intent upon a dozen problems at once and more than one site at a time, passionate always in a theory of archaeological practice to be understood as a historical *not* a natural science.

Grace Simpson's loyalty, Berlin's double echo and Tamara's mouse, Richmond's not unprejudiced unease, even Knox's stolid devotion, give the lie to an obscurity at the heart of Collingwood's thinking and his selfhood (both inseparable). The momentousness and celerity of his thought, which is the ground of this biography and the occasion for the so very welcome rediscovery of "the line of force" he released into the future, may be written out as a five-part invention. In the first part, set out in the two early books, he explicates the mutual embeddedness, the nature of progress, and the characteristic styles of each of the forms of knowledge. But as Kipling, surprisingly, said of *Speculum Mentis*, "the denouement is that there isn't any denouement—only deliquescence. . . . But Collingwood is tremendously interesting."[23] The long process of solidifying the liquefaction led him to the victory of history over all other sciences.

The second stage of the invention was therefore the figuring of question-and-answer logic; the third, the theory of the "re-enactment" of past thoughts, and this, in turn, of a piece with the

"encapsulation" theory of culture in the present; the fourth, the revelation that all thought is grounded in a metaphysics of the past which
shapes and transmits those "absolute presuppositions we have to
have if we are to think at all"; the fifth and last, foreshadowed but
muffled from the start, the unity of theory and practice, elusive, battled for, lost but essential, to thinker or to any other human agent.
As his health failed and his insomnia swelled in the 1930s, these
imperial themes pressed more and more irresistibly upon him.

The knot of obscurity thickened and clotted. The unity of knowledge and the integrity of a life must be made coterminous. This, I
suppose, is the struggle of the mind for monism, and every serious
scholar reaches a point in his or her career at which a decision must
be made about the attainment of such a thing. Collingwood, like
Ruskin, never doubted it. His life was given its integrity by the courage and sureness with which he pursued and, it may be, won his
prize. What I have called his five-part invention is only my way of
beginning to make his ascent to the top usable for later climbers,
with different equipment and new routes.

IV

In the summer of 1928 Collingwood went to stay with his friend
Vernon Blake at Le Martouret, a modest country house or *mas* near
Die, the pretty little market town where the river Drôme rises in the
Haute Savoie, as his father had described in his first book. Blake was
an English painter, friend of David Bomberg and part of that strong,
admirable movement in British painting of the day that had read
Clive Bell and Roger Fry, taken to heart the lessons of Cézanne, and
set to work to produce work that would combine Cézanne's severity
of colour and emphasis on plane with the wonderful magic they
found in the visions of Samuel Palmer. As always, Collingwood was
braced by the presence of works of art—such a good, strong phase
as it is, combining the duress of labour with the love made by art—
to wrestle once more with the unity of thought and action, the insep-
arability of theory and practice, the integrity of a life.

He was rewriting his lectures on the philosophy of history, which had so fired the young Dorothy Emmet, and, contemplating his efforts in recollection, referred to himself a trifle incredibly as "always a slow and painful thinker."[24] This severity was doubtless the result of a frustration all scholars will recognise at the blockage made in one's thought by an impassable problem. Time and again one finds it immovably in one's path; systematically, one procrastinates with it, writing passages of the work in hand that permit one to skirt or curve away from it until, with grim inevitability, it looms once more on the way ahead and must be faced.

At Die in 1928 one finds his extraordinary swiftness and elasticity of thought baffled in this way by the sheer scope of the sciences. The seeming impossibility of discovering the unity that must be there if human beings were indeed to make a science of their own affairs would then thwart applying knowledge of the forms of knowledge to the kind of self-knowledge that alone could turn history into progress, as the Enlightenment had promised. If we do not learn from the past—"and we cannot otherwise learn at all"[25]—we merely practise what Collingwood called "pseudo-history," a wandering narrative in which there is no conception of *purpose*, and therefore no exercise of mind. Contrariwise, he declared in his best-known aphorism "all history is the history of thought," which he took to mean that political theory is not an interminable anecdote summarising a sequence of remarks on politics made by consecutive theorists—by seven league boots from Plato to Nato, as the old joke has it—but is "the thought which occupies the mind of a man engaged in political work: the formation of a policy, the planning of means to execute it, the attempt to carry it into effect, the discovery that others are hostile to it, the devising of ways to overcome their hostility, and so forth."[26]

It is worth, in a biography such as this, remonstrating with Collingwood when he dismisses from the historian's consideration such "sensuous elements" of the historical context as the state as the size of a statesman's audience when he said what he said, or the cold and misery of the soldiers when the general took his fateful decisions. For Churchill's rhetoric in the House of Commons in 1940 turned precisely on the uncertain morale of his listeners, in the House and in the nation. That rhetoric was inseparable from the reasons for his policies. Reason and rhetoric were at one. By the same token, Truman's decision to drop the hideous atomic bomb on Hiroshima in August 1945 was deeply influenced by all the inexperienced president was truthfully told of the dreadful battles in the Philippines and the certainty of mass civilian opposition—"schoolgirls in the trenches"—to any invasion of Japan. The pitch of the statesman's voice (Churchill's in my example) and the agony of wounded men (on Iwo Jima) are formative of the history of the thoughts, so they are to biographical history.[27]

The source of such rediscovery is not, it must be emphasised, in cultivating one's powers of empathetic understanding. Empathy, no doubt, has its importance and its actuality.[28] Question-and-answer logic, the first step on Collingwood's historical hermeneutic, is, as we have already noted, a more cognitive motion of mind. Knowledge for the historian is not the ordering and verification of propositions and statements, but the derivation of these from questions to which they serve as answers.

It should be remarked in passing that on the way to making this case he was guilty, in Bernard Williams's eyes, of some "ill-advised and arrogant remarks . . . about what is ordinarily called 'logic.'" Williams was of the view that there is no particular need to follow Collingwood into his logic of question-and-answer, but only to agree that "every statement that anybody ever makes is made in answer to a question."[29] He goes on, "Every question involves a presupposition," but presuppositions will have to wait. Question-and-answer logic he took to be intrinsic to thought and deliberate in its advance. In puzzling out meaning, one is not guided by a vague and general interrogativeness of disposition (whereabouts did the legionaries build their living quarters?), but by a question specific to one's position on the site (is this the corner of the first barrack block?). Interpreting the answers of others to the questions they had put to experience is a matter of determining the question. Conduct is only contradictory when a person attempts contradictory answers to what we are sure is a single question. Consequently, truth may only be asserted of correct answers to identified questions. (This, to one's relief, gets rid of infantile discussions about so-called absolute truths.)

Collingwood is scornful of the received theories of truth at least for historical purposes: in the first such case, there is the correspondence theory, according to which a proposition corresponds exactly with a state of affairs, something the impossibility of which had caused Prichard such anguish. In the second case, he dismissed the coherence theory, by which token a proposition is true in that it is structurally "coherent" with related propositions of a formal kind (e.g., in Euclidean geometry). Lastly, in contemptuous undertone, he put aside the pragmatists and their gingerly criterion of "warranted assertability." Breezing past all this, what Collingwood commends is not so much a method or a technique for the historian of thought to follow as it is an understanding he or she will command of the *constitution* of the knowledge arrived at. What we know is constitutive of ourselves: historical self-knowledge (the construction of the Roman wall, the construction of Marx's *Capital*, the decline and fall of the British Empire) goes towards the statutes of the human constitution.

So what we know is fashioned out of the answers given and found adequate to the questions put to the little bit of experience in front of us. The painter in front of the Old Man of Coniston wants to catch the first light glinting on the shoulder of the mountain. There is a technique for rendering this with a highlight, a speck of white on the black of the stone. But this spot of white, now it's applied, is wrong. Not scientifically wrong, emotionally wrong. It is, let's say, too flashy an effect. It's not an answer. The painter, Vernon Blake perhaps, or Collingwood himself, who was still painting occasionally in 1928, although nearly always in water-colour, scrapes the patch of paint down.

If the answer had been right, it would have been in response to a particular question itself "part of a question-and-answer complex" true as a whole (the painting). It would also have been "a sensible or intelligent question, not a silly one," arising relevantly from its complex.[30] To be able to judge its truthfulness, you need to know quite a lot of the history involved, whether you are the painter or someone looking at the painting (*without* your hands in your pockets, what's more). The history of art, the history of metaphysics, the history of the Roman wall are the same kinds of intellectual venture, and we shall only summon up the temerity to face down Collingwood's terrific disdain when we add to the question-and-answer complex the necessity to determine enough of what the original agents felt as part of their thought. For it will become a premise of our revisions of Collingwood that all history is the history of thought inseparable from the moral sentiments that give it form.

There is, it should be added, a radical sociability implicit in question-and-answer logic. Collingwood had sorted out to his own satisfaction the clinching rebuttal of the "realists" in the manuscript of *Truth and Contradiction*, of which only one chapter remains.[31] This he wrote when off duty in Church Street, Kensington, in 1917. By 1928 he could see that his argument provided the first, great gateway to the planned city of historical reason. It freed the mind, on the one hand, from the charges that metaphysics is a trivial game of paradoxes ("the world is many and one") and, on the other, from the reductivism of the know-all realists, whose prime concern was to show how other people were wrong about everything. The strength of question-and-answer reciprocity (to avoid the inutility of "logic" in this context) is that truth may indeed be come at but is never complete. Future questions will not be the same as present ones and will in any case be thought by different people in unforeseen circumstances. Collingwood thus opened the way to his next, much trickier innovation, the "re-enactment" of past thoughts in the present.

Fifteen or so years later and after Collingwood's death, eighty miles east of Oxford, Wittgenstein was inaugurating his revolution in philosophy from a bare room above Trinity Street, Cambridge. His racy, conversational wisdom matches with a startling likeness Collingwood's ideas couched in such a very different idiom, though by a not dissimilar man.

> 241. "So you are saying that human agreement decides what is true and what is false"—It is what human beings *say* that is true and false; and they agree in the language they use. That is not agreement in opinions but in form of life.

242. If language is to be a means of communication there must be agreement not only in definitions but also (queer as this may sound) in judgements. This seems to abolish logic but does not do so. It is one thing to describe methods of measurement, and another to obtain and state results of measurement.[32]

Hence the sociability of inquiry, the congeniality of judgement, the intractability of truth.

V

The sociable Collingwood was the archaeologist, the solitary one the philosopher, or at least that is the readiest way to tell the story. For there are plenty of glimpses of a sociably contentious philosopher, amiably smiling at Prichard when that worthy would say, exasperated, "I wish you'd get off the fence," the fence being the only place to avoid being told by Prichard, a tormented Pyrrhonist searching for moral belief, why what you thought was erroneous before you had spoken. McCallum recalled his colleague's own delight in demonstrating his interlocutor's mistakes, saying in courteous repetition, "certainly, certainly" before going in ruthlessly, the Oxford and Cambridge way, to display the mistake and demolish the certainty. I am irresistibly put in mind of a piece of marvellous mimicry by Jonathan Miller, imitating an imaginary conversation between Bertrand Russell and G. E. Moore:

> "Moore," I said, "how many apples are there in that basket?"
> He smiled seraphically, as was his wont. "There are no apples in the basket."
> "Moore, are there some apples in that basket?" He shook his head.
> Finally, "Moore, are there apples in that basket?"
> "Yes."

After all, it was Collingwood himself who observed that most people regarded philosophy as a mere parlour game.

Archaeology, however, was not a parlour game. It was that undefined realm of life where gentlemanly hobbies become passions, formal scholarship melds with civic society, and the routine distinction between work and leisure dissolves into the sport of life, a game keenly played for the serious answers it yields to the demand for meaning, mostly of a reassuringly local kind. Coniston was Collingwood's second locality, and the home of his active, practical, public character. Throughout the second half of the 1920s, his father, well into his seventies, was growing progressively more infirm. For so many decades, the most energetic and tireless walker, painter, sailor, carpenter, excavator, writer, organiser of so much of Coniston's and Ambleside's cultural life, let alone that of University College, Reading, he had been slowly stricken by a series of small strokes that had blurred his speech but not his mind, and partly paralysed one leg and arm, confining him largely to Lanehead where nonetheless he worked, as his son wrote in an obituary, "with unabated firmness."[33] In the noble tradition of the localness of local history, there had long been a strong museum interest maintained at the Armitt Library in Ambleside. Its roots were in the Ambleside Book Club, founded in 1828 with Wordsworth a member, conjoined to the Ruskin library, which was founded and perpetrated with Gershom's indispensable help, in 1882. The money was supplied by another of those cultivated Ambleside women, Mary Louisa Armitt, with whom Gershom had long collaborated on the Parish Register Society,[34] and the Collingwoods all weighed in with their habitual display of civic-mindedness. For "any loyal member of a community wills the whole organisation of that community, not merely the little part of it which is in an immediate sense his own business."[35]

In 1929 the indomitable Antiquarian Society approached the Armitt Library to propose that one of its large, high-windowed rooms be allocated for a permanent archaeological display. On 10 May 1929 Collingwood wrote to his father:

> I think that if the Armitt Library is prepared to give a room to the Roman finds it is a good chance for displaying them and should be accepted on the main and indispensable condition that members of the public can obtain access to the collection. If this were done I should

be prepared to help as far as I could towards making the collection interesting and instructive by supplying such things as drawings, photographs, maps and perhaps even models.

He kept his word. The two minutely accurate models of Galava Fort now in the specially designed and new Armitt Museum and Library opposite the site are by his own hand, a hand first trained in such accomplishments by making papier mâché relief maps of Lakeland with his father thirty years before. Gordon Wordsworth, family friend, committee member, and grandson of the poet, coordinated things in Ambleside now that Gershom was immobilised, and the establishment of the display went slowly ahead. Collingwood prepared all the labelling cards in his beautiful calligraphy,[36] Herbert Bell, by then a photographer of renown, provided illustrations, and by the end of 1932 the room was ready.

Gershom had died suddenly but not unexpectedly on 1 October. At the last, he was finishing the proofs of a revised edition of his classic guide *The Lake Counties*. The same year, to his great pleasure, the publisher Edward Arnold reissued *Thorstein of the Mere* to some little acclaim. Gershom had dedicated this new edition to the poet Edward Thompson, Methodist minister, friend of Jawaharlal Nehru and redoubtable campaigner for Indian independence, another cause of Gershom's.[37] Gershom was buried beneath a low cross in Coniston churchyard, immediately next to Ruskin's monument, a fine imitation of the Northumbrian crosses his secretary spent so much time cataloguing.[38] Two years later, speaking according to tradition on the site and before the Antiquarian Society, his son paid the last of his many tributes to his father. The meeting was held beside the Bewcastle Cross in its memorable position just below Barron's Pike, on the western edge of the Cheviots, well to the northeast of Lakeland and a few miles beyond the wall and Roman jurisdiction. It was 19 June 1934, a gusty, slightly overcast day. The comrades of the society were scarfed and overcoated against Cumbria's uncertain summer. The high, clear, modulated voice rang out over the wind; the cross itself, even shorn of its crown as it is, towered over the little audience, its massive but slender lines setting off the three Christs in relief in their niches, the central Christ with long, wavy hair falling to his shoulders, the other three sides richly wrought in long, vinous coils punctuated by the figures of birds and intricately inwoven patterns.

> In asking me to describe this cross, the most beautiful work of ancient art that our district contains, and perhaps the finest extant masterpiece of early English stone-carving if both its intrinsic excellence and its relative completeness are taken into consideration, your committee was, I know, thinking of me not as an authority on the difficult problems of pre-Norman history and art, but as representative of the great scholar who for many years directed our Society's study of those problems. His loss has removed from among us the only man who could describe the Bewcastle Cross as it deserves to be described, with full justice done to its art, its archaeology, and its setting in the history of the age; and the only reason that could induce me to accept so difficult a task is the fact that, having watched him at work so closely and so long, I have learnt to see in these things a little of what he saw.[39]

"He was a man of strong affections and warm temper," Collingwood had already written, "his manner . . . full of courtesy and charm . . . and he always gave away whatever of value he possessed, as generously as he gave his time and his knowledge to all who asked for them."[40] He knew he was describing the life and character he wished to embody in his own.

But not only was Gershom's life inimitable, the social conditions that made it what it was had disappeared. Nobody could re-create the Coniston of 1900, nor do so much again from a house perched above a remote lake alongside barren fells ten hours' journey from Oxford. Robin took on many of Gershom's duties and put on his father's manners with them. But he was, even then, a renowned figure, in demand countrywide, eminent in the great university, frequently away from home not just for his "pernoctations" at Pembroke, but archaeologising, historicising, and writing interminably in France, Germany, Italy, Spain. He kept up family life and paternity, beekeeping, bookbinding (another craft he loved and mastered), sailing, camping (at Skipness), but rootedness, the value so unself-consciously lived by his father, himself a tough traveller, was much harder for Collingwood. He belonged to two Englands, not one; he was completely a European; he was called for to spread his ideas nationwide; in all this he presaged the internal émigré and wandering intellectual of our own day. The price of such experience is high; it is bought with all that a man hath.

VI

Housesteads, the excellent Hunter Davies says, "is the best Roman fort to be seen, not just on Hadrian's Wall but in the whole of Europe."[41] It traverses a narrow site running east-west on the wall just west of Hexham. As it is now, kept spick and span by English Heritage, it shows off the best of what might be called "field museum vernacular." That is to say, the disjuncture between the busy garrison fort it was for a full cohort of one thousand Belgian legionaries in the third century, crowded with soldiers and horses and delivery wagons, a shanty town of pedlars, *vivandières*, victuallers, smallholders outside its walls and, 1,700 years later, the quiet, tourist present is deliberately marked. The vernacular grammar is made up of well-mown turf running with suburban tidiness up to the scattered foundations of the various walls on show. These have been in places restored, so that the lines of the foundations are clear and clean. Up in the northeastern corner the outline and floors of the sixteen barrack buildings are plain and countable. In the centre, by the south gate, the foundations of the commanding officer's house make it easily possible to walk round the outline of a large villa, to pass beneath the long-since collapsed atrium into the inner courtyard, once tiled with a mosaic floor, now carpeted with cropped English turf. Westwards to the fortified ramparts, there is only turf, newly mown and today smelling of Maytime.

The whole place is not a symbol, it is an actualisation of question-and-answer inquiry, and the ordinary tourists, visiting in their thousands, must, insofar as they make the effort, attempt the re-

enactment of old thoughts (what's this bit of the commanding officer's house for? How did patrols cross the wall?), let alone re-enact
the thoughts of two centuries of archaeologists whose collective effort of mind is visible on the ground.

Collingwood himself, his pupil Richmond tells us,[42] only actually
excavated once on the wall itself, although he led the Cumbrian archaeologists on their pilgrimage to celebrate another ten years of
such excavation on 30 June 1930, addressing the faithful at the then
Newcastle branch of Durham University.[43] There was, however, not
a man or woman of archaeological bent but was aware of his authority, his enthusiasm, his "hard driving of the evidence." Richmond's
impressive candour about his teacher takes the measure of the man's
forcefulness and swiftness of insight as these qualities led him, sometimes too fast, to conclusions that he urgently desired both to be his
and to be done with, so that he could be off, returning to whatever
writing it was that he had left unfinished. His conviction "that to
pose a problem permitted its answer to be predicted was a product
of the study rather than the field. For the fieldworker excavation is
always a plunge into the dark." But this, as we learned from Grace
Simpson, is not only nonsensical about archaeology—only General
Pitt-Rivers leaped in the dark—it is wrong about Collingwood. He
was quick but not hasty; he was decisive but not impulsive. The
keenness of his practice in the field, with all its mud and perspiring
effort, is incontestable. What he then carried back to "the study" was
the record he had found of human activity, there to give it accommodation within the larger historical narrative to which it belonged. So
when Richmond, with a sardonic turn of a cliché, severely reproaches
Collingwood after one of his last major expeditions, to the prehis-
toric site at Penrith known as King Arthur's Round Table, we back
off a little: "There he had made up his mind what he was to find and
found it with fatal precision . . . he had fallen into a pit of his own
digging. . . . This was high tragedy."[44]

There is for Richmond when he wrote this more to the pit than
archaeological error. But that corner of our own diggings lies well
ahead. At the time of his father's death in 1932, Collingwood's was
the straight road ahead, whether for history in the field, in the li-

brary, or in the conduct of political life. His own tragedy was almost to comprehend how to think about these terrific topics, but to know he wouldn't have time to work it out. Yet he set himself nonetheless to do just that, and to write in a few years the *Summa Historica* that would lay the foundations of the future.

No doubt many of his admiring critics were right in saying, as Dorothy Emmet did, that "Collingwood's views on the development of thought make it appear more of a unity than it actually is."[45] Monism, the unity of mind, thought itself as a huge collective enterprise of humankind: these were the first premises of his intellectual formation, and he yearned to make them true. The long eclipse of metaphysics, effected in Oxford by the young blades, A. J. Ayer, J. L. Austin, and, from the Fens, Ludwig Wittgenstein, meant that neither philosophers nor their friends have had much to say about the unity of spirit of the collective mind for many a long day since 1932.

Yet the pull of such a vision remains. Men and women try to make sense of themselves and the world by seeing it whole, by devising a narrative of their personal integrity. It gets shy-making to say so, of course, but effort and desire persist. Our biographical point is that we will only understand how Collingwood helps to this momentous vocation by our following him, so far as we can, through the actualities of his daily round, thought and the passions that give it form.

In a marvellous poem about one of Collingwood's giant ancestors, Charles Tomlinson compresses one such famous occasion in the life of René Descartes into a few lines.

> Thrusting its armoury of hot delight,
>   Its Negroid belly at him, how the whole
> Contraption threatened to melt him
>   Into recognition . . .
>   . . . All leaned
> Into that frigid burning, corded tight
> By the lightlines as the slow sun drew
> Away and down. The shadow, now,
> Defined no longer: it filled, then overflowed
> Each fault in snow, dragged everything

Into its own anonymity of blue
Becoming black. The great mind
Sat with his back to the unreasoning wind
And doubted, doubted at his ear
The patter of ash and, beyond, the snow-bound farms,
Flora of flame and iron contingency
And the moist reciprocity of his palms.[46]

One cannot first comprehend and then use Collingwood's thought to think for oneself without questioning his questioning, seeing and hearing his equivalent of Descartes' stove in the reddish-brown sails of *Swallow* slapping above his head, replacing Descartes' deadly dualistic doubt with the affirmation of spades grating on Roman stones, and with the grave, worn, calfbound spines of the books lining the shelves in Duke Humfrey's Elizabethan library.

Figure 1. Lanehead, Collingwood family home.

Figure 2. Ruskin's home, Brantwood, overlooking Coniston Water.

Figure 3. Gershom: a self-portrait, 1886 (age thirty-two). Reproduced by kind permission of the Collingwood Society.

Figure 4. Collingwood's mother Dorrie. Reproduced by kind permission of the Collingwood Society.

Figure 5. One of Gershom's landscapes from Iceland, June 1897. Reproduced by kind permission of the Collingwood Society.

Figure 6. Schoolboy at Rugby, 1903–1908. Reproduced by kind permission of the Collingwood Society.

Figure 7. Undergraduate at Oxford, 1909–1912. Reproduced by kind permission of the Collingwood Society.

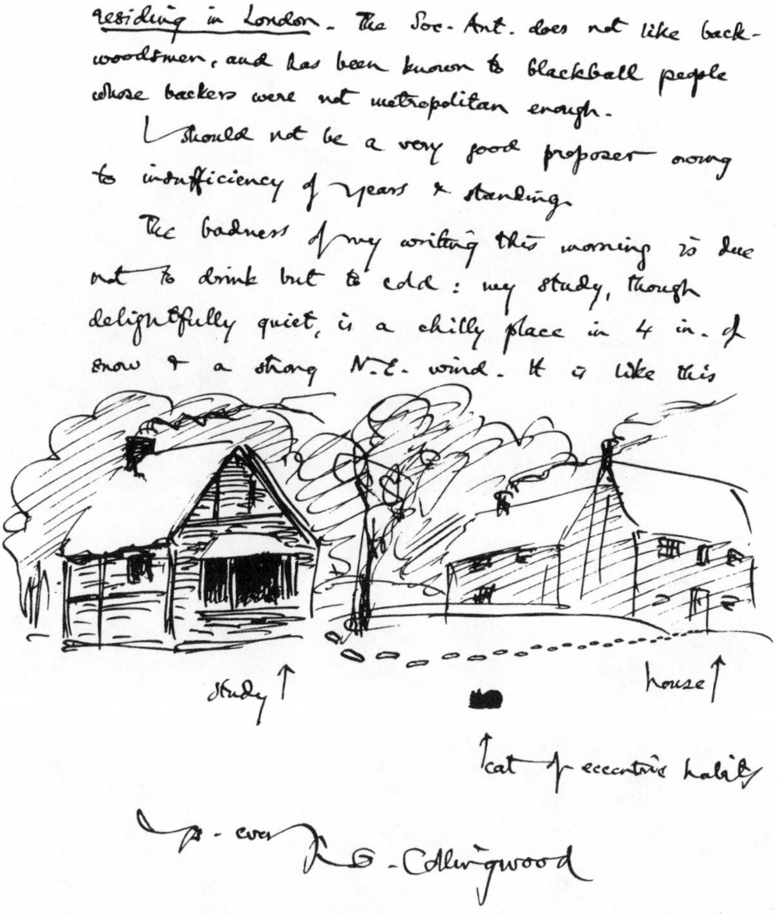

residing in London. The Soc. Ant. does not like back-woodsmen, and has been known to blackball people whose backers were not metropolitan enough.

I should not be a very good proposer owing to insufficiency of years & standing.

The badness of my writing this morning is due not to drink but to cold: my study, though delightfully quiet, is a chilly place in 4 in. of snow & a strong N.E. wind. It is like this

study ↑   house ↑

cat of eccentric habits

p - ever   R. G. - Collingwood

Figure 8. Letter to Mortimer Wheeler, 1924, with drawing of Collingwood's study at Stapleton's Chantry. Reproduced by kind permission of the Collingwood Society.

Figure 9. Stapleton's Chantry, Collingwood's home from 1920 to 1928. Photograph by Hilary Britland.

Figure 10. Taking a Roman rubbing, early 1930s. Reproduced by kind permission of the Collingwood Society.

R. G. Collingwood. Æsica. 3. VII. 30

Figure 11. Speaking to Cumberland and Westmorland archaeologists, June 1930. Reproduced by kind permission of the Collingwood Society.

Figure 12. Collingwood and his wife Ethel at a dig in 1935 (Ethel second from right). Reproduced by kind permission of the Collingwood Society.

Figure 13. Pembroke College in the 1940s. Reproduced by kind permission of McGowin Library, Pembroke College, Oxford.

Figure 14. The first mate of the *Fleur de Lys*. Reproduced by kind permission of the Collingwood Society.

Figure 15. The mule path from Santorini harbour.

Figure 16. W. G. and R. G. Collingwood's graves, Coniston churchyard.

6

The Idea of the Ideas: The New Science

In 1930 Oxford remained hardly larger than its medieval self, at least as far as the university was concerned. The staff lived in the red brick avenues only a few hundred yards north of the Parks, where the University XI played its cricket, and although by then the Morris works out at Cowley, a mile or so beyond Magdalen bridge, were going strong, there was plenty of road to be filled up. Even by the end of the decade, there were only two million cars in Britain, one for every twenty-four persons. In 1945 Oxford City Council asked the best town planner of the day, Thomas Sharp, what the city should do about itself, and in his masterly response he spoke, for sure, of "the turmoil of traffic" (the city had seen nothing yet) and observed that "Oxford was by no means a well-balanced city before the manufacture of cars began. It was too dependent on the University to be socially healthy," and he went on to regret the elongated compressions of its development, which made it six miles long and three miles wide, isolated the knolls of Cumnor and Hinksey, and packed all traffic, moving to whichever point of the compass, into the middle.[1]

In spite of assorted efforts at traffic first aid, those criticisms still hold, sixty years after Sharp first made them. But for the last eleven years of Collingwood's life in Oxford, it was still at its heart a city of bicycles and pedestrians. He stepped off the little local train after it had trundled up from North Moreton and walked to Pembroke in ten minutes. When he left the college to go to the Bodleian—its dull, stolid extensions were not built on the corner opposite the Clarendon building until 1937—he turned out of the college and into St. Aldates, stepped into the huge quadrangle of Christ Church and out at the back of the college into Merton Street, up Magpie Lane and past St. Mary's, the university church in which he gave sermons on a few occasions, across the cobbles of Radcliffe Square beneath the great bulk of the Camera, and into the lovely plainness of the courtyard in front of the library, its stone tablets on the walls solemnly naming the forms of philosophic knowledge (including metaphysics) for the edification of the scholar below.

He was a brisk, short, stocky figure like his father, limping hardly at all in spite of the stiff knee, small of bone but strong of muscle, an indomitable walker (and sailor), balding, for a few years neatly moustached (never a happy adornment), cordial and formal at once, greeting his pupils as he walked through the town—Ian Richmond, Tom Hopkinson, Bernard Miles, Michael Foot, John Mabbott, Kathleen Edwardes in particular.

Richmond came to the red brick house at 15 Belbroughton Road where the Collingwood family moved as its first occupants in 1928. He recalled, as we heard, his tutor's kindliness and sensitivity (no aloofness there) when he was in trouble, and he also recalled the man's practical skilfulness, his craftiness of hand and eye. "Sensitive and meticulous drawings from Collingwood's own pen" we know about, but to make copies of Roman inscriptions, "he mounted rubbings on a transparent screen, thence producing a black and white rendering. He drew *all* the important stones this way before his death. Who else possessed the genius for the task?"[2]

Hopkinson remained a friend long after making a very different kind of career in journalism from one implied by the zest for Aristotle, Descartes, and Hume that Collingwood inspired in him.

> His thick tweed suits looked like the product of some cottage industry, and from the far side of the quadrangle he might be supposed to have walked out of an illustration by Edward Lear. Across a desk, however, there was no mistaking the precision and quality of his mind, and though his voice was high-pitched, he had an actor's range and control over it. . . . In discussion he could explain a point by making a quick drawing, taking a musical instrument down and playing it . . .

his breadth of knowledge, his capacity for relating abstract speculation to everyday happenings, and his wit—which was not contrived
but a matter of immediate response—had made Collingwood's lectures so popular that they could no longer be held in Pembroke and
had been transferred to a college with a larger hall where they were
attended by many who were not studying philosophy but came simply
for enjoyment.[3]

All undergraduate essays done for Collingwood, Hopkinson says,
had to be properly researched and formally written and read out,
but seeing plainly enough that Hopkinson was more interested in
becoming a writer than a scholar, Collingwood expanded into the
role Oxford provided for its tutors in those days and "was ready to
talk about plays, novels, religion, love, or any other subject." He was
severe on pretentiousness and snobbery, "though without ever abandoning his attitude of urbane inquiry." Once, when Hopkinson referred deprecatingly to Henry Ford as certain to be a bore, Collingwood blandly inquired: "Really—is that your opinion? A man who
has changed the whole pattern of industry and developed an invention which is transforming social life—and will completely alter the
relationship between town and country which has lasted with com-
paratively little change for centuries . . . but for you he has no interest. Kindly explain your point of view."[4]

It's nice to discover that Collingwood encouraged Hopkinson to
be away from his work in Oxford over several weekends, even though
finals were looming, in order to play rugby for Lancashire. It's even
nicer to go into the rare books room in Pembroke College Library
and find a fine water-colour by Edward Lear presented to the college
in 1974 by Tom Hopkinson in memory of his tutor. Hopkinson by
then had long been a committed socialist of the class of 1939–1945,
and founder-editor of *Picture Post*, a British and Labour Party version of *Life*, its stories told partly in black-and-white photographs,
four or six to a big folio page, partly in terse, well-written journalese
below the illustrations. The stories, like the photographs, were chosen on the whole for what they revealed about the condition of Britain, to a readership with a lively social conscience, a modest patri-

otism, and a more-or-less Labour-voting picture of the world. It is a gratifying legacy of, among other things, Collingwood's teaching and an Oxford education between and on the way to wars, as it is a monument to social democratic journalism which the teacher so stoutly defended in the *Autobiography* and of which he had this proud glimpse before he died.

Hopkinson's closest comrade was a rangy lad called Bernard Miles, who later became actor, producer, pillar of the big British film industry when at its peak, and ennobled for his pains. MacCallum, remembering, as elderly teachers will, with advantages, wrote many years later to his wife of his distinguished alumnus that "Admittedly he was a difficult subject but I should have realised there was something a little bit exceptional, if a bit mad, and given him a course suitable for a fighting fourth. I might just have done it."[5]

Until recently, Oxford, unlike all other universities, did not split its second-class honours into the two divisions, upper and lower. A fourth was a not very honourable honours degree. But while Miles was, as he said, dazzled by Collingwood, he put all his efforts into the university's Dramatic Society, and when he appealed to his tutor for advice on a career, Collingwood fell back on the threadbare catch-all of public school housemasters and advised Miles to "do something with his hands."

He was far from finished with whoreson players, however. In 1931 a young student from Lady Margaret Hall called Kathleen Frances Edwardes began to attend Collingwood's philosophy lectures as part of her degree course in Modern Greats, or philosophy, politics, and economics, the course that gradually supplanted *Litterae Humaniores* (the original Greats) as the crown of Oxford's human sciences. She arrived at the university intending to study English, having been a pupil at Wycombe Abbey, one of the most stylish and venerable of English public schools for girls.[6] But she heard of the spellbinder, came, and was transfigured. She became a tutorial student, perhaps made the acquaintance of the clockwork mouse, was, like Bernard Miles, suborned into the Dramatic Society, was awarded a respectable third-class degree, and went off to the old Embassy Theatre in Eton Avenue near Swiss Cottage to be made into an actress at the

Central School of Speech and Drama (and to be followed there by a distinguished succession of English theatre dames). She was vivacious, a devoted admirer of the professor, and very pretty. Her father had been a mathematics teacher at Harrow, and her widowed mother lived in a handsome house on Lansdown Hill, just above the centre of Bath. She wasn't a student anybody could overlook, and Collingwood didn't.

II

His father's death in the autumn of 1932 brought Collingwood up sharp. Gershom had suffered a series of minor strokes and had always had high blood pressure. In May 1931 Collingwood wrote to T. M. Knox, his future editor, and another of his pupils eventually to be knighted for services to scholarship. (It remains a striking anomaly in the British academies that so many social democrats among its membership are still unembarrassed by accepting knighthoods elsewhere sold across the political counter.) In the letter, Collingwood reported a "serious illness" and in October 1931 he was "overhauled" by the doctor, prescribed "daily walks" (as though he had ever done anything else), and a month later wrote asking for leave.[7] The illness was chicken pox, caught from his children and a severe attack; Collingwood was convinced it was the source of his later strokes.

The permission for leave was given, but the freed time was hardly put to the purposes of normal convalescence. He promptly set off on a long, more or less archaeological tour to Catalonia in Spain and on to Rome, where Ian Richmond was by then director of the British School and where he stayed some weeks patrolling the new excavations of classical antiquity. Then he went on to his so well-loved Athens, taking the interminable train journey rather than the uncertain ferries: Rome to Milan, change at Milan for Padua and Trieste, then the slow trundle down the Balkans, and a long wait in Skopje before descending the long slope of Macedonia to Athens.

Collingwood called it a "breakdown," but he was writing all the way. He had always written prodigally, as we know. The heavy weight of teaching—forty hours a week during the twenty-four weeks of the Oxford terms—hardly deflected him from his writing, whether in the eyrie at the Chantry, in Belbroughton Road, or in college. In any case, as soon as term was over, he settled once more to maintain his amazing output, frequently writing for his personal edification and not for publication, just as frequently rewriting his lectures on behalf of the audience packed into a college lecture room, gratifyingly numerous to the eye but nonetheless limited to the tiny sphere of Oxford still in thrall to the minute philosophers. Joachim, Joseph, Prichard, Ross—they all knew how good Collingwood was, but they were held tight in the little ring of "the philosophers' teas" and the philosophers' customs. John Mabbott recounts an ineffable incident at a tea meeting to discuss a proposed international conference where no such conference had ever been held at Oxford before, and for entertainment for which, incidentally, there was no university money.

> It was suggested that the three philosophy professors should invite the conference to tea in the College garden of one of them. This was warmly welcomed when Joachim, Professor of Logic, had second thoughts. While he personally would be delighted to help in this way, he felt he could not agree as it would establish a precedent and impose on his successors in the Chair a duty which they might not accept as happily as he. A baffled silence followed, until it was suggested that the party should be given by Mr Joachim (*qua* Mr), Mr Smith (*qua* Mr) and Mr Prichard (*qua* Mr).[8]

Collingwood was far too courteous to burst out against these ditherings, at least until a very different temper was forced upon him by the history of the present. But he withdrew to his usual distance and set himself not so much a programme but a marshalling of the regiments of questions before him. His planning of his writing was rarely single-minded, rather it took off in a number of different directions, was interrupted by the deadlines for archaeological reports, book reviews, the insistent demands for references about new manuscripts, punctually responded to, of the University Press, and then revised as new, imperious, and unforeseen themes and topics gathered about his head and clamoured for his attention.

This seems to me the way to describe and understand the onward, hurried march of his thought, rather than to break it into three periods as Knox and others do. He drove several horses at once from a single seat and under varying control. He wrote everywhere, thriftily using the blank verso sheets of undergraduate essays, Clarendon Press headed paper, scraps of foolscap torn neatly across where the paper became vacant; wrote tumultuously, insomnia extending the day by several hours, his wife and children asleep elsewhere in the house, or alone at the college, gazing out at the moonlit turf, the college clock tolling the small hours until the darkness paled; wrote in a beautiful, fluid, unstoppable hand the distinctiveness of which only failed as his illness grew unignorable.

He ignored it all right during that Hilary term, while he wrote *An Essay on Philosophical Method*, the book he later described as being the only one with which he was wholly satisfied, as being fully prepared and polished for the press.[9] Bernard Williams, on the other hand, in his otherwise admiring essay dismisses it briskly as "in fact a dull and dated book, full of what are likely to seem now unhelpful distinctions and assimilations," although he qualifies this judgement by commanding "a marvellous section at the end about philosophical style."[10] This is chapter 10, "Philosophy as a Branch of Literature," to which we shall return.

Malcolm Knox, whom Collingwood once described as "my only real pupil," was of the view, however, that the *Essay on Philosophical Method* was Collingwood's best because it was purest, coolest, most serene and poised in manner, lucid in argument, wholly philosophical in content. Knox, however, is easy to cast as the Dogbery of philosophy, and at least to today's taste in these matters, Williams is more likely to be right. Yet *Philosophical Method* still pegs away at working out a coherent argument for the "scale of forms" to which large portions of *Speculum Mentis* were also applied.

From a little way off, the problem looks merely scholastic, a knot to be cut or untied in the theory of classifications. A. N. Whitehead, whom Collingwood much admired for his historicising of science, had praised Bacon for being the first thinker to grasp the key scientific precept as being not to classify, but to count. Collingwood stuck to classification nonetheless but distinguished philosophy from science as permitting, indeed requiring, overlapping classes. (This is like Wittgenstein's saying that an indistinct or blurred concept is often exactly what we need.[11])

Collingwood had prowled around the topic for the preceding several years. In a wonderfully contentious review of George Santayana's *The Realm of Essence* written in 1928, he praises the prose but is left distraught by the argument.

> The idea of essence is a very simple idea, and Mr Santayana has thought it out with the utmost lucidity, and expounded it with that elegance and clarity which are the admiration, envy and despair of other philosophical writers. Plato has accustomed us to think of essences, and to recognise in triangularity or justice a "form" (an essence, Mr Santayana would say) exemplified in triangular things or just actions, but having its own eternal being independently of anything or action whatever, "itself by itself." Mr Santayana would say that Plato was so far right, but would add that there is an essence, just as eternal, of blueness or dog-in-the-manger-ish-ness and even that there is an essence of the particular sound-group which I heard just now—the peculiar rhythm of raindrops on the window combined with the peculiar rise and fall of the wind's howl in the chimney—which was embodied in an actually existing thing, this morning's storm, exactly as justice may be embodied in an actual legal decision and, before and after being so embodied, has, exactly as much as that, its own proper eternal disembodied existence.[12]

"Essentialism" is nowadays, of course, identified with a quiver of self-righteous revulsion as the last refuge of scoundrelly idealism, but insomuch as it is another name for the scale of forms, this fighting volubility of Collingwood's is a matter of the heart. For Santayana claims that essentialism is a *psychological* necessity of the mind; psychologism is already his critic's deadliest enemy of rational thought. Santayana airily waves Kant away, turns the a priori categories of reason into human biology, and renders mathematics, science, and philosophy impossible.

The polemical manner makes for a sprightly piece of academic theatre. But Collingwood was out for blood. His adaptation of the scale of forms, winnowed first from Plato, then thickened up by Spinoza, finally and by way of the prizefight of all philosophy between Kant and Hegel, ending up as represented by the hand-made, three-dimensional miniature model of a Roman fort, was configured to map out philosophical thought as collective, progressive, and historical.

In this, it was presaged by religious thought, and one can see, over the final decade of his amazingly productive writing life, the struggle on Collingwood's part to explain and vindicate St. Anselm's celebrated "ontological proof" of the existence of God, made in Canterbury in the eleventh century. In an essay written in 1928, Collingwood retold as we have heard the famous tale about Anselm, when "a kindly critic pointed out that his proof was logically conclusive only to a person who already believed in God. . . . Anselm was not in the least disconcerted. "I believe," to quote his own words, "in order that I may understand; for this I know that unless I first believe I shall never understand."[13]

Collingwood's reverence towards religious belief is sustained up as far as his penultimate book, and in his extended correspondence with Gilbert Ryle in 1935. It is, you might say, personal, but its grounding is to be found in the theory of absolute presuppositions, yet to be made explicit. He might be taken, in an anachronistic leap, to be facing down that doughty atheist, Richard Dawkins, when he writes that "the scientific spirit is a spirit, not a dodge; it lives by living up to an ideal, not by inventing marketable gadgets."[14] Doing its best to drive religious belief into margins science cannot (yet) colonise, scientists (Dawkins, for instance)[15] fail to see just how serious a thing religion is, and that the common endeavour of both modes of thinking is to find, as Descartes did in the proof of his own existence, a point at which faith and reason coincide. When we do so, it transpires that the task of scientific reason is to determine the

details of the world according to its laws, and that—not in competition but in communality—it is the task of faith to picture the wholeness of all things, that which is "the cause of itself and of everything
in it." The proper sphere of faith is everything as a whole, it is what
we know, and it admits of no proof because (as Wittgenstein also
said) proof would be irrelevant as well as already being undis-
coverable. Practical faith, one could say, is the knowledge, for which
no proof is conceivable, that we are free.

The ambition of such thought is, as I said, close to that of
T. S. Eliot in *Four Quartets*. There, too, history and divinity become
interchangeable. In making history the source of both energy and
dissolution, Collingwood saves the day not for Christianity but for
faith. If present-day thinkers feel shifty in the presence of the concept, then just a little later Collingwood would simply refer them to
their absolute presuppositions.

The book on method cannot be assimilated to contemporary
postgraduate courses on that subject. (The very notion is gratifyingly
comic.) Collingwood was producing the line from F. H. Bradley's
classic and neglected *Presuppositions of Critical History* and, by way
of his own *Religion and Philosophy*, keeping philosophy itself queen
of the sciences by virtue of its practitioner's "theorising his own place
in the whole to which he is contributing."[16] To be doing this, however, each philosopher is "not merely adding another item to an inventory, he must be shaping afresh in his own mind the idea of philosophy as a whole."

This is some ambition, and to bring it off he has to situate his
newly gestated account of philosophy as historically constituted by
its predecessor forms of knowledge. Such a venture, whatever the
magnificence of Collingwood's definition in the book of "system,"
might now be condescended to as quaint, but that is a measure of
the switch in attention by philosophers away from "the real" and
towards "meaning." Hence, perhaps, the charge of datedness.

In *Philosophical Method*, however, the "datedness" is partly a consequence of its ponderous abstractions. Portentousness is never a
fault of his; to think these thoughts again, however, is not to be lost

as to their strangeness, so much as distraught by their pointlessness. *Why* tread the airy path he takes to the point at which he can say that "there are some grounds for saying that where we find expositions of a philosophical as opposed to a non-philosophical scale of forms we find the variable identified with the generic essence."[17] The answer is confined to the zoologist's handbook. His argument leads him here because that is what it was to speak philosophically in the idiom of his tradition, the very one that he was seeking to split open and, without destroying it, to turn its language and its character to quite new purposes and life-endeavours. Unless he completes the philosophy with its own history—which is what he does not do in the *Method*, in spite of the four brief entries on Socrates and co—he remains stuck with old and not new idealism. Surely he recognised this? That is what makes the book, compact and typically lordly as it is, a distinctive turning point in his thought, and makes the lectures on nature that follow something utterly new.

What is deeply important in *Philosophical Method* is *style* in that very strong sense implied in the old saw, *Le style, c'est l'homme*. Nietzsche, in *The Gay Science*, wrote, in the full quotation we have already touched on: "To give style to one's character—a great and rare art! It is practised by those who survey all the strengths and weaknesses of their nature and then fit them into an artistic plan until every one of them appears as art and reason, and even weaknesses delight the eye."[18] In quoting this passage I do not imply that philosophy is a mere expression of personality as opposed to being an attempt to tell the truth. But a thinker's style is inseparable from his or her capacity to tell the truth. It is in that sense that Collingwood's character and the success or otherwise of his philosophical career are one and the same. The style and character of his *Philosophical Method* are not (of course) untruthful; they are *interim*, now *and* then. (In *An Autobiography*, famous for its caustic as well as its colloquial style, he pretty well acknowledges this.) Offering a summative statement by way of a high-class textbook, he found he could not go on in the old way. He had to radicalise his own precept, and speak philosophy as history.

The bright young philosophical things at Oxford at this date were of a mind to dissolve these difficulties by roundly abandoning them. When their debonair leader, Freddie Ayer, published his heartless, trenchant, and daring work of demolition, *Language, Truth and Logic,* three years after *Philosophical Method,* the scale of forms, the system of ideal thought, the supreme "task of thinking out the idea of an object that shall completely satisfy the demands of reason" are all comprehensively dumped in the bin.[19] Collingwood saw what Ayer had done, all right. He overheard Prichard tutting to someone about Ayer's book while in Blackwell's one day and broke into the conversation to say, "Gentlemen, this book will be read when your names are forgotten." All the same, he later reckoned himself to have sufficiently rebuked Ayer, by quoting Samuel Alexander, whom he so revered, to the effect that metaphysics required "an attitude of natural piety."[20]

Ayer was nothing if not impishly impious, and Collingwood, not at all without impishness, writes in a style too filled with piety in the volume at hand. It is at its best and is most distinctively Collingwood's when, still serenely commending to his readers the validity of Anselm's ontological proof, he catches up the very heart of ethics and finds it at work in every human being puzzling out what best to do in the practical language of everyday moral thought. These wise and beautiful sentences themselves embody the activity of such thought as any one of us might attempt it, like a great poem creating as they are uttered the state of mind and feeling that they describe.

> [I]t must be borne in mind that the question how people think is not in any philosophical science separable from the question whether they think rightly or wrongly; . . . the moral ideal already exists as an ideal in the minds of all moral agents; . . . the science is both normative and descriptive; it describes, not action as opposed to ideas about action, but the moral consciousness; and this it is forced to describe as already being in some sense what it ought to be. This in turn will affect the account which it gives of action; for no theory of moral ideals is conceivable which does not admit that to some extent moral ideas affect action.[21]

Then he turns away, glancing at the hope we might rightly enter-
tain that the moral philosopher should himself display in his work
the virtues he describes, "sincerity, truthfulness, perseverance, courage, and justice." This is the lead I want to take in praising the marvellous final section of the book, "Philosophy as a Branch of Literature." For this presages in Collingwood's terms what we may expect
of his developing "style," which is to say the character of his character, or the form of his thought as manifested in the shape of his life.

He, however, refuses to allow that discursive prose might become
poetry. In this I believe him to be wrong. He permits that philosophy
shall be written in a literary not a scientific (because not a technical
nor an *experience-distant*)[22] language, that it must have the expressiveness, flexibility, and dependence on context that mark literature
with its domestic familiarity. In a way he was later to reject, he subor-
dinates history to philosophy since historians are there to be "consulted" and philosophers to be "followed" (in the sense of understood). Then he says: "A philosophical work, if it must be called a
poem, is not a mere poem, but a poem of the intellect. What is
expressed in it is not emotions, desires, feelings, as such, but those
which a thinking mind experiences in its search for knowledge; and
it expresses these only because the experience of them is an integral
part of the search, and that search is thought itself."

Emotions, etc., "as such" Collingwood assigns to poetry *tout court*.
But if I can show, as I try to do later, that T. S. Eliot's *Little Gidding*
and Collingwood's last works have a common subject and object,
then what this paragraph describes may be as much the property of
one kind of poem as another kind of historical or anthropological
inquiry.

It is a point to labour, as being the very purpose of writing a fully
historical biography; one, that is, that manages to re-create how a
life was lived and then takes its moral measure again, two generations
later. The mind searches for a style (in Nietzsche's usage), shaped and
reshaped by certain passions, which it struggles to make congenial to
thought, and applies this style to the comprehension of its experience
and the knowledge it will yield. The great stylists of philosophy
whom Collingwood briefly typifies in the book—"the classical ele-

gance of Descartes, the lapidary phrases of Spinoza, the tortured metaphor-ridden periods of Hegel"[23]—are stylish precisely because such are the accommodations these men found for their passions as these compelled and were harnessed by their thought.

III

The Times Literary Supplement, when the book was published, acclaimed it as "for all its brevity, one of the finest restatements in contemporary British philosophy of a Platonic and Hegelian metaphysic."

The Hegelians enjoyed a brief moment of resurrection in 1933, the very year in which their hero's name became associated with "Prussianness" and Nazism, thereafter to be, somewhat unjustly, tarnished for half a century. Michael Oakeshott published *Experience and Its Modes*, from the department of history, the most elegant, most graceful, and quietist of the major works of British idealism.[24] It was a moment at which the philosophical world was being made safe in Vienna, Oxford, and Cambridge for a severe and reductive positivism, advocated by Wittgenstein's amazing *Tractatus Logico-Philosophicus*, which burst out from nowhere and, once translated from the German, was the occasion for Bertrand Russell's rescuing the man of the day from an obscure schoolroom and installing him in Trinity. Logical positivism is the doctrine that the world is the sum of its (empirical) facts ascertainable in a symbolic code ground and polished into a mirror reflecting those facts as nearly as possible to how they really are. A. J. Ayer, as we saw, domesticated the Viennese school as well as giving it his own style of jaunty and *boulevardier* insouciance (moral judgements are like saying "Boo!"), and thereafter the way was clear in philosophy for John Austin to take everybody's minds off systematic and totalising theory and turn them to seeing, in his famous pun, how to do things with words.[25]

This little shower of dropping names must do for now to suggest just how radical a new direction for philosophy was pointed out across the 1930s, and indicate also that, as respectfully as Collingwood's and Oakeshott's two books were received, they were sailing together on a fading current (they met several times and Oakeshott promised Collingwood a book for the Clarendon Press; he delivered it in 1975). But both were explicit critics of the predominant scientism, and Oakeshott opens by saying that if we begin from the sciences, our conclusions can only be scientific.[26] He begins from "experience," present throughout his splendid book as large, authoritative, and undifferentiated.

For Oakeshott, all modes of intellectualising our experience, as history, science, art, are what he calls "arrests"; that is, they are blocks to the free flow of life, and therefore immediately abstract. In his account of historical experience, which Collingwood read with avid and approbatory disagreement,[27] he insists, as a good idealist should, on the ideational constitution of history. "History . . . cannot avoid the character of thought," the inevitability of human judgement turns the mere succession of events into a world, and not only a world in implying a narrative, "but a world of ideas." Oakeshott's historian is a scholar rather than a plain person, a scholar putting herself or himself under the stern discipline never to suppose that the past is like the present, but one for whom the knowability of the past moves it into the present, renders it mobile and changeable, varying as the evidence for it increases, obliging us to interpret and *believe* it differently.

This is nobly said, and Collingwood applauds him. But Oakeshott is fundamentally a verificationist. He separates theory and practice. Facts are always judgements, for sure, nor are they "immune to change"; but he refuses (in the grip, it may be, of a suppressed scientism) the mutual embeddedness of history and philosophy, of, indeed, *all* the modes of experience. In the end, he crowns "practical experience" queen of the modes, but even here Oakeshott separates thought and action. Ethics, for instance (and a pressing one for the horrible politics just coming into view in Spain, Italy, Germany) is practical, not historical; it is "the construction of a world of values," "an attempt to decide what we shall do and how we shall live."[28] Thus far, thus commonplace. But: "and casuistry may be said to be the goal of ethical investigation." This is Oakeshott's deep and, in the end, cynical Toryism. Ethics is historical, that is plain enough. It is also, as Collingwood argued in *Philosophical Method*, constructed out of its own self-criticism, made out of its making, written and enacted according to as good, true, and beautiful a story as may be made out of a life and out of all life.

Thus the sentimentalist to the cynic. Collingwood's own is stiffer medicine. By the end of the decade he could say with finality, "history is the only kind of knowledge"; writing about Oakeshott three years after *Experience and Its Modes* came out, his stern objection is to say:

> Oakeshott supposes that there is no third alternative to the disjunction that the past is either a dead past or not past at all but simply present. The third alternative is that it should be a living past, a past which, because it was thought and not mere natural event, can be re-enacted in the present and in that re-enactment known as past. If this third alternative could be accepted, we should get the result that history is not based on a philosophical error and is therefore not in his sense a mode of experience, but an integral part of experience itself.[29]

Oakeshott was not a copious writer. Although his three classics are each in their way canonical, even when enlarged by his occasional essays, they are a minor *oeuvre*. Collingwood wrote unstoppably, helped in a way by insomnia—when "pernoctating" in Pembroke, his light would sometimes be visible across the courtyard until the sun came up.

The family had reluctantly moved back into Oxford in September 1928, leaving Stapleton's Chantry with tearful regret on everybody's part, especially Bill's and Ursula's. The bees were given away and much of the carpenting abandoned; for 15 Belbroughton Road, another newly built and solid edifice of Oxonian red brick in the spacious enclave of staff houses off the Banbury Road, lent itself far less to the practical maintenance Collingwood learned at Lanehead. But the distance and the journey from North Moreton took too long; his duties in the city, the increasing demands on his presence in London and in the larger Europe, made it hard to sustain the good life as lived by the old statesmen-smallholders. So father and mother succumbed to social class presumption and paternal convenience, Bill was sent to board at Shrewsbury in 1932, Ursula to Roedean in 1934, and the Collingwoods became an urban, metropolitan household.

The life of its patriarch was now brimming with paper. On the death of his father and the cessation of his punctual and lengthy letters to Gershom, Collingwood was at once elected to the presidency of the Cumberland and Westmoreland Archaeological Society and intensified his efforts on behalf of the Roman display at the Armitt. There wasn't a day he didn't write or, reading, annotate what he read in fine detail, using any scrap of paper at hand, vacant strips torn neatly off any unfinished sheet of foolscap. (This thriftiness, learned at home, was of a piece with the care with which he always reused envelopes and wrapping paper.)

His remained a full, fulfilled, and local life. But from 1931 onwards it was also hard hit by illness and accident, as well as by his father's death.[30] In his illness of May 1931, Collingwood was in bed on and off for two or three days at a time and went to his doctor for his "overhaul" (as he put it to his father). The doctor found his blood pressure too high, his insomnia severe, his fits of dizziness ominous, stiffness in his left limbs, and his usual mixture of tiredness and hyperactivity perturbing (archaeological expeditions to Spain and Palermo impending); he fell back, as we heard in those unpharmaceutical days, on ruminative sagacity and the "daily walks."[31]

Collingwood remained no less active, but out of sorts. By November he was troubled enough by his health to write formally to the chair of his Faculty Board, David Margoliouth, the seventy-four-year-old professor of Arabic, to request leave of absence for the following term. This, with an adjustment to his stipend, was duly granted, and he duly filled his recuperative Hilary term of 1932 by writing, at a crammed-on pace, the first draft of the *Essay on Philosophical Method*. He knew of course that something serious was up, and that it was likely to be the same condition that caused his father's strokes and finally killed him. But Gershom had reached the age of seventy-eight, undiminished in mind if halt in movement, and his son had, naturally enough, every hope of matching him.

All the same, his correspondence of the period makes increasing reference to his ill health,[32] and from this time forward its menace sat always at his elbow. It was compounded by bad luck. In the snowy February 1934 he was cycling back from Pembroke up the badly lit Banbury Road when a car skidded slightly and knocked the forty-five-year-old off his bicycle. Writing to one of the editors at the Clarendon Press a few days later, naturally including the reader's report of a kind he had been writing for the press since 1926, he admits, "I was rather bashed about and here I am flat on my back for some time to come."[33] His arm was broken; he employed a shorthand secretary and carried on writing.

He was in the middle of an indiscriminate heap of work just about to assume definite and rugged outline. All his intellectual life he had sought the systematic and believable unity of theory and practice, mind and nature, which both his reading and the directly lived experience of country and city had settled in him as his deepest convictions. He had taught himself to be quizzical of such convictions but was gradually concluding that conviction be understood not so much as belief but as the constellation of "absolute presuppositions" which must be made if we are to live freely (let alone think rationally) at all. We make these "presuppositions" less as foundations of thought, more as the light of our being. "As lief get round the back of them as get round the back of the sun," as D. H. Lawrence put it a year or two before his death. Metaphysics was made up of them, and Collingwood's pledge, which he made to life as a gift of his natural piety, was to keep the great realm of metaphysical being illuminated, to prevent the positivists turning out its lights. He would defeat them by making metaphysics itself historical.

The year 1934 was therefore a crucial moment. He was a man well aware of the needfulness of authority. The definition of his vast labours required, as it does for anyone, not just a mind and its talents, but eminence and outline. This was the year in which J. A. Smith, his guide, confessor, and abiding friend, himself a gentle, good-humoured, ultimately diffident priest of metaphysics, retired from the great Waynflete Chair of Metaphysical Philosophy in which he had sat since 1910. His admiration for his former pupil, whom he introduced to Croce and Ruggiero, was enormous. Unable by protocol to be his man's advocate, he was held in widespread affection and his influence counted a lot.

Collingwood had applied in 1928, at a mere thirty-nine (generally thought too young in those days), for the White's Chair of Moral Philosophy, and he saw, as expected, Prichard appointed. The Waynflete was the brother chair and Collingwood its heir apparent, his only serious rival H. H. Price, the great Samuel Alexander from Manchester his referee; Joachim, Joseph, Prichard were all just as sure as well as nervous of his largesse of disposition and of his capability in office. Isaiah Berlin, bouncing with happiness, as well he might be, in his new post at All Souls, wrote to a friend: "We are in the throes of elections of philosophy professors, JA and Joachim are going, Collingwood and Price are nuclei, the slave market is heaving like a jelly and the logical positivists, Braithwaite, Ayer and such are spreading havoc wherever possible."[34]

Collingwood's last service to his college was in October 1934 in presenting drawings and a detailed plan for a proper library at the college, which was intended to retrieve the rare books from the master's lodgings, themselves adapted from Cardinal Wolsey's Almshouses only in 1927, and house the college's full stock in a new extension "end to end with the chapel and in the same style," with a paid assistant to the fellow in charge, which, for a tiny honorarium, had been Collingwood himself since he rejoined the college in 1919. Ayer subsequently applied for the vacancy at Pembroke but was turned down, as MacCallum immortally said, as being "too clever for Pemmy . . . his Jewish appearance also militates against him."[35]

So it was that on 24 March 1935 Collingwood wrote to the master of Pembroke with full feeling and his habitual, slightly overdone courtesy: "it is with the deepest regret and the liveliest sense of the good things I am abandoning, that I tender my resignation of my fellowship. . . . The happy life and friendships which I have enjoyed at Pembroke for so many years will always remain among my most precious memories and nothing can ever surpass or equal those experiences in my eyes." He offered to continue teaching, unreimbursed, his Pembroke students for the next term; his salary was then £825 per annum.

IV

The post entailed a move to Magdalen, the most gracious, rural, utterly beautiful of Oxford colleges, where the fellowship attached to the chair was held. The contrast with Pembroke, packed into the medieval streets behind St. Aldate's and St. Ebbe's, its tiny courtyards and handkerchief lawns snug and lovable for sure, but expressively diminutive and modest beside the showy constellations of Magdalen; its lovely bridge signalling its custodianship of the river; its strong medieval tower, visible across the city, marking the boundary of the university's city and the road out to the car works. Magdalen's proportions are those of an English country house of the grandest kind. You could put most of Pembroke into the first courtyard behind the Victorian curtain wall and in front of the magnificent fifteenth-century Gothic chapel. The college unfolds expansively into several more such handsome spaces, one of them closed on a little knoll at its end by the attractive college library built in 1850, while westwards, towards the Cherwell, beyond the superb New Buildings of 1733 with their twenty-seven bays and splendid arcade, you will find the college deer grazing in their own park, and you may now walk up, past the quiet herd, along the river to St. Catherine's, the Parks, and Music Meadow.

This spaciousness unrivalled in Oxford even by Christ Church standards went, in 1935, with ample college wealth and the assumptions to match. The college had a strong academic tradition in which philosophy figured largely;[36] its money rested easily beside its intellectual capital and the stupendous freedoms these ensured. Collingwood knew the college intimately, of course, from his twenty-five-year friendship with Smith, but his new appointment was not only a glowing triumph in itself—even the subdued indifference of Oxford to all academic officers took note of the Waynflete professor—it freed him from his punishing tutorial timetable ("forty hours a week") in term time, as well as taking his salary in a most welcome way well into four figures. Collingwood himself said wryly that when he became professor the audiences at the lectures dropped by half, which one takes with a pinch of salt, but the liberation for someone with the programme of writing he was gradually setting himself released a rush of sheer exhilaration.

As is the way with such milestones, he had sought to clear all unfinished tasks from his desk before the appointment fell due. The largest of these was his 350-page contribution to the Oxford History of England volume, *Roman Britain and the English Settlements*. His collaborator in this, writing the section on early post-Roman England, was J.N.L. Myres, thirteen years Collingwood's junior, father and son both friends, both archaeologists and gardeners. Collingwood liked Myres's passion for connecting the disciplines[37]—archaeology, geography, anthropology—which matched Collingwood's own, as did Myres's keen sense of humour; the joint volume remains a classic.

It is, naturally, a much enlarged sequel to his 1923 textbook; it is also his principal contribution to conventional history. After 1935 he went on doing archaeology, but this new volume, written as usual at great speed before he assumed his new duties (the preface is dated 14 January 1936), is his most substantial example of how to write the practical history on which he spent so many pages of theory. But then, as it was his life's work to protest, you cannot separate the two.

Roman Britain and the English Settlements is, therefore, from the start a cracking narrative set in a specific and local geography. Collingwood is at pains to cherish the toughness and continuity of Celtic culture, and its pallid survival into post-Roman times, and his mastery of such thin and (literally) scattered evidence as the distribution of coins as found across the country lends authority and vivacity to a tale wrung with such very hard labour out of holes in the ground dug and redug during a period of over a hundred years. As I have remarked, early history and the conditions of its production fairly force on us the truth that our history is collectively made, and then made again in its retrieval. It further compels on us the inanition of any doctrinaire claims about either historical materialism or idealism. Thought lies in the forts; the ideal and the material are indistinguishable, and there is simply no call to perspire over the primacy of one over the other.

Collingwood is writing total history a year or two before the *Annalistes* opened their revolution. Braudel was bravely conceiving the terrific scale of *The Mediterranean in the Age of Philip II* when Collingwood took the small space of Britain across half a millennium and told the several tales of its slow colonisation before the Romans came, the stormy and contradictory two arrivals of Caesar, the insurgencies of Caratacus and Boudicca, the making of the frontier in the North and of his beloved wall, and the uncertain end of empire, the slow and irregular withdrawals of rivalrous emperors, the spurts of prosperity, and his wonderful speculation on the myth of Arthur.

These latter few pages serve to announce at first glance an unfamiliar theme in Collingwood's work. His childhood education was full of the old Arthurian legends, thickened with Kipling's heady style, stretched by Gershom's love of the Icelandic sagas and William Morris's translation of them. J.R.R. Tolkien had come to Pembroke as colleague, is personally acknowledged in the 1936 *Roman Britain*, and was even then gestating his giant mythology, and painting the luscious water-colours of Cheddar Gorge and the Rock of Ages in Burrington Combe that would supply the landscapes first for *The Hobbit* in 1937 (much admired by Arthur Ransome) and then for his masterpiece, *Lord of the Rings*.[38] Folklore was an ardent interest of Collingwood's, which went deeper than hobbyhood and into selfhood. As he wrote fiercely in his notes: "To the educated man as such there is no pleasanter kind of self-flattery than the doctrine that folklore, the one cultural possession of the illiterate, is merely their perversion of what his own class has bestowed on them."[39]

The Arthurian legend was a proud rejection of these complacencies. There are, it seems, sufficient references to some such figure in the original ancient histories, including Bede's in the eighth century and, well before him, the monk Gildas's *De Conquestu Britanniae* and the *Historia Brittonum*. Collingwood resurrects Arthur as a fifth-century *condottiere*, who recruited and commanded a cavalry brigade when such a thing had vanished from late empire Britain; who knew how such a force, familiar with the still usable network of fast Roman roads, could roll up the invading Saxon infantry; protected as his men were, like the Roman military that had taught Arthur, by chain-mail and arm and leg guards, they could defeat the unarmoured Saxons however outnumbered the swift and mobile force might be.

Collingwood, moved by his historical sense and by his reverence for the truths hidden in the mists of legend, peers into them and descries what may have happened in "a country sinking into barbarism, whence Roman ideas had almost vanished; and the emergence of a single man intelligent enough to understand them, and vigorous enough to put them into practice by gathering around him a group of friends and followers, armed according to the traditions of civilised warfare and proving their invincibility in a dozen campaigns."[40]

Later in 1936, Collingwood pulled this action out of the book and elaborated it. He gave it as a paper to a college society, the Martlets, at his old college, University, in June.[41] He told his audience an affecting anecdote of an old man, not long before, accosting a party of archaeological diggers in Glastonbury and asking fearfully whether they had come "to take away the king." His smile as he recounted the anecdote was inseparable from the lump it caused in his throat, and causes in ours. Collingwood ended his talk: "If I am right, Arthur was the last Roman in Britain, the last man who understood Roman ideas and used them for the welfare and salvation of the British people. In their love of his name and their hope of his reappearance the British people have embalmed their memories of Roman Britain."

The Arthurian excursus is Collingwood's coda to the book. Its chords resound with many earlier such moments, each of them commemorating the sowing of the early (not the earliest) seeds of Englishness. He contrasts a Mediterranean work of town-dwellers with the northwest European way of finding beatitude and serenity not in the life of polis, forum, and agora, but in meadow and homestead. He quotes Gunnar in the *Burnt Njal* saga: "Fair is the Lithe; so fair that it has never seemed to me so fair; the cornfields are white to harvest and the home mead is mown; and now I will ride back home, and not fare abroad at all."[42] Home: the so powerful, so always-missing concept in the political theory of the professional. All the same, the Romans brought town planning to Britain, and he writes with unabated admiration of Silchester, by this time benefiting from another dozen years of scientific (question-and-answer) excavation

since he published his textbook. Collingwood makes the crucial revision to popular historiography that town life began to decline in the
late third century not because the Romans began to quit, but because
of raging inflation and the consequent corrective taxes on urban centres, which failed to staunch the devaluation and brought bankruptcy. Those, however, with sufficient estates around their villas
could live self-sufficiently, and life in the country houses—a veranda
to the front, a courtyard within, two wings, two corridors front and
back—throve until the brigands came.[43]

The book is happily punctuated by spirited little pen portraits,
which give the lie to any notion that archaeological history is a digging record, and that for the rest, the folk history is as good as it'll
get. The immortal pages of *1066 and All That* still strike a sonorous
chord in popular ignorance.

> For some reason the Romans neglected to overrun the country with
> fire and the sword, though they had both of these; in fact, after the
> Conquest they did not mingle with the Britons at all, but lived a semi-
> detached life in villas. They occupied their time for two or three hun-
> dred years in building Roman roads and having Roman baths; this was
> called the Roman Occupation, and gave rise to the memorable Roman
> law, "HE WHO BATHS FIRST BATHS FAST," which was a Good Thing,
> and still is. The Roman roads ran absolutely straight in all directions
> and all led to Rome. The Romans also built towns wherever they were
> wanted and, in addition, a wall between England and Scotland to keep
> out the savage Picts and Scots. This wall was the work of the memora-
> ble Roman Emperor Balbus and was thus called Hadrian's Wall. The
> Picts, or painted men, were so called to distinguish them from the
> Britons (see *supra, woad*).[44]

But Sellar and Yeatman can't quite match Collingwood on, say,
Governor Agricola, disagreeing with Tacitus, the governor's first
biographer:

> For all Tacitus's praise, he remains a somewhat unattractive character:
> an able man, evidently, both in the field and in administration; a man
> of sound judgement, and incorruptible; but cold, calculating, obsequi-

ous to authority, yet grudging in his submission; incapable of inspiring enthusiasm like Cerialis or reverence like Frontinus; in his last years, after a longer term of office in Britain than most, a man with a grievance, resenting his recall, living in gloomy retirement for safety's sake, and nursing his spleen.[45]

Perhaps the most majestic passage in the book, as well as the one that penetrates so much else of Collingwood's work, is as one might expect the chapter in book 3 on art. It is preceded, as the argument demands, by his earlier treatment of pre-Roman Celtic art and its vigorous flourishing just beyond the limits of the Belgic settlers who first drew the border of civilisation from the Wash to the Severn. Touchingly, Collingwood is standing up for his lifelong sympathy with the art of the North, when "Before the Roman conquest the Britons were a race of gifted and brilliant artists: the conquest, forcing them into the mould of Roman life with its vulgar efficiency and lack of taste, destroyed that gift and reduced their arts to the level of mere manufactures."[46] That artistry had crossed with the Belgic migrants of the third and second centuries BCE and struck root. It was characterised by the flowing and lambent line of its designs, rejecting naturalism, intent upon the lovely abstractions of curve and curlicue, the sweet flowering of volutes, medallions, stylised leaves, and flowers.

So there is a deep difference between the two schools, and British workmen could not resolve it (Collingwood points out the distinction between art and workmanship as anachronistic in Roman Britain). Yet, from time to time, little spasms of the old artistry break out (happily, in Northumberland and Cumbria), and this is the cue for Collingwood's theory of cultural survival and disjuncture: that British artists could never wholly reconcile themselves to Graeco-Roman naturalism and figuration; they *would* be off, swinging from their curvilinear abstractions. The symbolism of the former artistic tradition struggled to transmute the new naturalism into the old springing line. When Roman cultural energies failed and their reach no longer stretched so far, British artists, who had learned a little and forgotten much, returned at last to blow up the embers of their inheritance. The Bewcastle cross and the triumph of Lindisfarne, six hundred years in the future, are their resurrection.

Indeed, more than six hundred. Nikolaus Pevsner, in his pioneer classic, *The Englishness of English Art*, traces "the flaming line" from the amazing tracery on the west front of York Minster and the almost Almoravid curves and decoration of the north door of St. Mary Redcliffe in Bristol all the way through to the visions of William Blake.[47] The "flaming line" is, Pevsner thinks, an intrinsic characteristic of English art—nothing to do with racial temperament or pseudo-biology of that kind (as Collingwood said)—learned, taught, transmitted, and retained as native, formative, possessed, for two millennia. You might think of the flaming line as an artist's absolute presupposition.

There was one task left unfinished before Collingwood ascended the chair. Tormented and beset by the puzzle of the "scale of forms," no sooner had the *Essay on Philosophical Method* come out than he applied himself to the vindication and detailing of his argument about science. For it had come momentously to him that his ambition and avocation, growing and clarifying in the decade since *Speculum Mentis*, redirected by *Philosophical Method*, must be not so much to draw the map of knowledge as to plot the history of the ideas of knowledge as they came to know themselves *as* ideas. Oakeshott had helped to this realisation, but it was latent from the start, like Wordsworth's unapprehensible shapes, troubling his dreams and obstructing his sleep.

Therefore, during the second half of 1933, after a short summer holiday by himself visiting Vernon Blake in Die, and an even shorter one camping with the family in Scotland, he applied himself to the idea of nature as it directed the scientists to do what they did in the three definitive epochs of the Pythagoreans, the trinity of Bacon, Galileo, and Newton, and of modern physics.

He started out from his own strong sympathies with the Greek view that nature has a soul and a rational "mind" in which all living things participate to their own degree. He counterposed *and* derived from this the Cartesian view of nature as radically divided between matter and minds although ultimately connected in and by the being of God (a junction to be found, as Descartes rather desperately concluded, in the brain's pineal gland). Whatever minds could make of matter, the post-Cartesians knew for sure that matter worked not unlike the machines they had suddenly become so good at making. God was the omnipotent clockmaker, and the task at hand was to discover the design of the clock.

Evolutionary theory, in the hands of its many proponents as well as Darwin, placed nature in time and turned progress into its dominant value. History had meanwhile become a progressive science on its own account. Teleology took on a new life, the world was infinitely changeful and forever *becoming*, even if it ultimately would die. History and science found their theories and inventions, their regularities and discoveries, intertwined. Neither subject nor its object is ever at rest. Discoveries about the nature and speed of light at the turn of the nineteenth century left Newton's laws where they were for ordinary human motion but destroyed them for velocities at the speed of light. Hence the difficulty of conceptualising light itself: are its rays waves or particles? The same difficulty holds for all particle behaviour in all matter.

A. N. Whitehead and Samuel Alexander are Collingwood's two leading lights,[48] and he uses them with great confidence to conclude that the changeful idea of nature must, because of that very changefulness, be historical, and that therefore science can only be understood as a historical and an artistic contrivance. Alexander's prime importance for Collingwood is that he offers to keep open the road to God, even if God is "only a picture," however worth drawing, and himself a necessary creation of space-time.

Collingwood has too much of the "natural piety" he believes proper not just to philosophers and scientists but to humankind to permit this empirical heresy to Alexander, but his concluding declarations of transcendence over scientism is hardly at all theistic, only markedly Greek: "mind as we know it in man is something that has come to be what it is by developing functions belonging to life in general and even in the last resort to the inorganic world."[49] This formulation gathers science into that more comprehensive and comprehending form of thought to which all Collingwood's argument hereafter is to tend. He reproaches his heroes for retaining "a certain relic of positivism" that compels the belief that natural science is a progress towards unvarnished truth.

In 1686 the great Robert Boyle published *A Free Inquiry into the Vulgarly Received Notion of Nature*, and though they would never have been so rude as to repeat Boyle's phraseology, scientific philosophers of modern science place themselves in Boyle's column of troops. Collingwood, on the other hand, has all in common with the amazing Pierre Hadot, only thirty years his junior, for whom nature is itself a historical character, tricky, secretive, never finished with you even in a zero degree vacuum, and at all events nothing like the Cartesian ideal of a logical, rational system gradually revealing itself in the clear mirror of pure inquiry.[50] However his own argument may have helped Collingwood with his theism, his central conclusion is that "a scientific fact is a class of historical facts"; it is enjoined by his methods that somewhere encapsulated in Max Planck's way of writing equations will be traces of Newton's dynamics, that in Newton will remain traces of Kepler's cosmology, that in Kepler there is plenty left over from Aristotle, for after all the Greek title of Aristotle's *Physis* translates as "Nature."

Collingwood was writing *The Idea of Nature* from August 1933 until September 1934, when he first gave the work as lectures during the Michaelmas of that year.[51] For the whole of that period the conviction grew upon him and a few others that the new form of irrationalism emerging in Italy and Germany, formalised by Hitler's election victory on 30 January 1933, possessed hideous strength and menaced far more than Communist trade unionists and Jewish shop windows. He had given a welcoming party in his Belbroughton Road house to a young friend first made while visiting Germany. Adam von Trott zu Solz, charming, witty, cultivated, honourable patrician,[52] was guest of honour and a Rhodes scholar at Balliol. He said then, and many times thereafter, that his country was sick, that "there was a vast transformation going on . . . a kind of fateful historic mutation to which the ordinary categories did not apply, terrifying . . . but unintelligible [to his audience]."

There were sure to be some in that audience at the party who were not unsympathetic to the new German chancellor and the rejuvenation he was so clearly announcing as feasible for his country.[53] Britain had its deep Depression and Ramsay MacDonald; smart Fascist uniforms and black and gold banners were rousing enough symbols. Eleven years after the party, Adam von Trott was hanged by a wire in a cellar for his part in the 1944 plot to assassinate Hitler. As Collingwood finished the lectures on nature in 1934, the metaphysics of history was barging through the door, transforming the science of aeronautics, ballistics, explosives, radio, leading events from Versailles in 1919 to Warsaw in 1939. Collingwood piled his lectures together in August and took his wife and children camping on the Skipness estate.

V

Calling Collingwood (in the technical sense) an "idealist" seems reasonable enough for a man several of whose books have the word "idea" in the title. But that is only because the Titans of the nineteenth century divided thought into only two categories, idealism and materialism, and after the idealist had held the stage with Hegel's muscle and Kant's stamina for eighty years the materialists with the aid of Darwin, Marx, and Engels routed them and cleared the way for the positivists.

The real struggle, however, as it was Collingwood's life-task to affirm, was between science and history. In joining, or rather in his solitary way, leading this fight to the death, he had to put aside that translucent coolness and serene detachment for which Knox (and many others) praised *Philosophical Method*. His long illness had suggested time might be short—*timor mortis conturbat me*—the electoral landslides of Fascism were a dreadful portent in response to which serene detachment was quite inadequate. From the time of his assuming the Waynflete Chair (itself named after the metaphysical and contentious bishop of Winchester who founded Magdalen in 1458), the passions of his prose directed his thought in quite new ways.

There is an important lesson here for present-day theorists. Theory has taken much upon itself these past thirty years, and, with our subject at hand, it is noticeable that his titles either invoke "the Idea" or "the Principles," and principles do not compose theory, with its implied all-inclusiveness and explanatory finality. Neither do they provide rules to be followed. A principle, rather, is an originary bearing provided for the mind; it is a primary orientation for thought; it is formative of the faculty of reasoning on a particular subject and as such will vary from time to time. Insofar as a body of principles provides a foundation for coherent thinking, it is not a foundation one can get to the bottom of ("After that, it is elephants all the way down"). The absoluteness of its presupposition is shadowy and guarded.

In the play of principles, the passions form and inform the understanding. Passion has always been a difficulty for philosophers, and even Descartes' great essay on *The Passions of the Soul*, while paying homage to their power, leaves him with the old dualism, passion and reason.[54] Only now is that dualism melting into one. As the image of a personal God recedes from the Western academies, so too does the feasibility, let alone the desirability, of the "view from nowhere." If all moral and intellectual meditation and judgement must take place somewhere, and that somewhere is the spot on which the thinker lives and thinks, then having thought (including the re-enactment of the thoughts of others) sufficient unto the day will not be best accomplished by trying to expunge all feeling. It will be a matter having the feelings best suited to the occasion in which one finds oneself. The hermeneutician seeks for those feelings that best enfold or comprehend the (historical) experience in view. Right feeling and just interpretation unite in a single action of mind.[55]

7

"Fighting in the Daylight": Metaphysics against Fascism

On 28 October 1935 Collingwood gave his inaugural lecture as Waynflete professor. It was supposed to take place in Wren's grandly classical Sheldonian theatre, designed by the genius tyro when he was only thirty, and flanked by Duke Humfrey's Bodleian Library in the plain style and Hawksmoor's "grave and pretentious" Clarendon Building at the corner of Broad Street.[1] The trinity of buildings make up as formidably noble and vernacular a statement of British architecture as may be anywhere found, and a stage-frightening rostrum even for so practised a performer on which to pronounce on "The Historical Imagination." In the event, the occasion was moved to the Victorian clubland marble of the Examination Schools, where twenty-five years before Collingwood had sat for his scholarship.

All the same, the occasion, like all such in Oxford, was (and still is) produced by custom and ceremony with that slovenly dignity of local academic life that holds at poise pomp, circumstance, and self-amusement. The procession of university officers wound its way into the schools from the High Street, clad in hoods and habits, the vice-chancellor conducted to his throne by the bedels armed with their staves, bowing to them cap in hand before taking his seat. The university's orator, bowing also, rehearsed to his audience sitting in its Sunday best the accomplishments and record of the new professor who was finally given his cue, and Collingwood's high, clear, and beautifully modulated voice, the north country traces in its accent almost entirely lost to Oxford by now,[2] rang out under the high hammerbeam timbers and the gaze of oil-painted bishops and chancellors in their big gilt frames six feet above the heads of the three hundred listeners.

For a metaphysician, his topic, although tricky, was plainly within the bounds of everyday experience. His title was a deliberate statement of his vocation: the metaphysical professor must be, *as such*, a historian, and philosophers shall beware of pretending to live in a glassy essence untouched by time.

In a nonchalant manner, he announced the supercession of science by history, declared the authority of historian over history ("he is responsible for what goes in"), and that this revolution in thought must provide grounds for hope in human affairs. He is at pains to dismiss the commonsensible conception of history as a matter of received authorities setting down their memories of things, after which historians cut up these authoritative recollections and paste them into an intelligible order with a commentary. By this rulebook, the historian is bound by fidelity to his or her sources not to contradict or criticise but only to expound them.

Collingwood is of course courteously censorious of any such so-called method, voiding history of *thought*. The practice of mind that plays upon the past is imaginative, discovering implications left unvoiced by authority or unnoticed in the evidence. The force of the historical imagination is not "ornamental but structural." Collingwood goes on:

> The historian's picture of his subject, whether that subject be a sequence of events or a past state of things, thus appears as a web of imaginative construction stretched between certain fixed points provided by the statements of his authorities; and if these points are frequent enough and the threads spun from each to the next are constructed with due care, always by the *a priori* imagination and never by merely arbitrary fancy, the whole picture is constantly verified by appeal to these data, and runs little risk of losing touch with the reality which it represents.[3]

The a priori imagination is that movement of the mind whereby the historian (and biographer) applies it to a critical-creative making-of-connections between the fixed points of the dependable facts. In a favourite analogy of his, Collingwood compares his historian to the hero of the detective novels in which he had always taken such pleasure ever since his early encounters with Raffles and Sherlock Holmes. Thereafter his off-duty reading took in, naturally, Agatha Christie and a good deal of tenderness for Dorothy L. Sayers (whom he actually quotes in *The Principles of Art*). Her silly-ass-perfect-gentleman-intellectual-genius (first in *Literae Humaniores*, Cricket Blue), Lord Peter Wimsey, ministered in *Gaudy Night* with a faultless mixture of charm, snobbery, acumen, and a stirring love of the place to the susceptibilities of Oxford dons with just that mixture in the composition of their souls.

The good historian and the fictional detective think alike. From indications of the most suggestive kind—not so much the given as the found—each constructs an imaginary picture of what happened, an event conceived as the expression of the thoughts of those who acted it out. The facts, such as they are, are placed in an interpretative order by historian or detective. Their validation is consequence of the narrator's plausibility and imaginative forcefulness. The sources, the facts, or—such a final-sounding word—the *data* are only as good as the historical hermeneutician can make them. "The *a priori* imagination which does the work of historical construction supplies the means of historical criticism as well."[4] Thus the usual opposition between criticism and creation is dissolved. As imaginative works of art, novel and history are indistinguishable. As a mode of thought with its own principles, however, the history must be truthful, and its story must be true.[5]

It is nonetheless never finished. The historian brings everything of himself or herself to the task of interpretation, all the knowledge and experience that make up a mind and its spirit. But the work when it is done becomes part of the history of history, part of the process under study, seen not from a lofty historical peak outside everything (the view from nowhere) but from the only habitable somewhere there is, here, now, which is, if one is fortunate, the right moment to be pursuing one's particular inquiry. If historical luck holds, and if the historian's talents are adequate, then the consequence will be that act of resurrection on the page that is the reward of the art of history when consummated.

> And what the dead had no speech for, when living,
> They can tell you, being dead: the communication
> Of the dead is tongued with fire beyond the language
>   Of the living.
> Here the intersection of the timeless moment
> Is England and nowhere. Never and always.[6]

II

His inaugural lecture was the first of two imperial statements on the metaphysics and meaning of the two sorts of history: the facts of the past and their arrangement in the present as narrative. The year before his elevation to the chair, he was likewise raised up to a fellowship of the British Academy, the elite and oligarchic body that oversees the conduct and standards of British university life, conferring recognition by election only to those judged to have singularly contributed to their discipline (nowadays also allocating colossal research funds for those same purposes).

Its premises today are as towering, ostentatious, and classical as the Sheldonian, huger and less beautiful than Wren's because Victorian, and dominating St. James's Park and Palace at the very heart of British power and government. But Collingwood addressed his new fellow-fellows on 20 May 1936 in the sort of bare, blank meeting hall somewhere in Bloomsbury to which all extramural lecturers are accustomed. He told them too that history was become queen of the sciences and, however dull the scenery, he fairly matched the manner to the moment. "Self knowledge is desirable and important to man, not only for its own sake but as a condition without which no other knowledge can be critically justified and securely based."[7]

This was the largest and most ambitious statement on behalf of the intellectual life and its needful embodiment in the practice of history that anyone had made in the universities for a very long time. Bertrand Russell wrote with a comparable largesse, no doubt, but even his title did not prevent his snobbish countrymen from thinking of him as not quite *sound*. The scientists and the literati (apart from T. S. Eliot) were much fired by communism, J.B.S. Haldane and P.M.S. Blackett in science for instance, W. H. Auden and his fellow poets on the left, Stephen Spender and Louis MacNeice, in literature.

Collingwood, hardly at all a public figure of their eminence, untouched by the stirring music of Marxism, equally repudiating the revolting complacencies of English Toryism, spoke up for the missing "science of human affairs," for scholarly life and its application to historical knowledge as the single source of painfully acquired wisdom, as the needful measure of our own transience, as the steady reminder of the sheer differences from our own in the thought of other minds at other times as well as their continued, compelling, barely recognised presences "encapsulated" in our present. And to those latter-day agonisers over historical relativism, who say that if all human values are historically enunciated, temporally transient, and subsequently discredited, then life has no meaning at all, Collingwood implies, with appropriate nerve and calm, that the best you can do is live up to the best principles you can find in your history, grasping both their provenance and their mortality.

At the academy he began by putting down Locke, Hume, and even Kant for having sought a theory of human nature as prompted by the methods of natural and empirical science that had rolled on to such amazing successes since they were systematised in the seventeenth century. It is now that Collingwood feels able to declare with professorial authority that a new revolution in thought, comparable to that of seventeenth-century science, has been turning on the wheel of time for several decades, and in 1935 to announce, not for the first time, its advent: "whereas the right way of investigating nature is by the methods called scientific, the right way of investigating mind is by the methods of history."[8]

In human affairs there is no fixed repertory of forms of civic and political life (evolutionary biology, as Collingwood notes, suggests that nor is the repertory of nature so very fixed either). At this point, in what must have been a thunderclap for the professionals who were following and not dozing through his address, he gives us his central principle.

> The historian ... is investigating not mere events (where by a mere event I mean one which has only an outside and no inside) but *actions* ... his main task is to think himself into this action, to discern the thought of its agent. ... For history, the object to be discovered is not the mere event, but the thought expressed in it. To discover that thought is already to understand it. ... The history of thought, *and therefore all history,* is the re-enactment of past thought in the historian's own mind.[9]

This classic formulation had been gestating since he rewrote his philosophy of history lectures in southern France in 1928. In 1932 he had found for the first time a little-known work by the great metaphysician F. H. Bradley, whom he and Eliot so much admired. It was *The Presuppositions of Critical History,* was first published in 1874 and surely the source of Collingwood's crucial term of art.[10] Bradley pointed to those assumptions we are bound to be making— assumptions about reasons and causes, human conduct and routine obtuseness, imagination and the lack of it (he calls them "prejudications")—in taking inferences from evidence.[11]

This, as we shall see, is a crux in his main symphonic writing about history. But there is first a misconception, shared a bit surprisingly by Isaiah Berlin, to be cleared up. It is that the doctrine of the re-enactment of past thoughts involves some kind of empathic levitation of one's mind into the mind of the person who did the thinking in the first place. Much was made in a minor pedagogic movement of the 1970s of putting oneself imaginatively into some past period, which issued in pleasant little festivals of historical self-indulgence where local worthies of a thespian bent dressed up as blacksmiths in restored forges and as milkmaids with wooden pails. Whatever these capers did to interest schoolchildren in history (and it may have been plenty), they were nothing to do with thinking past thoughts.

Re-enactment counted as thought in its own right only insofar as the historian (and as Collingwood said, every one of us attempts proper historical thinking at frequent intervals in our lives, puzzling out family history or national politics) brings to bear on the original action his or her full intelligence and full knowledge: "It is not a passive surrender to the spell of another's mind; it is a labour of active and therefore critical thinking. The historian not only re-enacts past thought, he re-enacts it in the context of his own knowledge and therefore, in re-enacting it, criticises it, forms his own judgement of its value, corrects whatever errors he can discern in it."[12]

"All thinking," he says, "is critical thinking"; we criticise as we re-enact. Criticise, certainly, but Collingwood is also describing creative thought, as we normally use the word. For the strenuous discipline of learning "re-enactment" takes place as part of a historian's coming-to-awareness of the past in the present. Nor is this a metaphysical idea, or not at least as J. A. Smith or T. H. Green would have understood that word. It is an awareness of how the past lives in traces of itself "encapsulated" (Collingwood's key term) in later forms of the original.

Our present concept of the political state, for example, carries within its practices encapsulated versions of the state as a moral agent, sovereign over the people and at best their protector, as worked out by Thomas Hobbes immediately after the English Civil War. Moreover *his* concept of the state contained earlier encapsulations deposited by Renaissance thinkers, supremely Machiavelli, as they worked out their advice to the haughty princes of the Italian city-states. As Collingwood spoke his lecture, Hatchard's in Piccadilly three hundred yards up the road had on its shelves T. S. Eliot's just published poem, *Burnt Norton*. It begins:

> Time present and time past
> Are both perhaps present in time future,
> And time future contained in time past.
> If all time is eternally present
> All time is unredeemable.
> What might have been is an abstraction

Remaining a perpetual possibility
Only in a world of speculation.
What might have been and what has been
Point to one end, which is always present.

On Collingwood's account, like Eliot's, the past lives on in the present, and the historian justifies his craft, his art, and his guild as being each appointed to point out that present past and thereby make the present more intelligible. In the first instance, as he says, this turns the historian into a diagnostician,[13] which one certainly needs in order to know what's wrong. But what is one to *do*? Will the historian tell us this? In a marvellous plain passage in his classic of plain speakers, the *Autobiography*, written at top speed in the late summer of 1938, Collingwood gives a more direct and colloquial reply than was suitable for the formalities of inauguration.[14]

He there advises us that the acutest situations demand action without recourse to rules. Faced with such crises (a word to be careful of abusing), taking them with due seriousness, the hardest thing even for the best people is to refuse not only the seductive temptress Desire and Self-interest, but "the tempter whose disguise is so good most people hardly ever penetrate it at all. . . . Right Conduct,"[15] which was to say action according to the rules of convention, or duty, or even virtue. (Hard not to think that these strictures had for him a private application.) The purpose of history was then practical and rational; it was to find the past in the present, to understand backwards in order to plan forwards, to teach us, in order to know what to do next, how on earth we got into this mess in the first place.

He told the crowded auditorium that "all knowledge of mind is historical," for "history is the life of mind itself,"[16] and saying so professed, as it was the whole point of the ceremony to do, the highest claims and noblest significance for his avocation, and to do so contentiously: as he would later say, "fighting in the daylight" against the minute philosophers, whether of Cook Wilson's persuasion or from Carnap's New Wave sweeping in from Vienna.

For I have written, as well I might, of the gatherings in Oxford and London as academic life at its stateliest and academic intonation at its most audible. But in truth the bald, spectacled, and thickset figure on the podium was as isolated as he had ever been. The students may have flocked to hear him, but the best of the other philosophers were talking with animation and ardour in quite another vocabulary. Indeed, the incipient hero of the opening philosophical epoch, Ludwig Wittgenstein, had just then invented his subject-changing concept, the "language game,"[17] and Prichard's intent worrying out of the question of duty, pulling away at his scruffy moustache, or Joseph's prognaceous severity with contradiction,[18] were replaced by quite another scene.

That scene was dominated by a newcomer fellow of Magdalen called J. L. Austin, who arrived at the college in 1933. At this distance it is astounding that neither ever mentioned the other. Ayer and Austin became the great double act of the new, contemptuously anti-metaphysical and (again) minute attention to the nature of language. They also rejected the old realists' apparatus for the theory of perception and the grounding of knowledge. Ayer stood, with voluble wit and celerity, for positivism and the absolute necessity for verification; Austin, slower in speech and with a genius for searching out the fallibility of general propositions, the implausibility of dualising (he particularly disliked so-called antinomies, for example between universals and particulars, or descriptive and emotive terminology). He was, as they say, brilliant—brilliant in the dazzling play of his analysis, but tenacious, sure-footed, commonsensible, too, and witty in his many inventions.[19]

The group led by Ayer and Austin, joined by Berlin, Stuart Hampshire, and Donald Mackinnon, never numbered more than seven and was, like so many of the philosophical groups we have already met, "excessively self-centred" (Berlin's own words), interested only in their own competitive conversation, delighting in their cleverness. But as Berlin also says, only under the spell of such delight and held by such friendship does anybody discover intellectual happiness.

I do not think Collingwood was often happy like that. The isolation in which he worked was in part a consequence of his opposition to both the residual and emergent forms of dominant philosophy; it was also a consequence of self-imposed solitude, of the satisfaction he found in voyaging his own strange seas of thought alone. For sure, he took great delight—what teacher worth the name wouldn't?—in the admiration of his students, and more than one of the tiny minority of women students, especially if they were pretty, he had singled out for coffee and ices in Buol's. One of these, as he became interested in and, from time to time, infuriated by Freud, was a contemporary, not a student, and a subsequently distinguished child psychoanalyst from Poland called Margaret Lowenfeld with whom he dined once or twice in London (and with whom his name was linked in gossip of an affair);[20] another was Kathleen Edwardes, whom he rediscovered at her drama studies at the Embassy Theatre in West Hampstead and, as 1937 progressed, saw more and more often.

III

As his new office and the labour that he had set himself to make a complete exposition and revision of his philosophy of history coincided, the conviction grew upon him of a public duty to make these arguments and opinions tell in the great world outside Oxford, the political weather in which was turning so dark and looming. And yet his intellectual ambit, for all the largeness of his reputation among the couple of hundred or so of professional British philosophers, and for all the admiration he won from a few dozen lady-and-gentleman archaeologists in the county antiquarian societies, was extremely small. His most public forum was, as Stefan Collini puts it, "almost entirely as a book reviewer . . . in the local parish magazine" by which Collini means, not unfairly, the *Oxford Magazine*, the university's own little monthly review composed of book notices and topical essays by the locals.[21] But then, as Collini goes on to say, to men of Collingwood's Edwardian formation the only public that mattered was "a very small one, a "public" which could be encountered in person at high tables, at weekend house parties, on the governing councils of learned and public bodies, and in the reading rooms of clubs and professional associations" (pretty well closed to women).[22]

Collingwood never displayed any irony towards his secure position in the British class system nor awareness of his own occasional social class absurdities (for example, the comical moment in the *Autobiography* when he illustrates his argument about rules by telling us how a chap ought to deal with his tailor).[23] No doubt the physical effort of what the army used to call mucking-in when excavating as well as his enormous walks about Coniston, in the Haute Savoie, in Catalonia, and along the Rhine, his fluency in several tongues, as much as his moral qualities, all militated against Collingwood's ever becoming the sort of claustral and snobbish recluse the ancient universities have often made of their menfolk. I suppose his character and its sociable expression still belonged to the Wordsworthian and Ruskinian ideal: the self-reliant solitary and Lakelander "statesman," the mind with a message to any passerby prepared to listen. As Collini adds, in a kindly exculpation: "maybe just because he moved so little in circles of power and influence he was the more inclined to take the established channels of expression for granted: a truth laid out in the *Oxford Magazine* could seem like a truth made powerful in the world."[24]

So although one cannot doubt a new urgency in his writing coming through during 1936, his sense of how and where to express it was limited, naturally, by time and chance as well as by class and occupation. The *Autobiography*, written in 1938 when mortal illness became certain, represents his calm but desperate attempt to connect personal experience to public politics in a plain, affirmative idiom and with a dramatic mien. The assorted writings in *The Idea of History*, striking and unusual though it is as the only thing of its kind in the English literature of the period, are a medley of lectures for different purposes and did not in any case appear as a book until 1946, and then, as all its readers know, edited by Knox with a good deal of unjustified self-confidence.

While I think one can say that the almost forty thousand words of the never-finished *Principles of History*,[25] which were written early in 1939, represent Collingwood's maturest statement of his position, one further, rather desperate, sally demands our attention, exactly because it was the nearest he came to public journalism addressed to the frightful historical beast slouching towards Berlin, Rome, and Madrid to be born. It was written in 1936, entitled "Man Goes Mad," and (revealingly) never published.[26] This effort, prophetic, resolute, and afraid by turns, is in the mode we associate with our latter-day intelligentsia, "speaking truth to power" as the slogan has it, minatory, hostile to the revolutionary creeds of Communism and Fascism, seeking to call an enfeebled liberalism back to its own best attitudes. Where on earth could his warning go? He wrote the piece at his usual velocity (the manuscript is almost unemended), and then that was that for another fifty-three years.

Work was his refuge and writing his platform. Correct and formal as always in his official manners, he was living at full tilt. He had had more than a glimmering of the danger his health was in, and by 1937 he positively courted the danger his marriage was in, and did so by way of the beginnings of the courtship of Kathleen Edwardes. There is a good deal of well-bred swallowing to be found in the records of those who knew him well at this critical time. Richmond refers blankly to his "breakdown";[27] Knox does the same, putting everything down to the illness;[28] Mabbott remarks, by way of corroborating Collingwood's pedagogic principle that a student must always be sure what a thinker had really said by going to the original, that "Collingwood went off and was analysed [in 1937–1938]—the full fifty session process." But Mabbott goes on, "I fear it did him serious harm. It increased the introverted, defensive side of him, and I feel sure it contributed to his later breakdown."[29]

At about this same time, Collingwood was annotating Freud's *Totem and Taboo* with great dash and as part of his pioneering incorporation of anthropology into the comity of the human sciences. He is his usual brisk, at times devastating self, at once delighted and ruthless with his overpositivist and simplistic forebears. He scants, for instance, even the great early anthropologist A. C. Haddon in one tart aside: "to explain exogamy by jealousy would be like trying to explain fishing and hunting by reference to hunger."[30] And he is firmer still on Sir Edward Tylor's celebrated classic, *Primitive Culture*, for while praising Tylor as the great man no doubt he was, he rebukes him for falling into the error Tylor reproaches in others, to the effect that primitive peoples display a "low intellectual condition." Collingwood finds in Tylor the enormous condescension of posterity that disfigures so much of the human sciences, acquits savages of their imputed animism, and, in an immortal dictum, brings the subject at one bound up to the moment not of Evans-Pritchard but of Clifford Geertz.

> Stupidity and ignorance, invoked as causes, may explain (if we think "the explanation" a good one) why mistakes in general should be made; they can never explain why one particular mistake should be made out of all the infinity of possible mistakes.
>
> [For] the savage is not a consistent animist. Engaged in smelting copper for example, he does not command the copper to melt, he treats it quite scientifically, raising it to the right temperature by means of a furnace and bellows. We cannot logically explain this by saying that he is too stupid to be a consistent animist; for we have no reason, apart from what he does and says, to think him an animist at all.[31]

In each of his annotations of the anthropologists and of Freud in his guise as psychoanalyst of the primitive, Collingwood strikes the attitude we now take as a commonplace of method, let alone a gesture of politeness. That is, he allows no superiority of explanation to the human scientist over the beliefs of those people under study. Indeed, he takes the side of the primitives as against the scientists for misunderstanding the absolute presuppositions of the society to hand. "Thus, they concluded, magic is at bottom simply a special kind of error: it is erroneous natural science."[32]

Collingwood presaged this now customary stance in human inquiry by several decades, and he did so out of his strong and lifelong interest in and sympathy with the origins of systematic thought and theoretic explanations that are to be found in folklore, the historical science of the illiterate. That sympathy had been formed in him by his sisters and parents in childhood; it had been deepened, enlarged, and given roots in his archaeology, and the records it provided of the mingling of civilisations, their domestic science, and their local art, each symbolic of their theories of the world. Art itself, as he had argued in *Speculum Mentis*, is the earliest such theory, closest of the forms of knowledge to originary experience. When he moved from Pembroke for Magdalen, he left his ally Tolkien behind, working at his language of Middle Earth, painting those extraordinary water-colours of Cheddar Gorge and Burrington Combe transformed into the wilds of *Lord of the Rings*, and in 1937 finishing his great chil-dren's classic, *The Hobbit*.

So folklore and its scholarly archivist, the anthropologist, were near Collingwood's heart. King Arthur, we know, held it tight, and his profound admiration for Eliot's poem *The Waste Land* was given its depth and ardour by his familiarity with the resonant associations of folklore Eliot had learned from Jessie Weston and Sir James Frazer, and which Collingwood had first encountered on the Lakeland Fells, in the Icelandic sagas translated by William Morris, and in his fa-ther's bedtime stories. They were at the root of his Englishness, so it is only surprising that it took Collingwood until 1936 formally to join the Folklore Society in its solid Bloomsbury premises, to chair one or two of its meetings the following year, and in 1938 to lecture at the headquarters on magic in human life, much of his thought on that topic already having appeared in *The Principles of Art* and having been worked out in the unfinished book on folk tales.

His comrades in the antiquarian societies took for granted such familiarities; they still do, although a thinning out of the presence of fairy tales in the culture may indicate the thinning out also of English identity. But insofar as his passion for folktales was intrinsic to his north country version of freeborn Englishness, to the formation of his "statesman" politics, indeed to his Oxonian and social-class self-certainty and tinge of arrogance, it was also of a piece with his histor-ical and geographical frame of reference. He left Europe only once, for his convalescent journey to Java across the winter of 1938–39, but no one, *no one* can doubt his imperial cosmopolitanism, a calm certainty of self that was the ground of his courteous openness to the remotest zones of thought.

So it isn't easy to detect in his prose of these years, nor in his conduct, signs of the "breakdown" referred to by Richmond, Knox, and Mabbott. The strongest hint is given in a note of his own on love and moral crisis: "There are many crises in which we preserve a sense of our own rectitude; but that very fact shows that they are not moral crises; they are crises of desire or expediency or policy, where the knowledge that we are right supports us through our difficulties. In a moral crisis this knowledge fails us: a person whom it has never failed, has never faced a moral issue." Then Collingwood adds that it is only in such crises "that we set aside . . . even all questions of right and wrong . . . and try to discover what is the one thing we *must* do on pain of a kind of moral death or dissolution."[33]

With this characteristic candour before us, the decision to undergo fifty sessions of psychoanalysis looks as though it has much more to it than obedience to his own scholarly injunction always to make sure what a thinker really did say. He spoke, after all, with great respect of Freud as the doctor of the irrationality of the human soul. But in long years of hostility to the claims of psychology to be the natural science of the mind, Collingwood defended against all such delusive claims the primacy of philosophic history as the realm of reason and the custodian of truth.

His pepperiness with Freud, when Freud ventures into anthropology and savage minds, is itself an assertion of this primacy. Freud may be a remarkable diagnostician of the so far unknown liabilities of human intelligence to neurosis and therefore unreason. Made more aware of this danger, the individual may be better able to frame rational thought with comprehensible passions. But in supposing that Freud's methods will identify the burden of suppression beneath which the savage mind is groaning is a grotesque misapplication resting not on the evidence, but "read into it," "resting rather on the false assumption, implicit in the naturalistic method, that subject and object are external to each other and that each is the other's opposite."[34]

His exasperation with Freud is thus much more than a matter of correcting anthropological error. You could better say it was personal, especially when he turns fiercely to Freud to say: "The savage is *not* your patient. This is a new attitude towards the native: not the "damn nigger" attitude but the "lunatic" attitude. Savagery is now a mental disease to be cured by psychoanalysis!"[35] And he adds of

Freud's discussion of menstruation, with an endearing exasperation, "I transcribe this sentence in full because I can hardly believe my eyes! What the Devil does the man think he means?"

The strictures are unanswerable. All Collingwood wishes at this point to do is hold Freud to his own art and craft, which is "to wring from his patients secrets whose genuineness is vouched for either by their corroboration or by their restoration to health." It is this genius that Collingwood admires "only on this side of idolatry."[36] As patient of a Freudian (recommended by Margaret Lowenfeld) as well as critic of Freud, Collingwood was to search for the secrets of his unconscious in order to add them to his stock of self-knowledge. If there were a neurotic element in his feelings for Kathleen Edwardes in 1937 and 1938, he was determined to have it out in front of him, for his own sake and Ethel's. But the moral crisis of which his marriage was at the heart, which gathered to its turning point over these many months, could not be *answered* by psychoanalysis and was not a disease from which he could be restored to health. It could only be concluded, in his own words, by discovering what was the one thing he *must* do.

Nor can his personal circumstance be severed from the gathering storm over European history, least of all for a man for whom history is the alone substance and essence of human self-knowledge, and whose strange-sounding doctrine of re-enactment is not so much a method of inquiry as a condition of knowing anything, of tying the knot between knower and known.[37] The storm was about to surge unstoppably into the junction boxes of human reason, destroying that reason in the headquarters of Fascism, terrorising it in the terrible policy centres of Communism, and draining power out of the energy reserves of Liberalism. Any personal crisis could not fail to be linked to these violent disturbances. In April 1937 Collingwood was by himself, as usual, walking on the border of Catalonia; on the frontier's other side, just down the road in Barcelona, George Orwell was discovering at the same moment what it was like to "be in a town where the working class was in the saddle."

And it was the aspect of the crowds that was the queerest thing of all. In outward appearance it was a town in which the wealthy classes had practically ceased to exist.... Practically everyone wore rough working-class clothes, or blue overalls or some variant of the militia uniform. All this was queer and moving. There was much in it I did not understand, in some ways I did not even like it, but I recognised it immediately as a state of affairs worth fighting for.[38]

A few years before Franco resolved by the usual methods to restore cruelty and stagnation to Spanish politics, Collingwood and some friends were sitting drinking in a Catalonian wine shop and asked fellow-drinkers what the festival was in which they had just watched white-clad children singing peaceably. "Festival?" said they. "That was the Revolution."[39]

IV

Collingwood slowly discovered what he must do by means of his usual discipline; he wrote a new book. The book in question was *The Principles of Art*, and it replaces the little textbook he published with the Clarendon Press in 1925 as *Outlines of a Philosophy of Art*.[40] Of its nature, and of *his* nature at the age of thirty-six, his aesthetic philosophy had not begun to absorb the shock of the war and the extraordinary new forms of art that were to constitute modernism, and which both anticipated and were shaped by warfare. Art, however, remained the point at which a theoretic form of knowledge stood closest to the practice of everyday life. History, no doubt, comprehended practice the most fully and resolved it most truthfully, but with no duties except to truthfulness about its own expressiveness, art could speak most directly to and from the heart.

It is a striking thing about Collingwood's aesthetics that he can write of the heart in heartfelt ways without any disfiguration by the demotic, and without losing hold on his own high-mindedness. It is plainly a book in which he sets out to address his times, another attempt to enter from the academic wings and speak upon the public stage of what is past, or passing, or to come.

He had for many years, as one would expect, firm views about the condition of culture and the place of art in modern life. The marvellous pages in *The Principles of Art* praising Eliot's *The Waste Land* ring so true because he shared Eliot's vision of the degeneration of culture and the putrefaction of the commercial art produced to sell as modern culture.[41] Eliot's poem counterposes the dark images of the modern city, the collective sigh exhaled by its drooping multitudes of people, to the brief glow given off by the vanished splendours of the past, glimpsed along the river and then gone out. Eliot's mighty vision, derived from and comparable to that of Dante in the *Inferno*, which Collingwood had taught himself to translate at Rugby, diffused itself through the consciousness of that majority of the intelligentsia who, refusing Marxism and the intimations of mechanical immortality coming out of revolutionary Moscow, saw in modern culture only abject escapism and "the corruption of consciousness."[42] With a comparable commitment, F. R. Leavis's famous periodical *Scrutiny* had started off with a bang in 1932, calling for "an armed and conscious minority" to oppose the degeneration of taste and to recover, among the membership of tiny elites, a language with which to resist the slide into mass deturpation readable on every side.

Yet the style of Leavis's opposition was not high-pitched—he compiled, with his brave lieutenant, Denys Thompson, an inspiring school textbook to illustrate his case and to spark some critical recognition of its importance in sixth forms.[43] Eliot's poems, increasing in difficulty, nonetheless swelled even in 1942 into the lovely affirmation of *Little Gidding*. Collingwood had written, for sure, of the consequences for art of mechanisation, had utterly disparaged the cinema, and voiced the view, similar to Leavis's and Eliot's, that only in agrarian society and according to its natural rhythms can men and women live at peace with themselves and nature. All three men—like so many others—were fervent in their belief that only art could restore the great gaps torn open in popular culture by the savageries and primitivism of commerce and mass politics.

These atavistic melodies, these days, are both mocked and upheld: upheld by the *Daily Telegraph*, no doubt, but also by the volunteer armies of eco-warriors; mocked by the heartless hedonists of Big New Money and an international way of life owing allegiance to no geography or history but only to the bonus. But at this distance from Collingwood's essay,[44] let alone the wistful chorus of 1930s' agrarians mourning the loss of the folk arts of ploughing, wheelmaking, thatching, hayrick-building, there is no question of repair work. The agrarian order is gone, its survival, vigorous enough in its own way, is to be found in the almost universal practices of leisure-time gardening, the garden centres packed with customers, and their public conversation on *Gardeners' Question Time* and *Groundforce*, listened to and watched by millions.

Contemplating its certain demise, the only redemption for the unself-conscious arts of living sustained and renewed by domestic crafts and the inheritance of an expressive, courteous, and civic language would be the making of the formal arts themselves and their craft ancillaries: literature, painting, music, sculpture, theatre, embroidery, metalwork, wood carving. This was Ruskin's lesson and it is Collingwood's. Like Ruskin, and with as great a revulsion, he condemns as rotten the popular arts of industrialism, specifically football, radio, cinema. These are "amusement art," which is to say "a device for the discharge of emotions in such a way that they shall not interfere with the concerns of practical life."[45]

Amusement art is so organised and defined that the emotions it arouses cannot and must not spill over into practical life. (This separation, he insists, does not occur in children's make-believe, a phrase that misdescribes the child's working busily away at life-problems unhindered by the grown-ups, just as the adult artist does.) He also distinguishes between amusement art and art as magic, a useful and long-standing device whereby the magical acts (or arts) "generate in the agent . . . certain emotions considered necessary . . . for the work of living . . . the function of magic is to develop and conserve morale, or [when pointed at one's enemies] to damage it."

Propaganda is a version of magical art, and because magical art "is a kind of dynamo supplying the mechanism of practical life with the emotional current that drives it," it is a necessary part of every thriving and energetic society. In 1937 magical art was everywhere

on the advance, never more so than in the frightful theatre of
Nuremberg, but it was no less effective if slightly less brutal, as Collingwood points out, in the muscular Christianity and team sports
of the ancient public schools of England, their wardrobes, rituals,
honours, and acclamations.

Magical art is everywhere, and it may be good or bad. Amusement
art, however, is everywhere overwhelming and frequently vicious; it
conduces irresistibly (in a key formulation) to the "corruption of
consciousness" in its society. "The artist as purveyor of amusement
makes it his business to please his audience by arousing certain emotions in them and providing them with a make-believe situation in
which these emotions can be harmlessly discharged."[46]

Harmless is as harmless does. Collingwood's key instance of
amusement art in his contemporary society is pornography, a wholly
make-believe substitute in a society in which Aphrodite is no longer
a god but a toy, and (following Eliot) one in which "the instinctive
desire to propagate has been weakened by a sense that life, as we
have made it, is not worth living."

What he would make of today's adult film industry or the gleam-
ing limbs and curly pubes of the girls on the covers of the men-only
shelves in W. H. Smith's isn't hard to imagine. But there is something
too confident in these curses spoken over the bodies of amusement
art. After all, he is very rough with thrillers but was himself an avid
reader of detective stories and used their intellectual method, as we
saw, as a type of the historical inquiry he commended. There is also
something repugnant in the accents of a ruling-class professor (and
the Waynflete Chair must surely hold up such an occupant) ritually
denigrating the most popular art in history. The 1930s' slump was
barely over at this date, *The Road to Wigan Pier* was published that
year; small wonder that people took succour from amusement and
"escapist" art—there was so bloody much to escape from.

Nor is his disdain for popular taste conscious of secondary objec-
tions that official guardians of that taste have *always* denigrated the
latest popular form of expression; the Puritans simply shut down the
theatres out-of-hand, literary men in 1800 dismissed novels as trivial
entertainment fit only for women (recall how Jane Austen has to

defend them in *Northanger Abbey*), and in the 1930s the academics took it upon themselves to present the cinema as unimprovably bad for everybody because commercial, lacking any audience participation,[47] taking place in the dark, insufficiently effortful and otherwise marking the end of civilisation as we know it.

All of which mild mockery is not to ignore the fact that amusement art is indeed a corruptor of consciousness, nor to fail to see that as so many traditions that bind us to life have lapsed, a love of art and the health of art are all the more pressing concerns for the continuity of a civilisation that in 1937 was confronted by certain menace and possible extinction.

> What we are concerned with is the threatened death of a civilisation. That has nothing to do with my death or yours, or the deaths of any people we can shoot before they shoot us. It can be neither arrested nor hastened by violence. Civilisations die and are born not with waving of flags or the noise of machine guns in the streets, but in the dark, in a stillness, when no one is aware of it. It never gets into the papers. Long afterwards a few people, looking back, begin to see that it has happened.
>
> Then let us get back to our business. We who write and read this book are persons interested in art. We live in a world where most of what goes by that name is amusement. Here is our garden. It seems to need cultivating.[48]

He has already distinguished art from craft, important nowadays when both terms are being dissolved into the single catchall "skills" (or techniques). Craft is the deployment of chosen means and materials to a determinate end; art is the discovery of an unenvisageable end,[49] the means towards which disappear in their fulfilment as work of art.

That end, which the artist is only sure of when he or she sees or hears it *expressed* in a work that satisfies him or her, corresponds to something which artists have "in their heads," but which is knowable for what it is strictly as an achievement. This simple enough version of the artist's sense of completion resolves a paragraph in the book that has caused a lot of trouble and turned many readers off Collingwood as being far too much the idealist philosopher for whom ideas (by definition) are everything and life and work merely their epiphe-nomena. (This is a practical painter and musician writing.)

> If the making of a tune is an instance of imaginative creation, a tune is an imaginary thing. And the same applies to a poem or a painting or any other work of art. This seems paradoxical; we are apt to think that a tune is not an imaginary thing but a real thing, a real collection of noises; that a painting is a real piece of canvas covered with real colours; and so on. I hope to show, if the reader will have patience, that there is no paradox here; that both these propositions express what we do as a matter of fact say about works of art; . . . an artist's business is not to produce an emotional effect in an audience, but, for example, to make a tune. This tune is already complete and perfect when it exists merely as a tune in his head, that is, an imaginary tune. Next, he may arrange for the tune to be played before an audi-ence. Now there comes into existence a real tune, a collection of noises. But which of these two things is the work of art? Which of them is the music? The answer is implied in what we have already said; the music, the work of art, is not the collection of noises, it is the tune in the composer's head. The noises made by the performers, and heard by the audience, are not the music at all; they are only means by which the audience, if they listen intelligently (not otherwise), can reconstruct for themselves the imaginary tune that existed in the composer's head.[50]

There is admittedly something a bit clumsy in this. Collingwood is struggling to show how the work of art comes into being only in the encounter between artist and spectator. He has of necessity to draw on his own philosophical tradition to do this and not the mate-rialist tradition for which a painting is a matter of pigment on a flat surface, rendered into art by the assent of the right social institution. For Collingwood art (like history) is the "intelligent reconstruc-tion"[51] of the artist's intentions (the picture, the time, the thought) on the part of the artist, the spectator or the listener. Hence the pictures stacked against the wall as unsatisfactory answers to ques-tions at Lanehead; scanning them for the right realisation of the original idea, his father or his mother couldn't find it in what each had done.

This is the most familiar of our struggles to say what we really mean, and Collingwood, like Tolstoy in his similar effort to fix the nature of art,[52] finds putative works of art in any of our everyday efforts to tell a convincing story about some aspect of our lives, to express our feelings about it, to come at a truth that it has implied to us. The crux here (and Collingwood is miles away from the mistake) is not to suppose that successful expressiveness in art is a matter of the artist's so communicating the experience that we each share a perfect facsimile of it, feel the identical feelings, and think the identical thoughts.

What is at stake is not this happy communication of a private state of being from artist to audience. It is the joint reconstruction of the original ideas (again, "in the artist's head") as the painting, the music, the poem, or the film is reviewed, rethought, *criticised.* This is what criticism truly is, the effort to determine what the work means as an intentional action on the part of another person *or oneself.* Painters, for instance, will often talk about one of their paintings as if it had a life of its own and they must catch it on the hop to make it do what they want. Novelists frequently speak of a character's having her own wilful life and its being their artistic task to be sure that they have interpreted the creature's purposes aright. Wittgenstein must take the credit for breaking up the idea (propounded, among others, by Croce "with his hands in his pockets")[53] that art is experienced as the direct, intuitive communication of feeling from artist to audience. Wittgenstein says: "The temptation to say 'I see it like *this*,' pointing to the same thing for 'it' and 'this.' Always get rid of the idea of a private object in this way: assume that it constantly changes but that you do not notice the change because your memory constantly deceives you."[54]

There is something fundamental here about the common and collective action that is the making of art. Collingwood, I think, was more thorough about that than anybody else, and in being so, he is as firmly actual and tactile as he is, in the jargon, "expressivist." Art expresses, for sure, and what it expresses is the truth it finds in experience. This isn't—perhaps it is superfluous to add—something that one can carry away from a work as some kind of "absolute," a truth about life dissociable from the work to hand. The truth the artist wants to find is the truth about the experience as it is framed and made intelligible by the right emotions:

> [T]he artist presents us with a picture. . . . When he painted it, he was in possession of an experience quite other than that of seeing the colours he was putting on the canvass; an imaginary experience of total activity more or less like that which we construct for ourselves when we look at the picture. If he knew how to paint, and if we know how to look at a painting, the resemblance between this imaginary experience of his and the imaginary experience which we get from looking at his work is at least as close as that between the colours he saw in the picture and those we see; perhaps closer. . . . The imaginary experience which we get from the picture is not merely the kind of experience the picture is capable of arousing, it is the kind of experience we are capable of having. . . . We bring our powers of vision with us, and find what they reveal. Similarly, we bring our imaginative powers with us, and find what they reveal: namely, an imaginary experience of total activity which we find in the picture because the painter had put it there. . . . Thus a work of art proper is a total activity which the person enjoying it apprehends, or is conscious of, by the use of his imagination.[55]

These conclusions about the constitution of works of art as collaboratively established by the people making and remaking them emerge from Collingwood's strenuous account of the imaginative effort that goes into these labours of love. This effort is part "of an imaginative experience of total activity" and in a wonderful few paragraphs he describes just how total this activity is but does so by removing the faculty of sight from a painter. His example is Cézanne, and Collingwood brings out Cézanne's originality in this astonishing description:

> Then came Cézanne, and began to paint like a blind man. His still-life studies, which enshrine the essence of his genius, are like groups of things that have been groped over with the hands; he uses colour not to reproduce what he sees in looking at them but to express almost in

a kind of algebraic notation what in this groping he has felt. . . . His landscapes have lost almost every trace of visuality. Trees never looked like that; that is how they feel to a man who encounters them with his eyes shut, blundering against them blindly. A bridge is no longer a pattern of colour, . . . it is a perplexing mixture of projections and recessions, over and round which we find ourselves feeling our way as one can imagine an infant feeling its way, when it has barely begun to crawl, among the nursery furniture. And over the landscape broods the obsession of Mont Saint-Victoire, never looked at, but always felt, as a child feels the table over the back of its head.

Of course Cézanne was right. Painting can never be a visual art. A man paints with his hands, not with his eyes. The Impressionist doctrine that what one paints is light was a pedantry which failed to destroy the painters it enslaved only because they remained painters in defiance of the doctrine: men of their hands, men who did their work with fingers and wrist and arm, and even (as they walked about the studio) with their legs and toes. What one paints is what can be painted; no one can do more; and what can be painted must stand in some relation to the muscular activity of painting it.[56]

Vernon Blake had taught him to use a pencil in a sketch as if the paper were a slab of clay in which you were going to cut a relief, to find (like the sculptor) the shape hidden in its thick white texture. Collingwood takes this lesson off to the Florentine frescoes in the Brancacci chapel, marching into Masaccio's piazza and past the lovely colonnades where a heavily built and thick-bearded St. Peter is about his miraculous business.

The act of expression, as Ridley summarises things, is tied indissolubly to the medium through which it is achieved, and this is as physically, imaginatively true of music and poetry as it is of painting.[57] (It is most of all true, as Ruskin would have said, of the public art of architecture.) Expressiveness in art is the opposite of theoretic explanation, for "to describe a thing is to call it a thing of such and such a kind: to bring it under a conception, to classify it. Expression, on the contrary, individualises."[58]

So it is, I remind my readers, that a biography is always in danger of becoming mere description, of forgetting the old saw of creative writing classes, "show, don't tell," of failing Henry James's injunction, "dramatise, dramatise." Expression in the art of biography, as in all the other arts, individualises; in our master's voice, "*Expression is an activity of which there can be no technique*" (my italics), hence it is not an activity in the service of truth and truthfulness, it is those qualities actualised, individualised.

Thus the utter seriousness of art, for Collingwood and for us. It squeezes out, it eliminates the forces and passions that make for the corruption of consciousness. This latter monster, to my mind every bit as pervasive as when he turned the phrase in 1937, is that cancer of heart and mind that distorts the attention we would otherwise give to difficult or disagreeable ideas. This cancer of the mind sprouts cells of poisonous nullity, causing consciousness to make itself blind to those ideas that pain or frighten it, directing their growth into pendulous tumours of deathly inattention in which the imagination cannot seize the idea and consciousness itself as an efficacious instrument comes to a halt.

Collingwood makes a long detour through the history of the idea of ideas, agreeing with Hume that an idea is what consciousness makes of an impression. I do not propose to follow him down this road, beyond endorsing this declaration of the moral basis of mind: "A true consciousness is the confession to ourselves of our feelings; a false consciousness would be disowning them . . . soon we learn to bolster up this self-deceit by attributing the disowned experience to other people."[59] Spinoza is his master here, for whom the problem of ethics was the mastery of one's feelings such that *passio* (undergoing things) is transformed into *actio* (doing things). Once a passion is clearly understood it ceases to be a passion.

One may doubt this latter conclusion. One may think that, in a man as formidably honest with himself as Collingwood, these arguments may have acute personal relevance. The preface to *The Principles of Art* is dated 22 September 1937, and the place where it was written is given as West Hendred, a little village a mile or two away from Stapleton's Chantry, a long way from the family home

in Oxford but only a few miles up the road from Kathleen Edwardes
(by now an actress) and *her* home in Streatley. One cannot doubt
that when Collingwood writes that "the untruthful consciousness,
in disowning . . . its own experience . . . is shirking something which
its business is to face,"[60] he wouldn't allow any such evasion in his
own life.

His theory of the passions will come into greater prominence
when I turn to *The Principles of History*, never finished by his hand
and not without rough edges, but his most satisfactory treatment of
his life's topic and our most important contribution to the long effort by twentieth-century thinkers to discover a historical science of
human affairs and to persuade humankind of its primacy. But *The
Principles of Art* is, I think, Collingwood's most consummate work,
one that broke out decisively from the confines of academic philosophy and assumed the command and visibility of the first intellectual
importance. The true expressiveness that "art proper" demands
turns moral seeing from obscurity to clarity and *finds* the truth about
the moment of life that is its subject by way of its fidelity to its
medium. "Design technique"—the contemporary phrase—is of use
in this task only as teaching a respect for the medium (words, paint,
metal, gut strings, keyboard). True expressiveness is a moral discovery; the artist (and, as he and I said, all of us endeavour to be artists
in life at least some of the time) takes his or her pains in order to
find in what has been made a truthful realisation of an idea. That
idea will express both thought and the best feelings possible that
inform and embody it. Doing this well repels the evil (Collingwood's
word) of corrupt consciousness. This is good art, and insofar as an
artist (or a person) retains an uncorrupted consciousness, then the
marks of bad art are as hard and definite as stone.

The book is the grandest and most complete theory of art from
within the Romantic tradition that we have in the Anglophone or
European canon. Its tests of truthfulness in consciousness apply as
much to politics and history as to art; if corruption of consciousness
is widespread (it was then, it is now), "Intellect can build nothing
firm. Moral ideals are castles in the air. Political and economic systems are mere cobwebs. Even common sanity and bodily health

are no longer secure. *But corruption of consciousness is the same thing as bad art.*[61]

The manner is as much Ruskin's as his own. This is the intellectual as artist, the prophet armed. Conscious of his doubtful health, torn in his loyalties between home and away, he turned to face the immensity of the historical moment with his academic authority, the terrific breadth of his intellectual inheritance and command, and a quite new sense for a man of his formation of his civic and public responsibilities, and of the press of time.

V

Time pressed upon the blood vessels of his brain; on 8 February 1938, when *The Principles of Art* was in press, he wrote to his publishers to say, with typical briskness:

> On Saturday morning last I had a very slight stroke. I propose to make a rapid and satisfactory recovery, but granted that I do so I shall have to arrange matters rather differently in the future. My output of work will be very much smaller and I expect that it will be confined to what I consider to be the most immediately urgent philosophical problems. The remit should be a series of books more like *Principles of Art* than anything else I have written.[62]

It was hardly the case that he wrote less. There were at least seventeen hundred pages still to come; but he warned the Clarendon Press editors that he wouldn't be able to complete his directory of all the Roman inscriptions in Britain of which he had already taken thousands of rubbings. His archaeological work may already have begun to suffer if we believe Richmond, whose severity about the report his teacher had presented to his peers at King Arthur's Round Table at Penrith in the late summer of 1937 we have heard before ("this was high tragedy").

He had stayed on that occasion with Ethel at the Queen's Head in Tirril for a couple of nights in early July. Digging began at 8:00 a.m. (Mr. Cruddas the foreman), and the men had worked their way down three feet below the modern bottom. They found five hearths by 4:30 on the second day. Harold Joachim came to visit with his wife, and so did sister Ursula. Collingwood knew for sure what he would find and did. Uncontainable haste was upon him. There was everything to finish. There was a winter's heavy writing to do, and the fearsome shock of the stroke would only bring a short pause.

His recovery was to be neither rapid nor satisfactory. After some delay, his doctor dispatched him to a friend of Collingwood's, Tom Nelson in Harley Street, whose advice, like all doctors' advice, was optimistic enough about the "arterial spasms" (in his phrase) and that "Robin must do very much less."[63] He thought there was no reason why Collingwood should not live "another twenty years." He overbid by fourteen years.

Doing less meant doing lots, but differently. He had decided, as he pondered illness and marriage, to buy a yacht. The solitary practice of the art of sailing is the most exigent, the most physical, the most serene, and the most dangerous of those artful sports that compress into their forms a complete model of the human comedy. Since boyhood it had provided for Collingwood the hermitage in and from which he followed the vocation of his thought. Now, confronting mortal illness and the fierce pull of a love affair with a woman twenty years his junior, sailing not just at Coniston but on the open sea would provide the necessary discipline of art by means of which he could think out and live through this peripetaia of biographical passion, and turn that passion into action.

The yacht in question was built to order, a Z-class 3.3-tonner designed by Thomas Harrison Butler, an ophthalmologist who was also a self-taught yacht designer, and won a high reputation for designing small and famously sweet-handling yachts at a time when heavy weather helms for reaching (and heeling) were the convention. The sloop had a small, undependable two-stroke engine and was a short twenty-one feet nine inches in length, with a mainsail and a jib. Below, its owner would sit on either of the long, narrow bench bunks running down each side of the cabin with a bare inch or two above his head. She was stylishly tailored of oak and elm frames, and splined planking.[64] Obliged to find a name beginning with Z because of her class, Collingwood named her *Zenocrate,* or the power of Zeus, also occasionally bestowed upon the female form. The quotation from Marlowe's *Conquest of Tamburlaine* was a sardonic one much to Collingwood's taste, the more so given the sticky end to which Marlowe's hero came.

> Now walk the angels on the walls of heaven,
> As sentinels to warn the immortal souls,
> To entertain divine Zenocrate . . .
> Ah fair Zenocrate, divine Zenocrate,
> Fair is too foul an epithet for thee.

Under the doctor's orders issued in March, Collingwood had applied for sick leave for a year beginning with the Trinity term; it was promptly granted. On 23 May he sent one of his regular family postcards to his beloved sister Barbara, always "My Darling" in his letters, saying: "I join my ship tomorrow at Brentford, sail on Tuesday at 11.50am (high tide) . . . on Tu night I shall sleep at anchor somewhere in the Thames . . . through the Downs into the Channel."[65]

Even for someone of his sailing experience, it was no slight task to learn to handle his new craft, frail enough as she was, with no radio and a feeble engine if in trouble. He took a few days making shortish expeditions out of Gravesend Basin to acclimatise himself. On 31 May he had a late lunch at the Lobster Smack and heard from the landlord, an old ferryman, that "the wireless forecast is for gales in the south-west." Collingwood was aiming to cross the Channel, but if things became rough he would put in to Ramsgate and shelter until it passed. He intended to be away from home for at least three months.

By 9:00 a.m. *Zenocrate* was rounding Lower Hope Point on her way to sea while her captain took soundings where the Yantlet sand flats reach out several cables from the shore to trap any careless sailor cutting the corner on a falling tide. Then as the Medway opened up to starboard, he entered deep water, was swept past the Isle of Sheppey, its low cliffs catching the morning sun, by the Medway ebb. He was steering by compass southeast by east, the little oil lamp in its shiny new copper binnacle lighting the azimuth line along the compass card. Wind and tide were too strong to round North Foreland that morning; he made it back to Margate and moored in a jam-packed harbour, the wind clapping the halliards above his head, and there ate the sailor's staple of a bread and cheese lunch, having lost his glasses at anchor and found them again at low tide.

On the morning of 1 June he was up before 6:00, breakfasted on eggs fried on the little primus, and peered out of the cabin into strong rain and force 4 winds. He was eager to be properly at sea and happy and exultant in his new boat. He waited a few hours with seamanlike caution, however, and, when the wind abated slightly, allowed the ebb tide to take him, well reefed, east, fast, past the line of buoys marking Gore Channel and then out of the shelter of the North Kent coast as he rounded North Foreland, the very furthest tip of southeast England. He was now close to the point at which Caesar had made his first, unsuccessful landing in Britain, and with the wind veering south, the Goodwin Sands stretching menacingly close, the long history of maritime disaster crashed into his bows and filled the deep cockpit with twelve inches of thrashing sea.

The Times report of that night's weather brought news of snow across the Lake District, marquees blown away at Epsom races, trees blocking railway lines, and gales up to 90 mph all along the south coast. Lamb reports "a small but intense depression moving eastwards from the Channel mouth some 600 miles in the twenty-four hours from 1pm."[66]

On *Zenocrate* it was as much as the helmsman could do to hold the tiller and stop himself being thrown against the side of the cockpit. He was wearing oilskins but was drenched right through, the cabin was half-flooded, the boat pitching violently, the danger of a standing gybe breaking the mast immediate. There weren't many choices. Making either Dover or Ramsgate would demand prodigious feats of seamanship. The only thing to do seemed to be to heave to and let the current carry him south of the treacherous sands, hoping the gale would ease before he was swept right out into the Channel. Loose on the churning sea, *Zenocrate* no longer rode the waves but wallowed between their eight-foot crests; he needed to pump as a matter of utmost urgency and to lash the helm. Kneeling on the cockpit sole, he opened the cabin hatch as far as he dared for the flares secured on the rack just inside. He let off two to windward and managed to steady the little yacht enough to heave to.

The Deal lifeboat, as *The Times* reports, was one of seven out that night, and it took Collingwood in tow as *Zenocrate* "was driving ashore."[67] He later disclaimed to Tom Hopkinson that he had told the lifeboatman he believed he would founder at any moment. But then he had his pride as a sailor and rarely admitted to either error or failure. Indeed, he wasn't a man who much permitted what William Empson so well called "the mind's recoil upon itself"; he wrote, spoke, and lived with calm assurance, massive rectitude, swiftness of decision, an attractive levity of spirit and manner allied to a settled conviction as to his own rightness, in thought and conduct.

The stout frame of that integrity was under acute physical and emotional stress. On 29 July his log records his beginning *An Autobiography* still on board *Zenocrate*. On 28 August out at sea, a fresh stroke hit him. For two days he lay below on his bunk with a blinding headache, able to move only blunderingly. He was anchored in deep water. He could not sail.

Now he had his moral crisis. He was coming to the end of his fifty sessions of psychoanalysis, a process no so serious a person could undergo unshaken; he had unmistakably fallen in love with Kathleen Edwardes—it is the only phrase to describe the headlong recklessness with which a world-distinguished professor in the dead centre of 1930s' Oxonian respectability openly kept company with a beautiful actress and former student; he was stricken with mortal illness from which he could no longer "propose to make a rapid and satisfactory recovery."

The specialist, Tom Nelson, he returned to in early September knew already what sort of man sat on the other side of the desk. He counselled, as medical people did in those days, a long cruise, but one on which he should carry on writing. There was then a surgical procedure for too high blood pressure, one in which the nerve that contracts the blood vessels was cut. It was irrevocable. The patient declined it.[68] Collingwood duly arranged his cruise—six months to

Java and back, starting at the end of October—but fell to writing at once anyway.

The result was the 167 pages of his best-known and surely classic work, *An Autobiography*. Insofar as the story told in this biography is an extended gloss on his own story, quoted here many times already, I shall not treat it at great length. But it *is* a classic in the genre, written with a heat, a colloquialism, an assumption of a newly public but not conventionally academic manner, written also with a pungency and partisanship that caused his more timid colleagues at Oxford, when it came out in the summer of 1939, to murmur among themselves that Collingwood had gone over to the Communists.

He himself saw it more simply. "People certainly won't take the book in the spirit in which it is written, and a lot of them will be very angry. I wrote it because I was told that I was dying, and thought it time a few home truths began sitting on my lips."[69]

He began writing in late July and finished it in October, convalescing at Lanehead, by then his sculptor sister Barbara's home. She was his confidante, always, and his refuge. After Dorrie, her mother, died, Barbara Gnosspelius had looked after her father for the last four years of his life, similarly punctuated by a series of minor but progressively lethal strokes.

The book is the story of the thinker's thought, rapid in pace, brisk in manner, impassioned in feeling. Indeed, it sharply modifies (by its example) the theory of the passions propounded in *The Principles of Art*. There, Collingwood speaks of bringing the passions under control, of (with Spinoza) turning *passio* into *actio*, of a passion understood as a passion dispelled. Here, more winningly and as it seems to me more accurately, the emotions give thought its form. The larger and more comprehensive they are, the better chosen the distance from which they do their work, the truer and more permanent the thought.

So the scorn expressed for "the minute philosophers" clarifies and fixes the intellectual insight better than the glassy "objectivity" commended in *The Essay on Philosophical Method*. The Waynflete professor's vocation being mind and metaphysics, scorn and anger at the dereliction of duty displayed, as he judged, by his parent generation of philosophers, give his prose and thought a terrific zing, a

purity of an icy, accurate sort quite unlike the strenuous, tiny dis-
tillations of Prichard and company. In a rousing and lucid polemic,
Collingwood arraigns his prisoners not just with disappointing their
students, but with preparing the ground for what W. B. Yeats called
"the phantoms of hatred and the coming emptiness." In T. H.
Green's Oxford, young people on the threshold of life, perhaps of
public life, "had been told that by thinking about what they were
doing, or were about to do, they would become likely on the whole
to do it better; and that some understanding of the nature of moral
or political action, some attempt to formulate ideals and principles,
was an indispensable condition of engaging creditably in these activities themselves."[70]

T. H. Green's school of philosophers gave to Collingwood's father's generation of students "ideals to live for and principles to live
by"; the new doctrinaires left their students to drift on a tideless
ocean, "the dupes of every adventurer in morals or politics." If it
seems a bit hard to blame Cook Wilson or even Freddie Ayer for
intellectual helplessness when faced with Fascism, it is as well to
have recalled to us by a later chapter in *An Autobiography* just how
desperate things were, what Armageddon impended worldwide, how
threadbare its author's home civilisation looked after years of needless slump, of cowardly or greedy indifference (to India, to Abyssinia,
to Spain, to Czechoslovakia), of famine and plague and war.

Collingwood gathers and reassembles his fortifications for the
mind's protection against the phantoms of hatred: question-and-
answer logic, historicism as the method to attain the self-knowledge
of mind, the unity of theory and practice, the supercession of science
by history. Then, in a grand finale, he turns both reason and rhetoric
upon the moment of 1938.

It is in this conclusion that he most plausibly appears as one of
Britain's best, lost intellectuals of the 1930s. Yet this ringing sermon
occupies merely the last twenty pages of a brief autobiography submitted to the University Press in November 1938 to a rather mixed
reception, as many (including especially F. A. Lindemann, a man of
bellicose respectability and an experimental physicist, and W. D.
Ross, philosopher provost of Oriel) of the press's delegates being
indeed offended by his tone and undoubted *hauteur* as others (A. D.

Lindsay) were stirred and convinced by its moral sureness and political force. As Collini bluntly says, the periodicals for which he wrote, the very manners of his prose were "the print equivalent of those groups of conventionally suited gentlemen who met in the sorts of discussion and dining clubs which seemed so to proliferate in the years before the Second World War and who still managed to think of themselves as 'the country'—or at any rate as the part of it that really mattered."[71] As we saw, Collingwood attended several such groups in the 1920s, and although he speaks, a bit pharisaically, in the *Autobiography* of his growing isolation from his colleagues in the 1930s, there is no doubting his assumption of an audience out there (where "there" isn't much farther away than Broad Street and the High), divided amongst itself for sure, but needful, "mattering" to the country, at once certain of that country's significance and proud of it, as well as much afraid at its present pass.

So his rather moving statement of faith in parliamentary democracy and his malediction over the debasing of the yellow press are spoken for sure from a particular position in a social class. How could they not be? But their calm forcefulness sounds an appeal to a larger audience than could get into the Sheldonian. At this distance, with an even yellower press in Britain about which one can only feel shame, Collingwood's strictures look almost mild. And when he turns from the dizzy, delusive, and poisonous distortions of the press to the cowardice and cynicism of the then government, he brings together the unspoken patriotism of Lakelander "statesmen," their gritty independence, and a larger summons to high-minded (but reasonable) principles and resolute (but domestic) courage, which would have rung true to many more people than ever read it. He names for what it was the moral failure of parliamentary Britain when the Falangistes set the Spanish Army against the Spanish Parliament; when he looks homeward he finds a public mind corrupted but not unredeemable, an ineffectual but not a doomed democracy, and he pledges himself to oppose with all his strength systems of thought and forms of education that fail to provide, as they ought, "ideals to live for and principles to live by," ideals and principles which might be embodied in a free and intelligent press, which would vivify parliamentary debate, which would impel "professional thinkers" like himself to "break up the pose of detachment," to engage with a full awareness in the political struggle, "fighting not in the dark but in the daylight."

VI

You can see why some of the delegates and editors at the Clarendon Press were a bit rattled when they got the manuscript of *An Autobiography*. It wasn't so much the comical discrepancy between the realist philosophers as "propagandists of a coming Fascism" and the boots, banners, and tanks of Nuremberg that was the trouble; it was the effort at destruction of a whole class manner, what a later intellectual called "those quiet voices, the composed manners . . . that keep suggesting there is nothing whatever to hide: all is purest rationality and normality . . . the appearance of frankness, of that cool but always available politeness is the most effective collective disguise I have ever encountered, and for my own part I have given up asking it questions. I look for my answers in what they do."[72]

Back in the twenty-first century, it is easy to see why the *Autobiography* has remained in print pretty well since it first came out and is the best known of all Collingwood's work.[73] For all its veeringness between philosophy at Oxford and crisis in the European mind, it admonishes the reader to see thought in action, to respond eagerly to the fact that theory and practice are conjoined, not only to feel but to understand that history is all we have to learn from (God makes no appearance in *An Autobiography*), that public life is privately sanctioned and that the private citizen owes a public duty, and owes it in terms of his or her thoughts and ideas about the conduct of society.

Of course, another seventy years of individualism and all the companion "isms" of reach-me-down social explanation (consumerism, globalism, managerialism, narcissism) have eaten away at any picture of the common good, collective rationality, the good society, and so forth. But I will risk saying that Collingwood's biography rests above all upon the foundation of this single book. Without it, his work and life would signify much less to us; would be, that is, far less of an intelligible shape and force, such as to come through into our future with a distinctive, characterful, ardent presence. We know from this book what those qualities were that make him tell, not without a contradictory grandeur, in our lives and of those, let us say, no further forward than our grandchildren's.

8

The Valley of the Shadows: Java, Oxford, Greece

The stroke that Collingwood suffered while at sea on *Zenocrate* in August was more serious than that in February and more ominous. A transient ischaemic attack, once called apoplexy, indicates that the brain is not getting enough blood and therefore enough oxygen. Debris thrust upwards by high blood pressure from the carotid arteries into the tiny vessels that supply the brain becomes temporarily stuck, and a variety of symptoms follow, either major ones like impairment of arm or leg movements or of speech, or minor ones such as numbness of limb, pins and needles, blurred vision. This latest laid him flat, the symptoms only lasting briefly enough but the aftermath exhausting. Computer tomography scanning was still thirty-four years in the future; all that could be done in 1938 was to log the symptomatic patterns. There would be several more strokes to come, and then the last.

Earlier the same year, his friend and pupil Malcolm Knox, now a professor at the University of St. Andrews, who has always revered his teacher if a bit reprovingly, had successfully nominated Collingwood for an honorary doctorate, but much gratified though the recipient of course was, he was prevented by the illness from attending the ceremony and only met with Knox sometime later to have his hand shaken and receive his congratulations.

He was due to sail in late October on his restorative cruise from the Mersey to the Dutch East Indies, to do the Far Eastern sights, listen to gamelan concerts, watch the mummers, stay in a series of private houses with Dutch hosts, walk gently up the mountains, and, for his very peace of mind, continue to write.

Public life in Oxford would certainly be doing little for his peace of mind, or anyone else's. At the very end of September, Neville Chamberlain, prime minister, had solved to his own satisfaction "a quarrel in a faraway country between people of whom we know nothing" (as he unforgettably put it). As all the world knows, he did so by signing away, without that faraway nation's consent or even their attendance at the meeting, the *Sudetenland* of Czechoslovakia, thereby consigning it to Fascist Germany and its imperious chancellor. Chamberlain was rapturously received at Croydon airport and brazenly voiced his shameful slogan, "peace with honour," but the country was radically split and its name, not infrequently linked to perfidy, disgraced in the eyes of millions of its people.

There was by coincidence a parliamentary bye-election due in Oxford on 27 October. Some of the brightest as well as most public-spirited of the younger Oxford dons, progressive members of the Labour Party, petitioned A. D. (Sandy) Lindsay to oppose the Tory candidate (Oxford was reckoned a safe enough Tory seat) not for a political party but as an Independent standing on the issue of foreign policy.

Lindsay was a formidable choice. He had just completed a tour of duty as vice chancellor, he was master of Balliol, the most intellectually ferocious of Oxford's colleges (where Bill Collingwood was studying at the time), we have already encountered his name as a star pupil in *Literae Humaniores* ten years before Collingwood's time, a pillar of the T. H. Green tradition, high-minded, idealist in ethics as in philosophy, sympathetic to socialism and member of the Labour Party, eventually prime mover, founder, and first head of the egalitarian University of Keele.

It is a rare thing to have such a person as parliamentary candidate, and Lindsay took on the task with terrific bravura and iron principle but against all his inclinations except the call to duty. He was fifty-nine, he wanted a break, he was to visit his daughter in India, he said no, went to bed, and "woke up next morning, turned to his wife and said, 'Oh God, I've got to stand for Parliament.' "[1]

He was supported by assorted patriotic Tories in the university as well as others of the same kidney in Parliament (notably Harold Macmillan as well as Churchill, then a party outlaw), and the Oxford Union, the university undergraduates' mock parliament, passed a motion during the election campaign "That this House deplores the Government's policy of peace *without* honour."

The Liberal and Labour candidates, after some reluctance, agreed to stand down (Patrick Gordon Walker, the Labour man and a later cabinet minister, only with a bad grace). The heir apparent Tory, an invincibly sanctimonious and sharpshooting career politician of subsequent eminence called Quintin Hogg, prated of "thankfulness for the peace that has come . . . an opportunity . . . to create permanent peace in our time," words by which he remained apparently unhaunted during his thirty subsequent years in office.

For it is dismaying, even after seventy years, to report that Lindsay was defeated. The Tory majority was halved, however, and two very unexpected defeats for the craven government followed in bye-elections in Dartford and Bridgwater. Chamberlain's days in power were numbered. The students, including Edward Heath and Denis Healey, turned out to canvass for Lindsay, and so, unusually, did the staff, R. H. Tawney and John Austin among them. Collingwood, packing his bags for Java, wrote:

My dear Lindsay

I am leaving for the East tomorrow but I cannot go without sending you my deepest good wishes for your success in your candidature. I do not think that the country has ever in all its history passed through a graver crisis than that in which it is now involved. I am appalled by the apathy with which our situation is regarded by a great many of us and by the success which the government has had in keeping the country as a whole from knowing the truth. Your candidature shows that the spirit of English democracy is not extinct. I hope that it still survives among those who have to vote next week.[2]

The country's gravest crisis in its history? That seems still about right. He had just completed his analysis of these events in exactly the same spirit in the *Autobiography,* beside Coniston three weeks previously. Lindsay, incarnation of Collingwood's own moral tradition, produced the line, as he ought, from theory to practice. Collingwood left him to it.

II

Collingwood abandoned Oxford a week before polling day and left Britain to the care of the appeasers with every appearance of eager anticipation of his first ever extended departure from Europe, brief visits to his sister in Aleppo and to Jerusalem excepted. Favourite sister Barbara Gnosspelius came down from Coniston to see him off at Birkenhead where he arrived on 21 October. They dined at the Queen's, and he boarded Motor Vessel *Alcinous*, legendary mother of Ulysses' lover Nausicaa, Dutch registered out of Rotterdam, to be greeted by her grizzled, experienced captain, Mijnheer Koningstein of the Blue Funnel line, and to be up betimes the next morning to watch the tugs draw the ship out into the Mersey and begin the month's journey to Java.[3]

Cruises occupied a place on the homeopathic list of palliatives for general practitioners in the 1930s a little way below "daily walks." They released the patient from professional and domestic duties, provided daily doses of tranquil seascape, and were much believed to alleviate the symptoms of overwork and what is nowadays, in the no less credulous waiting rooms of folk medicine, diagnosed as stress.

MV *Alcinous* wasn't without stressfulness. But for a sailor rescued from *Zenocrate*, the white-painted little cabins with a single brass porthole and the solid metal bulkheads with their rows of rivets all part of the décor brought homeliness from home at once. Then, by the time the ship had raised Finistere on a "fine, clear night" two days later, Captain Konigstein had been made sufficiently aware of his distinguished passenger's compulsions to have rigged up an awning on his very own bridge where Collingwood began to write the *Essay on Metaphysics* as they entered the Bay of Biscay.

He had brought with him a little case of books, a *Collected Plays* of Racine among them, which he read right through, Racine's perilous balancing of taut alexandrine couplets holding back the desperate licence of transgression, of love and lust in Phèdre and Berénice perhaps answering something in his own heart. He also intended to teach himself Malay during the trip and brought a primer with him to that end, to stand in a small stack beside some Agatha Christie and Dorothy L. Sayers, Beatrice Webb's *Autobiography* (intellectual and beautiful doyenne of the Labour Party, "a very good and interesting piece of work"), Benedetto Croce, and "the illiterate autobiography of the exhibitionist vulgarian, M. Asquith, equally revolting from a literary and a moral point of view."

None of these bore upon the *Essay on Metaphysics*, to whose argument we shall return but of which he wrote, in his usual way, parts 1, 2, and 3B (about 50,000 words) in sixteen days of work without reference books or conversation. He was taking butobarbital, a strong soporific, for his insomnia, but it did not have an impact on his writing. The weather was hot, and in three days at the end of October, established on the lower bridge between Malta and Port Said, he polished off his fullest statement of his theory of absolute presuppositions and wrote his declaration of metaphysics as a historical science. By 3 November, interrupted by the sudden death of a fellow yachtsman and passenger, "Skipper" Lynam (as it happened, his son Bill's sometime headmaster at the Dragon School), also trying but failing to hold off mortal illness, whose papers Collingwood then undertook to sort out, he had done his demolition work on "the pseudo-science" of psychology.

He kept up this dedicated schedule as the ship made its calm and easy voyage through the Suez Canal, past "the extraordinarily savage and rocky" Arabian coast, eastwards out into "the smooth sea and gentle swell" of the Indian Ocean with Kant in his sights, until finally the rains came and he was driven into his cabin where his neighbours made a lot of noise and broke up his always broken sleep. On 17 November *Alcinous* entered Padang in Sumatra, and Collingwood sufficiently forgave his noisy neighbours to go with them and a couple of the engineers to "the flicks" (Anglophone of course) before sitting drinking in the Dutch club until the small hours. All of Indonesia was then the Dutch East Indies, slaughterously pacified by the Dutch Army in 1906 and thereafter pacific enough.

Alcinous made her leisurely way down the Sumatran coast before turning west through the Sunda Straits and docking at Batavia, now Jakarta. Jakarta in those days was pretty much as Singapore was, which is to say a huge, unplanned, jammed and untidy harbour front leading to its two demarcated districts, the one more or less a shanty town with the riot, colour, clutter, and unbelievably frail and battered shelters of native thousands in the manner of the imperial Orient, the other a miniature northern European capital with Victorian Gothic churches, embassies, clubs, hotels, all with stone porticos and steps and heavily rusticated dark stone walls. Collingwood enjoyed himself happily under the guidance of a former student and his wife who lived there and who showed him the sights for two or three days, including walks in the jungle, a trip to admire the three thousand-metre mountains, the Chinese temples, and to watch the fireworks of Islam's New Year.

He also picked up his mail. These people were indomitable letter-writers-and-answerers, and he found letters from Malcolm Knox, from sisters Barbara and Ursula, from his wife Ethel, and from Kathleen Edwardes. Naturally he replied to them all; there were plenty more to come from both Ethel and Kathleen. Home was Oxford, Coniston, even Streatley also, and as such foolish, passionate men always are, he was homesick in spite of himself, always checking for his mail in the poste restante, even while contented enough in the guise of tourist. He wound his way from Batavia the slender length of Java, emerging distinctly shaken by encounters with boy prostitutes and unappeased by its being explained to him that "tourists generally like buggery." There were hospitable and prearranged sojourns with various Dutch families, and on 7 December he crossed the straits in a little steamer to Bali.

Bali was at the time well on the way to becoming the boom-centre for tourists in search of the exotic, caught for ever in the *New Yorker* cartoon, when the breathy young American bursts into the travel agents to ask, "is Bali . . . er . . . still Bali?" Of course the number of tourists in 1938 was still tiny, and getting there took a very long time. But the matriarch of all anthropologists, Margaret Mead, was frequently on the island even then, with her husband Gregory Bateson, preparing the materials for their joint work on Bali,[4] and she had already done much in her work to persuade the cultivated classes of Britain and North America that the islands of the Indian Ocean were little Edens, particularly as to child-rearing and family life, the cheery little products of which, she fondly asserted, were healthily disinhibited (plenty of candid genital manipulation—this, as Collingwood ruefully knew, was the heyday of Melanie Klein), while being instructed in an emotional schedule oscillating between spurts of intense passion and long periods of expressionless passivity.

The theatres of Balinese life are its juiciest expressions of these intermittent "spurts," and Collingwood attended, as part of his anthropological fieldwork undertaken with characteristic thoroughness, displays of dance-and-trance, the unforgettable theatre of the hideous witch and the clowning dragon, and listened with far more than dutiful pleasure to gamelan concerts and recitations ("pentatonic scale ... highly wrought and satisfying music"), sometimes until four in the morning. And he attended several cockfights, now unmentionable except in the company of Clifford Geertz's famous essay,[5] originating in his visit to Bali in 1958, which unlocks the mystery of the cockfight, Balinese life at its most spurting, its central fact the cock in all senses, its meaning in its dramatic shape (blood, feathers, shrieks), its metaphoric content (your cock against mine), its social context (heavy gambling, passionate rivalry). I don't doubt that, folklorist as he was, Collingwood intuited some of these things.

He met and befriended an expatriate German artist called Walter Spies trying to paint with the childlike freedom of Chagal and Klee. Over three consecutive days in December, he attended a series of musical performances and dances, some lasting from late afternoon until after midnight, and picked up enough local knowledge to recognise *Gamboeh*. This is the ancestral shade from whom all Balinese dance-forms derive, whose voice is heard when, at temple feast or cremation, the mummers in their gold headdresses and brocaded robes are roused and transfigured as never before by magic strains

and clashes from the flutes and bells, dominating the rippling gam-
elans and lending the ceremony a weird, novel, and antique beauty.
Over lunch on the third day (17 December), "soup, rijstafel, yurn
cake, fruit, coffee. Good," he learned from Walter Spies that "the
compositions they were playing (one of amazing rhythmical complexity and terrific bravura) was a Balinese symphony which two
players had learned by heart in three days, and had taught to the rest
less than a week ago."

Collingwood lived during the time in Bali in that receptive, admiring, glad, and astonished frame of mind that belongs to the anthropological tourist and, in Bali especially, addles the brain of the
brightest visitor, even if Collingwood missed what Geertz calls "the
ground-bass of passionless horror" that becomes audible in Bali after
a longer stay.[6]

He wrote regularly to both Ethel and Kathleen, to Ursula, Barbara,
and his son Bill, and heard punctually back, took a trio of Dutch
steamers plying the northern coasts of the Indonesian islands towards Flores and Timor, was unwell for some days with the diarrhoea
that is also part of anthropological duties, walked indomitably in
heat until on 23 January he was badly bitten by a malignant insect
and severely infected so that he couldn't get his shoes on for a week.

The Collingwood found in this staccato, fairly detailed log is a
much more gregarious character than the compulsive writer-thinker
of his past few years. He falls easily into new company, is taken on
long walks and drives with new friends, photographs assiduously,
earnestly notes local agricultural methods as well as local artistry
(there is no word for art or artist in these parts, says Walter Spies).
He is untouched by the seasickness that flattens his fellow passengers
but on 1 February is reminded of the attentions of his grim companion when he feels his left leg trailing ("inhaled amyl nitrate in case,"
increasing oxygen to and dilating the blood vessels of the heart).
Then he went on as before, ignoring the other's presence.

Letters collected at Macascar on the isle of Flores included one
from his friend, Kenneth Sisam, the most senior editor at the
Clarendon Press, warning him that the delegates had the wind up
about the last chapter of the *Autobiography*, as being highly conten-

tious, splenetic about the government, censorious of Oxford philosophy, and generally liable to create a fuss, also advising that the proofs were on their way to the Far East. Collingwood was not so much unmoved as gratified by the impending row; it was why he wrote the book.

The correspondence with Sisam sent him back to his cabin desk. The *Essay on Metaphysics* was done, except for further revisions (which admittedly would involve him in rewriting whole chapters). Fired by sudden, bright energy, on 9 February he drafted a sketch for a new work, long in his mind and of a piece with what became *The Idea of Nature* and was already begun in *The Principles of Art.*

This was to be *The Principles of History*, now promoted over philosophy to top of the scale of knowledgeable forms. On berthing the next day back on the northern coast of Java, he checked into the hotel and started to write rapidly. He wrote for all of the following week, saying with exhilaration in a letter on 14 February to his son Bill at Balliol that it was to be the book by which he would be content to be remembered, the one he had it in him to write best, his "masterpiece."[7] His poisoned bites wouldn't heal; he kept to his room and wrote—wrote forty thousand words by early April.

By 21 February writing from 5:00 a.m., he was in the grip of the book. Irritated by noisy guests in his hotel, he took the Java Express back to Jakarta. He "had been long enough in Dutch East Indies." The next morning he booked a passage on SS *Rhesus*, leaving 4 March, wrote to Ethel to tell her so, and collected and began to check the proofs of the *Autobiography.* He spent the rest of his time in Jakarta rewriting the *Essay on Metaphysics*, did a bit of extravagant shopping (for "fairings" to take home), bought himself a hundred cigars for the journey, and duly sailed at 6:00 p.m. on 4 March, finding *Rhesus* a friendly ship, its passengers "all North Country people, thank God, and very sweet," and sealed his departure with a large gin with some of the officers.

He worked at the three books all the way home, rewriting the offending last chapter, no less on the offensive, of the *Autobiography*, disagreeably interrupted by a villainous lobster mayonnaise that upset the interiors of most passengers and officers, sharpening the metaphysics book, "playing with" *The Principles of History.* The food poisoning knocked him out for several days, but he kept at the proofs and wrote to Kenneth Sisam from Port Sudan to post them off and to say he knew there would be trouble. Letters from Ethel and Kathleen were at Suez to greet him, and he was still queasy and living off poached eggs at the end of March.

On All Fools' Day, with the Spanish mountains visible, listening to the Boat Race on the ship's wireless, he felt better. With Cape St. Vincent in sight, he wrote by way of its preface his farewell to the *Essay on Metaphysics* and began to brace himself for a homecoming that, in his divided state—pulled, in his reticent, self-contained way, between the fixed points of duty and desire, death and the onward drive of his mind—would be both glad and tormented. Tired and restored at once, he looked over the *Metaphysics* and reckoned that job well enough done, and *An Autobiography* on its way to make its little explosion among the three hundred or so professional philosophers in British universities, and at the very least to bear its honourable witness to the dishonour done to Britain's good name and the solidarity of democracies by a disgraced government.[8] As he set in italics in *New Leviathan,* "*A man's duty . . . is the act which for him is both possible and necessary: the act which . . . character and circumstance combine to make it inevitable . . . that he should freely will to do.*"[9]

III

The *Essay on Metaphysics* had pretty well been written in a first draft with few gaps by the time Collingwood reached Java, and after all the specialist had told him to rest by writing; his captain had constructed him his writing room; he had need (as we know Collini puts it)[10] neither of library nor of interlocutors but enjoyed the "perfect conditions" of solitude and monolocution.[11] By the Christmas of 1938 he had forty thousand words written; during November he wrote to the Clarendon Press, saying: "I have been for a long time contemplating a short book which should explain to the public what

Metaphysics is, what it is for, how it works, and why the various people who clamour for its abolition ought not to be listened to."[12]

His intended audience is, he says, "public," and indeed the book is in part written with touches of that not unattractive arrogance of *An Autobiography*, that go-to-blazes and colloquial polemic that makes its predecessor such a cracking read. At the same time, even allowing for its large and handsome typeface, the thing is 354 pages in length, formidably abstract in manner, its concrete examples of actuality taken from the works of other philosophers, and is assigned by its author in the blurb as second in a series of philosophical essays of which the 1933 essay on method was the first. If this is what it was for him to address a wider public and attempt its enlightenment, then it is plain just how badly the isolation of a too-technical language as well as the ingrained habits of his way of life had damaged his self-awareness and the simple knowledge of what other people can stand. The gregarious Collingwood and the "steel-blue, polished" solitary mocked with affection by Arthur Ransome were constantly transposing themselves in his being. He was pulled as strongly towards boisterous popularity and genial membership as he was towards his voyaging on strange seas of thought as well as the irresistible loneliness of the unplumbed and estranging ocean itself.

Hence the difficult mixture of the *Essay on Metaphysics*. His habitual poise is most ill-at-ease when he treats, from memory but with perfect accuracy, A. J. Ayer's disdainful repudiation of metaphysics in *Language, Truth and Logic* by which, as we heard, he was much impressed,[13] and which, in its swift, heartless, confident way, *did* address (and persuade) a common readership, catching just the crest of a wave of unbelief sweeping through the literary weeklies, the extramural classes as well as the bright young undergraduates.

Taking on Ayer and the logical positivists, Collingwood nonetheless convicts his opponents of mistaking presuppositions for propositions, for propositions ("that is a table," "this is a fact") are the positivist's sole business, and anything not a proposition is "meaningless," a judgement as to value being a mere expression of emotion. If you are betrayed by someone you love and trust, you might as well say "Boo!" "Boo!" would have the same standing and relevance as any moral elaboration of the matter.

Collingwood, as we may imagine, hated the argument while admiring the style. Ayer's scientific criterion for all propositions of "verifiability" fails to grasp the function in life of the "absolute presuppositions" we must make if we are to think at all. It is, moreover, worth adding at this point Collingwood's timely reservation on the use made, by philosophers in particular, of the pronoun "we,"[14] asking to know who "we" are, and answering that "our" identity is largely rhetorical, in some cases being those who think like the author (and are therefore in the right), in others those who don't (and are therefore in the wrong).

Ayer—for this is what it is to be a positivist—has not understood that he too has his "absolute presuppositions" that there is no verifying. Verifiability is itself one such. Metaphysics, on the other hand, deals in what cannot be verified but is a matter, as it would usually be put, of belief. But belief is an elastic condition, and presuppositions are not held in the way one holds a belief, say, in the goodness (or wickedness) of a certain class of persons, or a belief that dark thunderclouds presage rain, or even a belief that tomorrow is Thursday. One cannot, as I put it (with D. H. Lawrence) earlier, get around the back of an absolute presupposition; "as lief get round behind the sun." Collingwood's prime example is the positivists' presupposition that everything has a cause, and causation itself is intrinsic not to the practice of modern physics (then the most advanced form of science) but to the positivists' picture of what science is.

Collingwood returns with admiration in this argument to a paper Bertrand Russell had given to the Aristotelian Society "on the notion of a cause" back in 1912, and which he had read for himself in the last year of the war, when he was a junior making preparations, as the Allies at last broke through the German lines, for the Versailles Peace Conference. Russell pointed out that modern physics does *not* presuppose causation. Collingwood completes the dictum: the twentieth-century physics of Planck, Einstein, Rutherford, and (at work as he wrote) Heisenberg presupposed *laws*. All Collingwood's efforts at this point in the book (part 1) are to historicise metaphysics. This means that when he reports that Spinoza says that Nature is the same thing as God, this is not his "metaphysical doctrine" but a statement of "historical fact about the religious foundation of seventeenth-century natural science."[15] Absolute presuppositions are not components in an explicit theory; they are more like aspects of a culture, itself a concept that makes particular features damnably hard to pick out but whose presence in thought and conduct is as certain as the water one swims in.

Water is, however, analysable; even if once analysed into hydrogen and oxygen, it is no longer water. It is also thick and thin, heavier and lighter, salt and fresh, stagnant and flowing, all these attributes regulated by laws capable of formulation by human minds presupposing such things as, for their purposes, real. The idea of law (or a cause or, come to that, a God) is necessary for the time being, but not changeless. Indeed a main conclusion of this historical metaphysics is that nothing is changeless and that an absolute presupposition is unprovable. Descartes doubted everything until he got down to the *cogito*, the fact that he *thought*, and that he couldn't doubt that he thought was the presupposition he came down to, which turned out, as he discoursed upon method, to be pretty well absolute.

For, as Collingwood concludes, truth conditions cannot be demanded of absolute presuppositions. He was coming to much the same conclusions about proof and its lack of purchase upon the frameworks of thought as was Wittgenstein over the same years. Wittgenstein had already written in the *Tractatus*, "scepticism is not irrefutable, but obviously nonsensical when it tries to raise doubts where no questions can be asked,"[16] and then, in relation to the work posthumously published as *On Certainty*, he said: "Certain propositions belong to my 'frame of reference.' If I had to give *them* up, I shouldn't be able to judge *anything*."[17]

This is much the point of Collingwood's identification of absolute presuppositions. There has been much perspiration shed on what these confounded things are, and Rex Martin, in his admirable introduction to the *Essay on Metaphysics*, points out that question-and-answer logic seems like (but isn't) a "neat ground" for the claim that truth-tests don't help. Question-and-answer logic doesn't help because absolute presuppositions are neither question-posing nor answer-providing. Their purpose is to give form and meaning to the procedures of practical rationality in a given history. They are not, as Louis Mink supposes, "*a priori* concepts," which is not Collingwood's kind of language at all.[18] They are integral to the practice of a science, human or natural, inseparable from the actions that do the presupposing. Martin calls them "objective patterns or structures in our way of knowing . . . neither right nor wrong, true nor false, they just are."[19] Patterns? Perhaps. Collingwood calls them "constellations."

> I speak of a set of absolute presuppositions, because if metaphysics is an historical science the things which it studies, namely absolute presuppositions, are historical facts; and any one who is reasonably well acquainted with historical work knows that there is no such thing as an historical fact which is not at the same time a complex of historical facts. Such a complex of historical facts I call a "constellation." If every historical fact is a constellation, the answer to the question "What is it that such and such a person was absolutely presupposing in such and such a piece of thinking?" can never be given by reference to one single absolute presupposition, it must always be given by reference to a constellation of them.[20]

It is an argument much like Quine's in his landmark essay as positivist-against-the-positivists twenty years later, "Two Dogmas of Empiricism."[21] The facts find the order they do according to a whole and encompassing *set* of propositions and principles, each of which is no more than an element in a system. This set comprises the absolute presuppositions. These in their historical turn come under "strains," for where there is no strain there is no history.[22] The presuppositions the historian-metaphysician studies may be expected to be "consupponible only under pressure, the constellation being subject to certain strains and kept together by dint of a certain compromise or mutual toleration."[23] When history applies too much strain, the whole constellation shifts, after which the scientist (and, I would say, the ordinary citizen) never sees things that way again.

Unless, one might add, one is re-enacting old presuppositions. Rex Martin is of the strongly held view that no one can "re-enact" a presupposition because it is not an action, but background and context to actions. I cannot agree. Re-enacting a presupposition is surely the same as comprehending it, and such comprehension is the hoped-for result of someone else (the metaphysician or the anthropologist) explaining as a teacher does just what these distant people believed in order to perform the actions they did. I can't see how one could explain remote actions without some grasp of what used to be called—pre-eminently by Basil Willey—historical "background."[24] Foregrounding background was surely a key tactic in the historiographic revolution, and a necessary precondition of "re-enactment."

The historicising of metaphysics was, I claim, Collingwood's most radical idea. He was memorably scornful, both in *An Autobiography* and in *The Idea of History*, of mistaking the features of a historical moment as features of humankind at large, and as he said in the book at hand, it would be wearisome always to attach what he called "the metaphysical rubric" to every historical peculiarity one reports. Such a rubric—"in such and such a phase of scientific thought it is (or was) absolutely presupposed that . . ."—remains unrepeated but omnipresent. There are no "eternal" or "crucial" or "central" problems in metaphysics (nor, we shall be earnest in adding, in moral philosophy or politics).[25]

Saying so, however, has thrown several of Collingwood's admirers into fits. Poor old Knox shook his head over what he understood plainly was his master's dissolving of philosophy into history,[26] and Alan Donagan as well as Mink exhibit similar signs of distress.[27] The anxiety centres, as one would expect, on the danger that Collingwood, stern moralist, had endorsed relativism, or the doctrine that, histories and geographies being so drunkenly various, there is no choosing for the better amongst all their different ways of being peoples and societies. Eating people is wrong over here, and lunch over there.

We shall return to this argument at the end of the chapter. For now it will do to make three points. The first is that relativism does not demolish rationality and the human effort to be reasonable in practical life. The same relativist (the rational person) relativises what it is rational to hold true. Thus it was once rational to believe that the sun goes around the earth but is not now. The barmy relativist holds the same belief that it was true then, but is not now. This seems ludicrous. The second point at issue is that Collingwood's view of historical metaphysics was that it was progressive. Putting belief rather than knowledge as paramount in the study of mind, he saw the invention of the idea of progress as a decisive moment of improvement in the history of mind.[28] The third point is that, convinced that even though absolute presuppositions were historical and mutable, and that it followed that metaphysics was as changeable as all ancillary sciences—ethics, politics, physics, and the ideas of nature—this truth did not affect either scholar or plain person in their determination to live a life each can be proud of according to the moral and intellectual history in which each is placed.

History, he concluded, was on this showing "the process of development"[29] leading from one state of (thoughtful) affairs to another. When history as thought is infected by irrationalism, a fearful crisis portends, and Collingwood saw the life of civilisation as rising and falling according to the vigour, the coherence, the resilience of its systems of thought to "strain," and the adequacy and humour of its natural homeopathy such that it will expel any inclination to madness or unreason. Error in its homeopathy will destroy the body politic.

The metaphor is mine not his, but he was much exercised in the book by the threat of irrationalism in contemporary modes of thought, not only in the stricken minuteness and airy irresponsibility of the philosophers (were they going to say Boo! to Hitler?), but also in the advance of the science of psychology.

This was something of a personal crux. He had finished his year-long psychoanalysis shortly before he left for Java. He acknowledged psychology's great achievements as "the science of feeling,"[30] but he opposed with all his might its imperialist ambition to become the science of mind. Psychology offered to supplant logic by experimental-cognitive method, and in a brisk passage, Collingwood routs the great Spearman, and then in his most high-handed manner, dispatches psychology as "the propaganda of irrationalism," a debile medicine turning everything it taints into lethal sentimentality. Politics is then become (as in the press in Britain it has) the vehicle of mass emotion, religion the worship of pious feeling (nowadays "spirituality"), public debate the exchange of true confessions, and a moral preference is everywhere endorsed for intuition over practical rationality.

He speaks a long and convincing malediction over the culture of the day. The echoes seventy years later are deafening. He sweeps down abruptly from the thin air and ethereal abstractions of his defence of metaphysics onto a modest eminence from which to address the people: "If European civilisation is a civilisation based on the belief that truth is the most precious thing in the world and that pursuing it is the whole duty of man, an irrationalist epidemic if it ran through Europe unchecked would in a relatively short time destroy everything that goes by the name of European civilisation."[31]

The epidemic was at the gates all right. But there is nonetheless something too vertiginous in this swoop from unoxygenated abstraction to heavy-breathing polemics. Writing away headlong under his canopy on the bridge of the *Alcinous*, he didn't know where to stand and speak to a people who couldn't hear him anyway. Solitude and certainty, the passion to redeem his beloved country and continent, the knowledge of his own genius and his utter unawareness of his own parochialism whether in the quadrangle or the dig, rendered him unable to tie together a speakable idiom and the feelings needed to form it. His ambition, you might say, to write a prosaic *Four Quartets* hardened into the marmoreal chapters of part 3 on reasons and causes. The last, gallant, but helpless paragraph marks the moment at which, pushing back his chair in a cabin aboard SS *Rhesus* off Cape St. Vincent, he mocks his own intellectual predicament and has to leave it there.

The fate of European science and European civilisation is at stake. The gravity of the peril lies especially in the fact that so few recognise any peril to exist. When Rome was in danger, it was the cackling of the sacred geese that saved the Capitol. I am only a professorial goose, consecrated with a cap and gown, and fed at a college table; but cackling is my job, and cackle I will.[32]

IV

He still had his "masterpiece" in his knapsack. As he had added in his letter to Bill, "I suddenly began it quite unexpectedly, as my boat was approaching Soerabaja, and spent my whole time in that damnably hot town writing it as hard as I could."[33] In a letter to his archaeological colleague, the shoe magnate Gerald Simpson, written when he reached Oxford, he referred to *The Principles of History*—itself intended as a companion volume to what was to be published as *The Idea of History*—as "the book my whole life has been spent in preparing to write. If I can finish that, I shall have nothing to grumble at."[34]

This isn't the moment at which to debate once again the decisions of his executor, Malcolm Knox, in cutting so much out of *The Principles* when he edited *The Idea of History* for publication in 1946 (when there were in any case serious paper shortages). The criticisms have been justly and studiously made by the editors of *The Principles* after the thrilling discovery of the manuscripts, long believed lost, at Oxford University Press in 1995.[35] Our immediate concern is to locate these forty thousand words in the chronology of both life and work, and the one, as I have insisted throughout, as inextricably embedded in the other. For the fact is that Collingwood wrote the pieces we have at his usual speed and, it seems, with high excitement.

He wrote out a swift plan for the whole book and then plunged into the three long chapters entitled "evidence," "action," "nature and action" and three pages on "the past." Surprisingly also, for a man as concerned as he was to forestall publication after his death of anything he judged inadequate in what he had written, he had attached a note to Ethel authorising publication of the fragment if she thought fit. (It is worth adding that this note was added at some point after the last day at sea on which he worked on *The Principles*, which was 27 March, and that at that date, at least, no separation from his wife impended.)

The high ambition for the book is apparent even when the ground he is covering is much trodden by his own feet. In the section on evidence he is finally settling accounts with Cook Wilson, aligning inference with judgement, and establishing the authority of inductive thinking not as pointlessly proving what is unprovable but perfectly sufficient unto the day. He dispatches with what is now a familiar curse the repetitious banalities of "scissors-and-paste history," which is to say the writing up and pasting back of received testimony *tout court*, without asking what the testimony could have meant *then*, and not whether it was true or false. He returns, with obvious pleasure, to his own little sketch of a detective story, "Who Killed John Doe?," and uses it to establish the principles of historical detection, that intelligent compound of the pursuit of clues and the plausible ascription of intention to action that is the historian at work. And, borrowing Collingwood's own and frequent trope for a moment, if a postmodern somebody says to me that intentions are infinitely murky and therefore irrecoverable, I shall tell him that I cannot imagine how he manages to cope with the world for an instant.

Central to interpretation (whether by cop or by prof) is question-and-answer logic, which may be better thought of less with the daunting severity of the logician and more as a series of consequential inquiries arranged, so to speak, with the connectedness (and logic) of a tree-diagram. By now in happy rhetorical flight, Collingwood conjured the historian only "to ask questions which you think ... you are going to have evidence for answering" and ends ringingly:

> It was a correct understanding of this truth that underlay Lord Acton's great precept, "Study problems, not periods." Scissors-and-paste historians study periods; they collect all the extant testimony about a certain limited group of events, and hope in vain that something

will come of it. Scientific historians study problems; they ask questions, and if they are good historians they ask questions which they see their way to answering. It was a correct understanding of the same truth that led Monsieur Hercule Poirot to pour scorn on the "human blood-hound" who crawls about the floor trying to collect everything, no matter what, which might conceivably turn out to be a clue [as police searches unfailingly do]; and to insist that the secret of detection was to use what, with possibly wearisome iteration, he called "the little grey cells." You can't collect your evidence before you begin thinking, he meant: because thinking means asking questions (logicians, please note), and nothing is evidence except in relation to some definite question.[36]

He had conducted himself in this recital before, but rarely with such dash and scorn. He keeps up the manner and the high hand in his theory of significant action. Action expresses itself in language (including gesture—*Res Gestae* as he says), and "the business of language is to reveal thought."[37] For "That great and golden-mouthed philosopher, Samuel Alexander . . . wished philosophers to learn . . . the all-importance of time, 'the timefulness of things.' "[38]

It was hardly a topic of which Collingwood, in February 1939, could be unaware. As was his habit, he turned Alexander's injunction into a flourish of disdain towards "the faculty organisation in our universities, which automatically breeds nonsense," quoting Hobbes (from memory) on "the frequency of insignificant speech" in universities, at which most academics may burst into applause but not to the extent of dissolving their faculties.

Finally, and by way of a neat little thought experiment describing process and conclusion at an imaginary archaeological dig called "Highbury," he allows himself to have established as a truth his slogan that "all history is the history of thought," and—more audaciously—that in studying an embodied action (the building of a Roman fort) we are also studying and recovering the relevant emotions that the officer responsible for building the fort experienced.

This is an extension of Collingwood's argument about "essential emotions" in *The Principles of Art*, and it looks like an important concession to his hitherto conventional separation of reason and emotion. I will take the risk of saying that the thoughts of the fort-building officer were reciprocally formed by the emotions he felt while at his task, just as thought itself inflected the emotions and reordered them according to his understanding of what was to be done. Thus he felt apprehension at the danger of attack without sound camp walls around his troops, misery at the certainty of heavy rain in which to work (and a determination to build stoutly enough to keep the weather out), irritation that his men would try to shirk the heavy labour and just do enough to get by.

These feelings are inseparable from the thoughts. The one informs the other, without remainder. For the written history and my money, re-enactment (to use once again the confounded term left unused throughout *The Principles of History*) is a matter of matching thought to feeling and vice versa, each as formative as the other. The interpretative task is to bring the play of thought and feeling into an inferred pattern; the historian replays feeling and thought (much as a musician replays a score) within as large a comprehending framework of human sympathy as he or she is capable of.

I am repeating a position sketched earlier by way not only of suggesting the nature of historical interpretation as at once cognitive and emotional, but also to repudiate Collingwood's strictures against biography, which we have already encountered and which surely stem, I would say in passing, from misgivings about how his own might seem unless kept very strictly to the pages of his published work.

Sympathy and malice, even "gossip-interest" and "snobbery-values," are not without their little room in the house of history, and the beams of passion, even the vehement ones, as they shine upon the historical facts, will reveal many things that would not flash out under a greyer light. Sheer exasperation is a not infrequent emotion in Collingwood's pages and, we may be sure, his life; it isn't an irrelevant principle in writing and speaking history.

The fragment of *The Principles* culminates in a section on nature, much of it rehearsing the lectures of 1934, which Knox edited as *The Idea of Nature*. Its lesson is plain.

What man, at any stage of history, thinks of himself as dealing with, when we say that he is dealing with nature, is never nature as it is in itself but always nature as at that stage of history he conceives it. All history is the history of thought: and wherever in history anything called nature appears, either this name stands not for nature in itself but for man's thought about nature, or else history has forgotten that it has come of age, and has fallen back into its old state of pupilage to natural science.[39]

The bluntness of this is then filled out and given human form by a striking passage describing a terrified man crossing a devil-haunted pass in the mountains (one of many such tales heard by Collingwood on his Javanese rainforest walks) being told by a modern-minded historian not to be afraid of mere superstitions. The modern man has come to his certainties, in which he cannot help but believe, in "precisely the same way" as the man terrified of devils on the mountain path.

This isn't a case of Collingwood's handing victory to fanatic relativism. Progress and even emancipation were, on his account, ideas that arrived, or rather were composed during the eighteenth century, and given form and effectiveness by Hegel. What he is after with the man on the devil-haunted mountain is *freedom*: the man believes freely, and "The discovery that the men whose actions he studies are in this sense free is a discovery which every historian makes as soon as he arrives at a scientific mastery of his own subject."[40] Historical thought has thrown off the domination of natural science, whose propagandists among philosophers (the malignant motley of positivists and realists) had persuaded everybody that nature, including human nature, preceded history.

Many years later, Collingwood's impish opponent, Freddie Ayer, a man whose raffish charm and delightful quickness of mind he responded to warmly even as he repelled his thoughts, expresses surprise at the conclusion that "there can be no history of anything other than thought."[41] Collingwood's constitution of scientific history was fourfold: that it asked relevant and exact questions; that it asks these of "determinate men at determinate times"; that it maintains a "criteriological" rationality in its recourse to evidence; that its point is to enlarge humankind's knowledge of itself by telling it what it has done.[42] But Ayer can find no justification in these reasonable bromides for the claim about the thoughtfulness of history.[43]

What Ayer seems to me to be quite right about is in his objection to Collingwood's assertion that natural science in its absolute presuppositions is thereby committed to presupposing the Christian theism out of which, as the *Idea of Nature* shows, scientific principles and methods developed. What Collingwood gives no adequate account of is loss of belief in a presupposition, although such changes are exactly the evidence of the historical movement that is his subject.

Ayer is relaxed about pressing this charge; his is a volume of late ruminations on philosophers he has been interested by. But by the point at which Collingwood had finished *An Essay on Metaphysics* and the first third of *The Principles of History*, he was searching for a grand theory of history as a theory of mind-in-context, a way of envisaging the past in such a manner as to acknowledge its changefulness, and yet at the same time to discover from its chronicles an understanding of the present, thence to derive sufficient precepts for human conduct in present action.

Time and again he reverts to the error of supposing various versions of realism or materialism to be true. He praises Marx, for instance, for his genius in economic history and for his "fighting" propensities but also castigates Marx for trusting in nature and natural science to find the laws of that economics. "Any given natural science [is] an historical achievement" and then, as best suggesting where his thoughts now tended,

> If this is worked out carefully, then should follow without difficulty a characterisation of an historical morality and an historical civilisation, contrasting with our "scientific" one. Where "science" = of or belonging to *natural* science. A scientific morality will start from the idea of *human nature* as a thing to be conquered or obeyed: a historical one will deny that there is such a thing, and will resolve what we are into what we do. A scientific society will turn on the idea of *mastering*

people (by money or war or the like) or alternatively *serving* them (philanthropy). A historical society will turn on the idea of *understanding* them.[44]

This would have been a theory of a historical ethics, either the grandest conception in modern philosophy or the last gasp of Victorian idealism. But then he came home, and wrote no more.

V

Back in Oxford in April, sporting a fine nautical beard, pleasantly irresponsible with five months of his leave of absence still to run, Collingwood looked forward to the small notoriety that he happily anticipated when the *Autobiography* came out. The word had gone around that, what with leaks about his censures on government and university philosophy, his support of Lindsay the previous October, and the visible evidence of a beard such as such people were known to wear, that he had "gone over" to Communism, along with so many of the most civic-minded and idealistic of Oxford's students at the time.

One of these latter may stand for many. Frank Thompson, son of the poet, the professor of Indian history to whom Gershom dedicated *Thorstein of the Mere*, friend and supporter of Jawarhalal Nehru, was a Wykhamist poet and linguist (speaking, by the age of twenty-four, a dozen languages).[45] Tall, very handsome, ardent, and gifted, he was revolted by the government's treacherous indifference to depression at home and Fascist murder in Spain. He campaigned for Lindsay in the bye-election and joined the Communist Party with his Oxford sweetheart, Iris Murdoch, because it seemed the only organisation with any serious commitment to international solidarity and justice, and with a keen sense of the hideous strength of Fascism. (Frank Thompson took those allegiances with him as a liaison officer alongside the partisans in Bulgaria and was there executed by the Fascists in 1944.)

These ideals fairly glowed in Oxford in the summer of 1939, but Collingwood, just turned fifty, while recognising and sympathising with them in print, was hardly likely to follow them into the Communist Party. He was, however, exceptionally open, cordial, and responsive to the students. His closeness to Kathleen Edwardes, herself a Labour Party member, was of a piece with that strong part of his character that was cheerful, congenial, breezily abusive in the fraternal manner taught by Rugby School, then switching with endearing suddenness to earnest exchanges about art, music, sex, politics.

So it is no surprise to follow Collingwood one fine May morning out of his son Bill's rooms in Balliol, across to the window of Thornton's bookshop, then on the south side of Broad Street, and hear his being courteously accosted by a young American who happened also to be carrying "a large wireless set by one finger passed through a hole in its top." Collingwood's own account of this first meeting is unexpectedly fey, winningly so, I think, even though there is a comical jarring effected by his apparent ignorance of the slang meaning attributable to his playfulness.

> He stood on the pavement like a dancer . . . his light grey eyes . . . looked not at the surfaces of things but through them, so that (I thought) if he wished to leap through the stones and mortar of a building in order to grasp its soul he would know in advance where to leap. . . . That this young man was a fairy I knew when I first clapped eyes on him. There are rules for dealing with fairies; in particular, that you must play them as you play fish or women, by means of a certain guile or honourable (because expected) deceit, and that you must make them give you a sign that they are genuine, though naturally you must never ask for it.[46]

The playfulness of Lanehead with his sisters, of the magic kingdoms of Jipandland and Gialdahourgh, return in the recollection of one of the very happiest intervals of his life.

In front of him was Chadbourne Gilpatric, twenty-five years old at that date, product of Choate, one of the most select schools in New England, of Harvard, and then a Rhodes scholar at Oxford, fired by Collingwood to go to study philosophy both at Oxford, and until the United States declared war in 1941, back home, this time at Princeton. By 1950, as an officer for the Rockefeller Foundation, he was negotiating with Wittgenstein to try to support his work (Wittgenstein declined the help because "he couldn't promise to publish anything at present").[47] He was a grave and graceful young man; he captivated his interlocutor, who knew instantly that he would accept the proffered invitation to join the crew of young men sailing a battered schooner to Greece and the Cyclades.

Collingwood pretended he had his doubts, discussed matters further with Gilpatric in Magdalen, but having returned only on 7 April, undertook to set out to sea again on 27 June. One cannot here mistake the sense of a man in flight. He must have visited Kathleen at Streatley after his return—he had stayed with her at the end of the last summer,[48] before leaving for Java. He had had no further strokes since September 1938, but the impairment to his leg movement while on board ship did not augur well. He was in love with a very good-looking woman twenty-two years his junior who reciprocated his feelings. He was pretty certainly under sentence of death and just as certainly not a man to baulk at that fact. Two months more of physical effort, boisterous company, putative convalescence, and seaborne meditation on what it was he *must* finally do offered both respite and a punishing regime of self-examination. Sailing had always been the location for some of his deepest thought as well as his most fulfilling hours. The company of half a dozen sunny-tempered, studious, and high-spirited young men turned out to be much more than an agreeable background to thought; it brought, along with sun and sea and 250 litres of *vin ordinaire*, forty-two of the happiest days of his life.

Gilpatric was captain, always thoughtful for others, unselfish, serious to a degree but merry with it; Collingwood his first mate, sailing under the stars and stripes alongside a Canadian, Dick Ghiselin, two other Americans, Jack Golay and John Moore, a Harvard classicist; another Canadian, Ralph Collins, from Alberta and Harvard with a first in PPE, later Canadian ambassador to China; and a trio of English public schoolboys: Stephen Verney of Harrow and Balliol, later fighting with the Free French in North Africa and the Greek resistance in Crete, eventually a bishop; Robin McCurdy, ship's doctor and then naval surgeon, from Edinburgh and Balliol; and David

James of Eton and Balliol, who had sailed before the mast to Australia and back at the age of eighteen, later, inevitably, a naval officer of a heroic record at which from here one can only throw up one's hands in joyful wonder—wounded at sea, prisoner of war, escaped, made it home, awarded DSC, Arctic explorer, Tory MP of the old school for ten years in Dorset, married Baron Digby's daughter, six children, stately home; all that, *you* know.

There is no more immediate nor abject experience through which to dissolve strangers into shipmates than seasickness, and during the first hundred miles of the journey after leaving Antibes in the schooner *Fleur de Lys* the strong bonds of, first, queasiness and then a dreadful waiting, finally evacuation, united the crew every bit as much as the fierce activity of learning the character of the ship.

Which was wayward, indeed. She was a 48-ton Newfoundland Banks fishing boat with yachting adaptations, on loan from her owner but wretchedly maintained, her standing rigging slack and threadbare, pitiful in tools and equipment and with a diesel engine at once defective and obdurate. The compass worked badly, and all in all the shortcomings of the boat not only furnished the inexhaustible logkeeper with his main plot (Collingwood kept up his old ways and wrote his steady thousand words a day as a log of the voyage) but provided those happy catastrophes that are the making of a holiday.

They were moving slowly south, past Corsica, ultimately bound for the Straits of Messina six hundred miles south, discovering pretty soon that the pumps would have to be dismantled and put together again, and that all the batteries were run down. Terrific meals, perhaps austere to present tastes in ocean-going luxury—macaroni cheese, tinned beans from the immortal Heinz, spaghetti and mince in a thick brown gravy, tinned fruit, more cheese, hard tack biscuits once the bread ran out—were the best moments of many best moments (choral renderings of sea shanties bouncing back from any convenient cliff, swimming when becalmed, uncontainable high spirits and mutual mockery, the intense busyness of sailing a rather sluggish old tub). The crew was all by now rivalrously bearded, most of the time stark naked, its first mate, twice the age of everyone else on board, resourceful, ingenious, energetic, and occasionally frightening.

To improve the crew's dead reckoning and augment the lousy compass, First Mate Collingwood fashioned an azimuth instrument out of cardboard, cutting a disc with a hole in the middle to fit the compass glass and setting cardboard sights joined by twine at each end of the diameter. With this contraption they could take cross-bearings. The whole crew was struck solemn with respect at their First Mate's practical powers.

They had been by now a week at sea and lay off Stromboli trying to make their engines work. The engineer, Dick Ghiselin, like all marine engineers, loved his engine for its very mulishness, was made sad but sympathetic by its refusals, protected it from abuse by others, and never lost his temper with its dependable undependability.

Stromboli was pouring red-gold lava down its flanks and Collingwood on deck confessed to terror at the sight, while the captain below ("who has not yet altogether seen through me") read aloud to an attentive crew from *The Principles of Art*.[49] Then they stood in to Stromboli, took perilous soundings with Collingwood swinging the leadline, "singing out marks and deeps in a good round voice and a plausible order," and came soundly to anchor in four fathoms under the church of San Vincenzo, Collingwood feeling "like an accepted lover in the moment of his triumph." It was what he was.

The crew cheerfully endured the fatuous hyper-bureaucracy of Fascist Italian police in Stromboli, the younger members invaded the island for drink and high jinks, Dick Ghiselin, head cook and engineer, sprained an ankle, "but there is a high standard of heroism in this ship, and an hour after coming on board he was on duty again."[50]

That last remark catches much of what is so attractive about the expedition and about Collingwood himself to his youthful shipmates. He never lost his authority nor his congeniality and playfulness either. When, sternly in the role of first mate, he lost his temper with Ralph Collins for leaving a burning cigarette on the edge of the cabin roof, he later apologised not for the disciplinary point but for losing his temper,[51] and since the log was read aloud to an attentive crew every evening, he apologised in public.

Following Odysseus, they steered between Scylla the dreadful yelper with her six long necks each with three rows of teeth, and Charybdis sucking down the sea all black, of which Collingwood in his respectful way speaks with a discreet credulity, and docked at Messina, where the first mate and the captain remained on watch with their pipes and a pound of French tobacco, while the crew went boisterously ashore, "the lechers" as Gilpatric called them amiably, David James and McCurdy, the ship's doctor, setting off for a brothel, in McCurdy's case his "*prima volta*," for which "the prostitute . . . gave my tail a little kiss."[52]

They set course from Sicily for Greece, a shipful of philosophers arguing about Spinoza of an evening, listening to the log, reading aloud to one another the captain's latest find in American literature, *Moby Dick*, listening mesmerised to a very fast, completely fluent and accurate (the Waynflete professor assures us) history of ancient Greece from Minoan civilisation to the Roman conquest given unrehearsed by John Moore.

The temperature climbed as they sailed east, intensifying for the first mate an insomnia increased by the Diesel's water system so throbbing hotly through his cabin that until he was moved, he slept on deck. They passed Cephallonia and landed at Patras, and their teacher, anxious like any good teacher that the students shall love what he loves, was satisfied by all the signs of "the authentic *coup de foudre*. The landscape had done its stuff."[53] They celebrated, as all arrivals after hard journeys must be celebrated, with a massive seamen's lunch, 2:00 to 4:30: retsina and ice (that piney Greek wine which Kingsley Amis thought tasted of "strained cricket bats"), boiled chicken and rice, baked fish, fresh figs, oranges "soft as girls' lips" our man adds.

It was mid-July 1939, and various minor incidents suggested sinister Fascist mystery brewing in the Ionian sea—Italy had seized Albania, the Italian fleet steamed bullyingly past, heeling the *Fleur de Lys* until all the crockery fell out of the racks in the galley and smashed. But in an affecting little episode that takes a kind of measure of the seventy years since, Dick Ghiselin lost his spectacles overboard in port and found them retrieved and waiting for him at Athens ten days later.

Like all happy and capable crews, this one briefly embodied Collingwood's picture of the good society whereby, as he had put it in a telling aside earlier in the same year: "This eternal life of mind as taken up into the being of God can best be symbolised . . . by the life of a human society in which the differences between person and person are welded into unity by honourable dealing and loving intercourse."

The only and boorish villain in the tale was the infernal diesel engine. Its recalcitrance and hateful inefficiency are nonetheless the occasion for such calm and arduous labour, such gratifying admixtures of oil and sweat so that the engineer could pose unawares for a bronze statue of Vulcan himself, such tearing high spirits and jollity punctuated by much singing of sea shanties—"Farewell and adieu to you fair Spanish Ladies"—that it provides, as I said, that essential of the happy holiday, the comedy of misfortune.

At Delphi Collingwood was visiting his most sacred place, the invisible shrine of Socrates, secular saint of philosophers who had, "at Apollo's bidding, become the organ by which the corporate consciousness of the Greeks examined and criticised itself." This is the philosophers' vocation; I think philosophers would not put it with quite such exaltation today, but they would put it nonetheless. So too did the crew of the battered schooner.

In Olympia they put ashore for good the artist Herzl, waited for Denis Healey, who never turned up, and another American, Kermit Gordon, who did. At Katakolo, the southwestern spur of Peloponnesia (they were still sailing east, having come back south from Patra), they hobnobbed with another yacht, and Collingwood, as one of the chaps, called out to the dory, "tell them to hoist a pair of trousers if there are any women on board."[54] In Olympia they had made pilgrimage to the twilit temples; Collingwood collected his mail from the women in his life and heard that Chamberlain had renounced his agreement over Czechoslovakia with Hitler. On their departure, the damned diesel engine seized again so that, almost becalmed off Kythera, the island at the southern tip of Greece, Collingwood at the helm was able to meditate, with some personal pointedness, on the goddess Aphrodite whose home the island was.

> I do not imagine that the Greeks connected Kythera with Aphrodite because its landscape suggested to their minds the miseries and torments of a love-affair. But I thought of the *Hippolytus*, and reflected that they knew a good deal about the grimmer aspect of these things. It was curious, I reflected, that the very facts which caused Donne to renounce his belief that "there was some Deitie in love" were the facts which caused the ancients to fear, and do their best to understand, a power so formidable, so mighty for creation and for destruction.[55]

VI

There was in the cheerful, knockabout, jocular, and movingly serious conversation of the crew, which this splendid log reports, a certain consistency of theme. Of course, the young men were much of a wealthy social class, whether British or American—David James from Eton, Chadbourne Gilpatric from Choate, and they seem mostly to have been very much alike in their ideals and allegiances. They turned out, it would appear, as brave as anyone in the coming unpleasantness; they took their studies and their sailing with great seriousness; if these were representative of two ruling classes—and they were—there is much to be said for them. They put me in mind of the stricken hero of that great Powell and Pressburger movie, *A Matter of Life and Death*, made in 1945 precisely to dramatise questions of love and justice in the world war. Seated at the controls of a doomed Lancaster, certain he is about to die, the pilot describes himself to the beautiful American radio operator at the station who is trying to guide him in to land as "Conservative by upbringing, Labour by experience," and tops it off with a quotation from Walter Raleigh's "Passionate Man's Pilgrimage."

Collingwood's shipmates were of that cross-Atlantic formation, and two impressive episodes bring this out. During one of the evening forums daily held below deck with the ship at anchor, the Rhodes scholars fell to criticising Oxford for not giving them all they had believed it would as "a sort of bigger and better Harvard." Collingwood counterposed the tutorial (or face-to-face) teaching at Oxford to the seminar-and-lecture system of Harvard, the emphasis on breadth of reference in America, and depth of inquiry in England, and, listening but saying nothing, he concluded that:

> This difference is neither accidental nor superficial; it is rooted in the divergent American and English conceptions of society: the American conception more "democratic," attaching more importance to equality between man and man, and to the links which bind together the various parts of the social body; the English conception more "aristocratic," attaching more importance to excellence of a specialised kind, and less to the way in which that excellence may affect the lives of persons who do not share it.[56]

Attaching this thought to his new resolution to fight in the daylight, he was sure that English education (and "English" is the adjective he uses throughout) could do something urgent about the uncomprehending chasm ("a great evil") between the public and the learned class. He could not of course foresee that, seventy years later, the gap has been narrowed by the partial transformation of learning into a consumer commodity and an instrument for lifestyle and upward social mobility.

The second episode that makes for a kind of epiphany in the *First Mate's Log*, and is the high point of the book as it is the clearest expression of something central to Collingwood's worldview, concerns their arrival at the easternmost point of the voyage on the Cycladean island of Santorini (or Thira as it is now formally known).

There had been, on the last leg of the outward journey, the usual gloomy accidents transmuted into high comedy—the night "some of us throwing to the winds every law of morality ate rose jam with a spoon out of the tin," and finished it, what's more. There had been the memorable visit to the incomparable piles of the Acropolis in Athens where, sitting in the sun on one of the vast blocks of unkempt broken marble unarranged for the benefit of pious visitors at that date, Collingwood wrote home to Kathleen and Ethel. The doctor, faint with lust, had vanished into an Athenian brothel, and then into a monastery.[57] The first mate, captain, and engineer had a high old time crammed one by one in the hold repairing leaking water tanks, which threatened to kill the crew from thirst by emptying themselves as fast as they were filled (there was still the wine). After taking us wriggling and claustrophobic all around the tanks, the first mate rallies us, "All clear, Reader. You can come out." We leave, three men short (for Collins, Moore, and Golay had had to quit at Piraeus, the port for Athens), and by way of some heavy weather and an island stop or two, made the 150-odd sea miles to Santorini by midnight on 31 July. World war was five weeks away.

The approach to Santorini harbour was and is stupendous. Round about 1650 BCE the volcano erupted and a colossal crater opened up below the water of the bay whose gaunt cliffs rise four hundred metres sheer above the harbour in brown, black, and grey pumice striations. The only way up then was by mules, which still ply the winding track to the little town at the top. The crew stayed a few days, for Santorini was enchanting and, allowing for a bit of tourist tat, still is. Collingwood and Gilpatric set off on foot (it's about eight kilometres with a stiff pull at the end) for the best-known tourist visit, to the monastery of the Prophet Elijah.

> We went without haste, for the midday sun is hot in August. In answer to our wishes a small boy suddenly rose out of the ground in front of us, slipped into a vineyard on the left, and came back with two large clusters of grapes, which he solemnly bestowed upon us. Surely the people of Santorin have the prettiest manners in the world. All our crew had similar encounters to narrate: gifts of fruit by the wayside, invitations into strange houses where food and drink were set before them, sweet-smelling herbs offered in little posies. We thanked our benefactor and ate his grapes as we walked.[58]

At the monastery they met the chaplain, a Chaucerian figure, "full fat and in good point," his intense and fanatical deputy, two other monks, and the thoughtful, modest, authoritative, and hospitable archimandrite, Father Loukas, who led them in orthodox worship in the narrow little L-shaped chapel, still set about today by blackened frescoes and faded but ornate gilt fretwork with a strongly Byzantine feel to them.

The singing was very fine, the intense monk proved a fine tenor, the archimandrite a beautiful clear baritone, the singing in praise of God and the Panagia an honest job of work well done, for sure, but also achieving a purity and loveliness taught with great exactness by the tradition, and happily uncovering the talents to match. Collingwood was a Christian, as we know, and much moved; but the atheist with a proper musical education would be no less so. If art is indeed the expression in the medium at hand of truthful emotion, such music speaks to believer and unbeliever alike.

As the sun sank, the many bells of the island began to toll from their multiple white campaniles beside the beautiful blue domes that together comprise the metonymy of the Cyclades. The two sailors were to sleep not in the main chapel, which would not have been proper, but in a mortuary chapel beyond the gate. They found provided for them fresh bread, goats' cheese, tomatoes, a small bottle of the local wine made from mavrotragano grapes and now the island's biggest trade after tourism, and a dish of rosehip jam.

> We slept well on the black-and-white marble floor of our chapel. It must have been about midnight when I awoke and saw Gil standing in the doorway gazing out into the moonlight. The wind had gone. Twenty yards from the door grew a bush covered with pink flowers, a little like hibiscus. I do not know its name. The chapel was full of its sweet smell. Gil turned and lay down again beside me, and we went to sleep.[59]

Most of the crew also made a shorter visit to the monastery during their four-day sojourn. In the subsequent days, Collingwood assumed his full persona as teacher and taught them his central lesson: that such monks were not absurdly cloistered nor self-indulgent nor even useless according to the key modern criterion of social utility. The importance and vindication of their beautiful music, which only the occasional visitor ever heard, was not only to the islanders, who certainly believed that the monks' lives fitted into the patterns of meaning that issued as the fulfilment of a common good, but also that the way of that monastic life with its summit as being the beautiful act of worship was a good *in itself*—just as it was and is a good in itself that the pure mathematician shall pursue the truth and beauty of numbers wherever they lead.

Collingwood mounts at this juncture one of the most pungent of the critiques of modern utilitarianism, pursuing the infinite regress of the utility test (this is useful because it leads to that which is useful, which leads to that which is useful . . . and so on).[60] Sooner or later, something is worthwhile for its own sake. The way of life on the island into which the monastery fitted both centrally and remotely was plainly a good way. In being so at odds with the way of life even of such decent, worldly, probably agnostic, and much travelled modernists as the crew, it turns into an involuntary criticism of that other, wealthy, and mobile way of life, and might even have caused some of its participants to want to resign from it and hide away from its rough beastliness.

Collingwood can afford to be mocking and affectionate in a book like this; but he meant what he said and lived the principles of the argument. They are put in the appropriate diction in *The Principles of Art, The Essay on Metaphysics,* and of course *An Autobiography.* They are present in his deep loyalty to folklore as an encapsulation of past in the present, and in his lived conjunction of archaeology and history, Lakeland and Oxford. Indeed, his firm little lesson to his shipmate students brings out happily for my purposes just why and how the story of a thinker's thought may be read in his brief friendship with an Orthodox priest to whom he spoke classical Greek, and in his admonitions to the young men—admonitions that Ruskin and T. S. Eliot would have endorsed—to dissolve secularism and utilitarianism into a love of the past-in-the-present and to envision the common good as a web of many significances.

The six of them turned back westwards. It is painful to me to have to omit taking my reader through the many rich moments of the return journey, overlooking the coming-to-power of the Primus stove, first necessity of Coniston Water, when the gas ran out; or Robin McCurdy's being ceremonially flung into the Ionian on the occasion of his twenty-first birthday "to the accompaniment of song," or again "the futile gibberings" of the Sicilian policeman who rammed their boat with his launch.

These delights are commended to readers of the *Log*. The diminished crew was tired and apt to doze on duty. "One of us, counting our blessings, said we had been free from [the curse] of a man in love (he meant loquaciously in love, I suppose, for it is not to be thought that there is among us no man in love at all)."[61]

There was the first mate himself, after all. When the ship raised Vesuvius and made Naples on 20 August, Collingwood jumped ship and set off home by train, a familiar ride, Naples—Rome—Milan, there to pick up the Orient Express north to Calais and the packet to Dover. During the journey, Ribbentrop signed the mendacious nonaggression pact with Molotov. Hitler could now turn all his attention for the time being to western Europe. Collingwood took the train back to Oxford, and so to 15 Belbroughton Road, braced to meet his destiny.

VII

The monastery of Elijah is not a mid-nineteenth-century building, as Collingwood thought, but mid-eighteenth, a crude enough construction of concrete and stucco with high walls, overbearing gates, a grim little car park outside, and nowadays a dreadful, twelve-tone automated campanile set on the outer wall. The walk from the level plain below to the heights on which the monastery stands is as winding and punitive as ever, and on making the top one is shocked to find all the apparatus of a NATO listening station left over from the Cold War but now of course intently eavesdropping on radio noise from the Middle East. Hard by the entrance to the monastery stand the sentries and the usual striped military barrier, swinging up when drivers are passed on to the bleak, sealed box buildings beyond. North from the summit, you can see and hear the hefty tourist airbuses roaring into deceleration as they fetch the next load of tourists to shatter the silence on Mount Elijah. Below the mountain crest, there are visible the clumps of low-growing mavrotragano grapes, trained to a metre-wide tiara never more than thirty centimetres high, for the dry tramontane gales that sweep the Cyclades all winter and springtime would sear and tear out anything higher.

There could be no harsher way of seeing how completely the monastery life and its lessons of frugal goodness and orderly devotion have gone forever. One thinks back to Collingwood's intemperate endorsement of the bleak vision in Eliot's *The Waste Land*, when he wrote, with a dreadful desolation and certainty:

> The poem depicts a world where the wholesome flowing water of emotion, which alone fertilises all human activity, has dried up. Passions that once ran so strongly as to threaten the defeat of prudence, the destruction of human individuality, the wreck of men's little ships, are shrunk to nothing. No one gives; no one will risk himself by sympathising; no one has anything to control. We are imprisoned in ourselves, becalmed in a windless selfishness. The only emotion left us is fear: fear of emotion itself, fear of death by drowning in it, fear in a handful of dust.[62]

It is his conclusion to the book. He ends his commentary, as we have heard, by saying that the poem "describes an evil not curable by shooting capitalists or destroying a social system, a disease which has so eaten into civilisation that political remedies are about as useful as poulticing a cancer."

It's a remark of terrible force, yet now it just sounds raving. Less than three years later, writing in London during the Blitz, he speaks admiringly of how that same civilisation is indestructible by Hitler, just as Eliot at near enough the same moment was able to walk past *The Waste Land* into the lovely affirmations of *Little Gidding*. A little earlier in the same book Collingwood had written of a society in which sexual desire itself is disjoined from the wish to procreate, "weakened by a sense that life as we have made it is not worth living, and where our deepest wish is to have no posterity."[63] *Our* wish? Within two years, a dying animal himself and his country, as it seemed, facing immediate defeat by the Nazis, he fathered a daughter whose growing even into a little girl he was certain not to see.

One might say that in spite of his passionate conviction of the deturpation of culture, the loss of religious meaning, of the natural rhythms of an agrarian life, the hatefulness of modernism—all that, the old rhodomontade—his own absolute presuppositions were such as to make him stand up for good old life. So much in his last three finished books rings with an affirmation that the ancient imperfect democracy would win through, that the self-knowledge his nation had won out of the horrors, the boredom, and the glory of its history would, by way of the Slough of Despond, of Doubting Castle and the burning Pit where fiends "whisperingly suggested grievous blasphemies,"[64] pass in the end the test of the Lions and permit entrance into the House Beautiful.

So it is no use looking for a systematic and dovetailed political and philosophic vision in Collingwood's work. The thought of a great philosopher like Collingwood resembles more the architectures of his parent colleges, Pembroke and Magdalen, than that of a New Town like Milton Keynes. Probably there is never any point in contriving a perfect projection of the order of the books for the sake of biographical shapeliness. The unity he sought and I aim to reconstruct is the unity of his character in life and work, its style (in Nietzsche's strong sense), and that way of thinking and feeling he worked at constructing on the page, and which could then bring together the man and his history such that each comprehended the other.

It is a colossal ambition, of course, and in the end it breaks your heart. But not always the spirit. If that survives, the work and the man who made it live on in the lives and thought of those who follow. Which strong-sounding chord is not a finale; it merely returns us to that crux in the bequest of his thinking that he called "re-enactment": the re-enacting of past thoughts (in this case *his*) in a different present. A properly historical biography will so re-enact the thoughts that we understand what he meant then, when he said it; thereafter the right biography will make it possible to turn those thoughts, resurrected from so different a moment, into something practical and rational now.

Re-enacting the moral vision of *The Waste Land* in the twenty-first century isn't too difficult just because it is so wonderful a poem. Eliot matches his entirely rational verdict on the slaughterous ruins of postrevolutionary and postwar Europe in 1922 to the emotions that should accompany it.[65] The singleness of expression compels on us both passion and judgement. We take it on, but we do not have to take it down. Re-enacting is bracketed; we think and feel what is expressed as it is expressed and then turn to our affairs. The re-enacted thoughts match those affairs or don't. We decide accordingly.

Perhaps it helps to compare the doctrine of re-enactment to the concerns of musicians seeking to play the music of the past in the way in which the composer not only intended it to be played but was so constrained by the musical technology of the day that in some sense it *had* to be played that way.

The authenticity movement in music gathered pace about the middle of the twentieth century. It coincided with and was lent energy by the change in taste that returned early music to favour— the wonderful church and instrumental music of the Elizabethan Renaissance, welcomed back not for its religious content so much as for its purity and precision, the bare, living line of its melodies, its austerity when contrasted with the huge orchestral effects of the Romantic movement.

When this authenticity movement turned to the Baroque and, supremely, to Bach, it had to start again. Bach had been domesticated by the nineteenth century, his precision and rapidity softened, and his chords made more sumptuous than these new ears could permit. With a new kind of insistence on the artist's intentions and therefore a demand for a radical historicism in musical performance, playing Bach required the effort not only to restrict performance to the instruments of his day, but also to restore his notation as exactly as possible, "to re-enact past thought ... in the context of [the performer's] own knowledge and therefore, in re-enacting it, criticising it, form[ing] judgements of its value, correct[ing] whatever errors were discerned in it."[66]

Anthony Newman, in his performer's guide to Bach's music in particular and the Baroque in general, writes against the view that new developments in neuromuscular coordination mean that today's players are technically more resourceful than in Bach's day. He denies this. There may have been fewer virtuosi, but "they must have played with a skill equal . . . to today's best performers."[67] But there was and is *no* substitute for a "feel" or a "performance understanding" of the written notation that puts out of court the "exactly as written" school of thought. Couperin said that playing well depended on having "good taste," and the sources from Bach's time discuss in detail the importance of timing and rhythm, especially the articulation of the notes, the *rubato,* and "the additions to the text of the music," which is to say the symbolism for dynamics and the way the music "falls within time," which will make performance historically correct or not. The Baroque literature constantly refers to "good taste," "proper proportion," "good mediation" of tempi,[68] all the inexplicit conventions of a culture which the performer (and historian) must reconstruct in order to re-create (re-enact) the original correctly, that is, with as great fidelity as possible.

> Newman ends his player's guide by putting most of his money on the "affect": or proper energy . . . plus "good taste" . . . Baroque music is filled with many examples of "affect". . . . The question is to find the proper "affect" for each piece and . . . to bring out the primary energy and focus of the piece in the most direct way. It is above all a proper *rubato* that is necessary. . . . The selecting and identifying of strong measures, and of strong places within measures, is one of the most important creative problems to be solved. . . . There are often several possible solutions. The only impossible solution is that the music be played with metronomic regularity.[69]

It's pretty vague: the emphasis falls on such imponderable but definite qualities as "affect," propriety, taste, all products of dedicated familiarity with and a genius for the right "feel," for avoiding "metronomic regularity." Even then, there are "several possible solutions."

So it is with re-enacting thoughts. This is no arcane experiment with the historical imagination. It is hard enough, no doubt, but it does not really warrant the heavy perspiration of so much commentary by the Collingwoodians. Re-enactment is a matter of understanding the conventions of an historical argument in such a way as to recover the intentions of the writer. Those intentions will be apparent and re-creatable insofar as the writer writes well; well-made art, whether in prose, paint, or music, speaks with certitude.

At first sight this looks like a rebuttal of Wittgenstein's claim that you can't communicate private states of mind; but it isn't. These are public meanings uttered either in one of the languages of art, or in mere expression. The other person is properly understood (whether one's interlocutor is Plato, Hobbes, or the next-door neighbour) when they can say what they mean out loud, and we can understand them.[70] This past thought is then "encapsulated" in a new present, and we go to work on it accordingly.

This is Collingwood's first move in the making not so much of a method as "a science of human affairs." It has therefore a moral force. The past makes the present. As Louis Mink puts it in a neat little saw, we must understand backwards in order to think [or plan] forwards.[71] Re-enactment is no more than thinking what has been thought *exactly* as it was thought then, so that the historical past can yield its lessons of difference, contrast, comparison, and does so as its differently ground optics show us contrastive and contradictory signification. Hobbes's liberty is not ours, nor Cromwell's pacification, whether of the Irish or the Levellers. Yet both have deposited their residue in our political formation. Our applications of the science of human affairs starts with a sufficiency of these re-enactments, faithfully performed. This is the first form of the new science, history its content. Of itself, of course, it runs practice into theory. For history, the paramount form of theoretical knowledge, teaches understanding of how matters came to be the way they are. Duty, its corollary as dominant form of practical knowledge, teaches us freely to will what must be done.

9

The Passionate Man's Pilgrimage:
On Barbarism and Civilisation

Throughout most of the voyage in the Mediterranean and like so much else of the machinery of the *Fleur de Lys*, the radio had failed to work. Political news had been sparse, and the exuberance of Fascism was to be observed and detested only in the form of overdressed and underpaid bullies from the Italian and Sicilian police, as well as a few military Greeks from the wrong side wearing their preposterous skirts, pom-pom pumps, and bellhop hats. Once in Britain, the Americans quit Europe before the fighting began (they joined in all right, as we learned, once the Stars and Stripes were in), David James at once joined the navy, Stephen Verney an ambulance unit, Robin McCurdy qualified as a doctor in Edinburgh and joined the merchant navy on the Atlantic convoys, Dick Ghiselin volunteered for active service as soon as Canada declared war, and meanwhile Bill Collingwood joined the Royal Air Force on active service in 1940.

The remainder of the crew attended the first mate's lectures in the Michaelmas term. They heard him say this.

I think that you young people are better stuff than I and my contemporaries were. I say this not in my capacity as a professional pedagogue, but on the strength of what I have learnt by making friends out of school with people of your generation. And I would not say it at all—for it is dangerous praising people to their face—but for the fact that I am sickened and ashamed by the campaign of calumny which old people today are carrying on against the young and I think it is the part of an honest man to declare on which side he stands.[1]

The yellow press had been much put out by the various Oxford Union motions denigrating the Tory government, which was in any case quite unable to make the necessary preparations for a war economy and both irresolute and incompetent in deciding, in the very centre of the most acute crisis ever to face Britain, whom to choose as prime minister. Only when, after much vacillation, evasion, and shameful dodging about, Churchill was finally appointed on 13 May 1940, to the relief of the whole country, was there a leader who at least could name plainly to his people the only wages on offer.[2]

Political and personal crisis coincided in Collingwood's own life. For some little time he had been formulating, with an autobiographical scalpel, his thoughts on individual moral destiny. We have heard him warn against the siren blandishments even of "right conduct" itself (remembering also J. A. Smith's strictures on the English gentleman). If one traces a series of sampler commonplaces in Collingwood's lectures on moral philosophy as he rewrote them for 1940,[3] one can arrange them in such a way as to frame and explain the drastic domestic decision he was about to make.

I certainly do *not* say that this is what Collingwood himself was doing in those notes. Some of them, indeed, recur in muted and mutable form in *The New Leviathan*, there pitched, however, on the less urgent and more abstract level belonging to the kind of book it was to be. Nor am I essaying some scissors-and-paste history by way of aligning Collingwood's life-chronicle with the thoughts he happened to write down at the same time. On the contrary, over-hearing (or re-enacting) them makes it easier to recognise his tiny life-crisis in the midst of a gigantic continental crisis, and to associate his decision with the context of respectable Oxford life at that time, and what it would be for the Waynflete professor to leave his wife, the well-liked Ethel, sound mother and aunt, faithful communicant of the Cumbrian antiquarians, chair of a child welfare committee, to go to live a few miles out of town with a tall and beautiful young actress who was, it seems, fully braced to the common knowledge of her fifty-one-year-old lover's mortal ill health and brief expectation of life.

There are moral crises in which all the rules of life become a bankrupt currency; those who have experienced such a crisis, and have not forgotten what they experienced, know by experience that these rules are only contingent expressions of a single ultimate rule. But the experiences which force us into the presence of that rule are for most of us so rare, that philosophical argument will hesitate to appeal to them.[4]

And then, tersely: "rule abiding is a form of goodness . . . the mind is always to be, or rather to become, itself."

This following is a quotation already seen. In this situation, it bears repetition. It sounds like a paraphrase of Machiavelli on *virtu*:

It is only on the occasion of rare moral crises . . . that commonplace criteria cease to satisfy us and we are obliged to set aside all question of what we want to do, and question of utility or expediency, and even all question of right and wrong, and try to discover what is the one thing we *must* do on pain of a kind of moral death or dissolution.

Finally:

Scales of value change . . . if one generation feels its scale of values to differ from that of its fathers, it will have to rewrite history; what used to be thought failures it will think successes. . . . this revaluation . . . may seem a confession of failure . . . but that is not so . . . it is not a mere advancement of knowledge, it is an advancement in the whole moral attitude of humanity.

The moral language of sexual relationships was on the move in step with the growing tendency towards disbelief in The Fall among the intellectual classes. John Maynard Keynes, Collingwood's contemporary, had written blithely about this loss of belief years before, in a letter about Henry Sidgwick, another grand philosopher-patriarch of the generation before Keynes's and Collingwood's:

Have you read Sidgwick's life? It seems to be the subject of conversation now. Very interesting and depressing, and, the first part particularly, very important as an historical document dealing with the mind of the period. Really—but you must read it yourself. He never did anything but wonder whether Christianity was true and prove that it wasn't and hope that it was. . . . And then his conscience—incredible.

There is no doubt about his moral goodness. And yet it is all so dreadfully depressing—no intimacy, no clear-cut crisp boldness. Oh, I suppose he was intimate but he didn't seem to have anything to be intimate about except his religious doubts. And he really ought to have got over that a little sooner; because he knew that the thing wasn't true perfectly well from the beginning.[5]

Collingwood of course had kept hold of Anglicanism notwithstanding, although throughout the 1930s the necessity he had once found and affirmed in *Religion and Philosophy* and *Speculum Mentis* in Christianity's personal God had thinned out to become the vast transparency of Spinoza's God-as-and-in-Nature. But the value-change in the opposition between *eros* and *agape*, sexual desire and married love, was taking place at nontheological levels of passion and action. D. H. Lawrence, rightly enough, was and is taken to be prophet of this movement after *Sons and Lovers* came out in 1913, and his definition of his artistic purpose may be taken as indicative of the value-change coming in like a tide, first through the bodies and minds of the intellectual classes, then through everybody, only to be captured and corrupted for its own ends by market capitalism sometime after about 1970.

Lawrence wrote in a letter about *Lady Chatterley's Lover*, "I always labour at the same thing, to make the sex relation valid and precious, instead of shameful. And this novel is the furthest I've gone."[6] Collingwood had endorsed Eliot's *The Waste Land* as a vision of a world in which emotion was dead and the desire to propagate children extinguished because life seemed no longer worth living. He would bear his witness against such a death-in-life by going to live with Kathleen Edwardes, first in London and later in her own home in Streatley, and then by giving her their own child.

II

The decision to end a marriage of more than twenty years' duration, to cause the fearful distress certain to be felt by so steady a woman as Ethel, to gamble the estrangement of his children, to be the certain object of eager and excited gossip, enacted one version of being a "gloves-off philosopher" and of "fighting in the daylight" for what he believed he *must* do. The *Autobiography* had been a declaration of independence—independence, doubtless, of social conventions at the expense of truth to oneself, and by way of not permitting any separation between one's theory and one's practice. But he craved also the independence of the free thinker, of the philosopher who has broken from "the parlour game" of minute analysis and moved into the public realm, there to occupy his place in the agora and to speak to whomever listened of the mere anarchy being loosed upon the world.

The *Autobiography* had been his best effort in this direction. There the powerful feelings of impatience with his profession, of revulsion from his government, of contempt for his daily press, of certainty about his own genius, of anger at the foreshortening of his life, had focused his thought with a concision and energy that spontaneously generated the style the book demanded. Of itself it refutes the notion that a passionless purity of diction is the only art-speech for philosophers. It is caustic, clear, incisive, comic, and profound. If more academic journalism (a term of honour) had been like it at the time, the polity would have been in better health. But the only such toughness of manner and stubbornness of argument was to be found among the fellow travellers of the Left, and neither power elite nor people inclined that way. Lindsay had lost his protestant bye-election, and the Conservative government would blunder incompetently on until the last minute of May 1940 when the Nazi Tiger tanks were already at the gate.

Collingwood sought for but could not find the role of public intellectual. I suppose this was his tragedy. There was no passage he knew of, even from the ease and wisdom of such a plain-spoken book as *The Principles of Art*, to the kind of public address brought consummately off by Ruskin in the *Addresses to Working Men* and in the proceedings of the Guild of St. George. The nearest he could come to such a manner and the content to match was his tribute to Gershom's example in the *Autobiography*, the malediction spoken over minute philosophy as the presager of Fascism (and who shall say it wasn't?), and the unforgettable last chapter dedicating himself not to the class struggle, but to the struggle for a decent democracy.

He had one or two shots at writing in the manner called for. One was the recklessly titled "Man Goes Mad," which we have glanced at. The other was a short essay published in the house journal *Philosophy* in 1940, entitled "Fascism and Nazism."[7] He turns this, however, into his *idée fixe*: that liberal democracy can thrive only as the expression of a grounding on the foundations of Christian belief. The scale of forms, the groundedness of new knowledge in old, still throttles his thought; the historical fact, which he asserts but nowhere clinches, that the love of liberty and the hatred of tyranny ringingly upheld in English historiography rest on "the fact that God loved the human individual and Christ had died for him."[8] The idea that whatever such intellectual origins may indeed owe to dogmatic religion, they can nonetheless shake themselves clear not from the absolute presupposition of liberty but from its religious provenance, Collingwood rejects with scorn. With a touch of Eliot's fatalism, Collingwood asserts that "Religion is the passion which inspires a society to persevere in a certain way of life and to obey the rules which define it." Or a little earlier, "Take away Christian theology and the scientist no longer has any motive for doing what inductive thought gives him permission to do."[9]

The success of Fascism, he goes on, comes with its strange capacity to fire up its supporters with an ardour and fervour lost by wet old liberals. It has developed the cult of *Il Duce* and *der Führer*, and by drawing on pre-Christian and pagan passions still roaming in the spirit of Catholicism, reignited the fires of self-sacrifice and subservience carefully extinguished by old dissent and the Protestant ethic.

Collingwood adds a footnote to this remarkable manifesto, saying that it was a response to C.E.M. Joad, the popular philosopher-broadcaster who by way of the BBC's *Brains Trust* tried to do what Collingwood failed to do and bring moral and political philosophy to the aid of everyday life. Collingwood's essay in radical historicism (the absolutes of Fascism go back to the pre-Christian emperor Julian, as you might say) was his effort to support Joad.

During the essay he quotes the most famous passage of *Leviathan*, where Hobbes describes the "natural condition of mankind, the place of desolation, where there is no sovereign, no state or commonwealth, no rule of law . . . no account of time; no arts; no letters; no society; and which is worst of all, continual fear, and danger of violent death; and the life of man, solitary, poor, nasty, brutish, and short."[10]

"No account of time," so no history. Collingwood said not much about Hobbes in *The Idea of History*. Now he set himself, as he said in one letter, "to draw the bow of Ulysses." It is plain that, not without a certain appealing innocence, he saw it as his public duty, in order to put to rights public muddle. "When the war broke out I saw that the whole business was due to the fact that everybody concerned was in a completely muddled condition about the first principles of politics and, examining my own mind, I saw that I had plenty of ideas which it would be a public service to state."[11] And in much the same manner, he had written to Knox as he began the new work, to anticipate "intellectual bankruptcy" as a first consequence of war, and tell his favourite pupil that "people like you and me have a clear duty to prevent this if it can be prevented and to diminish the evil effects if it can't."[12] You can't say he was wrong to call it duty; but it's a large enough ambition.

The surprise is that he starts from Hobbes, not Spinoza or Hegel; surprising, that is, until one recalls Collingwood's Englishness, and as another anti-English and nomadic preacher, D. H. Lawrence, put it, also from the middle of a war, "my Englishness is my very vision."[13] Hobbes's grim materialism and his granite style chimed well with Collingwood's mood in 1940. He adapted the moral philosophy lectures he was giving that year to a new, bleak, extremely terse, and assertive mode of presentation on the page.

1.1 What is Man?

1.11 Before beginning to answer the question, we must know why it is asked.

1.12 It is asked because we are beginning an inquiry into civilisation, and the revolt against it which is the most conspicuous thing going on at the present time.

1.13 Civilisation is a condition of communities; so to understand what civilisation is we must first understand what a community is.

1.14 A community is a condition of men, in which are included women and children; so to understand what a community is we must first understand what men are.

1.15 This gives us the scheme of the present book: Part I, an inquiry into man; Part II, an inquiry into communities; Part III, an inquiry into civilisations; and Part IV, an inquiry into revolts against civilisation.

1.16 About each subject we want to understand only so much as we need in order to understand what is to be said about the next.

It fairly shook his admirers. Some of them put it down to the several vague explanations—illness, breakdown, and the rest—with which Knox, Richmond, Sisam, and company balanced their social embarrassment (about beards, adultery, radicalism) against their affection and admiration. Collingwood leaned hard on both the severity of form and the Hobbesian grandeur of reach in his subtitle: *Man, Society, Civilisation and Barbarism.*

The form itself is reminiscent to tourists of modern philosophy of Wittgenstein's early classic, the *Tractatus Logico-Philosophicus,* but of course the notation is familiar to anyone taking a first year course in logic. All the same, it is worth suggesting a convergence in the thoughts of the Austrian genius who was to dominate Anglophone philosophy for the next generation, and the greatest English philosopher of the prewar years. Collingwood as Waynflete professor was external elector to the Cambridge Chair of Philosophy for which Wittgenstein had applied in 1939. Keynes was his champion in Cambridge, clutching a first translation of Wittgenstein's greatest work, the *Philosophical Investigations,* and Wittgenstein himself, with his habitual self-deprecation, was convinced he wouldn't get the job because Collingwood was "a man who was sure to disapprove of Wittgenstein's work."[14]

In the event, Collingwood was away for the election, convalescing on his Javanese voyage, and anyway the result, on 11 February 1939, was a walkover for Wittgenstein. But it may be doubted whether the author of *The Essay on Metaphysics* and *New Leviathan* would have so disapproved of the *Philosophical Investigations*. They shared a joint conviction that propositions have no common essence and doubted that truth is a correspondence between proposition and fact. They were at one in rejecting an account of knowledge as a blank apprehension of the facts. They both argued that inner states were only knowable, by oneself and others, by the making of outer expression. And they both thought that to demand something called "proof" for everything one believes is to sentence oneself to sterility.[15]

It is in the final chapter, however, that I try to assess the importance or otherwise of early anticipations of later platitudes in thought. For now, it is only worth noting that brief passing one another of the two great philosophers, and to add that Wittgenstein would have seen nothing amiss in talking of barbarism and civilisation.

Collingwood does so boldly. It is a splendid book. Frederick Tomlin, his former student, is perhaps its most unqualified admirer, although David Boucher runs him close. Tomlin says:

> The fruit of years of reflection, *The New Leviathan*, like the *Principles of Art*, is the definitive contribution to its subject in our day. Nor is it merely a political treatise; it serves to rescue from oblivion some of Collingwood's ethical speculations, his refreshing views on education, and some important statements on the nature of language and the procedure of physical science. With the tremendous punch of its tabulated paragraphs, it is one of the most powerful, if the least "finished," of Collingwood's works. Given the author's extreme ill-health and the fact that much of the book was written during the blitz, its sustained mastery compels our admiration.[16]

It is noteworthy how many commentators remark on the very achievement of finishing a book at all when awaiting the next stroke, and certainly Collingwood didn't lack the courage, let alone the compulsion, necessary for the task. But after all, he had only been back from his convalescent cruise a few months when he was writing to the Clarendon Press to say he had to hand "36,000 words of more or less revised and final text."[17] It wasn't until the next stroke, which he suffered at the end of January 1941, that he himself thought that his intellectual powers might be impaired. As he said cheerfully in another letter to the press later that same year, only part 4 was written after that attack, "and so will contain any signs of battiness in the whole work."

There is plenty that sounds batty to our ears seventy years on, but he meant every word of it, and as he insisted himself the encapsulations of the past in the present may explode into utterly unforeseen eventualities. When, for instance, he comes to the incendiary section of his book, "civilisation as education," he straightly commits *all* education to the care of parents: "37.4. Plato is the man who planted on the European world the crazy idea that education ought to be professionalized; and, as if that were not enough, the crazier idea that the profession ought to be a public service."[18]

This is to go back to first principles with a Hobbesian vengeance, and the vengeance is taken on those *bien-pensant* worthies of the then Ministry of Education and their policy-makers in the London School of Economics who went on building the mountainous House of Schooling. That house is now become a vast conurbation, a national Panopticon endlessly measuring, barely suppressing, merely incarcerating. It does its best we all suppose, but "to ask even for a little of Cobbett's method [Gershom and Dorrie's kind of teaching] is to ask for the moon."

And yet. And yet today more parents than ever before—a tiny number, but rising—take the legal option to educate their children at home. Neither state nor the well-upholstered privileges of private education are going to go away this side of apocalypse, but Collingwood's scornful, racy dismissal of the efforts of all those teachers takes the measure of his book and its style.

It is written in what Edward Said calls "late style," as he exemplifies this from a range of artists working beside the oldest of civilised oceans, the Mediterranean: Euripides, Cavafy, *Death in Venice*, Venice herself with her gorgeous and garbage-strewn place in the European imagination, Ibsen, Wagner; then Said moves back north to consult late Beethoven, the last quartets and sonatas.

Late style, Said says (and never more so than in Beethoven) "is what happens if art does not abdicate its rights in favour of reality."

It is made by "an ego painfully isolated in the absolute," often "extremely careless and repetitive" in its characteristics, compressed, intransigent, difficult, nonchalant. "Lateness is being at the end, fully conscious, full of memory, and also even (even preternaturally) aware of the present. . . . Beethoven becomes therefore a figure of lateness itself, an untimely, scandalous, even catastrophic commentator on the present."[19]

Collingwood was as always writing philosophy as a branch of literature; he was "isolated in the absolute" but determined to brace transcendence against the quotidian, to be a poet and a man (like Wordsworth) speaking to men, and speaking to them of the world as it ought to be after he had had to leave it, which would be soon.

In the autumn of 1940, as the Nazis declared night-time Blitzkrieg after losing the Battle of Britain, Collingwood was living in a rented apartment in London in order to be with Kathleen Edwardes. He claims with modest pride in the preface to *New Leviathian* that "some degree of greatness, though I hardly know what, might be ascribed to a book written in great part not (as Hegel boasted) during the cannonade of Jena, but during the bombardment of London."

The book was his contribution to the war, for what else could a sick and ageing philosopher do except think and write clearly and truthfully, and point out the lies, the bullying, and the long-lived self-deceptions of the enemy's thought and action. This being so, it is less of a surprise to read his praise of the original *Leviathan* as a work of gigantic stature, and to find behind Hobbes's "grim features" and "the savage irony of his style how deeply he understood himself and his fellow men."[20] So he pits his own late style against Ulysses himself. It took confidence and not a little impudence.

He begins with the several topics of his 1940 lectures in moral philosophy, body, mind, feeling, hunger and love, utility, right, duty, on each of which he had been having his antirealist say for ten years. These pages are in the professional manner, and a bit of a plod. Here and there are to be found bold tips—"coming to know what you want is not to be done by reflection,"[21] "no man can become free by choosing,"[22] and his last word to Prichard, "A man's duty on a given occasion is the act which for him is both possible and necessary: the act which at that moment character and circumstance combine to make it inevitable, if he has a free will, that he should freely will to do."[23] It is only when we reach the section "Theoretical Reason" at the end of the first part that he begins to find his range and the right weight with which to load his tone. The section packs the whole history of rational inquiry into five pages; Nature has her means to her ends, teleology is intrinsic to her and to human self-images; the modern mind began when it softened teleology and hardened the rule of law, in nature and society; "history is to duty what modern science is to right" (what a zinging *mot* that is!); and the novelty of modernity that follows from this dictum is that "the object of scientific study is now become not nature but history."

He was now able, having got the moral keywords sorted out to his satisfaction, to give rein to a galloping combination of dense compression, free-floating dicta, truculent philippic (on psychology, on schools), terrific scorn (how about "Pacifism is warmongery complicated by defeatism"?),[24] and a glowing certainty of the coming victory of the civilised over the barbarians. Woven into these varied effects is a good deal of heavy-duty exposition, of "society as joint will" and the distinction between "society" and "community," which he needs for his argument but is unrelieved by illustration (which he rarely indulged), and ponderously delivered, as by the voice of the Sibyl.

Even so, it is strong stuff. The moralities of politics and quotidian goodness are distinct; government is "regularian," its office is to produce order, not economic efficiency (this would upset latter-day sentimentalists seeking an "ethical foreign policy"). There is a harshness in this to put one in mind of the recent revival of attention given to another bleak theorist, Carl Schmitt. Collingwood, however, considers "right" (in both a legal and a moral sense) and "duty" aspects of goodness,[25] and duty is integral to the very feasibility of rule, for "it is impossible for anyone actually to rule without feeling absolutely convinced that rule is duty."[26] That conviction was the product of the Roman Empire and its basis in law, and

39.92 Let us get this clear, for it is the most important thing in the book. *Law and order mean strength.* Men who respect the rule of law . . . are becoming day by day less liable to be bullied or threatened or cajoled or frightened into courses they would not adopt of their own free will by men who would drive them into doing things in the only way in which men can drive others into doing things: by arousing in them passions or desires or appetites they cannot control.

39.93 This is the lesson of history and . . . everybody knows it.[27]

This is Collingwood at his bluntest and of his most stony immovability. The dutiful student yields. But yielding is no good. Rightness entails rules, and the citizen's duty is to follow the rules. But "there are always conflicts between one way of life and another," and duty, under the instruction of conscience, is what one ought to do. What one then decides to do is up (or down) to the person in the case. He or she knows there *is* a duty, but what it is may be one of several possibilities, as well as another, better course of action still, which is, however, completely overlooked. Duty is not therefore an iron direction post, but an uncertain oscillation.

All this being part of Collingwood's hymn to his country and its civilisation in time of war, he disparages Kant's doctrine of the categorical imperative as so much "herd-marching" of a Teutonic kind. What he is determined to argue were it not for the fact that it is a very affirmative, not to say nonargumentative book, is for the certain presence of a collective will seeking to actualise a common good.

The family and marriage have become the basic units of community and society (although there have been other social contracts), and that unit becomes a society by the propagation of children. Collingwood is surprisingly rough with the conventional belief that the desire for children comes before the sexual permission granted by marriage, but then he adds, and proves his own with the child he made with Kathleen Edwardes, that "there is something distasteful about gratifying one's sexual desire for a woman without becoming the father of her children." It may be surmised that Kathleen had her predecessors in extramarital affairs (Margaret Lowenfeld for one), but this time was to be different. He meant it, and the baby was proof. "23.92 The facts of human infancy are dirtier and less picturesque ... than the fancies of Rousseau; but they are a safer foundation on which to build a science of the relations linking a man to his fellow men."[28]

Early in 1941 he suffered another stroke. He wrote to the London School of Economics to say that he would no longer be able to give the L. T. Hobhouse memorial lecture as scheduled, that it was already written, and asking that it be read by a member of staff on Collingwood's behalf.

It duly was. Old Etonian Alexander Maurice Carr-Saunders, director of the school, stood in to read the lecture (which the LSE published as a pamphlet) to a packed audience, before they all left to spend the night in the shelters. This was the section in *New Leviathan* headed "The Three Laws of Politics," which together enunciate Collingwood's theory of social classes, the formation of a ruling class's will, the qualities of rule-worthiness, and the appropriate reciprocity and its permitted freedom of play as between ruler and ruled.

This becomes an apology for social democracy in opposition to the sham democracy of Hitler's rule, whereby "a mob elevates to a position of supremacy over itself whatever is most devoid of free will, whatever can be entirely trusted to do what is dictated by the desires which the mob feels."[29] This is not a dogmatic (in spite of his dogmatism) but a historical guide to politics, and an explanation of the origins of contemporary tyranny and of the traditions that opposed it. Writing from London in the flat he was sharing with Kathleen Edwardes to his old archaeological co-digger and ally, the shoemaker Gerald Simpson, he had said a little time before, "I was away from home for a few days when your letter came, wishing to see for myself what the "greatest air force in the world" could do to London. The results are conclusive. Hitler can never beat us."[30]

He was proved right in the end, although there was a lot more air force to come, and terrible devastation with it. If the civilisation in which he put his historical faith was sure to win, it would finally be because of that singular version of it that had grown omnipotent across the Atlantic, a civilisation whose ultimate weapon for the creation of Armageddon was designed in America for the Allies by several German-Jewish-Americans, an Italian, a Dane, a Ukrainian, an Englishman, a New Zealander, as well as many others.[31]

Well, "a good cause is a cause of peace," as Collingwood says, but always an admirer of the misanthropy of Swift as well as the grimness of Hobbes, he adds, "the Yahoos are always here with us."[32] The Germans have thought themselves into a hatred of freedom and a state of herd worship—if it's a shock to read that said so straightly, remember Riefenstahl's *Triumph of the Will*—what is then at stake, as indeed it was in 1941, is whether the counterposing civilisation is historically well enough founded and sufficiently courageous and confident to win. Such a civilisation is founded on civility (this is no pleonasm); it avoids the use of force until forced to it, it will diminish as far as possible disparities of wealth between rich and poor (will it, indeed?), it will keep order and the rule of law, it will provide for peace and plenty.

These sound at first like unexceptionable bromides, until one remembers the hideous distortions of such natural hopes and expectations then being busily enacted across the rest of Europe, and one is taken up short by Collingwood's saying, "Peace is a dynamic . . . a strenuous thing,"[33] to be civilised implies "constantly overcoming one's own passions and desires by asserting oneself as free will" (we don't put it like that now, but we know what he means). Socialising means civilising, so down with school (this from a parent at Shrewsbury, Roedean, and the Dragon School). Then he reaches back to the tradition of liberty before liberalism[34] to commend in a civilisation that self-government among the ruled which the rulers are appointed to ratify and which is the ground of their authority.

With such a vision before us, barbarism, even if written about battily, doesn't stand a chance. Civilisation is too resourceful for one thing; barbarism lives to destroy, and it has to work itself up into a state of conscious hatred towards what it is seeking to destroy. (The jihadists of militant Islam at the present time are by this token barbarians.) But whatever damage the barbarian does, in the long run he cannot win.

41.7 What ensures the defeat of barbarism is not so much the enormous diversity of existing civilisations, too numerous for any
conqueror to dream of overcoming; it is the literally infinite
possibility of varying the nature of the thing called civilisation,
leaving it recognisable in this diversity; a possibility which will
be exploited as soon as success in a barbarian attack stimulates
the inventive powers of civilisation to look for new channels of
development.

41.71 For example, under the destructive energy of barbarism's first
onslaught it may seem dreadful that the monuments of civilisation in brick and mortar, in paint and canvas, in human customs and institutions, should be destroyed. But these things are
not civilisation itself, they are only examples of what it can do.
What made them once can make them again; their destruction
is a challenge to such remaking.[35]

He closes by arraigning four historical barbarians, the last a history
of the present: Saracens, Albigensians, Turks, and Germans. If there
is something a bit Anglocentric in all this, you can only say that in
1941 it was well earned. I do not myself think that there is. Primitive
tenth-century Islam was exigent, simple-minded, bred for the desert,
dismissive of literacy; the fourteenth-century Albigensians were
Manichean, antinomian, and lunatic; the fifteenth-century Turks
were simply murderous in the pursuit of territory; German barbarism, "thinking with your blood" in the Nazis' fatuous slogan, com-
pounds German history from Luther to Frederick the Great to Bismarck to Hitler in a condition of "herd-marching," of the worship
of "blood and iron," of incivility developed into mania.

He had spoken his last words on this or any topic, "a plain man
telling a plain story."[36] No need now to cackle his goose's warning.
The enemy was plain to see, and he had, in this heavy, veering, sometimes truculent, always dogged and compelling book, done all he
could to arm his small audience with the intellectual weapons its
history put into its hands.

III

The stroke at the end of January 1941 as London blazed around him at last persuaded Collingwood that he would have to resign his chair. He put in train the appropriate arrangements and sealed them in February by making Kathleen (known to everyone as Kate) pregnant. Mortal illness or no, modern contraception notwithstanding, he stuck to his beliefs about desire and procreation. At the beginning of April he and Ethel, with an indicative reluctance, began divorce proceedings, the sale of the Belbroughton Road house, and the division of their possessions,[37] some of the best furniture inherited from Skipness and Lanehead, all complicated by the fact that his sister Barbara Gnosspelius was still at the house, and Lanehead had changed little from the days when they were all children together. His professorial resignation was noted by the *Times* on 29 April, he resigned as a delegate at the press after thirteen years, and throughout all these weeks he was reworking and polishing the *New Leviathan* in order to send Kenneth Sisam the finished manuscript in August.

This brief chronicle indicates Collingwood's usual level of activity, but in these terms activity of a very painful kind—leaving a wife, leaving Oxford, battling with illness and with a book sure to be his last, leaving life too and with a child on the way, for he was by now very ill indeed. As he writes to his friend Wolfgang von Leyden, a German refugee philosopher whom Collingwood had helped spring from internment as an enemy alien on the Isle of Wight,

> There is much that I should like to talk to you about, but I cannot write except in a scrawl barely legible to myself and not at all to anyone else; and this machine which I am trying to use instead of a pen, is a tedious thing and difficult to keep under control. I should like to ask you to come and see me here [he is writing from Streatley]; it is not very far from Oxford; but then I can't talk except a little and stumblingly, like a man using a language to which he is strange.
>
> All this is explanation, not complaint. I lead an interesting, sufficiently active, and on the whole happy life. The work I watch myself

doing day by day to restore the adjustment of mind and body is I can't tell you how interesting, though mostly "unconscious": I congratulate myself that I have trained myself all my life to "keep on good terms with my own unconscious," as a psychologist once put it to me.[38]

Mind and body were never, alas, to be adjusted. The book was done, he was happy enough, like Mr. Valiant-for-Truth waiting for his summons, and the token, "That his Pitcher was broken at the fountain." His sister Barbara came fondly by slow wartime train to see him as she always had, and all three sisters were on good terms with Kathleen. There were few other visitors: Birley and Richmond were in uniform, Tom Hopkinson a war correspondent, Bernard Miles making AKC propaganda movies. But on 17 December 1941 baby Teresa arrived safely eleven days after the United States came into the war and thereby ensured that civilisation would, for the time being, turn back the tide of barbarism and provide the infant with a safe future.

The New Year turned, the Blitz was over, carpet bombing of the Ruhr by the RAF began, Collingwood signed off the preface to *New Leviathan* on 16 January 1942, and as the spring blossomed, he and Kathleen drove the few miles from Streatley to Reading and on 14 May were married at the Registry Office.

Almost at once, another severe stroke hit him, this time leaving him paralysed all down his left side and necessitating a wheelchair. Like every dying animal, there was only one place he wanted to be, and that was home. He said to Kathleen, "take me home to Lanehead to die,"[39] and they went, the old familiar journey, in trains packed with servicemen, frequently delayed by God knew what freight or troop movements blocking the route north, Didcot to Birmingham, Birmingham to Barrow, Barrow to Coniston, where they were greeted by the sweet and gracious features of sister Barbara, and driven in the dog cart (petrol rationing was severe) round the lake to the beloved house crowning its long slope down to the water.

There was still no electricity at Lanehead, the water laboriously heated from the boiler, and no telephone, as well as very little petrol. Robin was installed in a ground-floor room from which his wheelchair could be manoeuvred onto the terrace when the sun was out. There were still one or two elderly locals ready to do the chores and smuggle black-market chickens into the kitchen, and when *New Leviathan* came out it sold, to the surprise of the publisher, briskly and was cordially reviewed in the respectable weeklies. Kate's mother, Mrs Edwardes, the "tower of strength,"[40] came to stay for the duration and to help with the baby and the invalid, and a frugal, sufficiently beneficent order was constructed while the man waited for the end.

From the terrace he could watch the clouds moving east towards him from beyond the Old Man, see them form and reform exactly as Ruskin had seen them from the bluff only a little way down the lane, after he had launched upon those serpentine and engrossing speculations, part science, part worship, part the painter's attempt to translate observation into the rules of representation.

14. And in these figures, which, if we look up the subject rightly, would be but the first and simplest of the series necessary to illustrate the action of the upper cirri, the reader may see, at once, how necessarily painters, untrained in observance of proportion, and ignorant of perspective, must lose in every touch the expression of buoyancy and space in sky. The absolute forms of each cloud are, indeed, not alike, as the ellipses in the engraving; but assuredly, when moving in groups of this kind, there are among them the same proportioned inequalities of relative distance, the same gradated changes from ponderous to elongated form, the same exquisite suggestions of including curve; and a common painter, dotting his clouds down at random, or in more or less equal masses, can no more paint a sky, than he could, by random dashes for its ruined arches, paint the Coliseum.

15. Whatever approximation to the character of upper clouds may have been reached by some of our modern students, it will be found, on careful analysis, that Turner stands more absolutely alone in this gift of cloud-drawing than in any other of his great powers. Observe, I say, cloud-*drawing*; other great men coloured clouds beautifully; none but he ever drew them truly: this power coming from his constant habit of drawing skies, like everything else, with the pencil point.[41]

The beloved house enfolded Collingwood in safety, sister Barbara always, Ursula frequently present, the third, Dora, still in Aleppo but home for a while in 1942, the past of his childhood encapsulated in the familiarity of family opening into the still unknown and thrilling present of a new wife awaiting a new child. Kathleen as well as Barbara was a pianist, and breakfast was called, as it was by Dorrie fifty years before, by the clear notes of the baby grand piano telling the time according to Bach and Beethoven (Bach having by now replaced Beethoven at the centre of Collingwood's musical Pantheon).

The months turned summer into autumn, and by mid-December he was severely paralysed and almost speechless. He had put off until it was almost too late the preparations for a new will, and when it came to it, the form of words was devised by his solicitor William Heelis (whom Beatrix Potter had married) and read aloud to the invalid, "when he seemed thoroughly to understand the same." The document is very brief, leaving a thousand pounds to each of his children, and the rest from a net value of five thousand pounds to Kate. The will wrestles a little with Collingwood's instructions about publishing his remaining writings, leaving the decision to his wife and "a person nominated by the Clarendon Press." In the event, Malcolm Knox consulted Collingwood's wife only once. The will is authorised by a shaky cross, "Robin George Collingwood, his mark."

It was already bitter winter in the Lake District, the hills and lakes black and sodden with ice-cold rain. But there was plenty of wood to burn at Lanehead in order to make a sufficient wartime Christmas, lit by flames and oil lamps. Collingwood, by now barely stirring, was fading steadily away; he died on 9 January 1943, a short time before his fifty-fourth birthday. He was buried desolately three days later. His sister Barbara wrote in her diary:

> Funeral at Coniston 2.30 pm. A frightful day of dark and rain. There were no flowers, and no wreath but ours. The churchyard was muddy and wet; it poured steadily. The grave had been dug beside his parents' and with great difficulty. He had an unpolished coffin, and on the plate was the only name he came into the world with, Robin Collingwood (by my instructions).[42]

His brother-in-law, the Reverend Mark Luard Selby, Ursula's husband, officiated; Barbara had never quite approved of her brother's assuming the new name George after his baptism at Rugby. His first wife, Ethel, was eventually buried next to Gershom and Dorrie, in the grave next to her husband, when she died, aged ninety-four, in 1979. Neither of Collingwood's children with Ethel survived into old age. Their daughter died of unforeseen postnatal complications only six months after her father, and she too was buried beside him. Bill, after a solid career in the wartime RAF and British Airways, married Vera, a distinguished photographer, fell with complete abandon in love with somebody else, could see no way out, and killed himself in his garage by carbon monoxide poisoning in 1975.[43] Kate never remarried and lived the rest of her life with a woman companion. She became a teacher for the Workers' Educational Association and in Further Education, and a Labour councillor.

IV

During his last months at Lanehead, waiting and at times, one dearly hopes, directing his attention not towards the rushing end in sight, to tiny symptoms—this headache, that groping grasp—that might presage it, but towards the raging world and his brief, loving enclave within it, how did he reckon up his life?

> Think where man's glory most begins and ends,
> And say my glory was I had such friends.

Yeats's wonderful lines commemorate one glorious such portion of Collingwood's life: fewer friends, it may be, than his parents had, but abundance anyway: archaeologists, philosophers, students, curators, painters, carvers, naturalists, musicians; French, Spanish, German, Dutch; Coniston, Pembroke, Magdalen. This was the population of his own republic of letters, and he its consul-governor. The rollcall of his books stood as colonnade in the little city forum, the last one finished in the nick of time. *The Principles of History* remained, alas, a massive fragment; the Roman inscriptions would have to wait another twenty-four years for Richard Wright to finish them, but Collingwood's rubbings, copies, and annotations of the inscriptions already numbered five thousand (!) and stood as another large monument to his achievements.

The books spoke for themselves but have nonetheless been much spoken for in these pages.

> "The work is done," grown old he thought,
> "According to my boyish plan;
> Let the fools rage, I swerved in naught,
> Something to perfection brought."
> *But louder sang that ghost, "What then?"*[44]

"What then? sang Plato's ghost." Any such reckoning up as he made would see that his effort to shape the new science of human affairs was incomplete, the architecture rough-hewn, too often inconsequential, frequently adorned with a dead rhetoric. His heroic attempt to pull his work into the public realm and, even from the margins, to utter in a sane, affirmative speech such things as might purify the language of the tribe and rescue philosophy from the trivialities of its "parlour games" had been blocked by the limitations of his own historical experience, vitiated even by his own class arrogance and a vision of human possibility that, while never narrow, looked out from too high a mountain on the clouds of abstraction below. Given the high ambition, there is failure here; there is even tragedy.

Tragedy, the destruction of what is fine and noble by human malice or ugliness? And yet, reaffirming the possibility of victory even in failure. For failure is not defeat. The lines of force running through, gathered and laid down as veins of radical energy by Collingwood's life, the thought embodied in his actions, awaits its release as flame and power in a later generation. What I have insisted upon throughout the chronicle of his life as his Englishness, that of his multiplicity as scholar-sportsman-intellectual, reckless lover, artist, Lakelander statesman, freeborn Englishman, haughty Oxonian, is packed, like Ariel, into the vaults of possibility until the life surges through into a later history and geography and utterly changes actors in a brave or timorous new world, American, Indian, Chinese.

Who owns a biography? Does the matter of ownership even signify much, outside the redundancies of legislation around intellectual capital? That great poet, Edwin Muir, a man exactly Collingwood's contemporary, wrote in his *Autobiography* that "in themselves our conscious lives may not be particularly interesting." An autobiography, as the word declares, is only a particular sort of biography, another chronicle of a conscious life, written nonetheless because the biographer believes it indeed to be of interest, as I do this one. But Muir sets the ordinary domestic chronicle against another, much more distant and obscure horizon.

> What we are not and can never be, our fable, seems to me inconceivably interesting. I should like to write that fable, but I cannot even live it; and all I could do if I related the outward course of my life would be to show how I have deviated from it; though even that is impossible, since I do not know the fable or anybody who knows it. One or two stages in it I can recognise: the age of innocence and the Fall and all the dramatic consequences which issue from the Fall. But these lie behind experience, not on its surface; they are not historical events; they are stages in the fable.
>
> The problem that confronts an autobiographer even more urgently than other men is, How can he know himself? I am writing about myself in this book, yet I do not know what I am.[45]

Like Collingwood, Muir sees Christianity as supplying something for the locals at least of the essential form—the absolute presuppositions—of the fable, the conceptual shape it has to have in order to *be* a life. (For fear that people say, as they do, "that wasn't much of a life.") It must be part of the biographer's duty to render the fable, through however dark a glass. This is not a matter of a summary of the life at the end. The fable lurks in the chronicle, suddenly appearing at little climaxes, maybe, more likely moving, like Wordsworth's inapprehensible shapes, behind the settings and scenery of the life—the Lakeland mountains, say, or the architecture of Oxford, the presence of old history in a hole in the ground, the unpresuming closeness of young shipmates, a fountain pen scratching faintly on paper deep in the night at Pembroke College, the writer's reflection looking at him from the window the other side of the dark.

In 1984 the British writer Ian Hamilton set himself to write a biography of the famously reticent and reclusive American novelist, J. D. Salinger. Hamilton knew that Salinger would resist this plan, and he did, finally preventing publication of the full version by litigation. One judge's ruling that Hamilton made "fair use" of private letters, and that his book was "no act of commercial voyeurism or snooping into . . . a private life for commercial gain,"[46] was overturned by two others in the inviolable name of the right to privacy. Although much of the crucial letters' content had nonetheless appeared in newspapers, Salinger's suit was upheld by the asses of the law. Hamilton had to write a biography describing how he couldn't write a biography.

The protective obstacles around Collingwood are informal but not dissimilar. In 2003 I wrote to Collingwood's daughter (Kate's child), Teresa, saying I hoped to write her father's biography, setting out my credentials with well-deserved modesty. No reply. I tried again, recklessly saying that of course she would be offered the manuscript to edit as she saw fit. No reply. I solicited the help of three of my friends known also and quite well by Collingwood's daughter, one of them a very distinguished sociologist, her former professor and head of department (she was and is an academic at Oxford). All to no avail, indeed to no reply. In the meantime, with gratifying support from assorted referees, I had been awarded a two-year emeritus fellowship by the Leverhulme Foundation to write the biography.

In the meantime I had approached Collingwood's own publishers at Oxford University Press to ask for a contract. The proposal was duly sent out to readers who declared me unsuitable as not being a philosopher, not knowing enough about Hegelianism, not having ever written much about Collingwood. Quite shaken by this, I enlisted help from a former chief executive officer at Cambridge University Press who was much taken with the synopsis, and his efforts won the endorsement of the august house now my publishers.

By this time, I had adventitiously met with Collingwood's daughter. She confessed herself dissatisfied with what she saw as my picture of her father as "sportsman-intellectual," one of a long list of such hyphenations I had injudiciously suggested; she swiftly disappeared and ignored further letters. Since there is certainly an unseen stock of Collingwood's letters, perhaps totalling hundreds, this was a fierce disappointment. I was braced by my supporter from Cambridge saying that he thought I might find the lack of access a "liberation not a privation."

I tell this unedifying little tale in no vengeful spirit, but to give this book its context, to sketch something of its theory as issuing in its practice. Families, even at seventy years' distance, want to muffle the stories of their great ancestors until such time as the tale may be told without any of the crumpled demeanour or smell of mortality with which it was lived. Professional bodies of philosophers want to keep the re-enactment of pure thought as vacuum-packed and immunised as possible, in the case of Collingwood veering away with quite extraordinary fastidiousness from any of the facts of his life that made for his fable, whether the lengthy affair with Kate Edwardes (never mentioned in any of the commentaries) or the wide gap between his professed scorn for official education for children away from home, and the conventionality of dispatching his own son and daughter to expensive boarding schools.

Finding room for these things in the house of biography is then to limn the outline of the fable. In the case of a philosopher whose first precept directs us to the identity of theory and practice, not only are thought and feeling indissolubly linked, they take both form and content in tension with mere eventuality, transfiguring those events into experience, where that rather blank (but venerable) concept turns out to mean events-that-signify, significance being given by the collusion of our best thoughts and the best feelings that may inform them.

I am arguing for a view of Collingwood's life that retrieves him, as surely he would have wanted, from the parlour gaming prison-house of philosophy, and resituates him in a history, necessarily a history of private life and its presence in public thinking, a history also of how metaphysics may glow in the light of an ill-kept schooner in the Mediterranean as the gathering storm rolls in, on the face of a tombstone 1,800 years old, in the recollection of a mother's lovely face as she sang to a listening household, in the swift accumulation of pages of handwriting piling up towards a finished book, a set of answers to some sharp and pressing questions.

To have rendered these things on the page is not to have expounded a thinker's thoughts but to have dramatised a life. A biography—*this* biography—then attains the condition of art and further aspires to the condition of history. It is not likely that I have brought this off, but this is my ambition.

10

The Time of the Preacher:
Collingwood's Resurrection

Around 1984 the American country-and-western singer, Willie
Nelson, cut a new disc beginning with the song "The Time of the
Preacher." It starts

> It was the time of the Preacher
> In the year of 01
> And just when you think it's all over
> It has only begun . . . [1]

The preacher is the gun, and when Collingwood died the gun ruled
politics. While he wasn't exactly a gunslinging kind of scholar-
intellectual, the veering manner of his late style—from *An Autobiography* on—was clearly that of a man trying to make himself heard
over the noise of warfare. He *was* so heard; whatever the misgivings
at Oxford University Press and the startled drawing in of breath
around Oxford, the book struck a chord that resounded quietly
enough but well beyond the High; it was a fighting piece of work, it
was in the daylight, and it described the kind of gloves-off philosophy
to command the respect of the tough-egg philosophers of Marxism
who were its allies against Fascism.

When it was joined by the sibylline trenchancy of the *New Leviathan* and even by the bulky abstractions of the *Essay on Metaphysics*,
it was and remains clear that Collingwood intended a legacy of much
more than academic significance. When we now look at the extended
fragment of *The Principles of History*, as nobody has been able to do
until the day before yesterday when it was so thrillingly rediscovered

in the stacks at the Clarendon Building, the unmistakable manner, the fierce scorn, the earnest conviction, the charm and energy, all bear out the certainty that their author sought a high place from which to address the kingdoms of the world and the glory of them. Nobody can say why he broke off when at full gallop on *The Principles*. He was on his restorative cruise; he had just rewritten the last chapter of the *Autobiography* hardly in a way to reassure the ruffled delegates at the press, he was in fine literary form, and as the *First Mate's Log* also demonstrates, he felt happy, playful even, had been out of Oxford and mostly at sea since the end of May 1938, and was damned well going back to sea with the lads of the *Fleur de Lys* at the end of June 1939. *The Principles* could wait, and he would insert the *Log* into the gap before assuming the mantle of Hobbes and the preacher's voice.

I think it likely that he simply put the *Principles* aside, confident enough of his health for a while, cheerful in any case, excited, too, about Kate and his predicament, and confident of what would go into them. By the time he returned from Greece, war was declared and the gravity, the nontheoretic finality of the *New Leviathan* insisted on precedence.

Its fair success and that of the *Autobiography* notwithstanding, it was the philosophy of history that remained at the front of his admirers' minds. At his death, there were still two and a half years of total war to go, followed by acute privations (including paper rationing) for some years after that. In 1945, as the University Press began to resume some kind of publishing programme, Collingwood's presence was much in their minds; his arguments of five or six years previously looked pretty telling; even the alleged eradication of metaphysics looked much less complete after Belsen and Hiroshima, and Robert Oppenheimer a more rallying prophet than Freddie Ayer.

In these circumstances, the press cast about for an editor capable of ordering all the papers they supposed they held and as we know had, as they thought, the ideal man in Malcolm Knox. Collingwood had described him when Knox was only twenty-three as his best pupil, had supported him during his steady rise up the academic ladder at Oxford and St. Andrews, accepted the honorary doctorate

Knox had seen through the Scottish committees; he was eminent, competent, and confident.

It is hard nowadays not to feel sorry for Knox. He is so rightly convicted of sanctimonious error and sheer misunderstanding towards Collingwood. He ignored Kate, he disapproved of Collingwood's late style, he even destroyed some of the papers after transcribing them, but he was devoted and he was assiduous. So it was also that he took responsibility for the final version of *The Idea of Nature* and *The Idea of History*, which duly came out to some *éclat* in 1945 and 1946, the second almost immediately being awarded classic status and finding its way as a cogent influence into the work of some varied thinkers.

The anxiety of "influence" as exerted by thinker or writer on other thinkers and writers is, as is known by everyone, pervasive and unidentifiable. Nor is it clear what it is to speak of influence; as often as not, commentators detect influence where what is more accurately meant is that something in a later writer *reminds* the commentator in question of something about an earlier one. "The frequent result," as Quentin Skinner says, "is a narrative that reads like the opening chapters of the First Book of Chronicles." He goes on,

> Consider, for example, the alleged genealogy of Edmund Burke's political views. His aim in his *Thoughts on the Causes of the Present Discontents* was "to counteract the influence of Bolingbroke." Bolingbroke himself is said to have written under the influence of Locke. Locke in turn is said either to have been influenced by Hobbes, whom he must "really" have had in mind in the *Two Treatises*, or else to be concerned to counter Hobbes's influence. And Hobbes in turn is said to have been influenced by Machiavelli, by whom everyone was apparently influenced.[2]

Not that "influence" is a vacuous concept. It has essential relevance in our understanding of how ideas may be formed and, indeed, characters made. It is just that the concept is only applicable with great care; it is also indispensable, a mark of exactly that collective effort of creative mind that it was so much Collingwood's concern to detect and affirm.

It is therefore a matter of moment in estimating Collingwood's life-significance, to determine some of his direct influence. But there are two other ways in which a biography may judge importance and assign recognition. The first offers itself as a mapping of a series of familiar academic tasks and, indeed, labours of love. Under this heading, the biographer will provide a report on the industrial productivity brought into being by the subject at hand. There are whole volumes of lively interest about the Shakespeare, Machiavelli, or Henry James industries. It will only be just to Collingwood's name briefly to weigh the labours of those many men and women busily at work on the large archaeological site of his thought. Telling their names is one way of reckoning his continued presence, of coming to a valuation of his standing and of the degree of reinvestment of his intellectual capital.

Yet for much of the almost seventy years since his death, such reinvestment has not really penetrated beyond the boundaries of the active but still minor exchanges of the Collingwood industry itself. Commentary has led back into itself. The commentators converse largely with one another. It is as though the product of their labours is consumed only by other such producers; their nourishment is rarely gathered and absorbed into the food-chain of being and ideas, it cannot replenish the common good.

Such a judgement doesn't make the work pointless. All those with the necessary faith to work on and with Collingwood's life and thought (and the two as inseparable) can only keep going and trust that their reward will one day be to flourish in that new polity made possible by the reasons and passions of the tradition in which they stand with Collingwood.

After this roll-call, however, and after the conning of influence, there is the harder as well as the more exhilarating task of marking on the intellectual map "the line of force for transformation" (in Anderson's phrase I have three times invoked) that runs through Collingwood and on into his successors, including those who do not refer to his name. This is not a question of influence. It is the picking up of those historical messages which, in Arnold's great phrase, keep up communication with the future. I shall take two trios, partly by way of placing certain leading moral scientists of a more or less Collingwoodian persuasion against the intellectual horizon of the day, partly in order to suggest where we stand at the present in the contrivance of our "science of human affairs." The first such trio, composed of Thomas Kuhn, E. H. Carr and Charles Taylor, represents those who have come to conclusions similar to Collingwood's (in Carr's case, acknowledging indebtedness) about the historicality of human formation and the importance of establishing this truth as a commonplace of public thought. The second trio—Peter Winch, Quentin Skinner, Alasdair MacIntyre—count themselves explicitly heirs of Collingwood and, each in different ways, intend to apply his lessons two generations later to the construction of new "foundations of the future" upon which shall rise, it may be hoped, the science of human affairs.

This, finally, will provide the occasion for sketching out a version of such a thing as it might be assembled from those main components of method and metaphysics that Collingwood himself bequeathed to us, taking due regard at the same time of the extent to which those instruments of thought have dated, or remained both usable and real.

II

The Second World War left more than the cities of Europe in ruins. The right side won, but only just; the imperious claims made upon the Deity by the British national anthem and the more pious declarations of faith in Lutheran chorales were still being sung, but to emptying churches and with diminishing conviction. If one casualty of total war was a faith in Christianity, which could not survive the extermination camps nor Stalin's reign of terror, another was the blithe belief of the logical positivists that moral judgements amounted just to saying "boo!" to a blackshirt. Even A. J. Ayer himself had the honesty to admit as much, and there seemed to be as little to build on and up from the blitzed foundations of fundamentalist verificationism as from the broken walls and towers of the city of metaphysical reasoning. In politics, the battle was joined between two armies: on the one hand, existential Marxists marching to Sartre's stirring drumbeats in order to trample underfoot the Fascism always to be found in the secret gardens of the *bourgeoisie*; on the other, the victorious pragmatists of the United States taught a kindly salvation-through-liberal-capitalism, and set up Harvard University's Department of Human Relations and their allies in Chicago to accompany the Flying Fortress bases in West Germany and South Korea.

There wasn't much for metaphysicians to do. Back in Oxford and Cambridge, Ryle and Wittgenstein had demolished the long-lived psychology of Romanticism whereby human beings are divided into inner states and outer appearances and in which the key to understanding other people is to discover how they truly think and feel about the world. Wittgenstein showed his students, sitting in old deckchairs and on broken-down kitchen stools in a bare, floorboarded room in Whewell's Court, Cambridge, that we grasp other people's meanings in terms of what they say and how they use language to say it.[3] In unacknowledged tandem with Wittgenstein, John Austin was, as his famous book puts it, teaching *How to Do Things with Words*, and dividing the *practices* (rather than the functions) of language into three: the locutionary (propositional), perlocutionary (performative), and illocutionary (effective).

In these circumstances, deprived for the time being of "ideals to live for and principles to live by," Anglophone philosophers followed their dazzling teachers into a new, irresistible minuteness. Idealistic young men and women, looking for principles to live by, jumped ship and went to study English literature and history.

Passionate hearts attached to ardent minds seek out of necessity for a subject among the human sciences that will do them good. Theology was mortally ill; moral philosophy said to its students, as Collingwood reported it as saying half a century before, "I will tell you what acting morally is, but don't expect me to tell you how to do it."[4] When those same students sought to turn the ideals they now found in literary criticism and the history of democratic struggle into significant action and an honourable career, they were faced by the political immobilities of the Cold War and the scientific certitude of positivism.

In John Passmore's phrase, natural scientists had turned philosophers, and had done so since Russell came all-conqueringly forth.[5] The unorganised opposition to scientism, whether of Viennese or Oxbridge-and-London coloration, had been living rough in the Sherwood Forest of the outlaw human sciences—intellectual history, moral theory, literary criticism, archaeology, and anthropology— and had no alternative but to set to warrening the positivists from below, occasionally riding gallantly on guerrilla raids to attack the vast caravan of the enemy, laden as it was with chestfuls of government research money and dressed in the well-cut tabards of official ideology.

It is as members of this band of merry men that, for instance, Louis Mink published forty years ago his study of Collingwood's thought.[6] Now it would be impossible for me to round up the troops of the Collingwoodian tendency and say something not untrue and not unkind about each of them. I am here concerned only to treat them as symptomatic of the antipositivist guerrilla, and as keeping those humanly central arguments going in inauspicious weather.[7]

Mink does this nobly and, naturally, from a position on the margins of American thought. He takes the honorific term "logic" away from Collingwood's "logic of question-and-answer" and substitutes for it Aristotle's originary discipline, "hermeneutics," which is fine. He gets needlessly tangled up in trying to make absolute presuppositions into a priori concepts when Austin, as we saw, had showed him how needless this was, but he carries them forward nonetheless into "the grammar of action," using them to join institutional to individual explanations of conduct, and to discover in Collingwood's aesthetics an inclusive theory of language as of its nature always seeking higher-order ways of expressing itself as the unity of thought and emotion. In this search, art is first and last both end and means.

Collingwoodians must declare for monism. It doesn't win everybody's vote. Jan van der Dussen, writing in the Netherlands at another geographic liminal, advances steadily through the *oeuvre*, disregarding art, and making much of archaeology as *the* type of scientific history. Van der Dussen carefully excavates Collingwood's early endeavours as director of excavations at the Roman fort at Ambleside in 1913, adding the admiring detail that the diggings stretched over twenty-nine weeks of the four years, 1913, 1914, 1915, and 1920, and that Collingwood was present for all but four of them.[8]

Van der Dussen is following his subject along the trail of question and answer and pursues him across Borrans field to the edge of the lake while Collingwood determines whether a particular wall was a Roman quay, a breakwater, or a landing of another date, finally explaining the anomaly by proving that an Agricolan fort of turf and timber lay below the one ordered by Hadrian.[9] Thus history as science, the product of many hands and minds, and science as human, which is to say interpretative.

It is Rex Martin who, in a lifetime dominated by his earnest attention to Collingwood, most directly addresses the large question of, in his phrase, a science of human nature. Martin puts at the centre of any such science the task of the re-enactment of the thoughts of others, and the sheer unfeasibility of doing so successfully when frames of mind are so unalike as across histories and between geographies.[10] Collingwood dismissed the possibility of trans-historical generalisation about human nature. Yet he advocated as method a movement of mind requiring that a contemporary human nature in some sense occupied a past human nature. Martin writes, "since the principle of practical inference would itself have to be set aside as inapplicable, he would not even have a clear sense of how these notions could be applied to agents in the past."[11]

Martin's answer for the founding of "a discipline, if not a science of history" is to devise "a scheme of practical inference," according to which "qualitatively dissimilar instances" would be assimilated according to "material rules of intelligibility" from very different historical moments. These rules (Martin's "schema" is, so to say, a theorisation of rule-following) would, as a consequence of working towards general agreement about the practices of historians, provide "for objectivity of a sort" by assuming kinship in "a single family of such rules."[12]

This isn't the place to pursue so formidable an algebra. We shall take refuge in Clifford Geertz's haunting interpolation: "one of the significant mysteries of man's life in culture: how it is that other people's creations can be so utterly their own and so deeply part of us."[13] The point of these brief reviews is, after all, not to enter into the technicalities of the debate but to gesture towards a few of those figures who, without of themselves ever quite gaining the authority to return Collingwood to the mainstream of historical and philosophic thought, had the dedication and the talent to keep interest up, to sustain a debate on the work without which any future recovery of Collingwood's ideas would have to reach back over a long period of silence and neglect, and the task of restoration be made the much harder.

An absorbing conclusion to any biography is posthumous. What do we make of our hero now? This becomes an essay in a reach-me-down sociology of knowledge, and the last major contributor to the little enclave of Collingwoodians who have tended the flame in the hope that it will then be at hand to illuminate a much wider horizon is David Boucher. The praise due to his prodigious efforts, still very much in train, is such as cannot be tucked away in prefatory acknowledgement; those efforts are part of the biography. For sure, there is his admirable and timely guide to Collingwood's *oeuvre*, in which he presents Collingwood less as metaphysician and more as a political theorist, and successfully translates the high abstractions of sort-of-idealism into a tough secular liberalism.[14] *The New Leviathan* is therefore Boucher's culminating text (not at all the usual evaluation in 1989), the liberal theorists who succeeded T. H. Green such as Hobhouse and, indeed, Ruggiero being reproached by him for failing to connect community and family to the polity, and the final masterpiece providing a neo-Hobbesian account of authority as held on behalf of the common good by a steely and socially mobile elite.

The theory of mind is then a theory of the good society. The threat to civilisation came primarily, as Collingwood sees it in his last book, from the mindless predominance of scientistic thought, abominably distorted and ideologised by Soviet Marxism on one hand, and the crazed worship of militarism by Fascists on the other. Boucher expounds all this faithfully and bids farewell to a Collingwood taking his stand on the unity of metaphysics and the moral sentiments, a compound hardly recognisable as liberalism, at least of a variety promulgated by Sir Isaiah Berlin, canon of contemporary liberalism. In Boucher's version of Collingwood's hopeful vision, the victory of civilisation over barbarism would be declared by the social expression of a commonly understood and practical rationality. It is this goal that Collingwood's most impressive successors address in our own time.

Boucher's book, however, is only the first intimation of his importance to admirers of Collingwood. One of the most obscure but important of those admirers, a wealthy businessman named Bill Rieckman (who was introduced by some daring teacher while pursuing an MBA degree to the idea of absolute presuppositions in marketing), had offered Oregon State University about £100,000 on behalf of Collingwood studies. He was (indicatively) turned down, and after the founding of the Collingwood Society with the help of James Connelly, another stout defender of the faith, in 1989 an approach was made to St. Catherine's College, Oxford, which wanted a million pounds for a couple of rooms. Finally, by dint of Boucher's heroism, a centre was established at his university in Wales. Boucher and Connelly called into existence a society with substantial vice-presidencies; founded, edited, and developed the journal *Collingwood Studies*,[15] arranged its supporting conferences (including driving the bus for trips to Hardknott Fort); and tirelessly and devotedly gave themselves to the immense labours of maintaining these activities for almost twenty years.

This is no merely dutiful tribute. Boucher's own dutiful fidelity makes an indispensable link in the very survival of the social history of a philosopher's thought. The competition of ideas is as bloodstained and arbitrary a process as the survival and mutation of species. We cannot know how many thinkers and their thoughts have been, along with their lives, lost forever. The small domestic business and pleasure of journals, conferences, doctoral dissertations, all the commonplace life of the mind in action, provide a reassuring sign to the gloomy that a love of scholarship and an unselfinterested zeal for thought and its succour still brace themselves against the worst the Philistines can do.

III

Such is the strange catchall, culture, which builds continuity. The clutch of thinkers who follow depend on it. This review of their life-thinking must serve to indicate how Collingwood's "line of force" comes through to a changed world, how his ideas, couched in a different historical idiom and with absolute presuppositions other than our own, lives in the present, even, it may be, with greater powers of transformation than he could ever exert in his lifetime.

Scanning the intellectual landscape for signs and wonders that do not so much declare Collingwood's influence as give a glimpse of his aliveness to changes in the winds and tides of thought, one's eye is caught in 1962 by Thomas Kuhn's amazing book, *The Structure of Scientific Revolutions*.[16]

Its provenance lay in assorted French researches of the 1930s into early modern scientific inquiry, and, highly specialised though it was, it was clearly and beautifully written. There can hardly have been a single more signal explosion to shake the complacencies of positivism at the very heart of scientific certitude. It is noteworthy, moreover, that Kuhn pays tribute to the help and friendship of Stanley Cavell who, his rapturous praise for Cary Grant's movies notwithstanding, is surely the American philosopher closest to Collingwood in taste, manner, and heresy.

Neither in Cavell's work nor in Kuhn's can I find reference to Collingwood, but Kuhn provided a definitive account not only of certain absolute presuppositions that, in his idiom, constituted the "paradigms" of "normal science," but also caught those paradigms in the process of changing. It is perhaps worthy of note also that a prominent Collingwoodian, Stephen Toulmin, spotted the similarity in ideas but haughtily and wrongly described them as a "crude" "popularisation."[17] Kuhn wasn't "crude," he was bold. Taking as a first instance of such a change historical inquiry into the nature of light, Kuhn identifies Newton's defining role as gathering the conflicting and fissiparous theories of physical optics swirling about the competitive practices of late-seventeenth-century inquiry, and reordering them as "paradigm."

Newton's constitution of light was, of course, solidified and extended for a couple of centuries until Planck and Einstein inaugurated *their* revolutions and thought that light is "quantum-mechanical entities that exhibit some characteristics of waves and some of particles,"[18] but on the way to that stupendous discovery scientists accrued, more or less randomly according to Kuhn, all sorts of data that became more and more difficult to fit into the paradigm. "History suggests that the road to a firm research consensus is extraordinarily arduous,"[19] and that the displacement of one paradigm by another is resisted for a long time as scientists try to stick with the theories they know and understand, theories that fit their absolute presuppositions, until at last the weight of contrary evidence, piled against their present explanations, breaks down the walls of their resistance and sweeps them away.

It is at such moments that Kuhn's "paradigm-shift"—itself an invention that became a cliché so forceful were its implications—may be observed in detail. For our purposes, Kuhn's book reads like an extended and detailed elaboration of *The Idea of Nature*, but instead of merely marking out the three distinct epochs of scientific presuppositions, Kuhn plots the movement from one to another and provides a sociology of that uneven and erratic transition.

What does it matter if it is indeed true that Collingwood presages Kuhn in mutual ignorance? Only this: that Kuhn, in the next generation, provides new evidence that history explains science and not vice versa, and that perhaps our hero is right to say that history is now assuming its role as key to all our mythologies, and that the right theory of history will provide the guide to a practical rationality in social and scientific, as well as political life.

The first most direct and ambitious public statement of a Collingwoodian kind on the importance and coming-to-maturity of historical consciousness was that of E. H. Carr, when he gave the Trevelyan Lectures in Cambridge in 1961. Public lecture series at the old universities carried more weight in those days than they do now, and besides, Carr cut quite a public figure. Three years younger than Collingwood, he had been of course a star undergraduate (in classics, also of course), a brilliant recruit to the Foreign Office, a professor at the then University College Wales before, in a startling detour, becoming assistant editor at the *Times* and frequently author of its first leaders. He had taught himself Russian during his diplomatic peregrinations, and in 1945 he began his classic *History of Soviet Russia*, a thirty-year, fourteen-volume megalith with its author's own sympathy for Marxism carried in its genes, but also with its own absolute probity of spirit accompanied by the kind of explanatory completeness called for in *The Idea of History*.

There could hardly have been a more salutary medicine to be taken by Britain's exhausted political elite, tiptoeing towards the awful daring of its first majority Labour government, threatened by bankruptcy, incredulous of the end of empire, chilled to the bone in 1946 by the coldest winter for a century.

By 1961, when Carr spoke his lectures, it was goodbye to all that, and the country stood on the edge of astounding prosperity. But it did so, it may be, with some sense of the partisan beneficence of history, of all that it had done to others' harm (including Soviet Russia's) which once it took for exercise of virtue. If, at the least, a new historical awareness and a new industry on the part of a more collectively self-aware labour force in academic history could teach how to bring a better future out of a tormented past, then Carr's secular sermons serve to mark a moment at which such a change became possible.

So Collingwood is an early text in Carr's homilectics and is so because the rule of the historical facts as arranged for English self-congratulation had relaxed its grip exactly when "the facts seemed to smile on us less propitiously."[20] For Collingwood prescribed a philosophy of history concerned neither with "the past by itself" nor with "the historian's thought about it by itself," but with "the two things in their mutual relations." Then follows perhaps Collingwood's most life-pervading commonplace: "The past which a historian studies is not a dead past, but a past which in some sense is still living in the present."[21] This is our master's prime lesson: action expresses thought, hence the interpretation of action can only follow the re-enactment of the thought.

I have already suggested that for all the to-do by commentators on what it is to re-enact the thoughts of others, Collingwood did not mean anything exaggeratedly novel or difficult in the exercise. It is what we all do in trying to understand the actions of others with more or less of intelligent imaginativeness or obtuse partiality. Carr says so too.

> Much of what has been written in English-speaking countries in the last ten years about the Soviet Union, and in the Soviet Union about the English-speaking countries, has been vitiated by this inability to achieve even the most elementary measure of imaginative understanding of what goes on in the mind of the other party, so that the words and actions of the other are always made to appear malign, senseless, or hypocritical. History cannot be written unless the historian can achieve some kind of contact with the mind of those about whom he is writing.[22]

Carr's hope for historical education in the climate of 1961 is that it can teach a people some timely modesty about itself with regard to other peoples at a conjuncture when it was more than time due modesty was compelled upon it.

Carr has admonitions for Collingwood, whom he is the first critic to characterise as a relativist,[23] but we may put this down to Marx's getting the upper hand in his mind, Collingwood's firm conclusion in a number of places in his work being that while we can only think as we do in the relative contexts of a particular history (there is no "view from nowhere"), that fact in no way debars us from a greater historical intelligence than that shown by some past competitors, nor prevents our being more likely to be right about the past-in-the-present as it shapes our purposes than was the case with historically more ignorant predecessors.

Perhaps this banal and baffling thought may best be illumined by following a metaphor of Carr's own about the very idea of progress, and turning it to our account; perhaps in addition this pointing of the moral may persuade the reader to abandon the subjectivity-objectivity antinomy for ever, and to speak instead, if a bit mouthfil-lingly, of "historical intersubjectivity," or a neater neologism—"ret-rocognition" or some such—which I leave it to you to invent. What is meant is, in any case, Louis Mink's slogan, "understanding back-wards to think forwards," and that cannot be done without both the facts and the hermeneutics.

With the volumes not only of Marx but of Darwin in his study, Carr launches himself on the fifth of his lectures, "History as Prog-ress." He acknowledges, as after two hideous world wars he must, just how frail a belief in progress has become and notes how, even before the second of those wars, such a historical study as Spengler's *Decline of the West* attained best-selling status. But as he wrote, social reform in Britain had recently completed one of its most radical programmes, which, with the inauguration of the National Health Service and the welfare state, the wholesale nationalisation of bank-rupt utilities, the extension of free, secondary education for all chil-dren, and so forth, bore more than sufficient witness to a nation's belief in the reality of progress. And such a movement in different idioms was general all over Europe.

Carr makes fun, as Collingwood would certainly have done, of the so-called Whig Interpretation of History,[24] according to which, as goofy Dr. Pangloss almost taught, everything is for the best but is getting better anyway. Nonetheless he is resolute in holding on to a vision not of a nation, but of a world on the move, a colossal multi-tude not swimming aimlessly about but gathered into a kind of order, its ranks trooping in a long, errant line, now bending to one side or the other, sometimes doubling back on itself, but still discern-ibly *advancing*, becoming

> something in the future towards which we move, which begins to take shape only as we move towards it, and in the light of which, as we move forward, we gradually shape our interpretation of the past. This is the secular truth behind the religious myth that the meaning

of history will be revealed in the Day of Judgement. Our criterion is not an absolute in the static sense of something that is the same yesterday, today, and for ever: such an absolute is incompatible with the nature of history. But it is an absolute in respect of our interpretation of the past.[25]

There is furthermore something opportune about the vantage point, wherever it is, at which any one age finds itself when part of this massive march into the light and darkness of the future. As the great host moves more or less forward but intermittently doubling backwards, we may think of it, from our particular location, as passing close to earlier incarnations of our own society (or of another one) such that their past becomes suddenly visible and sharp-etched.

At such a coincidence, our historical moment is placed with accidental happiness close to another, past moment and able to recover that history with unusual clarity. Four decades ago, for example, this fortunate propinquity made it possible for gifted historians like Christopher Hill to write a new, rich, moving, and complex history of the English Revolution, and E. P. Thompson to do the same for the early nineteenth century. Something in the intellectual and moral temper of these authors—their egalitarianism, no doubt, their feeling for social justice, even their republicanism—made a new history of the Civil War and the Commonwealth, and of the moment of Peterloo, both more urgent and more immediate. So too the vast upheavals of the Second World War and its preliminaries helped rouse the great *annaliste*, Fernand Braudel, to compile his total history, *The Mediterranean in the Age of Philip II*.

This is no more than a glimpse of the revolution in historical consciousness of which Collingwood was the prophet and of which the Second World War, amongst so much destruction, may be thought of as the terrible parturition. Whether the march of progress, in Britain at least, has made such conjunctures by now less likely, for this or other nations or for historians, may be judged in the light cast by the monumental labours of a contemporary figure, Collingwoodian in ambition if not in allegiance.

Charles Taylor is a Canadian of a strong Anglophilia. In the 1950s as a research student in Oxford he was a leading figure of the then

New Left, a British group of intellectually spirited students and youngish teachers looking for a radical critique of a now resurgent capitalism while rejecting both the monstrosity of Stalinism and the stolid quietism of the British Labour Party. Taylor put a family legacy at the service of the movement's journal, *New Left Review*, and in a classic new study, *Hegel*, restored the old prophet to his rightful place as father of the human sciences.[26]

He then bent himself to turning Hegel's lessons into a form usable for the late twentieth century, joining Collingwood in a restoration of a sort of historical idealism to hermeneutics. In a classic essay, "Interpretation and the Sciences of Man,"[27] he did everything he could to dissolve the distinction between subjectivity and objectivity into the shared but necessarily relativised world of "intersubjectivity." He repeated the old, necessary injunctions against treating human conduct as a succession of mindless behaviours and insisted with a novel thoroughness on the explanation of action as being the interpretation of purposive meaning (or, as Collingwood would have preferred, *thought*). He added to this foundational effort to recast his intellectual inheritance another quite new statement, "Self-interpreting Animals,"[28] there contending for an interpretative procedure ordered according to the best and most relevant emotions that the interpreter is capable first of disciplining and then of bringing to the inquiry.

Armed with these powerful utensils, he produced his masterpiece, *Sources of the Self*, an extended account of the historical self-making of the modern character in its typical Western European and North American incarnations.[29] Taylor traces the strands of thought that mingle and intertwine in our daily selves—the doctrines of work (production) and of domestic life, especially marriage and the family (reproduction)—and rightly makes much of that key development in modern life whereby individuals seek so ardently for "expressivist" or Romantic satisfaction, that is, for hoping to find and live a happy match between passion and another person, between restfulness and a place (home), and—in a Collingwoodian turn—between a lifetime and a God (sometimes more vapourously, "the Good").

For one sharp critic, a later spokesman in this concluding chapter, this is the point at which "Taylor the moralist steps aside in favour of Taylor the protagonist of theism" and thereby disqualifies much of his conclusion.[30] Collingwood's ghost may have been applauding Taylor for his rooting of the modern in various versions of the Christian's spiritual inheritance, but for Skinner what is "astonishing is Taylor's failure to come to grips with the intellectual depth and reach of modern unbelief."[31]

Two decades later, no doubt, that deep unbelief has to face up to the renaissance of religious belief especially in its hate-filled fundamentalist and delirious forms; but intellectual disbelief has stood its ground. The commonest response to Taylor's return to a pacific Catholicism seems to be (it certainly is for me) a head-shaking incredulity.

Yet nothing can gainsay the unignorable grandeur of this book, nor the doggedness and courtesy with which he has nondoctrinally sought to accommodate, in a long series of quiet-spoken interventions, the noisy new adherents of the politics of recognition (Taylor's own phrase), of authenticity and identity. The answer of nonbelievers to the question, "what shall we *do* with such thoughts?" is much the same as with Collingwood: lean on the history, heed the moral judgements, ignore the presence of God. Collingwood, of course, said this was impossible, that the godless scientist would otherwise have no "motive" (curious word in this context) to analyse nature.

Taylor himself has proved sufficiently provoked by atheistical criticism to produce a monumental response. In *A Secular Age*, he not only returns to and elaborates his hostility to scientism but argues that dogmatic atheism is blank to the human need for spiritual meaning and epiphany and, in a way Collingwood would applaud, notes the "pressures" (like the "strains") that make resolution on the big questions about Being quite impossible to reach. At the same time, he is generous about the richness and resourcefulness of the secularism he criticises, now well over two centuries old. He analyses movingly and advocates strongly the success of new social forms created by Romantic individualism, its freedoms and its sense of the service due to others.[32]

One can find, it seems to me, in this large and magnificent intellectual achievement a latter-day embodiment of what Collingwood would have wanted for himself. Taylor's splendid career is without tragedy. He is an acclaimed public intellectual; in the 1960s he ran four times for the Canadian Parliament on behalf of a new party of the herbivorous Left; he is now turned to by his people for wise and ecumenical advice on the difficulties of multiculturalism, whether Francophil, Anglophone, Inuit. He writes copiously and all the time, like Collingwood. He is pungent on the weaknesses of liberalism, and his science of human affairs is historical, as Christianity is historical.

This being so, best to take him, like Collingwood, shorn of religion. Whatever the future of the clash of civilisations, European civilisation will continue to reject and put down barbarism, and confine religion to private life.

Given the statute, therefore, that religion cannot in its established churches bind societies together as a unifying presence, and this largely because its historical claims have become strictly incredible, Taylor's importance, like Collingwood's, lies in his historical method and in the courage with which he moves from method to morality. His politics is the product of deep changes in sensibilities shaped by Christianity. This is true of all of Western civilisation. That politics gives rise to our best inheritance, which is the conjunction of freedom allied to a civil conception of the common good. Radical historicism need make no pledge to save or destroy religion. It's nature herself that is cutting our time short and impelling humankind towards its terminus. History—scientific history—proves that. Collingwood's admonitions in *New Leviathan* about law and order meaning strength find their echo in Taylor, at this moment of human reckoning; so they do in those thinkers explicitly his heirs.

III

It is time to turn, as we approach our coda, to those present-day historical philosophers and scientists of human natures, who have not so much displayed an involuntary kinship with Collingwood, like Kuhn, or a sympathetic recognition of methodical approach, like

Carr, or a grand similarity of purpose, like Taylor, but have directly started out from some of his key ideas. There are three: Peter Winch, Quentin Skinner, and Alisdair MacIntyre. Obviously there could be many more in either of the two categories—the self-conscious heirs and those unaware of their similarity to Collingwood's work who nonetheless fit his purposes and predictions.

My three choices as sons and heirs are each much applauded as makers of the present shape of the human sciences and as powerful presences in what Clifford Geertz, in a strong essay, calls "The Way we Think Now."[33] Indeed, Geertz himself, who only died in 2006 and was long interested in Collingwood, could certainly stand in here as another such pillar of the community of human scientists were it not for the fact that I have tried to take his measure elsewhere and could only become repetitive if I tried again.[34] My three alternative figures stand in turn on the arc of human science as anthropologist, historian, and moralist.

Peter Winch does duty as anthropological worthy, in particular as pointing the moral from an early contention in the critique of positivism that how other people, in other times and places, think for themselves is only rarely how we do our thinking here and now.

In a footnote, Collingwood once quoted a remark of a rather barking kind by Britain's greatest anthropologist, Sir Edward Evan Evans-Pritchard, who intended it, I guess, as a paradox with which to shake up *bien pensant* social scientists who had never left North Oxford: "Let the reader consider any argument that would utterly demolish all Zande claims for the power of the oracle. If it were translated into Zande modes of thought [which is the same thing as saying, if it were translated into the Zande language] it would serve to support their entire structure of belief."[35]

Winch reaches what was then a shock and is now a triteness, that understanding other cultures must be, so far as possible, the result of an effort to think in and with their categories.[36] He quotes Collingwood who, as we saw, foresaw the extent of the alternative error, dismissing some anthropological explanations as masking "a half-conscious conspiracy to bring into ridicule and contempt civilisations different from our own."[37] Collingwood's accounts of magical art and how to understand it provide the theoretic core of Winch's idea of a social science.

This puts in place a quite straightforward version of re-enactment as the first stage of such a science. An event is circumscribed by the concept of action, and action expresses thought. To understand the action is to think the thought as the original agent thought it. The interpretation of the ideas of others is the point of Winch's social science. Globalisation hadn't been named as the new condition of modernity in 1958, but it was on its way. Reconstructing the context of the thoughts of others in order to understand them would offer the only way to turn back nations as they groped for progress or trekked sullenly away from it.

These are the principles of history as a theoretic discipline and, if you like to put it that way, of politics as a form of practical rationality.[38] As I said, principles are not synonymous with theory; they regulate inquiry, bringing its conclusions into the form of knowledge itself and ascribing value to that knowledge. Quentin Skinner, as he says himself, began his career with *The Idea of History* in his hand.[39] He recalls that as a schoolboy, preparing in his turn for a scholarship at Cambridge, "one text we were particularly advised to read was R. G. Collingwood's *The Idea of History.* I was fascinated by it, and I remember looking for others of his works and read them too, in particular his *Autobiography.*"

What Skinner found in Collingwood was threefold and familiar to anyone reading this book this far: there was first the insistence that historical study is the study of mind in action; second, that for such study to be *historical,* it could not pretend to be the study of "dateless wisdom in the form of universal ideas" but must give itself to the actualities of context and intention;[40] third, that in recovering the pastness of past thoughts, one is not in the ordinary sense furthering one's understanding of oneself, one is rather enabled to see how we might think and feel otherwise than as we do. The purpose of historical inquiry so defined is to erect a larger context of experience within which we may define and understand our own by attending to the disparity between it and the experience of others.

It is forty years since Skinner gave his conference paper "The Unimportance of the Great Texts"[41] and so roused his academic audience from their dogmatic slumbers by contending that their labours were built over a huge hole that a number stalked out in a huff and have been obliged, over the years, to return apologetically and admit that the boy, by 1997 the Regius professor, was right all along.[42]

His Collingwoodian argument has been that all political philosophers, including authors of the classics, were not trying to answer timeless questions on eternal exam papers, but to win an argument about matters of life and death immediately around them, by the power of reason if possible, of rhetoric if not. Skinner's first preoccupation was to return the history of ideas to *history*, which is to say that the great texts, like the lesser ones, belonged to contexts. In spite of what some parodists of his method have said,[43] this was not a programme to dissolve text into context, still less to deconstruct text into those forces of which the authors were so wholly unaware that they had no clear sense of what they meant and hadn't said it anyway. Skinner's plain blunt injunction was to assume that his key thinkers meant what they said. Adding J. L. Austin to Collingwood, he wished to pursue not only what they said, but what they were doing as they said it. Were they persuading, affirming, subverting, or revising, when they rehearsed their doctrines to decidedly touchy and unpredictable princes? Hobbes's truculence, More's innocence, Machiavelli's moral revisionism were all intentional devices purporting to win the intellectual day for their side.

This goes deep. For once you radically historicise author and argument in this way, you hit hard against their sheer incommensurability with contemporary certainties about what really matters. Skinner returns to the arguments of the past in order to bring back to the present disconcerting truths (true, that is, as being part of a factual historical record) about the way, for example, people in the Italian city-states of the early Renaissance thought about what is right rather than about rights, about the common good rather than private pleasure, about their duty to maintain the conditions of liberty rather than about their licence to do what they liked.[44]

This is not the tired old reactionary bromide saying that the past is a better place. It is an admonition to notice how we cannot use the past as the materials for self-congratulation in the present. It is also an inquiry into roads then opened up, but not taken subsequently. Liberty, before liberalism[45] got hold of it, was extolled by John Milton and James Harrington, during the great, lost opportunity of the English Commonwealth, as only being there to enjoy if the people were their own sovereign. None of this pussyfooting about "freedoms to . . ." and "freedoms from" with Isaiah Berlin: a citizen is only free when self-governing.

To speak so is to take Skinner's point and stick it into present ignorance with a coarse insistence quite at odds with his own, non-polemical courtesies. But one's excuse is that it is such a pleasure to find the vindication of scholarship at the present time so easy to make. As one reads Skinner's infinitely patient, detailed, strenuously plain-speaking prose in earnest reconstruction of long-dead arguments, one feels a gradual urgency thrilling through them, until one sees that he has brought off the miracle of resurrection all historians strive to perform. The old words are spoken again in the alien present. The calls to liberty, equality, or the common good are made by these weird-sounding men, and we shrink to see our own falling-off. It is impossible to resist naming one such moment in his work in which the past is made to hurtle into the present with a dizzy force. It is when Skinner is dealing with those well-paid American academics who persuaded themselves that Thomas More couldn't possibly have been recommending the abolition of private property.

> If private property is the source of our present discontents, and if our basic ambition is to establish a good society, then it seems undeniable to More that private property will have to be abolished. This means that, when he presents his description of Utopian communism in Book II, he must be taken to be offering a solution—the only possible solution—to the social evils he has already outlined in Book I. And this in turn suggests that, in giving *Utopia* the title of "the best state of a commonwealth," he must have meant exactly what he said.[46]

Like Collingwood, he too had found the study of the history of ideas both historically in error and socially in the margins. Braudel and the *Annalistes* had so far subordinated mind to geography and economics, that ideas were reduced to hardly more than adornments on the engines of power, and the only rivals to Marxism were the hard-boiled old realists led by Sir Lewis Namier and Hugh Trevor-Roper (subsequently ennobled as Lord Dacre for services to cynicism) for whom moral principles in politics were mere "flapdoodle" (Namier's word) and whose preferred way of disagreeing with "screaming radicals" was to "knock 'em on the nose" (Trevor-Roper). Against this philistinism, Skinner insists how politicians are obliged to use principle to justify expediency, and therefore move always in the forcefield of ethics.

In a way unparalleled in practices of academic pedagogy (and such as to make Collingwood's ghost wriggle with envy), Skinner has promulgated his approach in the lengthy and amazing series of textbooks published by his parent press and under his editorship as "Cambridge texts in the history of political thought."[47] By the time this enterprise was completed, there were more or less a hundred volumes in the series, which Skinner cheerfully referred to as "the intellectual historians' contribution to defeating Thatcherism," the point being not only that ideas matter intensely in history or, more in Collingwood's vein, that history is the history of thought (and not of making money), but also that unfamiliar ideas made to walk again from the past have a way of chopping down and out the latest wheeze of bright and heartless young fogeys announcing the end of history and the advent of the consumerist globe.[48]

There is not much for our comfort in Skinner's own vision of politics, only that we had better summon up for our self-protection Machiavelli's bleak vision of human nastiness (as Collingwood did Hobbes's) and tie our politicians, ever too attentive to the caprices of the market and its consumer preferences, to their own best picture of themselves as placed in the hands of the state, itself conceived as our best moral agent.

To talk like this at a time when the yellow press never stops foaming over the "nanny state" and worse, when the cheapest daily clichés refer to the omnipresence of Big Brother, is a risky business. But unless we contrive a state within the larger state of the European Union that can act for the best and not the most hateful parts of us and do so with our consent as well as our not unkindly indifference, then the runaway world will dash over the edge and disappear in a cloud of smoke. Collingwood's minatory words in a different world crisis did what little an academic philosopher can do to cackle a warning. Skinner's, explicitly following his lead and example, do the same and, I will risk saying, do so to greater effect. The line of force for transformation comes through with a brighter glow and a bigger charge of energy.

So it does in the last of these cartoons of Collingwood's nephews. In the stirring first chapter to his classic *A Short History of Ethics*, Alasdair MacIntyre puts down A. J. Ayer in accents any reader of this book will at once recognise. Ayer had said, like Cook Wilson before him, "All moral theories . . . insofar as they are philosophical theories, are neutral as regards actual conduct,"[49] and MacIntyre shared Collingwood's contempt for such a view. As he said at the time, "moral concepts change as social life changes" and, just as important for the sociologist MacIntyre is as well as the philosopher, "Moral concepts are embodied in and partially constitutive of forms of social life."[50]

This conception of moral principles as *constitutive* (that is, as shaping the human constitution in both a codifying and a dispositional sense) goes deep in MacIntyre's thought, is perhaps his single most important contribution to moral understanding, and is, of course, reminiscent of the Collingwood of both the *Essay on Metaphysics* and the *New Leviathan*. Even more familiarly, however,

> to analyse a concept philosophically may often be to assist in its transformation by suggesting that it needs revision, or that it is discredited in some way, or that it has a certain kind of prestige. Philosophy leaves everything as it is—except concepts. And since to possess a concept involves behaving or being able to behave in certain ways in certain circumstances, to alter concepts, whether by modifying existing concepts or by making new concepts available or by destroying old ones, is to alter behaviour.[51]

In a couple of interviews given twenty-five years later, MacIntyre said of that early book, "I should have taken as a central standpoint what I learned from R. G. Collingwood: that morality is an essentially historical subject matter and that philosophical inquiry, in ethics as elsewhere, is defective insofar as it is not historical." Then he adds, with regard to the relevance of autobiography to his moral theory, that actually to write one such, as opposed to living it and in living it making as much a work of art of it as one can, "you need either the wisdom of an Augustine or the shamelessness of a Rousseau or the confidence in one's own self-knowledge of a Collingwood. I fail in all three respects."

MacIntyre's biography defines his moral themes, as does everybody's, no doubt, but a moral philosopher's above all—that is the point of writing Collingwood's. So to know that MacIntyre was born in 1929 to devoutly Christian parents who were both doctors in rural Scotland is to find how he learned so early and so deeply to respect the strengths of a local, sufficient but never wealthy, strongly self-reliant, and informally self-governing community. He then attended an English private school, took his first and research degrees in philosophy and sociology at London, Manchester, and Oxford, and in 1957 joined the staff of the University of Leeds and the membership of the British New Left movement as himself of a fiercely marked Trotskyite stripe.

Trotskyism provided him with the ammunition to attack the manifold failures of liberalism (which must here be understood as taking in *most* of contemporary ethics; by this token American neoconservatives are ethical liberals). But he quit the party once he became convinced that state power, whether in the hands of tyrants or managers, always itself vanquishes those who offer to wield it, and that the only defence against power-without-value is for "plain people" to create value communally.

The quest for this goal begins while he was a youthful professor of sociology at the University of Essex, by way of his remarkable textbook, the methodological premise for which is that Aristotle's ethics of the Greek polity may only be understood in the context of the secure roles assigned to men (and only men, not women, aliens, or slaves) as citizens in public life. Thereafter MacIntyre analyses all moral theories in relation to the possibilities each creates not only to live a moral life but to do so within the social practices and traditions those theories can shape and embody.

He concludes that modern moral theories are incapable of building such institutions. In *Marxism and Christianity,* he brings out, in a pioneering interpretation, the way a new ethics may translate old and absolute presuppositions into a quite new framework: Marxism recasts the doctrines of the Fall, the struggle of good with evil, and the chance of redemption for a secular politics.[52] This announces his ultimate questions: how do traditions of rational enquiry become socially embedded? and, from which such traditions in the past may we learn, and which must be discarded as "incommensurable" or untranslatable into later frameworks? In other words, he took completely to heart Collingwood's lessons about question-and-answer hermeneutics: "The history of philosophy is still too often written as if it were exclusively a matter of theses and arguments. But we ought by now to have learned from R. G. Collingwood that we do not know how to state, let alone to evaluate, such theses and arguments until we know what questions they were designed to answer."[53]

The questions and the answers then become embodied in an argumentative tradition; the trouble with which latter concept, as MacIntyre says, is that it is regarded as the property of the intellectual Right, when in point of fact *all* argument forms itself gradually into a tradition, even the arguments of such sanctimonious antitraditionalists as the liberal managers of contemporary consumerism. MacIntyre's biographical and vocational purpose was therefore, from its beginning and as confirmed by his exceptional singlemindedness, to turn philosophy away from epistemological inquiry and linguistic analysis back to its traditional themes of the nature of human nature, of moral conduct, and of the point or meaning of human life. His signal contributions to this venture are threefold: first, to insist that ethical theory must be grounded in a particular sociology—codes of conduct are unintelligible outside the forms of life and culture that give them value, shape, and meaning. Second, to argue that modern ethics is catastrophically fragmented, the vacuities of liberalism its besetting delusion, and, third, that it is only by taking to heart the lessons of Aristotle on the good life and "human flourishing" that different societies can recover the modes of rationality needed in order to think clearly about morality.

In his most momentous book, *After Virtue,* he tackled the moral doctrines of modernity, in particular those of the managers who pretend to perfect freedom from moral doctrine and only aspire to efficiency, and those complementary stooges of demand management who subscribe to a sort of rinsed-out existentialism that clings to an empty ideal of antisocial individualism, truth-to-personal-feelings, and the vacuities of "choice." His ringing conclusion, expounded for the rest of his career, is that the dominant moral decisions of the day are incapable of rational justification or mutual resolution. The only restoration now feasible (one still latent in much human hopefulness) is, with Aristotle, to ground a life in the virtues of which one is truly capable. "The good life for man is seeking the good life for man," and it is to be lost or found in the narrative of one's truthfully told biography.

In speaking thus of good lives, MacIntyre puts away relativism of any slack-jawed sort. Certainly things are relative; it is the point of his life's work to ground moral philosophy in the historical changefulness of social life. What he takes from Collingwood and then lends his own Scottish Dominie's authority of tone, prose, and moral severity is that changeful as life may be, arbitrary and unfounded as beliefs often are, there remain better and worse ways to live, and some traditions are more of a help than others.

Long ago, MacIntyre quit both the Trotskyism and the Catholicism he had sought to reconcile in Collingwoodian ways along a scale of forms from religion to politics. In later life, he returned, like Charles Taylor, to the Church, and this gives his work a didacticism his secular admirers cannot share. All the same, no one who has got this far in this book and found its main character congenial can fail to respond to MacIntyre's call to the colours in an essay entitled "The Ends of Life and of Philosophical Writing."

There he writes mournfully of the kind of all-too-common academic philosophy that separates philosophic discussion from practical engagement with the ends of life. Such separation permits its conversationalists to pursue with every appearance of enthusiasm minute particulars in the course of argument and then, when they stop and resume everyday life, to vanish into the conventions of home and university without a backwards glance. This is what Collingwood dismissed as a "tedious and stupid parlour-game," and MacIntyre does the same. In doing so he has something urgent and, for us, pointed to say about philosophers' lives and how we might narrate and read them.

> Enough has now been said to suggest a remark about that well-established genre, the biography of philosophers, and that yet to be established genre, the history of philosophers (as contrasted with the history of philosophy). It is that both authors and readers of such biographies and such yet to be written histories would do well to attend to the relationship in the life of each philosopher between her or his mode of philosophical speech and writing and her or his attitude towards questions about the ends of life. Being a great philosopher is not at all the same thing as leading an exemplary philosophical life, but perhaps the point of doing philosophy is to enable people to lead, so far as it is within their powers, philosophical lives. And of course how individual philosophers work out in the detail of their lives the relationship between the ends of their philosophical writing and the ends of their lives always depends on a myriad of contingencies, so that any life may open up hitherto unimagined possibilities. And in this respect for anyone things may go either well or badly.[54]

IV

Dead reckoning is one of the arts of sailing; reckoning the lives of the dead is the art, the historical art, of biographising. Collingwood's bequest is the life in the thought, and this biography offers to reckon that up. But the use to which we put such a bequest takes the next step in the traditions he embodied. This might be, in part, a matter of living one's life not in emulation of his—his England has gone from sight although not from mind—but as being touched, or moved, or even directed by his.

Such motions are sure to be largely unconscious, at least until we wake to awareness. But inasmuch as his great ambition was to conceive a theory of practical reasoning worthy of the name of a science of human affairs, the final reckoning must be with just that: with a stab at outlining notes towards his supreme fiction.

It has already been suggested just how striking a coincidence it is that T. S. Eliot was publishing the greatest long poem in English of the twentieth century, *Four Quartets*, during the years that Collingwood was struggling to bring his historical metaphysics and its concomitant theory of practice to a finished maturity. His admirers tend naturally to sort his work into periods—the early one the period of English idealism, the second the period of historicising epistemology and reconstituting metaphysics as the point of philosophy, the third the period of his late style in which he went public, revised the theory of history, and provided his beleaguered civilisation with a harsher and more intransigent version of social democracy than poor old liberalism could manage by itself.

For sure the work is recognisable according to these divisions. But the onward motions of his thought criss-cross, overlap, start and stop, race ahead (and are even abandoned, like *The Principles of History*), pick up and drop themes and topics, double back, change tone, register, diction, and audience, while all the time being presented, on the whole, in the most poised and beautiful prose to be found in the British or American philosophy of the twentieth century. Implicit in this swift and darting passage is always the search for a unity that will bring knowledge and self-knowledge into alignment, that will lead straight from the right questions to enlightenment, and in such a way as to indicate what should be done as a consequence of what has happened. The subject and object of history will yield the knowledge of human selfhood in such a way that humankind will know what to do next.

This is not to wave fatuously towards some Panglossian theory of conduct in which the human mind is saved by humanly collective self-knowledge. The world is too much at its own throat for any such illusion. Rather, as James Connelly puts it, Collingwood aspires towards an argument which at its strongest would run from

(a) knowledge to (b) self-knowledge to (c) moral consciousness to (d) theory and practice. Collingwood does not provide this argument.... However, we might agree that Collingwood was right in maintaining that realists make a mistake in ethics. He might not have shown that there is a necessary relation between knowledge and ethical action ... but this does not prevent him maintaining the ... thesis that we are not committed to leave matters alone when we know them.[55]

Perhaps it isn't necessary to invoke necessity in the link between knowledge and action. Perhaps our intuition that there *must* be such a link, if we are to think and act coherently, will have to do. Some such conclusion was there to be pondered in the lines of *Four Quartets*, as these came out between 1935 and 1942.

> Time present and time past
> Are both perhaps present in time future
> And time future contained in time past.[56]

These things are also spoken in the same year in these lines, as Collingwood's two great historical addresses, "The historical imagination" and "Human nature and human history."

> Time past and time future
> Allow but a little consciousness.
> To be conscious is not to be in time
> But only in time can the moment in the rose-garden,
> The moment in the arbour where the rain beat,
> The moment in the draughty church at smokefall
> Be remembered.

This could be a dramatisation of Collingwood's philosophy of history. If it were, what should one actually do?

> Had they deceived us
> Or deceived themselves, the quiet-voiced elders?

[Why of course they had!]

> There is, it seems to us,
> At best, only a limited value
> In the knowledge derived from experience.
> The knowledge imposes a pattern and falsifies,
> For the pattern is new in every moment
> And every moment is a new and shocking
> Valuation of all we have been.[57]

"Oh, I see," one says then, "so that's why a theory of historical knowledge cannot provide a course in practical action." You know, if you are sufficiently thoughtful, what you don't know; you are fighting to recover what has been lost time and again, and now under conditions that seem unpropitious; to recover, that is, the right speech, to put down the wrong feeling, to find out once again that

> Love is most nearly itself
> When here and now cease to matter . . .

By the time Eliot came to publish *Little Gidding*, Collingwood had only a few months to live. Both historian and poet had found, in the frightful din of *Blitzkrieg*, a moment of extraordinary exhilaration. Eliot turned back for inspiration to that earlier cataclysm of English history, the Civil War, and finds, in Collingwood's noun, after "the rending pain of re-enactment / Of all that you have done, and been," that

> We cannot revive old factions
> We cannot restore old policies
> Or follow an antique drum.
> These men, and those who opposed them
> and those whom they opposed
> Accept the constitution of silence
> And are folded in a single party.[58]

Eliot's salvation comes no doubt out of the exiguous version of Christianity with which he ends. Probably so it did for Collingwood. At the present time, when Christianity is become one amongst many competitive creeds, religion is no longer an institution in command of the social system, thereby ensuring its unity; it is merely and at best a subordinate system articulated into the many such in society, holding it together or driving it apart. Once "religion" has become as plural as it is today, it either affirms its certainty more or less blindingly or it is softened and returned to locality by ecumenical efforts. Either way, the science of human affairs, if it is to be scientific and historical as the man says, can work only as a practical rationality, herbivorous not man-eating, hermeneutic not epistemological, political not religious.

It will start with question-and-answer logic where logic is less mathematical than pragmatic.[59] It will return text to context, events to their original sequence, meaning to what was meant in the past. It will retrieve, with one eye on T. S. Eliot, the encapsulations of the past living in the present, forever opening to new possibilities. It would thereby reverse the teaching of positivism that the mind can only move from the known to the unknown, and refuse a licence to psychology's boast that it has supplanted ethics. It will point out the unexpected presence of that past, it will specify the rules for action when such a past is indeed present, and hardest of all, identify those occasions when the rules won't fit, and intelligent improvisation, refusing the tempters "Desire, Self-interest, and Right Conduct," is the only action open. To act thus is certainly to act in history, and it is also to act out of and on one's self-knowledge. It is therefore to act as freely and as rightly as one knows how. A nation that does this (to go no further than the frontier) would have the chance of making a reasonable and a decent society. It would not, for example, go to war without understanding the history of the proposed belligerence; it would demand of its citizens their active presence in the practice of politics and would not suppose that they were no more than an aggregation of consumer choices; it would impose hardship and stern discipline upon itself when there were, as there are, apocalyptic horsemen of sun and tides, gales and floods, at the gate; its happiness would be gregarious not solitary, its wants modest not ravenous, its temper equable not overheated.

Such a picture of a society is not so very far outside the people's vision, nor that of most social democratic politicians. To aim for it is to be part of a long and noble tradition of democratic self-education and, indeed, political struggle in British society. There are many other travellers on the same road, but this book is attentive to the local making of an English, a British, and then an Anglophone tradition, as that was sustained in the lived thought of one slight but commanding figure. He died early, before his work was done. Time and chance turned his heroism into a tragedy with comic interludes. Like every hero of thought and action, "he is remembered with a start, by those who are not bad of heart."

The story of a life summons up a ghost. Ghosts warn of what is to come. Collingwood's ghost brings the past with him. It is up to us, whether philosophers, historians, or plain persons, to turn that past into a good enough, a livable future.

Abbreviations

A   *An Autobiography.* Oxford: Oxford University Press, 1939.

EM   *An Essay on Metaphysics* (1940). Revised edition with an introduction and additional material edited by Rex Martin. Oxford: Oxford University Press, 1998.

EPM   *An Essay in Philosophical Method.* Oxford: Oxford University Press, 1933.

EPP   *Essays in Political Philosophy.* Edited with an introduction by David Boucher. Oxford: Oxford University Press, 1989.

FML   *The First Mate's Log.* Oxford: Oxford University Press, 1940.

IH   *The Idea of History.* Edited by T. M. Knox. Oxford: Oxford University Press, 1946.

IN   *The Idea of Nature,* edited by T. M. Knox. Oxford: Oxford University Press, 1945.

NL   *The New Leviathan, or Man, Society, Civilisation and Barbarism.* Oxford: Oxford University Press, 1942.

PA   *The Principles of Art.* Oxford: Oxford University Press, 1938.

PE   *The Philosophy of Enchantment: Studies in Folktales, Cultural Criticism and Anthropology.* Edited by David Boucher, Wendy James, and Philip Smallwood. Oxford: Oxford University Press, 2005.

PH   *The Principles of History and Other writings in Philosophy of History.* Edited and with an introduction by W. H. Dray and W. J. van der Dussen. Oxford: Oxford University Press, 1999.

RB   *Roman Britain.* Revised edition. Oxford: Oxford University Press, 1932. Originally published in 1923.

RBES   *Roman Britain and the English Settlements.* With J.N.L Myres. Oxford: Oxford University Press, 1936.

RP   *Religion and Philosophy.* London: Macmillan, 1916.

SM   *Speculum Mentis or the Map of Knowledge.* Oxford: Oxford University Press, 1924.

Notes

Chapter 1. By Coniston Water

1. I owe much in this paragraph to William Empson, who understood how Freud illuminates Wordsworth. See *Some Versions of Pastoral* (London: Chatto and Windus, 1935). The first guidebook to the Lakes came out in 1774; it was William Hutchinson's *An Excursion to the Lakes*. See also "The Invasion of Tourism" in my *The Delicious History of the Holiday* (London: Routledge, 2000).

2. For much of these and subsequent details, I am most grateful to Dick Wakefield of Cheddington, and for an offprint of his pamphlet *The Collingwoods at Lanehead*, privately published, August 1993, with marginal corrections added by Janet Grosspelius. See also Teresa Smith (Collingwood's daughter), "R. G. Collingwood: The Ring of Thought," *Collingwood Studies* 1 (1994): 27–31, together with D. Boucher, J. Connelly and T. Modood, eds., *Philosophy, History and Civilisation: Perspectives on R. G. Collingwood* (Cardiff: University of Wales Press, 1995), chap. 1.

3. See W. Rybczynski, *Home: A Short History of an Idea* (London: Heinemann, 1988).

4. *A*, 1.

5. I take this and several other details from a long and informative letter to me from Janet Gnosspelius, R. G. Collingwood's niece, as well as from her marginalia comments on Wakefield, *The Collingwoods at Lanehead*.

6. *Children and Their Primary Schools*, 2 vols. (London: HMSO, 1967).

7. Panels of her flower paintings hang in Wallington Hall, Northumberland, home of the Trevelyans.

8. Tim Hilton, *John Ruskin: The Later Years* (New Haven: Yale University Press, 2000), 428ff.

9. London: George Allen, 1884.

10. W. G. Collingwood, *The Life and Work of John Ruskin*, 2 vols. (London: Methuen, 1893, revised 1911).

11. R. G. Collingwood, "Obituary: W. G. Collingwood," *Times*, 3 October 1932.

12. *A*, 34.

13. Both books reprinted in facsimile editions by Llanerch Publishers, Felinfach, Lampeter, 1989 and 1993.

14. First published by Titus Wilson of Highgate in 1909, reprinted by Llanerch Enterprises in 1990.

15. "Letters from Iceland," *Collingwood Studies* 3 (1996): 12.

16. Detail of the journey from Janet Gnosspelius's scale map in ibid., xi.

17. *Times*, 3 October 1932.

18. Hilton, *John Ruskin* 579ff.

19. A revised edition was published as he died in 1932. The book, often reprinted, was further revised with great tact by William Rollinson, republished by J. M. Dent, in 1988.

20. W. G. Collingwood, *The Lake Counties* (London: J. M. Dent, 1988), 45.

21. This account is paraphrased from *The Autobiography of Arthur Ransome*, ed. with a prologue and epilogue by Rupert Hart-Davis (London: Jonathan Cape, 1976), 80–81.

22. There is, for example, an Arthur Ransome Society in Japan.

23. Ransome, *Autobiography*, 81.

24. Hugh Brogan, *The Life of Arthur Ransome* (London: Hamish Hamilton, 1985), 42.

25. Ransome, *Autobiography*, 93.

26. Ibid., 96.

27. Ibid., 94.

28. T. Altounyan, *In Aleppo Once* (London: John Murray, 1969), 162.

29. When Arthur Ransome moved house from Lakeland to near Pin Mill in Suffolk, he offered the haulier a bed for the night. "Nay, Mr. Ransome," said the man with a shudder, "I want to get back to England."

30. John Henry Cardinal Newman, *The Idea of a University* (New York: Doubleday, 1959), 8–9.

31. *The Principles of History and Other Writings in the Philosophy of History*, ed. W. H. Dray and W. J. Van der Dussen (Oxford: Oxford University Press, 1999), 70.

32. *A*, preface, n.p.

33. *PH*, 71.

34. *PH*, 71–72.

35. Claire Tomalin, *Samuel Pepys: The Unqualified Self* (London: Viking Penguin, 2002).

36. The foregoing few sentences are sprinkled with phrases from Clifford Geertz's great essay, "Found in Translation: The Social History of the Moral Imagination," in his *Local Knowledge* (New York: Basic Books, 1983), 36–54.

37. Friedrich Nietzsche, *Beyond Good and Evil* (New York: Vintage, 1966), 118; *On the Genealogy of Morals* (New York: Vintage, 1968), 3:28.

38. J. P. Sartre, *Being and Nothingness*, trans. Hazel Barnes (London: Routledge and Kegan Paul, 1969).

39. Alisdair MacIntyre, *After Virtue: A Study in Moral Theory* (London: Duckworth, 1981), 207.

40. I have in mind Isaiah Berlin's title essay in his *The Crooked Timber of Humanity* (London: Hogarth Press, 1990).

41. MacIntyre, *After Virtue*, 208.

42. Friedrich Nietzsche, *The Gay Science* (New York: Random House, 1974), para. 290.

43. Alisdair MacIntyre, *The Tasks of Philosophy, Selected Essays* (Cambridge: Cambridge University Press, 2006), 1:132.

Chapter 2. Brought Up by Hand

1. *Signalling from Mars: The Letters of Arthur Ransome*, ed. Hugh Brogan (London: Jonathan Cape, 1997), 13 August 1917.

2. The concept and its sociology belongs to Erving Goffman. See his *Asylums: Essays on the Social Situation of Mental Patients and Other Inmates* (Harmondsworth: Pelican, 1968).

3. *A*, 8.

4. Thomas Hughes's celebrated novel, *Tom Brown's Schooldays*, presents a popular and idealised cartoon of Rugby in Arnold's day. It was first published in 1857.

5. See Roy Porter, *England in the 18th Century* (Harmondsworth: Penguin, 1985), 67ff.

6. Norbert Elias, *The Civilising Process*, 2 vols. (Oxford: Blackwell, 1969, 1982).

7. *A*, 9.

8. Details from Nikolaus Pevsner and Alexandra Wedgwood, *The Buildings of England: Warwickshire* (Harmondsworth: Penguin, 1966), 394–95.

9. Quoted in J. B. Hope-Simpson, *Rugby since Arnold* (London: Macmillan, 1967): 150.

10. As Jonathan Gathorne-Hardy fully describes, in *The Public School Phenomenon* (Harmondsworth: Penguin, 1979), chap. 8.

11. Eighteen such were appointed in the thirteen years before Collingwood arrived. *Rugby School Register 1824–1904*, ed. A. T. Mitchell (Rugby: subscription volume). I owe my copy to the generosity of Simon Bennett.

12. Jim Hunter, *The Flame* (New York: Pantheon Books, 1966): 40.

13. Thucydides, *History of the Peloponnesian War,* book 1, 10, 2 (London: Dent Everyman, 1983).

14. See for a selection Alan M. Boase, *The Poetry of France 1400–1600* (London: Methuen, 1964).

15. Hope-Simpson, *Rugby since Arnold,* 134.

16. Ibid., 167.

17. Reported in Christopher Hassall, *Rupert Brooke: A Biography* (London: Faber, 1972), 38–40.

18. *The Meteor,* 8 March 1917, 33, unsigned but attribution unmistakable.

19. *A,* 7.

20. Collingwood Papers, Pembroke College, Oxford, 15 May 1912.

21. *Dictionary of National Biography* (1941–1950), 168–70.

22. A point made by Adrian Stokes in *Stones of Rimini* (1934), republished by Schocken Books (New York, 1969), 59ff.

23. W. G. Collingwood, *Lake Counties,* 111.

24. See Alan Macfarlane, *The Origins of English Individualism* (Oxford: Basil Blackwell, 1979).

25. See Doreen Russo, *Charlotte Mason: A Pioneer of Sane Education* (Ambleside: Armitt Trust, nd).

26. Held and displayed by the Armitt Museum in Ambleside.

27. George Orwell, *The Lion and the Unicorn* (London: Searchlight Books, Secker and Warburg, 1941), reissued ed. Bernard Crick (Harmondsworth: Penguin, 1982), 39.

28. Splendidly commemorated in Jane Renouf, *The Lake Artists' Society: A Centenary Celebration* (Ambleside: Lake Artists' Society, 2004). See also Marshall Hall, *Artists of Cumbria: An Illustrated Dictionary* (Newcastle: Marshall Hall Associates, 1979).

29. Barbara carved the 1914–18 war memorial in Hawkshead.

30. I quote John Barrell's paraphrase of Ruskin in his *The Political Theory of Painting from Reynolds to Hazlitt* (New Haven: Yale University Press, 1986), 338–39. The original passage is in Ruskin's *Modern Painters* (London: Dent Everyman, 1913), 3:267, "The Moral of Landscape."

31. Joseph Conrad, *Three Novels: The Shadow Line* (London: Dent Everyman, 1945), 247.

32. Local colour borrowed from Christina Hardyment, *Arthur Ransome and Captain Flint's Trunk* (London: Cape, 1984).

33. The insolence positively celebrated in Horace Annesley Vachell's novel about Harrow, *The Hill* (London: Methuen, 1902).

34. James Morris, *Pax Britannica* (Harmondsworth: Penguin, 1979), 3:35ff.

35. Known respectively by the names of their chairs, *Newsom Report* (1963) and *Donnison Report* (1970).

36. A phrase taken from Perry Anderson, *Arguments within English Marxism* (London: Verso, 1980), 98.

Chapter 3. Oxford and the Admiralty

1. *A*, 10.

2. D. W. Harding, "The Hinterland of Thought," in *Experience into Words* (London: Chatto and Windus, 1963), 175–97. The lines from *The Prelude* occur in Book 1: ll. 395–400.

3. *A*, 13–14.

4. G.D.H Cole and Raymond Postgate, *The Common People 1760–1814* (London: Methuen, 1962), chap. 1.

5. Max Beerbohm, *Zuleika Dobson* (Harmondsworth: Penguin, 1952 [1911]), 107, 137.

6. Its contents surely those of Rat and Mole's picnic in *The Wind in the Willows* (published in 1908 and set a few miles down the Thames in Streatley). "There's cold chicken inside it," replied the Rat briefly, "coldtonguecoldhamcoldbeefpickledgherkinssaladfrenchrollscresssand widgespottedmeatgingerbeerlemonadesodawater—." "O stop, stop," cried the Mole in ecstasies: "This is too much." (London: Methuen, 1961), 13.

7. These passages will all be dealt with in their turn. They cover the period 1919–1938. The essay on country life and labour has never been published.

8. "The Roman Centurion's Song," in *A Choice of Kipling's Verse Made by T. S. Eliot* (London: Faber and Faber, 1950), 285–87.

9. I am drawing here on Alexander Nehemas, *Nietzsche: Life as Literature* (Cambridge: Harvard University Press, 1985).

10. See, for example, John Watson's essay, "German Philosophy and the War" (1916), reprinted in *The British Idealists*, ed. David Boucher (Cambridge: Cambridge University Press, 1997), 253–69.

11. Cook Wilson's lectures, manuscript fragments, and letters were posthumously published in two volumes as *Statement and Inference* (Oxford: Clarendon Press, 1926).

12. H. A. Prichard, "J. Cook Wilson," *Mind* (1919).

13. Cook Wilson quoted in ibid.

14. Quoted by John Passmore, *A Hundred Years of Philosophy* (1957) (Harmondsworth: Penguin, 1970), 241.

15. *A*, 20.

16. Published in *Mind* (1912), reprinted in Prichard's collection, *Moral Obligation* (Oxford: Oxford University Press, 1937).

17. I take much in this account from Alasdair MacIntyre's *Against the Self-Images of the Age* (London: Duckworth, 1971), 152–72. See also Bernard Williams, *Ethics and the Limits of Philosophy* (London: Fontana Collins, 1985), 180–82.

18. See Farquharson's memoir "Professor H. A. Prichard: Personal Recollections," *Mind* (1948).

19. I depend for this summary, and later, on Isaiah Berlin, *Vico and Herder: Two Studies in the History of Ideas* (London: Hogarth Press, 1976).

20. Passmore, *Hundred Years*, 299.

21. See James Patrick's graceful narrative, *The Magdalen Metaphysics* (Macon, GA: Mercer University Press, 1985).

22. J. A. Smith's lecture notes for these are in the Smith Papers, Magdalen College Library.

23. R. G. Collingwood, *Roman Britain* (Oxford: Clarendon Press, 1923 (here quoted in the revised edition of 1932), 24.

24. See Farquharson's memorial article in *Proceedings of the British Academy* (1915).

25. Pembroke College Papers 1912, 60/15/65.

26. Leibniz here paraphrases the first two paragraphs of the *Monadology* in his correspondence with Burcher de Volder in Leyden, 1698–1706.

27. McCallum Papers, Pembroke College, 38/1/29.

28. McCallum's words, Pembroke Library Papers, in relation to Patrick Campbell's memoir (1987).

29. These are Collingwood's own phrases from *The Principles of Art* (Oxford: Clarendon Press, 1938), 26. The argument is summarised with the help of Andrew Harrison, *Making and Thinking* (Brighton: Harvester Press, 1982).

30. Collected in a first such volume by R. P. Wright with R. G. Collingwood as *The Roman Inscriptions of Britain* (Oxford: Clarendon Press, 1965). Subsequent volumes have appeared since 1992.

31. George MacDonald, "Haverfield, Francis John, *DNB* 1912–1921" (1927 edition), 244–45. Haverfield's chief opus is *The Roman Occupation of Great Britain* (Oxford: Clarendon Press, 1924). See also the biography referred to: P.M.W. Freeman, *The Best Training Ground for Archaeologists: Francis Haverfield and the Invention of Romano-British Archaeology* (Oxford: Oxbow Books, 2007).

32. A point taken from David Pears, *What Is Knowledge?* (London: Allen and Unwin, 1972).

33. *A*, 27.

34. A.J.P Taylor, *English History 1914–1945*, *Oxford History of England* (Oxford: Oxford University Press, 1965), 52–55.

35. Letter to J. M. Knox, reprinted in *EPP*, 234.

36. A suggestion borrowed from William Johnston, *The Formative Years of R. G. Collingwood* (The Hague: Martinus Nijhoff, 1967), 10.

37. *A*, all annotations from pp. 28–33.

38. One chapter survives in Collingwood Papers, Bodleian, deposit 16. When it was submitted to Macmillan in 1916, (Sir) Henry Jones in his reader's report vigorously recommended publication. *EPP*, 230–31.

39. *A*, 43.

40. *RP*, 16–17.

41. *RP*, 29.

42. Janet Gnosspelius letter to author, 22 February 2005.

43. As a term of art he formalises this in *EM*, although he implies it long beforehand.

44. *RP*, 36.

45. *RP*, 43.

46. Collingwood quotes Anselm in Lionel Rubinoff, ed., *Faith and Reason: Essays in the Philosophy of Religion by R. G. Collingwood* (Chicago: Quadrangle Books, 1968), 135. Quoted by James Patrick, *Collingwood Studies* 7 (Cardiff: R. G. Collingwood Society, 2000): 29.

47. *RP*, 120–21.

48. Contributed to a collection edited by Canon Streeter, *Concerning Prayer* (London: Macmillan, 1916), reprinted in Rubinoff, ed., *Faith and Reason*.

49. See A. C. Bradley, ed., *Thomas Hill Green's Prolegomena to Ethics* (New York: Thomas Crowell, 1969), "The Moral Ideal and Moral Progress," 180.

50. Rubinoff, ed., *Faith and Reason*, 232.

51. Finally published as *Knowledge and Experience in the Philosophy of F. H. Bradley* (London: Faber and Faber, 1964). See James Patrick, "Eliot and the New Idealism, 1914–15," *Collingwood Studies*, 7 (2000).

52. F. R. Leavis, "Thought and Emotional Quality," in *A Selection from "Scrutiny,"* ed. F. R. Leavis (Cambridge: Cambridge University Press, 1968), 1:231.

53. *A*, 90.

54. Taylor, *English History 1914–1945*, 63.

55. A. N. Whitehead, *Science and the Modern World* (Cambridge: Cambridge University Press, 1925), 81.

56. First published in English in 1922.

57. Karl Popper, *The Poverty of Historicism* (London: Routledge and Kegan Paul, 1963).

Chapter 4. Against the Realists

1. *Proceedings of the Scottish Archaeological Society* (1922–23): 42:264ff. I am most grateful to Douglas Templeton for the references. See also Angus Graham, *Skipness: Memories of a Highland Estate* (Edinburgh: Canongate Academic, 1993).

2. Pembroke College Library, file 38/1/29, McCallum Papers.

3. Pembroke College, 61/7/3.

4. Pembroke Papers.

5. Robert Graves, *Goodbye to All That* (Penguin: Harmondsworth, 1960 [1929]), 238.

6. Pembroke College, 61/7/5, letter from Edmund Esdaille.

7. Evelyn Waugh, *Brideshead Revisited* (London: Everyman's Library, rev. ed., 1993 [1945]).

8. Ibid., 26.

9. Ibid., 27.

10. Harold Acton, *Memoirs of an Aesthete* (London: Hamish Hamilton, 1984 [1948]), 120–21.

11. Ibid., 134.

12. Much is made of it by George Steiner, *Lessons of the Masters* (Cambridge: Harvard University Press, 2003).

13. T. S. Eliot, "East Coker," in *Complete Poems and Plays* (London: Faber and Faber, 1969), 177.

14. Notes on "The Function of Metaphysics in Civilisation," Bodleian Papers, reel 6, dep 19/6–15.

15. Collingwood Papers, Bodleian, reel 8, dep 24/1–13, from which the observation about pessimism also comes. Reprinted in *EPP.*

16. John Donne, *Satyre III*, "On Religion," in *Complete Poems*, ed. H. Grierson (Oxford: Clarendon Press, 1912).

17. Reprinted in Alan Donagan, ed., *R. G. Collingwood: Essays in the Philosophy of Art* (Bloomington: University of Indiana Press, 1964), 5–41.

18. Ibid., 18.

19. Carritt was writing his *Theory of Beauty* (London: Macmillan, 1914) at the time, including a chapter on Croce.

20. Dates taken from James Patrick, "Eliot and the New Idealism: Poetry and History at Oxford 1914–1915," *Collingwood and British Idealism Studies* (2000): 1–31. See also John Brett Langstaff's memoir *Oxford 1914* (New York: Vantage Press, 1965).

21. See Dennis Mack Smith, *Mussolini* (London: Weidenfeld and Nicholson, 1981).

22. Peter Johnson, *The Correspondence of R. G. Collingwood* (Swansea: Collingwood Society, 1998), 85.

23. Collingwood and Croce met face to face for the first time in 1923. See G.R.G. Mure, "Benedetto Croce and Oxford," *Philosophical Quarterly* 4 (1954).

24. Collingwood Papers, Bodleian, reel 9, dep 26/2–10.

25. Ruskin, *Modern Painters*, preface to vol. 3.

26. *SM*, 90.

27. The quotation was first copied to me by Clifford Geertz. James Connelly identifies it as *IH*, 281.

28. G. Vico, *Scienza Nuova*, trans. T. Bergin and M. Fuch (New York: Cornell University Press, 1948), 331.

29. Benedetto Croce, *An Autobiography* (Oxford: Clarendon Press, 1927), 31.

30. Guido de Ruggiero, *A History of European Liberalism* (London: Oxford University Press, 1927).

31. Croce, *Autobiography*, 31.

32. Ibid., 65.

33. Published in a much criticised translation by Douglas Ainslie in 1920.

34. R. G. Collingwood, "Croce's Philosophy of History," *Hibbert Journal* 19 (1920–21): 263–78. Reprinted in W. E. Debbins, *R. G. Collingwood: Essays in the Philosophy of History* (Austin: University of Texas Press, 1965), 15.

35. Croce, *Autobiography*, 109.

36. Croce, Ibid., 85.

37. I follow Connelly's admirable essay, "Art Thou the Man: Croce, Gentile or de Ruggiero," in *Philosophy, History and Civilisation*, ed. Boucher, Connelly, and Madood.

38. Ruggiero, *European Liberalism*, 434–43.

39. I am much indebted here to Stefan Collini's excellent study of the period, *Liberalism and Sociology: L. T. Hobhouse and Political Argument in England 1880–1914* (Cambridge: Cambridge University Press, 1979).

40. In his essay of that title, "Practical Rationalities as Social Structures," *The MacIntyre Reader*, ed. Kelvin Knight (Cambridge: Polity Press, 1990).

41. Ruggiero, *European Liberalism*, 374–75. We shall return to this assertion by way of another latter-day Collingwoodian, Quentin Skinner, and his riposte to Isaiah Berlin, "The Third Concept of Liberty," *JPBA* (2002): 237–68.

42. Ruggiero, *European Liberalism*, 387.

43. Ibid., 442.

44. Collingwood Papers, Bodleian, reel 7, dep 21/11–32.

45. Janet Gnosspelius, letter to author.

46. Reprinted in *The Philosophy of Enchantment*, ed. D. Boucher, W. James, P. Smallwood (Oxford: Clarendon Press, 2005), 49–80.

47. *PE*, 21. He omits Wordsworth, born in 1770.

48. *PE*, 23–24.

49. E. P. Thompson lists all such occasions for Morris in his classic biography, *William Morris: Romantic to Revolutionary*, rev. ed. (London: Merlin Press, 1977). For Ruskin's diary of engagements, see Hilton, *John Ruskin*.

50. *SM*, 314–15.

51. I depend here and in several later places on David Wiggins, "Truth, Invention and the Meaning of Life," in his *Needs, Values, Truth* (Oxford: Basil Blackwell, 1991), 89–138.

52. Lined up in a canon by Boucher, *British Idealists*.

53. Bradley, *Thomas Hill Green*, 13–58.

54. *SM*, 311.

55. I have here as touchstone John Ziman's *Reliable Knowledge* (London: Routledge and Kegan Paul, 1972).

56. Above all, Hegel was derided by Karl Popper in *The Open Society and Its Enemies* (London: Routledge and Kegan Paul, 1952), 2:27–80.

57. *SM*, 65.

58. *SM*, 63.

59. *SM*, 87.

60. *SM*, 83.

61. *SM*, 118, and see the footnote on 108.

62. Clifford Geertz illustrates this difficulty in his account of street poets in his "Art as a Cultural System," in *Local Knowledge* (New York: Basic Books, 1983), 109–18.

63. See *From Max Weber*, ed. and trans. H. H. Gerth and C. Wright Mills (London: Routledge and Kegan Paul, 1948), 139ff.

64. *SM*, 148.

65. *SM*, 164.

66. *SM*, 173.

67. R. H. Tawney, *The Acquisitive Society* (London: G. Bell, 1921).

68. Richard Rorty, *Philosophy and the Mirror of Nature* (Oxford: Basil Blackwell, 1980).

69. *SM*, 208.

70. *SM*, 211.

71. Michael Young, *The Rise of the Meritocracy* (Harmondsworth: Penguin, 1951).

Chapter 5. On Hadrian's Wall

1. Collingwood Papers, Bodleian, reel 2.

2. *IH*, 274.

3. *RBES*, vii.

4. See, e.g., F. G. Simpson, *Watermills and Military Works on Hadrian's Wall: Excavations in Northumberland 1907–1913*, ed. Grace Simpson (Kendal: Titus Wilton, 1976).

5. *Times* obituary by John Wilkes, 15 November 1995. His house at Chesterholm is now headquarters of the Vindolanda Trust.

6. These details are mostly taken from the attractive pen-portrait in Hunter Davies, *A Walk along the Wall: A Journey along Hadrian's Wall* (London: Weidenfeld and Nicolson, 2000 [1974]).

7. *A*, 124.

8. Ibid.

9. *A*, 125.

10. *RB*, 6–7.

11. *RB*, 2–3.

12. David Hume, *The History of England* (London: Inskeep and Bradford, 1810).

13. I have in mind a long sequence of travesties and transvestites, from *I, Claudius*, for which I suppose Robert Graves's impecuniousness in 1930 was first responsible, to the truly awful *Rome* on the BBC in 2006.

14. *RB*, 8.

15. *RB*, 12.

16. *RB*, 83.

17. *A*, 140.

18. Dorothy Emmet became professor of philosophy at Manchester where she introduced the young Alasdair MacIntyre to Collingwood's work. The quotation is from her memoir, *Philosophers and Friends, 70 Years in Philosophy* (London: Macmillan, 1996), 9.

19. Tamara Talbot Rice, *Tamara: Memoirs of St. Petersburg, Paris, Oxford and Byzantium*, ed. Elizabeth Talbot Rice (London: John Murray, 1996), 103.

20. Isaiah Berlin, *Flourishing: Letters 1928–1946*, ed. Henry Hardy (London: Chatto, 2004), 44.

21. Ian Richmond, obituary entry, *Proceedings of the British Academy* 29 (1943): 476–80.

22. Grace Simpson, "Collingwood's Latest Archaeology Misrepresented," in *Collingwood Studies* 5 (1998): 109–19. See also her earlier paper, written with Stein Helgeby, in *Collingwood Studies* 2 (1995): 1–11.

23. Charles Carrington, *Rudyard Kipling: The Work and the Man* (London: Macmillan, 1985), 480. Carrington says the comment was made about the *Autobiography*. But Kipling died in 1936 and the *Autobiography* was not published until 1939. Boucher, omniscient in all such matters, tells us the remark was made about *SM*.

24. *A*, 107.

25. I am using the words of Quentin Skinner, a professed admirer of Collingwood, in his *Visions of Politics* (Cambridge: Cambridge University Press, 2002), 89.

26. *A*, 110.

27. This is forcefully evident in literary history. Everyone knows to avoid the solecism that biography explains the poetry. But biography restores vitality and precision to poetry otherwise faded by the passage of time.

28. Vigorously spoken for by Roger Poole in his *Towards Deep Subjectivity* (London: Allen Lane, 1972).

29. *EM*, 23. Williams's essay appears in his posthumous collection, *The Sense of the Past*, ed. Myles Burnyeat (Princeton: Princeton University Press, 2006), quotations on 352.

30. *A*, 38.

31. In the Collingwood Papers at the Bodleian.

32. Ludwig Wittgenstein, *Philosophical Investigations*, trans. G.E.M. Anscombe (Oxford: Basil Blackwell, 1953), 88.

33. *Times* obituary, 3 October 1932.

34. Armitt Library, ALM box 218.

35. *EPP*, 25. The observation comes from the 1929 lectures in moral philosophy.

36. His correspondence on these matters collected at the Armitt ALM, boxes 202 and 266. The labels are preserved in box 268.

37. Thompson's second son, E. P. Thompson (1924–1993), was the great historian; his first son, Frank, was shot while fighting with the partisans in Bulgaria in 1944.

38. W. G. Collingwood, *Northumbrian Crosses of the Pre-Norman Age*, facsimile ed. (Dyfed: Llanerch Enterprises, 1989 [1927]).

39. *PCWAAS*, 24 (1934): 1.

40. "In Memoriam," *PCWAAS* 34 (1933): 311.

41. Davies, *A Walk along the Wall*, 111.

42. Richmond, obituary entry, 478.

43. "Ten Years' Work on Hadrian's Wall," *CWAAS Transactions* 31 (1931).

44. Collingwood's interim report on the diggings (during 1937) appears in the *CWAAS Transactions* 38 (1938).

45. Emmet, *Philosophers and Friends*, 9.

46. Charles Tomlinson, "Descartes and the Stove," in *The Way of a World* (Oxford: Oxford University Press, 1969), 14–15.

Chapter 6. The Idea of the Ideas

1. Thomas Sharp, *Oxford Replanned* (London: Architectural Press, 1948), 73ff. "A Basis for Planning."

2. Richmond, *Proceedings of the British Academy* 779. He drew five thousand in the course of his career.

3. Tom Hopkinson, *Of This Our Time: A Journalist's Story* (London: Hutchinson, 1982), 85–86.

4. Ibid., 93–94.

5. MacCallum Papers, Pembroke College, 1 November 1968.

6. University registration document held at Lady Margaret Hall.

7. Letter to the author from Janet Gnosspelius, 16 February 2005; and letter dated 20 November 1931 to D. S. Margoliouth, chairman of board, Pembroke Papers.

8. John Mabbott, *Oxford Memories* (Oxford: Thornton's, 1986), 74.

9. *EPM* (1933).

10. Bernard Williams, *The Sense of the Past* (Princeton: Princeton University Press, 2006), 341–60.

11. Wittgenstein, *Philosophical Investigations*, para. 71.

12. *New Adelphi* 1 (1927–28): 357–60, collected in *Collingwood and British Idealism Studies*, by James Connelly (Cardiff: Collingwood Society, 2000), 7:86–89.

13. "Faith and Reason," published first as a pamphlet (London: Ernest Benn), then reprinted in *God in the Modern World*, ed. A. A. David (New York: Putnam, 1929). Also in Rubinoff, ed. *Faith and Reason*, 122–27. This quotation is from Rubinoff, p. 103.

14. Rubinoff, ed., *Faith and Reason*, 127.

15. Richard Dawkins, *The God Delusion* (London: Random House, 2006).

16. *EPM*, 184.

17. *EPM*, 61.

18. Nietzsche, *The Gay Science*, para. 290.

19. *EPM*, 125.

20. *EM*, 173.

21. *EPM*, 132.

22. Clifford Geertz's useful term in his *Local Knowledge* (New York: Basic Books, 1983), 57–58.

23. *EPM*, 213.

24. Michael Oakeshott, *Experience and Its Modes* (Cambridge: Cambridge University Press, 1933).

25. J. L. Austin's *How to Do Things with Words* wasn't published by Oxford until 1962, but the views on which it was based were first formed in 1939. It was in 1940 that he first gave his paper "The Meaning of a Word," to the Jowett Society in Oxford, with Collingwood present.

26. Oakeshott, *Experience and Its Modes*, 11.

27. *IH*, 151–59.

28. Oakeshott, *Experience and Its Modes*, 331–46.

29. *IH*, 158.

30. Johnson, *Correspondence of R. G. Collingwood*, 69. Knox MSS 37524/410, University of St. Andrews.

31. Details of visit to doctor supplied in a private letter from his niece, Janet Gnosspelius.

32. Johnson, *Correspondence of R. G. Collingwood*, 3, 5, 17, 42, 57, 69.

33. He was appointed a delegate to the press (i.e., trustee and executive adviser) in 1928 and resigned due to ill health in October 1941.

34. Berlin, *Flourishing*, 14 March 1935.

35. MacCallum Papers, Pembroke College.

36. Commemorated by James Patrick, *The Magdalen Metaphysics*.

37. Admired by Maurice Bowra in his *Memories* (London: Weidenfeld and Nicolson, 1966), 103.

38. I am grateful for this insight to Neville Grenyer, who has established the likeness by comparing 1920 air photographs of these areas with the paintings.

39. Collingwood Papers, Bodleian, reel 7, 21/4, folio 1.

40. *RBES*, 324.

41. Collingwood Papers, Bodleian, reel 7, 25/15. Discussed by Wendy James in *PE*, 56ff.

42. *RBES*, 187.

43. *RBES*, "Economy of the Villa," 220ff.

44. W. C. Sellar and R. J. Yeatman, *1066 and All That* (London: Methuen, 1930), 3–4.

45. *RBES*, 113–14.

46. *RBES*, 247.

47. First given in the Reith lectures of 1955. *The Englishness of English Art* (Harmondsworth: Penguin, 1964).

48. A. N. Whitehead, *Process and Reality* (London: Macmillan, 1929); Samuel Alexander, *Space, Time and Deity* (London: Routledge and Kegan Paul, 1920).

49. *IN*, 176.

50. In many books, most recently Pierre Hadot, *The Veil of Isis: An Essay on the History of the Idea of Nature* (Cambridge: Harvard University Press, 2006).

51. See Knox's prefatory note to *IN*, none of which was published until January 1945, much delayed by wartime paper shortages.

52. Isaiah Berlin's adjectives in *Flourishing*, 16 June 1934. See also Bowra, *Memories*, 306–7.

53. E.g., in Oxford at the time the Fascist Society, including E. C. Radcliffe, later Regis professor of divinity at Cambridge; Alan Lennox Boyd, president of the union; J. M. Tomes, president. See also Richard Griffiths, *Fellow-Travellers on the Right: British Enthusiasm for Nazi Germany 1933–1939* (Oxford: Oxford University Press, 1983).

54. I borrow in what follows from Philip Fisher, *The Vehement Passions* (Princeton: Princeton University Press, 2002).

55. These remarks anticipate much that is to come, and they depend on two admirers of Collingwood: Thomas Nagel, *The View from Nowhere* (Oxford: Oxford University Press, 1986), and Charles Taylor, "Self-interpreting Animals" in his *Human Agency and Language: Philosophical Papers* (Cambridge: Cambridge University Press, 1985), 45–74.

Chapter 7. "Fighting in the Daylight"

1. Pevsner's judgement in his *Oxfordshire: Buildings of England*, with Jennifer Sherwood (New Haven: Yale University Press, 1974), 256.

2. As his niece Taqui Altounyan tells us in her memoir, *Chimes from a Wooden Bell* (London: IB Tauris, 1990), 57.

3. *IH*, 241, 242.

4. *IH*, 245.

5. I have foreshortened Bernard Williams's argument, which I take it owes something to Collingwood's, in his *Truth and Truthfulness* (Princeton: Princeton University Press, 2001).

6. T. S. Eliot, *Little Gidding* (1942), in *Complete Poems and Plays* (London: Faber and Faber, 1969), 192.

7. *IH*, 205.

8. *IH*, 209.

9. *IH*, 213–15. Paul Pickering, on reading this, points to the likeness between Collingwood's formulation for detective and historian and a

passage in a handbook entitled *Criminal Investigation: A Practical Textbook for Magistrates, Police Officers and Lawyers*, adapted by John Adam and J. Collyer Adam (London: Norman Kendal, 1934). In a striking echo of our original, the author, Hans Gross says, "He (the investigator) must . . . reconstruct the occurrence, build up by hard labour a theory fitted in and coordinated like a living organism; just as on seeing the fruit he will recognise the tree and country of its growth, so from the scrutiny of the deed he can presume how it has been brought about, what has been the motives, and what kind of persons have been employed in it." (p. 34). The book was first published in 1906, when Collingwood was reading Conan Doyle at Rugby. I am very grateful for this insight to Professor Pickering.

10. I owe this detail and much more to A. F. Wilson's admirable monograph, "Collingwood's Forgotten Revolution," *Collingwood Studies* 8 (2001), 6–72.

11. F. H. Bradley, *Collected Essays* (Oxford: Oxford University Press, 1935), 1: 20–21.

12. *IH*, 215.

13. *A*, 101.

14. *A*, "The Foundations of the Future," 101–14.

15. *A*, 105.

16. *IH*, 219, 227.

17. This was recorded by several of his students in transcriptions of his lectures, collected and duplicated by hand as *The Blue Book* during 1934–35. Ray Monk, *Ludwig Wittgenstein: The Duty of Genius* (London: Vintage, 1991), chap. 16.

18. Bowra, *Memories*, 110.

19. I take much in this account from Isaiah Berlin, *Personal Impressions*, ed. Henry Hardy (London: Hogarth Press, 1980), 101–15.

20. I owe this suggestion (and much else on the invaluable disk he generously gave me) to Glenn Shipley. It is hinted at by the editors of her collected essays, *Child Psychotherapy, War, and the Normal Child*, ed. C. Unwin and J. Hood-Williams (London: Free Association Press, 1988).

21. Stefan Collini, "R. G. Collingwood," in his *Absent Minds: Intellectuals in Britain* (Oxford: Oxford University Press, 2006), 331–49.

22. Ibid., 340.

23. *A*, 104.

24. Collini, "R. G. Collingwood," 341.

25. Although he left a note attached to the manuscript for his first wife, Ethel, to say it could be published after his death.

26. Until a long extract appeared in *EPP* in 1989 and the full text in *PE* in 2005.

27. Richmond, obituary entry.

28. Knox, *Dictionary of National Biography* (London: Oxford University Press, 1943), entry for RGC. Also introduction to *IH*.

29. Mabbott, *Oxford Memories* 76.

30. Collingwood Papers, Bodleian, reel 6, 21/3.

31. *PE*, 147.

32. *PA*, 58. I am following the lead given by David Boucher's editorial essay in *PE*, lxiv–lxv.

33. Collingwood Papers, Bodleian, dep 8, reel 2, folio 49. These are the lectures on moral philosophy, rewritten in 1933.

34. *PE*, 182.

35. Collingwood Papers, Bodleian, reel 6, 21/5. See also *PE*, lxxviii–lxxix and 132–77.

36. *PE*, 169.

37. I copy out this aphorism from Boucher in *PE*, cv. Marjorie Grene's celebrated book, *The Knower and the Known* (London: Faber and Faber, 1969), makes extensive use of Collingwood.

38. George Orwell, *Homage to Catalonia* (Harmondsworth: Penguin, 1962 [1938]), 8–9.

39. *A*, 159.

40. The 1924 lecture notes for which are reprinted in *PE*, 48–80.

41. *PA*, 333–35.

42. I have in mind T. J. Clark's incomparable recreation of this moment in his *Farewell to an Idea: Episodes in the History of Modernism* (New Haven: Yale University Press, 1999), chap. 5.

43. F. R. Leavis and Denys Thompson, *Culture and Environment: The Training of Critical Awareness* (London: Chatto and Windus, 1933).

44. Reprinted in *PE*, 291–304, probably written in 1926 but everywhere present in *PA*. For the greatest threnodies on the vanishing countryside, see George Sturt, *The Wheelwright's Shop* (Cambridge: Cambridge University Press, 1934); Adrian Bell, *Corduroy* (Harmondsworth: Penguin, 1940); and many others.

45. *PA*, 78.

46. *PA*, 81.

47. *PA*, 323.

48. *PA*, 103–4.

49. Andrew Harrison's phrase in his *Making and Thinking* (Brighton: Harvester Press, 1973), on which I draw substantially in what follows.

50. *PA*, 139.

51. My phrase with reference to Richard Wollheim's treatment of the topic, in his *Painting as an Art* (London: Thames and Hudson, 1985): chap. 1.

52. Leo Tolstoy, *What Is Art?* (Oxford: Oxford University Press World's Classics Edition, 1965).

53. Benedetto Croce, *The Aesthetic as Science of Expression*, trans. Ainslie (London: Vision Press, 1967 [1920]), chap. 2, "Intuition and Art."

54. Wittgenstein, *Philosophical Investigations*, part 2, p. 207.

55. *PA*, 149–51. My elisions mostly follow Aaron Ridley in his *R. G. Collingwood: A Philosophy of Art* (London: Phoenix, 1998), 24.

56. *PA*, 144–45.

57. Ridley, *R. G. Collingwood*, 27.

58. *PA*, 112.

59. *PA*, 216–18.

60. *PA*, 219.

61. *PA*, 285, my italics.

62. Johnson, *Correspondence of R. G. Collingwood*, 25.

63. Janet Gnosspelius, letter to author.

64. Details of the yacht and of nautical knowledge assiduously provided by David Hornbrook (RNVR).

65. Johnson, *Correspondence of R. G. Collingwood*, 41.

66. H. Lamb, *Historic Storms of the North Sea, British Isles and North-west Europe* (Cambridge: Cambridge University Press, 1991), 166.

67. *Times*, 3 June 1938.

68. I owe these medical details to Sir Roger Bannister.

69. Letter to Kenneth Sisam, senior editor at the Clarendon Press, 22 March 1939. Johnson, *Correspondence of R. G. Collingwood*, 26–27.

70. *A*, 47.

71. Collini, *R. G. Collingwood*, 340, also 348, n. 16.

72. Raymond Williams, *Raymond Williams on Television*, ed., Alan O'Connor (London: Routledge, 1989), 157.

73. Collini, *R. G. Collingwood*, 338, suggests that this popularity is spurred on by the success of *The Idea of History*, but *An Autobiography* was the only one of his books reviewed by all the dailies and weeklies with review sections (a very interesting one by Rayner Heppenstall in the *New Statesman*, loud applause in the *Manchester Guardian, Scotsman, Spectator*).

Chapter 8. The Valley of the Shadows

1. Quoted from Drusilla Scott, *A. D. Lindsay: A Biography* (Oxford: Basil Blackwell, 1971), 243, but see the whole of chap. 14.

2. Ibid., 251.

3. Collingwood kept, as usual, a log of his journey, generously made available to me by David Boucher.

4. Gregory Bateson and Margaret Mead, *Balinese Character: A Photographic Analysis* (New York: New York Academy of Sciences, 1940–42), 2 vols.

5. "Notes on the Balinese Cockfight," in his *The Interpretation of Cultures* (London: Hutchinson, 1975).

6. Geertz, *Local Knowledge*, 51.

7. Quoted by W. J. van der Dussen, *History as a Science: The Philosophy of R. G. Collingwood* (The Hague: Nijhoff, 1981), 61.

8. I am aware that the revisionists of the right now suggest that Chamberlain bought essential time for British war production by the sellout in Munich. But a sellout is a sellout, and Hitler in any case stuck to his own timetable.

9. *NL*, 124.

10. Collini, *R. G. Collingwood*, 335.

11. *EM*, viii.

12. Johnson, *Correspondence of R. G. Collingwood*, 26.

13. The most telling rejection of this was by a pupil of Collingwood's, Frederick Tomlin, who tore the heart out of the book in his lethal review in *Scrutiny* 5, 2 (1936): 200–18.

14. Since taken by Bernard Williams in an unpublished brief paper entitled "The Force of 'We,' " given at the Dworkin-Nagel seminars, New York University, April 1989.

15. *EM*, 69.

16. Ludwig Wittgenstein, *Tractatus Logico-Philosophicus* (London: Routledge and Kegan Paul, 1922), 6.51.

17. Quoted by Ray Monk, *Ludwig Wittgenstein: The Duty of Genius* (London: Vintage, 1996), 557.

18. Nor J. L. Austin's, in his 1939 essay "Are There *a Priori* Concepts," with strictures on "bad habits encouraged by talk about concepts," J. L. Austin, *Philosophical Papers*, ed. J. O. Urmson and G. J. Warnock (Oxford: Oxford University Press, 1961), 18.

19. *EM*, xxxviii.

20. *EM*, 66. I am grateful to Mike Beaney, and the gift of his paper on presuppositional analysis, *Collingwood Studies* 2, 2 (2005): 2.

21. W.V.O. Quine, *From a Logical Point of View* (Cambridge: Harvard University Press, 1961), 37–46.

22. *EM*, 75.

23. *EM*, 76.

24. Basil Willey, *The Seventeenth Century Background* (London: Chatto and Windus, 1954).

25. *EM*, 72.

26. *IH*, x–xi.

27. Alan Donagan, *The Later Philosophy of R. G. Collingwood*, rev. ed. (Chicago: University of Chicago Press, 1985).

28. *IH*, particularly the sections on Hegel and Marx, and the mention of Darwin, p. 115. See also *IN*, 10–13.

29. *IH*, 169.

30. *EM*, chap. 10.

31. *EM*, 140.

32. *EM*, 343.

33. Quoted in van der Dussen, *History as a Science*, 61.

34. *PH*, lviii.

35. W. H. Dray and W. J. van der Dussen, *PH*, xi–lxxxvii.

36. *PH*, 37.

37. *PH*, 55.

38. *PH*, 56.

39. *PH*, 98.

40. *PH*, 181.

41. *IH*, 302.

42. Summarised from *IH*, 18.

43. A. J. Ayer, *Philosophy in the 20th Century* (New York: Random House, 1982), 191–213.

44. "Scheme for a Book: The Principles of History," *PH*, 246, dated 9 February 1939.

45. His story is told by his brother, E. P. Thompson, in *Beyond the Frontier* (Suffolk: Merlin Press, 1997), and by me in *The Cruel Peace: Everyday Life and the Cold War* (New York: Basic Books, 1992).

46. *FML*, 1–2.

47. Monk, *Ludwig Wittgenstein*, 565–66.

48. Janet Gnosspelius, letter to author.

49. *FML*, 28–29.

50. *FML*, 32.

51. *FML*, 112–13.

52. Robin McCurdy, *Past Imperfect* (Lewes: Book Guild, 2003), 89.

53. *FML*, 51.

54. McCurdy, *Past Imperfect*, 90.

55. *FML*, 79.

56. *FML*, 85–86.

57. McCurdy, *Past Imperfect*, 89.

58. *FML*, 136.

59. *FML*, 142.

60. Because *The First Mate's Log* is little known, the critique isn't mentioned by Bernard Williams in his identical attacks on utilitarianism, first

in J.J.C. Stuart and Bernard Williams, *Utilitarianism: For and Against* (Cambridge: Cambridge University Press, 1973).

61. *FML*, 176.

62. *PA*, 335.

63. *PA*, 85.

64. John Bunyan, *Pilgrim's Progress* (Oxford: Oxford University Press, 1964 [1678]), 81.

65. This is how the Californian poet and critic Yvor Winters, who died in 1969, would put it. There were marked similarities between Winters's and Collingwood's aesthetics.

66. *IH*, 215.

67. Anthony Newman, *Bach and the Baroque: A Performing Guide to Baroque Music with Special Emphasis on the Music of J. S. Bach* (New York: Pendragon Press, 1985), 17. See also Gary Tomlinson (who alludes to Collingwood), "The Historian, the Performer and Authentic Meaning in Music," in *Authenticity and Early Music*, ed. N. Kenyon (Oxford: Oxford University Press, 1988). I am grateful to James Connelly for this reference.

68. Newman, *Bach and the Baroque*, 20–21.

69. Ibid., 204. See also Thurston Dart (a giant of the authenticity movement) and his classic *The Interpretations of Music* (London: Novello, 1954).

70. I borrow here from Stanley Cavell, *Must We Mean What We Say?* (Cambridge: Harvard University Press, 1965).

71. Louis Mink, "History and Fiction as Modes of Comprehension," *New Literary History* 1 (1970): 545.

Chapter 9. The Passionate Man's Pilgrimage

1. Collingwood Papers, Bodleian, dep 8, reel 2, folio 67A. 1939–40 lectures.

2. Taylor, *English History*, 472–75.

3. Collingwood Papers, Bodleian, dep 8, reel 2.

4. Ibid., folio 49, headed "Dialectic of Rules," for this and the next two quotations.

5. Letter dated 27 March 1906, quoted by D. E. Moggridge, *Keynes* (London: Fontana/Collins, 1976), 13.

6. 12 April 1927. Reprinted in *D. H. Lawrence, Selected Literary Criticism*, Anthony Beal (London: Heinemann, 1955), 23.

7. Reprinted in *EPP*, 187–96.

8. *EPP*, 190.

9. *IH*, 255–56.

10. Thomas Hobbes, *Leviathan*, ed. John Plamenatz (London: Fontana/ Collins, 1962), 143.

11. Letter to the archaeologist Osbert Crawford, 14 April 1941. Cited in O.G.S. Crawford's memoirs, *Said and Done* (London: John Murray, 1955), 113.

12. To T. M. Knox, 6 January 1940. Knox Papers, St. Andrews University Library, 37524/430.

13. D. H. Lawrence, 21 October 1915 to Lady Cynthia Asquith, in *Selected Letters*, ed. R. Aldington (Harmondsworth: Penguin, 1950).

14. Monk, *Ludwig Wittgenstein*, 414.

15. I am grateful in these remarks for an unpublished paper by Simon Blackburn, "Some Wittgensteinian Themes in Collingwood," retained in the Pembroke College papers on Collingwood.

16. E.W.F. Tomlin, *R. G. Collingwood*, British Council Series, *Writers and Their Work* (London: Longmans Green, 1953), 42:34.

17. 11 March 1940. Johnson, *Correspondence of R. G. Collingwood*, 30.

18. *NL*, 311.

19. All these quotations are selected (and rearranged) from Edward Said, *On Late Style: Music and Literature against the Grain* (London: Bloomsbury, 2007), 137–60, 8–15.

20. *NL*, iv.

21. *NL*, 75.

22. *NL*, 91.

23. *NL*, 124, already quoted, as well it might be.

24. *NL*, 232.

25. In which view he found help from, as he always called him, "the Provost of Oriel," Sir David Ross, in his *The Right and Good* (1935).

26. I follow David Boucher here, in his classic exposition of *NL*, *The Social and Political Thought of R. G. Collingwood* (Cambridge: Cambridge University Press, 1989), 91ff.

27. *NL*, 332. Original italics.

28. *NL*, 176.

29. *NL*, 191.

30. 7 October 1940. Johnson, *Correspondence of R. G. Collingwood*, 107.

31. Their stories are finely told by Richard Rhodes, *The Making of the Atomic Bomb* (Harmondsworth: Penguin, 1986).

32. *NL*, 242–43.

33. *NL*, 334.

34. I borrow Quentin Skinner's title, *Liberty Before Liberalism* (Cambridge: Cambridge University Press, 1998), to which I return in the last chapter.

35. *NL*, 348.

36. *NL*, 387.

37. Letter from Bill to Janet Gnosspelius, 10 April 1941.

38. To W. von Leyden, 31 May 1941, quoted by von Leyden in his essay "Philosophy of Mind: An Appraisal of Collingwood's Theories of Consciousness, Language and Imagination," in *Critical Essays on the Philosophy of R. G. Collingwood*, ed. M. Krausz (Oxford: Clarendon Press, 1972), 20–21.

39. As reported verbatim in a letter to the author from Janet Gnosspelius.

40. Ibid.

41. John Ruskin, *Modern Painters* (London: J. M. Dent, 1913), 5:115–16.

42. Quoted in Patrick, *The Magdalen Metaphysics*, 162.

43. Letter from Janet Gnosspelius, 25 January 2005.

44. W. B. Yeats, "What Then?," in *Collected Poems* (London: Macmillan, 1961), 348.

45. Edwin Muir, *An Autobiography* (London: Methuen, 1964 [1940]), 49.

46. Ian Hamilton, *In Search of J. D. Salinger* (London: Heinemann, 1988), 204.

Chapter 10. The Time of the Preacher

1. Used as a diagetic theme in Troy Kennedy Martin's *Edge of Darkness*, the greatest work of art ever broadcast as BBC television drama. It was first broadcast in 1985, and Faber published the script in 1990.

2. Quentin Skinner, *Regarding Method: Visions of Politics* (Cambridge: Cambridge University Press, 2002), 1:75.

3. The details of the furniture taken, of course, from Norman Malcolm, *Ludwig Wittgenstein: A Memoir* (Oxford: Oxford University Press, 1962).

4. *A*, 48.

5. Passmore, *A Hundred Years of Philosophy* (Harmondsworth: Penguin, 1968), chapter 14.

6. Louis Mink, *Mind, History and Dialectic: The Philosophy of R. G. Collingwood* (Bloomington: Indiana University Press, 1969).

7. The story of antipositivism is excellently told by Richard Bernstein, *The Restructuring of Social and Political Theory* (Philadelphia: University of Pennsylvania Press, 1978). He does not, however, mention Collingwood.

8. Van der Dussen, *History as a Science.*

9. Ibid., 211–12; *PCWAAS*, 1916, 79–81.

10. Rex Martin, *Historical Explanation: Re-enactment and Practical Inference* (Ithaca: Cornell University Press, 1977).

11. Ibid., 220.

12. Ibid., 242–47.

13. Geertz, *Local Knowledge*, 54.

14. David Boucher, *The Social and Political Thought of R. G. Collingwood* (Cambridge: Cambridge University Press, 1989).

15. Subsequently *Collingwood and British Idealism Studies*.

16. Thomas S. Kuhn, *The Structure of Scientific Revolutions* (Chicago: University of Chicago Press, 1962).

17. Stephen Toulmin, introduction to the 1975 edition of *An Autobiography*.

18. Kuhn, *Scientific Revolutions*, 12.

19. Ibid., 15.

20. E. H. Carr, *What Is History?*, rev. ed. (Harmondsworth: Penguin, 1990 [1961]), 21. I am grateful to Martin Minogue for help with this passage.

21. *IH*, 218.

22. Carr, *What is History*, 24.

23. Quoting Knox's introduction to *IH*, xii.

24. First caricatured by Herbert Butterfield, *The Whig Interpretation of History* (Cambridge: Cambridge University Press, 1931).

25. Carr, *What is History*, 121.

26. Charles Taylor, *Hegel* (Cambridge: Cambridge University Press, 1975). He followed this with a compressed version adjusted to its different title, *Hegel and Modern Society* (1978).

27. Reprinted in his *Philosophical Papers*, 2 vols. (Cambridge: Cambridge University Press, 1985).

28. Collected in *Philosophical Papers*, vol. 1: *Human Agency and Language*, 45–76.

29. *Sources of the Self: The Making of Modern Identity* (Cambridge: Harvard University Press, 1989).

30. Quentin Skinner, "Who Are 'We'? Ambiguities of the Modern Self," *Inquiry* 34 (1990), 133–53.

31. Ibid., 148.

32. Charles Taylor, *A Secular Age* (Cambridge: Harvard University Press, 2007).

33. Geertz, *Local Knowledge*.

34. Fred Inglis, *Clifford Geertz: Custom, Culture, Ethics* (Cambridge: Polity Press, 2000).

35. *PA*, 8, n1. E. E. Evans-Pritchard, *Witchcraft: Oracles and Magic among the Azande* (Oxford: Oxford University Press, 1937).

36. Peter Winch, *The Idea of a Social Science and Its Relation to Philosophy* (London: Routledge and Kegan Paul, 1958).

37. Ibid., 103. *PA*, 62–65.

38. This would also be the occasion to discuss the classical work of John Pocock, forerunner to Skinner, but Skinner has a longer historical reach, and brevity demands ruthlessness.

39. Quentin Skinner, "On Encountering the Past: Interview with P. Koikkalainen and S. Syrjamaki," in *Finnish Yearbook of Political Thought* (University of Jyvaskyla, Department of History, 2002), 5:32–63.

40. Ibid., 38.

41. An early version of his "Meaning and Understanding in the History of Ideas," in ibid., 1:57–89.

42. Another early and important paper of his was published in Patrick Gardiner's collection *The Philosophy of History* (Oxford: Oxford University Press, 1974). The paper was Skinner's "Social Meaning and the Explanation of Social Action," and the first chapter of the collection was Collingwood's "Human Nature and Human History."

43. E.g., Jonathan Ree, "The Vanity of Historicism," *New Literary History* 22 (1991): 961–83.

44. Skinner's method (and Collingwood's) is explored, criticised, and developed by Mark Bevir in his excellent study, *The Logic of the History of Ideas* (Cambridge: Cambridge University Press, 1999).

45. This is the extended version of his Regius inaugural, "Liberty Before Liberalism," already referred to (Skinner, *Liberty Before Liberalism*).

46. Quentin Skinner, *The Foundations of Modern Political Thought* (Cambridge: Cambridge University Press, 1978), 262.

47. The most relevant of which for this book is David Boucher's *The British Idealists.*

48. As eponymously performed by Francis Fukuyama, *The End of History and the Last Man* (New York: Random House, 1994). A dozen years later, he took it all back.

49. A. J. Ayer, *Philosophical Essays* (London: Macmillan, 1975), 245.

50. Alisdair MacIntyre, *A Short History of Ethics* (London: Routledge and Kegan Paul, 1967), 1.

51. Ibid., 2–3.

52. Alasdair MacIntyre, *Marxism and Christianity* (London: Duckworth, 1969).

53. MacIntyre in K. Knight, *A MacIntyre Reader* (Cambridge: Polity Press, 1998), 199.

54. MacIntyre, *The Tasks of Philosophy,* 1:132.

55. See Connelly's excellent essay, "Character, Duty and Historical Consciousness," in *British Idealism: Moral, Social and Political Philosophy,* ed. W. Sweet (Exeter: Imprint Academic, 2007). I also borrow here (and quote)

from an unpublished paper by Connelly entitled "Knowing the Difference: Collingwood's Refutation of Realism."

56. T. S. Eliot, "Burnt Norton," 171.

57. Eliot, *Complete Poems*, 179.

58. Ibid., 196.

59. Richard Rorty's name must be invoked here, and his doctrine of edification. See his *Philosophy and the Mirror of Nature* (Oxford: Basil Blackwell, 1980).

Index

2001 SOURCES of FINANCING for SMALL BUSINESS

2001 SOURCES of FINANCING for SMALL BUSINESS

Herman Holtz

ARCO PUBLISHING, INC.
New York

Published by Arco Publishing, Inc.
215 Park Avenue South, New York, N.Y. 10003

Library of Congress Cataloging in Publication Data

Holtz, Herman.
  2001 sources of financing for small business.

  1. Small business — United States — Finance — Directories.
2. Venture capital — United States — Directories.
I. Title. II. Title: Two thousand one sources of financing
for small businesses. III. Title: Two thousand and one
sources of financing for small businesses.
HG4057.A286   1983   658.1'522   82-11366
ISBN 0-668-05468-9 (Cloth Edition)
ISBN 0-668-05470-0 (Paper Edition)

OTHER BOOKS BY HERMAN HOLTZ

Contents

Preface

One of the reasons the Small Business Administration (SBA) and others cite as a common cause of business failure is "undercapitalization." In plain English that means that the entrepreneur did not have enough money to do what had to be done to make a success of the enterprise. The lack of enough money may have restricted marketing and sales efforts to the extent of crippling the business — it does take money to put on a sales campaign. Moreover, the lack of enough money can precipitate other disasters that may be fatal to a business: The entrepreneur may be forced to pay excessively high prices for goods because there isn't enough capital to "buy right." In the case of a retail operation, the entrepreneur may have been forced into an undesirable location where the rent was cheaper. Or the entrepreneur may have been forced, in any or all of a myriad of other ways, to compromise what was best for what was cheapest — or even tried to make do without some vitally needed element of the enterprise.

It does "take money to make money" in at least some kinds of enterprise, although there are some enterprises that need little capital, at least initially. But even that is relative: one entrepreneur may consider $5,000 "no money at all," while that same sum may represent the difference between success and failure to another small entrepreneur. So when it comes to what is "enough," in capital, the word has different meaning for different individuals, according to each situation.

To those uninitiated in business funding, it might seem logical that it is far easier to raise $5,000 than $300,000. Strangely enough, the opposite is true in many cases, such as in arranging for business loans to be guaranteed by a government agency. The Small Business Administration, for example, makes some "direct" loans (lends federal money to the borrowers), and these are almost invariably in cases where the loan is too small to be attractive to a lending institution, such as a commercial bank.

This is not to say that the small-business borrower ought to immediately ask for ten times what is needed. That doesn't work, either: all business loans require ample explanation and justification, even when the government acts as your cosigner and guarantees the loan. But, as you will soon discover in these pages, there are many ways to finance a business, and the wise borrower selects the way that best suits the situation.

There is a sardonic jest, repeated so often that it is a cliche, that a bank lends you money only when you prove that you don't need it — that you have ample assets ("collateral") to ensure that the lender can collect what you owe, one way or another. That is, like most cliches, only partially true. Collateral does not always have to be negotiable or liquid assets, nor even a cosigner and guarantee of repayment. Acceptable collateral can be and often is your good name, a credible business program, an equity interest in your venture or proposed venture, or a few other things, rather than stocks and real property.

The world of finance — especially business finance — is a world unto itself, one about which most of us know little and rarely have reason to learn. But for the individual who wishes to undertake a business venture and needs to raise capital for it, it is a decided business asset to gain some knowledge of this world. Another business philosophy — no jest this — which is also repeated so often that it has become a virtual cliche, is nonetheless largely true. This cliche has it that smart businesspeople never use their own money to launch a business venture, but always use OPM — other people's money. I say "largely true" because although there are some cases where the entrepreneur does not have five cents of personal investment, that is the exception: in most cases, it is necessary for the entrepreneur to furnish start-up capital. It is usually much more difficult to persuade lenders to furnish all the capital. Lenders prefer that the entrepreneur show enough faith in the enterprise to share the risk by making a personal investment. Moreover, it is usually far easier to persuade others to lend money to or invest in an already operating (and successful) enterprise than one that is still on the drawing board.

Where an entrepreneur has taken his enterprise from a modest beginning to a multimillion-dollar success in a short time — and the business literature of today is full of such success stories — you may be reasonably sure that the entrepreneur managed to find substantial financing. It is all but impossible to grow to a large size without backing today and, conversely, in many enterprises (such as computers) today's dynamics are such that only the lack of financing can hold a company back from spectacular growth. That is, for some companies, rapid growth was all but inevitable, once the capital was made available.

For some enterprises, borrowing (debt financing) will raise enough capital to finance the growth. For other types of business, borrowing is simply inadequate, for one or another reason — in many cases, far more financing is required than can be raised by borrowing. In such cases, other means must be found for financing, usually investment or equity financing, although some firms have also achieved swift growth through franchising. (The McDonald hamburger chain is one such example.)

The statistics on new enterprises and their survival rate are depressing. As many as seven out of ten new businesses perish within the first year or two, according to reports by the United States Small Business Administration, the United States Department of Commerce, Dun & Bradstreet, and other organizations. It is not possible to say in what percentage of these cases "undercapitalization" was the sole or even the chief cause of the failure, but it is obvious that a successful working "partnership" between the investor(s) and the entrepreneur has often been the reason for success. The entrepreneur brings the business plan, the basic idea, and whatever other ingredients are necessary, while the investor(s) make(s) it possible for the entrepreneur's dream to come to life.

To a large degree, that's what financing is to an infant enterprise: the breath of life. It is in recognition of the importance of financing to a small, new business, plus the great difficulty most entrepreneurs have in financing their ideas, that the federal and state governments have created the socioeconomic programs to guarantee that small business can still survive in this late twentieth century, where big business dominates the business and industrial landscape. However, by far the greatest obstacle to finding financing for the new, small business is the lack of knowledge — not only the knowledge of how the world of finance operates, but where the many sources of help are. In a phrase, what the small entrepreneur needs to know is both where the money is and how to get it. Thousands of entrepreneurs who could not walk through the front doors of their local banks and get approval for business loans have found the capital they needed through a thousand other sources. It can be done.

That is what this book is all about: those "other" sources — where the money is and how to get it for your business.

HERMAN R. HOLTZ

Silver Spring, Maryland

2001 SOURCES of FINANCING for SMALL BUSINESS

Chapter 1

A Thousand Financial Backers

Just about everybody knows about banks and borrowing money from them, and a great many people know about the SBA – the Small Business Administration – and its lending programs. But those are only the beginning of capital sources.

THE GOLDEN RULE

The world of finance is heavily larded with anomalies and paradoxes — more, perhaps, than any other field of business activity. Banks and other lending institutions, for example, find success only in keeping their capital working — loaned out and earning interest from borrowers. Nevertheless, most banks and other lending institutions refuse far more customer-applicants than they accept. Probably no other business or industry turns away would-be patrons to anything like the same degree.

There is a "golden rule" in the financial community — probably circulated (ruefully) more among the borrowers than the lenders, which says, "Those who have the gold make the rules." That, of course, explains readily why banks can turn away so many applicant borrowers and yet have their money loaned out at highly satisfying interest rates most of the time: they have far more borrowers than they need, and can therefore choose the lowest risk loans among applicants.

BANKS ARE THE PRIMARY SOURCE OF THE MONEY

When the subject of financing and borrowing money comes up, most people think of banks and loan companies. However, although these are the obvious sources of capital, they represent only a fraction of all the possible sources and means for financing a small business. Moreover, walking through the front doors of a bank and submitting an application for a business loan is only one way of utilizing that potential financial resource: A large portion of the loans made by a typical bank are made via other means, such as through state and federal government loan and loan-guarantee socioeconomic programs, through brokers and other intermediaries, through venture capitalists — people who make a full-time business of investing money in what appear to be sound business enterprises, and through organizations set up under government programs to assist small business people

1

in getting their businesses launched and financed. In fact, the latter category alone represents many hundreds of sources.

For the most part, when you borrow money from any lending institution, you are borrowing directly or indirectly from the banks because loan companies, Small Business Investment Companies (SBICs), mortgage companies, and other lenders are almost invariably lending money they have themselves borrowed from banks. There are, of course, a few wealthy investors who use their own funds — who make a business of investing in ventures or use their own money to set up lending institutions of some kind, but they are very much the exception, not the rule. The chief difference is that when a bank lends money to you, it is you who furnishes whatever guarantees are furnished — collateral in the form of negotiable or liquid assets (assets readily convertible to cash); collateral in the form of a good credit record and a plan for investment of the money that appears sound and likely to enable repayment of the loan; or collateral in the form of cosigner guarantees by someone else who is most credit-worthy — whereas when the bank lends money to another lending institution, the bank is getting guarantees from an established business, often backed by mortgages on real estate, usually guaranteed by collateral of some kind, sometimes from more than one principal in the firm. In any case, when you borrow from one of these secondary lenders, your obligation for repayment is to that secondary lender, although the money probably came from a bank, with the secondary lender obliged to repay the bank, whether you pay or not.

Banking has become a complex business, with many state and federal laws governing what banks can and cannot do. That is one reason banks are so conservative: laws compel them to be conservative. The whole business of finance and economics has become a complex matter, since the United States Government became responsible for and in basic control of the country's economy, managing "money supply," and through that tool exerting enormous influence on interest rates, ease or difficulty of borrowing, and just about every other facet of the nation's credit and currency.

Today, American banks are generally regarded as bulwarks of integrity and dependability, with government guarantees of savings accounts in both banks and savings-and-loan institutions. Most of us deposit our money in the bank with confidence that it will be there waiting for us and available instantly to us whenever we want it. It wasn't always so. There was a time when banks were not at all safe and dependable, and many investors lost their savings through bank failures. There was a time, too, when banks issued their own paper money — banknotes, literally.

It goes back to a time when gold was the medium of exchange. However, one could not carry a great deal of gold around, and it was not exactly wise to "deposit" one's savings, in gold, under the mattress or in a hole dug in the ground. Those who were fortunate enough to have more gold than they could comfortably or safely carry on their person deposited it with a warehouse and got paper receipts, of course. One could then turn over some of these receipts to another party, in exchanges of any kind, and the other party could then go to the warehouse and claim the gold represented by the receipts. That was immediately a primitive kind of bank and paper money, and today's system is similar in principle, except that we no longer have a guarantee of gold, in exchange for the paper "receipts" (money). Of course, today only the federal government can coin and print money legally, a further control, which has brought stability to what was once a chaotic system.

The federal laws that govern banking permit the bankers to lend out money at a level (currently 85 percent of money on deposit) the government sets by law. The current law requires that the banks retain a 15-percent reserve — that the bank can show that at least

15 percent of all the money on deposit is in the possession of the bank to meet instantaneous demands. Other than that, the bank is free to lend out the money on deposit, at interest rates which are within the legal limits (which have been extremely high, in recent years). Within whatever requirements the federal laws place on the banks, however, each bank is free to set its own rules and conditions for lending money. For that reason, while there are some loans that probably no bank would risk, many borrowers turned down by one bank find their applications accepted by another.

The factors affecting the acceptance or rejection of a loan application are several — certainly more than one — which accounts for an applicant being rejected in one bank and accepted in another. First of all, there are certain fixed bank policies regarding loans, and your application may simply run counter to one of those policies. For example, a given bank may tend to specialize in financing certain kinds of business. Consequently, the bank officials who must discuss and pass judgment on the loans feel comfortable when the loan is for one of those enterprises they feel rather comfortable with, and which they believe they can evaluate well. But if you are applying for a loan for an entirely different kind of enterprise, those officials feel rather insecure about it — they are not familiar with your kind of enterprise, and they'd rather reject your application than make a judgment of which they are entirely unsure.

Another factor is how badly the bank wants business. Since the bank pays interest on deposits, it must keep that money working. If there is too much idle money in the vaults, there is greater pressure on the loan committee to approve as many loans as possible.

The recommendation of the loan officer with whom you discussed your application is another factor. Although this individual rarely has the final word — most loans go before a committee, with the loan officer's recommen-

dation — he does have some influence over the decision.

On the other hand, there are some things that would almost guarantee that any bank would reject an application. Here are a few of the factors that are definite "do's and don'ts" in applying for bank loans:

- Your application — what many in the financing profession call the "loan package" — must be complete, detailed, and persuasive. The bank's officials who review loan applications must be convinced that your business plan is sound, well-thought out, and likely to succeed, thus enabling you to repay the loan. Poorly prepared loan packages are among the leading causes of turndowns — perhaps *the* leading cause.
- You must furnish the "adventure" capital — start-up funding. Banks are not disposed to furnish start-up funding, nor 100-percent capitalization of any enterprise. (Exceptions to this are principally in government-backed programs.)
- Applications must be truthful. If you furnish false information and it is discovered to be false, turndown is almost certain. Adverse information may hurt your chances, but covering it up will hurt them more, whereas frank revelation and explanation is usually well received. This is just as true for any information you supply verbally, in an interview, as for written information in your application.

TYPES OF FUNDING

In general, there are three kinds of funding used by businesses. Many use all three kinds of funding, while others use only two of these:

Adventure financing, just referred to above, is the start-up money that almost every entrepreneur must furnish from his or her own resources. That does not exclude personal borrowing from friends and relatives, or even some equity financing in this manner — that is, selling an interest in your enterprise to friends and relatives, in some proportion to their investment. But however you raise this adventure money, you generally do so before you can approach a bank or other lending institution for additional financing with any hope of success.

Equity financing is possible, under certain conditions, to get adventure money and launch an enterprise. One way is as already mentioned, through selling shares in the enterprise to friends and relatives, on an informal basis. Another is to form a public corporation and offer stock to the general public, under the rules and regulations of the SEC (Securities and Exchange Commission) for public corporations offering stock. Still another approach is to sell an interest in the venture to individuals or organizations specializing is making such investments — "venture capitalists," as they are frequently called.

Debt financing is simply borrowing money from an individual or lending institution, for which you pay interest — a fee for the use of the money. As in the case of equity financing and adventure financing, there are a number of ways to use or apply debt financing to meet your financial needs. Here are a few, in principle (how-to details will be furnished later):

- Straight borrowing from banks and other sources of loans.
- Factoring or "selling receivables" to banks and others.
- Bank credit cards, such as VISA and MasterCard (a way to sell receivables, actually).
- Using trade credit (buying from suppliers "on terms").

OPM

The whole concept of using capital raised by borrowing and/or persuading others to invest in your enterprise is often referred to as using OPM (other people's money), and there are some wealthy entrepreneurs who believe that a business ought to be financed by OPM as a matter of sound business principle, even though they are perfectly capable of supplying all the financing they need out of their personal resources. Invariably, when they refer to OPM, they mean equity financing and debt financing. There is, however, still another way to use OPM, which I have yet to see mentioned by anyone writing on the subject of business financing. It is not available to everyone because it applies only to certain kinds of business. Yet, it is a factor to consider, if your enterprise can utilize this concept or if you are considering which of several alternative enterprises to undertake.

The United States Postal Service is one example of an enterprise — today, it is a quasi-official corporation, supposed to generate enough revenue to meet its own expenses without government subsidies — which uses the latter OPM I refer to here: advance payment by the customers.

Businesses generally operate on one or more of the following bases for exchange of goods or services for money:

- Cash on the barrelhead — payment upon delivery of goods or service.
- Credit — payment within some period following delivery of goods or service.
- Advance payment — cash before delivery of the goods or service.

It is the latter exchange, *advance payment,* that is still another kind of OPM, for you manage to use the customer's money to help finance your enterprise.

The Postal Service is an outstanding example of this kind of financing because it is paid *so far* in advance of delivering the service for which the customers pay. Every postage stamp in your pocket or desk drawer represents money the Postal Service has use of before they provide the delivery service you buy. If you use their other services and maintain a deposit account against which to charge your mailings, they have the use of that money, too, for some time before they provide the service. Every penny of account on the millions of postage metering machines in offices throughout the United States is advance payment the Postal Service uses. And all is interest-free!

Few other businesses can take advantage of advance payments as effectively as the Postal Service can. For most businesses who can use the advantage at all, the period in which they can use the money free of charge is far more limited. Still, it is true OPM financing, and used wisely it can add greatly to business profits.

Take the typical mail-order enterprise, for example. There are some mail-order houses who extend credit, but even those do not make all sales on credit terms: they do some percentage of their business on a "cash" basis. But it's not really the traditional cash basis because they receive the payment with the order, and don't fill the order immediately. Many will not ship the order for 30 days or more. Note how many mail-order catalogs and advertisements caution you to "allow 4 to 6 weeks for delivery." That means that the company has the interest-free use of your money for those weeks.

Other delivery services, particularly those who guarantee overnight delivery, require payment in advance, and have the use of the money for a short time before providing the service. Nevertheless, even that short time is a great advantage. And they usually have "deposit account" convenience offered to companies, too, and get the advantage of using that money for a while.

The United States Government Printing Office is another example of an organization offering "deposit accounts," which provides them the interest-free use of the customer's money.

Landlords require advance payment of rents, which means that each month's rent is OPM.

Businesses which provide custom services, such as printing, usually have a policy of requiring one-half the money due in advance, and many require full payment in advance. This is true for many service businesses, such as accounting, consulting, legal services, and other situations where a custom product is to be created or retainers are customary.

On the other hand, there are many entrepreneurs who fail to recognize the opportunities for meeting at least part of their financial needs through such methods, and therefore fail to take advantage of opportunities to get payments well in advance of delivering the goods or services paid for. Many enterprises now conducted on a cash basis, or even on credit, in many cases, can benefit from this, either by a change in policy or by inducements to pay in advance. Of course, many merchants do offer such inducements — bonuses or discounts for payment with the order. Such inducements might also be offered to encourage such things as deposit accounts to regular customers. Whenever a new product or service is to become available in the near future, prepaid, advance orders are often solicited by astute entrepreneurs, offering inducements of some sort.

INTEREST RATES FOR DEBT FINANCING

All debt financing entails interest payments of some kind. Much also entails additional fees, often called "service charges." These presumably are extra fees for bookkeeping, postage, and other items, whereas the interest fees are solely charges for the use of the money.

Interest rates have been so unpredictable these past few years as to be almost mysterious, and the financial experts warn us that little change can be expected soon. Over the past couple of years, the prime interest rate — that rate that the big banks charge their most-favored borrowers (supposedly!) — has tended to vary between 18 and 21 percent. Only a few years ago, that would have been usurious and illegal, and in fact a number of states have had to amend their usury laws to accommodate a legitimate prime rate of approximately 20 percent.

Many business failures — *small* business, primarily — have been attributed to this sharp rise in interest rates. An irony in the entire situation, is that while the prime rate is supposedly around 20 percent, almost all lending in the business world is being done at rates considerably below the prime rate. This suggests that it is most unlikely that the rate is the true prime rate. For example, it is nearly impossible to sell real estate and automobiles at such rates, so these commodities are being offered at rates usually in the mid-teens, and sometimes less. It is hardly likely that the major corporations are truly paying the banks 20 percent, when so much trading and credit transactions are taking place at well below that rate. Nevertheless, the interest rates today are intolerably high, driven there, presumably, by inflation. (However, if inflation is the primary cause of high-interest rates, the interest rates ought to vary with the term of the loan, and be relatively low for short-term loans.)

In any case, the small business owner must expect to pay high interest rates (probably 15 to 20 percent) for loans, and is well advised to seek financing methods other than straight long-term loans. (Alternatives and exceptions to this will be described, presently.)

Interest on credit card purchases made by your customers will generally cost you from three to six percent, depending primarily on your volume. This is the fee you pay for converting that charge purchase to immediate cash on deposit in your account. (The cardholder pays interest also on the credit purchase.)

Private factors — individuals who advance you money against your receivables every week or every month — tend to charge high interest rates plus service fees, particularly if they accept high-risk receivables without recourse (which latter term means that the factor accepts the loss if the creditor fails to pay, and has no recourse to you).

In general, interest rates vary with the degree of risk. It is for that reason that a small-loan company charges extremely high interest rates: they are accepting "unsecured" loans (loans with no collateral provided). This is the concept behind the "prime rate" idea: traditionally, the banks offered the lowest interest rates to the "blue chip" companies — those with AAA credit ratings and businesses considered to be extremely sound. (At one time, when the typical interest rate for a mortgage or automobile purchase was about six percent, the prime rate would be likely to be about three percent, and perhaps even lower, for certain loans.) Ironically, the situation is reversed today: loans are being made at rates far below what is being claimed by the banks to be the prime rate.

SPECIAL PROGRAMS

The government began programs a few years ago which were designed to ensure small-business survival. Later, additional programs were instituted, designed to aid "socially and economically disadvantaged minorities" gain a foothold as entrepreneurs, and recently some lip service has been paid to doing as much for women, although very little has actually been implemented, with regard to the latter vows. Among these "socioeconomic" programs have been those intended to make capital available to those for whom capitalization has always been a major obstacle. There are a number of basic programs, falling into two classes:

- Direct government programs, wherein the federal agencies and federal employees deal directly with the "clients" in providing services.
- Indirect progams, wherein the government provides federal funds and sometimes licenses, to private-sector organizations to provide the services and implement the programs.

The result is that there exist many hundreds of organizations — in fact, more than the hyperbolic "2,001" — to whom the entrepreneur can turn when and if the more traditional sources of capital cannot or will not provide capital.

There are somewhat similar programs of state and local governments, some of them funded in whole or in part by the federal government, and some funded by both government and private funds.

VENTURE CAPITALISTS

Venture capital — capital offered as investment, in return for equity interest in an enterprise — is also offered by a substantial number of firms organized for that purpose and funded entirely with private funds. Such firms are motivated by the prospect of profits. Although they, too, will want to be first convinced that the venture is soundly based and likely to succeed — that there is no excessive risk of losing money — that is not always enough to persuade the venture capitalist to invest his money. He is also motivated by the rate of return, and will not be interested in even the soundest enterprise if it does not show the promise of a large enough profit.

In this connection it should be noted that among venture capitalists there are those who will accept high risks, if the prospects for profits or capital gain are tempting enough, while there are other venture capitalists who are far more conservative, and will not accept added risk in return for the prospect of greater gain. In a sense, they are something like gamblers — venture capital is, in a large sense, always a gamble — in that there are "high rollers" and there are cautious investors. Obviously, the cautious investor is not going to develop much interest in what appears to be a high-risk enterprise, no matter how great the potential payoff is; conversely, the high-roller venture capitalist is not going to develop much interest in a venture that promises only a modest yield, no matter how low the risk.

Of course, it is necessary to understand this, especially when seeking funds from wealthy individuals or other private sources; there, you are far more likely to encounter the risk-taking, large-gain oriented capitalist than in the walnut-paneled offices of the Wall Street venture-capital firm.

WHAT IS IN THIS DIRECTORY/GUIDE

The primary purpose of this book is to guide you to the best financing sources for your needs. You must recognize that there is no such thing as "best" for everyone, for everyone's needs are different: what is best for you is not necessarily best for someone else. For example, equity financing might be ideal for another and be entirely wrong for you. Or, where another may be able to get a straight loan without difficulty, you may be compelled to resort to other means to meet your capital needs.

Some entrepreneurs also find it necessary or advisable to get financing from several sources, for one reason or another. Again, this book will provide at least some guidance in deciding what sources are best for your needs.

A great many sources are listed here, some of them what might be considered "conventional" and well-known sources, such as banks, but a great many are not at all well-known to anyone but those who seek them out. Listed herein are those most likely to be of use to the small-business owner or the individual seeking to launch a small enterprise. This is more than a directory or catalog, however; you will be advised to read the text passages also, which will help you use the directory sections most advantageously.

The directory listings have been separated by category. There are, for example, both federal and state government programs designed to help small business generally (in the name of preserving free enterprise, among other objectives) and minority entrepreneurs especially. In these programs, the governments may make direct loans, from government funds, to entrepreneurs, and they do so, in some cases — primarily where the amount required is relatively small and is not likely to interest a commercial bank. In most cases, the government agency guarantees the loan, which is made by a regular lending institution, such as a bank. In so doing, the government is actually your cosigner. Best known is the SBA (Small Business Administration) loan and loan-guarantee program, but — ironically enough — it is by no means either the only federal-government loan/loan-guarantee program, nor is it even the largest one. What many entrepreneurs need to know is that there are several other federal programs to which this directory guides the reader: the Farmers Home Administration (FmHA), United States Department of Agriculture program, which makes more loans for business purposes than for farm homes; the programs of the Department of Housing and Urban Development (HUD), which financed a great deal of the residential construction of recent years in the United States; and a number of other such programs.

Read the text in its entirety first. Then begin your study of those listings which appear most appropriate to your needs. Appropriateness of the listing and the sources is not the sole criterion, however. In some cases, although a source appears most appropriate, contingencies may bar it from being of use to you. For example, you may encounter a Small Business Investment Company (SBIC) that would have been exactly right for you, and discover that the company is "fully invested" — that it has loaned or invested all its available capital, and is therefore unable to help you. There are numerous other circumstances such as this, which make it necessary to resort to alternative sources.

For this reason, use this directory to develop your own *list* of potential capital sources, and rank-order them. Start with those closest to your area of operation, and be sure to include government sources. The probabilities are that you will have to go to a number of sources before you find the success you want. That is why this volume provides so many sources of help — well over 2,000.

Chapter 2

How to Find the Right Backer

There is an old saw in business that says, "There is a buyer for everything, if you wait long enough." This could be paraphrased as, "There is capital available for everyone, if you search long enough." In any case, there is ample evidence that even with "tight money," intelligent and informed effort produces results.

WHERE DO YOU FIT?

One reason for the many different ways of financing a business, and the many different organizations and programs, is simply that there are so many different kinds of needs. To some degree, the nature of your financing problem is inherent in you, as an individual, and in the kind of enterprise you seek to launch. For example, if you are a member of a minority recognized by the government as "socially and economically disadvantaged," the presumption is that it is automatically all but impossible for you to get a large bank loan, for that has been historical fact. Whole neighborhods — large sections of urban areas — have historically been "redlined" (automatically barred from borrowing) by banks, despite laws prohibiting the practice. It is rather well known that women have enormous difficulty in borrowing from banks, even for personal loans, let alone for substantial business investments. These are only two examples of the problems faced by many individuals in financing enterprises that require substantial capital.

The latter consideration is another factor: It is inherent in some enterprises that a great

deal of "front end" money (basic investment capital for start-up) is required, whereas some enterprises require little capital (relatively) to launch. Even with the best of credit-worthiness, and even with the best of business plans, it is difficult to raise millions of dollars by straight debt financing through bank loans. Yet, surprising as it may be, it is also difficult to get bank loans for business ventures when the loans requested are too small. Banks often believe that business loans of $25,000 or $50,000 are not large enough to be worth the paperwork and bookkeeping.

It is in recognition of these problems that so many different programs have been established, with so many different means and organizations to solve the financing problems of small business generally and minority-owned small business especially. (Not much more than sympathy has been extended, so far, to women who want to start or have started enterprises of their own.) It is assumed that big business does not have the problems of small business in capitalization, despite the fiscal crises of Chrysler, Lockheed, W. T. Grant, Korvette's, Robert Hall, and other large businesses that have run into financial difficulties and sometimes succumbed to them. (It is also by no means certain that financial aid would have helped these firms, despite the recovery of Lockheed.)

Consider, therefore, what sort of seeker after funds you are, in both the socioeconomic terms commonly recognized by the government today and in terms of the kind of enterprise you seek to finance. Consider the kind of funding ordinary business considerations dictate as most logical or most likely to be realizable. Consider, too, where the funds and the programs are and what they are — which appear designed for you, in your own set of circumstances.

This directory was conceived to help you do just these things — make the preliminary analyses so that you can make a reasonable judgment as to the "2001" sources of funding you are most likely to find useful, and then search out the individual agencies, institutions, or organizations you should solicit for help. The directory is therefore organized progressively:

- The general introduction and orientation.
- Help in initial analyses of your circumstances and needs.
- Description of the various agencies, institutions, programs, organizations.
- Listings, by nature of the organizations and programs.
- Reference data: some miscellaneous data and how-to instructions.

Before we go on to describe and explain the various programs in detail, let's discuss some of the terms already used and explain what they mean, so that you may judge which of these classes of entrepreneur or prospective entrepreneur you fit best.

ARE YOU "SMALL BUSINESS"?

For most purposes, businesses are "small" if they are not "dominant in their field" and do not exceed certain standards by which they are judged. The United States Small Business Administration (SBA) sets the size standards for the federal government, and each state that has a small-business program (most have some sort of program or are planning one) sets standards for its own purposes.

Some of the size standards will shock you, for they appear to be quite large in relation to what many of us think of as a small business. For example, the SBA has standards ranging as high as $8 million in annual sales volume, as the maximum size for some businesses to qualify as "small" and therefore to be entitled to certain special benefits. Where the number of employees is used as a standard, some of the businesses may have up to 500 employees before they stand to lose their "small-business" classification.

The states are a trifle more conservative, in general, but still classify many businesses doing several millions of dollars per year as small business. In any event, it would be a rare enterprise that did not qualify as a small business in its early days at least, as long as it is independently owned.

Both the federal government and the state governments — and even some of the local (city, town, township, and county) governments — have programs for small, minority owned, and women-owned businesses. Since some minority-owned businesses have grown quite large, in recent years the programs have been further qualified, by SBA at least, as designed to aid minority-owned *small* business.

The federal government has a surprisingly large number of agencies and programs designed to help small businesses and minority entrepreneurs, some of them fairly well known (SBA, for example), others not at all well known (Farmers Home Administration, for example). Both the federal and the state and local government programs are designed to provide a variety of services and kinds of assistance, but most include loans or loan-guarantee programs — both, in many cases. There are some private-sector programs, too, operating frequently with federal support, but sometimes funded privately. All these programs will be described and explained in greater detail (in terms of their financial-aid aspects) in the next chapter.

WHAT IS YOUR SOCIOECONOMIC STATUS?

In most federal programs today, a great deal of preference is given to those who qualify as members of what the law describes as "socially and economically disadvantaged minorities." These include — but, the federal announcements carefully stress, are not limited to — blacks, Asiatics, Hispanics, American Indians, Eskimos, and Aleuts. However, under the law as written, being a member of one of these minorities does not automatically qualify you, supposedly. You must demonstrate that you are also indeed, "socially and economically disadvantaged"! In practice, however, qualification is almost automatic for those who are clearly members of one of these minorities. On the other hand, individuals who did not belong to one of the named minorities have managed to qualify as belonging to a "socially and economically disadvantaged minority" for administrative purposes, at least. (Example: One Washington-area woman owner of an engineering services firm sued the SBA for denying her the desired status, charging that as a woman in the unaccustomed area of engineering, she should qualify; the court supported her position and arguments.)

Whether you are or are not a member of a minority that qualifies in toto, or whether you can qualify as an individual, appears to be largely a matter of how hard you will fight for the status and how good your lawyer is. Whether it is helpful to you to qualify is another matter, one you will have to judge for yourself, after you have had the opportunity to review all the programs and institutions listed in these pages.

Qualifying as a small business is another matter, and is quite easy to do, for most entrepreneurs starting a new enterprise or seeking financing for a young enterprise. Under the standards of most governments and programs, you are unlikely to reach big-business status for a few years. As far as loans are concerned, small business generally has a great many special resources, although minority entrepreneurs admittedly have many additional, special resources.

As far as government programs are concerned, there is little in the way of special programs for women entrepreneurs, although programs have been promised for several years. One problem is that the various trade groups of minority entrepreneurs have battled against any entitlement legislation for women entrepreneurs, on the grounds that little enough is provided for minority entrepreneurs, and even that would be further reduced by any new entitlement programs for women. However, there is a growing number of banks owned by determined women entrepreneurs, and those would logically be more sympathetic to applications from women than might the traditional male-owned banks.

There are also some special programs for special situations, such as help for the physically handicapped individual who wants to launch and operate a small business.

Chapter 3

The Big Uncle: Federal Agencies and Programs

One thing our government fails to do well is to publicize the astonishing scope of "federal domestic assistance," under which federal loan, loan-guarantee, and other local-aid programs are grouped, in a spread of programs offering almost $100 billion annually.

TYPES AND CLASSES OF FEDERAL PROGRAMS

Programs of the United States Government designed to aid business — usually directed at small business generally, and special groups in particular — are classified generally as "socioeconomic" programs. One of the basic concepts underlying such programs is that big business has grown so big and powerful in the United States that only the controlling hand of the federal government can preserve small business and free enterprise. Ostensibly, the various programs preserve for all the economic freedom to launch new and independent enterprises, despite the overpowering and dominant presence of big business. (Other objectives are to create and preserve jobs, especially in economically depressed areas, but these objectives are irrelevant to the purposes of this book, except as they explain the purposes of many programs in providing capital to businesses so that jobs are created or preserved.)

The various programs aid small businesses or beginning entrepreneurs attempting to start a small business through direct loans, loan guarantees, equity financing, and direct assistance in pursuing and winning financial help — e.g., aid in preparing loan packages, training, and guidance. This assistance is both direct — the federal agency and its staff provide the services — and indirect — the government funds and supports private-sector organizations who provide the services.

There is also a form of indirect financial support, in that federal agencies supply some services free of charge to those businesses who qualify. These services would otherwise cost the businesses money, so that their provision by the government without charge represents a form of financial support, indirect though it is. For that reason, some mention of these services will be made here, in describing and discussing federal programs.

The Small Business Administration

Undoubtedly the best known among all the federal agencies established to aid small business is the Small Business Administration, more popularly referred to as the SBA. With its central or headquarters office in downtown Washington, DC, SBA maintains ten regional offices and nearly a hundred field or district offices, so that every area of the United States is served by an SBA office within a reasonable distance.

The SBA is a relatively small organization, as federal agencies go, and is by no means the sole agency entrusted with major responsibilities regarding assistance to small business and preservation of free enterprise and entrepreneurial opportunity in the United States. Still, the large number of offices and far-ranging set of programs operated by SBA indicate the leading role played by the agency. Brief descriptions of SBA programs and activities relating to SBA financial assistance to small business follow.

SBA financial assistance takes the form of direct loans, guaranteed loans, and direct participation loans to small business. These can be for virtually any legitimate business purpose, and since 1976 "small business" has included farming enterprises in its definition, making farmers eligible for all SBA programs and benefits, if they qualify as "small."

SBA also operates programs of disaster assistance, under which financial assistance is provided to businesses and farmers who have suffered disasters — flood, drought, fire, earthquake, riots, and other such cataclysmic events.

Still other SBA financial-assistance programs help small businesses meet environmental and safety requirements of other federal agencies, such as the Occupational Safety and Health Administration (OSHA) and the Environmental Protection Agency (EPA)

SBA also supports small-business and minority-small-business assistance programs of state and local governments in several ways, including financing such programs through loans and loan guarantees.

An indirect SBA program which has been of material assistance to small and minority entrepreneurs is the Small Business Investment Company/Minority Small Business Investment Company (SBIC/MESBIC) program. In this program, SBA has licensed hundreds of private-sector organizations to provide both debt financing and equity capital (investment) in small businesses, aiding the SBICs and MESBICs by loans and loan guarantees that provide the SBICs and MESBICs leverage in creating pools of capital for long-term loans and investment in new ventures.

A more detailed and exhaustive explanation of the program will be presented in Chapter 6, where the organizations are listed.

SBA offers a wide variety of business publications, many free and others at nominal cost, as well as counseling and consulting services, training programs, seminars, and other assistance, such as direct help in developing "loan packages" (applications for loans). There are also programs to help small businesses win government contracts, and help in getting financing to ensure capability to perform on government contracts. Moreover, SBA will help small businesses who contract with the government in getting progress payments on government contracts.

Following is a directory listing of SBA offices, arranged geographically to facilitate locating the nearest or most convenient one for your use.

Alphabetical/Geographical Listing of All SBA Offices in the United States and Possessions

Alabama

908 S. 20th Street, Room 202
Birmingham 35205
(205) 254-1344
District Office

Alaska

1016 W. 6th Avenue, Suite 200
Anchorage 90501
(907) 272-5561
District Office

Federal Building & Courthouse
Fairbanks 99701
(907) 452-1951
Branch Office

Arizona

3030 N. Central Avenue
Phoenix 85004
(602) 261-3611
District Office

301 W. Congress Street
Tucson 85715
Post of Duty

Arkansas

320 West Capital
Little Rock 72201
(501) 378-5871
District Office

California

1229 N Street
Fresno 93712
(209) 487-5000
District Office

350 S. Figueroa Street
Los Angeles 90071
(213) 688-2956
District Office

2800 Cottage Way, Room 2535
Sacramento 95825
(916) 484-4726
Post of Duty

880 Front Street, Room 4-S-38
San Diego 92188
(714) 293-5440
District Office

450 Golden Gate Avenue
San Francisco 94102
(415) 556-7487
Regional Office (Region IX)

211 Main Street, 4th floor
San Francisco 94105
(415) 556-7490
District Office

Colorado

1405 Curtis Street, 22nd floor
Denver 80202
(303) 837-0111
Regional Office (Region VIII)

721 19th Street
Denver 80202
(303) 837-0111
District Office

Connecticut

1 Financial Plaza
Hartford 06103
(203) 244-3600
District Office

Delaware

844 King Street, Room 5207
Wilmington 19801
(302) 573-6294
Branch Office

District of Columbia

1441 L Street, NW
Washington 20416
(202) 653-6365
Central (Headquarters) Office

1030 15th Street, NW
Washington 20417
(202) 653-6979
District Office

Florida

2222 Ponce deLeon Boulevard
Coral Gables 33134
(305) 350-5521
District Office

400 W. Bay Street, Room 261
Jacksonville 32202
(904) 791-3782
District Office

700 Twiggs Street
Tampa 33607
(813) 228-2594
Post of Duty

701 Clematis Street
West Palm Beach 33402
(305) 659-7533
Post of Duty

Georgia

1375 Peachtree Street, NE
Atlanta 30309
(404) 881-4943
Regional Office (Region IV)

1720 Peachtree Rd, NW
Atlanta 30309
(404) 881-4325
District Office

Guam

Pacific Daily News Building
Agana 96910
777-8420
Branch Office

Hawaii

300 Ala Moana
Honolulu 96850
(808) 546-8950
District Office

Idaho

1005 Main Street
Boise 83702
(208) 384-1096
District Office

Illinois

219 S. Dearborn Street, Room 838
Chicago 60604
(312) 353-0355
Regional Office (Region V)

219 S. Dearborn Street, Room 437
Chicago 60604
(312) 353-4528
District Office

1 N. Old State Capitol Plaza
Springfield 62701
(217) 525-4416
Branch Office

Indiana

575 N. Pennsylvania Street
Indianapolis 46204
(317) 633-7000
District Office

Iowa

210 Walnut Street, Room 749
Des Moines 50309
(515) 284-4422
District Office

Kansas

110 E. Waterman Street
Wichita 67202
(316) 267-6311
District Office

Kentucky

600 Federal Plaza, Room 188
Louisville 40202
(502) 582-5971
District Office

Louisiana

1001 Howard Avenue, 17th floor
New Orleans 70113
(504) 589-2611
District Office

500 Fannin Street
Shreveport 71101
(318) 226-5196
Post of Duty

Maine

40 Western Avenue
Augusta 04330
(207) 622-6171
District Office

Maryland

8600 LaSalle Road
Towson 21204
(301) 962-4392
District Office

Massachusetts

60 Batterymarch Street, 10th floor
Boston 02110
(617) 223-2100
Regional Office (Region I)

150 Causeway Street
Boston 02114
(617) 223-2100
District Office

302 High Street, 4th floor
Holyoke 01040
(413) 536-8770
Post of Duty

Michigan

477 Michigan Avenue
Detroit 48226
(313) 226-6075
District Office

540 West Kaye Avenue
Marquette 49885
(906) 225-1108
Branch Office

Minnesota

12 S. 6th Street
Minneapolis 55402
(612) 725-2362
District Office

Mississippi

111 Fred Haise Boulevard, 2nd floor
Biloxi 39530
(601) 435-3676
Branch Office

100 W. Capitol Street
Jackson 39201
(601) 969-4384
District Office

Missouri

911 Walnut Street, 23rd floor
Kansas City 64106
(816) 374-3318
Regional Office (Region VII)

1150 Grand Avenue
Kansas City 64106
(816) 374-5557
District Office

1 Mercantile Tower
St. Louis 63101
(314) 425-4191
District office

Montana

301 S. Park Avenue
Helena 59601
(406) 449-5381
District Office

Nebraska

19th & Farnum Streets
Omaha 68102
(402) 221-4691
District Office

Nevada

301 E. Stewart Street
Las Vegas 89101
(702) 385-6011
District Office

50 S. Virginia Avenue, Room 308
Reno 89501
(702) 784-5477
Post of Duty

New Hampshire

55 Pleasant Street, Room 213
Concord 03301
(603) 224-4041
District Office

New Jersey

1800 E. Davis Street
Camden 08104
(609) 757-5183
Post of Duty

970 Broad Street, Room 1635
Newark 07102
(201) 645-2434
District Office

New Mexico

5000 Marble Avenue, NE
Albuquerque 87110
(505) 766-3430
District Office

New York

99 Washington Avenue, Room 301
Albany 12210
(518) 472-6300
Post of Duty

111 W. Huron Street, Room 1311
Buffalo 14202
(716) 846-4301
Branch Office

180 State Street
Elmira 14901
(607) 734-3961
Branch Office

401 Broad Hollow Road
Melville 11747
(516) 752-1626
Post of Duty

26 Federal Plaza, Room 29-118
New York 10007
(212) 264-1468
Regional Office (Region II)

26 Federal Plaza, Room 3100
New York 10007
(212) 264-4355
District Office

100 State Street, Room 601
Rochester 14614
(716) 263-6700
Post of Duty

100 S. Clinton Street
Syracuse 13260
(315) 423-5383
District Office

North Carolina

230 S. Tryon Street
Charlotte 28202
(704) 372-0711
District Office

215 S. Evans Street, Room 206
Greenville 27834
(919) 752-3798
Post of Duty

North Dakota

657 2nd Avenue N., Room 218
Fargo 58102
(701) 237-5771
District Office

Ohio

550 Main Street, Room 5028
Cincinnati 45202
(513) 684-2814
Branch Office

1240 E. 9th Street, Room 317
Cleveland 44199
(216) 522-4180
District Office

85 Marconi Boulevard
Columbus 43215
(614) 469-6860
District Office

Oklahoma

200 NW 5th Street, Room 670
Oklahoma City 73102
(405) 231-4301
District Office

Oregon

Federal Building
1220 SW 3rd Avenue
Portland 97204
(503) 221-2000
District Office

Pennsylvania

231 St. Asaphs Road
Bala Cynwyd 19004
(215) 597-3311
Regional Office (Region III)

231 St. Asaphs Road
Bala Cynwyd 19004
(215) 597-3311
District Office

100 Chestnut Street
Harrisburg 17108
(717) 782-3840
Branch Office

1000 Liberty Avenue, Room 1401
Pittsburgh 15222
(412) 644-2780
District Office

20 N. Pennsylvania Avenue
Wilkes Barre 18702
(717) 782-3840
Branch Office

Puerto Rico

Chardon & Bolivia Street
Hato Rey 00919
(809) 763-6363
District Office

Rhode Island

40 Fountain Street
Providence 02903
(401) 528-4580
District Office

South Carolina

1835 Assembly Street
Columbia 29201
(803) 765-5376
Post of Duty

South Dakota

515 9th Street, Room 246
Rapid City 57701
(605) 343-5074
Branch Office

101 S. Maine Avenue
Sioux Falls 57102
(605) 336-2980
District Office

Tennessee

502 S. Gay Street, Room 307
Knoxville 37902
(615) 637-9300
Branch Office

167 N. Main Street, Room 211
Memphis 38103
(901) 521-3588
Post of Duty

404 James Robertson Parkway
Nashville 37219
(615) 251-5881
District Office

Texas

3105 Leopard Street
Corpus Christi 78408
(512) 888-3011
Branch Office

1720 Regal Row, Room 230
Dallas 75235
(214) 749-2531
Regional Office (Region VI)

1100 Commerce Street, Room 3C36
Dallas 75242
(214) 749-3961
District Office

4100 Rio Bravo, Suite 300
El Paso 79902
(915) 543-7200
Branch Office

500 Dallas Street
Houston 77002
(713) 226-4341
District Office

222 E. Van Buren Street
Lower Rio Grande Valley — Harlingen 78550
(512) 423-8934
District Office

1205 Texas Avenue, Room 712
Lubbock 79401
(806) 762-7011
District Office

100 S. Wash Street
Marshall 75670
(214) 935-5257
Post of Duty

727 E. Durango, Room A-513
San Antonio 78206
(512) 229-6250
District Office

Utah

125 S. State Street
Salt Lake City 84138
(801) 524-5800
District Office

Vermont

87 State Street, Room 204
Montpelier 05602
(802) 229-0538
District Office

Virginia

400 N. 8th Street, Room 3015
Richmond 23240
(804) 782-2617
District Office

Virgin Islands

Federal Office Building, Room 283
Veterans Drive
St. Thomas 00801
(809) 774-8530
Post of Duty

Washington

710 2nd Avenue, 5th floor
Seattle 98104
(206) 442-5676
Regional Office (Region X)

915 2nd Avenue, Room 1744
Seattle 98174
(206) 442-5534
District Office

W. 920 Riverside Drive
Spokane 99210
(509) 456-3777
District Office

West Virginia

Charleston National Plaza
Charleston 25301
(304) 343-6181
Branch Office

109 N. 3rd Street
Clarksburg 26301
(304) 623-5631
District Office

Wisconsin

500 S. Barstow Street
Eau Claire 54701
(715) 834-9012
Post of Duty

212 E. Washington Avenue
Madison 53703
(608) 252-5261
District Office

517 E. Wisconsin Avenue
Milwaukee 53202
(414) 291-3941
Branch Office

Wyoming

100 E. B Street
Caspar 82601
(307) 265-5550
District Office

Department of Commerce

The United States Department of Commerce, while not an especially large agency of the government, has a great many programs and conducts many activities related to commerce and industry in the United States and between the United States and other nations. Two Commerce Department agencies of special interest, in connection with business financing, are the Economic Development Administration (EDA) and the Minority Business Development Agency (MBDA). The latter was formerly the Office of Minority Business Enterprise (OMBE).

EDA, since 1965 and until recently, conducted a multibillion dollar program of loans, loan guarantees, and grants to support economic development and create or conserve jobs, especially in those areas suffering high rates of unemployment and economic distress in general. Under its authority, loans and loan guarantees were furnished to many private-sector companies, large and small, and, together with grants, to many communities and local governments, for economic development.

At the time of this writing, the future of the EDA programs is not bright. The current Administration has announced its intention of dismantling the program and the EDA in its entirety before the end of fiscal 1982, and there is currently no way to predict whether or not this will come to pass. When questioned about this, EDA officials advised that, in the future, you should check with the nearest of the following Commerce Department offices to determine the status of the EDA:

EDA Office of Public Affairs
Department of Commerce
Washington, DC 20230
(202) 377-5113

105 N. 7th Street
600 Federal Reserve Bank Building
Philadelphia, PA 19106

1365 Peachtree Street, NE
Suite 700
Atlanta, GA 30309

175 W. Jackson Boulevard
Chicago, IL 60604

909 17th Street
Denver, CO 80202

221 W. 6th Street
Austin, TX 78701

1700 Westlake Avenue N.
Seattle, WA 98109

The preceding are regional offices of the EDA, out of which branch approximately fifty EDA field offices and representatives who have, until now, administered the EDA programs. EDA officials expect these regional offices to remain in operation for some time, irrespective of what happens to the EDA programs during the coming year.

A far more important program of the Commerce Department, for purposes of financing your business, is the Minority Business Development Agency. Originally the OMBE, MBDA is dedicated to assisting minority entrepreneurs establish and operate new enterprises successfully. In the case of MBDA, however, vitually the entire annual budget, approximately $50 million, and the effort are expended through a net of private-sector organizations funded and supported by MBDA principally, although some of the organizations also get funds from SBA and from private sources. For the most part, the organizations supported are nonprofit. A few existed previously for other purposes, but most organized especially and solely to function as MBDA-supported contractors to assist minority entrepreneurs. A few of the organizations so supported are bureaus of state and local governments — state and city OMBEs.

The organizations vary in that each is somewhat specialized. For example, some specialize in construction-related enterprises, while others are devoted principally to working with large corporations and governments to develop business opportunity for entrepreneurs.

A listing of the supported organizations and details of what they offer will be found in Chapter 6. Following, however, is a list of Commerce Department MBDA offices, arranged alphabetically/geographically to enable you to locate the closest of these approximately forty offices and officials.

Arizona

Elisama L. Embry
MBDA District Officer
2940 Valley Bank Center
Phoenix 85073
(602) 261-3502

Arkansas

Bobby T. Jefferson
MBDA District Officer
600 West Capitol Street, Room 234
Little Rock 72201
(501) 740-6169

California

Ramon V. Romero
MBDA Regional Director
San Francisco Region
15045 Federal Building
San Francisco 94102
(415) 556-7234, 7633

Linda M. Marmalejo
MBDA District Officer
15043 Federal Building
San Francisco 94102
(415) 556-6065

Larry D. Burton
MBDA District Officer
2500 Wilshire Boulevard
Los Angeles 90057
(213) 688-7157

Colorado

Emma Buck
MBDA District Officer
333 West Colfax Avenue, 3rd floor
Denver 80204
(303) 837-2767

District of Columbia

Luis C. Encinias
MBDA Regional Director
Washington Region
1730 K Street, NW, Room 420
Washington 20006
(202) 634-7897

MBDA District Officer
U.S. Department of Commerce, Room 5628
Washington, DC 20230
(202) 377-5098

MBDA Information Clearinghouse
U.S. Department of Commerce, Room 5714
Washington, DC 20230
(202) 377-2414

Florida

Michael D. Wallach
MBDA District Officer
216 Federal Building
Miami 33130
(305) 350-5054

Georgia

Charles F. McMillan
MBDA Regional Director
Atlanta Region
1371 Peachtree Street, NW, Suite 505
Atlanta 30309
(404) 881-4091, 3094

Eddie L. Blankenship
MBDA District Officer
908 20th Street, NE
Atlanta 30309
(404) 881-7609

Beverly M. Hargrove
MBDA District Officer
1371 Peachtree Street, NE
Atlanta 30309
(404) 881-7609

Hawaii

Yosef Patel
MBDA District Officer
P.O. Box 50189
Honolulu 96850
(808) 546-3796

Illinois

Stanley W. Tate
MBDA Regional Director
Chicago Region
55 East Monroe Street, Room 1440
Chicago 60603
(312) 353-0182

Jessie B. Deloch
MBDA District Officer
536 South Clark Street, Room 223
Chicago 60605
(312) 353-2410

Maryland

Robert Sewall
MBDA District Officer
Fallon Federal Building, Box 286
Baltimore 21201
(301) 962-3231

Massachusetts

R.K. Schwartz
MBDA District Officer
441 Stuart Street, 7th floor
Boston 02116
(617) 223-3726

Michigan

Carol R. Raymond
MBDA District Officer
535 Federal Courthouse Building
Detroit 48226
(313) 226-4835

Minnesota

Otto Murry
MBDA District Officer
108 Federal Courts Building
Minneapolis 55401
(612) 725-2044

Missouri

Chester E. Stovall, Jr.
MBDA District officer
3130 Troost Avenue
Kansas City 64109
(816) 374-3381

Richard Anderson
MBDA District Officer
1114 Market Street, Room 633
St. Louis 63101
(314) 425-6426

New Jersey

John W. Alexander, Jr.
MBDA District Officer
970 Broad Street, Room 1653
Newark 07102
(201) 645-6497

New Mexico

Rita E. Gonzales
MBDA District Officer
505 Marquette, NW, Room 1001
Albuquerque 87101
(505) 766-3379

New York

Ralph J. Perez
MBDA Regional Director
New York Region
26 Federal Plaza, Suite 36116
New York 10007
(212) 264-3263, 3485, 4741

Louis Muniz
MBDA District Officer
26 Federal Plaza, 36th floor
New York 10007
(212) 264-4382

Dolores D. McCarley
MBDA District Officer
1111 West Huron Street, Room 500
Buffalo 14202
(716) 846-4387

Ohio

Sandra Suliman
MBDA District Officer
666 Euclid Avenue, Room 600
Cleveland 44114
(313) 522-5404

Oregon

Erma L. O'Neale
MBDA District Officer
511 NW Broadway, Room 647
Portland 97209
(503) 423-4997

Pennsylvania

Alfonso C. Jackson
MBDA District Officer
W. J. Green Federal Building
600 Arch Street, Room 9436
Philadelphia 19106
(215) 597-9236

Robert L. Boulden
MBDA District Officer
614 Federal Building
Pittsburgh 15222
(412) 644-5882

Tennessee

MBDA District Officer
747 Kefauver Federal Building
Nashville 37203
(615) 251-5722

Texas

Richard Sewing
MBDA Regional Director
Dallas Region
1100 Commerce Street, Room 7B19
Dallas 75242
(214) 729-8001

Thomas H. Hawkins
MBDA District Officer
1100 Commerce Street, Room 7B26
Dallas 75242
(214) 729-0793

Victor Casaus (Temporary)
MBDA District Officer
    for New Orleans
1100 Commerce Street, Room 7B19
Dallas 75242
(214) 767-8001

Ben Chavez (Temporary)
MBDA District Officer
    for San Antonio
1100 Commerce Street, Room 7B19
Dallas 75242
(214) 767-8001

Bennie L. Hubbard
MBDA District Officer
2525 Murworth, Suite 105
Houston 77054
(713) 660-4497

Virginia

Freddie L. Jones
MBDA District Officer
Federal Building, Room 7010
Richmond 23240
(804) 771-2050

Washington

Rosa V. McDaniel
MBDA District Officer
2001 Western Avenue, Suite 150
Seattle 98121
(206) 442-2437

United States Department of Agriculture

The United States Department of Agriculture (USDA) is, not surprisingly, concerned primarily with farmers, farming, farming communities, and the problems associated with these. USDA is a sprawling organization, with almost innumerable agencies within its bureaucratic structure. Like many other federal agencies, USDA has programs offering financial assistance to both individuals and communities — state and local governments. Chief among these agencies, for our purposes, is the Farmers Home Administration, or FmHA, as it is popularly abbreviated. USDA explains FmHA:

The Farmers Home Administration (FmHA), an agency within the Department of Agriculture, provides credit for those in rural America who are unable to get credit at reasonable rates and terms.... Applications for loans are made at the agency's 2,200 local county and district offices, generally located in county-seat towns. A county or area committee of three individuals, at least two of whom are farmers, certifies or recommends as to eligibility of individual farm loan applications and amounts of loans and reviews borrowers' progress.

Take note of the typical justification for all government loans and loan-guarantees: they are made to individuals and organizations who, among other necessary qualifications, are unable to borrow money through conventional channels at acceptable rates and terms. Generally, this means that the applicant must provide evidence of being unable to borrow from banks and other lending institutions, and the generally accepted evidence of this is a turndown from a bank or other such institution, following a proper application.

FmHA loans fall into at least fifteen categories, under more than twenty-five programs. By no means do all programs and loans relate directly to agricultural needs and problems, nor need the applicant be a farmer to qualify for FmHA assistance. In fact, many FmHA loans, some quite sizable, have been made for industrialization in rural communities — that is, to finance enterprises in small towns. In short, USDA and FmHA identify as within their interests and missions the general welfare of all rural communities and residents, and have supported many enterprises which are only indirectly related, sometimes only tenuously related, to agriculture. Following are the chief loan categories, and brief descriptions relative thereto:

Operating loans: These loans are for owners of small ("not larger than family") farms. Funds may be used to buy equipment, livestock, feed, fertilizer, and other such needs. Also to ". . . provide operating credit to fish farmers; carry out forestry purposes; and develop income-producing recreation and other nonfarm enterprises." (There is the clear admission that FmHA financing is available for investing in such things as amusement parks, picnic grounds, and other "nonfarm enterprises.")

Interest rates on direct loans made by FmHA are set by the government since loans made by lending institutions, under FmHA guarantees, are negotiated between the lender and the borrower, with FmHA concurrence. Direct loans are limited to $100,000, under present law, and guaranteed loans to $200,000, with terms of loans up to seven years.

Youth project loans: These loans are for rural youngsters, ten to twenty-one, to finance income-producing projects. Interest rates are by annual formula; other terms are negotiated.

Emergency loans: These loans are designed to offset losses resulting from natural disasters, at 5 percent interest rates.

Economic emergency loans: These loans are to assist farmers, ranchers, and others in agriculture during local or general economic recessions. The limit on such loans is $400,000, with the total of all FmHA loans to any one individual limited to $650,000. Terms are as in most FmHA loans, except real estate loans (mortgages), which may be for forty years.

Farm ownership loans: These loans are intended to enable farmers to buy their farms or to enlarge or develop their property, for a term of up to forty years. The direct-loan limit is $200,000; the guaranteed-loan limit is $300,000. Interest rates are as in operating loans.

Loans to limited resource farmers: These loans are intended to help the farmer who is doing poorly, for one reason or another, such as lack of necessary farming skills or lack of suitable equipment. If loans are used to buy farm real estate, interest rates may start as low as 3 percent, for real estate loans, but not less than 6 percent, for production loans. Real estate loans are limited to $200,000, production loans to $100,000.

Soil and water conservation loans: These loans are for use in carrying out soil and water conservation projects for terms as long as forty years.

Recreation loans: These loans are expressly for converting all or part of the applicant's farm or ranch to income-producing recreational enterprises. Terms are the same as those for soil and water conservation loans.

Loans to Indian tribes: Indian tribes or tribal corporations may borrow to acquire lands for terms for up to forty years; interest rates are set by the government's cost of borrowing.

Loans to associations: Farmers and other eligible individuals may group in an association and qualify for loans to construct irrigation systems, drain farmland, build recreational facilities, and conduct other projects in their communities.

Rural housing loans: These funds are to assist those of low and moderate income in acquiring housing in open country and rural communities of not more than 10,000 population (or 20,000, where there is a pronounced lack of mortgage credit available). Loans may be used to buy, build, or repair homes, farm buildings, and building sites. The maximum term is thirty-three years, with periodically assessed interest rates. Cosigners are acceptable, and guaranteed loans are available, as well as direct loans. Builders may ask for "conditional commitments" from the agency, which are assurances to the builder or seller that if their houses meet FmHA standards, FmHA will make mortgage money available to qualified buyers. Loans are made to private nonprofit corporations, consumer cooperatives, state and local agencies, individuals, and organizations operating on a profit or limited-profit basis, to provide housing in rural areas for persons of low and moderate income.

Rural industrialization loans: Loans and loan guarantees are available to a variety of individuals and organizations, profit and nonprofit, to improve the economic conditions of rural communities. That includes funding the start-up, improvement, or development of business enterprises in communities of population up to 50,000, although priority is given to projects for communities with population of 25,000 or less. The FmHA guarantee on such loans is for 90 percent of the principal and interest, with interest rates negotiated between borrower and lender.

In describing the various programs in detail, FmHA urges anyone interested to consult the local telephone directory to find the FmHA county office number. If there is no listing, FmHA says, get in touch with either FmHA headquarters at USDA in Washington, DC, or the FmHA State Office. The latter are listed in the following directory. They are arranged in the alphabetical/geographical listing used elsewhere in this volume for your convenience in locating the office nearest you.

Farmers Home Administration State Offices

Alabama

Room 717, Aronov Building
474 S. Court Street
Montgomery 36104
(205) 832-7077

Alaska

P.O. Box 1289
Palmer 99645
(907) 745-2176

Arizona

Room 3433, Federal Building
230 N. First Avenue
Phoenix 85025
(602) 261-6701

Arkansas

5529 Federal Office Building
700 W. Capitol
P.O. Box 72203
Little Rock 72201
(501) 378-6281

California

459 Cleveland Street
Woodland 95695
(916) 666-3382

Colorado

Room 231, 2490 W. 26th Avenue
Denver 80211
(303) 837-4347

Delaware

151 E. Chestnut Hill Road, Suite 2
Newark 19713
(302) 573-6694

Florida

Room 314, Federal Building
401 SE 1st Avenue
P.O. Box 1088
Gainesville 32602
(904) 376-3218

Georgia

355 E. Hancock Avenue
Athens 30601
(404) 546-2162

Hawaii

345 Kekuanoa Street
Hilo 96720
(808) 961-4781

Idaho

Room 429, Federal Building
304 N. Eighth Street
Boise 83702
(208) 334-1301

Illinois

2106 W. Springfield Avenue
Champaign 61820
(217) 398-5235

Indiana

Suite 1700, 5610 Crawfordsville Road
Indianapolis 46224
(317) 269-6415

Iowa

Room 873, Federal Building
210 Walnut Street
Des Moines 50309
(515) 284-4663

Kansas

444 SE Quincy Street
Topeka 66683
(913) 295-2870

Kentucky

333 Waller Avenue
Lexington 40504
(606) 233-2733

Louisiana

3727 Government Street
Alexandria 71301
(318) 473-7920

Maine

USDA Office Building
Orono 04473
(207) 866-4929

Massachusetts

451 West Street
Amherst 01002
(413) 253-3471

Michigan

Room 209, 1405 S. Harrison Road
East Lansing 48823
(517) 337-6631

Minnesota

252 Federal Office Building and Courthouse
St. Paul 55101
(612) 725-5842

Mississippi

Suite 831, Federal Building
Jackson 39201
(601) 960-4316

Missouri

555 Vandiver Drive
Columbia 65201
(314) 442-2271, Ext 3241

Montana

Federal Building
P.O. Box 850
Bozeman 59715
(406) 587-5271, Ext 4211

Nebraska

Room 308, Federal Building
100 Centennial Mall North
Lincoln 68508
(402) 471-5551

New Jersey

1 Vahlsing Center
Robbinsville 08691
(609) 259-3136

New Mexico

Room 3414, Federal Building
517 Gold Avenue, SW
Albuquerque 87102
(505) 766-2462

New York

Room 871, U.S. Courthouse and
    Federal Building
100 S. Clinton Street
Syracuse 13202
(315) 423-5290

North Carolina

Room 514, Federal Building
310 New Bern Avenue
Raleigh 27601
(919) 755-4640

North Dakota

Room 208, Federal Building
P.O. Box 1737
Bismarck 58502
(701) 255-4011, Ext 4781

Ohio

Room 507, Federal Building
200 N. High Street
Columbus 43215
(614) 469-5606

Oklahoma

USDA Agricultural Center Office Building
Stillwater 74074
(405) 624-4250

Oregon

Room 1590, Federal Building
1220 SW 3rd Avenue
Portland 97204
(503) 221-2731

Pennsylvania

Room 728, Federal Building
P.O. Box 905
Harrisburg 17108
(717) 782-4476

Puerto Rico

Federal Building
Carlos Chardon Street
Hato Rey 00918
(809) 753-4481

South Carolina

Strom Thurmond Federal Building
1835 Assembly Street, Room 1007
Columbia 29201
(803) 765-5876

South Dakota

Room 208, Huron Federal Building
200 Fourth Street, SW
Huron 57350
(606) 352-8651

Tennessee

538 United States Courthouse Building
801 Broadway
Nashville 37203
(615) 251-7341

Texas

101 S. Main
Temple 76501
(817) 774-1301

Utah

Federal Building
125 S. State Street
Salt Lake City 84138
(801) 524-5027

Vermont

141 Main Street
P.O. Box 588
Montpelier 05602
(802) 223-2371

Virginia

Room 8213, Federal Building
400 N. 8th Street
P.O. Box 10106
Richmond 23240
(804) 771-2451

Washington

301 Yakima Street
Wenatchee 98801
(509) 662-4353

West Virginia

75 High Street
Morgantown 26505
(304) 599-7791

Wisconsin

1257 Main Street
Stevens Point 54481
(715) 341-5900

Wyoming

Room 1005, Federal Building
100 E. B Street
P.O. Box 820
Casper 82602
(307) 265-5550, Ext 5271

Department of Housing and Urban Development

The Department of Housing and Urban Development (HUD, as this department is generally referred to), has a charter and mission defined in its title: the provision of adequate housing, especially for low-income families, urban renewal in decaying urban areas, and related activities. In practice, this translates into a large number of financial-support programs for mortgagors and builders, as well as for individual families. Programs include a variety of loan-guarantee (plus a few direct-loan) programs, with the beneficiaries of such programs both the buyers and the sellers. Some idea of the range and diversity of the HUD programs may be gained from examination of the following program titles, which are representative of the approximately fifty HUD programs:

- Interest Reduction — Homes for Lower Income Families.
- Mortgage Insurance — Construction or Substantial Rehabilitation of Condominium Projects.
- Mortgage Insurance — Mobile Home Parks.

- Mortgage Insurance — Rental Housing for the Elderly.
- Operating Assistance for Troubled Multifamily Housing Projects.
- Mortgage Insurance — Nursing Homes and Intermediate Care Facilities.

In each case, those interested in applying for any of the HUD programs are urged to seek out the nearest HUD local or regional office and make inquiry there. The following list of HUD offices are arranged in alphabetical/geographical sequence to facilitate finding the one nearest you. There are ten regional offices, one for each federal region. Within each region are several area offices and service offices, and most regions also have a valuation and endorsement station. Ordinarily, inquiries should begin with a regional or area office. The central or headquarters HUD office address is as follows: Department of Housing and Urban Development, 451 Seventh Street, SW, Washington, DC 20410. Telephone is (202) 655-4000.

Department of Housing and Urban Development Offices

Alabama

Daniel Building
15 S. 20th Street
Birmingham 35233
(205) 254-1617
Area Office

Alaska

334 W. 5th Avenue
Anchorage 99501
(907) 271-4169
Area Office

Arizona

Arizona Bank Building
101 N. First Avenue, Suite 1800
Phoenix 85003
(602) 261-4434
Service Office

Arkansas

Union National Bank Building
One Union National Plaza
Little Rock 72201
(501) 378-5401
Area Office

California

2500 Wilshire Boulevard
Los Angeles 90057
(213) 688-5974/3836
Area Office

801 I Street
545 Downtown Plaza
P.O. Box 1978
Sacramento 95809
(916) 440-3471
Service Office

110 880 Front Street
P.O. Box 2648
San Diego 92112
(714) 293-5310
Service Office

450 Golden Gate Avenue
P.O. Box 36003
San Francisco 94102
(415) 556-4752
Regional Office (Region IX)

Suite 1600, 1 Embarcadero Center
San Francisco 94111
(415) 556-2238
Area Office

34 Civic Center Plaza
Santa Ana 92701
(714) 836-2451
Area Office

Colorado

2500 Executive Towers
1405 Curtis Street
Denver 80202
(303) 837-4513
Area Office

Connecticut

999 Asylum Avenue
1 Financial Plaza
Hartford 06103
(203) 244-3638
Area Office

Delaware

Delaware Trust Plaza
1800 Pennsylvania Avenue, Suite 604
Wilmington 19806
(302) 571-6330
Valuation and Endorsement Station

District of Columbia

Universal North Building
1875 Connecticut Avenue, NW
Washington 20009
(202) 673-5837
Area Office

Florida

3001 Ponce de Leon Boulevard
Coral Gables 33601
(305) 445-2561
Service Office

Peninsular Plaza
661 Riverside Avenue
Jacksonville 32204
(904) 791-2626
Area Office

700 Twiggs Street
P.O. Box 2097
Tampa 33601
(813) 228-2501
Service Office

Georgia

Richard B. Russell Federal Building
75 Spring Street, SW
Atlanta 30303
(404) 221-5136
Regional Office

Richard B. Russell Federal Building
75 Spring Street, SW
Atlanta 30303
(404) 221-4577
Area Office

Hawaii

300 Ala Moana Boulevard, Room 3318
Honolulu 96850
(808) 546-2136
Area Office

Idaho

419 N. Curtis Road
P.O. Box 32
Boise 83707
(208) 384-1992
Service Office

Illinois

300 S. Wacker Drive
Chicago 60606
(312) 353-5680
Regional Office

1 North Dearborn Street
Chicago 60602
(312) 353-6979/7660
Area Office

Lincoln Tower Plaza
524 South Second Street, Room 600
Springfield 62704
(217) 525-4083
Valuation and Endorsement Station

Indiana

151 N. Delaware Street
P.O. Box 7047
Indianapolis 46205
(317) 269-6303
Area Office

Iowa

259 Federal Building
210 Walnut Street
Des Moines 50309
(515) 284-4512
Service Office

Kansas

444 SE Quincy Street, Room 330
Topeka 66683
(913) 295-2662
Valuation and Endorsement Station

Kentucky

539 River City Mall
P.O. Box 1044
Louisville 40201
(502) 582-5251
Area Office

Louisiana

Plaza Tower
1001 Howard Avenue
New Orleans 70113
(504) 589-2062
Area Office

Federal Building
500 Fannin
Shreveport 71120
(318) 226-5385
Service Office

Maine

Federal Building and Post Office
202 Harlow Street
Bangor 04401
(207) 947-8410
Valuation and Endorsement Station

Maryland

Mercantile Bank and Trust Building
Two Hopkins Plaza
Baltimore 21201
(301) 962-2121
Area Office

Massachusetts

800 John F. Kennedy Federal Building
Boston 02203
(617) 223-4066
Regional Office

Bullfinch Building
15 New Chardon Street
Boston 02114
(617) 223-4111
Area Office

Michigan

McNamara Federal Building
477 Michigan Avenue
Detroit 48226
(313) 226-7900
Area Office

Northbrook Building, No. 11
2922 Fuller Avenue, NE
Grand Rapids 49505
(616) 456-2225
Service Office

Minnesota

6400 France Avenue, South
St. Paul 55435
(612) 725-4701/4801
Area Office

Mississippi

Federal Building, Suite 1016
100 W. Capitol Street
Jackson 39201
Area Office

Missouri

Professional Building
1103 Grand Avenue
Kansas City 64106
(816) 374-2661
Regional Office

Professional Building
1103 Grand Avenue
Kansas City 64106
(816) 374-4355
Area Office

210 North 12th Street
St. Louis 63101
(314) 622-4761
Area Office

Montana

Federal Office Building, Dwr 10095
301 South Park, Room 340
Helena 59601
(406) 449-5205
Service Office

Nebraska

Univac Building
7100 West Center Road, 3rd floor
Omaha 68106
(402) 221-9301
Area Office

Nevada

1050 Bible Way
P.O. Box 4700
Reno 89505
(702) 784-5356
Service Office

New Hampshire

New Federal Building
275 Chestnut Street
Manchester 03103
(603) 666-7670
Service Office

New Jersey

The Parkade Building
519 Federal Street
Camden 08103
(609) 757-5081/5085
Service Office

Gateway 1 Building
Raymond Plaza
Newark 07102
(201) 645-3010
Area Office

New Mexico

625 Truman Street, NE
Albuquerque 87110
(505) 766-3251
Service Office

New York

Leo W. O'Brien Federal Building
North Pearl Street & Clinton Avenue
Albany 12206
(518) 472-3567
Service Office

Suite 800, Statler Building
107 Delaware Avenue
Buffalo 14202
(716) 855-5755
Area Office

26 Federal Plaza, Room 3541
New York 10007
(212) 264-8086
Regional Office

26 Federal Plaza
New York 10007
(212) 264-0644
Area Office

North Carolina

415 North Edgeworth Street
Greensboro 27401
(919) 378-5363
Area Office

North Dakota

Federal Building
653 2nd Avenue North
P.O. Box 2483
Fargo 58102
(701) 237-5771
Valuation and Endorsement Station

Ohio

9009 Federal Office Building
550 Main Street
Cincinnati 45202
(513) 684-2884
Service Office

777 Rockwell
Cleveland 44114
(216) 522-4065
Service Office

New Federal Building
200 N. High Street
Columbus 43215
(614) 469-7345
Area Office

Oklahoma

200 NW 5th Street
Oklahoma City 73102
(405) 231-4181/4891
Area Office

Robert S. Kerr Building
440 South Houston Avenue
Tulsa 74127
(918) 581-7435
Service Office

Oregon

520 SW 6th Avenue
Portland 97204
(503) 221-2552/2561
Area Office

Pennsylvania

Curtis Building
625 Walnut Street
Philadelphia 19106
(215) 597-2528/2560
Regional Office

Curtis Building, Room 892
625 Walnut Street
Philadelphia 19106
(215) 597-2645
Area Office

Fort Pitt Commons
445 Fort Pitt Boulevard
Pittsburgh 15219
(412) 644-2802
Area Office

Puerto Rico

Frederico Degetau Federal Building
United States Courthouse
Carlos E. Chardon Avenue
Hato Rey 00918
(809) 753-4201
Area Office

Rhode Island

330 John O. Pastore Federal Building
Providence 02903
(401) 528-4351
Service Office

South Carolina

Strom Thurmond Federal Building
1835-45 Assembly Street
Columbia 29201
(803) 765-5591
Area Office

South Dakota

119 Federal Building
400 S. Phillips Avenue
Sioux Falls 57102
(605) 336-2980
Service Office

Tennessee

1 Northshore Building
1111 Northshore Drive
Knoxville 37019
(615) 637-9300, Ext 1222

100 N. Main Street
Memphis 38103
(901) 521-3367
Service Office

One Commerce Place, Suite 1600
Nashville 37203
(615) 251-5213
Service Office

Texas

2001 Bryan Tower, 4th floor
Dallas 75201
(214) 749-1601
Area Office

221 West Lancaster Avenue
P.O. Box 2905
Fort Worth 76113
(214) 749-7401/7406
Regional Office

221 West Lancaster Avenue
P.O. Box 2905
Forth Worth 76113
(214) 749-3233
Service Office

Two Greenway Plaza East
Houston 77046
(713) 226-4335
Service Office

514 Courthouse and Federal Office Building
1205 Texas Avenue
P.O. Box 1647
Lubbock 79408
(806) 762-7265
Service Office

Washington Square
800 Dolorosa
P.O. Box 9163
San Antonio 78285
(512) 229-6800
Area Office

Utah

125 S. State Street
P.O. Box 11009
Salt Lake City 84147
(801) 524-5237
Service Office

Vermont

Federal Building
Elmwood Avenue
P.O. Box 989
Burlington 05402
(802) 951-6274
Valuation and Endorsement Station

Virginia

701 East Franklin Street
Richmond 23219
(804) 782-2721
Area Office

Washington

Arcade Plaza Buiding
1321 Second Avenue, Stop 329
Seattle 98101
(206) 442-5414/5415
Regional Office

Arcade Plaza Building
1321 Second Avenue, Stop 429
Seattle 98101
(206) 442-7456
Area Office

920 Riverside Avenue West
Spokane 99201
(509) 456-4571
Service Office

West Virginia

Kanawha Valley Building
Capitol & Lee Streets
P.O. Box 2948
Charleston 25301

(304) 343-6181, Ext 321
Service Office

Wyoming

Federal Office Building
100 East B Street
Casper 82602
(307) 265-5550
Valuation and Endorsement Station

MISCELLANEOUS FEDERAL PROGRAMS

Several other federal agencies operate programs of financial assistance to small business, although these tend to be in rather specialized areas. For example, there is the Overseas Private Investment Corporation (OPIC), designed to assist American investors in investing profitably in about eighty developing countries, while also contributing to the economic well-being of the foreign countries. The OPIC program includes at least two loan and loan-guarantee programs. Information about the OPIC programs may be requested by writing or calling OPIC:

Overseas Private Investment Corporation
1129 20th Street, NW
Washington, DC 20527
Attention: Office of Public Affairs
Telephone: (202) 632-1854

The agency makes available upon request and without charge the following information publications:

Annual Report

Guide for Executives of Smaller Companies
Smaller Business: A Directory of Services for U.S. Investors in Developing Nations
Investment Insurance Handbook
TOPICS (OPIC's newsletter)

A toll-free number is also provided for small businesses to use, in calling for information: (800) 424-OPIC.

The United States Department of Energy, which may ultimately be disbanded, although most of its functions will live on in other federal agencies, also offers a few financial-support programs:

- Small Hydroelectric Power Project Feasibility Studies (direct-loan program).
- Geothermal Loan Guarantees (loan-guarantee program).
- Electric and Hybrid Vehicle Loan Guaranties (loan-guarantee program).

Probably most veterans are aware that the Veterans Administration (VA) offers a number of benefits, among them loan and loan-guarantee programs. Details of such programs are available from VA regional offices.

Veterans Administration Regional Offices

Alabama

474 S. Court Street
Montgomery 36104

Alaska

P.O. Box 1288
Juneau 99802

Arizona

7th Street & Indian School Road
Phoenix 85102

Arkansas

1200 W. 3rd Street
Little Rock 72206

California

11000 Wilshire Boulevard
Los Angeles 90024

2022 Camino Del Rio North
San Diego 92161

211 Main Street
San Francisco 94105

Colorado

Denver Federal Center
Denver 80220

Connecticut

450 Main Street
Hartford 06103

Delaware

1601 Kirkwood Highway
Wilmington 19805

District of Columbia

941 N. Capitol Street, NE
Washington 20421

Florida

P.O. Box 1437
St. Petersburg 33731

Georgia

730 Peachtree Street, NE
Atlanta 30308

Hawaii

P.O. Box 50188
Honolulu 96850

Idaho

550 W. Fort Street
Boise 83724

Illinois

P.O. Box 8136
Chicago 60680

Indiana

575 N. Pennsylvania Street
Indianapolis 46204

Iowa

210 Walnut Street
Des Moines 50309

Kansas

5500 E. Kellog Street
Wichita 67218

Kentucky

600 Federal Place
Louisville 40202

Louisiana

701 Loyola Avenue
New Orleans 70113

Maine

Togus 04330

Maryland

31 Hopkins Place
Baltimore 21201

Massachusetts

John F. Kennedy Federal Building
Boston 02203

Michigan

477 Michigan Avenue
Patrick V. McNamara Building
Detroit 48226

Minnesota

Federal Building
Fort Snelling
St. Paul 55111

Mississippi

1500 E. Woodrow Wilson Avenue
Jackson 39216

Missouri

1520 Market Street
St. Louis 63103

Montana

Fort Harrison 59636

Nebraska

1000 Centennial Mall N.
Lincoln 68508

Nevada

1201 Terminal Way
Reno 89520

New Hampshire

275 Chestnut Street
Manchester 03103

New Jersey

20 Washington Place
Newark 07102

New Mexico

500 Gold Avenue, SW
Albuquerque 87102

New York

111 W. Huron Street
Buffalo 14202

252 7th Avenue at 24th Street
New York 10001

North Carolina

251 N. Main Street
Winston-Salem 27102

North Dakota

Elm Street N.
Fargo 58102

Ohio

1240 E. 9th Street
Cleveland 44199

Oklahoma

125 S. Main Street
Muskogee 74401

Oregon

1220 SW 3rd Avenue
Portland 97204

Pennsylvania

5000 Wissahickon Avenue
Philadelphia 19101

1000 Liberty Avenue
Pittsburgh 15222

Philippines, Republic of

Manila (APO San Francisco, CA 96528)

Puerto Rico

San Juan (Barrio Monacillos, GPO
Box 4867, 00936)

Hato Rey (U.S. Courthouse and
    Federal Building
Carlos E. Chardon Street, 00918)

Rhode Island

321 S. Main Street
Providence 02903

South Carolina

1801 Assembly Street
Columbia 29201

South Dakota

2501 W. 22nd Street
Sioux Falls 57101

300 N. Dakota Avenue
Sioux Falls 57101

Tennessee

110 9th Avenue S.
Nashville 37203

Texas

2515 Murworth Drive
Houston 77054

1400 N. Valley Mills Drive
Waco 76710

Utah

125 S. State Street
Salt Lake City 84113

Vermont

White River Junction 05001

Virginia

210 Franklin Road, SW
Roanoke 24011

Washington

915 Second Avenue
Seattle 98174

West Virginia

502 8th Street
Huntington 25701

Wisconsin

342 N. Water Street
Milwaukee 53202

Wyoming

2360 E. Pershing Boulevard
Cheyenne 82001

Chapter 4

Smaller Uncles: The State Agencies

In the aggregate, state and local government programs are probably greater than are federal programs, although even less well known. In addition, under the philosophy of the current Administration, these programs are likely to grow.

WASHINGTON, DC, ESTABLISHES A PATTERN

Inspired by the federal government examples, most of the fifty states have set up or announced their intention of setting up programs for small business, minority entrepreneurs, and women entrepreneurs. A number of the states have included, among their programs, loan and loan-guarantee provisions, along the lines of the SBA and Department of Commerce programs. To date, such programs have been announced by twenty-eight states and United States possessions, including the following:

Alaska	Maryland
California	Massachusetts
Connecticut	Michigan
Delaware	Minnesota
Hawaii	Mississippi
Illinois	Missouri
Indiana	Montana
Kentucky	New Hampshire
Maine	New Jersey

North Dakota	Tennessee
Ohio	Texas
Oklahoma	Vermont
Oregon	Puerto Rico
Rhode Island	Virgin Islands

The information available on these programs, at this time, like the programs themselves, is almost infinitely variable: in some cases the programs are quite extensive and detailed information is provided; in other cases, the programs are somewhat vague and general, and the information is therefore of the same character. In a few cases, the state plans a program and may even have passed enabling legislation, but has not yet formulated the plans fully. The information offered here is therefore not uniform, but reflects what the state has been able to offer.

For that reason, the reader would be well advised to press inquiries in his or her own state, and as many names, addresses, and telephone numbers as were available have been supplied here to assist the reader in beginning the quest, where there is insufficient information presented here.

In a number of cases, states offer other kinds of assistance to small businesses in general and minority- or women-owned business in particular. In some cases these other services are either tantamount to financial help (providing free services which have tangible value) or will provide indirect financial assistance, such as aiding the entrepreneur in making up a suitable loan package and finding the best sources for funding. Therefore, this chapter indicates generally other programs available in the various states, even in those which currently do not have active loan or loan-guarantee programs.

In some cases, state governments have been awarded federal funds to carry out programs, as in the case of federally funded OMBE — Office of Minority Business Enterprise — bureaus in state governments. These are included in a separate listing of organizations supported by the Minority Business Development Agency within the federal government's Department of Commerce.

In a study of the economic climate for small business in each state (*INC*. Special Report: STATE BUSINESS CLIMATES, *INC*. magazine, October 1981), *INC*. magazine researchers took into account many factors — tax burdens, tax breaks, labor supply, capital resources (including loan programs), and other kinds of support offered to small business. They employed a formula to rate each state on a scale A to F, but also determined the top ten states in each of several categories, including capital resources and small business commitment. Those states which made it into both these lists included the following: California, New York, Massachusetts, Connecticut, and Minnesota. Among these, all except New York have state loan programs. However, the study included the availability of small-business loans as only one factor in evaluating capital resources; other factors included the availability of funds for business use from other sources, including banks and SBICs (Small Business Investment Companies licensed by the Small Business Administration).

In evaluating the small-business-support factors, the study took into account the existence of procurement programs, assistance offices, advisory boards, and legislative committees for the encouragement and active assistance to small business.

In alphabetical ratings, the five states listed above as having been included in both "top ten" lists were rated as follows: California: A; New York: B; Massachusetts: B; Connecticut: C; and Minnesota: A. New York, Massachusetts, and Connecticut rated less than "A" because they lagged in other categories of evaluation, such as tax rates and tax breaks, labor supply, average labor rates, and matters other than the financial resources available to small business.

ALABAMA

Alabama offers a single program of assistance to small business, which includes aid in winning state procurement contracts and subcontracts from larger, prime contractors. For information:

> Clyde Chatman
> Office of State Planning
> 3734 Atlanta Highway
> Montgomery, AL 36130
> (205) 832-6400

ALASKA

Alaska has comprehensive loan programs and a small-business assistance office.

1. Small Business Revolving Loan Fund. Small business is defined as one with not more than 200 employees and not more than $10 million in annual gross sales, and which is independently owned. (Subsidiaries or divisions of larger companies do not qualify.) Funds may be used to acquire, finance, refinance, or equip business. Both direct and participation loans are included.

Terms and Conditions

1) Direct loans:
   Maximum $50,000
   Interest rate (per annum)   9.5 percent

2) Participation loans:

Minimum bank participation	25.0 percent
Maximum State portion	$500,000
Interest, bank portion	Current bank rate
Interest, state portion	9.5 percent

3) Term of loans: 15 years

II: Commercial Fishing Revolving Loan Fund.

This fund may be used to repair, restore, or upgrade existing vessels and equipment; for the purchase of entry permits and equipment; and for the construction and purchase of vessels. For the Commercial Fisherman, defined as a state resident for the preceding five years, who has held a limited entry permit, commercial fishing, or crew member license for at least one of those five years, and who has participated actively in fishing during that period.

Terms and Conditions

1) Direct loans:

Limited entry permit loans, maximum	$500,000
Interest	9.5 percent
All other loans, maximum	50,000
Interest	9.5 percent

2) Participation loans:
   (Limited entry permit loans not eligible; other loans as follows.)

Maximum bank participation	25.0 percent
Interest	Current bank rate
Maximum state portion	500,000
Interest	9.5 percent

3) Term of loan: 15 years

III: Tourism Revolving Loan Fund.

This fund may be used to finance facilities which provide goods or services to tourists while they are in Alaska.

Terms and Conditions

1) Direct loans:

Maximum	$50,000
Interest	9.5 percent

2) Participation loans:

Maximum bank participation	25.0 percent
Interest	Current bank rate
Maximum State portion	$3,000,000
Interest	9.5 percent

3) Term of loans: 20 years

IV: Fisheries Enhancement Revolving Lc Fund.

This fund may be used to pl construct, and operate a hatchery facility a preconstruction activities necessary to obtai permit. A hatchery is defined as a facility the artificial incubation of salmon eggs, wh may include the means for the raising of you salmon.

Terms and Conditions

1) To qualified regional association or local association approved by a regional association; maximum per project	$3,000,000
2) To nonprofit hatchery corporation, maximum per project	300,000
3) Interest per annum	9.5 perc
4) Term of loan	25 years

V: Child Care Facility Revolving Lo Fund:

This fund may be used to constru renovate, and equip child care facilities in t state to meet licensing requirements or meet Department of Education certificati requirements. A child care facility is defin as an establishment principally designed provide care for children not related by bloc marriage, or legal adoption, including but r limited to family day-care homes and scho(for children of preschool age.

Terms and Conditions

1) Maximum, per single child care facility	$30,000
Interest, per annum	7 perc
2) Term of loan	10 years

VI: Residential Care Facility Revolvi Loan Fund.

This fund may be used construct, renovate, and equip resident care facilities to meet licensing standards. residential care facility is defined as a fost home, group home, or institution whi provides 24-hour, nonmedical care for depe dent adults not related by blood, marriage, legal adoption to the owner, operator, manager of the facility.

Terms and Conditions

1) Maximum, per loan		$20,000
Interest, per annum		7 percent
2) Term of loan		10 years

VII: Historical District Revolving Loan Fund. This fund may be used to restore, improve, rehabilitate, or maintain a structure in a historical district or of importance in state or national history. The term "historical district" is defined as referring to one approved as such by a local historical district commission and by a majority of the members of the Historic Sites Advisory Committee.

Terms and Conditions

1) Direct loans:		
Maximum		$50,000
Interest		7.5 percent
2) Participation loans:		
Maximum bank participation		25.0 percent
Interest	Current bank rate	
Maximum State portion,		
per building or structure		$100,000
Interest		7.5 percent

(Note: State participation in all loans in the aggregate for any one historical district may not exceed $1,500,000.)

VIII: Alternative Technology and Power Resource Revolving Loan Fund. This fund may be used to purchase, construct, and install alternative power resources and for the development and implementation of more efficient, less costly, less energy intensive, and more appropriate technologies. An alternative technology and power resource is defined as a means for developing energy production utilizing energy sources other than fossil or nuclear fuel, including but not limited to wind, water, and solar power devices. Also included are the development and implementation methods of energy production, waste disposal, recycling, food production, transportation, building design, and industrial enterprise which may be more efficient, less costly, and less energy intensive than those methods currently utilized and which are appropriate to the Alaska environment.

Terms and Conditions

1) Maximum per project		$10,000
Interest, per annum		9.5 percent
2) Term of loan		20 years

The address furnished to make formal application or pursue further details of any of these programs is as follows:

> Ms. Sharon Taylor, Director
> Division of Business Loans
> Department of Commerce and
>   Economic Development
> Pouch D
> Juneau, AK 99811

Other assistance, including the preparation of information for the loan package, is offered by another State bureau:

> Donald M. Hoover
> Division of Economic Enterprise
> Department of Commerce and
>   Economic Development
> 675 7th Avenue, Station A
> Fairbanks, AK 99701
> (907) 452-8182

ARIZONA

Arizona has no loan program and no formal small-business programs at this time, although the state does report some efforts to assist small business through the Arizona Office of Economic Planning and Development (OEPAD), and has designated an employee of the OEPAD Economic Development Section as the formal State Liaison with the small-business community:

> Clint E. Johnson
> Office of Economic Planning
>   and Development
> 1700 W. Washington, Room 400
> Phoenix, AZ 85007
> (602) 255-5374

ARKANSAS

Arkansas has no loan programs, although the legislature did create a Department of

Economic Development in 1979, and one of that Department's divisions is dedicated to assisting small business, which is principally an information and referral service at this time. Contact:

C. A. Hamilton, Director
Small Business Assistance Division
Arkansas Department of
    Economic Development
1 State Capitol Mall
Little Rock, AR 72201
(1-800) 482-9659

CALIFORNIA

California offers a number of programs, including a loan program, a procurement program, and a small-business-assistance program. Brief descriptions of the programs are the following:

Small-Business Loans. Eligibility is confined to businesses meeting the federal (SBA) standards for small business or farm. The applicant must be a for-profit enterprise, and loans may be any of a wide variety, such as short- or long-term, for floor-planning inventory, for revolving credit, for bonds, and multiple other needs. As in the case of federal loan and loan-guarantee programs, the applicant must demonstrate an inability to borrow from conventional sources. The information provided by the state government does not prescribe any specific lending limits, and says, in connection with terms and conditions, that loan periods may vary from one to seven years, and interest rates will vary, according to the prime rate, generally running a point or two above prime. Loans may be for start-ups, but these are not favored because of the high risk associated with new starts. Borrowers should have equity, but corporations (the state carries out the loan programs through regional development corporations, which the state backs) may consider guaranteeing loans under other circumstances. (Loan guarantees cover 90 percent of the loan.)

Employment Incentive Loans. Loans may also be made to firms which do not qualify as small business if the loan will result in jobs for fifteen or more youths or persons living in economically disadvantaged areas of California.

Regional Development Corporations. The three regional development corporations through which the state conducts its loan and loan-guarantee programs are as follows:

California Regional
    Small Business Development Corporation
369 Hayes Street
San Francisco, CA 94112

Areas of service: statewide; concentration in Northern California.
Specialization: business loans.

California Rural
    Small Business Development Corporation
2006 N. Fine Street, Suite 104
Fresno, CA 93727
(209) 252-0321

Areas of service: statewide; although concentration in rural areas.
Specialization: financial packaging, using maximum of private and public financing and guarantees.

Pacific Coast Regional
    Small Business Development Corporation
1930 Wilshire Boulevard, Suite 414
Los Angeles, CA 90057
(213) 484-2900

Areas of service: statewide, although concentrates on southern California.
Specialization: business loans.

Procurement Small-Business Assistance. Contact for procurement services for small business:

James H. Exum
(916) 322-5060
(in Department of General Services)

COLORADO

Colorado has no loan program listed, although it does offer management and technical assistance to small business through a center jointly funded by the state and the federal government. Among the services offered are financial counseling. Contact:

Bill Scott, Director
The Small Business Assistance Center
University of Colorado
Campus Box 434
Boulder, CO 80309
(303) 492-8211

CONNECTICUT

Connecticut offers a number of programs, including loan programs, which the state describes as follows:

I: Small Contractors' Revolving Loan Fund. This fund may be used only for labor and materials to perform on specific contracts. Limit $100,000 or labor and material costs of contract, whichever is less. Term is not more than twelve months after initial disbursement, the interest rate is one percent above the interest rate paid by the State of Connecticut on the latest general obligation bonds issued prior to the date of the loan commitment. To qualify, contractors must have been in operation and doing business in the state for not less than one year prior to application, and must have had principal offices and place of business in Connecticut for at least one year prior. Gross revenues must be not more than $1 million annually.

II. Connecticut Product Development Corporation. The Connecticut Product Development Corporation (CPDC) is a quasi-public corporation which will furnish capital to develop new products. Ordinarily, CPDC will furnish 60 percent of the capital needed; the developer is expected to furnish the remaining 40 percent. The normal terms call for payment of a five percent royalty to CPDC, after the new product is marketed successfully. State funds are to be used solely for development costs.

III. Umbrella Revenue Bonds. These are for major industrial developments, and represent state-backed mortgages, in effect — long-term financing after project completion. (The company must arrange its own construction financing.) The interest rate is not more than 0.5 percent over the interest rate paid by the Connecticut Development Authority, which administers the program. The following are the terms:

	Land & Building	Related Machinery	Pollution Control
Maximum Cost Coverage (percent)	90%	80%	80%
Maximum Loan Amount	$850,000	$500,000	$800,000
Maximum Term	25 years	10 years	10 years

The contact furnished by the state, in the Office of Small Business Affairs, located within the Connecticut Department of Economic Development, is as follows:

Frank Silva
(203) 566-4051

A second contact offered, as the state's Business Ombudsman in the Department of Economic Development, is as follows:

Graham Waldron
(203) 566-7035

Connecticut also offers small-business assistance in winning a share of state contracts, as part of the state's procurement program.

DELAWARE

Delaware reports only a loan program without furnishing details. To seek information, contact one of the following offices:

Commerce Department
800 N. French Street
Wilmington, DE 19801
(302) 571-4610

Administrative Services Department
Governor Bacon Health Center
Delaware City, DE 19706
(302) 834-4512

FLORIDA

The State of Florida reports the existence of a small-business assistance office, lists no business-loan program, and offers few details. For more information, inquire of the following:

John Kraft
Office of Business Assistance
Executive Office of the Governor
Tallahassee, FL 32301
(904) 488-9983

General Services Department
515 Larson Building
Tallahassee, FL 32303
(904) 488-1194

Commerce Department
Collins Building
Tallahassee FL 32304
(904) 488-3104

HAWAII

Hawaii reports the existence of loan programs, as follows:

I: Capital Loan Program. May be used to finance plant construction, conversion, expansion, acquisition of land for expansion, purchase of equipment, machinery, supplies, materials, or for use as working capital. Eligibility: qualification as small business, under SBA standards. Limit is $50,000 at 7.5 percent interest, maximum term is twenty years.

II: Small Fishing Vessel Program. May be used for the purchase, construction, renovation, maintenance, and repair of small fishing vessels, as defined by statute. All other terms similar to those of Capital Loan Program, except the term is ten years. Contact:

Doreen Shishido
Department of Planning
    and Economic Development
250 South King Street
Honolulu, HI 96813
(808) 548-4616

IDAHO

Idaho reports no small-business programs, although the state offers the following contact as an active supporter of small business in Idaho:

Lloyd D. Howe, Administrator
Division of Tourism and
    Industrial Development
Capitol Building
Boise, ID 83720
(208) 384-2470

ILLINOIS

Illinois offers several programs to aid small business, including an assistance office, a procurement program, and a loan program. The latter is administered by the Illinois Industrial Development Authority (IIDA), with the principal purpose of creating jobs in areas of high and persistent unemployment. The information supplied does not specify that the business must qualify as a small business to make application, but the amounts of money available and offered suggest that the program would be of primary usefulness to small business. Loans may be for not more than 25-year terms and have, so far, varied from a low of $16,000 to a high of $150,000. The state suggests that its program is most suitable as part of joint funding with federal funds. The fund is a revolving one, which is, of course, a major factor in determining how many dollars are available at any given time. The interest rate is described as the equivalent of the yield of United States Government bonds of similar maturity, rounded to the nearest 0.5 percent per annum. Contact:

Illinois Industrial Development Authority
400 East DeYoung
P.O. Box 397
Marion, IL
(618) 997-6318

Other contacts for Illinois programs are given:

Peter J. Censky, Director
Illinois Office of Business Services
180 N. LaSalle
Chicago, IL
(312) 252-2923
Hotline number: (800) 252-2923

Sam W. Wright
Small Business Coordinator
Department of Administrative Services
Stratton Office Building, Room 802
Springfield, IL 62707
(217) 782-2249

INDIANA

Indiana lists assistance and loan services without details. For information:

Mark Hedegard, Ombudsman Office
Forms Management Division,
  Commission on Public Records
503 State Office Building
Indianapolis, IN 46204
(317) 232-3376

Commerce Department
State House
Indianapolis, IN 46204
(317) 232-8800

Administration Department
State Office Building
Indianapolis, IN 46204
(317) 232-3053

IOWA

Iowa does not list any kind of state program of business loans or loan guarantees, but does report the existence of the Iowa Business Development Credit Corporation (IBDCC), with only the following information about it:

Interest rates: Negotiable
Terms: Loans available to $300,000 (most average $100,000 to $150,000), with ten-year maturity.
Purposes/limitations: May be used to pay for machinery, equipment, accounts receivable, land, buildings, and working capital.
Fee: $100
Contact: Iowa Business Development Credit Corporation, (515) 281-3592.

Iowa also reports the establishment of a general Office of Ombudsman, with the following contact:

Iowa Citizens' Aide Office
State Capital
Des Moines, IA 50319
(515) 281-3592

KANSAS

Kansas offers a procurement program, with the avowed goal of awarding at least ten percent of the state's procurement to small businesses, but provides no contact.

KENTUCKY

Kentucky offers small business a variety of programs, including loans, procurement, and small-business assistance. The state's loan program is linked to its Appalachian regions, but the state also describes a private-sector venture capitalist:

I: Kentucky Appalachian Enterprise Development Loan Program. This program is administered by the Kentucky Development Finance Authority (KDFA), to encourage the expansion of existing or establishment of new small enterprises in the forty-nine Eastern Kentucky counties covered by the Appalachian Regional Commission. Any private person or corporation may apply for a loan under this program, to establish or expand such an enterprise. However, the enterprise must create new, non-coal-related jobs in the region. Applicants must be other than public, quasi-public or private nonprofit organizations, and must be unable to get financing from conventional sources. The program is designed specifically for high-risk, front, or venture capital to entrepreneurs who have exhausted other sources, but who are yet credit-worthy and can demonstrate the ability to repay the loan in terms of management skills and credit standing. Specific limits and interest rates are not specified. Contact:

Kentucky Development Finance Authority
State National Bank Building, Suite 300
Frankfort, KY 40601
(502) 564-4554

II. Kentucky Highlands Investment Corporation. The Kentucky Highlands Investment Corporation (KHIC) is a private, nonprofit, business-financing organization which serves nine counties of Southeastern Kentucky (Bell, Clay, Clinton, Harlan, Jackson, McCreary, Rockcastle, Wayne, and Whitley). The corporation finances young or new start-up companies, principally, and works closely with the entrepreneurs to create new jobs in these counties. KHIC participates with banks, federal agencies, and the KDFA in loans, most of which range from $50,000 to $350,000, for long-term subordinated debt and equity capital. Terms and interest are negotiated individually.

Other contacts suggested by the state are all in the following state organization:

Small Business Development Section
Small and Minority Business
    Development Division
Kentucky Department of Commerce
Capital Plaza Tower
Frankfort, KY 40601

The specific names and titles within the above organization are these:

Floyd Taylor, Director
    (502) 564-2064

Colin Phillips, Assistant Director
    (502) 564-2074
Patsy Wallace, Business Development Officer
    (602) 564-2074

LOUISIANA

Louisiana lists only a procurement program and small-business assistance office. The following contacts are furnished:

Andrew Flores, C.I.D.
Assistant Secretary
Office of Commerce and Industry
(504) 342-5361

Nadia Goodman
(504) 342-5366

Mitchell Albert, Director
Louisiana Office of Minority
    Business Enterprise

MAINE

Maine offers both loan and loan-guarantee programs, which the state describes as follows:
I: Maine Guarantee Authority Programs (MGA)
1) The Loan Guarantee Program provides guarantees up to 90 percent of the value of real property or 75 percent of the value of machinery and equipment, and of recreational projects. The maximum MGA can guarantee is $2.5 million. Loans are usually guaranteed up to 25 years for real estate and ten years for equipment. Special attention is given to fishing ventures, with guarantees for 80 percent of the value of vessel construction for a twenty-year term.

MGA is allowed by statute to guarantee up to $40 million in loans. The funds come from local banks and other lenders. For more information, inquirers are asked to write or call MGA:

Maine Guarantee Authority
The State House
Augusta, ME 04333
(207) 289-3095

2) The MGA Revenue Bond Program is one in which MGA is empowered to issue state-level industrial bonds. Details of this are also available from the MGA.

II: Maine Small Business Loan Authority. The Authority operates two loan programs, one for small business generally, and the other expressly for veterans who seek business loans. The two programs are nearly identical in terms and conditions. The applicant must be a Maine resident for at least six months prior to the application, plan to locate the business within the state, and choose an in-state bank or other lending institution. (The program is a guarantee program, rather than a direct-loan program.) If applying under the special provisions for veterans, the applicant can get forms for certifying eligibility by writing to the following:

Bureau of Veterans Services
Camp Keys
Augusta, ME 04333

Otherwise, all questions and requests should be addressed to the following:

Maine Small Business Loan Authority
Community Drive
Augusta, ME 04333
(207) 289-2094

3) The Maine Development Foundation is an independent, nonprofit corporation, established to foster and encourage growth in the State of Maine. It operates the Maine Capital Corporation as an investment company providing equity and long-term subordinated debt financing for Maine companies. Contact:

Maine Development Foundation
John E. Menario, Chairman
Nathaniel H. Bowditch, President
1 Memorial Circle
Augusta, ME 04333
(207) 622-6345

MARYLAND

Maryland has a small-business assistance office, a procurement program, and a loan program. No specific information about the loan program is offered, but those interested are referred to the following contact:

Norman Holmes
The World Trade Center
Suite 2223
Baltimore, MD 21202
(301) 383-7877

For other small-business and minority entrepreneur assistance, contacts offered are these:

Gordon Byrd
Office of Business Liaison
1748 Forest Drive
Annapolis, MD 21401
(301) 269-3727

Doug Sands
Office of Minority Business Enterprise
(Same address)
(301) 269-2682

MASSACHUSETTS

Massachusetts has a comprehensive array of programs for the support of small-business and minority enterprise, including loan programs. Following are descriptions of the loan provisions.:

I: Massachusetts Technology Development Corporation (MTDC). MTDC provides both start-up capital and technical assistance to small, innovative, technology-based enterprises, with the goal of aiding their development until they are well enough established to attract capital on their own merits. Both debt financing and equity financing methods are used, and MTDC offers both direct loans and loan guarantees. Contact:

Massachusetts Technology
Development Corporation
131 State Street
Boston, MA 02109
(617) 723-4920

II: Massachusetts Business Development Corporation (MBDC). MBDC offers loans to enterprises who cannot get all their needed funding from conventional sources, by accepting collateral not ordinarily acceptable to conventional lending institutions. MBDC also provides guidance and related assistance to businesses seeking financing. Contact:

Massachusetts Business
Development Corporation
1 Boston Place
Boston, MA 02108
(617) 723-7515

III: Mass Capital Resource Company (MCRC). MCRC is funded privately by a group of domestic life insurance companies, with a projected total investment fund of $100 million. The limit for any single loan is $5 million, with a term of five years, with interest rates to be determined at time of loan. Contact:

Mass Capital Resource Company
11 Beacon Street
Boston, MA 02108
(617) 367-3960

IV: Business Management Planning Guide. One of the many services the Commonwealth of Massachusetts offers small business is aid in preparing business plans and financial packages necessary to obtaining loans and venture capital. This is known as the "Business Management Planning Guide," part of the management-assistance program. Contact:

Department of Commerce & Development
Business Information Center/Network
  (BIC/NET)
100 Cambridge Street
Boston, MA 02202
(617) 727-0478

The above department also operates a Business Service Center, at the same address, with a toll-free number — (1-800) 632-8181 — and a general small-business office. Contact:

Mr. John Ciccarelli
Department of Commerce & Development
Division of Small Business Assistance
(617) 727-4005

MICHIGAN

Michigan has no loan program, although it does have a small-business procurement program and other services designed to aid small business, including guidance and aid in planning and preparation to seek loans or venture capital. Contacts:

Burt Jones, Director
Small Business Development Division
Office of Economic Development
Michigan Department of Commerce
P.O. Box 30225
Lansing, MI 48909
(517) 373-0637   *In-state:* (800) 292-9544

At the same address and telephone numbers:

Henry Patino, Business Services
  Consultant
Paul Rice, Small Business Finance
  Consultant

MINNESOTA

Minnesota has small business assistance services and small business procurement preference, but no loan programs. Contact for other services:

Ms. Dolores (Dee) Kauth
Department of Economic Development
480 Cedar Street
St. Paul, MN 55101
(612) 296-5011

MISSISSIPPI

Mississippi has developed a set of programs, including a loan program, to support small business. The loan program is one of loan guarantees, intended to encourage private-sector lenders to aid the expansion of existing businesses and the development of new enterprises in the state. Terms and conditions of the existing program are as follows:

1) Lending limit is $100,000 per loan, at current rate of interest, and for ten-year term.
2) The state guarantees maximum of 74 percent of the loan, charges a fee of 1 percent per annum of the guaranteed portion of the loan.

The contact furnished for this program is as follows:

> Buddy Mitcham
> (601) 354-6487

The state government also offers a number of training services, publications, and other aid to entrepreneurs. Contacts for these:

Entrepreneurship Development Workshops
P.O. Drawer 2470
Jackson, MS 39205

Mr. Van Evans, Manager
New Ventures Branch
Research and Development Center
(601) 982-6531

MISSOURI

Missouri's principal service to small business appears to be a loan program which the state lists but about which they provide no information. Contact:

> Thomas A. Monks, Manager
> Richard V. Jeffrey, Program Assistant
> Existing Business Assistance
> Division of Community and
>   Economic Development
> Jefferson City, MO 65102
> (314) 751-4855

MONTANA

Montana offers a loan program, procurement programs, and other services to in-state industry, through its Office of Commerce and Small Business Development. The state's loan program is intended, however, principally to match federal funds or attract federal funds. For more details, contact:

> John Lopach, Director
> Office of Commerce and Small Business
>   Development
> Governor's Office, Room 212
> Capitol Station
> Helena, MT 59601
> (406) 449-3923

NEBRASKA

Nebraska offers no programs for small business at this time, other than an office for general assistance. Contact:

> C.L. "Chuck" Elliott, C.I.D.
> Director
> Department of Economic Development
> Division of Industrial Development
> P.O. Box 94666
> 301 Centennial Mall South
> Lincoln, NE 68509

NEVADA

Nevada offers no business-assistance programs.

NEW HAMPSHIRE

New Hampshire lists a loan program, but offers no information about the claimed program nor any contact.

NEW JERSEY

New Jersey offers several programs, including loan programs. These are described as follows:

1) Revenue raised through tax-exempt bonds issued by the New Jersey Economic Development Authority may be used to finance manufacturing,

industrial, and other economic activities, including land purchase, construction, and purchase of equipment and machinery. Contact:

> Frank Mancini
> (609) 292-1800

2) Loan guarantees are offered for repayment of loans and used for purchase of fixed business assets, such as land, buildings, machinery, and also for debt refinancing and purchase of inventory. Contact:

> John Walsh
> (609) 292-1800

3) Small loans are available also for uses similar to those listed above, but applicants must be owners and operators of existing retail businesses located in neighborhood shopping districts of urban areas. Contact:

> Leroy Johnson
> (609) 292-1800

NEW MEXICO

New Mexico offers no programs for small business, but offers some general assistance through the following contact:

> Miriam McCaffrey
> Existing Industry Liaison
> Economic Development Division
> Santa Fe, NM 85703
> (505) 825-5571

NEW YORK

New York lists no loan programs, but does offer some other services to small business. Contact:

> Raymond R. Norat, Deputy Commissioner
> Division of Ombudsmen and Small
>   Business Services
> 230 Park Avenue
> New York, NY 10017
> (212) 949-9303
>
> > (or Richard A. Drucker,
> > Assistant Deputy Commissioner)

NORTH CAROLINA

North Carolina does not list a loan program, although some assistance in obtaining financing is promised. Contact:

> Mr. Albert H. Calloway
> Assistant Director
> Business Assistance Division
> North Carolina Department of Commerce
> 430 N. Salisbury Street
> Raleigh, NC 27611
> (919) 733-7980

NORTH DAKOTA

North Dakota offers no programs, program descriptions, or contacts for small business, although the state government has indicated the existence of a loan program.

OHIO

Ohio offers several small-business programs, including a loan program, but furnishes no information about the loan program. Contact:

> Gordon N. Waltz
> Manager
> Small Business Assistance Office
> (614) 466-4945

OKLAHOMA

Oklahoma offers a loan program in the form of mortgage loans to small manufacturers. Proceeds may be used to purchase land, buildings, or equipment. Interest rate at time of information was listed at 8 to 10 percent. No direct loans are made to industry. The maximum loan is $1 million. Contact:

> John R. Baker, Jr.
> Loan Officer
> P.O. Box 53424
> Oklahoma City, OK 73152
> (405) 521-2182

OREGON

Oregon offers small-business assistance, and loans, including a special loan program for small businesses developing renewable-energy projects. For information:

> Allan R. Mann
> (503) 373-1200
>
> Department of Energy
> (503) 378-3732
>
> Commerce Department
> Labor and Industries Building
> Salem, OR 97310
> (503) 378-4100
>
> Department of General Services
> 1225 Ferry Street, SE
> Salem, OR 97310
> (503) 378-4516

PENNSYLVANIA

Pennsylvania does provide subsidized-interest loans below market rates through the Pennsylvania Development Authority, but no details are furnished. Contact:

> Ms. Densey Juvonen, Director
> Small Business Service Center
> South Office Building, Room G-13
> Harrisburg, PA 17120
> (717) 787-3003

RHODE ISLAND

The State of Rhode Island offers several financing programs for small business through its Department of Economic Development. The Department handles all the details. Following are brief descriptions of the programs:

1. The Rhode Island Port Authority and Economic Development Corporation uses tax-exempt bonds to provide financial aid for the construction, acquisition, and renovation of industrial plants and equipment, under a 100-percent financing package.
2. The Rhode Island Building Authority issues mortgage insurance, backed by the state, guaranteeing the repayment of mortgage loans, with banks and other financial institutions providing the funds. By law, the Industrial Foundation of Rhode Island, a nonprofit industrial foundation (or other nonprofit industrial foundation), must hold title to the property or equipment, and the borrower then lease-purchases the property from the foundation. This plan can be used to finance new construction or renovate existing plants. The state provides 90-percent guarantees on first mortgages on real estate, 80 percent on equipment or machinery.
3. Representatives of the Department will assist applicants in getting financing in other ways, if the above programs are not suitable to their needs. Contact:

> Mr. Joseph C. Lombardo
> Department of Economic
>   Development
> One Webosset Hill
> Providence, RI 02903
> (401) 277-2601

SOUTH CAROLINA

South Carolina lists no small-business programs.

SOUTH DAKOTA

South Dakota lists no small-business program.

TENNESSEE

The Tennessee Industrial Development Authority (TIDA) offers financial assistance in the form of both loan guarantees, up to $250,000, and assistance in getting financial support from other sources. Contact:

> Rick Nally, Director
> 1021 Andrew Jackson Building
> Nashville, TN 37219
> (615) 741-1381
> In-state: (800) 342-8470

Office of Minority Business Enterprise
Roger Ligon, Director
1025 Andrew Jackson Building
Nashville, TN 37219
(615) 741-2545
In-state: (800) 342-8470

TEXAS

Texas claims a loan program for small business, but provides no description or contact:

UTAH

Utah offers only a small-business assistance office. Contact:

Mr. Norman V. Hall
Business Development Coordinator
No. 2 Arrow Press Square, Suite 260
165 South West Temple
Salt Lake City, UT 84101
(801) 533-5325

VERMONT

Vermont lists a loan program, administered by the Vermont Industrial Development Authority (VIDA). The program permits loan proceeds to be used for the acquisition of land, buildings, machinery, and equipment, and includes both a loan-guarantee component and a direct-loan component. Contact:

Robert Y. Justis, Jr.
Manager
(802) 828-2384

Still another program attempts to strengthen small businesses with small, low-interest loans up to $2,500. Contact:

Vermont Economic Opportunity Office
Montpelier, VT 05602
(802) 241-2450

VIRGINIA

Virginia offers only a small-business assistance office. Contact:

John Harris
The Virginia State Office of
    Minority Business Enterprise
Virginia State University
Petersburg, VA 23803
(804) 786-5560

WASHINGTON

Washington offers procurement and assistance programs only. Contact:

Douglas Clark
(206) 753-5614

WEST VIRGINIA

West Virginia does not have a small-business loan program, but does have a West Virginia Economic Development Authority, which has funds for financing up to fifty percent of the cost of land and buildings for manufacturing and warehousing, at four percent interest (at time of the information release). Contact:

Ms. Eloise Jack, Director
Small Business Service Unit
Governor's Office of Economic and
    Community Development
Building 6, Suite B-564
Capitol Complex
Charleston, WV 25305
(304) 348-0010

WISCONSIN

Wisconsin has no listed loan programs.

WYOMING

Wyoming lists no small-business programs.

PUERTO RICO

Puerto Rico indicates the existence of a loan program, but provides no details or contacts.

VIRGIN ISLANDS

The Virgin Islands offers both direct loans and loan guarantees, through its Small Business Development Agency (SBDA). Direct loans are made, up to $100,000, and commercial loans are guaranteed, up to $300,000. Contact:

Ulric F. Benjamin
Director
Small Business Development Agency
P.O. Box 2058
St. Thomas, VI 00801
(809) 774-1331

Chapter 5

The Venture Capitalists

As used here, "venture capital" refers to risk capital, invested in an enterprise by those seeking to earn income, increase capital, or both. Usually, to get such capital, you have to not only give up some of your equity in the enterprise, but also share control, to at least some extent.

WHAT IS A VENTURE CAPITALIST?

Venture capital is money *invested* in (rather than loaned to) an enterprise. It entails more risk than a loan does, compensated for by the potential for earning more profit than simple interest. Typically, venture capital represents equity financing: the supplier of the capital acquires an equity interest in the venture. This definition fits capital raised through the sale of stock — "going public" — but the stockholder is not ordinarily considered to be a "venture capitalist." Typically, that term is generally reserved for the individual or organization engaged in a full-time business of making substantial investments — "backing" — in enterprises, usually new enterprises. That is, the capital investment is generally made either before business operations actually begin or shortly thereafter. Therefore, whereas a lending institution studies the entrepreneur and the enterprise to determine the risk only — the probability that the entrepreneur will be able to repay the loan on schedule — the venture capitalist studies the proposition and the people involved to estimate both the risk and the probable rate of return. The venture capitalist is not in the lending business — although some venture capital organizations are *also* lending institutions — but wants to make long-term investments which will provide income and, it is hoped, will also add to available capital by providing capital gains.

There is one other feature generally associated with venture capitalists: in most cases, the venture capitalist wants to participate in the enterprise — in management, that is — to reduce the risk and be able to offer help when needed, on the one hand, and take remedial or preventive action when needed, on the other hand. Venture capitalists therefore often insist on at least some measure of control, such as one or more seats on the Board of Directors.

WHY TURN TO VENTURE CAPITALISTS FOR MONEY?

At first glance, it seems as though the venture capitalists ought to be a last or next-to-last resort, since raising venture capital normally dilutes the entrepreneur's control and, in all probability, venture capital will ultimately cost much more than would a straight business loan. However, there are at least these reasons for considering and going to venture capitalists:

Bank loans are not easy to get, even when you have collateral or security of some kind. Yet, the enterprise that banks are reluctant to lend money for may be one that in which venture capitalists are not hesitant to invest. Thus, one excellent reason for turning to venture capitalists is simply that you may be able to get the money there that you couldn't get from banks.

In some cases, you can get some of the money you need from banks, but not all of it. Therefore, you may wish to see if you can get all of it or additional funding from venture capitalists.

With interest rates as high as they are, bank loans are not cheap at all, and may offer no advantage, as far as the cost of money is concerned.

WHO ARE THE VENTURE CAPITALISTS?

Today, those described as venture capitalists range across a wide spectrum, from wealthy individuals to large organizations, from divisions of lending institutions to nonprofit corporations and foundations, and from small revolving funds backed by state and local governments to large organizations licensed and backed by the United States Government. In recent years, it has become big business — virtually an industry in itself. The venture capitalists licensed by the federal government (by SBA, specifically) alone number over 600 organizations nationally, for example, and there are many others operating entirely independently.

HOW VENTURE CAPITALISTS MAY SPECIALIZE

Some venture capitalists will take an interest in and consider investing in almost any kind of enterprise, but most tend to specialize to at least some extent. Usually, the tendency to specialize is geared to what the venture capitalist feels most comfortable with. A venture capitalist may therefore restrict interest to only certain kinds of enterprise or to only certain geographical areas — or both. Among those licensed by the SBA, for example, are those expressing preference for investments in manufacturing, R&D, transportation, or retailing. (In fact, there are twelve classifications of preference among these SBA-licensed organizations.)

SMALL BUSINESS INVESTMENT COMPANIES

A number of venture capitalists, many of them licensed by the SBA as SBICs and MESBICs (Small Business Investment Companies and Minority Enterprise Small Business Investment Companies), specialize in and restrict their loans and investments to small businesses. These companies fall into several general groups. Most SBICs are independent enterprises, often organized especially to take advantage of the government licensing, under the SBA sponsorship. One great advantage to applicants, with this kind of firm, is that it is relatively small and the entrepreneur can talk and deal directly with the principals, in many cases. Others are subsidiaries of banks or other institutions. Many are specialty investors, as suggested earlier, interested in only one kind of investment, such as real estate or oil.

Among the typical arrangements these companies make, in capitalizing enterprises, are straight loans, straight loans with options to buy stock, purchases of preferred stock, and sometimes even a buyout.

Since these SBA-licensed SBICs and MES-BICs were first established, starting nearly 25 years ago, they have made over 50,000 loans and investments, disbursing over $3 billion. SBICs and MESBICs, like banks and other venture capitalists, do not make loans or investments carelessly. Quite the contrary, they investigate the business proposition as carefully as possible. Disbursing money is their business, and they want to make loans and investments, but they must, of course, minimize their risks as much as possible. There are, therefore, certain "right" ways and "wrong" ways of going about seeking loans or equity funding. One thing that is a must, whether you are approaching a bank or a venture capitalist, and whether you are seeking a loan or backing, is a proper "loan package" (application) or proposal. (Venture capitalists tend to talk about "proposals," rather than "loan packages," when discussing applications for business financing, especially when the entrepreneur is seeking venture capital, rather than a loan.)

THE BUSINESS PLAN

The heart of any application or proposal is the business plan. It is agreed, among those involved professionally in business financing, that by far the vast majority of turndowns for financing are due to the lack of a proper business plan. It is on the basis of the business plan that the venture capitalist or lender, whichever, evaluates and estimates the soundness of the projected enterprise and the probability of repayment and business success — that is, the risk, which is the inverse of success. Not only is the lack of a proper business plan an insurmountable obstacle to making an adequate estimate, it is an indicator that the entrepreneur has not planned thoroughly — in itself an alarming circumstance, suggesting that the entrepreneur is not a good planner.

Don Dible, author of *Up Your OWN Organization!* (The Entrepreneur Press, California 1971) explains this most strikingly, in describing how he managed to get his book on the market, despite his lack of funds for manufacturing the book:

Having written the book, Dible investigated the printing and binding field — book manufacturing, in fact — and decided to have his book manufactured by a Michigan firm. He departed for Michigan from his home in California, and discussed his need with the head of the printing firm. He explained that he had no capital, but had plans for distributing the book and needed some time to pay the printing and binding bill.

The printer turned him down flatly, saying he absolutely could not offer terms to an individual with no credit rating or track record as a business.

Dible talked on, explained that he had come all the way from California, pleaded with the printer to at least listen to his (Dible's) business plan. He managed to persuade the printer to give him an hour for that presentation.

When Dible had finished, the printer looked at him thoughtfully. "That's without a doubt the best, most thoroughly thought-out and well-developed business plan I've ever seen." He paused, and then said, "I'll tell you what I'll do, Mr. Dible. You stay in town overnight and make that same presentation tomorrow morning to my staff, and I'll print your book on credit."

Such is the power of a good business plan. (See Chapter 6 for an explanation of what a good business plan includes.) No matter how good a salesman you may be personally, your written business plan is likely to be far more effective than anything you can say, if it is a good one. If it is not a good one, it is likely to nullify any personal selling you do.

GETTING HELP IN WRITING PROPOSALS AND APPLICATIONS

Not everyone is capable of preparing all the paperwork in its proper form. A great many entrepreneurs find it advisable, even necessary, to retain someone — a consultant specialist — to prepare the business plan and assemble the proposal or other material. In fact, there are many people who are specialists in this field — financial consultants, brokers, and middlemen — who offer their services. Unfortunately, many of these are also unscrupulous scoundrels, who mislead their clients and who, in fact, perpetrate fraud in what they promise and what they do. There are others who are well-intentioned, but unable to deliver on what they promise.

What such people do, in general, is called "loan packaging," and most of those who offer such a service are also financial consultants or brokers — middlemen — who arrange loans, usually for a small percentage of the value of the loan, such as one or one and one-half percent, but sometimes more or less, depending on the size of the loan.

The danger signs are these: "Guaranteeing" that the loan will be made and/or demanding a sizable fee up front for preparing the paperwork. This does not mean, of course, that a consultant you call in to prepare a business plan or write a proposal is automatically trying to defraud you by charging you a fee for his or her work — if he or she is a consultant in such work and is charging you entirely for the preparation of the "paper." If, however, the individual is a financial broker, who is going to be paid a percentage of the loan as a fee for the work, that is a different story: financial brokers do not ordinarily get paid up front, and certainly do not get paid *both* for the "loan packaging" and getting the loan. It's one or the other: you either pay some agreed-upon fee for assistance in preparing all the paperwork you need or you pay a middleman fee.

WHAT VENTURE CAPITALISTS WANT

Venture capitalists are realists. They do not expect their investments to begin paying off immediately, especially not when they are funding a new enterprise. They will, in fact, even invest in existing companies which are showing losses at the time. Most are looking for a profit, or at least a breakeven operation, within two to three years. (The shorter the time required to reach the stage of profitability, the more likely the capitalist is to invest, of course.) In general, the pattern is along these lines:

A start-up — a company just being or very recently organized: breakeven in one to two years, profit in two to three years.

A company approaching breakeven at the time: Profit in one to two years.

A company in existence two to three years, still a year or more from breakeven or profit: treated much as a start-up.

Few venture capitalists are interested in investments or loans of less than $100,000, although there are some exceptions to this, and many prefer investments running into at least several hundreds of thousands.

It appears that most venture capitalists do not favor dealing with brokers or other "middlemen," although there are some noteworthy exceptions. There are many cases in which middlemen find sources of capital investment when the entrepreneur is unable to do so. However, for the most part, venture capitalists prefer dealing directly with principals.

In some cases, cash flow is a major consideration. That is, cash flow as distinct from sales, receivables, and profitability. Even a company earning substantial profits can be cash poor and require financing receivables, or even financing needed expansion. It's important to distinguish such things as negative cash flow — spending more cash than the firm is taking in at the time — from losses. It's not unusual for a company to have a negative cash flow, while the backlog of receivables is growing well beyond the breakeven. This should be shown clearly in any application or business plan as a need for more operating capital.

Most venture capitalists will insist on some management control, as already noted. However, the venture capitalist does not want to be overly involved in the daily management of the client company, and looks for evidence of a strong management team. In fact, in many cases the venture capitalist will regard this as one of the most critical factors affecting the final decision as to whether to make the investment or not.

At least one major venture capitalist has declared that he is most adversely impressed by certain indicators, which he considers to be danger signs. Among these are an oversize and overly luxurious office for the company president; having the entrepreneur working overtime to impress him (the venture capitalist) with elaborate luncheons at expensive restaurants or clubs; failure by the entrepreneur to bring up past mistakes and anticipated problems, with comments on what he is planning to cope with these issues; overly long and unnecessarily elaborate proposals; and any other evidence that the entrepreneur is trying hard to impress the venture capitalist or is not highly cost-conscious.

IS VENTURE CAPITAL THE WAY FOR YOU TO GO?

Here are a few guidelines to help you determine if (1) yours is a venture that is "right" for venture capital, rather than for a straight loan, and (2) if venture capitalists are likely to be interested in your venture:

Growth Potential: Venture capitalists will invest in small businesses, of course, but "small" is a relative term. The odds are that the bigger your *potential* for growth — between at least $10 million and $20 million within a few years — the more attractive it will be to a venture capitalist. Of course, a consideration is going to be not only the individual growth potential of the enterprise you project, but the nature of the industry — whether it, the industry, appears to be a fast-growing one.

Management: The loner, starting the typical founder company, is not usually as attractive to an investor as a company with a management team whose members can point to impressive track records of success.

Objectives: Unless it is your specific objective and intention to grow to some substantial size, a loan may be far more suitable than venture capital. Make sure you have set your sights high enough.

Plans: You should have a five-year plan that includes cash-flow projections as well as projections of sales, financial requirements, profits, and other factors which reflect a thought out plan.

Personal Goals: To attract venture capital, you should be willing to grow in a direction and manner that permits the investor to get out, with gains, in five to eight years. That means that you must consider whether you are willing to go public, sell out later, share ownership, or whether it is important to you to hold your company closely and run everything yourself.

DIRECTORY LISTING OF VENTURE CAPITALISTS

Following is a listing of over 600 venture capitalists, arranged in the alphabetical/geographic format used elsewhere in this book. The majority of those listed here are SBICs and MESBICs, and all make investments in small businesses. Wherever possible, the entries have been coded, as follows.

Explanation of Codes
Preferred Limit for Loans or Investments
A — up to $100,000
B — up to $250,000
C — up to $500,000
D — up to $1 million
E — over $1 million

Investment Policy
* — will consider either loans or investments
** — prefers to make long-term loans
*** — prefers financings with right to acquire stock interest

Industry Preferences
1. Communications and movies
2. Construction and development
3. Natural resources
4. Hotels, motels, and restaurants
5. Manufacturing and processing
6. Medical and other health services
7. Recreation and amusements
8. Research and technology
9. Retailing, wholesaling, and distribution
10. Service trades
11. Transportation
12. Diversified

SBIC: Small Business Investment Company, committed to making all investments in small companies.

MESBIC: Minority Enterprise Small Business Investment Company, committed to concentrating its main investment in businesses owned and operated by recognized minority members (Blacks, American Indians, Eskimos, Asiatics, Hispanics primarily, but not to the exclusion of others, under the law).

Venture Capital For Small Businesses

Alabama

Benson Investment Company, Inc.
William T. Benson, President
406 S. Commerce St.
Geneva 36340
(205) 684-2824

Coastal Capital Co.
David C. De Laney, Inv. Mgr.
3201 Dauphin St., Ste B
Mobile 36606
(205) 476-0700
SBIC   C*12

Commercial Investment Resources
Neal Andrews, Jr., President
19 W. Oxmoor Road
Birmingham 35209
(205) 870-8880
MESBIC

First SBIC of Alabama
David C. De Laney, President
3201 Dauphin St., Ste. B
Mobile 36606
(205) 476-0700
SBIC   C*12

H & T Capital Corp.
John R. Bloom, President
PO Drawer Q
Montgomery 36105
(205) 288-6250

Western Financial Capital Corp.
Dr. Frederic M. Rosemore, President
306 Temple Ave. No.
Fayette 35555
(205) 932-3528
SBIC   B*6, 12

Alaska

Alaska Renewable Resources Corp.
Wayne C. Littleton, President and CEO
Box 828
Anchorage 99510
(907) 279-5602
E*3

Alyeska Investment Co.
Roy N. Goodman, Manager
1815 S. Bragaw St.
Anchorage 99504
(907) 270-9584
MESBIC   A*2, 4, 9, 10

Arizona

American Business Capital Corp.
Leonard A. Frankel, President
3550 N. Central, Ste 1305
Phoenix 85012
(602) 277-6259
SBIC   A***12

Associated Southwest Investors, Inc.
Fausto Miranda, General Manager
114 W. Adams, Ste 628
Phoenix 85003
(602) 253-6263
MESBIC

Arkansas

First SBIC of Arkansas, Inc.
Fred C. Burns, President
702 Worthen Bank Building
Little Rock 72201
(501) 378-1876
SBIC   A***12

Kar-Mal Venture Capital, Inc.
Tommy Karam, President
610 Plaza West
Little Rock 72205
(501) 661-0010
MESBIC B***9

Small Business Investment Capital, Inc.
Mr. C.E. Toland, President
10003 New Benton Highway
Little Rock 72203
(501) 455-2234
SBIC A***9

Venture Capital, Inc.
Charles E. Sims, President
Box 1343, 975 Tower Building
Little Rock 72203
(501) 374-9977
MESBIC

California

Asset Management Capital Co.
Franklin Johnson, Jr., President
1417 Edgewood Drive
Palo Alto 94301
(415) 321-3131

Atalanta Investment Capital Corp.
(See main office, New York, NY)
141 El Camino Drive
Beverly Hills 90212
(213) 273-1730

BankAmerica Capital Corp.
Steven L. Merrill, President
555 California St.
San Francisco 94104
(415) 622-2271

Bay Area Western Venture Capital Group,
   Inc.
Jack Wong, Secretary/Treasurer
383 Diablo Road, Ste 100
Danville 94526
(415) 820-8079
MESBIC B***2, 8

Brantman Capital Corp.
Mr. W.T. Brantman, President
Box 877
Tiburon 94920
(415) 435-4747
A***4, 5, 6, 7, 8, 9, 10, 11, 12

Brentwood Capital Corp.
Timothy M. Pennington, Gen. Ptnr.
11661 San Vincente Boulevard
Los Angeles 90049
(213) 826-6581
SBIC　2***1, 3, 5, 6, 8, 10, 12

Bryan Capital Corp.
John M. Bryan, President
235 Montgomery St.
San Francisco 94104
(415) 421-9990

Builders Capital Corp.
Victor Indiek, President
2716 Ocean Park Boulevard
Santa Monica 90406
(213) 450-0779
SBIC　C*12

Business Equity & Development Corp.
Ricardo J. Olivarez, President
1411 W. Olympic Boulevard, Ste. 200
Los Angeles 90015
(213) 385-0351
MESBIC B*5, 12

California Northwest Fund, Inc.
Kirk L. Knight, Managing Director
Ken E. Joy, Managing Director
H. DuBose Montgomery, Managing Director
3000 Sand Hill Road
Menlo Park 94025
(415) 854-2940
SBIC　D*12
Branch Office: NY

California Partners
William H. Draper, III, President
Two Palo Alto Square
Palo Alto 94304
(415) 493-5600
SBIC　A***8

Capital Formation Consultants, Inc.
John H. Rohan, President
177 Front Street, Suite F
Danville 94526
(415) 820-8030
12.

Chinese Investment Corp. of Calif.
Rosa Leong, President
1017 Wilshire Boulevard
Los Angeles 90017
(213) 482-0752
MESBIC

Citicorp Venture Capital, Ltd.
William T. Comfort, Chairman
44 Montgomery St.
San Francisco 94104
(415) 954-1155

City Capital Corp.
Morton Heller, President
2049 Century Park East
Los Angeles 90067
(213) 273-4080

Continental Association of Resolute
　　　Employers (C.A.R.E.)
James M. Stump, VP
555 Northgate Drive
San Rafael 94903
(415) 999-0930

Continental Capital Corp.
Frank G. Chambers, President
555 California St.
San Francisco 94104
(415) 989-2020
C***1, 5, 6, 8

Crocker Capital Corp.
Charles Crocker, President
111 Sutter St.
San Francisco 94104
(415) 983-2156

Crocker Ventures, Inc.
John M. Boyle, VP
#10 Montgomery St.
San Francisco 94104
(415) 983-7024
SBIC　B***1, 5, 8, 11

Crosspoint Investment Corp.
Max S. Simpson, President
1015 Corporation Way
Box 10101
Palo Alto 94303
(415) 964-3545
SBIC   B***1, 5, 8

Developers Equity Capital Corp.
Larry Sade, President
9201 Wilshire Boulevard, Ste. 204
Beverly Hills 90210
(213) 278-3611
SBIC   B*2, 4, 6, 11

Early Stages Co., The
William Lanphear, President
244 California St.
San Francisco 94111
(415) 986-5700
D*1, 5, 6, 7, 9, 10, 12

EDVESTCO, Inc.
William C. Edwards, President
150 Isabella Ave.
Atherton 94025
(415) 421-9990

Equilease Capital Corp.
(See main office, New York, NY)
315 S. Beverly Drive
Beverly Hills 90212

Equitable Capital Corp.
John C. Lee, President
855 Sansome St., Ste. 200
San Francisco 94111
(415) 434-4114
MESBIC   B*12

First SBIC of California
Timothy Hay, President
333 S. Hope St.
Los Angeles 90071
(213) 613-5215
SBIC

Florists' Capital Corp.
Christopher M. Conroy, President
10514 W. Pico Boulevard
Los Angeles 90064
(213) 204-6956
SBIC   D***9, 12

Fong Venture Capital Corp.
Walter S. Fong, President
2245 Park Town Circle
Sacramento 95825
(916) 481-7606
MESBIC

Foothill Venture Corp.
Russell B. Faucett, President
2049 Century Park East
Los Angeles 90067
(213) 556-1222
C***1 thru 12

Grocers Capital Co.
William Christy, President
2601 S. Eastern Ave.
Los Angeles 90040
(213) 728-3322
SBIC   B**9

H&R Investment Capital Co.
Herman Christensen, President
801 American St.
San Carlos 94070
(415) 365-4691

Howden, Walker, & Weinress, Inc.
Fred J. Howden, Jr., President
484 Prospect St., Box 2768
La Jolla 92038
(714) 459-3761
E***12

HUB Enterprises, Ltd.
Richard Magary, General Manager
5874 Doyle St.
Emeryville 94608
(415) 653-5707
MESBIC   A*2, 5, 6, 8, 10, 12

IBSI Capital Corp.
Mel L. Bacharach, President
765 Bridgeway
Sausalito 94965
(415) 331-2262
C***1, 5, 8, 9, 10, 12

Imperial Ventures, Inc.
Richard D. Robins, VP and Gen. Mgr.
9920 La Cienega Boulevard
Inglewood 90301
(213) 649-3886

International American Arab Investment
 Corp.
Ray Moore, J. Hamad
8383 Wilshire Boulevard, Ste. 1001
Beverly Hills 90211
(213) 272-4440

Jermyn Venture Capital Corp.
J. Barry Kulick, President
190 N. Canon Dr., #400
Beverly Hills 90210
(213) 550-8819

Krasne Fund for Small Business, Inc.
Clyde A. Krasne, President
Box 5257
Beverly Hills 90210
(213) 274-7007
SBIC A**2, 12

Lasung Investment & Finance Co., Inc.
Jung S. Lee, President
3121 W. Olympic Boulevard, #201
Los Angeles 90006
(213) 384-7548
MESBIC A*4

Lucky Star Investment Co.
Sinclair Louie, President
665 Grant Ave.
San Francisco 94108
(415) 982-5729
SBIC C*2, 4, 5, 6, 9, 10

Marwit Capital Corp.
Martin W. Witte, President
The Marwit Building
180 Newport Center Dr., Ste. 200
Newport Beach 92660
(714) 640-6234
SBIC D***1, 2, 4, 5, 6, 8, 10, 12

MCA New Ventures, Inc.
Robert B. Braswell, Chairman and President
100 Universal City Plaza
Universal City 91608
(213) 508-2937
MESBIC B*1, 5, 7, 12

Merrill, Pickard Capital Co.
Steven L. Merrill
Jeff Pickard
650 California St., 31st Flr
San Francisco 94108
(415) 397-8800
SBIC E***1, 5, 6

Mitchell & Pierce
J.H. Mitchell, Jr., Prin.
10th Flr Penthouse
1605 W. Olympic Boulevard
Los Angeles 90015
(213) 381-3947

Nelson Capital Corp.
(Branch Office; Main Office: NY)
Norman Tulchin, Chairman
1901 Ave. of the Stars, Ste. 584
Los Angeles 90067
(213) 556-1944
SBIC D**12

Novus Capital Corp.
Errol M. Gerson, President
5670 Wilshire Boulevard
Los Angeles 90036
(213) 932-4051/4077
SBIC C*2

Oceanic Capital Corp.
Robert C. Weeks, President
350 California St.
San Francisco 94104
(415) 398-7677
SBIC C*1, 5, 8

Opportunity Capital Corp.
J. Peter Thompson, President
100 California St., Ste 714
San Francisco 94111
(415) 421-5935
MESBIC   B***1, 3, 5, 6, 9, 12

Oxford Capital Corp.
Richard R. Lorenz, President
3700 Wilshire Boulevard
Los Angeles 90010
(213) 381-8743
SBIC   B***12

Pan American Investment Co.
Spencer W. Hoopes, President
350 California St., #2090
San Francisco 94104
(415) 398-7677
SBIC   D***1, 5, 6, 8

PBC Venture Capital, Inc.
Richard Robins, VP and Inv. Mgr.
1408 18th St., Box 6008
Bakersfield 93386
(805) 395-3555
SBIC   B***1, 5, 8, 12

Professional SBIC
David M. Zerner, President
9100 Wilshire Boulevard
Beverly Hills 90212
(213) 274-5821
SBIC

Risk Capital Funding, Inc.
Myron J. Hale, President
16055 Ventura Boulevard
Encino 91316
(213) 986-8840

Rodi, Pollock, Pettker, Galbraith & Phillips
Michael P. Ridley, Esq.
6112 W. Sixth St., Ste. 1600
Los Angeles 90017
(213) 680-0823

Roe Financial Corp.
Martin J. Roe, President
9000 Sunset Boulevard
Los Angeles 90069
(213) 275-4723
A***9, 12

Round Table Capital Corp.
Richard Dumke, President
601 Montgomery St.
San Francisco 94111
(415) 392-7500

San Joaquin Capital Corp.
Chester W. Troudy, Exec. VP
Box 2538
Bakersfield 93303
(805) 323-7581
SBIC   D***2, 5

San Jose Capital Corp.
H. Bruce Furchtenicht, President
130 Park Center Plaza, Ste. 132
San Jose 95113
(408) 293-8052
SBIC   B***1, 5, 6, 8

San Marino Capital Corp.
Lee H. Stein, VP
57 Post St., #813
San Francisco 94104
(415) 781-1313
C***1, 3, 5, 6, 8, 11, 12

Small Business Enterprises Co.
Steven L. Merrill, President
555 California St.
San Francisco 94104
(415) 622-2582
E***1, 3, 5, 6, 7, 8, 11, 12

Solid Capital Corp.
Lusing Ty, Chief Financial Officer
652 Kearny St., Ste. 1 & 2
San Francisco 94108
(415) 434-3371
MESBIC   A*2, 4, 9, 12

Southern Calif. Minority Capital Corp.
Onie B. Granville, President
2651 S. Western Ave.
Los Angeles 90018
(213) 731-8211
MESBIC   C*2, 4, 6

Space Ventures, Inc.
Leslie R. Brewer, General Manager
3901 MacArthur Boulevard, Ste. 101
Newport Beach 92660
(714) 851-0855
MESBIC   B***1, 2, 4, 5, 7, 8, 9, 10, 11, 12

TELACU Investment Co.
Gilberto Padilla, President
1330 So. Atlantic Boulevard
Los Angeles 90022
(213) 268-6745
MESBIC   B*5, 9, 10, 12

Union Venture Corp.
Brent T. Rider, President
445 So. Figueroa St.
Los Angeles 90071
(213) 687-6959
SBIC   E***1, 3, 5, 6, 8, 12

Unity Capital Corp.
Frank W. Owen, President
362 30th St. "B"
San Diego 92104
(714) 295-6768
MESBIC   C***2, 4, 5, 9, 12

Warde Capital Corp.
Thomas R. Warde, President
8929 Wilshire Boulevard
Beverly Hills 90211
(213) 657-0500

Warde Capital Corp.
(See main office, Beverly Hills)
3440 Wilshire Boulevard
Los Angeles 90005

Washington Capital Corp.
(See main office, Seattle, WA)
601 University Ave., Campus Commons
Sacramento 95825
SBIC   D*12

Walden Capital Corp.
Arthur S. Berliner, President
303 Sacramento St.
San Francisco 94109
(415) 391-7225

Wells Fargo Investment Co.
Robert G. Perring, President
475 Sansome St.
San Francisco 94111
(415) 396-3293
D*1, 3, 5, 6, 8, 12

WESTAMCO Investment Co.
Leonard G. Muskin, President
8929 Wilshire Boulevard, Ste. 400
Beverly Hills 90211
(213) 652-8288
SBIC   B*2, 3, 5, 8, 9, 12

West Coast Venture Capital
Gary W. Kalbach, Gen. Ptnr.
10440 So. DeAnza Boulevard, Ste. D-2
Cupertino 95014
(408) 996-2702
SBIC   C***1, 5, 8

Western Bancorp Venture Capital Co./First
    Interstate Capital, Inc.
David B. Jones, President
707 Wilshire Boulevard, Ste. 1850
Los Angeles 90017
(213) 614-5903
SBIC   D***12

Colorado

Associated Capital Corp.
Rodney J. Love, President
5151 Bannock St.
Denver 80216
(303) 534-1155

Central Investment Corp. of Denver
(Main ofc Northwest Growth Fund, Inc, MN)
Blaine E. D'Arcey, General Manager
7625 W. 5th Ave., Ste. 202N
Lakewood 80226
(303) 232-3018
SBIC   D***12

Colorado Growth Capital, Inc.
Nicholas H.C. Davis, President
950 17th St., #1630
Denver 80202
(303) 629-0205
SBIC   B*1, 3, 7, 8, 9

Colorado SBIC
Melvin J. Roberts, President
918 17th St., Box 5168
Denver 80202
(303) 222-0465
SBIC

Denver Ventures, Inc.
Stanley Perea, President
4142 Tejon St.
Denver 80211
(303) 433-8636

Enervest, Inc.
Mark Kimmel, President
7000 East Belleview Ave., #310
Englewood 80111
(303) 771-9650
SBIC   C***1, 3, 5, 6, 7, 8, 12

Equilease Capital Corp.
(See main ofc: New York, NY)
120 Bryant St.
Denver 80219

Stephenson Merchant Banking
A. Emmet Stephenson, Jr., Sr. Ptnr.
899 Logan St.
Denver 80203
(303) 837-1700
D*1, 2, 3, 5, 6, 8

Connecticut

AB SBIC, Inc.
Adam J. Bozzuto, President
School House Road
Cheshire 06410
(203) 272-0203
SBIC

Activest Capital Corp.
William N. Vitalis, President
Box 76
Cornwall Bridge 06754
(203) 672-6651
SBIC   A*2, 4

All State Venture Capital Corp.
Thomas H. Brown, Jr., President
830 Post Rd. E.
Westport 06880
(203) 226-9376

APCO Capital Corp.
S. David Leibowitt, President
63 Broad St.
Milford 06460
(203) 877-5101

Asset Capital and Management Corp.
Ralph Smith, President
608 Ferry Boulevard
Stratford 06497
(203) 375-0299
SBIC   A*1, 2, 6, 9

Beacon Partners
Leonard Vignola, Jr., Managing Ptnr.
111 Hubbard Ave.
Stamford 06905 (Branch ofc in NY)
(203) 348-8858
D*1, 4, 5, 6, 9, 11, 12

Business Ventures, Inc.
Gerald Clark, General Manager
226 Dixwell Ave.
New Haven 06511
(203) 776-6889
MESBIC

Capital Assistance Corporation of
    Connecticut
Robert A. Foisie, President
33 Brook St.
West Hartford 06110
(203) 232-6118

Capital Resource Co. of Connecticut
I. Martin Fierberg, President
345 N. Main St., Ste. 304
West Hartford 06117
(203) 232-1769
SBIC   A*12

Cominvest of Hartford, Inc.
Robert W. Beggs, President
18 Asylum St.
Hartford 06103
(203) 246-7259
MESBIC   A*12

Dewey Investment Corp.
George E. Mrosek, President
101 Middle Turnpike W.
Manchester 06040
(203) 649-0654

First Connecticut SBIC, The
James Breiner, Chairman
David Engelson, President
177 State St.
Bridgeport 06604
(203) 366-4726
SBIC   D*1, 2, 5, 6, 9, 12
(Branch ofc: NY)

First Miami SBIC
Irve L. Libby, President
293 Post Road
Orange 06477
(203) 799-2056
SBIC   A**1, 2, 7, 10, 12
(Main ofc: North Miami, FL)

Foster Management Co.
John H. Foster, President
1010 Summer St.
Stamford 06905
(203) 348-4385
SBIC   C***1, 3, 5, 6, 8, 11

Hartford Community Capital Corp.
Rodney N. Pakus, Manager
70 Farmington Ave.
Hartford 06101
(203) 728-2507
MESBIC   A*1, 5, 9

Manufacturers SBIC, Inc.
Louis W. Mingione, Executive Director
310 Main St.
East Haven 06512
(203) 469-7901
SBIC   A*12

Marcon Capital Corp.
Martin Cohen, President
49 Riverside Ave.
Westport 06880
(203) 226-7751
SBIC   C**1, 12

Northern Business Capital Corp.
Joseph Kavanewsky, President
Box 711
South Norwalk 06856
(203) 866-1000
A**12

Nutmeg Capital Corp.
Leigh B. Raymond, VP
35 Elm St.
New Haven 06510
(203) 776-0643
A*5, 9, 10, 12

Regional Financial Enterprises, Inc.
Robert M. Williams, Chairman
1111 Summer St.
Stamford 06905
(203) 356-1730
SBIC   D*1, 3, 5, 6, 8, 12

Small Business Investment Co. of
     Connecticut
Kenneth F. Zarrill, President
c/o E&F Construction Co.
505 Sylvan Ave.
Bridgeport 06604
(203) 367-3282
SBIC   A**12

Swedish Industrial Development Corp.
Tord Carmel, President
600 Steamboat Road
Greenwich 06807
(203) 661-2500
A*8, 12

Delaware

Whisman & Associates, P.A.
Ms. Carolyn J. Fausnaugh, CPA
4005 Kennett Pike
Wilmington 19807
(302) 652-3346

District of Columbia

Allied Capital Corp.
George C. Williams, President
David Gladstone, Exec. VP
1625 Eye St. NW
Washington 20006
(202) 331-1112
SBIC   C*1, 2, 4, 5, 6, 8, 9, 11, 12
(Branch ofc: Ft. Lauderdale, FL)

Broad Arrow Investment Corp.
Mr. C.N. Bellm, President
1701 Pennsylvania Ave., NW
Washington 20006
(202) 452-6680
MESBIC   A*5, 9, 12
(Main ofc: Morristown, NJ)

Capital Investment Co. of Washington
Jayrel Goldberg, President
1010 Wisconsin Ave., NW #900
Washington 20007
(202) 298-3214
SBIC   A*6, 12

Columbia Ventures, Inc.
Richard Whitney, President
1828 L St., NW
Washington 20036
(202) 659-0033
FULLY INVESTED SBIC
(Branch ofc: Jackson, MS)

Continental Investors, Inc.
Lac Thrantong, President
2020 K St., NW, Ste 350
Washington 20006
(202) 466-3709
MESBIC   A*12

Destan Capital Corp.
Frank J. DeFrancis, Chairman
4340 Connecticut Ave., NW
Washington 20008
(202) 362-1896

Fulcurm Venture Capital Corp.
Steven L. Lilly, President
2021 K St., NW, Ste. 714
Washington 20006
(202) 833-9590
MESBIC   C***1, 5, 8, 9, 11

Greater Washington Investors, Inc.
Don A. Christensen, President & Treasurer
1015 18th St., NW
Washington 20036
(202) 466-2210
SBIC   B***1, 5, 8, 12

Housing Capital Corp.
George W. DeFranceaux, Chairman
1133 15th St., NW
Washington 20005
(202) 857-5757

Malcolm Bund & Associates
Malcolm Bund, President
1111 19th St., NW, Ste. 301
Washington 20036
(202) 293-2910
E*1, 5, 7, 12

Minority Investment Co.
Fred Sims, President/Director
1019 19th St., NW
Washington 20036
(202) 785-3035
MESBIC

MODEDCO Investment
Joseph Jackson, President
1120 Connecticut Ave., NW
Washington 20036
(202) 452-1030
MESBIC   B*1, 2, 5, 8

Morrison & Foerster
Tino Kamarck
1025 Connecticut Ave., NW
Washington 20036
(200) 466-6060

Florida

Allied Capital Corp.
George C. Williams, President
Warren Miller, Reg. VP
1614 One Financial Plaza
Ft. Lauderdale 33394
(305) 763-8484
SBIC   C*1, 2, 4, 5, 6, 8, 9, 11, 12
(Main ofc: Washington DC)

Allied Investment Developers, Inc.
Robert V. Milberg, President
1200 Biscayne Boulevard
Miami 33132
(305) 358-8010
MESBIC

Atlantic American Capital Corp.
J. Patrick Michaels, Jr., President
Lincoln Center, Ste. 851
5401 W. Kennedy Boulevard
Tampa 33609
(813) 877-8844
B***1

Burger King MESBIC, Inc.
D.R. Christopher, President
7360 N. Kendall Drive
Miami 33156
(305) 596-7305
MESBIC   A***4

Corporate Capital, Inc.
Jerry Thomas, President
2001 Broadway
Riviera Beach 33404
(305) 844-6070

CUBICO, Ltd.
Anthony G. Marina, President
7425 NW 79th St.
Miami 33136
(305) 885-8881
MESBIC   B*12

First American Lending Corp.
G.M. Caughlin, President
1200 N. Dixie Highway, Box 1449
Lake Worth 33460
(305) 582-3322
MESBIC   A*12

First Miami SBIC
Irve L. Libby, President
1195 NE 125th St.
North Miami 33161
(305) 891-2534
SBIC

First Miami SBIC
Irve L. Libby, President
250 S. Ocean Boulevard, Ste. 18-D
Boca Raton 33432
(305) 392-4424
(Main ofc: North Miami)
SBIC

First North Florida
J.B. Higdon, President
1400 Gadsden St.
Quincy 32531
(904) 627-7188

Florida Crown MESBIC
George Bishop, Executive Director
604 Hogan St.
Jacksonville 32202
(904) 354-1776, Ext. 339
MESBIC

Gulf Coast Capital Corp.
Oscar M. Tharp, President
70 N. Baylen St., Box 12790
Pensacola 32575
(904) 434-1361
SBIC   A***2, 10

Industrial Development Corp. of Florida,
   The
Ray C. Barton, Exec. VP
801 N. Magnolia Ave., Ste. 218
Orlando 32803
(305) 841-2640

Interstate Capital Corp.
Wm. C. McConnell, Jr., President
701 E. Camino Real, Ste. 9A
Boca Raton 33432
(305) 395-8466
B***1, 5, 8

J & D Capital Corp.
Jack Carmel, President
12747 Biscayne Boulevard
North Miami 33181
(305) 893-0303
SBIC   C*10, 12

LeBaron Capital Corp.
Roy Hess, President
4900 Bayou Boulevard
Pensacola 32503
(904) 477-9733

Market Capital Corp.
Mr. E.E. Eads, President
Box 22667
Tampa 33622
(813) 248-5781
SBIC   A***9, 11

Massachusetts Capital Corp.
David Harkins, President
Warren Miller, Reg. VP
1614 One Financial Plaza
Fort Lauderdale 33394
(305) 763-8484
SBIC   B***1, 3, 5, 6, 10, 11, 12
(Main ofc: Boston, MA)

Quiet SBIC, The
Edward Gray, III, VP
105 E. Garden St.
Pensacola 32501
(904) 434-5090
SBIC   A*12

Servico Business Investment Corp.
Gary O. Marino, President
2000 Palm Beach Lakes Boulevard, Ste. 1000
West Palm Beach 33409
(305) 689-5031
SBIC   A*12

Small Business Assistance Corp.
Charles S. Smith, President
2612 W. 15th St.
Panama City 32401
(904) 785-9577
SBIC   B*4

Southeast SBIC, Inc.
C.L. Hofmann, President
100 S. Biscayne Boulevard
Miami 33131
(305) 577-4680
SBIC   C***1, 5, 6, 8, 12

Suwanee Capital Corp.
William Lovell, Chairman
1010 E. Adams St.
Jacksonville, 32202
(904) 355-8315

Universal Financial Services, Inc.
Norman N. Zipkin, CEO
225 NE 35th St., Ste. B
Miami 33137
(305) 573-6326
MESBIC   A*12

Urban Ventures, Inc.
William Wynn, Jr., President
4680 NW 7th Ave.
Miami 33127
(305) 754-4701
MESBIC   A*4, 5, 6, 7, 9, 10, 12

Venture Capital Corp. of America
Richard A. Osias, President
4875 N. Federal Highway
Fort Lauderdale 33308
(305) 772-1800
SBIC   B***12

Verde Capital Corp.
Jose Dearing, President
6701 Sunset Drive, Ste. 104
Miami 33143
(305) 666-8789
MESBIC   B*1, 2, 5, 11, 12

Georgia

Affiliated Investment Fund, Ltd.
Samuel Weissman, President
2225 Shurfine Drive
College Park 30337
(404) 766-0221
SBIC   A**9

Arthur Young & Co.
Michael R. Thomas, Ptnr. & Dir. Financing
235 Peachtree St., NE, Ste; 1900
Atlanta 30043
(404) 577-8773
*12

Business Development Corp. of Georgia, The
Mike Johnson, Exec. VP
558 South Omni International
Atlanta 30303
(404) 577-5715
D**5, 6, 8, 9, 10

CSRA Capital Corp.
Allen F. Caldwell, Jr., President
Box 11045, 1058 Calussen Road, Ste. 102
Augusta 30907
(404) 955-4313
SBIC   B***2

CSRA Capital Corp.
(See main ofc: Augusta)
1401 W. Paces Ferry Road, NW
Atlanta 30327
(404) 231-1313
SBIC   B***2

ECCO MESBIC, Inc.
Gloria Gardner
Central Administration Building
Mayfield 31509
(404) 465-3201
MESBIC   A*2, 5, 6, 7, 9, 11

Enterprises Now, Inc.
Joseph Lowery, President
2001 Martin Luther King, Jr. Drive
Ste. 404-C
Atlanta 30310
(404) 753-1163
MESBIC   A*12

Equilease Capital Corp.
(See main ofc: New York, NY)
22-61 Perimeter Park
Atlanta 30309

Fidelity Capital Corp.
Alfred F. Skiba, President
180 Interstate No. Parkway, Ste. 400
Atlanta 30339
(404) 955-4313
SBIC   C*1, 2, 5, 11

First American Investment Corp.
Clifton Hofman, President
300 Interstate North
Atlanta 30339
(404) 434-1234
D***2

Investor's Equity, Inc.
Ronald W. White, Managing Director
3517 First National Bank Tower
Atlanta 30303
(404) 523-3999
SBIC   B***1, 2, 3, 4, 5, 6, 8

Mome Capital Corp.
James A. Hutchinson, President
234 Main St.
Thomson 30824
(404) 595-1507
A*2, 4, 5, 9

Peachtree Capital Corp.
David W. Howe, president
1611 Gas Light Tower
Peachtree Center
Atlanta 30303
(404) 522-9000
SBIC   A***12

Phillips J. Hook & Associates, Inc.
Phillips J. Hook, President
5600 Roswell Road, Ste. 300
Atlanta 30342
(4044) 252-1994
E*12

Rio Investment Corp.
John Mock, President
1415 Industry Ave.
Albany 31702
(912) 435-3575

Southeastern Capital SBIC
J. Ray Efird, President
100 Northcreek, Ste. 600
3715 Northside Parkway NW
Atlanta 30327
(404) 237-1567
SBIC   B***12

Sunbelt Funding Corp.
Charles H. Jones, President
Box 7006
Macon 31298
(912) 742-0177
MESBIC   A*12

Hawaii

Capital Formation Consultants, Inc.
John H. Rohan, President
1720 Ala Moana Boulevard, Suite 1506B
Honolulu 96815
(808) 949-0544
12

Pacific Venture Capital, Ltd.
Dexter J. Taniguchi, President
1505 Dillingham Boulevard
Honolulu 96817
(808) 847-6502
MESBIC   A*12

Small Business Investment Co. of Hawaii, Inc.
James W.Y. Wong, Chairman
1575 S. Beretania St.
Honolulu 96826
(808) 946-1171
SBIC   A***2, 12

Idaho

First Idaho Venture Capital Co.
Jack L. Winderi, President
Box 1739
Boise 83701
(208) 345-3460
SBIC   B**12

Illinois

Abbott Capital Corp.
Richard E. Lassar, President
120 S. LaSalle St., Ste. 1100
Chicago 60603
(312) 726-3803
SBIC   C***5, 6, 8, 10

Adams Street Capital, Inc.
Marvin A. Marder, President
1866 Sheridan Road
Highland Park 60035
(312) 368-0077

Advance Growth Capital Corp.
Charles F. Sebastian, President
9355 W. Joliet Road
LaGrange 60526
(312) 352-2650

Agribusiness Capital Co.
James W. Eerickson, President
1401 N. Western Ave.
Lake Forest 60045
(312) 295-6300

Amoco Venture Capital Co.
Mr. L.E. Schaffer, President
200 E. Randolph
Chicago 60601
(312) 856-6523
MESBIC   B*12

Cap-Form, Inc.
John H. Rubel, President
327 S. LaSalle St.
Chicago 60604
(312) 939-6070

CEDCO Capital Corp.
Frank W. Brooks, President
Joseph W. Miller, VP
180 N. Michigan Ave., Ste. 333
Chicago 60601
(312) 984-5971
MESBIC   A***12

Certified Grocers Investment Corp.
Carl D. Nipp, President
4800 S. Central Ave.
Chicago 60638
(312) 585-7000

Chicago Community Ventures, Inc.
Ms. Phyllis George, President
108 N. State St., Ste. 902
Chicago 60602
(312) 726-6084
MESBIC   B***12

Chicago Equity Corp.
Morris Weiser, President
One IBM Plaza, Ste. 2424
Chicago 60611
(312) 321-9662
SBIC   A***12

Claremont/LaSalle Corp.
Steven B. Randall, President
29 S. LaSalle St.
Chicago 60603
(312) 236-5888
SBIC   D***1, 3, 5, 6, 7, 8, 12

Combined Opportunities, Inc.
Mr. E. Patric Jones, Assist. VP
300 N. State St.
Chicago 60610
(312) 266-3091
MESBIC   B*1, 5, 12

Continental Illinois Venture Corp.
John L. Hines, President
231 S. LaSalle St., Ste. 1617
Chicago 60693
(312) 828-8021
SBIC   E***1, 3, 5, 6, 8, 9, 11, 12

Equilease Capital Corp.
(See main ofc: New York, NY)
2400 E. Devon
Des Plaines 60018

Evergreen Capital Corp.
(See main ofc: Houston, TX)
208 S. LaSalle St.
Chicago 60604

First Capital Corp. of Chicago
John A. Canning, Jr., President
One 1st National Plaza, Ste. 2628
Chicago 60670
(312) 732-5400
SBIC   E***12

Frontenac Capital Corp.
David A.R. Dullum, President
208 S. LaSalle St.
Chicago 60604
(312) 368-0047
SBIC   C***1, 5, 6, 8, 12

Golder, Thoma & Co.
Stanley C. Golder, Gen. Ptnr.
120 S. LaSalle St.
Chicago 60603
(312) 853-3311
E***1, 3, 5, 6, 8, 11, 12

Heizer Corporation
Mr. E.F. Heizer, Jr., Chairman
20 N. Wacker Drive
Chicago 60606
(312) 641-2200
SBIC   E***1, 3, 5, 6, 7, 8, 11, 12

Kirkland & Ellis
Jack S. Levin
Edward T. Swam
200 E. Randolph Drive
Chicago 60611
(312) 861-2000

Nelson Capital Corp.
Irwin B. Nelson, President
8550 W. Bryn Mawr Ave., Ste. 515
Chicago 60631
(312) 693-5990
SBIC   D**12
(Main ofc: New York, NY)

NIA Corp.
Charles Davis, VP
2400 S. Michigan Ave.
Chicago 60601
(312) 842-6523

North American Capital Group, Ltd.
Gregory I. Kravitt, CEO
201 N. Wells St., Ste. 2300
Chicago 60606
(312) 372-7711
C***5, 6, 9, 10, 12

SB Management Investors, Inc.
Kenneth Eaton, President
17 E. Chestnut
Chicago 60611
(312) 943-0750

Spectrum Capital, Ltd.
William C. Douglas, Gen. Ptnr.
208 S. LaSalle St.
Chicago 60604
(312) 236-5231
C***1, 5, 6, 8, 9, 10

Tower Ventures, Inc.
Mr. R.A. Comey, President
Sears Tower, BSC 9-29
Chicago 60684
(312) 875-0583
MESBIC   B*12

United Capital Corp. of Illinois
Jack K. Ahrens, VP
United Center, State & Wyman Sts.
Rockford 61101
(815) 987-2179
SBIC   C***1, 5, 6, 8

Urban Fund of Illinois, The
Mr. E. Patric Jones, President
300 N. State St.
Chicago 60610
(312) 266-3050
MESBIC   B*12

Woodland Capital Co.
James W. Erickson, President
1401 N. Western Ave.
Lake Forest 60045
(312) 295-6300
SBIC   C***12

Indiana

Eastside Community Investments, Inc.
Thomas R. Creasser, II, President
3228 E. 10th St.
Indianapolis 46201
(317) 633-7303
C***5

Indiana Capital Corp.
Samuel A. Rea, President
5612 Jefferson Boulevard West
Fort Wayne 46804
(219) 432-8622
B***5, 6, 10, 12

Indianapolis Business Investment Co.
Holton Haves, President
5750 N. Michigan Road, NW
Indianapolis 46208
(317) 259-4125
MESBIC

Michiana Venture Capital Co.
Richard M. Lynch, President
207 Dixieway N., Ste. 120
South Bend 46637
(219) 277-1803
B*5, 12

Minority Venture Co.
Frederick L. Howard, General Manager
Box 606, Knute Rockne Memorial Building
Notre Dame 46556
(219) 283-1115
MESBIC

Tyler Refrigeration Capital Co.
William P. Linnen, President
2222 E. Michigan Boulevard
Michigan City 46360
(616) 683-0263

Iowa

A.G. Capital Corp.
Robert Metge, President
701 SE Shurfine Drive
Ankeny 50021
(515) 964-7300
A*9

R.W. Allsop Capital Corp.
Robert W. Allsop, President
1241 Park Place NE
Cedar Rapids 52402
(319) 393-6911
SBIC   D***1, 5, 6, 12
(Branch ofcs: KS, WI, MO)

MorAmerica Capital Corp.
Jerry M. Burrows, President
300 American Building
Cedar Rapids 52401
(319) 363-8249
SBIC   D***12
(Branch ofcs: MO, WI)

Pappajohn Capital Resources
John Pappajohn, President
2116 Financial Center
Des Moines 50309
(515) 244-5746

Kansas

R.W. Allsop Capital Corp.
Larry C. Maddox
35 Corporate Woods, Ste. 229
9101 W. 10th St.
Overland Park 66210
(913) 642-4719
SBIC   D***1, 5, 6, 12
(Main ofc: Cedar Rapids, IA)

Kansas Venture Capital, Inc.
George L. Doak, President
First Nat'l Bank Towers
One Townsite Plaza, Ste. 1030
Topeka 66603
(913) 233-1368
SBIC   A***5

Kentucky

Equal Opportunity Finance, Inc.
Frank P. Justice, Jr., President
9502 Williamsburg Plaza
Louisville 40222
(502) 423-1943
MESBIC   A*12

Financial Opportunities, Inc.
Gary J. Miller, General Manager
981 S. 3rd St.
Lousiville 40203
(502) 584-1281
SBIC   A*9

Mountain Ventures, Inc.
Frederick J. Beste, III, President
911 N. Main St., Box 628
London 40741
(606) 878-6635
SBIC   D***12

Louisiana

Business Capital Corp.
David R. Burrus, President
1732 Canal St.
New Orleans 70112
(504) 581-4002
MESBIC   D*12

CADDO Capital Corp.
Thomas L. Young, Jr., President
820 Jordan St., Ste. 504
Shreveport 71101
(318) 424-0505
SBIC   D***3, 5, 12

Capital for Terrebone, Inc.
Hartwell A. Lewis, President
1613 Barrow St., Box 1868
Houma 70361
(504) 868-3933
SBIC   A**12

Capital Resources Corp.
W. Denis O'Connell, President
1624 Letitia St.
Baton Rouge 70808
(504) 387-0806

Commercial Capital, Inc.
Mr. F.W. Pierce, President
200 Belle Terre Boulevard (Main office)
Covington 70433
(504) 892-4921, Ext 261
SBIC   A*1, 2, 4, 6, 7, 9, 10, 12

Commercial Capital, Inc.
c/o Northlake Insurance, Inc.
Bogue Falaya Plaza Shopping Center
Covington 70433
(See main ofc: Covington)

Commercial Capital, Inc.
c/o Central Progressive Bank
1809 W. Thomas
Hammond 70401
(See main ofc: Covington)

Commerical Venture Capital Corp.
William H. Jackson, President
329 Texas St.
Shreveport 71101
(318) 226-4602

Dixie Business Investment Co.
Steve K. Cheek, President
Box 588
Lake Providence 71254
(318) 559-1558
SBIC   A**12

EDICT Investment Corp.
Gregory B. Johnson, Exec. VP
2908 S. Carrollton Avenue
New Orleans 70118
(504) 861-2364
MESBIC   A**12

First SBIC of Louisiana
Mrs. Alma O. Galle, President
2852 Carey St., Box 1336
Slidell 70459
(504) 561-0017/641-2604
SBIC   A*12

First Southern Capital Corp.
John H. Crabtree, Chairman and President
Box 14205
Baton Rouge 70898
(504) 769-3004
SBIC   D***1, 5, 12

Greater New Orleans Investment Co.
Thomas E. Smith, Jr., President
210 Baronne St., Ste. 1140
New Orleans 70112
(504) 581-6982
B***5, 7, 8, 12

Gulf South Venture Corp.
Robert Aulston, President
821 Gravier St.
Commerce Building, Ste. 1100
(504) 561-2120
MESBIC A*12

Louisiana Equity Capital Corp.
G. Lee Griffin, President
451 Florida Street
Baton Rouge 70801
(504) 389-4421
SBIC   C**5, 9

Louisiana Venture Capital Corp.
Ben Johnson, President
315 North St.
Natchitoches 71457
(318) 352-9138

Royal Street Investment Corp.
William D. Humphries, President
618 Baronne St.
New Orleans 70113
(504) 588-9271
SBIC   B***12

SCDF Investment Corp.
Rev. Albert McKnight, President
1006 Surrey St.
Lafayette 70501
(318) 232-7672
MESBIC   B***2, 5, 9, 10, 12

Savings Venture Capital Corp.
David R. Dixon, Exec. VP
6001 Financial Plaza
Shreveport 71130
(318) 686-9200
SBIC   B**12

Venturtech Capital, Inc.
Mr. E.M. Charlet, President
Ste. 602, Republic Tower
5700 Florida Boulevard
Baton Rouge 70806
(504) 926-5482
SBIC   B***1, 6, 8

Maine

Great Northern Capital Corp.
Barry Goldman, President
97A Exchange Place
Portland 04111
(207) 773-1817

Maine Capital Corp.
Lloyd D. Brace, Jr.
VP & Director of Finance
One Memorial Circle
Augusta 04330
(207) 623-1686
SBIC   B*1, 2, 3, 5, 8, 11, 12

Maryland

Albright Venture Capital, Inc.
William A. Albright, President
8005 Rappahannock Ave.
Jessup 20794
(301) 799-7935
MESBIC   A*2, 4, 9, 10, 11, 12

Baltimore Community Investment Company
James Crockett, President
1925 Eutaw Place
Baltimore 21217
(301) 669-2863
MESBIC

Broventure Co., Inc.
Williiam Gust, President
Two Hopkins Plaza
Baltimore 21201
(301) 727-4520
D***1, 5, 6, 8, 11

Development Credit Corp. of Maryland
Mr. W.G. Brooks Thomas, President
40 W. Chesapeake Ave., Box 10629
Towson 21204
(301) 828-4711
C**12

Real Estate Capital Corp.
(Main ofc: Bala Cynwyd, PA)
9823 Central Avenue
Largo 20870
(301) 336-2345

Massachusetts

Advent Capital Corp.
David D. Croll, Chairman and CEO
111 Devonshire St.
Boston 02109
(617) 725-2301
SBIC   E*1, 3, 5, 6, 8, 12

Alta Capital Corp.
William P. Egan, President
175 Federal St.
Boston 02110
(617) 482-8020
SBIC   D*1, 6, 9, 12

Atlas Capital Corp.
Herbert Carver, President
55 Court St., Ste. 200
Boston 02108
(617) 482-1218
SBIC   B**12

Boston Hambro Corp.
Edwin A. Goodman, President
One Boston Place
Boston 02106
(617) 722-7055
SBIC   D*1, 2, 3, 5, 6, 8, 12
(Branch ofc: NY)

Business Achievement Corp.
Julian H. Katzeff, President
1280 Centre
Newton Centre 02159
(617) 965-0550

Capital Publishing Corp.
Stanley E. Pratt, President
Box 348, 2 Laurel Ave.
Wellesley Hills 02181
(617) 235-5405

Charles River Resources, Inc.
Richard M. Burnes, Jr., President
133 Federal St.
Boston 02110
(617) 482-9370

Chestnut Capital Corp.
David D. Croll, Chairman and CEO
111 Devonshire St.
Boston 02109
(617) 725-2302
SBIC   E*1, 3, 5, 6, 8, 12

Claflin Capital
Thomas M. Claflin, II
30 Federal St.
Boston 02110
(617) 426-6505

Cohasset Capital Corp.
Grant Wilson, President
4 Tupelo Road
Cohasset 02025
(617) 383-0758
SBIC   A***1, 2

Devonshire Capital Corp.
David C. Croll, Chairman and CEO
111 Devonshire St.
Boston 02109
(617) 725-2300
SBIC   E*1, 3, 5, 6, 8, 12

East Boston Community Develop. Corp.
Salvatore J. Colombo
130 Condor St.
East Boston 02128
(617) 569-5590

Equilease Capital Corp.
(See main ofc: New York, NY)
393 Totten Pond Road
Waltham 02154

Find & Ambrogne
Arnold M. Zaff
133 Federal St.
Boston 02110
(617) 482-0100

First Capital Corp. of Boston
George Rooks, President
100 Federal St.
Boston 02110
(617) 434-2442
SBIC   D***1, 3, 5, 6, 8, 9

First United SBIC, Inc.
Alfred W. Ferrara, VP
135 Will Drive
Canton 02021
(617) 828-6150

Greater Springfield Investment Corp.
Charles Rees, General Manager
121 Chestnut St.
Springfield 01103
(413) 781-7130
MESBIC   A***12

Hellman, Gal Capital Corp.
Frederick W. Hellman, Chairman
1 Federal St.
Boston 02110
(617) 482-7735

International Film Investors (LP)
(See main ofc: New York, NY)
1 Federal St., #1400
Boston 02110

Massachusetts Business Development Corp.
Fred F. Stockwell, President
One Boston Place
Boston 02108
(617) 723-7515
C**2, 5, 8

Massachusetts Capital Corp.
David Harkins, President
Christopher Lynch, VP
75 Federal St.
Boston 01945
(617) 426-2488
SBIC   B***1, 3, 5, 6, 10, 11, 12
(Branch ofc: Ft Lauderdale, FL)

Massachusetts Venture Capital Corp.
Charles Grigsby, President
59 Temple Place
Boston 02111
(617) 426-0208
MESBIC   B***12

New England Enterprise Capital Corp.
Z. David Patterson, VP
28 State St.
Boston 02106
(617) 742-0285
SBIC   C***1, 5, 6, 8, 10, 12

Northeast Small Business Investment Corp.
Joseph Mindick, Treasurer
16 Cumberland St.
Boston 02115
(617) 267-3983
A**12

Pace Consulting Group, Inc.
Mr. W.L. Welling
60 Hickory Drive
Waltham 02154
(617) 890-1910

Palmer Organization, The
Steven Ricci, William Congleton
183 Essex St.
Boston 02111
(617) 423-4355

Prime Capital Corp.
Jason Rosenberg, President
10 Commercial Wharf, S.
Boston 02110
(617) 723-2103

Schooner Capital Corp.
Vincent J. Ryan, Jr., President
77 Franklin St.
Boston 02110
(617) 357-9031
SBIC   B***1, 3

Transatlantic Capital Corp.
Bayard Henry, President
60 Batterymarch St., Rm. 728
Boston 02110
(617) 482-0015
SBIC   C***1, 5, 6, 8, 10

Urban National Corp.
Edward Dugger, III, President
195 State St.
Boston 02109
(617) 723-8300
C****1, 3, 5, 6, 8

UST Capital Corp.
Stephen R. Lewinstein, President
40 Court St.
Boston 02108
(617) 726-7260
SBIC   A*1, 2, 3, 5, 6, 8, 11

Venture Capital Fund of New England, The
Farrell, Healer & Co.
Richard A. Farrell, President
100 Franklin St.
Boston 02110
(617) 451-2575
C***1, 5, 8, 12

WCCI Capital Corp.
Ms. Deborah G. Nurse, VP
791 Main St.
Worcester 01610
(617) 791-0941
MESBIC   A***12

Worcester Capital Corp.
W. Kenneth Kidd, VP
446 Main St.
Worcester 01608
(617) 853-7508
SBIC   A***5, 8

Yankee Capital Corp.
Richard F. Pollard, President
175 Federal St.
Boston 02110
(617) 482-1041

Michigan

DBT Capital Corp.
John D. Berkaw, President
211 W. Fort St.
Detroit 48231
(313) 222-3907
SBIC   C***5, 6, 8, 12

Doan Resources Corp.
Ian R.N. Bund, VP
110 East Grove
Midland 48640
(517) 631-2471
SBIC   C***1, 5, 6, 8

Federated Capital Corp.
Louis P. Ferris, Jr., President
20000 W. Twelve Mile Road
Southfield 48076
(313) 559-0554
SBIC   A**12

Independence Capital Formation, Inc.
Walter M. McMurtry, Jr., President
1505 Woodward Ave., Pierson Building
Detroit 48226
(313) 961-2470
MESBIC   B*1, 5, 8, 9, 11

Metro-Detroit Investment Co.
William J. Fowler, President
18481 W. Ten Mile Road
Southfield 48075
(313) 557-3818/19
MESBIC   A**9

Michigan Capital & Service, Inc.
Joseph F. Conway, President
740 City Center Building
Ann Arbor 48104
(313) 663-0702
SBIC   C***1, 3, 5, 6, 8, 12

Motor Enterprises, Inc.
James Kobus, Manager
General Motors Building, Rm. 6-248
3044 W. Grand Boulevard
Detroit 48202
(313) 556-4273
MESBIC   A*9

Mutual Investment Co., Inc.
Timothy J. Taylor, Tresurer
17348 W. Twelve Mile Road, Ste. 104
Southfield 48076
(313) 552-8515
MESBIC   A*9

PRIME, Inc.
Jimmy N. Hill, President
1845 David Whitney Building
Detroit 48226
(313) 964-3380
MESBIC   B*12

Tyler Refrigeration Capital Corp.
Gary J. Slock, Chairman
1329 Lake
Niles 49120
(616) 683-1610
SBIC   A*2

Minnesota

Community Investment Enterprises, Inc.
Donald Soukop, President
7515 Wayzata Boulevard
Minneapolis 55426
(612) 544-2754
D***1, 5, 8

Consumer Growth Capital, Inc.
John T. Gerlach, President
430 Oak Grove
Minneapolis 55403
(612) 874-0694
SBIC   C***1, 4, 5, 10, 12

Control Data Capital Corp.
John F. Tracy, President
8100 34th Ave. S.
Minneapolis 55440
(612) 853-6537
SBIC   B*1, 5, 6, 8, 12

Eagle Ventures, Inc.
Thomas M. Neitge, VP
700 Soo Line Building
Minneapolis 55442
(612) 339-9694
SBIC   C***1, 5, 6, 7, 8

First Midwest Capital Corp.
Alan K. Ruvelson, President
Ste. 700 Chamber of Commerce Building
15 S. 5th St.
Minneapolis 55402
(612) 339-9391
SBIC   B***1, 5, 6, 8, 9, 10, 12

Northland Capital Corp.
George G. Barnum, Jr., President
613 Missabe Building
Duluth 55802
(218) 722-0545
SBIC   B***12

North Star Ventures, Inc.
Terence W. Glarner, Exec. VP and Gen.
    Mgr.
Ste. 1258, NFC Building
7900 Xerxes Ave., S.
Minneapolis 55431
(612) 830-4550
SBIC   C***1, 5, 6, 7, 8, 12

Northwest Growth Fund, Inc.
Robert F. Zicarelli, Chairman
1730 Midwest Plaza Building
801 Nicollet Mall
Minneapolis 55402
(612) 372-8770
SBIC   D***12
(Branch ofcs: Lakewood, CO & Portland, OR)

Pathfinder Venture Capital Fund
Mr. A.J. Greenshields, Ptnr.
7300 Metro Boulevard, Ste. 585
Minneapolis 55435
(612) 835-1121
SBIC   E***1, 5, 6, 8

Paulucci Venture Capital Corp.
Mike Paulucci, President
525 Lake Ave. S.
Duluth 55806
(218) 723-5472
MESBIC

Peat, Marwick, Mitchell & Co.
Kevin J. O'Connor
1700 IDS Center
Minneapolis 55402
(612) 341-2222

P.R. Peterson Venture Capital Corp.
Mr. P.R. Peterson, President
7301 Washington Ave., S.
Edina 55435
(612) 941-8171
SBIC   A***6, 8

Retailers Growth Fund, Inc.
Cornell L. Moore, Chairman and President
5100 Gamble Dr., Ste. 380
Minneapolis 55416
(612) 546-8989
SBIC   A*9

Shared Ventures, Inc.
Howard Weiner, President
4601 Excelsior Boulevard, Ste. 411
Minneapolis 55416
(612) 925-3411
SBIC   A*12

Westland Capital Corp.
Robert S. Dunbar, President
2021 E. Hennepin Ave.
Minneapolis 55413
(612) 331-9210
B*1, 5, 6, 9, 10

Mississippi

Columbia Ventures, Inc.
(See main ofc: Washington, DC)
809 State St.
Jackson 39201
FULLY INVESTED SBIC

DeSoto Capital Corp.
William B. Rudner, President
8885 E. Goodman
Olive Branch 38654
(601) 895-4145
SBIC   A***12

INVESAT Corp.
J. Thomas Noolin, President
162 E. Amite St., Ste. 204
Jackson 39207
(601) 969-3242
SBIC   C*12

INVESAT Capital Corp.
J. Thomas Noolin, President
1414 Deposit Guarantee Plaza
Jackson 39201
(601) 969-3242
MESBIC

Sun Delta Capital Access Center, Inc.
Charles Bannerman, President
819 Main St., Ste. 588
Greenville 38701
(601) 335-5291
MESBIC   B*12

Vicksburg Small Business Investment Co.
David L. May, President
First National Bank Building, Box 852
Vicksburg 39180
(601) 636-4762
SBIC   A*5, 9, 12

Missouri

R.W. Allsop Capital Corp.
Robert L. Kuk
111 W. Port Plaza, Ste. 600
St. Louis 63141
(314) 434-1688
SBIC   D***1, 5, 6, 12
(Main ofc: Cedar Rapids, IA)

Atlas Small Business Investment Corp.
Ronald Jarvis, Jr., President
1617 Baltimore
Kansas City 64108
(816) 471-1750

Bankers Capital Corp.
Raymond E. Glasnapp, President
4049 Pennsylvania, Ste. 304
Kansas City 64111
(816) 531-1600
SBIC   A*12

Equilease Capital Corp.
(See main ofc: New York, NY)
7700 Clayton Road
St. Louis 63117

First Missouri Dev. Finance Corp.
Jerry Stegall, Exec. VP
1411 Southwest Boulevard, Ste. B
P.O. Drawer 1745
Jefferson City 65102
(314) 635-0038
C   **2, 5

Intercapco West, Inc.
Thomas E. Phelps, President
7800 Bonhomme
Clayton 63105
(314) 863-0600
SBIC   A***1, 2, 3, 5, 6, 8, 9, 11, 12

MorAmerica Capital Corp.
Rex E. Wiggins, Reg. VP
Ste. 2724A, Commerce Tower
911 Main St.
Kansas City 64105
(816) 842-0114
SBIC   D***12
(Main ofc: Cedar Rapids, IA)

Nebraska

Community Equity Corp. of Nebraska
William C. Moore, President
5620 Armes Ave., Ste. 109
Omaha 68104
MESBIC　A**12

Nevada

Universal Investment Corp.
Bernard M. Nemerov, President
300 S. Curry St.
Carson City 89701
(702) 883-7585

Westland Capital Corp.
Morton B. Phillips, Chairman
100 W. Grove St., Ste. 550
Reno 89509
(702) 826-6307
SBIC　B*12

New Hampshire

Hampshire Capital Corp.
Philip G. Baker, President
48 Congress St., Box 468
Portsmouth 03801
(603) 431-1415
SBIC　A***5, 9, 12

New Jersey

Broad Arrow Investment Corp.
Mr. C.N. Belim, President
Box 2231-R
Morristown 07960
(201) 766-2835
MESBIC　A*5, 9, 12
(Branch ofc: Washington, DC)

Capital SBUC, Inc.
Isadore Cohen, President
143 E. State St.
Trenton 08608
(609) 394-5221

Delaware Valley SBIC
(See main ofc: Philadelphia, PA)
Plaza Apts.
Atlantic City 08201
SBIC

Engle Investment Co.
Murray Hendel, President
35 Essex St.
Hackensack 07601
(201) 489-3583
SBIC　A*12

Eslo Capital Corp.
Leo Katz, President
485 Morris Ave.
Springfield 07081
(201) 467-2545
SBIC　A**12

Gunther, Talcott & Benson, Inc.
Stephen G. Janick, III, President
P.O. Dwr 130, 190 Goodwin Ave.
Midland Park 07432
(201) 447-6020
A*12

Lloyd Capital Corp.
Solomon T. Scharf, President
77 State Highway #5
Edgewater 07020
(201) 947-6000
SBIC　C*2, 4, 6, 9, 12

Main Capital Investment Corp.
Sam Klotz, President
818 Main St.
Hackensack 07601
(201) 489-2080
SBIC　A***1, 2, 3, 4, 7, 10, 12

Monmouth Capital Corp.
Eugene W. Landy, President
125 Wyckoff Road, Box 35
Eatontown 07724
(201) 542-4927
SBIC　B*12

Quidnet Capital Corp.
Stephen W. Fillo, President
909 State Road
Princeton 08540
(609) 924-7665
SBIC   C***12

Rutgers Minority Investment Co.
Louis T. German, President
92 New St.
Newark 07102
(201) 648-5287
MESBIC   A*5, 9

New Mexico

Albuquerque SBIC
Albert T. Ussery, President
Box 487
Albuquerque 87103
(505) 247-4089
SBIC   A***12

Associated Southwest Investors, Inc.
John R. Rice, President
2425 Alamo SE
Albuquerque 87106
(505) 842-5955
MESBIC   B*1, 5, 6, 8, 12

First Capital Corp. of New Mexico
Ms. Shirley A. Williams, President
8425 Osuna Road NE
Albuquerque 87112
(505) 292-2300
SBIC   A*12

Fluid Capital Corp.
George T. Slaughter, President
200 Lomas NW, Ste. 527
Albuquerque 87102
(505) 243-2279
SBIC   B*2, 12

Franklin Corp., The
Herman E. Goodman, President
4209 San Mateo NE
Albuquerque 87102
(505) 243-9680
SBIC   D***1, 5, 6, 7, 8, 11, 12
(Main ofc: New York, NY)

New Mexico Capital Corp.
Mr. S.P. Hidalgo, II, Exec. VP
2900 Louisiana Boulevard NE, Ste. 201
Albuquerque 87110
(505) 884-3600
SBIC   C*12

Southwest Capital Investments, Inc.
Martin J. Roe, President
8000 Pennsylvania Circle NE
Albuquerque 87110
(505) 265-9564
SBIC   A*5, 10, 12

Venture Capital Corp. of New Mexico
Ben Bronstein, Chairman
5301 Central Ave. NE, Ste. 1600
Albuquerque 87108
(505) 266-0066
SBIC   B***12

New York

Adler & Company
James R. Swartz, Ptnr.
280 Park Ave.
New York 10017
(212) 986-3010
***1, 2, 3, 4, 5, 6, 7, 8, 9, 10, 11, 12

American Asian Capital Corp.
Howard Lin, President
79 Wall St., Rm. 907
New York 10005
(212) 422-6880
MESBIC

AMEV Capital Corp.
Martin S. Orland, President
Two World Trade Center, #9766
New York 10048
(212) 775-1912
SBIC   D***1, 4, 5, 6, 9, 10, 12

Armistad DOT Venture Capital, Inc.
Percy E. Sutton, Chairman and President
801 Second Ave., Ste. 303
New York 10017
(212) 573-6600
MESBIC   C*5, 8, 11

A.J. Armstrong Co., Inc.
Robert Spitalnic, VP
850 Third Ave.
New York 10022
(212) 826-3172

Arthur Young & Co.
Dennis Serlen, Ptnr.
277 Park Ave.
New York 10172
(212) 922-3010

Atalanta Investment Co., Inc.
L. Mark Newman, Chairman
450 Park Ave.
New York 10022
(212) 832-1104

BanCap Corporation
William L. Whitely, President
155 E. 42nd St.
New York 10017
(212) 687-6470
MESBIC   B***1, 3, 5, 12

Basic Capital Corp.
Paul Kates, President
32 W. 39th St.
New York 10018
(212) 944-9874
A*12

Beacon Partners
Leonard Vignola, Jr., Managing Ptnr.
733 Third Ave., Ste. 901
New York 10017
(212) 265-0177
D*1, 4, 5, 6, 9, 11, 12
(Main ofc: Stamford, CT)

Beneficial Capital Corp.
John J. Hoey, President
645 Fifth Ave.
New York 10022
(212) 752-1291
SBIC   A*3, 12

Bohlen Capital Corp.
Harvey Wertheim, President
230 Park Ave.
New York 10169
(212) 288-9535
SBIC   D***1, 3, 5, 6, 8

Boston Hambro Corp.
Edwin A. Goodman, President
17 E. 71st St.
New York 10021
(212) 288-7778
SBIC   D*1, 2, 3, 5, 6, 8, 12
(Main ofc: Boston, MA)

BT Capital Corp.
James G. Hellmuth, President
280 Park Ave.
New York 10017
(212) 692-4840
SBIC   D*12

California Northwest Fund, Inc.
Dr. Yung Wong, Managing Director
230 Park Ave., 3rd Floor
New York 10017
(212) 935-0997
SBIC   D*12
(Main ofc: Menlo Park, CA)

Capital for Future, Inc.
Jay Schwamm, President
635 Madison Ave.
New York 10022
(212) 759-8060
B**2

Capital Formation MESBIC, Inc.
Robert Hammerquist, Executive Director
5 Beekman St.
New York 10038
(212) 349-3650
MESBIC

CEDC MESBIC, Inc.
John Kearse, President
106 Main St.
Hempstead 11550
(516) 292-9710
MESBIC   A*12

Central New York SBIC, Inc.
Robert E. Romig, President
351 S. Warren St.
Syracuse 13202
(315) 478-5026
FULLY INVESTED

Chase Manhattan Capital Corp.
Robert Hubbard, President
1411 Broadway, 4th floor
New York 10018
(212) 223-7046
D*1, 5, 7, 8, 11

Cineffects Capital Corp.
Joseph J. Macaluso, President
115 W. 45th St.
New York 10036
(212) 575-5161

Citicorp Venture Capital, Ltd.
William T. Comfort, Chairman
399 Park Ave., 20th floor
New York 10043
(212) 559-1127
SBIC   C***12

Clarion Capital Corp.
(See main ofc: Cleveland, OH)
2 Penn Plaza
New York 10001

Clinton Capital Corp.
Mark Scharfman, President
35 Middagh St.
Brooklyn 11201
(212) 858-0920
SBIC   C***12

CMNY Capital Co., Inc.
Robert Davidoff, VP
77 Water St.
New York 10005
(212) 437-7078
SBIC   B***1, 5, 6, 7, 8, 9, 10, 12

Coalition SBIC
Carlos H. Lugo, President
1270 Avenue of the Americas
New York 10020
(212) 399-0229
MESBIC   A*12

College Venture Equity Corp.
Francis M. Williams, President
William A. MacDougall, VP
1222 Main St., Box 791
Niagara Falls 14301
(716) 285-8455
SBIC   A*12

Collier Enterprises
Miles C. Collier, Managing Ptnr.
Fred F. Nazem, Managing Director
655 Madison Ave.
New York 10021
(212) 752-0771
D***1, 2, 3, 5, 6, 8

Cornell Capital Corp.
Barry M. Bloom, President
8-B Main St.
East Hampton 11937
(516) 324-0408
SBIC   D*4, 12

CR Development Corp.
Alex Goodwin, President
717 Fifth Ave.
New York 10022
(212) 935-9600
D***12

Ray Dirks Research
John Muir & Co.
Robert Sterling, Jack Silver
61 Broadway
New York 10006
(212) 747-8300
E***12

EAB Venture Corp.
Richard C. Burcaw, President
Mark R. Littell, VP & Treas.
90 Park Ave.
New York 10016
(212) 437-4182
SBIC   C*1, 3, 5, 6, 8, 10, 12

Edwards Capital Corp.
Edward H. Teitlebaum, President
215 Lexington Ave.
New York, NY 10016
(212) 686-2568
SBIC*12

Engle Investment Co.
Murray Hendel, President
135 W. 50th St.
New York 10020
(212) 757-9580
SBIC   A*12
(Main ofc: Hackensack, NJ)

Equico Capital Corp.
Carlos R. Evering, Exec. VP
1211 Avenue of the Americas, Ste. 2905
New York 10020
(212) 921-2290
MESBIC   C***12

Equilease Capital Corp.
Norbert Weissberg, President
750 Third Ave.
New York 10017
(212) 557-6800

Equitable SBIC
David Goldberg, President
350 Fifth Ave., Ste. 5805
New York 10118
(212) 564-5420
SBIC   A*6

Equitable Life Community Enterprise Corp.
H.H. Mackey, III, President
1285 Avenue of the Americas
New York 10019
(212) 554-4978
MESBIC

ESIC Capital, Inc.
George H. Bookbinder, President
110 E. 59th St.
New York 10022
(212) 421-1605
SBIC   C**12

E S One Capital Corp.
Harvey J. Wachtel, President
400 Madison Ave.
New York 10017
(212) 750-9711

Exim Capital Corp.
Victor Chun, President
290 Madison Ave.
New York 10017
(212) 683-3200
MESBIC   A***5

European Development Capital Corp.
Harvey J. Wertheim, President
230 Park Ave., Ste. 1260
New York 10017
SBIC   D***1, 3, 5, 6, 8

Fairfield Equity Corp.
Matthew A. Berdon, President
200 E. 42nd St.
New York 10017
(212) 867-0150
SBIC   B***1, 5, 7, 9, 10, 12

Fifty-Third Street Ventures, Inc.
Alan J. Patricof, Chairman
1 East 53rd St.
New York 10023
(212) 753-6300
SBIC   D***1, 3, 5, 6, 8, 12

First Century Partnership II
c/o Smith Barney, Harris Upham & Co.,
    Incorporated
1345 Avenue of the Americas
New York 10501
(212) 399-6107
C***8, 12

First Connecticut SBIC, The
James Breiner, Chairman
David Engelson, President
680 Fifth Ave.
New York 10019
(Main ofc: Bridgeport, CT) SBIC

First Wall Street SBIC, Inc.
John W. Chappell, President
767 Fifth Ave., Ste. 4403
(212) 355-6540
New York 10153

FNCB Capital Corp.
John Murphy, Assist. VP
399 Park Ave.
New York 10022
(212) 559-1127

Foster, Hickman & Zanglein
John W. Hickman, Corporate
Eric W. Zanglein, Institutional
Raymond J. Foster, Private
183 East Main St.
Rochester 14604
(716) 232-3320
D***12

Franklin Corp., The
Herman E. Goodman, President
1 Rockefeller Plaza
New York 10020
(212) 581-4900
SBIC   D***1, 5, 6, 7, 8, 11, 12

Fundex Capital Corp.
Howard Sommer, President
525 Northern Boulevard
Great Neck 11021
(516) 466-8550
(212) 895-7361
SBIC   C**12

Hanover Capital Corp.
Daniel J. Sullivan, President
233 E. 62nd St.
New York 10021
(212) 752-5173
SBIC   B*12

Harrison Capital, Inc.
Mr. W.T. Corl, President
2000 Westchester Ave.
White Plains 10650
(914) 253-7845
D***1, 5, 6, 8

Heller Capital Services, Inc.
Jack A. Prizzi, Exec. VP
200 Park Ave.
New York 10166
(212) 880-7198
SBIC   E*1, 3, 5, 6, 7, 8, 9, 11, 12

Ibero-American Investors Corp.
Emilio Serrano, Gen. Mgr.
954 Clifford Ave.
Rochester 14621
(716) 554-7420
MESBIC   A***5, 9, 12

Intercoastal Capital Corp.
Herbert Krasnow, President
380 Madison Ave.
New York 10017
(212) 986-0482
SBIC   D*1, 2, 4, 5, 6, 7, 10, 11, 12

Intergroup Venture Capital Corp.
Ben Hauben, President
230 Park Ave.
New York 10169
(212) 661-5428
SBIC   A*12

International Film Investors, Inc.
Neil Braun, VP–Finance
595 Madison Ave.
New York 10022
(212) 310-1500
SBIC   E***7

Irving Capital Corp.
J. Andrew McWethy, Exec. VP
1290 Avenue of the Americas, 3rd flr.
New York 10019
(212) 922-8790
SBIC   E***1, 3, 5, 8, 9

Japanese American Capital Corp.
Stephen Huang, President
120 Broadway
New York 10271
(212) 964-4077
MESBIC   B*2, 4, 12

Korean Capital Corp.
Ms. Min ja OH, President
222-48 Birmington Parkway
Bayside 11364
(212) 224-5891
MESBIC   C*12

Ladenburg, Thalmann & Co., Inc.
Barry A. Bloomfield
540 Madison Ave.
New York 10022
(212) 940-0188

Lake Success Capital Corp.
Herman Schneider, President
5000 Brush Hollow Road
Westbury 11590
(516) 997-4300

Lincoln Capital Corp.
Martin Lifton, President
41 E. 42nd St., Ste. 1510
New York 10017
(212) 697-0610
SBIC   C*2, 12

Marwit Capital
(See main ofc: Newport Beach, Ca)
6 E. 43rd St.
New York 10017
(212) 867-3906
SBIC

Medallion Funding Corp.
Alvin Murstein, President
86 Glen Cove Road
East Hills 11576
(212) 682-3300
MESBIC   A*11

Medallion Funding Corp.
(Branch ofc)
205 E. 42nd St., Rm. 2020
New York 10017
(212) 682-3300

Mid-Atlantic Fund, Inc.
Austin Muscowitz, President
9 W. 57th St.
New York 10019
(212) 421-3940

Midland Capital Corp.
Michael R. Stanfield, Managing Director
Robert B. Machinist, Managing Director
110 William St.
New York 10038
(212) 577-0750
SBIC   E*1, 3, 12

Minority Equity Capital Co., Inc.
   (MECCO)
Patrick Owen Burns, President
275 Madison Ave., Ste. 1901
New York 10016
(212) 686-9710
MESBIC   C***1, 5, 6, 9, 12

M & T Capital Corp.
Harold M. Small, President
One M & T Plaza
Buffalo 14240
(716) 842-4881
SBIC   C***12

Multi-Purpose Capital Corp.
Eli B. Fine, President
31 S. Broadway
Yonkers 10701
(914) 963-2733
SBIC   A*1, 2, 3, 4, 5, 6, 7, 8, 9, 10, 11, 12

Nelson Capital Corp.
Irwin B. Nelson, President
591 Stewart Ave.
Garden City 11530
(516) 222-2555
SBIC   D**12

New Oasis Capital Corp.
James J.H. Huang, President
114 Liberty St., Ste. 404
New York 10006
(212) 394-2804/5
MESBIC   B*12

Noro Capital Corp.
Harvey Wertheim, President
230 Park Ave.
New York 10169
(212) 867-9535
SBIC   D***1, 3, 5, 6, 8

North American Capital Corp.
Stanley P. Roth, President
131 Jericho Tpke., Ste. 401
Jericho 11753
(516) 997-6800
D***12

North Street Capital Corp.
Ralph L. McNeal, Sr., President
250 North St., TA-2
White Plains 10625
(914) 683-6306
MESBIC   A***1, 5, 11, 12

NYBDC Capital Corp.
Marshall R. Lustig, President
41 State St.
Albany 12209
(518) 463-2268
SBIC   A***5

Percival Capital Corp.
George A. Simpson, President
300 E. 42nd St., 2nd floor
New York 10017
(212) 953-1540

Pines Venture Capital Corp.
Robert H. Pines, President
2 World Trade Center
New York 10048
(212) 432-1660

Pioneer Capital Corp.
William Bergesch, President
1440 Broadway, Rm. 1967
New York 10018
(212) 594-4860
MESBIC   A***12

Pioneer Investors
James G. Niven, President
113 E. 55th St.
New York 10022
(212) 980-9090
SBIC   C***1, 3, 5, 6, 8

Preferential Capital Corp.
Bruce Bayroff, Secretary–Treasurer
16 Court St.
Brooklyn 11241
(212) 855-2728

Printers Capital Corp.
Herbert Brandon, President
16 Court St.
Brooklyn 11241
(212) 430-0750

Rand SBIC, Inc.
Donald A. Ross, President and CEO
2600 Rand Building
Buffalo 14203
(716) 853-0802
SBIC   A*12

Realty Growth Capital Corp.
Lawrence A. Benenson, President
575 Lexington Ave.
New York 10022
(212) 755-9044
SBIC   A**11

Research & Science Investors, Inc.
Harvey Wertheim, Cydney Meltzer
230 Park Ave., Ste. 1260
New York 10169
(212) 867-9535
D***5, 6, 8, 12

Royal Business Funds Corp.
Mr. I.S. Goodman, Exec. VP
60 E. 42nd St., Ste. 2530
New York 10165
(212) 986-8463
SBIC   A*12

R & R Financial Corp.
Mr. Imre J. Rosenthal, President
1451 Broadway
New York 10036
(212) 790-1400
SBIC   A*12

Peter J. Schmitt Co., Inc.
Denis G. Riley, Manager
678 Bailey Ave.
Buffalo 14206
(716) 825-1111
SBIC   A***5, 8, 9

Sherwood Business Capital Corp.
Lewis R. Eisner, President
770 King St.
Port Chester 10573
(914) 937-6000
SBIC   B**12

Sherwood Business Capital Corp.
Lewis R. Eisner, President
230 Park Ave.
New York 10169
(212) 661-2424
SBIC   B**12
(Main ofc: Port Chester, NY)

Situation Ventures Corp.
Sam Hollander, President
126 13th St.
Brooklyn 11215
(212) 438-4909

Allan E. Skora Associates
Allan E. Skora
500 Fifth Ave., Ste. 2305
New York 10036
(212) 691-9895

Small Business Electronics Investment Corp.
Stanley Meisels, President
60 Broad St.
New York 10004
(212) 952-7531
SBIC   A**12

Southern Tier Capital Corp.
Irving Brizel, President
55 S. Main St.
Liberty 12754
(914) 292-3030
SBIC   A*2, 4, 9, 12

Sprout Capital Corp.
L. Robert Johnson, President
140 Broadway
New York 10005
(212) 943-0300
SBIC   D***1, 3, 5, 6, 8, 9

S & S Venture Associates, ltd.
Donald Smith, President
352 7th Ave.
New York 10001
(212) 736-2423

Tappan Zee Capital Corp.
Jack Birnberg, Exec. VP
120 N. Main St.
New City 10956
(914) 634-8890
SBIC   C**12

Taroco Capital Corp.
David Chang, Predsident
120 Broadway
New York 10271
(212) 964-4210
MESBIC   B 2, 4, 5, 6, 7, 8, 9, 10

Telesciences Capital Corp.
George E. Carmody, President
135 E. 54th St.
New York 10022
(212) 935-2550
SBIC   B***1, 8

TLC Funding Corp.
Phillip G. Kass, President
200 E. 42nd St.
New York 10017
(212) 682-0790
SBIC   B**1, 4, 5, 7, 9, 10, 11

Transportation SBIC, Inc.
Melvin L. Hirsch, President
122 E. 42nd St., 46th Floor
New York 10168
(212) 986-6050
MESBIC   A**11

Van Rietschoten Capital Corp.
Harvey Wertheim, President
230 Park Ave.
New York 10169
(212) 867-9535
SBIC   D***1, 3, 5, 6, 8

Vega Capital Corp.
Victor Harz, President
10 E. 40th St.
New York 10016
(212) 685-8222
SBIC   C*12

Venture SBIC, Inc.
Arnold Feldman, President
249–12 Jericho Turnpike
Bellerose 11426
(212) 343-8188
SBIC

Wachtung Capital Corp.
Thomas S.T. Jeng, President
111 Broadway, Rm. 2002
New York 10006
(212) 227-4597
MESBIC   A*2, 4

E.M. Warburg, Pincus & Co., Inc.
Robert S. Hillas, VP
Rodman W. Moorhead, III, VP
277 Park Ave.
New York 10172
(212) 593-0300

Welsh, Carson, Anderson & Stowe
Patrick J. Welsh, Russell L. Carson
45 Wall Street
New York 10005
(212) 422-3232
E***1, 3, 5, 6, 8, 12

J.H. Whitney & Co.
630 Fifth Ave.
New York 10111
(212) 757-0500

Winfield Capital Corp.
Stan Pechman, President
237 Mamaroneck Ave.
White Plains 10605
(914) 949-2600
SBIC   C*12

Wood River Capital Corp.
Richard M. Drysdale, President
767 Fifth Ave., 27th floor
New York 10053
(212) 750-9420
SBIC   D***1, 5, 6, 8, 12

North Carolina

Business Development Corp. of North
    Carolina, The
Gary M. Underhill, President
Box 10665, 505 Oberlin Road
Raleigh 27605
(919) 828-2331
D**5

Delta Capital, Inc.
Alex Wilkins, President
202 Latta Arcade
320 S. Tryon St.
Charlotte 28202
(704) 372-1410
SBIC   C***12

Heritage Capital Corp.
J. Randolph Gregory, President
2290 Jefferson First Union Plaza
Charlotte 28282
(740) 334-2867

Kitty Hawk Capital, Ltd.
Walter Wilkinson, President
2195 First Union Plaza
Charlotte 28282
(704) 333-3777
SBIC   B***1, 5, 6, 9, 12

Lowcountry Investment Corp.
(See main ofc: Charleston Heights, SC)
Vernon Ave.
Kinston 28659

Northwestern Capital Corp.
Clyde R. Brown, President
924 B St., Box 310
North Wilkesboro 28650
(919) 667-2111

Peat, Marwick, Mitchell & Co.
Edgar R. Wood, Jr., Ptnr.
1800 First Union Plaza
Charlotte 28282
(704) 372-4300

Vanguard Investment Co., Inc.
James F. Hansley, President
309 Pepper Building
Winston Salem 27101
(919) 724-3676
MESBIC   B*1, 5, 6, 11, 12

North Dakota

First Dakota Capital Corp.
David L. Johnson, VP
52 Broadway
Fargo 58102
(701) 237-0450
SBIC   A***12

Ohio

Aegis Group, The
John H. Kreinbihl, Exec. VP
Alan D. Johnson, Sr. VP
42 East Gay St.
Columbus 43215
(614) 463-1111

Banc One Capital Corp.
James E. Kolls, VP
100 E. Broad St.
Columbus 43215
(614) 461-5832

Capital Funds Corp.
Richard Berndt, Chief Investment Officer
127 Public Square
Cleveland 44114
(216) 861-4000

Clarion Capital Corp.
Peter Van Oosterhout, President
The Chesterfield
1801 E. 12th St., Rm. 201
Cleveland 44114
(216) 687-1096
SBIC   D***2, 3, 5, 12

Community Venture Corp.
Si Sokol, President
88 E. Broad St., Ste. 1520
Columbus 43215
(614) 228-2800

Dayton MESBIC, Inc.
Charles Jones, Secretary–Treasurer
40 W. 4th St.
Dayton 45402
(513) 223-9405

Dycap, Inc.
Mr. A. Gordon Imhoff, President
Ste. 1980, 88 E. Broad St.
Columbus 43215
(614) 228-6641
SBIC   A*1, 3, 6, 12

Evergreen Capital Corp.
(See main ofc: Houston, TX)
3 Commerce Park Square
23200 Chagrin Boulevard
Cleveland 44122

Fourth Street Capital Corp.
Robert H. Leshner, President
508 Dixie Terminal Building
Cincinnati 45202
(513) 579-0414

Glenco Enterprises, Inc.
Dr. Lewis F. Wright, Jr., VP
1464 E. 105th St.
Cleveland 44106
(216) 721-1200
MESBIC   A***12

Greater Miami Investment Service, Inc.
Emmett B. Lewis, President
3131 S. Dixie Drive, Ste. 505
Dayton 45439
(513) 294-6124
SBIC   A***5, 8

Gries Investment Co.
Robert D. Gries, President
2310 Terminal Tower Building
Cleveland 44113
(216) 861-1146
SBIC   B***12

Intercapco, Inc.
Robert B. Haas, Exec VP
One Erieview Plaza
Cleveland 44114
(216) 241-7170
SBIC   C***12

Miami Capital Corp.
Ken K. Feinthel, President
106 W. Ash St.
Piqua 45356
(513) 773-9777
B*12

National City Capital Corp.
Michael Sherwin, President
National City Center
1900 E. Ninth St.
Cleveland 44114
(216) 575-2491
SBIC   C***12

Scientific Advances, Inc.
Charles G. James, President
1375 Perry St.
Columbus 43201
(614) 424-6161
D***1, 5, 6, 8

SHV Investment Fund
Edwin T. Robinson, President
644 Linn St.
Cincinnati 45203
(513) 621-4014
D***3, 9, 10, 11

Tamco Investors SBIC, Inc.
Nathan H. Monus, President
375 Victoria Road, Box 1588
Youngstown 44501
(216) 792-3811
SBIC   A*9

Tomlinson Capital Corp.
Donald R. Calkins, VP
3055 E. 63rd St.
Cleveland 44127
(216) 271-2103
SBIC   A***12

Oklahoma

Activest Capital Corp.
George J. Recods, Chairman
6212 N. Western
Oklahoma City 73118
(405) 840-5597

Alliance Business Investment Co.
Barry M. Davis, President
500 McFarlin Building, 11 E. 5th St.
Tulsa 74103
(918) 584-3581
C***3, 5, 11, 12
(Branch ofc: Houston, TX)

American Indian Investment Opportunities,
    Inc.
James Wahpepah, President
555 Constitution St.
Norman 73069
(405) 329-3737
MESBIC

Bartlesville Investment Corp.
Mr. J.L. Diamond, President
Box 548
Bartlesville 74003
(918) 333-3022
SBIC   A***2, 3, 12

First Oklahoma Investment Capital Corp.
Gary Bunch, Sr., VP
Box 25189
Oklahoma City 73125
(405) 272-4338
SBIC   B***12

First Venture Corp.
Jon R.K. Tinkle, President
Venture Building, The Quarters
Bartlesville 74003
(918) 333-8820

Henderson Funding Corp.
C.A. Henderson, President
2629 NW 39th Expressway
Oklahoma City 73112
(405) 947-5746

Investment Capital, Inc.
James J. Wasson, President
300 N. Harrison, Box 1071
Cushing 74023
(918) 225-5850
SBIC   B*2

Oklahoma Capital Corp.
William T. Daniel, Chairman
2200 Classen Boulevard, Ste. 540
Oklahoma City 73106
(405) 525-5544
SBIC   A*6

Southwest Venture Capital, Inc.
Mr. D.J. Rubottom, President
1920 First Place
Tulsa 74103
(918) 583-4663
SBIC   A*8, 11, 12

United Business Capital, Inc.
Carl Sherman, Treasurer
1 E. Main, Box 322
Idabel 74745
(405) 286-7652

Utica Investment Corp.
David D. Nunneley, President
1924 S. Utica
Tulsa 74104
(918) 749-9976
SBIC   A***12

Oregon

Cascade Capital Corp.
Wayne B. Kingsley, VP
3018 First National Tower
1300 SW 5th Ave.
Portland 97201
(503) 223-6622
SBIC   D***12
(Main ofc: Northwest Growth Fund, Inc.,
    Minneapolis, MN)

First Farwest Capital Fund, Inc.
C.M. Armstrong, President
400 SW 6th Ave., Box 4162
Portland 97208
(503) 224-7740

Northern Pacific Capital Corp.
John J. Tennant, Jr., President
Box 1530
Portland 97207
(503) 245-3147
SBIC   B***5, 11

Washington Capital Corp.
1335 SW 5th Ave.
Portland 97201
(503) 243-1850
SBIC   D*12
(Main ofc: Seattle, WA)

Pennsylvania

Alliance Enterprise Corp.
Richard H. Cummings, Jr., President
2000 Market St., 2nd floor
Philadelphia 19103
(215) 972-4230
MESBIC   B***1, 5

American Venture Capital Co.
Knute C. Albrecht, President
Ste. 122, Blue Bell W.
Blue Bell 19422
(215) 278-8905
SBIC   B***12

Capital Corporation of America
Martin M. Newman, President
1521 Walnut St.
Philadelphia 19102
(215) 563-7423

Central Capital Corp.
Robert A. Rupel, VP
1097 Commercial Ave., Box 3959
Lancaster 17604
(717) 569-9650
SBIC   B*12

Cottman Capital Corp.
Richard Silva, President
575 Virginia Ave.
Fort Washington 19034
(215) 628-9540
MESBIC

Equilease Capital Corp.
(See main ofc: New York, NY)
1 Parkway Center, Rm. 213
Pittsburgh 15222

Fidelity America SBIC
Howard I. Green, President
2 Penn Center Plaza
Philadelphia 19102
(215) 568-3550
SBIC

Greater Philadelphia Venture Capital Corp., Inc.
Wilson E. DeWald, VP
225 S. 15th St., Ste. 920
Philadelphia 19102
MESBIC   B***12

Osher Capital Corp.
Mr. L. Cantor, President
Wyncote House
Township Line & Washington Lane
Wyncote, PA 19095
(215) 624-4800
SBIC   C***5, 6, 8, 9, 10, 12

Pennsylvania Dev. Credit Corp.
Mr. C. Drew Moyer, Exec. VP
212 Locust St.
Harrisburg 17101
(717) 234-3241
SBIC   B***5

Pennsylvania Growth Investment Corporation
William L. Mosenson, President
1000 RIDC Plaza
Pittsburgh 15238
(412) 281-1403

Poole Capital Corporation
Henry F. Poole
19 S. Pine St., Box 887
Doylestown 18901
(215) 348-9810

Progress Venture Capital Corp.
Ira Wells, President
1501 N. Broad St.
Philadelphia 19122
MESBIC   A*12

Real Estate Capital Corp.
William J. Levitt, Jr., President
111 Presidential Boulevard
Bala Cynwyd 19004
(215) 569-4401

Sharon Small Business Investment Co.
H. David Rosenblum, President
385 Shenango Ave.
Sharon 16146
(412) 981-1500
SBIC

TDH Capital Corp.
Mr. J. Mahlon Buck, President
Box 234, Two Radnor Corporate Center
Radnor 19087
(215) 297-9787
SBIC   C***12

Puerto Rico

CREDI-I-F.A.C., Inc.
Manuel L. Prats, Investment Advisor
Banco Cooperativo Plaza, Ste. 1001
Ave. Ponce deLeon #623
Hato Rey 00917
(809) 765-0070
MESBIC   A*12

First Puerto Rico Capital, Inc.
Mr. Eliseo E. Font, President
52 McKinley St., Box 816
Mayaguez 00708
(809) 832-9171
MESBIC   B**12

North American Investment Corp.
Mr. Santiago Ruiz Betancourt, President
Box 1831
Hato Rey 00918
(809) 754-6177
MESBIC   B*1, 5, 9, 12

Venture Capital Puerto Rico, Inc.
Manuel L. Prats, President
Banco Cooperative, Ste. 602
Hato Rey 00917
(809) 751-8040/8138
MESBIC   A*12

Rhode Island

Industrial Capital Corp.
Mr. A.A.T. Wickerman, President
111 Westminster St.
Providence 02903
(401) 278-6770
SBIC   C***12

Narragansett Capital Corp.
Arthur D. Little, Chairman
40 Westminster St.
Providence 02903
(401) 751-1000
SBIC   E***1, 5, 6, 12

South Carolina

Carolina Venture Capital Corp.
Thomas H. Harvey, III, President
Box 3110
Hilton Head Island 29928
(803) 842-3101
SBIC   B*1, 2, 4, 7, 8, 12

Charleston Capital Corp.
Mr. I.J. Futeral, VP
Box 30895
Charleston 29407
(803) 723-6464
SBIC   A***2, 9, 10

Falcon Capital Corp.
Mona G. Sokol, President
100 Broad St.
Charleston 29401
(803) 723-8624
A*12

Floco Investment Co., Inc., The
Milton Picard, Chairman
Box 216
Scranton 29561
(803) 389-2731

Lowcountry Investment Corp.
Joseph T. Newton, Jr., President
4444 Daley St., Box 10447
(803) 554-9880

Reedy River Ventures
John M. Sterling, President
Box 8931
Greenville 29604
(803) 233-2374
SBIC   B***12

Tennessee

Capital Services & Resources, Inc.
Charles Y. Bancroft, Treasurer
5159 Wheelis
Memphis 38117
(901) 761-2156
MESBIC   D*1, 4, 5, 6, 9, 11, 12

Chickasaw Capital Corp.
Wayne J. Haskins, President
Box 387, 67 Madison
Memphis 38147
(901) 523-6404
MESBIC   A**12

C & C Capital Corp.
Mr. T. Wendell Holliday, President
531 S. Gay St., 14th floor
Knoxville 37901
(615) 637-0521
SBIC   A***12

Financial Resources, Inc.
Milton C. Picard, Chairman
Ste. 2800, Sterick Building
Memphis 38117
(901) 761-3410
SBIC   A*12

Tennessee Equity Capital Corp.
Richard Kantor, President
4515 Poplar Ave., Ste. 222
Memphis 38117
(901) 761-3410
MESBIC   E***12

Texas

Alliance Business Investment Co.
Leon Davis, Chairman
2660 South Tower, Pennzoil Place
Houston 77002
(713) 224-6611
SBIC   C***3, 5, 11, 12
(Main ofc: Tulsa, OK)

Allied Bancshares Capital Corp.
D. Kent Anderson, President
808 Travis
Houston 77002
(713) 224-6611
SBIC   C*3, 5, 10, 12

Bow Lane Capital Corp.
Stuart Schube, President
2411 Fountainview, Ste. 250
Houston 77079
(713) 977-8882
SBIC   D***12

Brittany Capital Corp.
Robert E. Clements, President
2424 LTV Tower
Dallas 75201
(214) 742-8810
SBIC   A***1, 3, 6, 8

Cameron Financial Corp.
A. Baker Duncan, President
1410 Frost Bank Tower
San Antonio 78205
(512) 223-9768

Capital Marketing Corp.
Nathaniel Gibbs, Chairman
9004 Ambassador Row, Box 225293
Dallas 75222
(214) 638-1913
SBIC   D**9

Central Texas SBI Corp.
Walter G. Lacy, Jr., President
Box 829
Waco 76703
(817) 753-6461

CSC Capital Corp.
William R. Thomas, President
12900 Preston Road, Ste. 700
Dallas 75230
(214) 233-8242
SBIC   C***1, 3, 5, 6, 8, 9, 11, 12

Dallas Business Capital Corp.
Edgar S. Meredith, Sr., VP
5646 Milton St.
Dallas 75206
(214) 691-0711

Diman Financial Corp.
David S. Willis, President
13601 Preston Road, 717E
Dallas 75240
(214) 233-7610
SBIC   A*2, 3, 5, 8

Energy Assets, Inc.
Mr. L.E. Simmons, VP
1800 S. Tower, Pennzoil Place
Houston 77002
(713) 236-9999
SBIC   A*3

Energy Capital Corp.
Herbert F. Poyner, Jr., President
953 Esperson Building
Houston 77002
(713) 236-0006
SBIC   E*3

Enerpex Corp.
Norman J. Singer, President
One Houston Cir., Ste. 1506
Houston 77002
(713) 759-1522
C**3, 8

Enterprise Capital Corp.
Paul Z. Brochstein, President
4635 Southwest Freeway
Houston 77040
(713) 626-7171
C*2, 5, 12

Evergreen Capital Corp.
Jeffrey Garvey, Exec. VP
7700 San Felipe
Houston 77063
(713) 783-5003

First Bancorp Capital, Inc.
George F. Baum, Jr., President
100 N. Main St., Box 613
Corsicana 75110
(214) 874-4711

First Business Investment Corp.
Albert J. Prevot, President
1508 Niels Esperson Building
Houston 77002
(713) 225-1027

First Capital Corp.
John R. Payne, President
7100 Grapevine Highway, Ste. 105
Fort Worth 76118
(817) 284-0166

First City Capital Corp.
William E. Ladin, President
One West Loop S., Ste. 809
Houston 77027
(713) 623-6151
SBIC   A***12

First Dallas Capital Corp.
Eric C. Neuman, President
Box 83385
Dallas 75283
(214) 744-8050
SBIC   D***1, 3, 5, 11

First Texas Investment Co.
Lynn D. Rowntree, President
2700 S. Post Oak, Ste. 250
Houston 77056
(713) 629-5512
A***2, 5, 8, 9, 10, 12

Great American Capital Investors
Albert Dillard, President
1006 Holliday
Wichita Falls 76301
(817) 322-5554
SBIC   A***12

The Grocers SBIC
Milton Levit, President
3131 E. Holcombe Boulevard
Houston 77021
(713) 747-7913
SBIC A**9

Hixon Venture Co.
Michael Bell, President
341 Milam Building
San Antonio 78205
(512) 225-3053

Hixon Venture Co.
J.E. McAleer, VP
709-E Mockingbird Towers
1341 West Mockingbird Lane
Dallas 75247
(214) 634-1544

Livingston Capital, Ltd.
J. Livingston Kosberg, President
5701 Woodway
Houston 77057
(713) 977-4040
SBIC D***12

Mapleleaf Capital Corp.
Edward B. Scott, President
7500 San Felipe, Ste. 100
Houston 77063
(713) 975-8060
SBIC D**3, 8

Mercantile Dallas Corp.
J. Wayne Gaylord, Sr., VP
Box 222090
Dallas 75222
(214) 741-1469
SBIC E*3, 5, 12

MESBIC Financial Corp. of Dallas
Walter W. Durham, President
7701 N. Stemmons Freeway, Ste. 850
Dallas 75247
(214) 637-0445
MESBIC C***12

MESBIC Financial Corp. of Houston
Richard Rothfeld, President
717 Travis, Ste. 600
Houston 77061
(713) 228-8321
MESBIC B*12

MESBIC of San Antonio, Inc.
William A. Fagan, Jr.
2300 W. Commerce
San Antonio 78207
(512) 225-4241
MESBIC A***1, 4, 5, 11

Permian Basin Capital Corp.
Douglas B. Henson, President
303 W. Wall, Box 1599
Midland 79702
(915) 685-2000
SBIC A***5, 12

Rainbow Capital Corp.
Mr. W.A. Anderson, Jr., President
1470 One Allen Cir.
Houston 77002
(713) 757-0461
SBIC A*2, 3, 5, 11

Red River Ventures, Inc.
Thomas H. Schnitzius, President
2050 Houston Natural Gas Building
Houston 77002
(713) 658-9806
SBIC B***1, 3, 5, 6

Republic Venture Group, Inc.
Robert H. Wellborn, VP
Box 225961
Dallas 75265
(214) 653-5078
SBIC D***12

Retail Capital Corp.
William J. Broschma, President
13403 Northwest Freeway, Ste. 160
Houston 77040
(713) 462-8517
SBIC A**9

Rice Country Capital, Inc.
William H. Harrison, Jr., President
100 Commerce, Box 215
Eagle Lake 77434
(713) 234-2506
SBIC   A*12

Rice Investment Co.
Alvin Diamond, Secretary
3200 Produce Row
Houston 77021
(713) 652-2015

Rust Capital, Ltd.
Jeffrey C. Garvey, Exec. VP
605 Brazos, Ste. 300
Austin 78701
(512) 479-0055
SBIC   C*1, 5, 12

San Antonio Venture Group, Inc.
William A. Fagan, Jr., President
2300 W. Commerce
San Antonio 78207
(512) 223-3633
SBIC   A***1, 3, 4, 5, 6, 11

SBIC of Houston, The
William E. Ladin, President
1510 Niels Esperson Building
Houston 77002
(713) 223-5337
SBIC   A*12

Southern Orient Capital Corp.
Mr. Min-Hsiung Liang, President
2419 Fannin, #200
Houston 77002
(713) 225-3369
MESBIC   A*12

Southwestern Venture Capital of Texas, Inc.
Mr. J.A. Bettersworth, President
113 S. River St., Ste. 108, LaPlaza Building
Seguin 78155
(512) 379-2258
SBIC   B*2, 3, 5, 12

South Texas SBIC
Arthur E. Buckert, Treasurer
120 S. Main St., Box 1698
Victoria 77091
(512) 573-5151
SBIC

Texas Capital Corp.
W. Grogan Lord, Chairman
2424 Houston Natural Gas Building
Houston 77002
(713) 658-9961
SBIC   C***12

Trammell Crow Investment Company
Henry Billingsley, President
2001 Bryan Tower, #3900
Dallas 75201
(214) 747-0643
SBIC   A*12

TSM Corp.
Joe Justice
444 Executive Center Boulevard, Ste. 237
El Paso 79902
(915) 533-6375
SBIC   A*12

West Central Capital Corp.
Howard W. Jacob, President
440 Northlake Ctr., Ste. 206
Dallas 75238
(214) 348-3969
SBIC   A***2, 4, 5, 6, 12

Zenith Capital Corp.
Andrew L. Johnston, Secretary–Treasurer
5150 N. Shepherd, Ste. 218
Houston 77018
(713) 692-6121
SBIC   A*12

Vermont

Mansfield Capital Corp.
Stephen H. Farrington, President
Box 986, Mountain Road
Stowe 05672
(802) 253-9400
SBIC   A*2, 9, 11, 12

SBIC of Vermont, Inc.
Robert B. Manning, President
121 West St.
Rutland 05701
(802) 775-3393
SBIC

Vermont Investment Capital, Inc.
Harold Jacobs, President
Rte. 14, Box 84
South Royalton 05068
(802) 763-8878
SBIC   A*12

Virginia

East West Investment Co.
Doug Bui, President
6723 Whittier Ave., Ste. 206-B
McLean 22101
(703) 821-6616
MESBIC   A**4, 12

First Colonial Investment Corp.
M.G. Robertson, President
Pembroke Four, Virginia Beach Boulevard
Virginia Beach 23463
(804) 499-8201
MESBIC

Inverness Capital Corp.
Harry Flemming, President
424 N. Washington St.
Alexandria 22314
(703) 549-5730
SBIC   C***12

Lowry, Thetford & Associates
J. Scott Lowry, Ptnr.
211 The Strand
Alexandria 22314
(703) 836-4422
E***1, 5, 6, 8, 11, 12

Metropolitan Capital Corp.
Fred Scoville, President
2550 Huntington Ave.
Alexandria 22193
(703) 960-4698
SBIC   A***12

Nordyke & Associates, Ltd.
H. William Nordyke, President
8027 Leesburg Pike, Ste. 412
Vienna 22180
(703) 893-5800
D*12

Norfolk Investment Co., Inc.
Kirk W. Saunders, President
201 Granby Mall Building, Ste. 515
Norfolk 23510
(804) 623-1042
MESBIC   B*5, 9, 12

Professional Capital Corp.
Ronald E. Billes, President
1121 Arlington Boulevard
Arlington 22209
(703) 528-2844
MESBIC

Tidewater Small Business Investment Corp.
Robert H. Schmidt, Chairman
1106 Maritime Tower
234 Monticello Ave.
Norfolk 23510
(804) 627-2315
SBIC   B**5

Virginia Capital Corp.
Robert H. Pratt, President
Box 1493
Richmond 23212
(804) 644-5496
SBIC   B***12

Washington

Capital Designs, Ltd.
Dale H. Zeigler, President
1940 116th Ave., NE, Box 3500
Bellevue 98009
(206) 455-3037

Capital Resource Corp.
Theodore M. Wight, General Manager
1001 Logan Building
Seattle 98101
(206) 623-6550
SBIC   D***1, 5, 6, 7, 8, 12

Market Acceptance Corp.
Archie E. Iverson, President
1718 NW 56th St., Ste. B
Seattle 98107
(206) 782-7600

MESBIC of Washington, Inc.
Tukashi Mukai, General Manager
120 23rd Ave. E.
Seattle 98112
(206) 325-7633
MESBIC

Model Capital Corp.
Jerome Page, President
105 14th Ave.
Seattle 98122
(206) 447-3799
MESBIC

Northwest Business Investment Corp.
C. Paul Sandifur, President
929 W. Sprague Ave.
Spokane 99204
(509) 838-3111

Northwest Capital Investment Corp.
Dale H. Zeigler, General Manager
1940 116th Ave., NE, Box 3500
Bellevue 98009
(206) 455-3049
SBIC   D***12

Seafirst Capital Corp.
Steven G. Blanchard, VP and General
    Manager
Fourth & Blanchard Building
Seattle 98121
(206) 583-3278
SBIC   C*5, 9

Trans-Am Bancorp, Inc.
Harold T. Wosepka, President
3211 NE 78th St.
Vancouver 98665
(206) 574-4749

Washington Capital Corp.
James F. Aylward, President
David A. Kohls, VP
1417 Fourth Ave.
Seattle 98101
(206) 682-5400
SBIC   D*12
(Branch ofcs: OR, CA, WA)

Washington Capital Corp.
(See main ofc: Seattle)
North 920 Washington
Spokane 99201
(509) 326-6940
SBIC   D*12

Washington Trust Equity Corp.
Alan Bradley, President
Washington Trust Financial Center
Spokane 99210
(509) 455-4106
SBIC   C*12

Wisconsin

R.W. Allsop Capital Corp.
Gregory B. Bultman
815 E. Mason St., Ste. 1501, Box 1368
Milwaukee 53201
(414) 271-6510
SBIC   D***1, 5, 6, 12
(Main ofc: Cedar Rapids, IA)

Bando–McGlocklin Investment Co., Inc.
Salvatore L. Bando, President
13555 Bishops Crt., Ste. 225
Brookfield 53005
(414) 784-9010
SBIC   B**5, 9

Bankit Financial Corp.
Roy D. Terracina, Exec. VP
733 N. Van Buren St.
Milwaukee 53202
(414) 271-5050

Capital Investments, Inc.
Robert L. Banner, VP
515 W. Wells St.
Milwaukee 53203
(414) 273-6560

CERTO Capital Corp.
Howard E. Hill, President
6150 McKee Road
Madison 53711
(608) 271-4500
SBIC   A**9

MorAmerica Capital Corp.
H. Wayne Foreman, Reg. VP
Ste. 333, 710 N. Plankinton Ave.
Milwaukee 53203
(414) 276-3839
D***12
(Main ofc: Cedar Rapids, IA)

REC Business Opportunities Corp.
Duane Johnson, General Manager
316 5th St.
Racine 53403
(414) 637-8893
MESBIC

SC Opportunities, Inc.
Robert L. Ableman, VP and Secretary
1112 7th Ave.
Monroe 53566
(608) 325-3134
MESBIC   A***9

77 Capital Corporation
Sheldon B. Lubar, President
3060 First Wisconsin Center
777 E. Wisconsin Ave.
Milwaukee 53202
(414) 291-9000
SBIC   C*3, 5, 8, 12

Super Market Investors, Inc.
John W. Andorfer, President
Box 473
Milwaukee 53201
(414) 453-8200
SBIC   A**9

Wyoming

Capital Corp. of Wyoming, Inc.
Larry McDonald, Exec. VP
Box 612, 145 S. Durbin, Ste. 201
Casper 82602
(307) 234-5438
SBIC   A*12

COMMERCIAL CREDIT AND FACTORS

Among the 15,000 commercial banks in the United States (26,000, if we include all branch offices in the count) are myriad special divisions for factoring and otherwise servicing the financial needs of businesses, especially small businesses. There are also a number of finance companies, factoring companies, and other lending institutions organized especially to serve special financial needs of small businesses. The following listed institutions include commercial banks and many other financial service institutions who belong to a national organization, headquartered in New York City. The organization and its address is as follows:

National Commercial Finance
Conference, Inc.
One Penn Plaza
New York, NY 10001
(212) 594-3490
Leonard Machlis, Executive Director

Alabama

Amsouth Financial Corporation
Thomas J. Tucker, President
P.O. Box 2545
Birmingham 35202
(205) 326-5788

Arizona

The Budd Leasing Corporation
C.L. Gehring, Sr. Vice President
3003 N. Central Avenue, #1214
Phoenix 85012
(602) 264-4420

California

AVCO Commercial Corporation
John B. Patterson, Dir. Commercial
      Financing
620 Newport Center Drive
Newport Beach 92660
(714) 640-5200

Bank of the Orient
Thomas M. Chin, Vice President
233 Sansome Street
San Francisco 94104
(415) 781-6565

Bay Area Financial Corporation
Kenneth Pingree, Jr., Vice President
606 Wilshire Boulevard, Suite 604
Santa Monica 90401
(213) 451-8445

Business Loans, Inc.
Lawrence M. Kohn, President
1100 Glendon Avenue, Suite 759
Los Angeles 90024
(213) 824-5001

Commercial Funding
Alice E. DeLong, Secretary/Treasurer
1101 S. Robertson, Suite 101
Los Angeles 90035
(213) 273-3232

Commonwealth Financial Corporation
William F. Plein, President
3505 Broadway
Oakland 94611
(415) 658-4426

Crocker Commercial Services
Division of Crocker Bank
Robert R. Van Dyke, Sr. Vice President
595 Market Street
San Francisco 94105
(415) 477-8087

Financial Guild of America
Byron D. Hafner, President
5730 Uplander Way, Suite 103
Culver City 90230
(213) 641-9200

The Foothill Group, Inc.
John F. Nickoll, President
2 Century Plaza, Suite 600
2049 Century Park East
Los Angeles 90067
(213) 556-1222

Globe Business Credit, Inc.
Robert W. Brophy, President
480 Lytton Avenue
Palo Alto 94301
(415) 321-7170

Manalis Finance Company
Lowell B. Delbick, Partner
17141 Ventura Boulevard
Encino 91316
(213) 872-0193

Security Pacific Business Credit, Inc.
Barry I. Newman, Chairman of the Board
10089 Willow Creek Road
Scripps Ranch Business Park
San Diego 92131
(714) 587-6150

State Financial Corporation
Irving S. Reiss, President
100 Glendon Avenue, Suite 753
Los Angeles 90024
(213) 208-2200

U.S. Bancorp Financial
P. Anthony Yasiello, Executive VP
One Wilshire Building, Suite 2500
Los Angeles 90017
(213) 622-3820

Union Bank
Jack L. Myers, Sr. Vice President
445 S. Figueroa Street
Los Angeles 90071
(213) 687-6957

Washington Acceptance Corporation
I. William Zweben, President
1180 S. Beverly Drive
Los Angeles 90035
(213) 553-8595

Wells Fargo Bank
Peter F. Burns, Vice President
3130 Wilshire Boulevard
Los Angeles 90010
(213) 683-7173

Colorado

Seafirst Commercial Corporation
Charles Overson, President
Irongate Executive Plaza, Suite 102
777 South Yarrow
Lakewood 80226
(303) 989-6711

Connecticut

Barclays American/Business Credit, Inc.
James T. Verfurth, Executive VP
111 Founders Plaza
East Hartford 06106
(203) 528-4831

CBT Business Credit Corporation
(Affiliate of Connecticut Bank & Trust
    Company)
Paul Borden, President
100 Constitution Plaza
Hartford 06115
(203) 244-5223

Citytrust
Henry N. Kraver, Vice President
961 Main Street
Bridgeport 06602
(203) 384-5051

Colonial Business Finance Corp.
Joseph J. Gillooley, Jr., President
101 South Main Street
Waterbury 07620
(203) 574-7215

General Electric Credit Corp.
Robert E. Koe, VP and General Manager
260 Long Ridge Road
Stamford 06902
(203) 357-4540

Hartford National Bank & Trust Co.
Secured Lending Department
Arthur R. Beeman, III, Vice President
777 Main Street
Hartford 06115
(203) 728-2000

E.F. Hutton Credit Corporation
Harvey Leibowitz, Vice President
Greenwich Office Park I
Greenwich 06830
(203) 629-3025

Merchants Bank & Trust Company
Leonard R. Volpe, Vice President
59 Wall Street
Norwalk 06852
(203) 852-5507

Pitney Bowes Credit Corporation
Henry B. Vess, VP Marketing & Field
    Operations
72 Heights Road
Darien 06820
(203) 655-7761

State National Bank of Connecticut
Joseph Iannuccilli, First VP
One Atlantic Street
Stamford 06901
(203) 356-0499

Florida

Barnett Bank of Jacksonville, N.A.
John B. Logan, Vice President
100 Laura Street
Jacksonville 32202
(904) 791-7450

Southeast First National Bank of Miami
Robert E. Lerch, Jr., Vice President
100 South Biscayne Boulevard
Miami 33131
(305) 577-3198

Georgia

Citizens & Southern Financial Corp.
Charles S. Mitchell, Senior VP
33 North Avenue, NE
P.O. Box 4095
Atlanta 30302
(415) 491-4610

The First National Bank of Atlanta
William T. Deyo, Jr., Group Vice President
P.O. Box 4148
Atlanta 30302
(404) 588-5469

Trust Company Bank
J. Thomas Humphries, Sr. Vice President
P.O. Box 4955
Atlanta 30302
(404) 588-7711

Illinois

Albany Bank & Trust Co., N.A.
Joseph J. Briganti, President
3424 West Lawrence Avenue
Chicago 60625
(312) 267-0614

Associates Business Loans
Russell B. Donahue, Senior Executive VP
55 East Monroe Street
Chicago 60603
(312) 781-5858

Continental Illinois National Bank and Trust
    Company of Chicago
Commercial Finance Divsion
Philip M. Lewin, Vice President
231 South LaSalle Street
Chicago 60693
(312) 828-9080

Exchange National Bank of Chicago
Walter M. Macur, Senior VP
130 South LaSalle Street
Chicago 60603
(312) 781-8484

The First National Bank of Chicago
Joseph F. Guiffre, Vice President
One First National Plaza
Chicago 60670
(312) 732-3175

The Harris Trust & Savings Bank
Neal Elkin, Vice President
111 West Monroe Street
Chicago 60690
(312) 461-6580

National Acceptance Company of America
Frank R. Bergen, Vice President
105 West Adams Street
Chicago 60603
(312) 621-7500

Puritan Finance Corporation
Lawrence A. Sherman, President
One North LaSalle Street
Chicago 60602
(312) 372-8833

Kentucky

First National Bank of Louisville
Charles Reeves, Sr. Vice President
101 South Fifth Street
Louisville 40201
(502) 581-4200

Maryland

Commercial Credit Business Loans, Inc.
Frank J. Medeiros, President
300 St. Paul Street
Baltimore 21202
(301) 332-7963

The Finance Company of America
Louis Eliasberg, Jr., President
Munsey Building
Baltimore 21202
(301) 752-8450

The First National Bank of Maryland
William A. Quade, Jr., Senior VP
25 South Charles Street
P.O. Box 1596
Baltimore 21201
(301) 244-3709

Maryland National Affiliates Corp.
Alfred I. Puchner, President and CEO
120 East Redwood Street
Baltimore 21203
(301) 244-6740

Mercantile Safe Deposit & Trust Co.
Donald J. Trufant, Vice President
Two Hopkins Plaza
P.O. Box 1477
Baltimore 21203
(301) 237-5781

Massachusetts

Atlantic Corporation
Rubin Epstein, President
55 Court Street
Boston 02108
(617) 482-1218

Boston Financial & Equity Corp.
Adolf J. Monosson, President
P.O. Box 68, Kenmore Station
Bsoton 02215
(617) 437-1100

General Discount Corporation
Lawrence R. Seder, President
60 State Street, Suite 1800
Boston 02109
(617) 227-0900

JSA Financial Corporation
David E. Torrey, President
40 Court Street
Boston 02108
(617) 726-7100

New England Merchants National Bank
Leo R. Breitman, Senior VP
28 State Street
Boston 02106
(617) 742-4000

Shawmut Credit Corporation
William S. McLaughlin, President
One Federal Street
Boston 02110
(617) 292-3572

Worcester County National Bank
Judson J. Mohl, Vice President
446 Main Street
Worcester 01608
(617) 853-7342

Michigan

American Business Finance
Alfred F. Ryan, Senior VP
1190 First National Building
Detroit 48226
(313) 962-8600

Dimmitt & Owens Financial, Inc.
Clifford G. Dimmitt, President
3250 West Big Beaver Road
Troy 48084
(313) 643-6084

Minnesota

Banco Financial Corporation
John H. Olson, President
780 Northstar Center
Minneapolis 55402
(612) 372-7988

Diversified Discount & Acceptance
    Corporation
M.B. White, President
Northwestern Federal Building
Minneapolis 55403
(612) 339-8958

FBS Business Credit, Inc.
John E. McCauley, President
200 Soo Line Building
P.O. Box 522
Minneapolis 55480
(612) 370-4990

Industry Financial Corporation
J. Fred McCandless, Senior VP
444 Lafayette Road
St. Paul 55101
(612) 222-7792

Republic Acceptance Corporation
Fred (Bucky) Weil, Jr., President
P.O. Box 1329
Minneapolis 55440
(612) 333-3121

Missouri

ITT Commercial Finance Corporation
Melvin F. Brown, President
Suite 800, Community Federal Center
12555 Manchester Road
St. Louis 63131
(314) 821-7750

New Jersey

Chase Commercial Corporation
Stephen C. Diamond, President
560 Sylvan Avenue
Englewood Cliffs 07632
(201) 223-7006

Fidelity Commercial Finance Corp.
William J. Cardew, President
765 Broad Street
Newark 07101
(201) 676-6661

The First Jersey National Bank
Michael J. Palermo, Vice President
2 Montgomery Street
Jersey City 07303
(201) 547-7000

First National State Bank of New Jersey
Robert J. Corcoran, Vice President
550 Broad Street
Newark 07102
(201) 565-3705

Franklin Commercial
Division of Franklin State Bank
Thomas P. Smyth, Vice President
P.O. Box 293
Somerset 08873
(201) 745-6045

Heritage Commercial Finance Co.
Frank Sannella, Jr., President
Broadway and Cooper Streets
Camden 08101
(609) 964-2030

John J. McDermott Co., Inc.
John J. McDermott, Chairman of the Board
900 Route 9
Woodbridge 07095
(201) 750-0350

Midlantic Commercial Company
Division of Midlantic Banks, Inc.
A. Robert Lange, President
1455 Broad Street
Bloomfield 07003
(201) 266-8385, (212) 964-4478

Midlantic National Bank
Robert A. Klein, Senior VP
2 Broad Street
Bloomfield 07003
(201) 266-6110

The Trust Company of New Jersey
Robert J. Figurski, Vice President
33 Journal Square
Jersey City 07306
(201) 420-2808

New York

Abrams & Company, Inc.
Burton Abrams, President
400 Madison Avenue
New York 10017
(212) 355-4646

Ambassador Factors Corporation
George J. Colon, Senior VP
1450 Broadway
New York 10018
(212) 221-3000

Bank Hapoalim
Harris F. Epstein, Vice President
10 Rockefeller Center
New York 10020
(212) 397-9650

Bank Leumi Trust Company of New York
Harold Morrison, Vice President
1430 Broadway, 8th floor
New York 10018
(212) 832-5152

Bankers Trust Company
BT Factoring & Finance Division
Richard L. Solar, Vice President
1775 Broadway
New York 10019
(212) 977-6123

Brancorp Factors
Jack Lindner, President
1440 Broadway
New York 10018
(212) 840-2552

CBT Factors Corporation
Herbert A. Schattman, President
1040 Avenue of the Americas
New York 10018
(212) 944-1100

Century Factors, Inc.
Stanley Tananbaum, President
444 Fifth Avenue
New York 10018
(212) 221-4400

CF International, Inc.
Barry J. Essig, Executive VP
One Penn Plaza
New York 10001
(212) 239-7100

CIT Commercial Finance Co.
Vito "Vic" J. Ascatigno, Executive VP
650 Madison Avenue
New York 10022
(212) 572-6373

The Chase Manhattan Bank, N.A.
Frank J. Donahue, Vice President
1411 Broadway
New York 10018
(212) 223-7009

Chemical Bank, Factor and Finance Division
Andrew G. Tepper, Vice President
110 East 59th Street
New York 10011
(212) 750-7048

Citicorp Industrial Credit, Inc.
Frederick S. Gilbert, Jr., Executive VP
450 Mamaroneck Avenue
Harrison 10528
(914) 899-7540

Commercial Funding, Inc.
Alan A. Fischer, President
230 Park Avenue
New York 10017
(212) 661-4848

Commercial Trading Co., Inc.
Richard J. Tucker, President
1440 Broadway
New York 10018
(212) 840-8600

Congress Financial Corporation
Robert I. Goldman, President
1133 Avenue of the Americas
New York 10036
(212) 840-2000

European American Bank & Trust Co.
Eugene Campbell, Vice President
600 Old Country Road at Glen Cove Road
Garden City 11530
(212) 437-4652

FNB Financial Company
Gabe E. Romeo, Senior VP
Two Pennsylvania Plaza
New York 10001
(212) 239-1800

General Commercial Acceptance Co.
William T. Blumberg, Partner
2 Overhill Road
Scarsdale 10583
(914) 723-0857

Gibraltar Corporation of America
Herbert C. Hurwitz, Chairman
350 Fifth Avenue
New York 10001
(212) 868-4400

Hempstead Bank
George Stofsky, Vice President
40 Main Street
Hempstead 11550
(516) 560-2362

Walter E. Heller & Co.
Herbert E. Ruben Senior VP
200 Park Avenue
New York 10017
(212) 880-7154

Intercontinental Credit Corp.
Barry M. Weinstein, Vice President
2 Park Avenue
New York 10016
(212) 481-1800

Investors Lease Corporation
David J. Tananbaum, President
200 Park Avenue, Suite 228E
New York 10017
(212) 697-4590

Irving Factors Corporation
Joseph A. Grimaldi, President
One Penn Plaza
250 West 34th Street
New York 10001
(212) 239-5030

Irving Trust Company
Commercial Finance Department
Robert M. Grosse, Vice President
201 East 42nd Street
New York 10017
(212) 922-7100

William Iselin & Co.
Thomas A. Savage, President
357 Park Avenue South
New York 10010
(212) 481-9400

KB Business Credit, Inc.
John D. McCormick, President
450 Park Avenue
New York 10022
(212) 832-7200

Lazere Financial Corporation
Affiliated with Connecticut Bank & Trust Co.
Monroe R. Lazere, President
60 East 42nd Street
New York 10017
(212) 573-9700

Lincoln First Commercial Corp.
Robert E. Stark, Senior VP
1325 Franklin Avenue
Garden City 11530
(516) 248-1380

Manufacturers Hanover Commercial Corp.
Francis X. Basile, Executive VP
1211 Avenue of the Americas
New York 10036
(212) 575-7300

Marine Midland Bank-New York
Richard W. Parker, Senior VP
One Marine Midland Center
Buffalo 14240
(716) 843-2424

Meinhard-Commercial Corporation
Carroll G. (Peter) Moore
Vice President and General Counsel
9 East 59th Street
New York 10022
(212) 572-6346

Milberg Factors, Inc.
Leonard L. Milberg, President
99 Park Avenue
New York 10016
(212) 697-4200

The Mint Factors
Charlotte Mintz, Partner
215 Park Avenue South
New York 10003
(212) 254-2377

National Bank of North America
Commercial Finance Department
Austin Ludlow, Vice President
592 Fifth Avenue
New York 10036
(212) 730-6000

Nelson Capital Corporation
Irwin B. Nelson, President
591 Stewart Avenue
Garden City 11530
(516) 222-2555

Republic Factors Corporation
Robert S. Sandler, Executive VP
355 Lexington Avenue
New York 10017
(212) 573-5500

Rosenthal & Rosenthal, Inc.
Melvin E. Rubenstein, Executive VP
1451 Broadway
New York 10036
(212) 790-1418

The Slavenburg Corporation
Vincent P. Arminio, President
One Penn Plaza
New York 10001
(212) 564-8600

Standard Financial Corporation
Louis J. Cappelli, Executive VP
540 Madison Avenue
New York 10022
(212) 826-8050

Summa Capital Corporation
Howard A. Schulder, President
350 Fifth Avenue
New York 10018
(212) 244-1200

James Talcott Factors
William R. Gruttemeyer, President
1633 Broadway
New York 10019
(212) 484-0333

Textile Banking Co., Inc.
Joseph E. Mariani, President
51 Madison Avenue
New York 10010
(212) 481-3000

Todd Leasing Corporation
Robert L. Krause, President
350 Fifth Avenue, Suite 628
New York 10001
(212) 947-0505

Trefoil Capital Corporation
Gerald Blum, President
One Penn Plaza
New York 10001
(212) 736-3515

U.S. Capital Corporation
Martin Albert, President
525 Northern Boulevard
Great Neck 11021
(516) 466-8550

USI Capital & Leasing Corporation
Alphonse F. Fantuzzo, VP—Operations
733 Third Avenue
New York 10017
(212) 682-8500

United Credit Corporation
Leonard R. Landis, President
10 East 40th Street
New York 10016
(212) 689-9480

Webster Factors, Inc.
Alter Milberg, President
11 Middle Neck Road
Great Neck 10021
(516) 466-0200

Winfield Capital Corporation
Stanley Pechman, President
237 Mamaroneck Avenue
White Plains 10605
(914) 949-2600

Zenith Financial Corporation
Paul Singer, President
The Towers
111 Great Neck Road
Great Neck 11021
(516) 487-0320

North Carolina

Associates Commercial Corporation
Norris S. Griffin, Executive VP
400 South Tryon Street
Charlotte 28285
(704) 373-0466

Barclays American/Commercial, Inc.
Edward L. Boyd, President
201 S. Tryon Street, Box 31307
Charlotte 28231
(704) 372-8700

Colonial Acceptance Corp.
Charles G. Johnson, Executive VP
117 N. Main Street
P.O. Box 946
Mount Holly 28210
(704) 827-5853

First Factors Corporation
Earl N. Phillips, Jr., Executive VP
101 S. Main Street
P.O. Box 2730
High Point 27261
(919) 855-8055

First Union Caesar Corporation
James B. Wolf, President and CEO
First Union Plaza CORP-8
Charlotte 28288
(704) 374-6061

NCNB Financial Services, Inc.
Dan J. Crowley, President
1 NCNB Tower
P.O. Box 30533
Charlotte 28230
(704) 374-5087

Northwestern Bank
Business Finance Division
F. Gareth Beshears, Vice President
315 9th Street
P.O. Box 1347
North Wilkesboro 28659
(919) 667-2111

Southern National Financial Corp.
Preston L. Fowler, III, Executive VP
P.O. Box 33849
Charlotte 28233
(704) 377-5611

Wachovia Bank and Trust Co., N.A.
Richard J. Dorgan, Senior VP
P.O. Box 3099
Winston-Salem 27102
(919) 748-6201

Ohio

Beneficial Commercial Corporation
Ingo J. Kozak, Vice President
Holiday Park Towers, Suite 219
644 Linn Street
Cincinnati 45203
(513) 241-8822

Oklahoma

First Oklahoma Commercial Corp.
David H. Pendley, Senior VP
120 N. Robinson, Suite 1225 West
Oklahoma City 73125
(405) 272-4693

Oregon

First Interstate Commercial Corp.
Anthony E. Migas, President
1515 SW 5th Avenue, Suite 880
P.O. Box 1899
Portland 97207
(503) 225-7181

Northwest Acceptance Corporation
Frank J. O'Connor, President
Orbanco Building, 21st floor
1001 SW Fifth Avenue
Portland 97204
(503) 222-7920

Pennsylvania

Allegheny International Credit Corportion
Charles C. Maupin, President
One Allegheny Square, Suite 880
P.O. Box 6958
Pittsburgh 15212
(412) 562-4086

BA Commercial Corporation
Ronald P. Tweedy, President
1105 Hamilton Street
Allentown 18101
(215) 437-8265

Central Penn National Bank
John H. Van Dusen, Senior VP
Central Penn National Building
5 Penn Center Plaza
Philadelphia 19101
(215) 854-3900

Equimark Commercial Finance Co.
Gerard B. Knell, President
Equimark Bank Building
Two Oliver Plaza
Pittsburgh 15222
(412) 288-5010

The First National Bank of Allentown
William M. Holls, Jr., Vice President
645 Hamilton Mall
Allentown 18101
(215) 439-4548

Girard Bank
Walter Einhorn, Vice President
1 Girard Plaza
Philadelphia 19101
(215) 585-2160

Hamilton Bank
Robert A. Rupel, Vice President
P.O. Box 3959
Lancaster 17604
(714) 569-8731

Mellon Bank, N.A.
Alaric R. Bailey, Jr., Vice President
Mellon Square
Pittsburgh 15230
(412) 232-4100

PNB Commercial Finance Corp.
Alexander M. Gusdorff, Jr., President
1900 PNB Building
Philadelphia 19107
(215) 568-4604

Pittsburgh National Bank
Ronald L. Lambert, Vice President
P.O. Box 340700-P
Pittsburgh 15265
(412) 355-4922

Westinghouse Credit Corporation
Sylvan N. Mack, Manager Commercial
    Finance
650 Smithfield Street
Pittsburgh 15222
(412) 255-4140

Rhode Island

Old Stone Bank
James V. Rosati, Vice President
150 South Main Street
Providence 02901
(401) 278-2000

Rhode Island Hospital Trust National Bank
David F. Wall, Vice President
One Hospital Trust Plaza
Providence 02903
(401) 278-8391

Tennessee

First American Commercial Finance, Inc.
Charles McMahan, President
First Amtenn Center
Nashville 37237
(615) 748-2607

First Tennessee Bank, N.A. Memphis
Commercial Finance Division
Joseph D. Hardesty, Jr., Vice President
165 Madison Avenue
P.O. Box 84
Memphis 38101
(901) 523-4633

General Innkeeping Acceptance Corp.
E. Tucker Dickerson, President
3760 Lamar Avenue
Memphis 38195
(901) 362-4426

Union Planters National Bank
H. Morgan Brookfield III, Vice President
P.O. Box 387
Memphis 38147
(901) 523-6848

Texas

Armco Industrial Credit Corp.
David C. Schad, President
225 LBJ Business Park
2995 LBJ Freeway
Dallas 75234
(214) 247-7044

Capital Commercial Finance Corporation
John H. Ray, Jr., President and CEO
1801 Main Street, Suite 300
P.O. Box 2524
Houston 77001
(713) 658-8658

First City Financial Corporation
Lawrence C. Blanton, President
1111 Fannin
Houston 77002
(713) 658-6724

First National Bank in Dallas
Stephen Fisher, Senior VP
P.O. Box 83711
Dallas 75283
(214) 744-7238

KBK Financial, Inc.
Doyle Kelley, President
P.O. Box 61463
Houston 77208
(713) 224-4791

Mercantile Texas Credit Corp.
Ray G. Torgerson, President
2100 Mercantile Commerce Building
1712 Commerce Street
Dallas 75201
(214) 698-5719

Metro Factors, Inc.
Henry G. Wichmann, President
Royal Center Tower, Suite 216
11300 North Central Expressway
Dallas 75234
(214) 363-4557

Miller, Martin and Company
Richard Miller, President
2677 First International Building
P.O. Box 328
Dallas 75221
(214) 748-8373

Wells Fargo Business Credit
Thomas D. Drennan, President
12700 Park Central Drive, Suite 505
Dallas 75251
(214) 386-5997

Utah

Asset Funding Incorporated
Thomas Tony "Tom" Christopulos, President
57 West 200 South, #501
Salt Lake City 84101
(801) 521-6550

M.B.C.H., Inc.
Randy J. Bushnell, Senior VP
4590 Harrison Boulevard
Ogden 84403
(801) 394-3431

Virginia

Bank of Virginia
Harold F. Stierhoff, Senior VP
11011 West Broad Street Road
P.O. Box 25970
Richmond 23260
(804) 771-7404

United Virginia Bank
John K. Sheranek, Vice President
P.O. Box 26665
Richmond 23261
(804) 782-5458

Wisconsin

First Wisconsin Financial Corp.
Frank R. Quinn, President
622 North Cass Street, Suite 200
Milwaukee 53202
(414) 765-4492

Lakeshore Commercial Finance Corp.
Lawrence R. Appel, President
610 North Water Street
Milwaukee 63202
(414) 273-6533

Marine National Exchange Bank of
    Milwaukee
Commercial Finance Division
Phillip C. Strobel, Vice President
111 East Wisconsin Avenue
P.O. Box 2033
Milwaukee 53201
(414) 765-3000

Canada

Accord Business Credit, Inc.
Gerald S. Levinson, Vice President
1440 St. Catherine Street West, Room 310
Montreal, Quebec H3G 1R8
(514) 866-2711

Aetna Financial Services, Ltd.
Denis G. Higgins, President
4150 St. Catherine Street West
Montreal, Quebec H3Z 1X8
(514) 935-8585

Bank of Montreal
Current Asset Finance Division
19th Floor, First Canadian Place
King Street
Toronto, Ontario M5X 1G6
(416) 867-5313

Mirabel Factors Corporation, Inc.
Danny Aronoff, President
50 Cremazie West, Suite 811
Montreal, Quebec H2P 1A6
(514) 382-2000

Mexico

Factoring Banamex, S.A. DE C.V.
Oscar H. Castro, General Director
Av. Insurgentes Sur No 1189-90
Piso
Mexico D.F. 12
Tel. 559-5688

FOUNDATIONS

A foundation is a nonprofit organization (ordinarily incorporated as such) established by a company or wealthy individual to make grants, loans, and render other assistance for what the foundation deems to be worthy causes. Foundations are usually oriented toward some specific sphere, and in that sphere will provide funds for scholarships, fellowships, ventures, research, and other activities believed to be in furtherance of the foundation's purposes. Foundations are, in short, philanthropic institutions, usually endowed by extraordinarily wealthy individuals (such as John D. Rockefeller, Sr. and Andrew Carnegie), sometimes during their lifetimes, sometimes after their death, by bequests in their wills.

Although there are an estimated 30,000 foundations in the United States, many are quite small and were created primarily for the purpose of perpetuating a name or other such purpose — some, even, for the purpose of collecting funds for other purposes. Listed here are a number of those having substantial size (assets ranging over one-half million dollars, at least). Although most foundations do not limit their actions to their local geographic areas, it is always best to try those nearest you. Even when the nearest ones are not suitable for your needs, the staff can often suggest a more suitable foundation for you. However, there are some sources of information on what each foundation does — its programs and policies. These are open to the public without charge, and it is probably a good idea to visit one of these, if possible:

The Foundation Center
888 Seventh Avenue
New York, NY 10019

The Foundation Center
1001 Connecticut Avenue, NW
Washington, DC 20036

Donors' Forum
208 LaSalle Street
Chicago, IL 60604

The lists included here identify hundreds of foundations and trust funds located throughout the United States, but there are still many more whose names you can discover at the above information centers.

Note, in studying the following directory listings, that many foundations have been dedicated in the name of a private individual, while others are dedicated to philanthropies in the name of a business or industrial organization. In many cases, the same individual or organization has endowed more than one foundation, usually with a different charter or mission for each one.

Foundations tend to be most numerous in New York City, perhaps not surprisingly, but there are also many foundations in California, Texas, Ohio, Illinois, Massachusetts, Missouri, Wisconsin, Pennsylvania, and other populous and industrialized states or centers of commerce — essentially, wherever individuals and companies have amassed great wealth.

Where large corporations establish foundations, the mission of the foundation is typically directed towards fields related to the business of the corporation, although not necessarily. Andrew Carnegie gained his wealth in the steel industry, but is probably best known, as far as his philanthropies are concerned, for endowing many public libraries. It is therefore necessary to investigate any foundation you seek aid from to determine how they normally disburse their grants and gratuities, and what kinds of activities they seek to foster and encourage.

Foundations, government agencies, and many other institutions disburse billions of dollars annually in thousands of programs. With this amount of activity, change is constant, and the dynamics of the system have spawned a mini-industry: the maintaining and furnishing of accurate, up-to-date information on the institutions, their programs, and the current status of the various programs. Chapter 6 offers a bibliography of books and periodicals to assist you in this area.

Representative Sampling of United States Foundations

Alabama

The Mitchell Foundation
Box 1126
Mobile 36601

The William H. and Kate F. Foundation
Box 2592
Birmingham 35202

David Warner Foundation
Box 2028
Tuscaloosa 35401

Arizona

The Butz Foundation
RFD 1, Box 831
Prescott 86301

General Time Foundation
Box 13749
Phoenix 85002

Marshall Foundation
Box 3306
Tucson 85700

Arkansas

The Inglewood Foundation
1809 Beechwood Road
Little Rock 72207

The Murphy Foundation
Murphy Building
El Dorado 71730

The Donald W. Reynolds Foundation, Inc.
920 Rogers Avenue
Fort Smith 72901

Trinity Foundation
Box 7008
Pine Bluff 71601

California

Alameda County Community Foundation
Wells Fargo Bank
415 20th Street
Oakland 94604

Bank of America Foundation
Bank of America Center
San Francisco 94120

Bechtel Foundation
50 Beale Street
San Francisco 94119

The Mary A. Crocker Trust
233 Post Street, Suite 600
San Francisco 94108

Crown–Zellerbach Corporation
One Bush Street
San Francisco 94119

The Ernest Gallo Foundation
Box 1130
Modesto 95353

The Samuel Goldwyn Foundation
1040 N. Formosa Avenue
Los Angeles 90046

The William Randolph Hearst Foundation
Hearst Building
San Francisco 94103

The W.R. Hewlett Foundation
1501 Page Mill Road
Palo Alto 94304

Conrad N. Hilton Foundation
9990 Santa Monica Boulevard
Beverly Hills 90212

The Bob and Dolores Hope Charitable
    Foundation
10346 Moorpark Street
N. Hollywood 91602

The Henry J. Kaiser Family Foundation
300 Lakeside Drive
Oakland 94604

Foundation of the Litton Industries
9370 Santa Monica Boulevard
Beverly Hills 94104

North American Rockwell Corporation
    Charitable Trust
2300 Imperial Highway
El Segundo 90245

102 Foundation
500 East Commercial Street
Los Angeles 90012

The David and Lucille Packard Foundation
26580 Taaffe Avenue
Los Altos Hills 94022

John W. Porter Trust
Bank of America
120 East Fourth Street
Long Beach 90801

Price Foundation, Inc.
1314 N. Euclid Avenue
Upland 91786

The Simon and Virginia Ramo Foundation
9777 Wilshire Boulevard, Suite 915
Beverly Hills 90212

Riverside Foundation
5795 Palm Avenue
Riverside 92506

The Ellen Browning Scripps Foundation
Scripps Building, 525 C Street, Rm. 306
San Diego 92101

Foundation Funds of Norton Simon, Inc.
3440 Wilshire Boulevard, Suite 1216
Los Angeles 90005

Southern Pacific Foundation
One Market Street, Rm. 874
San Francisco 94105

Jules and Doris Stein Foundation
100 Universal City Plaza
Universal City 90036

The T.I. Corporation of California
    Foundation
433 S. Spring Street
Los Angeles 90013

Union Oil Company of California Foundation
461 S. Boylston Street
Los Angeles 90017

U.S. Motors Foundation
26 Harbor Island
Newport Beach 92662

Western Gear Foundation
Box 182
Lynwood 90262

Whittier Foundation
1300 W. Fourth Street
Los Angeles 90017

Colorado

The Denver Foundation
650 17th Street, Rm 808
Denver 80202

Gates Foundation
999 S. Broadway
Denver 80217

The Goodwin Foundation
Box 570
Grand Junction 81501

The Midwest Oil Foundation
1700 Broadway
Denver 80202

The Thatcher Foundation
Box 156
Pueblo 81002

Van Hummell–Howard Foundation
444 Sherman Street
Denver 80203

Connecticut

American Can Company Foundation
American Lane
Greenwich 06830

Concordia Foundation
Hartford National Bank & Trust Company
Hartford 06115

The Cuno Foundation
The Home National Bank & Trust Co. of
    Meriden
Meriden 06450

The Charles A. Dana Foundation, Inc.
Smith Building
Greenwich 06830

General Electric Foundation
1285 Boston Avenue
Bridgeport 06602

Koopman Fund, Inc.
17 Brookside Boulevard
W. Hartford 06107

The Maguire Foundation, Inc.
One Atlantic Street
Stamford 06901

The New Haven Foundation
One State Street
New Haven 06511

The Stone Trust Corporation
Box 1505A, Yale Station
New Haven 06510

United Aircraft Foundation
400 Main Street
E. Hartford 06108

R.T. Vanderbilt Trust
569 Sasco Hill Road
Southport 06490

The Wahlstron Foundation, Inc.
53 Ridgeway Road
Easton 06612

Delaware

The Carpenter Foundation, Inc.
9462 Nemoura Building
Wilmington 19898

The Christiana Foundation
1121 Wilmington Trust Building
Wilmington 19801

Eleutherian Mills–Hagley Foundation, Inc.
Box 3630, Greenville Branch
Wilmington 19807

Atwater Kent Foundation, Inc.
Box 1070, 100 W. 10th Street, Rm. 1008
Wilmington 19899

The Pren–Hall Foundation, Inc.
229 S. State Street
Dover 19901

The Ware Foundation
3908 Kennett Pike, Greenville
Wilmington 19807

District of Columbia

The Alvord Foundation
200 World Center Building
Washington 20006

John Edward Fowler Memorial Foundation
1025 Vermont Avenue, NW, Suite 400
Washington 20005

Frank R. Jelleff Charitable Trust
American Security and Trust Company
15th Street and Pennsylvania Avenue, NW
Washington 20013

The Kiplinger Foundation, Inc.
1729 H Street, NW
Washington 20006

Resources for the Future, Inc.
1755 Massachusetts Avenue, NW
Washington 20036

Guy T. Steuart Foundation
4646 40th Street, NW
Washington 20016

Florida

The Bay Branch Foundation
2737 E. Oakland Park Boulevard, Suite 202
Fort Lauderdale 33306

Conn Memorial Foundation, Inc.
1016 Wallace S. Building
Tampa 33602

Alfred I. duPont Radio Awards Foundation
The Florida National Bank of Jacksonville
Jacksonville 32203

The Poynter Fund
Box 625, 490 First Avenue South
St. Petersburg 33731

Rainforth Foundation
300 Ponce deLeon Boulevard
Coral Gables 33134

Winn–Dixie Stores Foundation
Drawer B. West Bay Station
5050 Edgewood Court
Jacksonville 32203

Georgia

Atlanta Foundation
Box 4148
Atlanta 30302

Metropolitan Foundation of Atlanta
1311 Healey Building
Atlanta 30303

Community Enterprises, Inc.
151 E. Main Street
Thomaston 30286

The James M. Cox Foundation of Georgia, Inc.
10 Forsyth Street, NW
Atlanta 30303

Crystal Foundation
Crystal Springs Textiles, Inc.
Chickamauga 30707

Franklin Fund, Inc.
First National Bank Building, 24th floor
Atlanta 30303

Rich Foundation, Inc.
45 Broad Street
Atlanta 30302

Hawaii

F.C. Atherton Trust
Box 3170
Honolulu 96802

Harold K.L. Castle Foundation
Kaneohe Ranch
Kaneohe, Oahu 96744

Charles M. and Anna C. Cooke Trust
Box 2634
Honolulu 96803

Mary D. and Walter F. Frear Eleemosynary
   Trust
Box 2390
Honolulu 96804

Idaho

The Margaret Cobb Alshie Trust, Inc.
119 N. 9th Street
Boise 83702

C.C. and Henrietta W. Anderson
   Foundation, Inc.
Box 7525, 200 N. 3rd Street
Boise 83707

Boise Cascade Corporation Foundation, Inc.
Box 200
Boise 83701

Laura Moore Cunningham Foundation
1109 Warm Springs Avenue
Boise 83702

Tarteling Foundation, Inc.
Box 1428
Boise 83701

Illinois

Abbott Laboratories Fund
1400 Sheridan Road
North Chicago 60064

The Allstate Foundation
Allstate Plaza F-3
Northbrook 60062

The Allyn Foundation, Inc.
120 S. LaSalle Street
Chicago 60603

Alsdorf Foundation
3200 W. Peterson Avenue
Chicago 60645

American Gage and Machine Company
   Foundation
853 Dundee Avenue
Elgin 60120

American National Bank and Trust Company
   of Chicago Foundation
LaSalle Street at Washington
Chicago 60690

Amsted Industries Foundation
3700 Prudential Plaza
Chicago 60601

The Aurora Foundation
32 S. Water Street
Aurora 60504

Blum–Kovler Foundation
500 N. Michigan Avenue
Chicago 60611

Borg–Warner Foundation, Inc.
200 S. Michigan Avenue
Chicago 60604

Boynton–Gillespie Memorial Fund
Box 245
Sparta 62286

The Bruning Foundation
1800 West Central Road
Mount Prospect 60058

Caterpillar Foundation
600 W. Washington Street
East Peoria 61611

The Centralia Foundation
Old National Bank
Centralia 62801

Chapin–May Foundation of Illinois
209 S. LaSalle Street, Suite 1150
Chicago 60604

The Chicago Community Trust
10 S. LaSallle Street
Chicago 60603

Chicago Title and Trust Company
    Foundation
111 W. Washington Street
Chicago 60602

Container Corporation of America
    Foundation
One First National Plaza
Chicago 60670

Continental Bank Charitable Foundation
231 S. LaSalle Street
Chicago 60690

The Cuneo Foundation
2242 S. Grove Street
Chicago 60616

John Deere Foundation
John Deere Road
Moline 61265

The A.B. Dick Foundation
5700 W. Touhy Avenue
Chicago 60648

Marshall Field & Company Foundation
111 N. State Street
Chicago 60690

First National Bank of Chicago Foundation
38 S. Dearborn Street
Chicago 60690

Robert W. Galvin Foundation
9401 W. Grand Avenue
Franklin Park 60131

Gardner–Denver Foundation
Gardner Expressway
Quincy 62301

Genesco Foundation
Central Trust & Savings Bank
Genesco 61254

The Hoover Foundation
Box 330
Glencoe 60022

Illinois Tool Works Foundation
8501 W. Higgins Road
Chicago 60611

International Harvester Foundation
401 N. Michigan Avenue
Chicago 60611

The Joyce Foundation
One N. LaSalle Street, Rm. 2901
Chicago 60602

The James S. Kemper Foundation
Mutual Insurance Building
Chicago 60640

Leslie Fund, Inc.
2600 N. Western Avenue
Chicago 60647

The Lumpkin Foundation
117 S. 17th Street
Mattoon 61938

Robert R. McCormick Chaitable Trust
435 N. Michigan Avenue
Chicago 60661

McGraw Foundation
333 W. River Road
Elgin 60120

Midas–International Corporation Foundation
33 N. Dearborn Street
Chicago 60602

The Moline Foundation
Moline National Bank
Moline 61265

Moorman Company Fund
1000 N. 30th Street
Quincy 62301

The Nalco Foundation
180 N. Michigan Avenue
Chicago 60601

The Northern Trust Company Charitable
    Trust
50 S. LaSalle Street
Chicago 60690

The Albert Pick, Jr. Fund
20 N. Wacker Drive
Chicago 60606

Polk Brothers Foundation
8311 W. North Avenue
Melrose Park 60160

Pullman Inc. Foundation
200 S. Michigan Avenue
Chicago 60604

The Quaker Oats Foundation
Merchandise Mart Plaza, Rm. 345
Chicago 60654

R.F. Foundation
130 East Elm Street
Sycamore 60178

The Sears–Roebuck Foundation
303 E. Ohio Street
Chicago 60611

The Siragussa Foundation
William S. Baltz
3800 Cortland Street
Chicago 60647

Square D Foundation
205 S. Northwest Highway
Park Ridge 60068

Staley Foundation
The Citizens National Bank of Decatur
Decatur 62525

Standard Oil (of Indiana) Foundation, Inc.
910 S. Michigan Avenue
Chicago 60680

Stilwell Foundation
715 W.C.U. Building
Quincy 62301

W. Clement and Jessie V. Stone Foundation
2720 Prudential Plaza
Chicago 60601

Swift and Company Foundation
111 W. Jackson Boulevard
Chicago 60604

Curt Teich Foundation
1733 W. Irving Park Road
Chicago 60613

United Air Lines Foundation
Box 66100
Chicago 60666

Victor Foundation
3900 N. Rockwell Street
Chicago 60618

Walgreen Benefit Fund
4300 Peterson Avenue
Chicago 60646

Wieboldt Foundation
29 S. LaSalle Street
Chicago 60603

Willkie Brothers Foundation
254 N. Laurel Avenue
Des Plaines 60016

Indiana

Associated Investment Company Foundation,
    Inc.
Associates Building
South Bend 46615

Ayres Foundation, Inc.
115 W. Washington Street
Indianapolis 46204

Ball Brothers Foundation
Ball Brothers Company
Macedonia Avenue South
Muncie 47302

Baxter Foundation
5676 N. Pennsylvania Street
Indianapolis 46220

Chicago Tile Supply Foundation
905 North West Boulevard
Elkton 46514

The EPH Foundation
Essex Wire Corporation
1601 Wall Street
Fort Wayne 46804

First Bank and Trust Company Foundation,
    Inc.
133 S. Main Street
South Bend 46601

Stanley W. Hayes Research Foundation, Inc.
Box 304
Richmond 47374

The Honeywell Foundation, Inc.
Box 432
Wabash 46992

The Indaianapolis Foundation
615 N. Alabama Street
Indianapolis 46204

Irwin–Sweeney–Miller Foundation
301 Washington Avenue
Columbus 47201

Liberty Fund, Inc.
3520 Washington Boulevard
Indianapolis 46205

Lilly Endowment, Inc.
914 Merchants Bank Building
Indianapolis 96204

The Lincoln National Life Foundation, Inc.
1301 S. Harrison Street
Fort Wayne 46801

The Martin Foundation, Inc.
500 Simpson Road
Elkhart 46514

Moore Foundation
6161 Crow's Nest Drive
Indianapolis 46208

Iowa

The Bohen Foundation
1716 Locust Street
Des Moines 50303

Gardner Cowles Foundation
Register and Tribune Building
Des Moines 50304

Kinney–Lindstrom Foundation
405 First National Bank Building
Mason City 50401

The Knalba Foundation
800 Paramount Building
Des Moines 50309

Wahlert Foundation
16th and Sycamore Streets
Dubuque 52001

Kansas

Cessna Foundation, Inc.
5800 E. Pawnee Road
Wichita 57218

N.W. Dible Foundation
9914 Oak Ridge Drive
Overland Park 66212

Garvey Foundation
300 West Douglas Street
Wichita 67202

The Mission Fund
5707 Oakwood Road
Shawnee Mission 66208

Kentucky

Appalachian Fund, Inc.
Box 2277, College Station
Berea 40403

Ashland Oil Foundation, Inc.
1409 Winchester Avenue
Ashland 41101

Courier–Journal and Louisville Times
    Foundation, Inc.
525 W. Broadway
Louisville 40202

Crounse Foundation
2626 Broadway
Paducah 42001

Highbaugh Foundation, Inc.
509 W. Market Street
Louisville 40202

Ralph E. Mills Foundation
Box 410, 414 Ann Street
Frankfort 40601

The WAVE Foundation, Inc.
Box 1000
Louisville 40201

Louisiana

The Callicott Foundation
Box 1511
Baton Rouge 70821

Coughlin Saunders Foundation, Inc.
Box 5485
Alexandria 71301

The Frost Foundation
Box 3387
Shreveport 71103

The Helis Foundation
912 Whitney Building
New Orleans 70130

Heymann–Wolf Foundation
1201 Canal Street
New Orleans 70112

Libby–Dufour Fund
Box 61540
New Orleans 70160

Six Foundation
521 Royal Street
New Orleans 70130

The Wheless Foundation
Box 1119
Shreveport 71102

Maryland

The A.S. Abel Company Foundation, Inc.
Calvert and Centre Streets
Baltimore 21203

The Baker–King Fund, Inc.
John T. King, II
27 Warrenton Road
Baltimore 21210

Commercial Credit Companies Foundation,
    Inc.
30 St. Paul Place
Baltimore 21202

The Allen Dickey Foundation, Inc.
W.J. Dickey & Sons, Inc.
Oella 21116

Fairchild–Hiller Foundation
William A. Jackson
Sherman Fairchild Technology Center
Germantown 20767

Giant Food Foundation, Inc.
6900 Sheriff Road
Landover 20785

The Hutzler Fund, Inc.
212 N. Howard Street
Baltimore 21201

S. Kann Sons Company Foundation, Inc.
2707 Lawina Road
Baltimore 21216

The Maryland National Foundation, Inc.
10 Light Street
Baltimore 21203

Middendorf Foundation, Inc.
309 Keyser Building
Baltimore 21202

Massachusetts

The Acushnet Foundation
Box 916
New Bedford 02742

American Optical Company Foundation
14 Mechanic Street
Southbridge 01550

Roger W. Babson Charitable Trust
Leonard Spangenburg
90 Broad Street
Babson Park 02157

The Boston Foundation
390 Commonwealth Avenue
Boston 02115

The Braitmayer Foundation
Box 122
Marion 02378

The Cambridge Foundation
99 Austin Street
Cambridge 02139

The Cornerstone Charitable Foundation
New England Merchants National Bank of
    Boston
28 State Street
Boston 02107

Fidelity Foundation
35 Congress Street
Boston 02109

The Gillette Charitable and Equitable
    Foundation
Paul G. O'Friel
Prudential Tower Building
Boston 02199

The Heald Foundation
10 New Bond Street
Worcester 01606

Henderson Foundation
892 Worcester Street
Wellesley 02181

Henry Hornblower Fund, Inc.
160 Franklin Street
Boston 02110

The Keystone Charitable Foundation, Inc.
50 Congress
Boston 02109

Edwin H. and Helen M. Land Foundation,
    Inc.
163 Brattle Street
Cambridge 02138

The Pilgrim Foundation
1106 Main Street, Rm 13
Brockton 02401

The Sheraton Foundation
470 Atlantic Avenue
Boston 02110

The United–Carr Foundation
4600 Prudential Center
Boston 02199

Warren Benevolent Fund, Inc.
Box 36
Ashland 01721

Michigan

Besser Foundation
150-B N. State Street
Alpena 49707

Burroughs Foundation
6071 Second Avenue
Detroit 48232

Chrysler Corporation Fund
341 Massachusetts Avenue
Highland Park 48231

Detroit Community Trust
The Detroit Bank and Trust Company
201 West Fort Street
Detroit 48231

Herbert H. and Barbara C. Dow Foundation
2301 West Sugnet Road
Midland 48640

Earhart Foundation
902 First National Bank Building
Ann Arbor 48108

Max M. and Marjorie S. Fisher Foundation,
    Inc.
2210 Fisher Building
Detroit 48202

Benson and Edith Ford Fund
1400 Buhl Building
Detroit 48226

Ford Motor Company Fund
The American Road
Dearborn 48121

Gerber Baby Foods Fund
405 State Street
Fremont 49412

Grand Rapids Foundation
780 Old Kent Building
Grand Rapids 49502

Harder Foundation
1580 First National Building
Detroit 48226

Herrick Foundation
2500 Detroit Bank and Trust Building
Detroit 48226

Hudson–Webber Foundation
1206 Woodward Avenue
Detroit 48226

Kalamazoo Foundation
7000 Portage Road
Kalamazoo 49001

W.K. Kellog Foundation
400 North Avenue
Battle Creek 49016

Augusta C. Kendall Foundation
707 Post Building
Battle Creek 49014

La-Z-Boy Chair Foundation
Box 149, 1284 N. Telegraph Road
Monroe 48161

The Greater Lansing Foundation
Box 300
Lansing 48902

The Loutit Foundation
Grand Haven 49417

The Lyon Foundation, Inc.
Box 858
Detroit 48231

Monroe Auto Equipment Company
    Foundation
Monroe 48161

Morley Brothers Foundation
115 N. Washington Avenue
Saginaw 48607

Charles Stewart Mott Foundation
500 Mott Foundation Building
Flint 48502

Plym Foundation
Star Building
Niles 49120

The Power Foundation
989 Forest Road, Barton Hills
Ann Arbor 48105

Whirlpool Foundation
North Shore Drive
Benton Harbor 49022

The Whiting Foundation
901 Citizens Bank Building
Flint 48502

Minnesota

Andersen Foundation
Andersen Corporation
Bayport 55003

The Andreas Foundation
Sheraton-Ritz Building
Minneapolis 55415

Baker Foundation
510 Baker Building
Minneapolis 55402

The Cargill Foundation
1200 Cargill Building
Minneapolis 55402

Central Exchange Foundation
1185 N. Concord Street
South St. Paul 55075

John and Elizabeth Bates Cowles Foundation
425 Portland Avenue
Minneapolis 55415

DeLuxe Check Printers Foundation
2199 N. Pascal Avenue
St. Paul 55113

Grain Terminal Foundation
1667 Snelling Avenue North
St. Paul 55101

Groves Fund
40 Washington Avenue South
Minneapolis 55401

Honeywell Funds
2701 Fourth Avenue South
Minneapolis 55408

The Hormel Foundation
Austin 55912

The Hubbard Foundation
3415 University Avenue, SE
Minneapolis 55414

Ingram Foundation
First Trust Company of St. Paul
322 Minnesota Street
St. Paul 55101

The Minneapolis Foundation
1020 Chamber of Commerce Building
15 S. 5th Street
Minneapolis 55402

Minnesota Mining and Manufacturing
Foundation, Inc.
3-M Center
St. Paul 55101

The Morse Foundation
Northwestern National Bank
7th Street and Marquette Avenue
Minneapolis 55402

Onan Family Foundation
403 Alworth Building
Duluth 55802

The Paulucci Family Foundation
525 Lake Avenue, South
Duluth 55802

The Phillips Foundation
700 Builders Exchange Building
Minneapolis 55402

The Southways Foundation
930 Dain Tower
Minneapolis 55402

Mississippi

Feild Company Operative Association, Inc.
405 First Federal Building
Jackson 39201

Missouri

American Investment Company Foundation
8251 Maryland Avenue
St. Louis 63105

Anheuser–Busch Charitable Trust
721 Pestalozzi Street
St. Louis 63118

Brown Shoe Company Charitable Trust
Box 354
St. Louis 63166

Butler Manufacturing Company Foundation
7400 E. 13th Street
Kansas City 64126

The Chance Foundation
210 N. Allen Street
Centralia 65240

Commerce Foundation
Box 248
Kansas City 63105

Emerson Electrical Manufacturing Company
Charitable Trust
8100 West Florissant Avenue
St. Louis 63136

Hallmark Educational Foundation
Box 437, 25th & McGee Trafficway
Kansas City 64141

Interco, Inc. Charitable Trust
1509 Washington Avenue
St. Louis 63166

The Jackes Foundation
11737 Administration Drive
St. Louis 63141

Mag Foundation
10 Main Center, Suite 2100
Kansas City 64105

Edward Mallinckrodt, Jr., Foundation
Second and Mallinckrodt Streets
Kansas City 64105

McDonnell Foundation, Inc.
Box 516
St. Louis 63166

Mercantile Trust Company Charitable Trust
721 Locust Street
St. Louis 63101

Monsanto Fund
800 N. Lindbergh Boulevard
St. Louis 63166

Nichols Company Charitable Trust
310 Ward Parkway, Country Club Plaza
Kansas City 64112

The Pillsbury Foundation
Box 187
St. Louis 63166

Ralston Purina Charitable Trust
835 S. Eighth Street
St. Louis 63102

Sachs Fund
5540 West Park Avenue
St. Louis 63110

St. Louis Union Trust Company Charitable
　　Trust
510 Locust Street
St. Louis 63101

Shoenberg Foundation, Inc.
314 N. Broadway, Rm 1210
St. Louis 63012

John S. Swift Company, Inc. Charitable Trust
2100 Locust Street
St. Louis 63101

Tension Envelope Foundation
819 E. 19th Street, 5th Floor
Kansas City 64108

Union Electric Company Charitable Trust
James J. Beisman
Box 87
St. Louis 63166

Montana

Fortin Foundation of Montana
Box 1555
Billings 59103

The Treacy Company
Box 1699
Helena 59601

Nebraska

The Bay State Foundation
First National Bank
Mitchell 69357

Cooper Foundation
325 Stuart Building
Lincoln 68508

Kiewit Foundation
The Omaha National Bank
1620 Farnam Street
Omaha 68102

The Lincoln Foundation, Inc.
215 S. 15th Street, Rm. 108
Lincoln 68410

The Steinhart Foundation, Inc.
Nebraska City 68410

Nevada

Alexander Dawson Foundation
Box 2714
Las Vegas 89104

Max C. Fleischmann Foundation
Box 1871, 195 S. Sierra Street
Reno 89505

New Hampshire

The Barker Foundation, Inc.
Box 328
Nashua 03060

Cogswell Benevolent Trust
875 Elm Street
Manchester 03101

Putnam Foundation
Box 323
Keene 03431

The Spaulding–Potter Charitable Trust
95 N. Main Street
Concord 03301

New Jersey

The Atlantic Foundation
501 George Street
New Brunswick 08903

The Bergen Evening Record Fund
150 River Street
Hackensack 07602

Bristol–Myers Fund
225 Long Avenue
Hillside 07205

The Brook Foundation, Inc.
Box 263
Orange 07051

The Emil Buehler Foundation, Inc.
207 Union Street
Hackensack 07601

Campbell Soup Fund
375 Memorial Avenue
Camden 08101

Russell Colgate Fund, Inc.
15 Exchange Place
Jersey City 07302

The Fidelity Union Foundation
765 Broad Street
Newark 07102

Freas Foundation, Inc.
75 Chestnut Ridge Road
Montvale 07645

The Hoffman–LaRoche Foundation
Box 278
Nutley 07110

The Hoyt Foundation
Half-Acre Road
Cranbury 08512

The Huber Foundation
Box 414
Rumson 07760

The International Foundation
Box 101
Englewood 07631

Robert Wood Johnson Foundation
142 Livingston Avenue
New Brunswick 08902

The Large Foundation
117 Main Street
Flemington 08822

The Lindberg Foundation
General Drafting Company, Inc.
Convent Station 07961

Thomas J. Lipton Foundation, Inc.
800 Sylvan Avenue
Englewood Cliffs 07632

The Merck Company Foundation
Rahway 07065

The Newspaper Fund, Inc.
Box 300
Princeton 08540

The Plainfield Foundation
202 Park Avenue
Plainfield 07061

The Rogosin Foundation
115 Spier Avenue
Allenhurst 07711

Turrell Fund
15 S. Main Avenue
East Orange 07018

Vahlsing Foundation, Inc.
550 Broad Street, Rm. 1601
Newark 07102

The Willits Foundation
731 Central Avenue
Murray Hill 07974

New Mexico

The Helene Wurlitzer Foundation of New
    Mexico
Box 545
Taos 87571

New York

ASAR Company Foundation
120 Broadway
New York 10005

The Abelard Foundation, Inc.
575 Madison Avenue
New York 10022

The Aeroflex Foundation
560 W. 42nd Street
New York 10036

Agric Development Council, Inc.
630 Fifth Avenue
New York 10020

Ailborn Foundation, Inc.
29 W. 53rd Street
New York 10019

Allen Foundation
30 Broad Street
New York 10004

Allied Chemical Foundation
1411 Broadway
New York 10018

Allied Stores Foundation, Inc.
401 Fifth Avenue
New York 10016

Allyn Foundation, Inc.
Box 22
Skanateales 13152

Altman Foundation
361 Fifth Avenue
New York 10016

American Airlines Foundation
633 Third Avenue
New York 10017

American Conservation Association, Inc.
30 Rockefeller Plaza, Rm. 5425
New York 10020

American Metal Climax Foundation, Inc.
1270 Avenue of the Americas
New York 10020

The Vincent Astor Foundation
320 Park Avenue
New York 10022

The Atlantic Richfield Foundation
717 Fifth Avenue
New York 10022

Axe–Houghton Foundation
320 Park Avenue
New York 10022

H.L. Bache Foundation
100 Gold Street, 5th floor
New York 10038

The Baird Foundation
Box 55, Station B
Buffalo 14207

Banbury Fund, Inc.
100 Wall Street
New York 10005

Bankers Trust Company Foundation Trust
280 Park Avenue
New York 10017

The Theodore H. Barth Foundation, Inc.
530 Fifth Avenue
New York 10036

Irving Berlin Charitable Funds, Inc.
T. Newman Lawler
500 Fifth Avenue
New York 10036

Sara J. Bloomingdale Foundation
641 Lexington Avenue, 29th floor
New York 10022

The Samuel Bronfman Foundation, Inc.
375 Park Avenue
New York 10022

The Brokdale Foundation
110 E. 42nd Street
New York 10017

Bruner Foundation, Inc.
60 E. 42nd Street
New York 10017

The Buffalo Foundation
812 Genessee Building
Buffalo 14202

CBS Foundation, Inc.
51 W. 52nd Street
New York 10019

The C.I.T. Foundation, Inc.
650 Madison Avenue
New York 10022

Caritas Fund
Nathaniel Field & Company
521 Fifth Avenue
New York 10017

Carnegie Corporation of New York
437 Madison Avenue
New York 10022

Carrier Corporation Foundation, Inc.
Carrier Parkway
Syracuse 13201

Chase Manhattan Bank Foundation
1 Chase Manhattan Plaza
New York 10005

Cities Service Foundation
70 Pine Street
New York 10005

The Clark Foundation
30 Wall Street
New York 10005

The Coe Foundation
225 East 57th Street
New York 10022

The Coleman Foundation
551 Fifth Avenue
New York 10022

The Cole Foundation
983 Park Avenue
New York 10028

The Commonwealth Fund
1 East 75th Street
New York 10021

The Continental Corporation Foundation
80 Maiden Lane
New York 10038

Corning Glass Works Foundation
Corning 14830

The Cowles Charitable Trust
Cowles Communications, Inc.
488 Madison Avenue
New York 10022

Crouse–Hinds Foundation, Inc.
Wolf and Seventh North Streets
Syracuse 13201

Crowell, Collier and Macmillan
866 Third Avenue
New York 10022

Deering Milliken Foundation
1045 Avenue of the Americas
New York 10018

Dun & Bradstreet Foundation, Inc.
99 Church Street
New York 10007

Eastman Kodak Charitable Trust
343 State Street
Rochester 14650

Esso Education Foundation
49 West 49th Street
New York 10020

First National City Bank Foundation
399 Park Avenue
New York 10022

The Ford Foundation
320 East 43rd Street
New York 10017

Foundation for the Needs of Others, Inc.
1 Wall Street, Suite 4100
New York 10005

Frank C. Gannett Newspaper Foundation,
Inc.
55 Exchange Place
Rochester 14614

General Telephone and Electronics
Foundation
730 Third Street
New York 10017

Gibbs Brothers Foundation
Gibbs and Cox, Inc.
21 West Street
New York 10006

Gilman Foundation, Inc.
111 West 50th Street
New York 10020

Gimbel–Saks Foundation, Inc.
Gimbel Brothers, Inc.
1275 Broadway
New York 10001

The Glickenhaus Foundation
100 Dorchester Road
Scarsdale 10585

John Golden Fund, Inc.
274 Madison Avenue
New York 10016

Goldman Sachs Fund
55 Broad Street
New York 10004

The Grant Foundation, Incorporated
130 East 59th Street
New York 10022

The Griffis Foundation, Inc.
8 Hanover
New York 10004

The Grolier Foundation, Inc.
575 Lexington Avenue
New York 10022

The Handmacher Foundation, Inc.
533 Seventh Avenue
New York 10018

Haxton Fund, Inc.
Central Trust Co.
44 Exchange Place
Rochester 14614

The Hearst Foundation, Inc.
959 Eighth Avenue
New York 10019

Hendrickson Brothers Foundation, Inc.
63 N. Central Avenue
Valley Stream 11582

Hess Foundation, Inc.
51 West 51st Street
New York 10019

Heublein Medical Foundation, Inc.
Edward J. Ennis
8 West 40th Street
New York 10019

Hickrill Foundation, Inc.
40 Wall Street, Rm. 5814
New York 10005

High Wind Fund, Inc.
Byram Lake Road
Mount Kisco 10549

Holmes Foundation, Inc.
122 East 42nd Street, Rm. 3612
New York 10017

The Howard Foundation, Inc.
200 Petersville Road
New Rochelle 10801

International Paper Company Foundation
220 East 42nd Street
New York 10017

Irving One Wall Street Foundation, Inc.
1 Wall Street
New York 10015

The Ivy Fund, Inc.
65 Broadway, Rm. 1921
New York 10006

The Knapp Fund, Inc.
460 Park Avenue, 14th floor
New York 10022

Samuel H. Kress Foundation
221 West 57th Street
New York 10019

Kurtz–Deknatel Foundation
46 Woodmere Boulevard
Woodmere 11598

The Lapkin Foundation
320 Central Park West
New York 10025

Larsen Fund, Inc.
Time–Life Building, Rm. 3436
New York 10020

Esteé and Joseph Lauder Foundation, Inc.
767 Fifth Avenue
New York 10022

Leviton Foundation, Inc.
236 Greenpoint Avenue
Brooklyn 11222

The Levitt Foundation
Lake Success 11043

The Link Foundation
80 East 42nd Street, Rm. 301
New York 10017

Manufacturers Hanover Trust Company
    Foundation
350 Park Avenue
New York 10022

Manufacturers and Traders Trust Company
1 M&T Plaza
Buffalo 14240

Marine Midland Foundation, Inc.
241 Main Street
Buffalo 14203

The Martin Foundation, Inc.
26 West 56th Street
New York 10019

The Marx Foundation, Inc.
1407 Broadway
New York 10018

The Andrew W. Mellon Foundation
140 East 62nd Street
New York 10021

Mohasco Memorial Fund, Inc.
57 Lyon Street
New York 12010

Morgan Guaranty Trust Company of New
    York Charitable Trust
23 Wall Street
New York 10015

The National Lead Foundation, Inc.
111 Broadway
New York 10006

The New World Foundation
100 East 85th Street
New York 10028

The New York Community Trust
415 Madison Avenue
New York 10017

New York Foundation
4 West 58th Street
New York 10019

The New York Times Foundation
229 West 43rd Street
New York 10036

Nichols Foundation, Inc.
150 Williams Street
New York 10038

Norwood Foundation, Inc.
50 West 44th Street
New York 10036

Olin Foundation, Inc.
99 Park Avenue, 16th floor
New York 10016

Orentreich Foundation for the Advancement
    of Science, Inc.
909 Fifth Avenue
New York 10021

The Overbrook Foundation
730 Fifth Avenue
New York 10019

The Pinkerton Foundation
100 Church Street
New York 10007

The Pope Foundation
136 West 52nd Street
New York 10019

Price Waterhouse Foundation
60 Broad Street
New York 10004

The Prospect Hill Foundation, Inc.
The Sperry and Hutchinson Company
330 Madison Avenue
New York 10017

The Quaker Hill Foundation
J.P. Stevenes, Jr.
1460 Broadway
New York 10036

R.T.A. Incorporated
John B. Madden
59 Wall Street
New York 10005

Reader's Digest Foundation
Pleasantville 10570

The Reeves Brothers Foundation, Inc.
1071 Avenue of the Americas
New York 10018

Research Corporation
405 Lexington Avenue
New York 10017

The Robert Alan Foundation, Inc.
666 Fifth Avenue
New York 10019

The Rosenthal Foundation
17 East 49th Street, Rm. 905
New York 10017

Helena Rubinstein Foundation, Inc.
261 Madison Avenue
New York 10016

Soloman Brothers and Hutzler Foundation,
    Inc.
1 New York Plaza
New York 10004

The Sexauer Foundation
10 Hamilton Avenue
White Plains 10601

The Evelyn Sharp Foundation
700 Fifth Avenue
New York 10019

Shell Companies Foundation, Inc.
50 West 50th Street, Staff Office
New York 10020

Samuel S. Shubert Foundation, Inc.
234 West 44th Street
New York 10036

The Starr Foundation
102 Maiden lane
New York 10005

State Bank of Albany Foundation
69 State Street
Albany 12201

The Statler Foundation
Statler–Hilton Hotel, Suite 508
Buffalo 14202

The Stauffer Chemical Company Foundation
299 Park Avenue
New York 10017

Stern Fund
21 East 40th Street
New York 10016

J.P. Stevens and Company, Inc. Foundation
1185 Avenue of the Americas
New York 10036

The Surdna Foundation, Inc.
35 East 72nd Street
New York 10021

The Switzer Foundation
75 West Street, Rm. 808
New York 10006

Community Foundation of Syracuse and
    Onandaga County, Inc.
107 James Street
Syracuse 13202

Louis Comfort Tiffany Foundation
1083 Fifth Avenue
New York 10028

The Tinker Foundation
550 Park Avenue
New York 10021

Twentieth Century Fund, Inc.
41 East 70th Street
New York 10021

Uniroyal Foundation
1230 Avenue of the Americas
New York 10020

United Brands Charities, Inc.
245 Park Avenue
New York 10017

United States Trust Company of New York
45 Wall Street
New York 10005

van Amerigen Foundation, Inc.
509 Madison Avenue
New York 10022

W.U.I. Foundation, Inc.
26 Broadway
New York 10004

The Western New York Foundation
Main Place Tower, Suite 2300
Buffalo 14202

The Wheelan Foundation, Inc.
370 Seventh Avenue
New York 10001

The Fanny R. and Grace K. Wurlitzer
    Foundation, Inc.
The Wurlitzer Company
North Tonawanda 14120

North Carolina

Mary Reynolds Babcock Foundation, Inc.
102 Reynolds Village
Winston–Salem 27106

The Belk Foundation
308 East 5th Street
Charlotte 20202

Blue Bell Foundation
355 Church Court
Greensboro 27401

Burlington Industries Foundation
Box 21207, 301 N. Eugene Street
Greensboro 27420

The Burroughs Wellcome Fund
3030 Cornwallis Road
Research Triangle Park 27709

The Cannon Foundation, Inc.
Box 467
Concord 28025

Carolina Steel Foundation
Box 21848
Greensboro 27420

Chatham Foundation, Inc.
Elkin 26621

The Dover Foundation, Inc.
Dover Mill Company
Shelby 28150

Hickory Community Foundation, Inc.
Box 350
Hickory 28601

Hilldale Fund, Inc.
Box 20124
Greensboro 27420

Myers–Textiles Foundation, Incorporated
Box 699
Gastonia 28502

Piedmont Publishing Company Foundation
Box 3099
Winston–Salem 27102

Salisbury Community Foundation, Inc.
Box 1377
Salisbury 28144

Ohio

Acme–Cleveland Foundation
170 East 131st Street
Cleveland 44108

The Allyn Foundation
2211 S. Dixie Avenue
Dayton 45409

Armco Foundation
703 Curtis Street
Middletown 45042

The Barnitz Fund
The Barnitz Bank
Middletown 45042

Champion Paper Foundation
Knightsbridge
Hamilton 45011

The Greater Cincinnati Foundation
1302 Gas and Electric Building, 4th and Main
    Streets
Cincinnati 45202

Cincinnati Milacron Foundation
4701 Marburg Avenue
Cincinnati 45209

Greater Cleveland Associated Foundation
700 National City Bank Building
Cleveland 44114

The Cleveland Electric Illuminating
    Foundation
Box 5000
Cleveland 44101

The Columbus Foundation
100 East Broad Street
Columbus 43215

The Corbett Foundation
1501 Madison Road, Suite 410
Cincinnati 45227

The Crosley Foundation
6609 Loiswood Avenue
Cincinnati 45224

Dana Corporation Foundation
4100 Bennett Road
Toledo 43601

The Davis Foundation
Box 1558
Columbus 43216

The Dayton Foundation
1785 Big Hill Road
Dayton 45439

Firestone Foundation
1225 West Market Street
Akron 44313

The General Tire Foundation, Inc.
1708 Englewood Avenue
Akron 44309

The B.F. Goodrich Fund, Inc.
500 S. Main Street
Akron 44316

Goodyear Tire and Rubber Company Fund
1144 East Market Street
Akron 44316

Gould Foundation
17000 St. Clair Avenue
Cleveland 44110

Charles F. Kettering Foundation
5335 Far Hills Avenue, Suite 300
Dayton 45429

Libbey–Owens–Ford Philanthropic
    Foundation
811 Madison Avenue
Toledo 43624

Lincoln Electric Foundation, Inc.
22801 St. Clair Avenue
Cleveland 44117

The Lubrizol Foundation
29400 Lakeland Boulevard
Wickliffe 44092

Marathon Oil Foundation, Inc.
539 S. Main Street
Findlay 45840

The NCR Foundation
Main and K Streets
Dayton 45409

Nationwide Foundation
246 N. High Street
Columbus 43216

The Needmor Fund
The Toledo Trust Company
245 Summit Street
Toledo 43603

The O'Neill Brothers Foundation
21111 Chagrin Boulevard
Cleveland 44122

The Perkins Charitable Foundation
401 Euclid Avenue, Rm. 480
Cleveland 44114

The Polk Foundation
Box 967
Dayton 45401

Premier Industrial Foundation
4415 Euclid Avenue
Cleveland 44103

The Proctor and Gamble Fund
301 E. 6th Street
Cincinnati 45202

Reeves Foundation
307 East Iron Avenue
Dover 44622

Republic Steel Corporation Educational and
    Charitable Trust
Republic Building
Cleveland 44115

The Rike Foundation
Box 977
Dayton 45401

The Scripps–Howard Foundation
1100 Central Trust Tower
Cincinnati 45202

The Sherwin–Williams Foundation
101 Prospect Avenue, NW, 12th floor
Cleveland 44115

Second Sohio Foundation
The Standard Oil Company
Midland Building
Cleveland 44115

The Stark County Foundation
618 Second Street, NW
Canton 44703

TRW Foundation
23555 Euclid Avenue
Cleveland 44117

Oklahoma

The First National Foundation, Inc.
Box 25189
Oklahoma City 73125

Harris Foundation, Inc.
1300 Colcod Building
Oklahoma City 73102

Kirkpatrick Foundation, Inc.
1300 N. Broadway
Oklahoma City 73103

McCasland Foundation
Box 400, McCasland Building
Duncan 73533

The McGee Foundation
K-McGee Building
Oklahoma City 73102

The Merrick Foundation
Box 998
Ardmore 73401

Oklahoma Gas and Electric Company
    Foundation, Inc.
Box 321
Oklahoma City 73101

Pan American Petrol Foundation, Inc.
Box 591
Tulsa 74102

Pioneer Foundation
Box 1748
Oklahoma City 73101

Price Foundation, Inc.
Box 1111
Bartlesville 74003

Sarkeys Foundation
4400 N. Lincoln Boulevard
Oklahoma City 73105

Tulsa Royalties Company
3229-A S. Harvard Avenue
Tulsa 74135

Oregon

The Autzen Foundation
Box 3709
Portland 97208

The Carpenter Foundation
Box 816
Medford 97501

The Collins Foundation
909 Terminal Sales Building
Portland 97205

Georgia-Pacific Foundation
900 SW 5th Avenue
Portland 97204

The Swindells Foundation
6317 SW Hamilton Street
Portland 97201

Tektronix Foundation
Box 500
Beaverton 97005

Wheeler Foundation
1104 Executive Building
Portland 97204

Pennsylvania

Alcoa Foundation
Alcoa Building
Pittsburgh 15219

American Bank and Trust Company of
Pennsylvania Foundation
36 N. 6th Street
Reading 19601

The American Foundation, Inc.
1532 PNB Building
Philadelphia 19107

The Annenberg Fund, Inc.
Box 750, 250 King of Prussia Road
Radnor 19088

The Arcadia Foundation
105 E. Logan Street
Norristown 19401

W.M. Armistead Foundation, Inc.
Ayer Building, West Washington Square
Philadelphia 19106

Bank of Pennsylvania Foundation
50 N. 5th Street
Reading 19601

Barra Foundation, Inc.
1910 Packard Building
Philadelphia 19102

Beneficia Foundation
Creek Road
Athyn 19009

Board of Directors of City Trusts
City of Philadelphia
1601 Spring Garden Street
Philadelphia 19103

Breyer Foundation, Inc.
1600 Locust Street
Philadelphia 19103

The Bulletin Contributorship
30th and Market Streets
Philadelphia 19101

Carborundum Charitable Foundation
2600 Neville Road
Pittsburgh 15225

Carnegie Hero Fund Commission
1932 Oliver Building
Pittsburgh 15222

City Stores Foundation, Inc.
8th and Market Streets
Philadelphia 19105

The Crels Foundation
Box 77
New Holland 17557

The Dentists' Supply Company Foundation,
    Inc.
Arthur W. Tinkham
500 W. College Avenue
York 17404

Dolfinger–McMahon Foundation
1617 Land Title Building
Philadelphia 19110

Samuel S. Fels Fund
2 Penn Center Plaza
Philadelphia 19102

The Albert M. Greenfield Foundation
Bankers Securities Building
Philadelphia 19107

The Grundy Foundation
1825 Fidelity Building
Philadelphia 19109

Harsco Corporation Fund
Camp Hills 17011

The M.S. Hershey Foundation
9 W. Chocolate Avenue
Hershey 17033

Houghton–Carpenter Foundation
303 W. Lehigh Avenue
Philadelphia 19133

The Lovett Foundation, Inc.
1630 Locust Street
Philadelphia 19103

Oxford Foundation, Inc.
55 S. 3rd Street
Oxford 19363

The Philadelphia Foundation
1400 S. Penn Square
Philadelphia 19102

Pitcairn–Crabbe Foundation
1417 N. American Rockwell Building
Pittsburgh 15222

The Reidler Foundation
642 Grant Street
Hazelton 18201

The Rockwell Foundation
400 N. Lexington Avenue
Pittsburgh 15208

The SICO Foundation
15 Mount Joy Street
Mount Joy 17552

Smith, Kline & French Foundation
1500 Spring Garden Street
Philadelphia 19101

Stackpole–Hall Foundation
19 N. St. Marys Street
St. Marys 15857

Frank Strick Foundation
765 Moredon Road
Meadowbrook 19046

Union Benevolent Association
10 W. Chestnut Hill Avenue
Philadelphia 19118

United States Steel Foundation, Inc.
600 Grant Avenue
Pittsburgh 15230

Zurn Foundation
1801 Pittsburgh Avenue
Erie 16502

Puerto Rico

The Luis A. Ferré Foundation, Inc.
16 Real Street
Ponce 00731

Rhode Island

Carol Foundation
249 Roosevelt Avenue
Pawtucket 02865

The Federal Products Foundation, Inc.
1144 Eddy Street
Providence 02901

Meehan Foundation
803 Turks Head Building
Providence 02903

The Textron Charitable Trust
909 Howard Building
Providence 02903

South Carolina

The Arcadia Foundation
Arcadia 29320

The Arkwright Foundation
Box 5565
Spartanburg 29301

Belk–Simpson Foundation
Box 969
Greenville 29602

The Daniel Foundation
Daniel Building
Greenville 29601

Woodside Mills Foundation
Box 6126, Station B
260 S. Pleasantburg Drive
Greenville 29606

South Dakota

Hatter Scheidt Foundation, Inc.
Box 939, 302 Capitol Building
Aberdenn 57401

Tennessee

American Snuff Company Charitable Trust
Box 387
Memphis 38101

Bernal Foundation
1400 8th Avenue North
Nashville 37202

The Dixie Yarns Foundation
Box 751
Chattanooga 37401

The Evans Foundation, Inc.
540 McCallie Avenue
Chattanooga 37402

Tonya Memorial Foundation
1033 Volunteer Building
Chattanooga 37402

Texas

Bank of Southwest National Association of
    Houston Foundation
Box 2629
Houston 77001

The Bass Foundation
1150 Mercantile Dallas Building
Dallas 75201

The Cullen Foundation
500 Jefferson Building, 19th floor
Houston 77002

Dallas Foundation
1501 Pacific Street
Dallas 75201

Davidson Family Charitable Foundation
1004 Continental Life Building
Fort Worth 76102

Ken W. Davis Foundation
600 Mis-Continental Building
Fort Worth 76102

The DeBakey Medical Foundation
700 Chamber of Commerce Building
Houston 77002

The DeGolyer Foundation
211 North Ervay Building, Suite 1008
Dallas 75201

The Fain Foundation
607 Hamilton Building
Wichita Falls 76301

The Fasken Foundation
414 W. Texas Avenue
Midland 79701

The Favrot Fund
8383 Westview Drive
Houston 77055

The Fentress Foundation
900 Franklin Avenue
Waco 76701

The Haggar Foundation
6113 Lemmon Avenue
Dallas 75209

Humble Companies Charitable Trust
800 Bell Avenue
Houston 77002

The H.L. Hunt Foundation
1401 Elm Street, 29th floor
Dallas 75202

The Johnson City Foundation
Box 1209, 10th and Brazos Streets
Austin 78767

The Kayser Foundation
1006 Main Street
Houston 77002

Meadows Foundation, Inc.
Meadows Building, 9th floor
Dallas 75206

Menil Foundation, Inc.
3363 San Felipe Road
Houston 77019

The Moody Foundation
704 Moody National Bank Building
Galveston 77550

Candace Mossler Corporation
918 Houston First Savings Building
Houston 77002

Rogers Brothers Foundation, Inc.
Box 1310, 595 Orleans Street
Beaumont 77704

Texas National Resources Foundation
515 Busby Drive
San Antonio 78209

Vale–Asche Foundation
1300 Main Street, Suite 421
Houston 77002

The Vaughn Foundation
553 Park Heights Circle
Tyler 75701

The Zale Foundation
3000 Diamond Park
Dallas 75247

Utah

Ruth Eleanor and John Ernest Bamberger
        Memorial Foundation
1401 Walker Bank Building
Salt Lake City 84111

Hogle Foundation
132 S. Main Street
Salt Lake City 84101

Vermont

Cone Automatic Machine Company
        Charitable Foundation
6 Everett Lane
Windsor 05089

Virginia

Dan River Mills Foundation
Box 261
Danville 24541

The F.E.B. Foundation
Box 1838
Richmond 23215

The Flagler Foundation
510 United Virginia Bank Building
Richmond 23219

The Mars Foundation
1651 Old Meadow Road
McLean 22101

Miller and Rhoads Foundation, Inc.
517 E. Broad Street
Richmond 23219

The Norfolk Foundation
400 Roysten Building
Norfolk 23510

Norfolk Shipbuilding and Drydock
    Corporation Charity Trust
Box 2100
Norfolk 23501

Richard S. Reynolds Foundation
Reynolds Metals Building
Richmond 23218

Washington

The Bloedel Foundation, Inc.
Rte. 8, Box 8818
Bainbridge Island 98110

The Boeing Company Charitable Trust
Box 3707
Seattle 98124

Medina Foundation
1616 Norton Building
Seattle 98104

Pacific Car and Foundry Company
    Foundation, Inc.
Box 1518
Bellevue 98009

The Seattle Foundation
1425 4th Avenue
Seattle 98101

Spokane Foundation
Box 1516
Spokane 99210

The Tenzler Foundation
Box 1493
Tacoma 98401

Weyerhauser Company Foundation
Tacoma 98401

West Virginia

Herscher Foundation, Inc.
Box 3939
Charleston 25322

Bernard McDonough Foundation, Inc.
325 7th Street
Parkersburg 26101

Wisconsin

Allen–Bradley Foundation, Inc.
1201 S. Second Street
Milwaukee 53204

Allis Chalmers Foundation, Inc.
Box 512
Milwaukee 53201

Beloit Foundation, Inc.
423 Bluff Street
Beloit 53511

Briggs and Stratton Corporation Foundation,
    Inc.
3300 N. 124th Street
Milwaukee 53201

Bucyrus–Erie Foundation, Inc.
100 Milwaukee Avenue
South Milwaukee 53172

Cutler–Hammer Foundation
4201 N. 27th Street
Milwaukee 53126

DeRancé, Inc.
7701 W. Blue Mound Road
Milwaukee 53213

First Wisconsin Foundation, Inc.
743 N.Water Street
Milwaukee 53202

Fort Howard Paper Foundation, Inc.
Box 130, 1919 S. Broadway
Green Bay 54305

The Johnson's Wax Fund, Inc.
1525 Howe Street
Racine 53402

Kearney and Trecker Foundation, Inc.
11000 Theodore Trecker Way
West Allis 53214

Kimberly–Clark Foundation, Inc.
North Lake Street
Neenah 53956

Koehring Foundation
770 N. Water Street
Milwaukee 53202

Kohler Foundation
Kohler 53044

Ladish Company Foundation
5481 S. Packard Avenue
Cudahy 53110

Oscar Mayer Foundation, Inc.
Box 1409, 910 Mayer Avenue
Madison 53701

Miller High Life Foundation, Inc.
4000 W. State Street
Milwaukee 53201

Milwaukee Foundation
110 E. Wisconsin Avenue
Milwaukee 53202

Neese Foundation
One St. Lawrence Avenue
Beloit 53511

Oskosh Foundation
Box 280
Oskosh 54901

Presto Foundation
National Presto Industries, Inc.
Eau Claire 54701

Rex Chainbelt Foundation, Inc.
4701 W. Greenfield Avenue
Milwaukee 53201

Schlitz Foundation, Inc.
235 W. Galena Street
Milwaukee 53201

Walter Schroeder Foundation, Inc.
741 N. Milwaukee Street, Rm. 300
Milwaukee 53202

Sola Basic Foundation, Inc.
Box 753
Milwaukee 53201

The Aytchmonde Woodson Foundation, Inc.
Box 65
Wausaw 54401

Charles W. Wright Foundation of Badger
    Meter, Inc.
4435 W. Brown Deer Road
Milwaukee 53223

The Ziegler Foundation, Inc.
400 Division Street
West Bend 53095

GOING PUBLIC

There is one way to generate capital which does not have to be repaid and which does not require the borrower to surrender control: attract the public's money by selling stock in your company. This is selling off some of your equity—the buyer of stock is *investing* in your company, in the hope of gaining both income (dividends) and capital gains (appreciation in the price of the stock). You are not really borrowing from the public (if you want to do that, you sell bonds, rather than stock), so you do not have to pay anything back, and you need pay dividends on the stock only when the company's earnings are such as to justify dividends.

You can legally issue stock for almost any legitimate purpose—to finance a new enterprise, make additional investments, refinance assets, meet current bills, or almost anything else. Theoretically, there is no limit to the amount of stock you may issue or the amount of money you can raise this way.

Of course, success in raising money this way depends on how successful you are at *selling* the stock you issue. Since you must be a corporation to go public, there are a number of legal requirements, both federal and state, with which you must comply. Going public does entail a certain amount of legal work as well as some specialized knowledge of how to market stock. Most corporations, unless they have some special arrangements to make a "private placement," engage the services of an underwriting firm, which specializes in selling new stock issues.

Not every brokerage firm underwrites stock issues, although by far the majority of the well-known, larger brokerages do, especially those in New York City. (The regional brokerages, in other cities, may or may not also underwrite issues). The following list is by no means a complete list of underwriters, and it is advisable, if you are considering an issue of stock, to check with a local brokerage. (They may be helpful in guiding you to a source of venture capital, even if they do not handle underwriting of stock issues or they think that it is unadvisable for you.)

Stock Underwriters

California

Bateman, Eichler, Hill, Richards
700 S. Flower Street
Los Angeles 90017
(213) 625-3545

Birr, Wilson & Co., Inc.
155 Sansome Street
San Francisco, CA 94104
(415) 983-7700

Hambrecht & Quist
235 Montgomery Street
San Francisco 94104
(415) 433-1720

Mitchum, Jones & Templeton, Inc.
612 S. Flower Street
Los Angeles 90017
(213) 488-0561

Morgan, Olmstead, Kennedy & Gardner,
   Inc.
606 S. Olive Street
Los Angeles 90014
(213) 625-1611

Roberts, Scott & Co., Inc.
1 Wilshire Boulevard
Los Angeles 90017
(213) 620-9060

Robertson, Colman & Siebel
235 Montgomery Street
San Francisco 94104
(415) 999-2050

Seidler, Arnett & Spillane, Inc.
445 S. Figueroa Street
Los Angeles 90017
(213) 624-4230

Shuman, Agnew & Co., Inc.
650 California Street
San Francisco 94108
(415) 981-0900

Stern, Frank, Myer & Fox, Inc.
606 S. Olive Street
Los Angeles 90014
(213) 623-7222

Colorado

Boettcher & Co.
828 17th Street
Denver 80202
(303) 629-2020

Delaware

DuPont, Glore, Forgan, Inc.
DuPont Building, Delaware Avenue
Wilmington 19801
(302) 656-9911

Laird, Inc.
100 W. 10th Street
Wilmington 19801
(302) 656-7741

District of Columbia

Ferris & Co., Inc.
1720 I Street, NW
Washington 20006
(202) 293-4500

Katz, Needelman & Co., Inc.
600 New Hampshire Avenue, NW
Washington 20037
(202) 965-4600

Wachtel & Co., Inc.
1000 Vermont Avenue, NW
Washington 20005
(202) 347-9588

Florida

First Equity Corporation of Florida
100 W. Kennedy Boulevard
Tampa 33602
(813) 223-1421

Raymond, James & Associates, Inc.
6090 Central Avenue
St. Petersburg 33707
(813) 381-3800

Georgia

Johnson, Lane, Space, Smith & Co., Inc.
1000 Commerce Building
Atlanta 30303
(404) 523-3692

The Robinson–Humphrey Co., Inc.
2 Peachtree Street, NW
Atlanta 30303
(404) 581-7111

Varnedoe, Chisolm, Skinner & Co., Inc.
1 Bull Street
Savannah 31401
(912) 236-5561

Illinois

Bacon, Whipple & Co.
135 S. LaSalle Street
Chicago 60603
(312) 782-3100

William Blair & Company
135 S. LaSalle Street
Chicago 60603
(312) 236-1600

The Chicago Corporation
208 S. LaSalle Street
Chicago 60604
(312) 855-7600

Sears, Sucsy & Co.
100 W. Monroe Street
Chicago 60603
(312) 726-1331

Woolard & Co., Inc.
135 S. LaSalle Street
Chicago 60603
(312) 346-4600

Maryland

Robert Garrett & Sons, Inc.
South and Redwood Streets
Baltimore 21203
(301) 685-7600

Massachusetts

Amadon Corporation
31 Milk Street
Boston 02109
(617) 482-6775

Breck, McNeish and Nagle, Inc.
3 Center Plaza
Boston 02108
(617) 742-5757

Burley, Harkins and Funk, Inc.
1 Boston Place
Boston 02108
(617) 723-6930

F.S. Moseley & Co.
50 Congress Street
Boston 02109
(617) 482-1300

Tucker, Anthony and R.L. Day
74 State Street
Boston 02109
(617) 523-2000

Michigan

William C. Roney & Co.
2 Buhl Building
Detroit 48226
(313) 963-6700

Minnesota

Craig–Hallum, Inc.
133 S. 7th Street
Minneapolis 55402
(612) 332-1212

Piper, Jaffray & Hopwood, Inc.
115 S. 7th Street
Minneapolis 55402
(612) 371-6111

Missouri

B.C. Christopher & Co.
4800 Main Street
Kansas City 64112
(816) 932-7000

Reinholdt & Gardner
506 Olive Street
St. Louis 63101
(314) 231-6640

Nebraska

First Mid-America, Inc.
1221 N. Street
Omaha 68501
(402) 474-3300

New York

Agio Capital Corporation
2 Broadway
New York 10004
(212) 363-8747

Allen & Company, Inc.
30 Broad Street
New York 10004
(212) 422-2600

Alpha Capital Ventures, Inc.
575 Lexington Avenue
New York 10022
(212) 688-5620

Andresen & Co.
140 Broadway
New York 10005
(212) 363-6300

Milton D. Blauner & Co.
115 Broadway
New York 10006
(212) 227-7626

Blyth, Eastman, Dillon & Co., Inc.
1 Chase Manhattan Plaza
New York 10005
(212) 770-8561

A.T. Brod & Co.
39 Broadway
New York 10006
(212) 422-5900

Burnham & Co., Inc.
60 Broad Street
New York 10004
(212) 344-1400

Cannon, Jerold & Co., Inc.
77 Water Street
New York 10005
(212) 344-1010

Clark, Dodge & Co., Inc.
140 Broadway
New York 10005
(212) 676-5151

Coenen & Co., Inc.
280 Park Avenue
New York 10017
(212) 661-4550

Coggeshall & Hicks, Inc.
1 Liberty Street
New York 10005
(212) 425-4100

Collins Securities Corporation
26 Beaver Street
New York 10004
(212) 425-4087

F. Eberstadt & Co., Inc.
61 Broadway
New York 10006
(212) 480-0800

Epstein, Parker, Carmel & Gaer, Inc.
1350 Avenue of the Americas
New York 10019
(212) 489-1150

Estabrook & Co., Inc.
80 Pine Street
New York 10005
(212) 944-7800

Faherty & Swartwood
70 Pine Street
New York 10005
(212) 248-6690

S.D. Fuller & Co.
26 Broadway
New York 10004
(212) 943-0066

Globus, Inc.
1345 Avenue of the Americas
New York 10019
(212) 582-5200

Grimm & Davis, Inc.
15 William Street
New York 10005
(212) 943-7960

Halle & Stieglitz, Inc.
52 Wall Street
New York 10005
(212) 797-2534

Hayden Stone, Inc.
767 Fifth Avenue
New York 10022
(212) 350-0500

Ladenburg, Thalmann & Co., Inc.
25 Broad Street
New York 10004
(212) 422-8570

Lehman Brothers
1 William Street
New York 10004
(212) 269-3700

Loeb, Rhoades & Co.
42 Wall Street
New York 10005
(212) 530-4000

Lombard, Nelson & McKenna, Inc.
111 Broadway
New York 10006
(212) 267-6100

S.D. Lunt & Co.
Marine Trust Building
Buffalo 14203
(716) 854-4035

Carl Marks & Co., Inc.
77 Water Street
New York 10005
(212) 437-7100

Morgan, Kennedy & Co., Inc.
5 Hanover Square
New York 10004
(212) 248-1480

New Street Ventures
50 Broadway
New York 10004
(212) 483-8650

New York Securities Co., Inc.
1 New York Plaza
New York 10004
(212) 425-2800

Oppenheimer & Co.
1 New York Plaza
New York 10004
(212) 825-4000

Phillips, Appel & Walden, Inc.
111 Broadway
New York 10006
(212) 064-9000

R.W. Pressprich & Co., Inc.
80 Pine Street
New York 10005
(212) 483-1100

C.B. Richard, Ellis & Co.
5 Hanover Square
New York 10004
(212) 944-0500

L.F. Rothschild & Co.
99 William Street
New York 10038
(212) 425-3300

Seiden & deCuevas, Inc.
110 Wall Street
New York 10005
(212) 747-0775

Shaskan & Co., Inc.
67 Broad Street
New York 10004
(212) 344-4950

Shields Securities Corporation
44 Wall Street
New York 10005
(212) 785-2400

F.S. Smithers & Co., Inc.
1 Battery Park Plaza
New York 10004
(212) 943-3300

C.E. Unterberg, Towbin & Co.
61 Broadway
New York 10006
(212) 425-3090

Van Alstyne, Noel & Co.
4 Albany Street
New York 10006
(212) 233-2000

White, Weld & Co., Inc.
1 Liberty Plaza
New York 10006
(212) 285-2000

Winkler, Cantor, Pomboy & Co.
485 Madison Avenue
New York 10022
(212) 371-2400

Winmill, Jones & Walker, Inc.
63 Wall Street
New York 10005
(212) 962-6500

Wood, Walker & Co.
63 Wall Street
New York 10005
(212) 944-7870

North Carolina

Interstate Securities
2700 NCNB Plaza
Charlotte 28280
(704) 379-9000

Ohio

The Clariden Corporation
1812 East Ohio Building
Cleveland 44114
(216) 241-1920

J.N. Russell, Inc.
Investment Plaza
Cleveland 44114
(216) 696-4242

Pennsylvania

Bache & Co., Inc.
1336 Chestnut Street
Philadelphia 19107
(215) 665-5596

Bullseye Associates
2900 U.S. Steel Building
Pittsburgh 15219
(412) 566-1234

Butcher and Singer, Inc.
1500 Walnut Street
Philadelphia 19102
(215) 985-5000

Dean Witter & Co.
5 Penn Center Plaza
Philadelphia 19102
(215) 985-5000

Delphi Capital Corp.
1700 Market Street
Philadelphia 19103
(215) 568-6001

Elkins & Co.
1700 Market Street
Philadelphia 19103
(215) 568-1975

Janney, Montgomery, Scott, Inc.
5 Penn Center Plaza
Philadelphia 19103
(215) 665-9200

Reynolds Securities, Inc.
1700 Market Street
Philadelphia 19103
(215) 568-3301

Salomon Brothers & Hutzler
1700 Market Street
Philadelphia 19103
(215) 568-3329

Suplee–Mosley, Inc.
1700 Market Street
Philadelphia 19103
(215) 665-8000

Texas

Earp, Kenney & Smith, Inc.
1600 Republic National Bank Building
Dallas 75201
(214) 741-3571

Eppler, Guerin & Turner, Inc.
2001 Bryant Tower Building
Dallas 75201
(214) 744-0511

First of Texas, Inc.
1800 Houston Natural Gas Building
Houston 77002
(713) 224-3033

Schneider, Bernet & Hickman, Inc.
2400 First National Bank Building
Dallas 75270
(214) 748-1201

Virginia

Wheat/First Securities, Inc.
707 E. Main Street
Richmond 23219
(804) 649-2311

Wisconsin

Robert W. Baird & Co., Inc.
777 E. Wisconsin Avenue
Milwaukee 53201
(414) 765-3500

Chapter 6

Special Help

Several sources of help in pursuing financing, plus some useful references, reminders, refreshers, and things you probably never knew before.

A MAJOR EFFORT TO HELP MINORITIES

Over the past quarter century concern about minority enterpreneurs has set in among legislators at all levels of government — federal, state, and local. With the federal government taking the lead, many socioeconomic programs have been devised to aid small business generally and "socially and economically disadvantaged" minority entrepreneurs especially. Among these programs is one headed by the Minority Business Development Agency (MBDA) of the United States Department of Commerce, formerly the Office of Minority Business Enterprise and more widely referred to as OMBE (pronounced AHM-BEE). With an annual budget of approximately $50 million, this agency supports a large number of agencies in the private sector (primarily nonprofit organizations, some already in existence, others formed especially for this purpose) to provide free services to minority entrepreneurs. A major objective of the program has been, from its inception, to help minority entrepreneurs find financing for their ventures, and the success of the program was measured largely by the number of clients so aided and the total

amount of dollars made available as loans and equity capital. In its more recent image, reorganized as MBDA, the agency tends to focus interest on the encouragement of technological and research and development (R&D) firms owned and operated by minority entrepreneurs, although financing assistance continues to be a major objective of MBDA service programs.

Originally, the program supported (funded) a number of state- and local-government bureaus dedicated to aiding minority entrepreneurs, and organized as "State OMBEs" and "City OMBEs," which were then part of the approximately 250 organizations supported under OMBE and, later, MBDA funding. Too, many of the organizations were highly specialized, and concentrated on various kinds of support activities, such as construction industries, business opportunity development, and so forth, and the organizations were so designated by the Department of Commerce. However, changes have come about during the current Administration, and the MBDA now lists only 89 organizations funded by MBDA, and shows no state or city OMBEs in the listings, although some of the states and cities have managed to continue supporting their OMBE organizations with their own funds.

Today, MBDA explains its activities in these words:

MBDA Coordinates and monitors minority business support in the public and private sectors, and manages a national network of business service organizations which offer management counseling to minority entrepreneurs. The business service organizations receive operating funds from MBDA through Federal contracts and grants, and report client services to MBDA.

Business Service counselors advise minority owners in areas such as marketing, accounting, personnel management, and business training. They help owners to secure Federal and private sales, and to assemble financial packages for submission to lenders. MBDA does not make loans.

Business services are offered free of charge to current minority business operators and those considering starting a business.

Executive Order 11625 defines a minority business enterprise as follows: ". . . a business enterprise that is owned or controlled by one or more socially or economically disadvantaged persons. Such disadvantage may arise from cultural, racial, chronic economic circumstances or background or other similar cause. Such persons include, but are not limited to, Negroes, Puerto Ricans, Spanish-speaking Americans, American Indians, Eskimos, and Aleuts."

It is noteworthy that the definition of disadvantaged minorities is not restricted to the enumerated classes. It is also not mentioned here that the law is not interpreted to mean that a person belonging to one of the listed categories of minorities is not automatically "disadvantaged," but must demonstrate that such disadvantage actually exists in his or her individual case. (In practice, however, no one has ever had the slightest difficulty qualifying as long as he or she did, in fact, belong to one of the groups listed.) On the other hand, individuals not belonging to one of those groups may undertake to prove that he or she is disadvantaged and entitled to qualify for assistance, and some individuals have done so.

Because so much change is taking place in the MBDA programs, as in many other government agencies and programs, MBDA is not able to supply the detailed information it has in the past about the organizations it supports, which are available and funded to aid minority entrepreneurs. Whatever information has been made available appears here, in the following lists. However, for more detailed and more up-to-date information, it would be wise to check with the nearest Department of Commerce MBDA office. (See Chapter 3 for listings.)

Before the recent changes and reorganization, the specialties practiced by MBDA-funded organizations included these, among others:

- BMD — Business Management Development — training and counseling.
- BRC — Business Resource Center — marshaling community resources.
- CCAC — Construction Contractor Assistance Centers — especially bonding help.
- LBDO — Local Business Development Organizations — counseling and guidance.
- MB&TA — Minority Business and Trade Associations.

The preceding is only a partial listing; there were many more, originally. This is not to say that all have disappeared; quite the contrary, a few of the organizations still tend to specialize to at least some extent. But for the most part, today, MBDA-funded support organizations tend to be what MBDA terms General Business Service Centers, providing a variety of services.

MBDA-Funded Organizations

The following is the most up-to-date list of MBDA-funded organizations available at this time and reports whatever information is currently available about these organizations, as reported by the Commerce Department's Minority Business Development Agency. The names of many of the organizations listed here identify them as business service centers, trade associations, business development centers, or other specialists, but the old codes (BSC, MB&TA, BDC, etc.) are no longer used. In fact, the only abbreviation encountered commonly in the new MBDA listings is "GBS," for General Business Service, which reflects the current trend to establishing MBDA General Business Service Centers.

List of MBDA-Funded Organizations

Alabama

Birmingham Business Service Center
Harold Gilchrist, Project Officer
Steiner Building
15 N. 21st Street
Birmingham 35201
(205) 252-3682

Arizona

Navajo Small Business Development
  Corporation
Joseph Hardy, Project Manager
P.O. Drawer 1
Fort Defiance 86504
(602) 729-5763

Arkansas

Little Rock Innocept GBS Center
Darnell R. Finsey, Project Officer
1200 West Park Drive, Suite 305
Little Rock 72204

California

United Indian Development Association GBS
  Center
Suzanne Johnson, Report Contact
1541 Wilshire Boulevard, Suite 307
Los Angeles 90017
(213) 483-1460
(Branch offices pending for Northern and
  Southern California.)

Operation Second Chance GBS Center
Wesley Jefferson, Report Contact
341 West Second Street, #1
San Bernardino 92401
(714) 884-8764

Cardinal Management Associates GBS
  Center
Ken Tahedo, Report Officer
2500 Wilshire Boulevard, Suite 1016
Los Angeles 90057
(213) 385-1335

Cardinal Management Associates
Oxnard/Santa Barbara GBS Center
Victor Fontaine
515 South Street
Oxnard 93030
(805) 486-4701

Confederation of Agriculture
Albert Oliverez, Project Officer
2212 N. Main Street
Salinas 93906
(408) 443-4550

Santa Clara GBS Center (RMC Group)
Jose Placencia, Project Manager
2700 Augustine Drive, Suite 242
Santa Clara 94501
(408) 980-0371

Price Waterhouse GBS Center
G. William Dauphinais, Project Manager
819 19th Street, Suite 102
Sacramento 95814

Price Waterhouse GBS Center branch offices:
  245 Arkansas Street
  Vallejo 94590
  (707) 554-8816

  2291 West March Lane
  Stockton 95207
  (209) 474-3553

NEDA, Inc.
David A. DeCima, Project Manager
1094 Cudahy Place, Suite 120
San Diego 92110
(714) 275-3512

Business Development Center of Southern
    California
Cleveland O'Neill
2651 South Western Avenue, Suite 300
Los Angeles 90018
(213) 731-2131

Arthur D. Little Associates San
    Francisco/Oakland GBS Center
Carol Lowe, Administration Coordinator
4 Embarcadero Center
San Francisco 94111
(415) 981-2500

Branch Office:
  James Lowery & Associates GBS Center
  Richard McClire
  333 Hegenberger Road, Suite 315
  Oakland 94150
  (415) 632-0696

Cal State University Fresno
CSUF Business Service Center
Sherry Steinhardt, Coordinator
Maple & Shaw Avenue
Fresno 93740
(209) 294-2298

Branch Office:
  Cal State Bakersfield Business Service
    Center
  Phillip Sanchez, Program Director
  9001 Stockdale Highway, Science
    Building 2, Room 165
  Bakersfield 93309
  (805) 833-2263

Business Development Center of Santa Ana
Cleveland O'Neill, Project Manager
2700 N. Main Street
Santa Ana 92801
(714) 667-8200

Salinas General Business Service Center
Stephen L. Frank, Project Manager
119 East Alisal
Salinas 93901
(408) 754-2246

Colorado

Gallegos Research Group
Terry Gallegos, Project Director
4100 West 38th Avenue
Denver 80212
(303) 458-0221

Connecticut

Burgos & Associates Connecticut GBS
    Center
Rodney Little, Project Officer
234 Church Street, Suite 803
New Haven 06510
(203) 773-9377

District of Columbia

Leevy, Redcross & Company
Stan Straughter
Mercury Building, Suite 400
1015 20th Street, NW
Washington 20036
(202) 634-3987

Native American Consultants, Inc.
Bill Hallett/Tom Fields, Project Manager
725 Second Street, NE
Washington 20002
(202) 528-7100

Greater Washington Iberio-American
    Chamber Construction Center
Wayne Frost, Project Manager
1633 16th Street, NW
Washington 20009
(202) 387-0275

Florida

North and Central Florida Business Service
    Center
Evelyn Moore, Administrative Officer
750 S. Orange Blossom Trail, Suite 215
Orlando 32805
(305) 841-2036

North & Central Florida Business Service
    Center
Benjamin Norman, Administrative Officer
137 East Forsyth Street, Suite 303
Jacksonville 32202
(904) 354-8168

Southeast Florida GBS Center
Mario Meneses, Project Manager
2929 SW 3rd Avenue
Miami 33129
(305) 854-4212

Fort Lauderdale GBS Center
Arward Bassut, Assistant Project Manager
2880 West Oakland Park Boulevard,
    Suite E-17
Fort Lauderdale 33311
(305) 486-0961

West Palm Beach GBS Center
Alfred Jones, Assistant Project Manager
2240 Palm Beach Lake Road, Suite 105
West Palm Beach 33409
(305) 656-6911

North & Central Florida Business Service
    Center
George B. Smith
1918 West Cass Street
Tampa 33606
(813) 253-3600

Georgia

Georgia Business Service Center
Eugene Campbell, Project Officer
75 Piedmont Avenue, NE, Suite 256
Atlanta 30303
(404) 586-0973

Savannah Business Service Center
205 Congress-Whitaker Building
31 West Congress Street
Savannah 31402

Illinois

Chicago Economic Development Co. GBS
    Center
Webster Daniels, VP Operations
180 N. Michigan Boulevard, Suite 333
Chicago 60601
(312) 984-5979

Branch Offices:
    CEDCO, Inc.
    1711 East 71st Street
    Chicago 60649
    (312) 684-8420

    CEDCO, Inc.
    Gladys Rodriguez
    5636 N. Western Avenue
    Chicago 60645
    (312) 334-7693

Indiana

H. A. Taylore GBS Center
Ben Garrett, Report Contact
475 South Broadway, Suite 507
Gary 46402
(219) 882-6116

Indianapolis Business Development
    Foundation
John P. Cox, Report Contact
1 Virginia Avenue
Indianapolis 46204
(317) 639-6131

Kentucky

Tennessee/Kentucky Business Service Center
835 West Jefferson Street, Suite 103
Louisville 40202
(502) 589-7401

Louisiana

Marcon GBS Center, Shreveport
Talmadge Mitchell, Project Officer
4700 Line Avenue, Suite 119
Shreveport 71106
(318) 861-2065

NEDA, Inc.
Margaret Dupont, Project Officer
3308 Tulane Avenue, Suite 200
New Orleans 70119
(504) 682-2611

Baton Rouge Innocept GBS Center
Morgan L. Dring, Project Officer
1821 Wooddale Court, Suite 110
Baton Rouge 70806
(504) 925-1313

Maryland

Baltimore Business Service Center
    (Commercial Credit)
Bob Bonnell, Project Officer
22 West Padonia Road, Suite 152-C
Timonium 21093
(301) 561-1800

Massachusetts

Small Business Development GBS Center
Frank Cruz
15 Court Square, Room 900
Boston 02108
(617) 723-8520

Minnesota

Minnesota Chippewa Tribe
Barbara Ragor
2344 Nicollet
Minneapolis 55404
(612) 871-5940

Minneapolis/St. Paul GBS Center
    (Commercial Credit)
Darvin Schauer, Project Director
5241 Viking Drive
Bloomington 55435
(612) 893-4203

Mississippi

Tennessee-Tombigbee Construction
    Contractor Assistance Center
Esther Harrison, Director
605 North Second Avenue, Suite 301
Columbus 39701
(601) 328-3251

Missouri

Maxxam GBS Center
Donald Maxwell, Project Director
1026 Forrest Drive
Kansas City 64106
(816) 421-4498

Maxxam Consulting GBS Center
Charles Bussy, Project Officer
4144 Undell Boulevard
St. Louis 63101
(314) 534-4144

Nevada

NEDCO GBS Center
Rob Egans, Report Coordinator
618 East Carson
Las Vegas 89101
(702) 384-3293

New Jersey

North New Jersey Business Service Center
    (Paterson/Newark/Jersey City)
James H. Blow, Project Officer
60 Park Place
Newark 07102

New Mexico

El Paso/Las Cruces GBS Center
Irene Huerra
First National Bank of Dona Anna County
    Building, Suite A26
Las Cruces 88001
(505) 524-4666

NEDA, Inc.
Anna Mueller, Project Officer
501 11th Street, NW
Albuquerque 87102
(505) 766-2668

All Indian Development Association
Bob Johnson, Executive Director
1015 Indian School Road
Albuquerque 87197
(505) 247-0371

New York

Brooklyn General Business Service Center
Pamela Polk-Hart, Program Manager
105 Court Street, Suite 403
Brooklyn 11201
(212) 773-0225

Planning Assistance Consultants, Inc.
Donald Lee, Project Manager
250 Delaware Avenue, Suite 4
Buffalo 14202
(716) 842-0750

Burgos & Associates
McKinley Howell
349 East 149th Street
Bronx 10451
(212) 665-8083

Minority Business Service Center of
    Rochester, Inc.
Salvador Maldonado
460 State Street, Suite 402
Rochester 14608
(716) 546-1930

Opportunity Development Associates GBS
    Center
Morton Silver
12 Heywood Street
Brooklyn 11211
(212) 522-5620

Burgos & Associates Long Island GBS Center
Sam Alverez, Project Director
150 Broad Hollow Road
Melville 11747
(516) 549-5454

Arawak Consulting Center
George Konstandt, Project Director
210 East 86th Street
New York 10028
(212) 737-9865

Burgos/Murtha/Gainza GBS Center, Queens
Henry Paulo/Beverly Moore
90-04 161st Street
Jamaica 11432
(212) 658-2227

Burgos/Murtha/Gainza GBS Center,
    Manhattan
Fernando Gainza
342 Park Avenue South
New York 10016
(212) 679-5998

North Carolina

Eastern Band of Cherokee Indians
Mike Lackey, Project Officer
P.O. Box 1200
Cherokee 28719
(704) 479-9335

North Carolina Business Service Center
William Hodges, Project Officer
4300 6th Forks Road
Raleigh 27619
(919) 781-6144

North Dakota

North Dakota Minority Contractors
    Association
3315 South Airport Road
Bismarck 58501

Oklahoma

Marcon GBS Center, Tulsa
Rita Abdulkareem, Project Officer
411 South Denver
Tulsa 74103
(918) 584-0650

Oklahoma Business Development Center
G. M. Dodson, Project Officer
1500 NE 4th Street, Suite 101
Oklahoma City 73117
(405) 235-0430

Oklahomans for Indian Opportunities
Iola Hayden, Executive Director
555 Constitution Avenue
Norman 73069
(405) 329-3737

Oregon

Impact, Inc. GBS Center
Grace Gallegos, Project Manager
8959 Southwest Barbur Boulevard, Suite 102
Portland 97219
(503) 245-9253

Pennsylvania

Leevy, Redcross & Company Business
    Service Center
G. Medina, Project Coordinator
1405 Locust Street, Suite 1515
Philadelphia 19102
(215) 545-0832

Branch Office:
    Business Planning Group (Spanish
    Merchants)
    G. Medina, Coordinator
    2825 North 5th Street
    Philadelphia 19102
    (215) 739-2911

Greater Pittsburgh Business Development
    Center
Pat Gibbs, Project Coordinator
429 Forbes Avenue
Pittsburgh 15129
(412) 255-6379

Puerto Rico

Associacion Productos de Puerto Rico
Oscar Prieto Morgado, Project Officer
GPO Box 3631
San Juan 00936
(809) 753-8484

South Carolina

South Carolina GBS Center, T. R.
    McConnell & Co.
Lisa Kocher, Project Officer
2611 Forest Drive, Suite 115
Columbia 29204
(803) 256-4076

Charleston, South Carolina Business Service
    Center
B. Generette, Project Officer
8740 Northpark Boulevard, Suite 108
Charleston 29406
(803) 572-4884

Greenville, South Carolina Business Service
    Center
Lynn Bigby, Project Officer
Suite 1104, Bankers Trust Building
Greenville 29601
(803) 233-3320

Tennessee

Tennessee/Kentucky Business Service Center
T. Augustus Hill, Director
830 E. H. Crump Boulevard
Memphis 38126
(901) 523-2220

Tennessee/Kentucky Business Service Center
404 James Robertson Parkway, Suite C
Nashville 37219
(615) 256-2687

Fort & Associates GBS Center
Lewis S. Fort, Executive Director
1835 Union Avenue, Suite 425
Memphis 38104
(901) 726-5492

Texas

Marcon GBS Center, Fort Worth
Ann Hughes, Project Officer
4420 West Vickery Boulevard
Fort Worth 76107
(318) 429-7781

Marcon GBS Center, Lubbock
Larry Lucero, Project Officer
8212 Ithaca, Suite E3
Lubbock 79423
(806) 793-0089

Coastal Bend Business Service Center
Ruben Lerma, Project Officer
4343 South Padre Island Drive, Suite 310
Corpus Christi 78411
(512) 855-3951

Dallas Minority Business Center
Efrain Sanchez, Project Officer
3737 Noble, Suite 450
Dallas 75204
(214) 528-1550

Houston/Galveston Innocept GBS Center
Cowperwood Regency
Terry McClellan, Project Officer
6001 Savoy, Suite 111
Houston 77036
(713) 789-6742

Beaumont/Port Arthur/Orange Innocept GBS
    Center
Joseph LeBlanc, Project Officer
905 Memorial Highway
Nederland 77627
(713) 724-0784

McAllen/Harlingen Innocept GBS Center
Dr. Barremore Brown, Project Director
Patterson Building
1319 North 10th Street
McAllen 78501
(512) 686-2263

El Paso/Las Cruces GBS Center
Carlos Restrepo, Director
P.O. Box 13165
El Paso 79912
(915) 581-2732

Avante GBS Center
Bill Johnson, Project Director
411 West 13th Street
Austin 78701
(512) 478-4051

Avante GBS Center
Joyce Sedillo, Project Director
1901 Corpus Christi Street
Laredo 78041
(512) 724-8308

Reporting Office for Avante:
Avante International System Corp.
    Consultant Service Grant
Abigail Antuna, Project Director
830 NE Loop 410, Suite 305
San Antonio 78209
(512) 828-6411

San Antonio Business Center
Bank of San Antonio
John Yoggerst, Program Director
1 Romano Plaza, Suite 311
San Antonio 78205
(512) 226-9953

Utah

NEDA, Inc.
Joe Pacheco, Project Director
195 East 6100 South
Murray 84107
(801) 268-8991

Virginia

Commercial Credit Business Center
Ron Eagle, Project Officer
7th & Franklin Streets, Suite 1316
Richmond 23219
(804) 780-3881

Boone, Young & Associates
United Virginia Bank Building
5 Main Plaza East, Suite 1620
Norfolk 23510
(804) 627-5254

Washington

Sites & Company GBS Center
Norm Ziegler, Project Manager
200 6th Avenue, Suite 1810
Seattle 98101
(206) 624-5897

Wisconsin

H. A. Taylor GBS Center
Henry Taylor, Project Director
536 West Wisconsin Avenue
Milwaukee 53203
(414) 276-7669

PROPOSALS AND BUSINESS PLANS

Your success in getting a loan approved or persuading a venture capitalist to invest money in your enterprise is heavily dependent on preparation. Make no mistake about it: your own traits as a persuasive salesperson are important, of course. It certainly helps to be affable, personable, sincere, alert, and have all those personal traits that make the other fellow find you an attractive and honest human being. Yet, the final decision as to whether to lend you money or invest with you is going to depend far more on what you have prepared on paper — your loan package, business plan, proposal, or whatever you choose to call it.

The gentleman who spent over a year raising the $3 million he needed to launch RF Monolithic, Clinton Hartman, believes that you have to really lay it on the line with your venture capitalist. Tell him what your dreams are — how big you plan to be, where you intend to take your company. This is no time for modesty or bashfulness, Hartman counsels, and he is one of many who agree that nothing is of greater importance in raising money than the business plan.

Kenneth Gjemre operates a sixteen-store discount book chain. He advocates that you "level" with your banker — "undress" in front of him, as you would with few others, if you want him to believe in you and your business dreams.

Planning is the distinguishing trait of the successful entrepreneur. Good planning is necessary for the success of the enterprise, so it is not too surprising that lenders and venture capitalists tend to judge you and your chances for success by the quality and thoroughness of your planning. Of course, they also need to examine your detailed business plan so that they can make a value judgment on your chances for success — on the probability that you will be able to repay the loan or make a suitable return on investment.

A typical business plan must reflect your best estimates of all the major factors of any business enterprise, such as capital investment (front-end money needed), operating costs, sales, profit and loss projections, and cash-flow projections. Many beginning entrepreneurs make the mistake of failing to distinguish between profits and cash flow.

WHAT IS A BUSINESS PLAN?

The nature and importance of the business plan become much easier to grasp when we analyze the business plan philosophically, to determine just what it really is. That can be best determined by asking ourselves: "Just what is it we want the business plan to *do* for us?"

The answer to that question depends on where and how you are using your business plan. When you are using it to begin actual preparations for or actually operating your new business by it, you want it to be the key to success — the road map for running your business. Therefore, your business plan is the means to success in planning and operating your company.

In this book we are talking about finding the money you need for business purposes, and the business plan or proposal (many use the two terms interchangeably, but here the business plan is defined as the heart of the proposal) is therefore a *sales presentation*. Its main purpose, when you are seeking a loan or capital investment in your enterprise, is to gain the approval of others, to *sell* them on your success.

Bear in mind that bankers and venture capitalists are not neophytes in the business world, nor are they bumpkins. Quite the contrary, they are invariably experienced and usually sophisticated, alert, and intelligent business people who could not survive long in their professions if they were anything else. They will therefore scrutinize your business plan most carefully and with an almost automatic skepticism. (This is the result of having reviewed so many defective business plans, to which they had to say "no.") If they can shoot holes in your plan, they most certainly will; if you have flaws in your business plan, they will certainly uncover them. Prepare your business plan with the expectation that it must stand up under the most rigorous efforts to find and reveal its weaknesses, if any. Only when reviewers are unable to find any serious weaknesses do they begin to become impressed and to find you and your plans credible. For example, you must somehow validate any figures you use, to show where they came from. This is not to say that you may not prepare your own estimates; reality usually requires you to develop estimates. Be prepared to show the reasonable basis for those estimates. Better yet, explain in your proposal how you arrived at those estimates and why you deem them reliable projections.

THE CONTENT

Historians report that when Abraham Lincoln was asked for his opinion on how long a man's legs ought to be, he responded, "Long enough to reach the ground." In that same vein, when I am asked what ought to be *in* a proposal or business plan I am usually tempted to say, "Whatever it takes to sell your proposition or get your loan approved." Although I can offer you here some general guidelines and even many detailed specifics, each case is unique, and you should use your own judgment as to what is necessary to demonstrate that your plan is viable and entails no unusual risk.

One thing you should consider first is what prospective lenders and investors typically want to know about you and your plans. Here are what some venture capitalists and bankers have observed:

Extremes: Anyone who receives proposals in quantity or on a regular basis soon discovers that many proposals represent an extreme, at one end or the other: some applicants submit only a page or two of explanation and justification for huge loans or investments, while others will prepare proposals that one venture capitalist has described as resembling the *Encyclopedia Britannica*. The size of the proposals frequently have little or no relationship to what's in them: ponderous proposals of hundreds of pages often contain little information of value that could not have been presented in ten pages. Instead, they are heavily larded with footnotes, tables, copies of material taken from other documents, and otherwise appear to reflect a belief that the venture capitalist or banker evaluates a proposal by its weight, rather than by its content.

What the recipient of a proposal wants is a specific, detailed plan, with precise figures, specific justifications for predicting success, and some *evidence* of sound and realistic planning. There was, years ago, a television cowboy who was a fast-drawn gunman, played by Walter Brennan. In each episode, as others tried to contest him in a shootout, Brennan warned his antagonist off with an explanation of how fast he was and how dangerous it would be to test him. He always concluded his explanation with these words: "No brag; just fact." One fatal weakness of many proposals is that they are "No fact; just brag." They make many elaborate *claims,* use many adjectives, but furnish few *facts.* The reader of the proposal does not judge the soundness of his investment in your enterprise by your claims, but only by the facts you can offer.

Make your proposal as long as it needs to be to tell the story — present all the pertinent facts — and no longer. Don't stint; make it long enough to do the job properly, but no longer than that.

Some proposals go to extremes in other ways. Some are sloppily prepared: typed carelessly, copied with equal carelessness, and delivered with coffee stained and dog-eared pages. Others are overdone, with fancy typesetting and printing, expensive binders, and other evidence of extravagance. Find the middle road, which is a clean, businesslike proposal that shows the evidence of careful preparation, but also shows some evidence of cost-consciousness.

Evasions: Some proposals never come to grips with the problems, attempting to convince the reader that there are and will be no problems. Whether this is self-deception, indicating that the proposer is entirely green and naive, or a conscious effort to lull the reader into a false sense of security, it doesn't work.

Unevenness of presentation: Some proposals go into elaborate detail about certain aspects of the plan, rush hurriedly by others, without heed to the relative importance of the areas. That is, a most-critical factor may be disposed of in a brief paragraph, and a fairly trivial consideration is covered by a full five pages of copy. Such a presentation reveals those matters hastily swept under the carpet

as the areas on which the proposer is most unclear or has failed to do the research and spend the time to develop the information. Worse yet, the proposer may be trying to avoid areas that hold nothing but bad news.

Venture capitalists look hard at problems, and want to know what they are likely to be and what you propose to do about them. They are automatically suspicious of the "no problems whatsoever" proposal.

Basis for success: It is essential that your proposal explain exactly *why* the proposed enterprise is going to be a success. Success is more than the mere avoidance of failure and is more than planning to avoid mistakes and do everything "right." Every investor is looking for tomorrow's Xerox Corporation — the sleeper that grows in a few years to become an industrial or commercial giant. Your proposal needs to consider and address *why* your product or service will sell. Is it better — faster, cheaper, more reliable, more convenient, or otherwise "more than" — a competitive product or service? If so, prove it. Is it something brand new? If so, what will it do? Who will buy it? Why will they buy it? Find the "sex appeal" in your proposition and make sure you have explained it clearly.

Management: Every investor or lender knows that a business venture depends heavily on management for its success. Be sure to identify your management assets — who will do what, how they are qualified to do whatever they are going to do. If you do not possess the proper "paper" qualifications (e.g., experience), make sure that you are going to have someone aboard who does have those qualifications.

Use of capital: Explain exactly why you need the money and how you will use it and manage it. Unless you are in or are going into one of those rare businesses that generate instant money up front and carry no accounts, you will soon have a great deal of money "on the street" — outstanding in delivered goods or services and on your books as "receivables," but not in your bank account as available cash. Bear firmly in mind, too, that the more successful you are in generating sales, the more money you are going to have tied up in that manner. That is, the more successful you are, the more you are going to need operating capital. Your proposal must show that analysis of capital required to cover all receivables — unless you plan to discount these at the bank or factor them in some manner. In today's high cost of money, the interest alone is an excellent argument for raising capital and an excellent reason for demonstrating to a potential investor that ample return on investment is possible by simply avoiding borrowing to cover receivables.

Control: Make up your mind at the outset that getting equity financing — venture capital, as the term is used here — means giving up not only some portion of ownership, but also some portion of control. It's the price you have to pay to get the capital you need, but the way to regard this is that it is far better to have a portion of something successful than all of something struggling to even stay alive. So often, it comes down to that.

THE FORMAT

There is no universal format for a proposal or business plan, although some banks will ask you, in applying for a loan, to fill out an elaborate set of forms, which in themselves constitute a virtual proposal and business plan. However, bear in mind that there are certain parallels between the written presentation and a personal presentation. Just as a lender or prospective investor would be adversely impressed by a hesitant, stumbling visitor who appeared unable to get to the point, so will that individual be adversely impressed by a proposal that rambles on and on and takes so long to get to the point that the

reader is no longer sure that he knows what the point is. A suitable format is therefore one that makes a crisp, businesslike presentation, gets to the point promptly, and makes the point absolutely clear. However, since the proposal *is* a sales presentation, there are other considerations.

To sell anything at all, you must focus your presentation on what the product or service you offer will do for the buyer — the selfish, what's-in-it-for-me reason for buying. In the case of a loan application, the buyer — the banker, in this case — wants to earn interest, probably would like to do business repeatedly with you, but does not want to take excessive risk. Obviously, all bankers are trying to keep all their available funds loaned out under the lowest risks possible. Bankers have no trouble finding borrowers: the demand for bank money — loans — almost always exceeds the supply. So what the prospect wants, in this case, is a low-risk borrower, one who is almost certainly going to be able to repay the loan. This illustrates the critical need to show the almost-certain success of your venture.

The situation is about the same with an investor or venture capitalist. All venture capitalists receive more proposals than they can possibly accept, and they try to select those most certain to succeed, of course. So, again, the main thing you must sell is the certainty of success or the almost complete absence of risk.

There is, however, this one difference between these two prospective "buyers" and what they want: both want low-risk propositions and both therefore are much interested in evaluating your prospects for success. The banker, however, is primarily concerned with the probability that you will be able to repay the loan, and only secondarily concerned with the prospect that you might become a large business and therefore an important bank customer. The venture capitalist is much more concerned with the possibility of getting in on the ground floor of a new IBM, and will certainly pay close attention to whatever you have to say about the long-term growth prospects for your venture.

Translating this into a written presentation, the proposal designed to back up a loan package is almost identical with one designed to interest investors, but it would be good tactics to dramatize growth prospects as much as possible, if you are seeking venture capital.

In either case, the point is that a proposal is something like the carrot dangled before the donkey's eyes to persuade him to move: in any sales presentation — including a proposal — it is good salesmanship to explain the benefits of what you offer as early in the presentation as possible and remind the prospect of the benefits as often as possible.

One way to do this is to include in your proposal, before the body of the proposal, an abstract or summary, in which you present the highlights (presumably; actually, this is best used to present all the most compelling arguments for acceptance).

The following sections describe the elements most often needed in a business plan or proposal, with such comments as are necessary to explain them.

Introduction

Introduce yourself, your associates, if there are other principals, and your proposed venture briefly, with the observation that details will follow. If at all possible, use something attention-getting here, something to persuade the reader to *want* to read on. (He probably will read on because it's his business, but it helps if you capture interest here so that the reader is eager to see what else you have to say.) Present your concept or enterprise in a capsule form, concentrating on its most attractive aspects. If you truly believe that your proposition has important growth prospects, say so: don't be bashful here. If you think that you are the new Texas Instruments, say so plainly and promise that the reader will get substantiating evidence and information in

the pages to follow. If you believe that your proposition will revolutionize the computer industry or cut printing costs by one-half, say so. Be as dramatic and/or offer as many attractive "teasers" here as possible. Don't deceive your reader; make only those promises you expect to be able to deliver on later in your proposal. This point is of utmost importance.

Explain, in this introduction, what the proposal will offer, in general: telegraph the "goodies" to come. On the other hand, don't give all the goodies away here; bear in mind two show business axioms: save something for the encore, and always leave them wanting more. Each page ought to pique the reader into wanting to see what is on the next page.

For example, suppose that there is a traditional problem associated with the kind of enterprise you are proposing, but you have devised some revolutionary method for coping successfully with this problem. Explain this in the introduction and assure that you will reveal your plan.

Discussion

In many cases, a general discussion of the proposed business, industry, or proposition is required to set the stage properly. You might, for example, wish to explain how you conceived the idea and on what basis you predict success — especially if your idea is a novel one or a foray into an already crowded field. If much research went into developing your plan, say so and explain the research. No modesty here: take all the credit due you.

This section ought to lead logically to the next section, which is the business plan proper. It should show that your specific business plan is a most logical approach, under whatever circumstances you covered in your discussion. The next items are specifics in this section of your proposal — specifics of the business plan.

The Basic Business Proposition

Explain specifically and in detail, if you have not already, exactly what it is you are going to sell, to whom, and in what manner. (Example: a new kind of soft drink to teen-agers, through normal distribution channels, with a brief characterization of the new drink.) This serves as an introduction to this section of the proposal. Details follow.

The Management Team

Explain who will do what in the top responsiibilities of the management team and the qualifications of each individual.

How the Venture Will Be Organized

Your organization plan, covering all relevant functions, such as purchasing (if that is a major need), marketing and sales (not the same thing!), manufacturing, packaging, distribution, advertising, and whatever else is a major function for the business you propose.

Outside Services

If you plan to use outside services for important functions — data processing and consulting, for example — provide specifics here: what tentative arrangements have you made or what investigations?

Incorporation

What kind of corporation have you set up or do you plan to set up? Who are the directors or proposed directors? What original funding have you provided? (How much of your own money or that of other principals is already invested or available to invest?)

Markets

What, where, who are your markets and prospects? Describe them in detail. Be as accurate and detailed here as possible; it's one of the most critical areas and one you are likely to be cross-examined about — if your proposal is adequate in this area.

A discussion of markets includes profiling your prospective customers — again, in some detail. It includes, also, your plans for reaching those prospects. You can't sell the greatest bargain in the history of mankind if you can't reach — meaning that you manage to put your proposition in front of — those who have use for what you offer.

Marketing/Sales Plans and Projections

You have explained generally how you plan to reach your prospects. Now lay out your marketing and sales plans in some details, and make some estimates or projections of sales for short-, intermediate-, and long-term futures.

The Numbers

All of these factors have to be supported by numbers. You need profit and loss statements, cash-flow projections, sales projections, payroll projections, and others, if you are not yet in business. If you are already in business and seeking fresh capital, you need to report all the above, with projections of what you will do with the infusion of additional capital. In any event, you do need all these figures, and they have to be based on some kind of verifiable reality, not on wishful thinking or casual wild guesses.

Miscellaneous

There may be other data required, depending on the nature of the proposed enterprise. For example, if it is a labor-intensive enterprise, especially if it requires highly skilled labor or labor that happens to be in short supply, it is necessary to discuss this in your business plan: Who will handle recruiting and how? If there are any special requirements which are critical to the success of the enterprise, acknowledge these in your proposal and present clear plans for handling the needs successfully.

Summary Proposal

You may have to submit your proposal to a large number of venture capitalists before you find the right one — or the right one finds you. The fact that one or even several venture capitalists have rejected your proposition does not necessarily mean that it is unsound (you should try to get those who turn you down to explain their reasons, so that you can make corrections to your business plan, if necessary). You may very well have to try a great many. (More than one entrepreneur has spent a year and even more in the quest, before finding the right source of capital.)

If your proposal is a fairly substantial one you may wish to make up an abstract or an abbreviated version to submit, for exploratory purposes, with the full proposal going to anyone who expresses some interest in seeing it. This need not be a large document, since you will explain in it that it is a brief abstract, and the full proposal is available on request.

Physical Considerations

It is not necessary to go to large expense in producing your proposal. Today's office copiers produce copies so well that it is often difficult to tell which is the original and which the copy, and sometimes the copy is even better than the original. Thus, an office copier is perfectly satisfactory for reproduction.

Proposals can be typed on electric typewriters, which are abundantly available today in every office.

Binding can be by any of the common methods for inexpensive binding: a corner staple or two side staples, for the small proposal; a plastic spiral binding for larger proposals; or any of the patent binders readily available in office-supply stores.

If you need help with this, most of the now-familiar "copy shops" can help you with any portion of the copying and binding process.

Special Considerations

One point that has not really been made yet is so important that it deserves a separate discussion. It is this: You may very well have some special reason for expecting success in your venture. If so, it is important that you dramatize it properly and make it abundantly clear to the reader of your proposal. Here are some examples of such special considerations:

Sales and Marketing

You may have one or more important accounts "practically in your hip pocket." It does happen, quite often, that an entrepreneur is able to do this — in fact, the existence of guaranteed major business may be the very reason for launching the enterprise. If something like this is the case in your own business prospects, you most certainly want to feature this fact prominently in your proposal. Be warned, however, not to bluff or make claims about having accounts promised to you if you can't validate those claims. If your proposal is predicated, in whole or even in part, on such a claim, you may be sure that any venture capitalist is going to want to verify that claim in some manner. Even a banker is likely to ask you to validate that claim somehow. Validating it may make getting the loan or venture capital "a piece of cake" — but be sure that you can validate it.

The same consideration applies to any other important feature of your proposal. Here are some of the things that show up, from time to time, as major features of proposals which, if they can be verified, make it far easier to get approval of loan or venture-capital applications:

- Any kind of sales and marketing asset that is obviously a great asset — not only promised accounts and even signed orders, but outstanding individuals in any key position of management, including sales and marketing, production, packaging, or other important function.
- A contract already signed that needs to be financed or, as is sometimes the case, an actual agreement to award you a contract, upon satisfactory evidence of "financial responsibility" which means enough capital to handle the job.
- A guarantee of other funding, which is enough to cover only part of your requirement and is contingent on your being able to get the rest of the capital you need.
- An exclusive of any kind, which is decisive for success: exclusive rights to some patent, exclusive sources of supply, exclusive franchise, or other such asset which is virtually "bankable."

GRANT PROGRAMS AND SOURCES

At the time of this writing, the Reagan Administration has begun to make some reductions in federal programs, including several which furnish funds for business enterprises, although Congress has thus far been unwilling to support a major cutback in the many grant programs. There are, currently, well over 1,000 programs of "federal domestic assistance," of which the majority are programs involving cash payments, some

of them intended for business uses. These programs are listed and described in an annual publication of the Government Printing Office, the *Catalog of Federal Domestic Assistance*. At this time, the price of this annual volume is $20, which includes a mid-year supplement every year, updating the listings in the main volume. The publication is available from the Government Printing Office bookstores. Following, are other publications and sources, with explanations of each.

The ORYX Press Grant Information System offers information on government and private sources of grant funds, with names of various organizations pertinent. For more information write to them at the following address:

The ORYX Press
7632 East Edgemont Avenue
Scottsdale, AZ 85257

The following organization is a nonprofit membership organization, which mails members monthly information on current grant programs and activities, and offers to help members win grants, among several other services. Reportedly, the organization has information on all government and private-sector granting organizations:

Funding Sources Clearinghouse, Inc.
2600 Bancroft Way
Berkeley, CA 94704

Another organization offering information and services relative to grants is the following:

The Grantsmanship Center
1015 West Olympic
Los Angeles, CA 90015

ABOUT FOUNDATIONS

Like other organizations, foundations sometimes "go out of business," and new foundations appear also. Following are other publications which offer information about foundations:

CALIFORNIA

A Guide to California Foundations, Peter D. Abrahams, Julie T. Casson, and Dennis B. Daul; Common College, Woodside, CA.

CONNECTICUT

A Directory of Private Foundations in the State of Connecticut, edited by John Parker Huber; Eastern Connecticut State College Foundation; Willimantic, CT.

DISTRICT OF COLUMBIA

The Guide to Washington, DC Foundations, by Margaret T. deBettencourt; Guide Publishers, Washington, DC.

MAINE

A Directory of Foundations and Charitable Trusts in the State of Maine, edited by John Parker Huber, Eastern Connecticut State College Foundation; Willimantic, CT.

MICHIGAN

Directory of Selected Michigan Foundations and Charitable Trusts, Michigan League for Human Services, Lansing, MI.

NEW HAMPSHIRE

A Directory of Private Foundations in the State of New Hampshire, edited by John Parker Huber, Eastern Connecticut State College Foundation, Willimantic, CT.

OHIO

Charitable Foundations Directory and supplement, *Ohio Charitable Foundations Directory*; Office of the Attorney General, State of Ohio, Columbus.

OREGON

Directory of Foundations and Charitable Trusts Registered in Oregon, compiled and edited by Virgil D. Mills, Dept. of Justice, State of Oregon, Portland, OR.

RHODE ISLAND

A Directory of Foundations and Charitable Trusts in the State of Rhode Island, edited by John Parker Huber, Eastern Connecticut State College Foundation, Willimantic, CT.

VERMONT

A Directory of Foundations and Charitable Trusts in the State of Vermont, edited by John Parker Huber, Eastern Connecticut State College Foundation, Willimantic, CT.

VIRGINIA

Virginia Directory of Private Foundations, Divison of State Planning and Community Affairs, Commonwealth of Virginia, Richmond, VA.

GETTING OUTSIDE HELP

There are a large number of individuals who represent themselves as "financial consultants" or "financial brokers." For the most part, these are individuals who are, in fact, brokers: they are middlemen, who know a number of sources to apply to, in an effort to help you get the loan or venture capital you seek, for which service they receive a brokerage fee. There are also those who call themselves "finders" and who work for a "finder's fee," also a small percentage of the money involved in the transaction.

One difference between the financial consultant or broker and the finder is that the former almost invariably works on behalf of the individual seeking the funds, and is paid by that individual, whereas the finder may be working in behalf of either party and gets paid by whichever party signed an agreement to pay for the service. This is either the service of finding the funding or the service of finding a good investment, for there are investors who will commission finders to locate good investments for them.

One word of caution, mentioned earlier but worth repeating: Be wary of any such person who demands "front money," or guarantees results. No one can guarantee results; there are too many imponderables in every case. Advance fees are sometimes justified, but only when they are clearly for some necessary service, such as preparing a proposal, legal fees, or other such expenses. Never pay someone a commission on a promised loan or investment. Legitimate and ethical financial brokers and consultants do not demand up-front commissions.

One way to find individuals offering such services is through one of the many newsletters carrying advertisements for such services. In fact, in some cases, these newsletters carry advertisements placed by the lenders or investors directly. One that carries many such notices every month is this one:

Business Opportunities Digest
301 Plymouth Drive, NE
Dalton, GA 30720
(404) 259-6035

Another publication is called *Moneyfax,* and is published by Richard Brisky, as the monthly newsletter of his organization, The National Association of Financial Consultants. Each month, Brisky offers news and other information about financial matters, and runs the classified advertisements of his members. These notices are listed under such headings as "CAPITAL AVAILABLE" and "CAPITAL WANTED," but some of the notices offer factoring services or buying receivables, real estate investments, and other related services. For details:

Richard K. Brisky
The National Association
    of Financial Consultants
Box 1
Ischua, NY 14746
(716) 557-8900

Useful information on financing ventures is also offered frequently in two monthly, "slick paper" magazines sold on the newsstands:

INC.
38 Commercial Wharf
Boston, MA 02110
(617) 227-4700

Venture, The Magazine for Entrepreneurs
Venture Magazine, Inc.
35 West 45th Street
New York, NY 10036
(212) 840-5580

Many other notices appear in weekly tabloids circulated nationally, and in several newsprint magazines. Unfortunately, some of these are "come ons," and if getting the money you need appears to be too easy to be true, it almost surely is.

There are, of course, also many business brokers, people who serve as middlemen in buying and selling businesses. These people advertise frequently in the classified advertising sections of newspapers, and it is not difficult to compile a list of business brokers from such advertisements. You can then pursue with such brokers the possibility of finding potential investors or factors, for any active business broker is an excellent source of such information.

One newspaper of special interest, in this regard, is the *Wall Street Journal,* the most widely circulated and widely read daily financial journal in the country. The *Journal* carries many advertisements offering to buy and sell businesses, investment opportunities, and investment opportunities wanted. Anyone seeking venture capital is well advised to peruse the many listings in the *Wall Street Journal,* although there are other sources.